W9-ASG-080

WOMEN AND RELIGION IN AMERICA

Women and Religion in America

Volume 2: The Colonial and Revolutionary Periods

ROSEMARY RADFORD RUETHER

ROSEMARY SKINNER KELLER

Harper & Row, Publishers, San Francisco

Cambridge, Hagerstown, New York, Philadelphia
London, Mexico City, São Paulo, Sydney

 For information address Harper & Row, Publishers, Inc., 10 East 53rd Street, New York, NY 10022. Published simultaneously in Canada by Fitzhenry & Whiteside, Limited, Toronto.

FIRST EDITION

Designed by Jim Mennick

Library of Congress Cataloging in Publication Data

(Revised for volume 2)
Main entry under title:

WOMEN AND RELIGION IN AMERICA.

Includes bibliographical references and index.
1. Women in Christianity—Addresses, essays, lectures. 2. Women and religion—Addresses, essays, lectures. 3. Women—United States—Religious life—Addresses, essays, lectures. I. Ruether, Rosemary Radford. II. Keller, Rosemary Skinner.

BR515.W648 1981 280'.088042 80-8346
ISBN 0-06-066829-6 (v. 1)

ISBN 0-06-066832-6
LC #80-8346

83 84 85 86 87 10 9 8 7 6 5 4 3 2 1

To our husbands

HERMAN J. RUETHER

and

ROBERT P. KELLER

with grateful appreciation for their support of our work over many years

Contents

Acknowledgments

Many scholars have contributed their time and expertise to make possible this volume, which gathers together the story of women of diverse cultures, religious traditions, and races in the colonial and revolutionary periods of the Americas. Not only the women who gathered and edited the documents and wrote the introductory essays are responsible for this work; in addition, each author has benefited from help from many scholars and libraries.

We would like to thank the Friends' Historical Library at Swarthmore College for photos and materials on early American Quakerism. Thanks also go to Herbert A. Wisbey, Jr., of Elmira College, whose letters helped us to obtain permission to reproduce the portrait of Jemima Wilkinson held by the Yates County Historical Society of New York.

We wish to acknowledge the many people who helped translate the documents included here: Odile Hellman and John Hellman, who translated texts on Quebec history from Old French into modern English; Ernest Prelinger, who assisted in the translation of texts on the Moravians and the Ephrata Community from the original German; Ruth Morales, who did the English translation from eighteenth-century Spanish of the poem "Dialogue with God," by Sor Paula de Jesus Nazareno.

We wish to thank John L. Kraft, Historic Site Administrator of the Pennsylvania Historical and Museum Commission at Ephrata Cloister for selecting and making archival material available; and Vernon H. Nelson, Archivist, the Moravian Archives, Bethlehem, Pennsylvania, for his assistance with Moravian materials. For materials on French Canada, we wish to thank Dr. Kathryn M. Bindon; Dr. Lionel Rothkrun of Concordia University in Montreal; and Dr. André Sanfaçon, of the University of Laval in Quebec City. We also thank Sr. Florence Bertrand, Archivist, Congregation of Notre Dame, Montreal; Sr. Frances Kerr, Historian, Religious Hospitallers of St. Joseph, Montreal; Sr. Estelle Mitchell, Historian, Grey Nuns, Montreal; and Dom Guy Marie Oury, O.S.B., Chaplain, Priory of the Immaculate Heart of Mary, Westfield, Vermont, for their help in interpreting French Canadian materials.

We wish to thank Arch McLean for his excellent work in reproducing most of the photos that appear in this volume, and David Himrod of the

Garrett-Evangelical Theological School Library for his many labors in obtaining sources and bibliographic information.

We thank the staff and fellows of the Newberry Library Center for the History of the American Indian, as well as Charlotte Heth, Pauline Turner Strong, Linda Hogan, Jennifer H. Brown, and Francis Jennings, for their numerous suggestions and textual criticism of the American Indian material.

Grateful acknowledgment is made to the following archives, authors, and publishers for permission to reprint texts or photos:

"Respuesta a Sor Filotea de la Cruz," by Sor Juana Inez de la Cruz: permission to reprint the translation from Margaret Sayers Piden, translator.

La Revolucion pedagogica en Nueva Espana, vol. 2, pp. 65–66, 187: permission to reprint from the author, Pilar Foz y Foz.

Minute Book of the Bray Associates, vol. 1, pp. 180, 186, 243; vol. 2, pp. 71–72: permission to reprint from the Society for Promoting Christian Knowledge, London.

The Letterbook of Eliza Lucas Pinckney, pp. 51–53, 100–101: permission to reprint from the University of North Carolina Press, Chapel Hill, NC.

The Education of the Heart: The Correspondence of Rachel Mordecai Lazarus and Maria Edgeworth, pp. 6, 14–15: permission to reprint from the University of North Carolina Press, Chapel Hill, NC.

William Gaston Papers, no. 272: reprinted by permission of the Southern Historical Collection of the University of North Carolina at Chapel Hill, NC.

Chronicon Ephratense, pp. 160–165, and the *Paradisisches Wunder-Spiel,* p. 360: permission to translate and print from the Archives of the Ephrata Cloister, Ephrata, Pennsylvania.

The Life Story of Martha Powell, The Bethlehem Diary, vol. 1, pp. 230–231, *The Diarium des Ledigen Schwestern Chors in Lidiz, Personalia Unserer am 24ten Nov. 1755 an der Mahoney von denen feindlichen Indianern martyrisierten Geschwister:* permission to translate and print from the Archives of the Moravian Church, Bethlehem, Pennsylvania.

Records of the Moravians in North Carolina, edited by Adelaide L. Fries, Douglas Letell Rights, Minnie J. Smith, and Kenneth G. Hamilton, vol. 2, pp. 715, 767, 825, 826, 827, 895: permission to reprint from the North Carolina Division of Archives and History, Raleigh, NC.

"Quaker Women's Meetings," published in *Signs Magazine,* Autumn, 1975, pp. 235–245: permission to reprint from the editors, Milton Speizman and Jane Kronick, from the publisher of *Signs Magazine,* The University of Chicago Press, and from the Philadelphia Yearly Meeting of the Religious Society of Friends, holders of the original document.

Extracts from The Wilkinson Papers, film 357: permission to print from the Cornell University Press Historical Archives.

"My Resting Reaping Time," by Sarah Osborn: permission to reprint from the editor, Mary Beth Norton, and from the publisher of *Signs Magazine,* The University of Chicago Press.

Excerpts from the Letters of Abigail Adams: permission to reprint from the Massachusetts Historical Society.

Title page of the Hymnal of the Ephrata Cloister Sisterhood by Petronella: permission to reproduce from the Historical Society of Pennsylvania.

Portrait of Martha Laurens Ramsay: permission to reprint from the Carolina Art Association, Charleston, SC.

Portrait of George Whitefield preaching: permission to reprint from the National Portrait Gallery, London.

Portrait of Rebekah Sewall: permission to reprint from Columbia University Press.

Gravestone of Sarah Swan: permission to reprint from the Columbia University Press.

Portraits of Abigail and John Adams: permission to reprint from the Massachusetts Historical Society, Boston, Massachusetts.

Drawing of Anne Hutchinson: permission to reprint from the New York Public Library.

Drawing of Indian women sowing corn: permission to reprint from the New York Public Library.

Etching of Quaker woman speaking: permission to reprint from the Library of Congress.

Portrait of Jemima Wilkinson: permission to reprint photo from Herbert A. Wisbey's *Pioneer Prophetess,* granted by Herbert A. Wisbey and by the Village Board of the Village of Penn Yan, New York.

Sculpture of Mary Dyer: permission to reproduce photo by the Philadelphia Annual Meeting of the Religious Society of Friends.

Palou's *Life of Fray Junipero Serra,* pp. 118–119: permission to reprint from the Academy of American Franciscan History.

Louis Deliette, *Memoir of De Gannes concerning the Illinois Country,* pp. 352–354, 369–371: permission to reprint from the Illinois State Historical Society.

"Slave Dance": permission to reprint from the Abby Aldrich Rockefeller Folk Art Collection, Williamsburg, Virginia.

Portrait of Elizabeth Freeman by Susan Sedgwich: permission to reprint from the Massachusetts Historical Society, Boston, Massachusetts.

Painting of "Rachel Weeping": permission to reprint from the Philadelphia Museum of Art, Philadelphia, Pennsylvania.

Etching, Shaker religious dancing: permission to reprint from the Shaker Museum, Old Chatham, New York.

Etching, Moravian group wedding: permission to reprint from Old Salem Inc., Winston-Salem, North Carolina.

Portrait, Mercy Otis Warren: permission to reprint from the Museum of Fine Arts, Boston, Mass.

Broadside by a Daughter of Liberty: permission to reprint from the New York Historical Society.

Portrait, Sarah Franklin Bache: permission to reprint from the Metropolitan Museum of Art, New York City.

Absalom Jones and Richard Allen, *Negro Protest Pamphlets,* p. 9: permission to reprint from The Ayer Company, successors to Arno Press.

The Carolina Chronicle of Dr. Francis Le Jau, pp. 67–68, 80–81: permission to use from the University of California Press.

The Letters of Eleazar Wheelock's Indians, ed. James Dow McCallum, pp. 230–231: permission to reprint from the Dartmouth College Library and the University Press of New England.

Introduction

The American colonies in the seventeenth and eighteenth centuries were the stage for a vast overseas expansion and settlement of European peoples. At the beginning of this period, the Spanish and Portuguese held the upper hand, closely followed by the French, but, by the eighteenth century, English colonization was setting limits to the North American expansion of the rival European powers. In this documentary history of women and religion in colonial and revolutionary America, we wish to illustrate the cultural pluralism of the colonial scene. This was a world, first of all, of Indians of many tribes and cultures who were being displaced, Christianized, and destroyed, culturally and physically, by European expansion. It was a world of competing visions of Christian renewal—Spanish Catholic, French Catholic, Puritan, Quaker, and German Pietist—each jostling to establish its claims upon the New World. Meanwhile, the black Africans, another conquered people, were being introduced as slaves into the colonies. Religion played an overt role in all of these colonization dramas. It was an integral part of each European group's claim to be the divinely ordained instrument of God, both to settle and to evangelize the New World.

In this documentary history, we have sought to chart women's role in the drama of colonization. What was the role that each of the dominant visions of religious renewal assigned to women? In what ways did each vision offer conflicting messages, at once encouraging and repressing new egalitarianism? How did this Christian zeal affect women among the Indians—or women among the Africans, brought to the Americas in chains? To catch even a glimpse of the role of women in this complex, intercultural story demanded the collaboration of many experts. Those who have ably brought us the story of New England Puritanism, the best-researched part of the colonial drama, seldom have even a glancing knowledge of the history of New Spain or of Quebec. They view Indians from the settler's perspective, not from the Indian's perspective. Stories of black Africans, of the Southern colonies, and of the sectarian groups are typically neglected as well. We hope that, through this documentary history, we can open up this wider stage of the drama of colonization and understand something of women's religious life within each of these many stories. Constructing this history required diverse research skills—the ability of one scholar to read seventeenth-century French, another to read Spanish from the same period, a third to read German script, these documents often being in handwritten form.

But the problem of sources involved more than translation. Almost all Indians lacked written forms of communication. Blacks also, with a few exceptions, were illiterate. Even among the European settlers, most women were illiterate. In the case of the Indians, we were triply handicapped by Eurocentric, Christian, and male biases. One is indeed looking through a glass darkly in trying to reconstruct the religious experiences of Indian women through sources from male Europeans who viewed Indians as savages without "true religion" and who were even less likely to understand, or even to notice, the roles played by women in those cultures.

Where sources actually written by women are abundant—such as the letters and writings of Spanish Catholic or French Catholic nuns, or the diaries of Southern plantation wives—one must read between the lines of a piety that rigidly assigned subordinate roles to women, if one is to try to imagine the actual meaning of these religious expressions for them. Only occasionally among the documents of this period do we get obscure or forthright assertions of women's own rights to autonomous religious self-definition. Yet those hopeful stirrings are there, stimulated first by the renewal movements of the Reformation and Counter-Reformation, and again by the Enlightenment and the American Revolution, only to be, again and again, betrayed by church and political leaders who wanted to rally the support of women for reforms, renewals, and revolutions, but did not want to extend the benefits of these changes to them.

The first chapter in the book is appropriately devoted to the group whose history in the Americas predates the European conquest: the American Indians. The chapter is coauthored by Jacqueline Peterson, an historian of the American Indian Studies Department of the University of Minnesota, and Mary Druke, an anthropologist and Associate Director of the Project for a Documentary History of the Iroquois, Newberry Library, Chicago. Peterson, who teaches the history of Indian-White relations, and Druke, an Iroquoian specialist, are collaborating in a pioneering effort to document some aspects of American Indian women's religious imagery and life before Christianization and, also, the effects of Christianity upon them. This is a body of material of great sensitivity for American Indian peoples today, and Peterson and Druke have profited by association with a number of American Indian scholars in crafting their chapter.

Peterson and Druke show the diverse roles played by American Indian women in tribal religious life. Their documentary task was particularly difficult because the travelers and missionaries, who are the sole written source for this period, were not able to recognize as "religious" many

Indian practices, since what religion meant to Indians was not what it meant to Europeans. Thus, it was often only by happenstance that they mentioned female participation in rituals. Even more difficult for Europeans to imagine were female forms of divine power or "gods." In documenting American Indian women's religious life, Peterson and Druke must often present fragmentary allusions which give us only a glimpse of that other world which was so foreign to the European mentality.

The impact of Christianization on American Indian women is documented not only in this first chapter, but in several other chapters that discuss the French Canadian, the Hispanic, and the Moravian settlements. Peterson and Druke try to look at Christianization from the American Indian side. Here we see that Indians often assimilated Christian symbols into their existing world view, so that what these symbols meant to Indians was quite different from what they meant to European Christians. This practice still continues today, as Christian and "traditional" Indians try to bridge the gap made between them by the missionaries and to maintain a coherent Indian world view.

Each of the various Christian churches vied for the souls of American Indians and imposed upon them their diverse religious cultures. Thus Indians were not just Christianized. They were turned into Counter-Reformation French Catholics in Quebec, Counter-Reformation Spanish Catholics in Mexico, German-speaking Moravian Brethren in Pennsylvania, English Puritans in New England, and so forth. Each European nation and sect justified its divine mission in part through its claims to evangelize the Indians. So, we find Indian women going through an astonishing plurality of metamorphoses throughout the chapters of this history, as each church group claimed evangelistic success in making over Indians in its own cultural image. When we read an account from a French nun describing how an Indian woman became a perfect model of French Catholic piety, we must always remember that such an account tells us little or nothing about how the Indian woman herself might have fitted this new identity into her traditional identity in ways hidden from her European mentors.

Asunción Lavrin, who is Associate professor of History at Howard University and has written extensively on women in colonial Mexico, especially on the role of nuns and nunneries during that period, has provided the chapter on women in Spanish America. Much of her story is about women in religious orders, for they were the literate class of women in New Spain. The women Lavrin documents were primarily upper-class Spanish or Creole (Spaniards born in the colonies), although there were some convents for women of the Indian aristocracy as well. But the cultural world of Amer-Indians has disappeared entirely. Christianity and Spanish Catholic culture are identical in these documents.

The convent offered Spanish American women a sphere of assured social respect, comfort, some autonomy, and education. The brilliant

Renaissance humanist scholar and poet Sor Inés de la Cruz chose a religious life over marriage, thereby indicating her own judgment that, of the two options open to "respectable" women in her culture, the former offered her a larger sphere for intellectual development. But even the convent proved narrow and repressive confines for a truly gifted woman. The tragedy of Sor Inés was that her culture really had no place for a woman of her talents, nor would the story have been much different if she had been born in Puritan Massachusetts or colonial Montreal.

The Quebequois Canadian story is much more overtly the drama of French and Indians. The Indians figure in this story both as menacing enemies and as allies and converts. Here again, it is the religious life that offered the larger scope for the talents of an independent woman who wished to pursue education, adventure, and high commitment to Christian ideals. French women who came as pioneering missionaries and founders of religious orders in New France were the product of a synthesis of the French Renaissance and the Catholic Counter-Reformation. This imbued them with a spirit of zeal and readiness for heroic self-sacrifice. They observed the American Indian world they encountered with the curiosity of Renaissance science and the assured confidence of an absolutist Catholic faith. They brought to their task a spirituality at once intellectual and intensely emotional and a practical administrative competence in the midst of often harrowing conditions. The chapter on French Canada was written by Christine Allen, who teaches philosophy at Concordia University in Montreal. Allen consulted widely with French Canadian historians in the development of her material (see Acknowledgments).

Rosemary Skinner Keller, Associate Professor of Religion and American Culture at Garrett-Evangelical Theological Seminary and a specialist in women and family history in Revolutionary America, has authored the chapter on women in Puritan New England. In her story, the latent conflict between church renewal and the patriarchal subordination of women by religious authorities is brought out into the open. The women of Puritan New England were the product of a dissenting culture which was at war with the established Anglican Church of the English Reformation. The splintering of the English Reformation into a bewildering array of competing sects reflected the conflicts of social classes as well as religious viewpoints. In this atmosphere of incipient civil war, women often took the initiative to gather dissenting congregations, call ministers, and assert their own rights to preach and to administer churches. Dissenting ministers encouraged such independence in women when the foe was the established Church.

However, once they themselves became the ministers of the established Church of New England, women of this type became seen as a threat to social and ecclesiastical order. Puritan theory assigned a positive but limited place to women as helpmeets to their husbands and co-authorities over children and servants, under their husbands. It encouraged the active piety of lay women, as docile recipients of Puritan preaching and piety. But it had little place for the woman whose religious experience bypassed ministerial authority and who sought to define her own faith. For the Puritan, the woman who dissented from the authority of minister, magistrate, or husband was both a heretic and a presumptive witch. She was a heretic because her place in society had been divinely ordained and revealed in Scripture, so for her to rebel against it was to rebel against God and God's revealed Will. She was probably a witch because only the presence of the promptings of the Devil could explain such insubordination in a woman.

It is in the context of this conflict between the two sides of Puritan theory about women and the actual social realities of women in Puritan New England that Keller interprets the heresy and witch trials that swept across the Massachusetts Bay Colonies from the mid-1700s until the end of that century. She shows that these two kinds of trials were not isolated cases, but were interconnected. They must be interpreted against the background of a dramatic struggle between the spirit of autonomy released by the dissenting wing of the English Reformation and a male leadership that had no place in their theology or society for women who applied this autonomy to themselves.

By the end of the century, the heresy and witchcraft trials had abated, perhaps less because their presuppositions were discredited than because the ministry had won its struggle to repress women and to place them within its own definition of their place in society and the church. Here we find the Puritan preacher encouraging the active lay piety of women in the congregation, so long as women took their cues from the preacher and confined their evangelizing zeal to the private sphere of home and family.

This settled domestic piety of women is the world we enter in the story of the religious life of Southern women told by Alice Mathews, Professor of History at Western Carolina University, Cullowhee, North Carolina. Most of these Southern women belonged to the established Anglican Church, although there were also Catholic women in Maryland, Jewish women in the Carolinas, and an increasing number of women attracted to dissenting churches. The religious role of women was fixed and limited. Women were to encourage a devout but moderate piety within the limits of their homes as mentors of children and servants. They were also expected to evangelize their own husbands discreetly, although they were not to take authority over them, but instead be prepared to endure with patience the impious, unfaithful, and even abusive husband.

The ambiguity of the relationship between these white Christian wives and black slaves is suggested in Mathews's account. In theory, the white women were to see their servants as a part of their households and extend their evangelizing nurture to them, so that mistress, children, and servants would all kneel together in prayer at the close of day. In fact, many slaves preferred to become Baptists or Methodists, attracted both to the more lively styles of worship and to the greater communal autonomy found in the dissenting churches. White women were caught in between the male religious and social authorities and the enslaved black world. They were themselves victims of its hierarchical social order, but also agents of it, who struggled, not always successfully, to enculturate their slaves in its values.

The chapter on black women in colonial America, developed by Lillian Webb, Chair of the Department of Religion and Philosophy at Clark College in Atlanta, Georgia, takes us to the other side of this story of enslaved Africans in colonial America. Webb also tries to give us a glimpse of the alternative religious and social values brought by black women from their non-Christian background in West Africa. The struggles of missionaries to repress what they regarded as sexual immorality among black slaves often reflected, in fact, these alternative social assumptions of West Africans. The increasing tendency of colonial Christianity to idealize women as the "religious and moral sex" seldom was extended to black women. They were regarded as naturally immoral, "beastly," and little fitted to Christian religiosity. Indeed, many plantation owners resisted the demands of churches and missionary societies to evangelize the Africans because they feared that baptism would give slaves the rights of emancipation. It remained for the Christian theologians to argue that the Scriptures allowed slavery, and so it was compatible with Christianity to baptize a person and yet hold as slaves those who were regarded as lacking full human status.

Nevertheless, African women adopted Christianity with alacrity. With the disintegration of African communal identity, the adoption of Christianity offered the only hope for black mothers to find a new identity for themselves and their children. During the first Great Awakening, blacks flocked particularly to the Methodists and Baptists, attracted, among other things, to the antislavery message that was at least hinted in these circles, although as Webb shows, even the Quakers were seldom forthright in their opposition to slavery as an institution. Even the dissenting churches, however, seldom extended full and equal fellowship to their black converts, and so, by the end of the colonial period, American black Christians were beginning to break with these churches and to found black congregations and denominations. Although preaching authority was not officially extended to women even in black churches, black women began to find ministerial roles as missionaries, charitable workers, and educators within these black denominations.

In the diverse American religious scene of this period, the heirs of the radical Reformation also were to be found. From the English in the seventeenth century there flowed Quaker missionaries, exponents of radical spiritualist Puritanism. From Germany came a diversity of Pietist sects, often adopting communal social forms and some of them practicing celibacy. These groups were more experimental in their theology and social practices toward women. The Quakers, through their co-founder, Margaret Fell, and her daughters, developed a theology and exegesis of women's spiritual equality. They advocated women's rights both to preach and evangelize and to participate in church administration. The Quakers preserved and developed the emancipatory trends of dissenting Puritanism. Not surprisingly, they were drawn into confrontation with the Puritan authorities in Massachusetts, who were engaged in repressing these emancipatory trends in their own Christian social order. The sufferings of Quaker women in this struggle with Puritan theocracy forms a heroic chapter of early Quakerism in America.

Among the German Pietist sects, the Ephrata community of Pennsylvania and the Moravian Brethren were two notable types. In both, women had a fixed and settled place. The forthright confrontation with religious authority found in the Puritan and Quaker context finds no echo among these German groups. Yet, the German sects also extended a large sphere to women's religious and administrative abilities through their communal social order. We also find in these sects experimentation with the doctrines of God and anthropology that had its roots in the Christian mystical and gnostic traditions. God was believed to have a feminine as well as a masculine side, and celibacy was seen as restoring androgynous wholeness to fallen humanity, according to the founder of the Ephrata community, Conrad Beissel (in turn, dependent on the German mystical writer, Jacob Boehme).

A similar theology was also held by the Anglo-American Shakers, who were led to the American shores by Mother Ann Lee in 1786. For the Shakers, too, God was androgynous. They took this idea a step farther by arguing that there must be a female as well as a male Messiah to represent redeemed humanity and the dual aspects of God. The American Revolution offered a scene of social conflict in which radically new religious voices were heard. Among them was the New England preacher, Jemima Wilkinson, who, after her "resurrection" experience, styled herself the "Universal Public Friend" and claimed messianic authority to preach God's final word of redemption in the "last days."

These Anglo-American women of radical sectarian groups shows us the emancipatory hopes released by the English Reformation and renewed again during the American Revolution. In contrast to established patriarchal theory, which continued to be espoused by established forms of Protestantism, these groups suggested that women might claim equal spiritual authority and even become the chosen instruments of God to preach salvation and found churches of the new millennial order. The chapter on utopian and sectarian women was coauthored by Rosemary Radford Ruether, Georgia Harkness Professor of Applied Theology at

Garrett-Evangelical Theological Seminary and the Graduate Council with Northwestern University, and Catherine Prelinger, editor of the Franklin Papers, Yale University. Ruether gathered the material on the English sectarian groups, and Prelinger both researched and translated the material on the German groups.

The evangelical revival that swept the American churches in the eighteenth century revived some of the emancipatory potential of radical Christianity that was found earlier among the antinomian Puritans and the Quakers. Revivalism also bypassed established ecclesiastical authority by stressing direct personal experience of God's redeeming grace. In this drama of repentance and conversion, social distinctions melted away. Women, unequal in society, were spiritually equal before God as repentant sinners and as recipients of divine grace. Rosemary Skinner Keller edited the Wesleyan material of this chapter, while Martha Blauvelt, Professor of History at St. Benedict College in St. Joseph, Minnesota, developed the material on the evangelical traditions that flowed from Puritanism.

In these documents on the evangelical and revival movements in American Christianity, we see accentuated the trend that was beginning in late seventeenth-century and early eighteenth-century Puritan preaching. The religious image of women was shifting from the late medieval emphasis on women's "carnality" and dangerous propensities to witchcraft to an increasing stress on woman's spiritual and moral superiority. Woman came to be seen as the more naturally religious gender, who must take the primary responsibility in the home for evangelizing her children and uplifting her husband from the secular and impious influences of the world. A new symbolism was beginning to attach itself to the growing separation between women's sphere in the home and the male public world. The home and the female sphere became the place of religion, while the world became the realm of nonreligion.

This growing stress on woman's moral superiority, her greater religiosity, and her role as domestic evangelist created mixed messages for women in the evangelical movements. Woman was, at once, man's spiritual equal and, in some ways, his superior and yet his social subordinate. This created conflicting directions for woman's role in the church. On the one hand, woman's piety was still seen as directing her voluntarily to accept her subordination in the church and in society. On the other hand, the stress on her religiousness and evangelizing mission tended to break these limits and to direct her ministry into a widening sphere that led her away from the family circle into prayer circles of friends and finally to organize and even preach at revival meetings. Early Methodism, particularly, gave these mixed messages of the evangelical movement to women and gives us intimations of those evangelical women of the Wesleyan tradition who, in nineteenth-century America, would increasingly claim the right to preach.

The documentary history ends with a chapter on women and civil religion in the American Revolution. Here we see the rationalist traditions of the Enlightenment mingled with evangelical fervor to suggest an image of the American nation as a divinely appointed instrument of political emancipation. As "Daughters of Liberty" who aided the American army with their sewing bees and fund-raising, women were enthusiastic supporters of the revolutionary struggle. Yet, again, as in the Reformation, the ideology of equality, shaped by men in their conflicts with established authority, was not intended to be extended to women and other dependent persons. White, propertied males were the subjects of that "equality of human nature," from which, according to the Declaration of Independence, there flows equal civil rights. The pleas of Abigail Adams to her husband, John Adams, at the Constitutional Convention, to "remember the ladies" went unheeded. Thus, both evangelical revival and revolutionary liberalism planted seeds whose promise for women would not bear fruit for another century.

The period between the Reformation and the American Revolution thus illustrates the conflicting possibilities for women fostered by these movements of religious renewal and social reorganization. Women enthusiastically responded to and participated in the renewal movements, helped to evangelize Indians, and to settle a new continent. But the emancipatory messages of these movements were contradicted by growing restrictions on the actual social mobility and economic roles of women from a sixteenth-century feudal, peasant, and merchant society into nineteenth-century industrialization. Women's role in the home would become more restrictive. Women would lose some of the power and skills they had had as feudal noble women, peasant manufacturers, and merchant entrepreneurs. Instead, they would be directed to narrower and more intensive roles as wives and mothers in the home. Religious piety would, at once, exalt women's piety and seek to restrict it to this shrinking world. The evangelical mandate to women to evangelize and the liberal ideology of human rights only hinted in the late eighteenth century at a rebellion of women against this diminishing sphere, which would be led by the female heirs of these movements in nineteenth-century America.

American Indian Women and Religion

JACQUELINE PETERSON
AND MARY DRUKE

INTRODUCTION

By 1800, a sizeable percentage of the estimated nine million American Indian men, women, and children who had originally inhabited what was to become the continental United States had felt the impact of the European invasion. Along the eastern seaboard, the Gulf coast, and in California, many of these peoples had ceased to exist as communities or tribal entities—devastated by epidemic diseases, wars of conquest, enslavement, and forced dispersal. Those who survived, and their descendants, had endured familiar, if not friendly, relations with the carriers of a Christian European culture and mentality since the mid-sixteenth century, when France and Spain secured tentative outposts in Florida, the Carolinas, and the desert Southwest. Such contact generated an enormous literature among the colonizing nations. Throughout the seventeenth and eighteenth centuries, explorers, travelers, military leaders, colonial administrators, and settlers, as well as a small army of zealous Catholic and Protestant missionaries—nearly all of them male—penned their impressions of North America's original peoples.[1]

These accounts, in the absence of a comparable literature written by the American Indian people themselves, constitute one of the few narrow windows through which we can view and understand the early religious beliefs and practices of native women. North American indigenous societies effectively utilized oral communication and, in some cases, mnemonic pictographs[2] to record and transmit sacred traditions, but not until their contact with Christian missionaries did they perceive alphabets and writing as necessary inventions. During the seventeenth and eighteenth centuries, the number of Indian people, particularly women, who chose to employ this mode of communication was small. Thus, while the following collection of documents presents a primary "first-hand" view, that view is, with a single exception (Document 19), from the vantage point of the outsider.

The stranger as observer was not always unsympathetic. In fact, many Europeans, who, despite their national and religious squabbles, shared a common cultural and intellectual tradition, were fascinated by North American Indian peoples. Yet, they were clearly unprepared for and bewildered by the more than four hundred geographically distinct and culturally unique bands, tribes, and confederacies. While their accounts reveal that they paid considerable attention to native lifeways and traditions, the narratives are nonetheless confused, given to fanciful illusion and distortion, and are marked, nearly always, by ethnocentric bias. Not surprisingly, sexual bias is also deeply imbedded in the early accounts. While male writers paid some slight heed to the sexual division of labor and to native women's economic roles and physical appearance, the lives of these women, both their individual and their collective concerns and activities, haunt only the shadows of the written record, to be glimpsed largely through inference and careful sifting.

What does come as a surprise is the relative lack of informed understanding garnered by Christians during these two hundred years about Native American beliefs and practices in the realm of what the western Europeans termed "religion."[3] Disinterest undoubtedly accounted for part of this neglect. Yet more potent explanations might be explored. By the lights of Christian believers in "the one true faith," the indigenous Americans were regarded first as heathens (lacking knowledge of "the Word") and later, when they rejected the Christian message, as pagans or infidels. Thus, while an occasional observer was impressed by the sophistication of native philosophy, cosmology, and medicine (Document 1), more typically Europeans groped for parallels with Christian sacred meanings (Document 2), ridiculed mere "superstitions," deplored "devil worship," or concluded that native peoples had no religion at all.

The intellectual baggage of the seventeenth- and eighteenth-century Europeans did not include notions about cultural relativity, and even the most inquisitive Europeans, impeded by the language barrier, failed to grasp the complexities and subtleties of Indian philosophy and ritual practice. Moreover, Indian religions often encompassed many areas of life, such as healing and political ritual, seldom associated in precisely the same way with Judeo-Christian concepts of the religious sphere. Rarely did missionaries and travelers encounter what seemed *to them* the denominators of a true religious system: a fixed and permanent place of worship (church or temple) adorned by permanent sacred objects; a priesthood; organized cults; a written liturgy or holy book; regularized forms of mass worship, penance, and prayer; or a religious calendar. Even when they did confront such aspects, especially among the sedentary horticulturists and townspeople of the Southeast and Southwest, they saw through a glass darkly.

Admittedly, they received little help. Spiritual formulators and sacred leaders of American Indian societies quickly recognized the threat posed by Christianity and its attendant culture and ranked themselves among the earliest and most ardent opponents. Much of what has been termed "religion" in Indian North America was shrouded in secrecy after European contact, and those men and women who would have been the most able instructors were the least likely to share their sacred knowledge and, with it, their power.

ALL THE WORLD WAS SACRED: TRADITIONAL BELIEFS AND PRACTICES

Despite these many limitations, reference to a rich corpus of surviving native oral tradition allows for partial reconstruction and a few tentative generalizations about the nature of native religions and the relationship of American Indian women to them. As suggested earlier, American Indian religious thought and practice did not occupy a clearly bounded "separate sphere" of "sacred" activity whose limits were easily identifiable to outsiders. Instead, for many seventeeth- and eighteenth-century American Indian societies, all the world was both sacred and alive or, at the very least, potentially sacred—that is, capable of being infused with power and vital influence in ways mysterious and unpredictable to human beings, worthy of awe and fear.

Similarly, the descriptive categories imposed by western scholars, such as animism, animatism, and totemism, have increasingly proved less useful as cultural differences in cognitive perception are recognized. What does seem clear, however, is that all Indian societies were profoundly reverential in their attitudes toward the world around them. Some had fully developed spiritual cosmogonies; all possessed sacred traditions, ceremonies, and rituals, many of them marvelously elaborate. Moreover, in nearly all of these aspects, women figured prominently. In fact, it would appear that American Indian women enjoyed greater opportunity for independent religious thought and ceremonial participation than did their American and European counterparts until at least the mid-nineteenth century.

The mental picture of the cosmos conceived by many North American Indian societies was composed of two or, more often, three layers: an astral heaven or sky, an earthly plane, and an underworld. Unifying the layers of the cosmos in both time and space was a sacred pillar or tree of life, its roots stretching deep into the underworld and its branches holding up the sky dome. The symbolic representation of cosmic unity appeared often in indigenous North America in a ceremonial context as a sacred pole. In its two-dimensional form, long before Christianity made its appearance on the continent, the symbol of the universe was written by native peoples as a cross, a cross within a circle, or simply as a circle which encompassed the four cardinal points or direction.[4]

In the beginning, the original inhabitants believed, there had been only a void, a sky world, or a primal sea. In some sacred traditions, a Creator, usually associated with the astral world, especially the sun, and usually, although not always, represented as male rather than female, thought or spoke the middle world into existence. But, more often, a sky person mated with a woman who fell from the sky and who, as Earth Mother or Grandmother, brought forth the various life forms. The earth itself emerged from the underworld, sprang from the body of the Creator or Earth Mother, or was gathered from the sea by an Earth Diver and built upon the back of a turtle (Document 3). The tasks of resolving opposition in the world and instructing the original human beings in how to live was undertaken by the Earth Mother's twin sons (in the Iroquois tradition) or by an other-than-human person—a Trickster or culture hero.[5]

Cosmological traditions varied widely in Indian North America, but common to many Indian societies was the belief in a creative force associated with the awesome powers of nature and the sky. Speculation about the creation and supplications addressed directly to the Creator usually appear to have been reserved for a small number of religious philosophers and practitioners who, through heredity, training, or intellectual bent, had acquired the necessary esoteric knowledge and leisure time to ponder origins and forces beyond the realm of human understanding. The religious formulators of seventeenth- and eighteenth-century Indian North America may have included a number of women.[6]

More pervasive, and more directly related to the daily concerns of native men and women, was the belief that after the creation the Earth Maker distributed or diffused his or her power so that all of life—heaven, earth, and the underworld—were imbued with the potential of that spiritual genius (Document 4). Thus, the Siouan term *wakan* or the Algonquian term *manitou* might refer to the Creator, but it also referred to the wonderful power released by the creation, which might be observed in the drenching storms caused by the Thunderbirds, in the successful prophecies of a priest or shaman, in a curative plant, or in a stone that moved.[7]

Common as well are traditions about the mating of sky with earth and the association of vegetal productivity with Earth Mother's body. For farming peoples especially, the holy triad—corn, beans, and squash—was often believed to have sprung from the first earth woman's body, and much ritual centered around her. Not surprisingly, Earth Mother's power was sometimes linked with the moon, since lunar calculations figured importantly in the planting, gathering, and harvesting of food crops and because women's mysterious flow of life substance occurred at monthly intervals (at "moon time").[8]

Even among hunting peoples, who tended to reckon the most influential sacred force as male and to regard menstruating women as harmful to the hunt, success in the food quest might be linked to a woman. According to Father Hennepin (Document 4), at least one informant (whose tribal affiliation is, unfortunately, unclear) portrayed the Keeper of the Game as female. This supernatural Keeper was most likely cast in the image of a menopausal woman, a status virtually required of female shamans associated with the hunting of animals. Hunters, their wives, and their families felt an intimate kinship with the animal world. In primordial time, animals spoke and thought as humans, and it was believed that their souls might still be offended if the proper ritual prayers, offerings, and respects were not made before taking or preparing game for food. Hunting peoples depended upon animals for survival. It was a blessing that the animals gave themselves to their human brothers and sisters. But the spiritual Keeper or keepers of various species beheld human conduct. When respect for animal relatives was forgotten or withheld, the Keeper might retaliate by withdrawing game animals or by inflicting disease.[9]

The separate but complementary roles of native men and women in securing and preparing subsistence were evident in religious practice as well as in sacred traditions. For those American Indian groups dependent upon horticulture or the gathering of wild fruits and vegetables—tasks ordinarily allocated to women—an annual calendar of rituals and ceremonies keyed to planting, ripening, and harvesting was observed. William Bartram (Document 5) witnessed one of the more widely practiced ceremonies of this type: the firstfruits, Green Corn Ceremony, or, as it was known among Muskhogean tribes of the Southeast, the Buskito or Busk.

Annual ceremonies of renewal and thanksgiving were celebrated throughout Indian North America and, among hunting peoples, were most often associated with astral phenomena such as the summer and winter solstices. The sequence and content of such ceremonies, some of them ritual dramas, and the roles and responsibilities of women within them, varied enormously. At base, however, all were designed to restore balance, both within the community and with the powers of the cosmos, and to ensure the well-being of the group—its harmony, fertility, abundance, long life, and freedom from disease. Although women might be physically separated from men and even barred from observing portions of these ceremonies, they did fast, purify themselves and their household domains, join in sacred songs and dances, and prepare the celebration feast that almost always followed a sacred ceremony. In some instances—for example, among matrilineal horticulturists, where women were highly esteemed, and in communities where female artisan sodalities fashioned sacred objects from wampum, quill, or, later, beads—women owned and conducted religious rituals, exclusive of men.[10]

Whether sex-specific or communitywide affairs, these calendrical ceremonies and ritual dramas were repetitive and surrounded with elaborate and sometimes highly esoteric paraphernalia and symbolism. They had to be learned, often through many years of training under a ritual specialist or priest, usually a family or clan elder. Rarely did such elders unite to form a priesthood that transmitted a uniform body of sacred knowledge. Rather, American Indian religious celebrations tended to reflect the reciprocal responsibilities of the various components of society, whether these components were families, clans, age- or sex-based groups, or classes. Each group might own a unique set of sacred symbols and ceremonial roles and, through a hereditary religious leadership, instruct its youthful members, both male and female, in their secret meanings. While seventeenth- and eighteenth-century Europeans almost universally described such priestly instructors as male, we can probably assume that women learned their ceremonial roles and spiritual attitudes from elder female relatives.

Group ceremonialism reinforced and strengthened the bonds of the community to the otherworldly powers upon which it was dependent; but sacred knowledge and blessings could also be sought through other means. Even socially stratified tribes or confederacies, such as the Timucuans of seventheeth-century Florida, whose calendrical observances and priestly prerogatives were not easily suppressed by Franciscan missionaries, shared a belief in the individual's ability to acquire spiritual aid and power through visions and dreams. Most European observers noted the importance of dreams and visions in American Indian religious practice. Indeed, the individual quest for spiritual understanding, protection, and power through waking or sleeping visions probably was the single most common attribute of North American Indian religions.[11]

Visions instructed. They brought men and women face to face with the Sacred in its many appearances, but usually embodied by a known other-than-human entity, such as an eagle, a bear, or a medicinal plant. In many groups, visions inspired the sympathy or pity of a "guardian spirit," which shared its particular powers and attributes with the human supplicant and which instructed him or her to prophesy, to cure illness and disease, to divine the source of game (Document 7), social stress, tribal enemies (Document 6), or the heart's desire. The intensity of this relationship between a spiritual protector and teacher and a human brother or sister was reflected and memorialized by personal emblems, such as tattoos and medicine bags, and by personal offerings and public feasts.

Members of hunting societies, especially, paid keen attention to the content and meaning of dreams, and they fasted for visions just as other societies sought priestly counsel as a means of knowledge and succor in times of crisis. In general, however, the first and most important vision quest, often intertwined with the search for a "guardian spirit," coincided with adolescence and/or puberty. At this juncture of the life cycle, boys and girls were encouraged to black their faces and fast and isolate themselves in order to moderate the forces that might otherwise buffet, manipulate, or destroy them, by acquiring the blessings of a spiritual ally. For males, success was critical. Unless they acquired spiritual resources and grew in power, men would fail as hunters and warriors; they would be denied wealth and respect; they would not be able to fend off disease and death.

For women, the vision quest was a natural outgrowth of the fasting and seclusion that accompanied their first menses. Since menstruating women radiated so much power as to be avoided by all, except other menstruating women or menopausal women, we might assume that something akin to "religious contemplation" was at least a monthly event. Among American Indian societies where women lived in extended households, and where menstrual cycles are believed to have occurred simultaneously, the periodic retreats to a menstrual lodge may have represented a communal growing in power and a sharing of womanly knowledge.[12]

Claude Dablon was nonetheless surprised to discover that both young Ottawa men and women were encouraged to seek spiritual aid through prolonged fasting and isolation (Document 8). Indian women, it was commonly believed by outsiders, neither concerned themselves with manly pursuits nor needed the strong spiritual guardians sought by men. Denis Raudot's rendition of Dablon's description implied that women, when dreaming, sought "weaker spirits," for love medicine or assistance in affairs of the heart and home. It is true that women were primarily occupied with mastering the household arts, with easy childbirth, and with rearing healthy children who would support them in old age. Yet, the dreams and visions of Net-no-kwa (Document 7), herself a skilled hunter, trader, and leader, and of the young Illinois woman (Document 6) might suggest the contrary. The dream recalled by Oshahgushkodanaqua (Mrs. Susan Johnston) indicates that some women of forceful personality, perhaps the eldest females or the daughters of respected leaders, sought and received blessings from spiritual allies that catapulted them into a larger domain (Document 9). As the wife of a senior trader and the daughter and granddaughter of influential chiefs, Oshahgushkodanaqua gained prominence among both the Lake Superior Ojibwa and the fur-trading community. She was sought out and esteemed for her guidance, wisdom, and generosity.[13]

The powers women acquired through dreams and visions, as well as those granted to them by their guardian spirits, were employed in various contexts. American Indian societies generally did not draw rigid distinctions between religion and medicine, so that female herbalists, midwives, and doctors practicing psychosomatic medicine were regarded as religious specialists, along with those termed shamans, whose powers included prophecy and spirit possession. Since illness and disease were traceable to supernatural causes, the ability to cure was a demonstration of sacred skills (Document 10).

Native doctors and shamans often formed associations and "medicine societies" into which new members were initiated through payment, training, and the demonstration of spiritual abilities (Document 11). Such societies illustrate the pragmatic bent of North American Indian peoples. European observers missed the point when they ridiculed powwows and medicine men and women for their fantastic pyrotechnic displays, shaking tents, sleight of hand, and shooting-and-life-renewal ceremonies (Document 10). These were *demonstrations* of sacred power, but they were not the ultimate demonstration, which was in the successful cure, the true prophecy, or an old age free of disease. The demand for visible proofs from native religious leaders undoubtedly rid American Indian societies of charlatans, but it opened the door to other, alien demonstrations of sacred power from Christianity's representatives.

INDIAN WOMEN AND CHRISTIANITY

The first Europeans that North American Indian peoples encountered were rarely men or women of the cloth intent upon saving heathen souls. Rather, the Indians' first contacts were with fishermen, traders, travelers, and slavers, whose materialistic aims superseded religious concerns. Nonetheless, native peoples quickly noted that these Europeans had been blessed by certain powers—manifested in wonderful objects whose source was mysterious, such as metal weapons, tools, and vessels, and ornamental glass beads, rosaries, gold rings, and mirrors. Among some American Indian peoples, especially in the Northeast, the objects themselves were initially perceived as the repositories of sacred power, and their ownership was valued for the power that was thus transferred to humans.[14]

The arrival of Catholic priests and nuns and Protestant missionaries gave American Indian peoples an opportunity to learn about and thus to tap the source of Europeans' apparent power. Generally, however, their impressions of European religious spokesmen were guarded.[15] These were strange religious leaders indeed: some, like the Franciscans, humbled themselves, eschewed outward symbols of influence, were willing to act like slaves and to do women's work, and did not marry. However, insofar as they were able to demonstrate that they owned medicine, to cure, to prophesy, and to produce miraculous occurrences through visions and prayers, they were a force to be reckoned with and, possibly, to be followed.

It is in this sense that Christian missionaries posed a vital threat to traditional American Indian leaders. Initially, however, native intellectuals and wise men and women proved more than capable of countering the claims of superiority advanced by Christian missionaries (Document 12). Older American Indian women, especially, spoke from experience and knowledge in defense of traditional beliefs and practices, even when they had integrated the sacred power objects of Europeans, such as rosary beads, into their religious repertoire (Document 13).

Missionaries, nonetheless, appear to have made many of their earliest gains among the female sex, notably children, adolescents, and women in their childbearing years. At least among semisedentary, horticultural town dwellers and those peoples who practiced a mixed economy, women and children were the likeliest subjects of missionary interest, since the subsistence activities of adult males often took them on extended hunting expeditions. A captive audience was not tantamount to wholesale conversion, however. The initial inability of missionaries and potential converts to converse in more than a rudimentary fashion and to translate their religious beliefs into each other's language suggests that Christian inroads were often superficial.

It seems likely that American Indian peoples responded most positively to Christianity when a convergence of religious symbolism or ceremony revealed itself. We have already noted that certain European power objects, both religious (such as rosaries) and secular (such as playing cards) could add to the store of sacred paraphernalia revered by American Indian peoples without disrupting traditional beliefs. Native religious leaders reinterpreted and breathed new meanings into alien objects, treating them as ritual enhancements and enrichments rather than as heralds of change or decay. Even where American Indian women and men actively requested baptism, they often expressed their belief in the power of Christianity in culturally specific terms. The California woman who based her request on the conviction that the Franciscans could fly, for example, did so in great seriousness. Among southern California coastal peoples, the sacred powers of male and female shamans came from visions induced by drinking toloache (*Datura meteloides*). One of the characteristics of this hallucinogenic experience was the ability, or seeming ability, to fly (Document 14).[16]

Similarly, the Mansa women of northern New Mexico miraculously approached the Christian cross as if it had the power to cure or bring blessings (Document 15). But were they responding to a Christian symbol or was Fray Benevides's reception warmed by the planting of a familiar sacred pole, a tree of life? And when southern California women brought gifts of seeds and milk and offered their breasts to paintings of the Virgin and Child shown them by the Franciscan missionaries, were they responding to the image with Christian devotion, or were they experiencing it as a powerful image of maternal fertility?[17]

The significance of food—both prayers for and offering of—in the religious observances of American Indian peoples has already been suggested. Much ceremonial activity and vision questing was devoted to appeals for rain, abundant harvest, successful hunting, and freedom from pestilence and disease. Similarly, traditions concerning an afterlife usually included a description of a world where all of these requests were granted. Thus, when the prayers of Christian converts or missionaries were successful in achieving desired results, Christianity could convince nonbelievers, as demonstrated by the influence a group of Iroquois women exerted over their non-Christian Algonquian hunter husbands (Document 16).

On the other hand, the female converts of the lower Mississippi Valley described by Hennepin (Document 17) were incredulous when they discovered that the Christian conception of heaven did not include food or material comforts. It was sad enough that Christian baptism sent Indian women to a French heaven, without family or friends. But when the hope for greater abundance in a non-Indian afterlife was removed, baptism lost its meaning and appeal.

The initial tendency of North American Indian peoples to graft selective aspects of Christianity onto their own religious traditions was widespread and, in fact, continues today. However, many Indian men and women exhibited a far greater willingness than European Christians to attempt to penetrate the mysteries of an alien religion. A number of seventeenth- and eighteenth-century American Indian women turned to Christianity with a fervor and intellectual intensity so convincing as to astound Euro-American missionaries and lay observers. Some of these women achieved a modest renown, and one, Catherine Tekakwitha, is treated in Chapter 3 of this book. All shared in common an active quest for Christian understanding and grace—whether through a rigorous education under a priest, minister, or nun, through self-mortification, fasting, and prayer that culminated in a conversion experience akin, perhaps, to the quest for a "guardian spirit," through vows of chastity, through good works, through persistent efforts to convert family and friends, or through a combination or all of the above. The intelligence of female converts is revealed in Experience Mayhew's life history of Jerusha Ompan (Document 18). However, the full force of the intense soul-searching and questioning that was characteristic of the young women who attempted to live as Christian Indians is most clearly brought home by the letter penned by a Narragansett student at Eleazar Wheelock's mission school in Lebanon, Connecticut (Document 19).

As Indians became more familiar with Christian religious ideology, they also became capable of confronting the whites with their failure to practice their own religious precepts. This is illustrated in a story of Indian women who requested the right to speak at the Council of the Six Nations with the American government in western New York (1794). In response to an earlier visit by a woman preacher, Jemima Wilkinson, to the council, in which she had called upon the Indians to repent of their sins, the Indian women called upon the whites to repent of their much more grievous sins in oppressing the Indians and depriving them of their lands (Document 20).

In the dialogue between two Oneida matrons, one a devout Christian and the other, her cousin, a traditional believer, we see the degree to which seventeenth- and eighteenth-century Indian communities could accommodate, as they do today, traditional religious expressions and practices, Christianity, and a combination of beliefs drawn from many quarters, held by men and women living side by side (Document 21).

Indian women sowing seeds in coastal Florida in corn ritual. [Drawing by Jacques Le Moyne (1564), a member of the Huguenot expedition, first published by Theodor de Bry, *America,* Part II, 1591. Reprint, from *A Concise History of the American People* (Oxford University Press: 1977), p. 4.]

Several persons who embrace virginity and chastity. Sketch by Père Claude Chauchetière, from his manuscript annual report of the mission of Sault St. Louis (Caughnawaga), dated 1686. [Courtesy of Archives Departmentales de la Gironde, Series H, Jesuites, Bordeaux, France.]

A woman, probably Minnesota Ojibwa, secluded in her "Menstrual Lodge," some distance from her family's bark-covered lodge. [A watercolor painted by Seth Eastman. Courtesy of the James Jerome Hill Reference Library, St. Paul, Minnesota.]

Oshagushkodanaqua (Susan Johnston), daughter of the Lake Superior Ojibwa leader Waubojeeg, and wife of trader John Johnston. [Portrait in oil attributed to Charles Bird King. Courtesy of Buffalo and Erie County Historical Society, Buffalo, New York.]

Women and men dancing and singing at a great feast of North Carolina Algonquian-speaking Indians. Three virgins, dancing and embracing one another, are depicted in the center of this watercolor by John White (1585). [Courtesy of Manuscripts, British Library, London, England.]

March of the Towisas or Sisters of the Three Sisters. The Towisas is a Seneca Iroquois Indian society of women who offer thanks to the spirits of the Three Sisters (Corn, Bean, Squash). [Sketch by Seneca, Jesse Cornplanter (1905). Courtesy of Manuscripts, New York State Library, Albany, New York.]

A sketch of an Indian baptism, probably in Bethlehem, Pennsylvania, showing Indian women on one side of the congregation and Indian men on the other. [Courtesy of the *North American Moravian,* Bethlehem, Pennsylvania.]

Documents: American Indian Women and Religion

---

1. *Indian Cosmology and Culture*
2. *The Separation of Men and Women in Indian Ritual*
3. *The Female as Creator in Indian Religion*
4. *The Mistress of all Animals*
5. *Women's Roles in the Green Corn Ritual*
6. *The First Dream Vision of a Female Adolescent*
7. *The Bear Vision of an Indian Mother*
8. *Women, Too, Enter the Quest for the Personal Guardian Spirit*
9. *The Vision Quest of an Indian Woman*
10. *The Female as Creator and Healer Among the Algonquins*
11. *A Demonstration of Power by Medicine Men and Women*
12. *The Old Ones Defend the Indian Ancestral Traditions*
13. *A Contest Between a Missionary and a Medicine Woman*
14. *An Indian Woman Seeks Baptism*
15. *The Christian Cross Worshipped as the Tree of Life*
16. *The Successful Hunt and the Prayers of Indian Christian Wives*
17. *The Christian Heaven, a Lean and Lonely Place for Indians*
18. *The Fervent Piety of an Indian Woman Convert*
19. *The Anxious Doubts of an Indian Woman in a Mission School*
20. *Indian Women Exhort the Whites to Repent of Their Sins*
21. *Mother-right and Christian Baptism Among the Oneidas*

Document 1: Indian Cosmology and Culture

John Lederer, a German explorer and traveler, arrived in Virginia in the 1660s and, in 1669 and 1670, made three trips into the Piedmont region of Virginia and the Carolinas. In his account of his travels, Lederer described and gave his impressions of many aspects of the culture of Indians (Algonquian, Iroquoian, Souian, and Uchean speakers) who inhabited the region. Although, at times, he romanticized and, in some cases, even gave incorrect information, his report is generally a valuable record of Indian life. The account of beliefs included here pertains to Souian speakers. It indicates a link, related to women, between cosmology and social organization, and it expresses Lederer's respect for the people whose beliefs are described.[18]

They worship one God, Creator of all things, whom some call Okaec, others Mannith: to him alone the high priest (or *Periku,*) offers sacrifice; and yet they believe he has no regard to sublunary affairs, but commits the government of mankinde to lesser deities (as *Quiacosough* and *Tagkanysough*), that is, good and evil spirits: to these the inferiour priests pay their devotion and sacrifice, at which they make recitals, to a lamentable tune, of the great things done by their ancestors.

From four women (viz. Pash, Sepoy, Askarin, and Maraskarin) they derive the race of mankinde; which they therefore divide into four tribes, distinguished under those several names. They very religiously observe the degrees of marriage, which they limit not to distance of kindred, but difference of tribes, which are continued in the issue of the females: now for two of the same tribe to match, is abhorred as incest, and punished with great severity.

Their places of burial they divide into four quarters, assigning to every tribe one: for, to mingle their bodies, even when dead, they hold wicked and ominous. They commonly wrap up the corpse in beasts skins, and bury with it provision and householdstuff for its use in the other world. When their great men die, they likewise slay prisoners of war to attend them. They believe the transmigration of souls: for the angry they say is possest with the spirit of a serpent; the bloody with that of a wolf; the timorous, of a deer; the faithful, of a dog, etc., and therefore they are figured by these emlemes.

Elizium, or the abode of their lesser deities, they place beyond the mountains and Indian Ocean.

Though they want those means of improving human reason, which the use of letters affords us; let us not therefore conclude them wholly destitute of learning and sciences: for by these little helps which they have found, many of them advance their natural understandings to great knowledge in physicks, rhetorick and policie of government. . . . (Three ways they supply their want of letters: first by counters, secondly by emblemes or hieroglyphics, thirdly by tradition delivered in long tales from father to son, which being children they are made to learn by rote.) . . . I have been present at several of their consultations and debates, and to my admiration have heard some of their seniors deliver themselves with as much judgment and eloquence as I should have expected from men of civil education and literature.

Document 2: The Separation of Men and Women in Indian Ritual

The separation of men and women in ritual was common among North American Indians. Dr. Francis Le Jau, a missionary for the Society for the Propagation of the Gospel, stationed at South Carolina Parish of St. James's Goose Creek, observed this among Muskhogean-speaking people (Lower Creek or Apalachi) and sought to know the reasons for it. The parallels with Christianity in the explanation that he was given should not be accepted without skepticism. Although it cannot be said that there are no parallels between Christianity and American Indian religions, often those noted either represent over-zealousness on the part of missionaries to find parallels (so that, as a consequence, meaning is distorted) or indicate previous familiarity of particular Indians with Christianity. It is likely that the person from whom Le Jau obtained his information had had contacts with Roman Catholic missionaries. Within many North American Indian cultures, ritual separation of men and women relates to distinct realms of power and expertise that distinguish between men and women in these cultures.[19]

I see Our free Indians, and several come to see me, when they fix their Abode near me, for they are perpetually changing places to get food, having no provisions laid up. Could we make them capable to understand what is meant by Words commonly used by us when we speak of Religion, we would find them others than We imagine; or could we understand their meaning; As they grow acquainted and familiar and can trust to one, they disclose surprising things. . . . Three Weeks ago my Indian Neighbours that live upon and near our Glebe Land had a dance which they keep Yearly from time immemorial for three days together, in the day time the Men dance by themselves, the Women for that time are absent and never come near till the three days are over; but those Women keep their dance among themselves by Night. As I asked one of the Men the reason of that Separation, he told me 'twas to remember a time wherein Man was made alone and there was no Woman; but after, God took somewhat out of Man and made the Woman; asking what it was God took; the Man put his hand upon his breast and somewhat there, and then called it a Bone: My Wife presently named a Rib, the Indian smiled and said Yes.

In a letter of a later date, Le Jau wrote about the same subject.

. . . my Indian Neighbours have surprising notions; I discovered with one that is very free with us about a dance they lately had, wherein the Women were absent, he told me 'twas because Man was a time without Woman and God took something out of Man to make Woman; during that Festival which returns yearly with many others, the Women eat nothing all day and are hid.

Document 3: The Female as Creator in Indian Religion

Father Louis Hennepin, a Recollect missionary, basing his writing on his travels in New France in 1679–1680, provides an example of the roles of women in American Indian origin accounts. The Iroquoian account described here depicts the world as being created on a turtle's back—a belief found in Southeast Asia as well as in North America.[20]

A rather curious story is related among them. They say that a woman descended from heaven and remained sometime fluttering in the air, unable to find a spot to rest her foot. The fish of the sea having taken compassion on her, held a council to deliberate which of them should receive her; the Tortoise presented himself and offered his back above the water. This woman came to rest and make her abode there. The unclean matter of the sea having gathered around this tortoise, a great extent of land was formed in time, which now constitutes America. But as solitude did not at all please this woman, who grew weary of having no one to converse with, in order to spend her days a little more agreeably than she was doing, a spirit descended from on high, who found her asleep from sorrow. He approached her imperceptibly, and begot by her two sons, who came out of her side. These two children could never, as time went on, agree, because one was a better hunter than the other, every day they had some quarrel with each other, and they came to such a pitch that they could not at all bear one another; especially one who was of an extremely fierce temper, conceived a deadly envy of his brother, whose disposition was completely mild. This one unable to endure the ill treatment which he continually received, was at last obliged to depart from him and retire to heaven, whence as a mark of his just resentment he from time to time makes the thunder roar over the head of his unhappy brother. Sometime after the spirit descended again to this woman and had by her a daughter, from whom have come the mighty nation which now occupies one of the largest parts of the world. There are some other circumstances, which I do not remember, but fabulous as this story is, you can not fail to discern in it some truths. The woman's sleep has some analogy with that of Adam; the estrangement of the two brothers bears some resemblance to the irreconcilable hatred which Cain had for Abel, and the thunder pealing from heaven, shows us very clearly the curse which God pronounced upon that merciless fratricide.

Document 4: The Mistress of All Animals

Although Hennepin rarely identified the tribal source of much of the information he gathered, the beliefs described here probably were those of Algonquian speakers from eastern Canada or the northern Great Lakes region, whose primary subsistence activity was hunting. Note the emphasis upon dreams and visions, the generalized belief in sacred power, and the personal emblems representative of a relationship with a guardian spirit.[21]

They recognize some sort of genius in all things. They all believe in a Master of Life, but apply the idea differently. Some have a crow which they always carry with them, and which they say is the master of their life. Some an owl, others a bone, a sea shell or some thing else of the kind. When they hear an owl hoot, they tremble and draw sinister omens from it. They put faith in dreams; they go into their vapor baths in order to obtain fair weather to take beaver, to kill animals in the hunt. They do not give beaver or otter bones to the dogs. I asked the reason; they answered me that there was a spirit in the wood which would tell the beavers and otters, and that after that they would take no more. I asked them what a spirit of this kind was. They replied that she was a woman who knew every thing, and was the mistress of all hunting. It must always be remarked that as I have said, most do not believe all this.

Document 5: Women's Roles in the Green Corn Ritual

The distinction and complementarity of men and women in ritual may be seen in the following description of the Busk, or Green Corn ritual, among the Creek in southeastern North America. William Bartram traveled in North and South Carolina, Georgia, and eastern and western Florida during 1765 and 1766.[22]

When a town celebrates the busk, having previously provided themselves with new cloaths, new pots, pans, and other household utensils and furniture, they collect all their worn-out cloaths and other despicable things, sweep and cleanse their houses, squares, and the whole town, of their filth, which with all the remaining grain and other old provisions, they cast together into one common heap, and consume it with fire. After having taken medicine, and fasted for three days, all the fire in the town is extinguished. During this fast they abstain from the gratification of every appetite and passion whatever. A general amnesty is proclaimed, all malefactors may return to their town, and they are absolved from their crimes, which are now forgotten, and they restored to favour.

On the fourth morning, the high priest, by rubbing wood together, produces new fire in the public square from whence every habitation in the town is supplied with the new and pure flame.

Then the women go forth to the harvest field, and bring from thence new corn and fruits, which being prepared in the best manner, in various dishes, and drink withal, is brought with solemnity to the square, where the people are assembled, apparelled in their new cloaths and decorations. The men having regaled themselves, the remainder is carried off and distributed amongst the families of the town. The women and children solace themselves in their separate families, and in the evening repair to the public square, where they dance, sing and rejoice during the whole night, observing a proper and exemplary decorum: this continues three days, and the four following days they receive visits, and rejoice with their friends from neighbouring towns, who have purified and prepared themselves.

Document 6: The First Dream Vision of a Female Adolescent

This brief description of an adolescent female's vision which occurred during the isolation and fasting that accompanied the first menses demonstrates that, at least among the Illinois tribes, women as well as men were urged to acquire dream guardians and the gifts of prophecy. Note the explanation by the medicine men of the girl's partial success in predicting the outcome of her brothers' war party. While the young French observer condemned the girl as "foolish" to fast until she could no longer stand up, there is no indication that the Illinois found this unusual, even for women. Are we witnessing, here, the debut of a respected medicine woman?[23]

They fear the women and girls when they have the malady to which they are all subject. Because of this, opposite every cabin there is another which offers very close quarters for two persons and to which they retire during all the time they are in this condition, with a kettle, a spoon, and a dish. No one enters except such as are in the same condition. When they need anything they come to the door to ask for it. When it is the first time, they make themselves cabins in the wilderness at a distance of more than ten arpents from the village, and all the girls' relatives advise them to abstain from eating and drinking as long as they are in this condition, telling them that they see the devil,* and that when he has spoken to them they are always happy and achieve the gift of great power as regards the future. I saw a

*A spirit that the writer, probably Louis Deliette, interpreted from a Christian perspective, as a "devil."

young girl of sixteen who was foolish enough to remain six days without eating or drinking and whom it was necessary to carry back to her cabin, after thoroughly washing her of course, because she was not able to stand up. She made all her relatives believe that she had seen a buffalo, which had spoken to her, and that her two brothers who were leading a party on the warpath against the Iroquois would make a successful attack without losing any life. They did indeed make a successful attack, as she had said, but one of the two brothers was killed. All the medicine men said she had been right, because the attack had succeeded, but that apparently she had not fasted all the time that was necessary, which was the reason why the devil had lied in a part of what he had said to her, since she had performed only part of what she ought to have seen.

Document 7: The Bear Vision of an Indian Mother

Tanner, a white captive taken by the Shawnee in Kentucky in 1787 when he was seven years old, was sold several years later to an Ottawa woman, Net-no-kwa, whom Tanner described as a principal chief. That she was a formidable woman, a successful hunter and trader as well as a visionary, is apparent in the following passage which relates how the old woman, a widow with two adolescent sons, persuaded Tanner to kill his first bear. The year is about 1795, and the locale is the juncture of the Red and Assiniboine Rivers, the site of present-day Winnipeg.[24]

After we had remained about three months in this place, game began to be scarce and we all suffered from hunger. The chief man of our band was called As-sin-ne-boi-nainse, (the Little Assinneboin,) and he now proposed to us all to move as the country where we were was exhausted. The day on which we were to commence our removal was fixed upon, but before it arrived our necessities became extreme. The evening before the day on which we intended to move, my mother talked much of all our misfortunes and losses, as well as of the urgent distress under which we were then labouring. At the usual hour I went to sleep, as did all the younger part of the family; but I was wakened again by the loud praying and singing of the old woman, who continued her devotions through great part of the night. Very early on the following morning she called us all to get up, and put on our moccasins and be ready to move. She then called Wa-me-gon-a-biew to her, and said to him, in rather a low voice, "My son, last night I sung and prayed to the Great Spirit, and when I slept, there came to me one like a man, and said to me, 'Net-no-kwa, to-morrow you shall eat a bear. There is, at a distance from the path you are to travel to-morrow, and in such a direction, (which she described to him,) a small round meadow, with something like a path leading from it; in that path there is a bear.' Now, my son, I wish you to go to that place, without mentioning to any one what I have said, and you will certainly find the bear, as I have described to you." But the young man, who was not particularly dutiful, or apt to regard what his mother said, going out of the lodge, spoke sneeringly to the other Indians of the dream. "The old woman," said he, "tells me we are to eat a bear to-day; but I do not know who is to kill it." The old woman, hearing him, called him in, and reproved him; but she could not prevail upon him to go to hunt. The Indians, accordingly, all moved off towards the place where they were to encamp that night. The men went first by themselves, each carrying some article of baggage; and when they arrived where the camp was to be placed, they threw down their loads and went to hunt. Some of the boys, and I among them, who accompanied the men, remained with this baggage until the women should come up. I had my gun with me, and I continued to think of the conversation I had heard between my mother and Wa-me-gon-a-biew, respecting her dream. At length, I resolved to go in search of the place she had spoken of, and without mentioning to any one my design, I loaded my gun as for a bear and set off on our back track. I soon met a woman belonging to one of the brothers of Taw-ga-weninne, and of course my aunt. This woman had shown little friendship for us, considering us as a burthen upon her husband, who sometimes gave something for our support; she had also often ridiculed me. She asked me immediately what I was doing on the path, and whether I expected to kill Indians, that I came there with my gun. I made her no answer; and thinking I must be not far from the place where my mother had told Wa-me-gon-a-biew to leave the path, I turned off, continuing carefully to regard all the directions she had given. At length, I found what appeared at some former time to have been a pond. It was a small, round, open place in the woods, now grown up with grass and some small bushes. This I thought must be the meadow my mother had spoken of; and examining it around, I came to an open place in the bushes, where, it is probable, a small brook ran from the meadow; but the snow was now so deep that I could see nothing of it. My mother had mentioned that when she saw the bear in her dream she had, at the same time, seen a smoke rising from the ground. I was confident this was the place she had indicated, and I watched long, expecting to see the smoke; but wearied at length with waiting, I walked a few paces into the open place, resembling a path, when I unexpectedly fell up to my middle into the snow. I extricated myself without difficulty, and walked on; but remembering that I had heard the Indians speak of killing bears in their holes, it occurred to me that it might be a bear's hole into which I had fallen, and looking down into it, I saw the head of a bear lying close to the bottom of the hole. I placed the muzzle of my gun nearly between his eyes, and discharged it. As soon as the smoke cleared away, I took a piece of a stick and thrust it into the eyes and into the wound in the head of the bear, and being satisfied that he was dead, I endeavoured to lift him out of the hole; but being unable to do this, I returned home, following the track I had made in coming out. As I came near the camp, where the squaws had, by this time, set up the lodges, I met the same woman I had seen in going out, and she immediately began again to ridicule me. "Have you killed a bear, that you come back so soon, and walk so fast?" I thought to myself, "how does she know that I have killed a bear?" But I passed by her without saying anything, and went into my mother's lodge. After a few minutes, the old woman, said, "My son, look in that kettle, and you will find a mouthful of beaver meat, which a man gave me since you left us in the morning. You must leave half of it for Wa-me-gon-a-biew, who has not yet returned from hunting, and has eaten nothing to-day." I accordingly ate the beaver meat, and when I had finished it, observing an opportunity when she stood by herself, I stepped up to her and whispered in her ear, "My mother, I have killed a bear." "What do you say, my son?" said she. "I have killed a bear." "Are you sure you have killed him?" "Yes." "Is he quite dead?" "Yes." She watched my face for a moment, and then caught me in her arms, hugging and kissing me with great earnestness, and for a long time. I then told her what my aunt had said to me, both going and returning, and this being told to her husband when he returned, he not only reproved her for it, but gave her a severe flogging. The bear was sent for, and, as being the first I had killed, was cooked all together, and the hunters of the whole band invited to feast with us, according to the custom of the Indians. The same day, one of the Crees killed a bear and a moose, and gave a large share of the meat to my mother. For some time we had plenty of game in our new residence. Here Wa-me-gon-a-biew killed his first buffalo, on which occasion my mother gave another feast to all the band.

Document 8: Women, Too, Enter the Quest for the Personal Guardian Spirit

The Jesuit Relations *are a rich source of information about the traditional religious beliefs and customs of numerous North American Indian societies east of the Mississippi River prior to 1760. Claude Dablon's description of the Ottawa quest for a guardian spirit accords well with many other accounts, some of them derived from the early nineteenth century.*[25]

It [the quest] consists in each one's making for himself, in his early years, a god which he reverences then for the rest of his days, with superstitious and ridiculous veneration. It is this which they believe to be the sole author of their good fortune in all their enterprises of war, fishing, and hunting; and so they wear its ineffaceable hieroglyphic—marking on their skin, as with the graver, the representations of the Divinities that they have chosen.

Now this is the way in which they create the Divinity. When a child has reached the age of ten or twelve years, his father gives him a lesson, imparting to him the necessary instructions for finding out what will be his god thenceforth.

First, he has him fast for several days, in order that, with his head empty, he may the more easily dream during his sleep; for it is then that this fancied god is bound to reveal himself to him, so that the sole object of all their ingenuity and all their exertions is to see in their sleep something extraordinary, which then takes for them the place of a Divinity.

Accordingly, when morning has come, the father questions his son very seriously and with great secrecy, on all that has occurred during the night. If nothing has appeared to him, the fast must be begun again, and followed up until finally something is formed in the empty brain that represents to him either the Sun or Thunder, or something else about which he has often been talked to; and, immediately upon awaking, he tells the good news to his father, who confirms the image in his thoughts. Consequently, after he has been brought up from infancy in this belief and has continued all his life to honor this god of his imagination with divers sacrifices and many feasts which are held in his honor, it is almost impossible to free his mind of this cursed superstition when he has grown old in it, or even passed some years.

At first we believed that it was only the young boys who were brought up in these stupid notions; but we have since learned that the little girls also are made to fast for the same purpose; and we find no persons more attached to these silly customs, or more obstinate in clinging to this error, than the old women, who will not even lend an ear to our instructions.

Document 9: The Vision Quest of an Indian Woman

Mrs. Anna Jameson, writer, art critic, proponent of women's rights, and the founder of the institution of Sisters of Charity in England, was born in Ireland in 1794. She spent only slightly more than a year in Canada, from December of 1836 through the Spring of 1838. However, during that time, she traveled to America and, at Mackinac Island, met Jane Schoolcraft, the wife of Henry Rowe Schoolcraft and the daughter of Oshahgushkodanaqua (Susan) and John Johnston, a prominent Irish fur trader at Sault Ste. Marie until his death in 1828. The Schoolcrafts arranged for Mrs. Jameson to visit the Johnston family, where she was adopted as a daughter by the Ojibwa matriarch, herself the daughter of Waubojeeg, chief of the LaPointe (Wisconsin) band of Ojibwa. Mrs. Jameson was a perceptive and sympathetic observer, and what follows is a rare account of an adolescent female vision quest. The passage of some forty years and

Oshagushkodanaqua's familiarity with Christianity subsequent to her marriage may have colored the account; however, it reveals a powerful female personality with strong spiritual inclinations.[26]

Mrs. Johnston relates that, previous to her marriage, she fasted according to the universal Indian custom, for a guardian spirit: to perform this ceremony, she went away to the summit of an eminence, and built herself a little lodge of cedar boughs, painted herself black, and began her fast in solitude. She dreamed continually of a white man, who approached her with a cup in her hand, saying, "Poor thing! why are you punishing yourself? Why do you fast? Here is food for you!" He was always accompanied by a dog, which looked up in her face as though he knew her. Also she dreamed of being on a high hill, which was surrounded by water, and from which she beheld many canoes full of Indians, coming to her and paying her homage; after this, she felt as if she were carried up into the heavens, and as she looked down upon the earth, she perceived it was on fire, and said to herself, "All my relations will be burned!" But a voice answered, and said, "No, they will not be destroyed, they will be saved;" and she knew it was a spirit, because the voice was not human. She fasted for ten days, during which time her grandmother brought her at intervals some water.

When satisfied that she had obtained a guardian spirit in the white stranger who haunted her dreams, she returned to her father's lodge, carrying green cedar boughs, which she threw on the ground, stepping on them as she went. When she entered the lodge, she threw some more down upon her usual place (next to her mother) and took her seat. During the ten succeeding days she was not permitted to eat any meat, nor anything but a little corn boiled with a bitter herb. For ten days more she ate meat smoked in a peculiar manner, and she then partook of the usual food of her family.

Document 10: The Female as Creator and Healer Among the Algonquins

Postmenopausal women, as well as men, were healers among the Algonquian-speaking people of Martha's Vineyard. Medicinal beliefs and practices were often an integral part of Native American religions. They were frequently deemed strange and categorized as satanic by Euro-Americans or zealous Christian converts who did not understand, or rejected, the rituals involved. Daniel Gookin, a pietistic New Englander, was quick to condemn the unfamiliar and to praise Indians who, according to him, adopted Christian rituals such as fasting and communal prayer, which are often similarly classified by unbelievers as a charade. Gookin's ethnocentric religious perspective did little to allow him to appreciate or understand the religion of the people with whom he had contact.[27]

There are among them certain men and women, whom they call powows. These are partly wizards and witches holding familiarity with Satan, that evil one; and partly are physicians, and make use, at least in show, of herbs and roots, for curing the sick and diseased. These are sent for by the sick and wounded; and by their diabolical spells, mutterings, exorcisms, they seem to do wonders. They use extraordinary strange motions of their bodies, insomuch that they will sweat until they foam; and thus continue for some hours together, stroking and hovering over the sick. Sometimes broken bones have been set, wounds healed, sick recovered; but together therewith they sometimes use external applications of herbs, roots, splintering and binding up the wounds. These powows are reputed, and I conceive justly, to hold familiarity with the devil; and therefore are by the English laws, prohibited the exercise of their diabolical practices within the English jurisdiction, under the penalty of five pounds—and the procurer, five pounds—and every person present, twenty pence. Satan doth strongly endeavour to keep up this practice among the Indians; and these powows are factors for the devil, and great hinderers of the Indians embracing the gospel. It is not small discouragement unto the Indians in yielding obedience unto the gospel, for then, say they, if we once pray to God, we must abandon our powows; and then, when we are sick and wounded, who shall heal our maladies?

Document 11: A Demonstration of Power by Medicine Men and Women

The probable author of this memoir, Louis Deliette, was a French officer stationed among the Kaskaskia in Miami and Peoria of the Illinois Country in the late seventeenth century. Although not always sympathetic, he was a keen observer of women as well as men. This early account of a medicine society, whose demonstration of sacred power lay in the ability to bring apparently mortally wounded members back to life, suggests that the Grand Medicine Society, or Midewiwin, which flourished throughout the region during the eighteenth century, had tribal rather than Christian roots. Note that the "shooting" ritual is intended to persuade followers, since members were primarily concerned with curing the sick and, probably, prophecy. Deliette was no doubt correct in his belief that powerful medicine men and women were feared as well as respected.[28]

Those who heal such wounds pass for manitous and inspire fear in the young men, and especially in the young girls, whom they often seduce, owing to their weakness in believing that these men might cause their death by blowing medicine upon them, because of which they dare not refuse.

They have also an extraordinary and ridiculous manner of inspiring belief in the infallibility of their remedies, which, however, has quite the effect they wish on the minds of the young. Two or three times in the summer, in the most attractive spot in their village, they plant some poles in the ground, forming a sort of enclosure half an arpent square, which they furnish with mats. All of them, the medicine men and the medicine women, remain for the time being in the cabin of one of their confreres, waiting for all this to be arranged, and planning together what to do in order more easily to hoodwink the young people and keep alive the faith in their magical powers, both for the rewards which they get for attending to the sick and also with a view to keeping the younger generation under their influence when they wish them to do something for the security of their village or the repose of their wives and children. After these preliminaries, they enter gravely into this enclosure, their dresses trailing, having their *chichicoya* in their hands and carrying bearskins on their arms. They all sit on mats which are spread for them. One of them rises, the *chichicoya* in his hand, and speaks in a chant before the whole assembly: "My friends, today you must manifest to men the power of our medicine so as to make them understand that they live only as long as we wish." Then they all rise and, waving the *chichicoya,* chant: "This buffalo has told me this, the bear, the wolf, the buck, the big tail"—each one naming the beast which he particularly venerates. Then they sit down again, still shaking the gourd. Immediately three or four men get up as if possessed, among them some who resemble men who are on the point of dying. Their eyes are convulsed, and they let themselves fall prostrate and grow rigid as if they were expiring. Another falls also, and rises with an eagle's feather in his hand, the barbs of which are reddened and form a figure suggesting that he has been wounded therewith, but has been saved from the consequences by his medicines, and wishes to inject it into the body of one of the band, who then falls to the ground and expels a quantity of blood from his mouth. The medicine men rush to give him help, tear away the feather which issues an inch out of his mouth, spout medicine all over his body, and then have him carried off with great solemnity to his cabin, where he is treated like men who have been poisoned. They make him swallow a quantity of drugs, and five or six of them lay hold of him and pull him by the arms and legs, uttering loud yells. They shake him for a long time in this manner without his coming to; finally he vomits a quantity of water, and they at the same moment throw down a little rattlesnake. A medicine man picks it up and shows it to the spectators and chants: "Here is the manitou that killed him, but my medicine has restored him to life." The whole assembly come like people filled with amazement to see this serpent and chant: "Medicine is the science of sciences."

Document 12: The Old Ones Defend the Indian Ancestral Traditions

Many observers noted that the old men and the women among the Indians proved least susceptible to Christian influence. That these Indians were not merely "superstitious," however, is amply demonstrated here by their clever and well-reasoned response to Hennepin's claim to superior knowledge based on the biblical word and the European's ability to write. Note as well the Indians' respect for age.[29]

There are some among them more superstitious than others, especially the old men and the women, who adhere stubbornly to the traditions of their ancestors, so that when they are told that they have no sense, that they ought not to cling to such follies, they ask us: "How old are you? You are only thirty or forty years old and you pretend to know what you are saying. You may know very well what is going on in your country, because your old men have told you, but not what occurred in ours before the French came." We told them in reply, that we know all by means of writing. These Indians ask: "Before you came into these lands where we are, did you know that we were there." We are obliged to say No. "Then you do not know everything by writing, and it does not tell you everything."

Document 13: A Contest between a Missionary and a Medicine Woman

An example of the role of a woman as a power-holder among Algonquian-speaking Indians (Micmac) is presented in the following selection from the writings 1676–1677 of a Recollect missionary, Father Chrestien le Clercq. Particularly interesting is le Clercq's description of the transformation of rosary beads from distinctly Christian objects into objects of power by the Indian woman and by others to whom she gave them. These rosary beads were viewed as repositories of power and treated as such—the attribution of power resting upon beneficial results associated with the objects.[30]

As our Indians perceive that much honour is accorded to the missionaries, and that they have given themselves in respect and reverence the title of Patriarch, some of these barbarians have often been seen meddling with, and affecting to perform, the office and functions of missionary, even to hearing confession, like us, from their fellow-countrymen. So therefore, when persons of this kind wish to give authority to that which they say, and to set themselves up as patriarchs, they make our Gaspesians believe that they have received some particular gift from heaven, as in the case of one from Kenebec, who said that he had received an image from heaven. This was, however, only a picture which had been given him when he was trading with our French.

It is a surprising fact that this ambition to act the patriarch does not only prevail among the men, but even the women meddle therewith. These, in usurping the quality and the name of *religieuses,* say certain prayers in their own fashion and affect a manner of living more reserved than that of the commonality of Indians, who allow themselves to be dazzled by the glamour of a false and ridiculous devotion. They look upon these women as extraordinary persons, whom they believe to hold converse, to speak familiarly, and to hold communication with the sun, which they have all adored as their divinity. Not long ago, we had a famous one of them who, by her extravagant superstitions, encouraged the same in these poor Indians. I had an extreme desire to see her, but she died in the woods without the baptism that I had the intention to give her if I had been so happy as to render her worthy of it. This aged woman, who counted more than a hundred and fourteen years since her birth, had as the basis for all her ridiculous and superstitious devotions, some beads of jet, which were the remains of an unthreaded rosary. These she carefully preserved and gave them only to those who were her friends, protesting to them, meanwhile, that the gift which she gave them had come originally from heaven, which was always continuing to give her the same favour just so many times as she, in order to worship the sun, went out from her wigwam and rendered it her homage and adoration. "I have only, then," said she to them, "to hold up my hand and to open it, in order to bring down from heaven these mysterious beads, which have the power and the property not only of succouring the Indians in their sicknesses and all their most pressing necessities, but also of preserving them from surprise, from persecution, and from the fury of their enemies." . . . This imposture, then, that these rosary beads came from heaven, was so well received by those who gloried in possessing some of them, that such persons preserved them as they did the things which they held most dear in the world; and it angered these persons beyond endurance to contradict them in a foolishness which passed in their esteem for something divine and sacred. Such was the sentiment of an Indian woman who had asked baptism of me, and whom I instructed to this end during my winter at Nipisiguit. She had, as a relative of that woman patriarch, five mysterious rosary beads which she kept wrapped up with much care. She showed them to me, wishing to persuade me that it was a present which Heaven had made to this pretended *religieuse.* The trait of superstition which I perceived in this catechumen made me resolve to defer her baptism, though I acquainted her of the obstacle which she had raised thereto by her false and foolish idea concerning these rosary beads, which had come from France. And I told her that if she had as much eagerness for baptism as she had testified to me, she could give me no more obvious proofs of it than by placing these beads in my hands. She was a good deal surprised by this discourse. She promised me, however, although in a somewhat faint-hearted manner, that she would do everything I desired in this matter. She let me see them, and when I had them in my hands, I wondered at the simplicity of this creature. I hid one of them, and of the five which she had given me, I returned to her only four. She asked me, much embarrassed, where the fifth was? I pretended to be ignorant of the number which she had given me, and made as if to seek among the branches of fir upon which I was then seated. This catechumen, as well as her whole family, being then persuaded that I had inadvertently dropped this mysterious bead, she herself, together with all the others, made a search for it so thorough that there remained nothing in the wigwam which was not moved several times from its place. I had some trouble to keep serious when I saw all this amusing disarrangement of the housekeeping; and little was necessary to make me burst into laughter when an old Indian woman, considering that all these researches were in vain, commenced to complain of the little care I had taken to preserve so precious a thing. She told me, with tears in her eyes, that she had a mortal regret for a loss so considerable; that it was very easy to see that this bead had come from Heaven, since it had vanished from their wigwam so suddenly in order to fly into the womb of the sun, from which it would descend a second time when the woman patriarch had made her usual prayer: that all incredulous as I had seemed up to that time to everything the Gaspesians had told me as to the holiness of that aged woman, and of the familiar conversation which she had daily with God, she would, however, make me understand the truth thereof when we went in the spring, as we were proposing, to the wigwam of this woman patriarch, where I should find without fail the bead which I had lost. She repeated the same thing to me during several days, and with so much importunity that I wondered at her folly and her superstitions. The most convincing reasons that I adduced to undeceive her were useless; for, closing her ears to everything I could say to inspire more correct sentiments in her, she railed against me with so much anger and violence that I judged it suitable to undeceive her at once, and to convince her of the error in which she was, something which was quite easy for me when I showed her the rosary bead and the surprising error for which she was responsible. She was extremely surprised, and frankly admitted to me that she had no sense. They all profited by my instructions, and our catechumen gladly gave me the four other beads, which she had kept carefully among her most important possessions. Some of our French, who had been in the wigwam of this aged Gaspesian woman, assured me that she held also in singular veneration a King of Hearts, the foot of a glass, and a kind of medal, and that she worshipped these trifles with so much respect that she prostrated herself before them as before her divinities. She was of the Cross-bearer nation, as it was easy to see by her own cross, which she had placed in the most honourable part of her wigwam, and which she had beautified with beadwork, wampum, painting, and porcupine quills. The pleasing mixture thereof represented several and separate figures of everything which was in her devotions. She placed it usually between her and the French, obliging them to make their prayers before her cross, whilst from her side she made her own prayers, according to her custom, before King of Hearts and her other divinities. These the Indians buried with her after her death, convinced as they were that she would go to be a patriarch in the other world, and that she would not have the fate of other mortal men in the Land of Souls. For these dance without ceasing at their arrival, and are always in a continual movement, whilst she would enjoy a perpetual repose, and a happy tranquility.

Document 14: An Indian Woman Seeks Baptism

The first in a chain of Spanish missions in California was established at San Diego in 1769, after considerable resistance on the part of local Ipai and Tipai (Diegueno) peoples. The woman described below was a member of one of these groups or, possibly, of the Luiseno, who resided further to the north in the San Clemente vicinity. The text describes the importance of "flying" in the sacred beliefs of Southern Californian peoples. However, the document also demonstrates the effectiveness of oral tradition as a history-recording device. While Southern Californian Indian peoples may have seen Franciscan friars, or at least heard of them as a result of trading ties with peoples in the Southwest, the only other time that Spaniards had set foot in the San Diego area was as a result of a reconnaissance voyage up the California coast made by Juan Rodriguez Cabrillo in 1541, more than two hundred years earlier.[31]

According to what those friars told me, there was among those Indians a woman named Agueda, so ancient that in appearance she seemed to be about a hundred years old. She came, asking the fathers to baptize her. When they inquired of her why she wanted to become a Christian, she answered that when she was young she heard her parents tell of a man coming to their lands who was dressed in the same habit the missionaries wore. He did not walk through the land, but flew. He told them the same things the missionaries were now preaching. Remembering this, she had determined to become a Christian. Unwilling to give credence to this old woman, the fathers made inquiries among the neophytes, who unanimously declared that that was just what their ancestors had told them, and that it was handed down as a tradition among them.

Document 15: The Christian Cross Worshipped as the Tree of Life

Benavides was Spanish custodian of New Mexico and commissary for the Spanish Inquisition from 1623 to 1629. He brought with him, to the northern territory, twelve new missionaries to join the fourteen who were already laboring in New Mexico in 1625, and he was active in the province until his replacement arrived in 1629. The document describes his first contact with the Mansa nation of the Rio del Norte, a puebloan group which was removed to the vicinity of El Paso, Texas, in 1659 in an effort to secure their conversion to Catholicism. Although Benavides was himself aware of the effectiveness of gifts which might be perceived and used as power objects, he seems to have missed the traditional sacred meanings which Mansa women apparently attached to the "sacred tree."[32]

I cannot refrain from telling at this time what happened to me the first time I passed through this nation. Some Indians took me to their ranchería and, after having regaled them with bells, rattles, feathers, and beads of different colors, for the Catholic king orders that we be furnished with things of this kind so that we may convert them peacefully and that they will gladly hear the word of the Lord from us, I made a cross the length of a lance and set it up in the center of the ranchería. Then, as best as I could, I explained to them that if they worshipped this holy symbol with all their hearts they would find therein the aid for all their needs. Falling on my knees, I kissed it. They all did the same. With this my soul was comforted greatly, for it was the first cross that they had adored in this place. Among others, there came an Indian woman with a toothache; with much devotion she held open her mouth with her hands and put her teeth close to the holy cross. Another, in the pains of childbirth, touched the holy tree with her body. From the comfort and joy with which they departed, I have great faith in the divine majesty who would work there His miracles in confirmation of His divine word, without considering the unworthiness of the minister who preached it. The devil speaks in person to this nation in diverse disguises, but the blessed fathers came out of it unharmed, although amid great dangers.

Document 16: The Successful Hunt and the Prayers of Indian Christian Wives

The following selection was taken from the Jesuit Relations, the reports of Jesuit missionaries, which were published contemporaneously in France as tools for encouraging contributions to missions by convincing people of the need for them and the success of the efforts made. It focuses on the interplay of traditional Indian and Christian beliefs in the late seventeenth century. The Iroquois hunters, finding that traditional rituals for acquiring game were not proving effective, turned to another potential source of power—the rituals and prayers of their Christian Algonquian wives.[33]

. . . a band of Iroquois passed the winter among the Algonquins, and no disagreement was noted between those two Nations, hitherto the most haughty and most hostile peoples under Heaven. . . .

Now, not only have they come to a good understanding, but the Algonquins were so well pleased with their hosts that they permitted the widows and girls of their Nation to marry some Iroquois men. And you would say that God approved of these alliances; for, when these Newly-married men were out hunting with their Christian wives, and found neither game nor venison, they said to them: "For some days now we have been coursing these great forests without finding anything. Why do you not pray to him who made the animals to give us some for our food, since you are acquainted with him?" Those good women began to pray, and asked God for something to eat as a Child would ask its Father. Strange to relate, although these Hunters had beaten up all the region around their Cabins without finding anything, yet the very next day, in the same district, they came upon and killed a large Elk. They were astonished at this, and were filled with wonder at the effect of the Christians' prayer, and at the goodness of their God.

Document 17: The Christian Heaven, a Lean and Lonely Place for Indians

Hennepin illustrates below that many North American Indian groups had a well-formulated conception of an afterlife, whose primary attributes were sociability, abundance, and freedom from pain. Where such beliefs converged with the Christian description of heaven, baptism and conversion may have been positively sought. On the other hand, this selection suggests that the Christian heaven was regarded as a separate place from that for which American Indian peoples were destined. Anxiety over lack of friends, family, and ample food, as well as fear of physical retaliation by whites in the afterlife and the possibility that heaven might turn out to be what Christians described as hell, are all evident here.[34]

They believe in the immortality of the soul, and they say that there is a very delicious country towards the west, where there is good hunting. There you can kill all kinds of animals, as much as you wish. It is to this place that the souls go, so that they hope to see each other all together there. But they are more ridiculous in saying that the souls of kettles, guns, steels, and other arms which they put in the graves of the dead, go with the dead to serve their use there.

One day a girl having died after baptism, her mother saw one of her slaves at the point of death. She said: "My daughter is all alone in the country of the dead among the French, without kindred, without friends, and here it is Spring. She will have to plant some Indian corn and squashes. Baptize my slave that she may also go to the country of the French and serve my daughter." A woman being at the point of death cried out: "I will not be baptized, for the Indians who die Christians, are burnt in the country of souls by the French." Some say that we baptize so that we may have them as slaves in the other world. Others ask whether there is good hunting in the land to which we wish them to go. When we reply that men live there without drinking and eating. "Then, I do not wish to go there," they say, "because I want to eat." If we add that they will not feel any want of eating or drinking, they put their hand on their mouth, saying: "You are a great liar. Can any one live without eating?"

Document 18: The Fervent Piety of an Indian Woman Convert

In brief biographical sketches of Indian converts to Christianity, Experience Mayhew presents accounts of a number of women. Of particular interest in the following selection is evidence of the questioning, inquisitive mind of Jerusha Ompan, an Algonquian-speaking woman who lived on Martha's Vineyard and had been raised as a Christian. Such intellectualizing was not uncommon—nor was it peculiar to Mayhew's reporting, as the next two documents will also indicate.[35]

JERUSHA OMPAN, who died in Tisbury September 18, 1711.

This *Jerusha Ompan* was a Daughter of religious Parents, *viz. Josiah Pammpan,* and *Ruth* his Wife, of the said Place, he the said *Josiah* being sometimes imployed dispensing the Word of God to his Country men on *Martha's Vineyard.*

The Parents of this young Woman taught her to read while she was young: she was also instructed in her Catechism, and as I have been informed, had much good Counsel by her Parents given to her.

And as she had a competent Measure of Knowledge in the things of God, so she soon appeared to have a serious regard to them. She seemed to have the Fear of God in her Heart, while she was but a young Girl, was very dutiful to her Parents, and was not known to be given to any Vice. She never much affected going to Huskings and Weddings, and if at any time she went to them, she would be sure to come home seasonably, not tarrying too long, as the Generality of Persons did.

She was a Person of very remarkable Industry, labouring daily with her Hands for her Livelihood. . . .

She did not appear to affect gay and costly Clothing, as many of the *Indian* Maids do, yet always went clean and neat in her Apparel, still wearing such things as were suitable to her own Condition and Circumstances.

She delighted much in going to the Assemblies of God's People, and used to attend the Exercises in them with a very becoming Sobriety, as both my self and others have frequently observed; and at the Conclusion of them she used to hasten home to the Place of her own Abode, and not to go a visiting to other Places. And when she was not her self to go to Meeting, she used to quicken others in the Family to do so, telling them, that there was no need for them to stay at home when she did.

She much delighted in reading her Books, and if she could not get time in the Day, she would not ordinarily fail of reading in the Night; and for that End always used to be provided with something to make a Light withal. . . .

She was deeply concerned how she might approve her self to God under a sore Trial wherewith she was for some time exercised, and did more than once with much Affection and many Tears, ask to be advised how she should govern her self in the Case that did distress her; and having received the best Counsel she could get, she carefully followed it, committing her Cause to God, and relying on him in a way of well-doing; and so doing, found his Grace sufficient for her. What her Trial in particular was, I think not convenient to relate, only will say it was what was no Fault in her.

She used to ask serious Questions in Matters of Religion, as particularly of one she enquired, Whether *Adam* had Free-will before his Fall, and how his Sin came to be imputed and propagated to his Posterity, and how we might be delivered from it? And, lastly, how she ought to order her Prayers with respect to it? . . .

Some of her Relations that survive her, do testify concerning her, that she was a serious and faithful Reprover of their sinful Miscarriages, and that she did often give them good Counsel: particularly one of her Brothers, that was younger than she, gives this Testimony concerning her; and says also that she used to instruct him in his Catechism.

She was about 29 Years old before she dy'd; and tho she had had some Offers of Marriage made to her, yet she would accept of none of them, alledging to her Friends as the reason of her Refusal, that of the Apostle in the first Epistle to the *Corrinthians, Chap. vii. The unmarried Woman careth for the Things of the Lord, &c.*

Her Discourses were during that time very pious and edifying; particularly she declared, that she saw no Beauty in the most desirable things and Enjoyment of this World, and wished that all her Relations and Friends had the same Sentiments concerning them as she had. She talked of Heaven as a Place of transcendent Excellency and Glory, and manifested earnest Desires of going to that Place. She declared, that if she were clothed with the Righteousness of Christ, that would entitle her to the Blessedness which was to be enjoyed in the Kingdom of God; and that *his Resurrection* would preserve her from a State of Sin and Death, to an eternal Life of Glory. She exhorted her Relations and Visitors to be diligent Seekers of God, and to depart from all Iniquity. . . . Some of the Expressions which she used, her Father having penn'd in *Indian,* and put into my Hand, I shall here insert in *English,* and they are these which here follow, "I beseech thee, O my God, to pardon all my Sins before I die; for I now know that I shall not recover, and live any longer in this World; nor are my Desires after any of the things here below; but I do most earnestly crave thy pardoning Mercy, thro' the Death of thy Son Jesus Christ.

"For verily thy Death, O Christ, is sufficient for the Salvation of my Soul from Death, when the time of my Death cometh. And when I die, I beseech thee, O my Redeemer, to receive my Soul, and raise it up to thy heavenly Rest. Thus have Mercy on me, O my God; and then I know when my time ends in this World, I shall be exceedingly happy in thine House for ever."

Document 19: The Anxious Doubts of an Indian Woman in a Mission School

The following letter is the one source in this collection of documents actually written by an Indian woman. Sarah Sinons (Sarah Simon), a Narragansett Indian, was attending a mission school established by Eleazar Wheelock in Lebanon, Connecticut, when she wrote this letter in 1769. It is clear that Sarah was a young woman with a searching, questioning mind and that she did not just passively accept Christianity.[36]

I have been this Some time back thinking upon things of Religion; and I think thay do not look So plain to me as I have Seen them and I have great many weicked thoughts and I donot know what I Shall do if I donot ask Sombodys advise about it for I feel very bad about it; I have thought a quite while that I would Come and talk with the Dr but then I thought again that it will not do me any good; for I have talked with the Dr grant many times and if I do not mind them words that had been already Said to me I Shall have the more to answer for; So I thought I would not go no where to here any thing or no ask any qu[ns] about any but I fear it is the works of Saton; and I have mind it till I am undone for Ever and I believe that Satan is besser with me than anybody els in this world Even when I go to Read he taks all my thoughts away upon Somthing Els and many temptations he las before me I thought I never would not till any body of it but as I was at home this after noon all alone I was thinking about thise things and wondering what I Should do. and I thought of a book I had Read onse that when any one was at lost about any thing they must go to there minster and inquire of them and these will lead you into it, and then I think it is my duty to Come and take your advise, and I what want to know is this am I uncurenble or not; the devil is jest Redy Sometimes to make me think that becase I have made a perfertion and do not alwas keep upright. and it seems to me all the true Christan never meats with Such a Struggle with Saton as I do and So that maks me fear that I am no Christan becase the Devil is So bese with me more than he is with any one Els. for when I go to try to pray he till me that it will not do any good nither will it merat any thing so he trys Every thing to put me back and o what Shall I do it Seam to me I Could writ all this night to you if it would do any good but I fear it will not. So I Desire to Subscrib my Silfe your most humble and Ever Dutyfull Searvent Sarah Sinons.

Document 20: Indian Women Exhort the Whites to Repent of Their Sins

William Savery, a Quaker Missionary, recorded his visit, as well as that of the heretical ex-Quaker woman preacher Jemima Wilkinson (see chapter 7), to the Indian Council of the Six Nations at Canandaigua in 1794. Here he describes how the Indian women, having heard of Wilkinson's sermon exhorting the Indians to repent, requested permission to deliver a similar sermon to the whites.[37]

A message was received, informing us that the Indians were collected. We went to council, whither Jemima and her disciples followed us, and were placed in the centre . . . [Colonel Pickering] introduced us, their old friends the Quakers, as having come forward at their [the Indians'] request, and with the approbation of the President. We then read the Address from Friends, Jasper Parrish interpreting, which they received with frequent expressions of *entaw* or approbation; and afterwards Clear-Sky said, they were glad to see us among them, and thanked us for our speech. It is however expected that they will give us a more full answer before the treaty is over. Immediately after we had read our speech, Jemima and all her company kneeled down, and she uttered something in the form of prayer, after which she desired to speak, and liberty not being refused, she used many texts of scripture, without much similarity or connexion. . . . Captain John, an Indian chief, visited us, and had much to say, about the many deceptions which had been practised upon them by the white people; observing, that however good and honest white men might be in other matters, they were all deceivers when they wanted to buy Indian lands; and that the advantages of learning which they possessed, made them capable of doing much good and much evil. . . . Being about to proceed to business, a request was made from three Indian women to be admitted to the council and deliver their sentiments, which being granted, they were introduced by Red Jacket. He addressed himself to the sachems and warriors, desiring their indulgence of the women, and also to the commissioner, enforcing their request by observing, that the other day one of our women had liberty to speak in council. He was then desired to act as orator for the women, and deliver to the council what they had to say. The substance of this was, that they felt a deep interest in the affairs of their nation, and having heard the opinions of their sachems, they fully concurred in them, that the white people had been the cause of all the Indians' distresses; that they had pressed and squeezed them together, until it gave them great pain at their hearts, and that the whites ought to give them back the lands they had taken from them. That one of the white women had yesterday told the Indians to repent; and they now called on the white people to repent, for they had as much need as the Indians, and that they should wrong the Indians no more.

Document 21: Mother-right and Christian Baptism Among the Oneidas

This selection demonstrates the juxtaposition of Christian and traditional believers among the Oneida Indians in 1800. It indicates also the importance of matrilineage among the Oneida, and its relation to the role of Christian women as liaison persons to the missionary, Samuel Kirkland, in pressing for the baptism of children, despite Kirkland's objection to this exercise of mother-right.[38]

I shall give a sketch of the speech of Waulee, wife of Anthony Soonooghleyon, a mere nominal Chief, a man of no talents: his wife is considered as one of the female Sachems. She is entitled to this distinction partly from talents & partly by inheritance, her mother being esteemed thirty years ago one of the most sensible women in the nation. Her husband was a professed pagen & continued so till his death, which was more then ten years after his wife's:

"Father, I have heard you. I am glad once more to hear your speech directed to me personally. I shall now open my mouth & speak freely. I have heretofore tho't that you neglected me & gave my family up for lost, abandoned to wickedness & contempt of the gospel of Jesus. You took no notice of me for many years, except the ordinary salutation on meeting together. You made no inquiry, how it was with my soul, & whether I had really forsaken Jesus, & forgotten all promises & professions of love to him & his religion. This has been a heavy weight upon my heart, in addition to all the troubles I have had with my family, & has sometimes almost sunk me down. I know the failings of my husband. I know his prejudices & the party with which he too often associates: I know too his weakness. He can do more than I can. I have felt the burthen of the family & the instruction of my Children to be entirely upon myself. I have exhorted them & counselled them. I have also exhorted many of the young women of my Clan, agreeably to the maternal relation in which I stand to them. I have not been discouraged, notwithstanding intemperance has come in upon us like a flood since the last summer. I know there have been evil reports in regard to some of my family that were tinged with the spirit of revenge, that has broken the peace of so many families.

And now, father, what has been my behavior during these troubles? I have kept up a more constant watch over my family, particularly over my eldest son, who will be now & then overcome strong drink. But he has not appeared to be revengeful, & has expressed no wish to become a *man-killer.* Whenever I have heard of his being in company at a drinking frolic, I have run with speed & accosted him with maternal authority and affection: My Son! quit this place & company, & return with your mother. He would instantly reply: Mother, I thank you. Do you return home & I will overtake you. And behold he has fulfilled his word on such occasions & has overtaken me before I could reach my house. He has never spurned at my reproof. Father, during all these afflictions I have looked to God. He perfectly knows my heart, my pains & my distresses.

Father, you know my general conduct & my trials. You remember what was my conduct when many years ago my son was murdered here upon the plain, within sight of the place of worship! " She was so affected as to be obliged to pause for some minutes. "Father, you know he was my darling son by my first husband. You know he was the flower of the whole town, & accused tho' falsely of having imbibed something of the tory spirit (as it was called) & to have been aceessary someway or other to the burning of our church. Oh that envious rival! of my darling son! On yonder plain, walking by his side with all the appearance of friendship, he drew the knife & gave him the *fatal stab.* Father, what was then my behaviour? You exhorted me not to indulge a spirit of revenge, but to commit myself to God. I did so. I never despised or rejected one of your counsels. Since that time I have ever remembered your advice & that comforts me in all my troubles.

Father, you have mentioned the pleasant days we enjoyed here before the revolution, when my mother was living, whom you say was esteemed the first & most influential woman in the nation. *I well remember them.* Ah! how then did you love me and how then did I love you! I never offended you in any instance so far as to incur your permanent displeasure or be considered unworthy of reproof. I wish if possible to see those days restored. I thought hard of you about a year from this present month when you refused to baptize my Child, my orphan Child. You made objections to the surviving parent, the father, who was indeed not married. But what has the father to do with the Child? The mother, just before her death, requested me to be a mother, to that Child. And mothers, agreeably to our customs, have a right to dispose of their Children. It is true, they were not married, which was an objection. But there was something very singular in this match. They agreed to take each other & live together as man & wife. After they had a child, the father proposed their being married by the minister agreeably to the words of the holy book. She refused. She again refused! He asked her if she did not love him. She replied by no means, that she loved him well enough, but that since the death of her first husband, she had a covenant in her heart, secretly, never to be married again by a minister commissioned by the word of the holy book. Soon after she died. She must have had some impression upon her mind, indicating the shortness of her life, or God in this signal manner punished her for that secret covenant she had made in her heart. The orphan Child I must give up to Jesus, & it must bear his name, or I cannot have peace. I will take care of as many Children as god shall give me or commit to my trust."

The matrons continue to exhort & counsel those who are under their care. The maternal affection seems far to transcent the paternal. I shall notice Kanwauganhlka's otherwise Margaret's, talk with several persons yesterday. It will shew the diversity of opinion which prevails among them. There is a young married couple belonging to her clan who have not lived happily together for some time. The woman is generally supposed to be in fault. She is fond of frolics & dancing, being herself very gay. Her husband has sometimes accompanied her & waited till a late hour before he proposed their return & she has replied that he might return home alone. Her mother rather upholds her in these irregularities. The husband, Wooloongh by name, is grieved at them, for he loves his wife & fears that she will draw him aside, as well as hurt herself. He has professed his belief in the doctrines of Christianity & wishes to have his child baptized & to practice all the Christan duties: but he feels reluctant to this great undertaking without the help & company of his wife: he also thinks some acknowledgement is due from her, & that she has good reason to repent. These arguments were urged by Margaret upon the mother of Wooloongh's wife. She replied with spirit to Margaret as follows (as she herself relates.): "Cousin, I have heard your long talk, I think my daughter is as good as the other young women that have had no more experience than she has. She is lively & likes to associate with her equals & former companions. For my part, I don't well like these rigid notions of some Christians. There is as much said against the communicants (of which number you are one) as of any others. They seem to be like a company of Children who need continually to be whipped with rods."

"Forbear a moment," replied Margaret, "you say we are whipped with twigs or rods; this is very true, & we deserve to be cudgelled that we don't do better & are not more holy & faithful as we ought to be,

& should be, if our hearts were right with god; besides we ought to esteem this beating our glory, for christians in old times & even the apostles of our Lord Jesus were beaten a thousand times more than we are, yet they rejoiced with god. Let these things be as they may, Cousin, according to the word of the holy book, the *man* is the Chief: he is head over the woman: the woman is the *little one,* or inferior. The man may, if he pleases, have his child baptised without any regard to the woman. But, Cousin, let us change sides for a moment. Suppose your daughter was a believer, & would have her Child baptised & her husband was *no where* [This word *no where,* in Indian gaughgauweregan, is properly an Indian phrase & very emphatically implies an uncertain indeterminate character & also want of judgment.], half pagan, half Christian. What would be your mind in this case, cousin? answer." "Why indeed, cousin, I should wish her husband to do right. But for my part I can't get along with so many difficulties: besides ministers don't agree."

Women and Religion in Spanish America

ASUNCIÓN LAVRIN

One of the avowed purposes of the conquest of America by Spain was the transfer of Christianity to the New World. The church took a preeminent part in the process of conquest and acculturation of the indigenous peoples, and the transfer of cultural and ethical values from the mother country to the new settlements. The close relationship between the church and the state allowed the former to participate in shaping, and executing, many policies that affected both sexes and all social classes, as befitted an institution which had both spiritual and political power.

In the early sixteenth century, after the political and religious unification of Spain, and prior to the Reformation, the Catholic Church in that country had started a process of internal reform aimed at regaining the spirit of the primitive Christian church through the strengthening of its spirituality and the betterment of the quality of its regular and secular members.[1] These reforms affected the female orders, which originated in the medieval period and had, by the 1700s, achieved a well-established place within the structure of the church. By far the most influential woman in the Spanish church of the sixteenth century was Santa Teresa de Jesús, who singlehandedly, and against considerable odds, reformed the Carmelite Order and restored respectability to female conventual life.[2] Earlier in the century, Beatriz de Silva had obtained ecclesiastical approval for the Conceptionist Order, which became extraordinarily popular in Spain and Spanish America.[3]

Another dynamic force behind conventual life in that century was the concept of *recogimiento,* the withdrawal or seclusion within the self in order to obtain a mystical union with God.[4] Some of the greatest mystics and religious writers practiced *recogimiento,* and even unorthodox theological offshoots, such as *alumbrados* and *quietists* partook of this concept.[5] *Recogimiento* and mysticism, however, could become dangerously close to Erasmian or Protestant doctrines, insofar as they endorsed direct communication with God. Thus, although mysticism remained a very important element of Spanish religiosity, the Counter-Reformation church stressed new elements that became the mark of post-Tridentine Roman Catholicism: the cult of the Virgin Mary and the saints, the emphasis on "deeds" or works toward perfection, since grace alone could not suffice to earn salvation, and the essential acceptance of the church as intermediary between God and humankind.

For members of the church, three "ways" or forms of religious experience were fundamental for achieving the final union with God: the "purgative" way, which implied discipline and sacrifice; the "illuminative" way, in which the soul gained a vision and understanding of God; and the "unitive" way, or final experience of God. In the sixteenth and seventeenth centuries, both the religious literature—popular or erudite—and the practice of religion reflected the mixture of the concepts of *recogimiento* and the acceptance of the Counter-Reformation tenets of discipline, deeds, and faith.

The female orders, spurred partly by Santa Teresa's reforms and partly by the prevailing religious ideas, strengthened the concept of enclosure, or total dissociation, from the world and the search for individual salvation through prayer, spiritual exercises, and physical penitence. Beyond this personal emphasis, the prayers of nuns were considered beneficial to their relatives, friends, and the community at large, as forms of intercession before God or the saints. Within the theological currents that prevailed in the late sixteenth and seventeenth centuries, the founding and rapid spread of nunneries in Spanish America is understandable. Conventual life was popular for several reasons. In addition to the strong spirituality of the period and the strength of the Counter-Reformation church, there was a rapid increase in the number of marginalized women during the postconquest period. These women were the offspring of impoverished conquistadors or unsuccessful settlers. Because they were members of the social elite, marriage to men of lesser stations in life was unacceptable. Lacking the means to carry on independent lives or find suitable husbands, these women entered convents or other types of sheltering institutions as their only option for achieving respect and protection. This solution was accepted and encouraged by both lay and religious authorities, and endorsed by the crown.

Thus, the foundations of convents had definite socio-economic meaning and represented the will of the community, as well as the crown and the church. Any given female monastery reflected the personal efforts of one or several founders and involved the full commitment and support of the city or town in which it was located. City councils and private citizens sought the creation of convents not only as centers of spirituality, but also as places for the protection and education of their women. Ultimately, these convents also became status symbols, since large towns with prestigious and wealthy patrons were the most successful in obtaining permission for foundations.[6] Because of the special rights of patronage granted by Pope Alexander VI (1493, 1501) and Pope Julius II (1508) to the Spanish crown, the latter, assisted by the Council of the Indies, had the right to supervise the process of foundation and all the nonspiritual activities of the regular and secular churches (Document 1).[7]

Nunneries were started in mid-sixteenth-century New Spain (Mexico) barely thirty years after the conquest. In 1536, the first bishop of Mexico, Fr. Juan de Zumárraga, requested that either *beatas* (devout women) or professed nuns be sent to Mexico to teach Indian women and to establish the foundations of Christian life through their example. Even though the concept of convents for Indian women did not prosper, the Conceptionist Order established its first convent for daughters of conquistadors and settlers around 1550. In Peru, the Augustinian convent of La Encarnación emerged around 1561 from a *recogimiento* (retreat house) established in 1558.[8] Soon enough other orders followed: Franciscans, Dominicans, Carmelites, Brigidittes, Hieronimites, and so forth. This geographical expansion was sustained for two and a half centuries by the branching out from one area to another with peninsular founders in the sixteenth century, but largely through nuns born and trained in the New World.

As convents spread throughout Spanish America, they became the enclave of the socio-ethnic elite formed by women of Spanish descent. Indian women were excluded, with few exceptions, on the grounds that they were neophytes in Christianity. Women of mixed blood were unacceptable due to the stigma ascribed to their interracial origins. The substantial cash dowry required as a requisite for profession reinforced the difficulties faced by the non-elite, which included poor white aspirants.[9] However, the discalced branches of several orders, which would accept aspirants without a dowry, were introduced to accommodate girls in that situation. This policy of racial exclusivity remained in force until the eighteenth century, when convents for the profession of Indian nobility were established in New Spain (Document 2).[10] Although such convents excluded plebeian Indians, the last of them, founded in 1811, broadened its social base and accepted Indian postulants from all social classes. It also belonged to a teaching order, reflecting the changing attitudes of a period much under the influence of the Enlightenment (Document 3).[11]

Candidates for profession were never lacking in any convent, and some aspirants waited for years to profess, especially since some orders allowed only a fixed number of nuns for each convent. Nuns were held in great reverence, having deep emotional appeal for the general public. Women were perceived as being more fragile in personal character and possessing less intellectual power than men. However, they were also believed to be more capable of intuitive knowledge and of generating a great moral strength, if properly guided. In the religious state, women conquered their weaknesses, directed by the church, which nurtured their natural inclination to modesty and piety.[12] Becoming a nun was part of an accepted spiritual frame of mind. Theologians waxed on the chosen state of the virginal bride of Christ and extolled it as superior to the married state. Under the theologians' influence and that of their confessors, the call to religion was heard by many, even among those who could not surmount the ethnic or economic obstacles raised by the church itself. To remedy this situation, the alternative of *beaterios* or *recogimientos* was made available. *Beatas* were women who made simple vows to live retired, devout, and chaste lives. *Recogimientos,* incorporating the concept of seclusion, were institutions where women, whether or not they called themselves *beatas,* lived together and helped each other economically, under the spiritual guidance of friars or priests.

The Third Orders, lay branches of the regular orders that permitted women to profess with simple vows, revocable by the prelate, were yet another possibility for women who wished to engage in religious life and pious practices (Documents 4, 5).[13] Confraternities or sodalities, founded by the laity for the purposes of fostering the cult of a patron saint and giving each other mutual help, accepted women from all classes in the area.[14] Thus, their membership comprised a broad spectrum of ethnic and socio-economic female members. These alternative institutions, open to the rich and the poor, to the free and the enslaved, to the black or the Indian, countered the heavy elitist character of the nunneries. It is significant that neither of the two women saints of South America were professed nuns. Santa Rosa de Lima (1586–1617; canonized in 1669), was a member of the Dominican Third Order. Born into a poor family, she had the opportunity of entering a convent with the help of some protectors, but she felt that a divine sign had directed her to remain in the world. Santa Mariana de Jesús (1618–1645; canonized in 1950), daughter of a wealthy family in Quito, did not belong to any religious association, although she wore a black habit very similar to that of the Society of Jesus, to which she felt a great affinity. She ministered to the poor from a retreat built in her own home.[15]

The education of women contained elements that echoed those of religious life, to which it could lead directly under the appropriate circumstances. The main components of such education were piety, devotion, and the tasks regarded as proper for the female sex. Counter-Reformation ideas popularized the concepts of devotion and shelter as an appropriate response to the challenges posed by the world to the female sex. While most women could not choose life in a convent, as the ultimate and most perfect shelter, their ties to the church were firmly established in childhood through their education and continued to sustain them throughout their lives. It was not uncommon for girls to be under the guidance of a spiritual director from the age of seven or eight, while they fully shared the devotional practices of the family. Many mothers led their offspring into the church, out of piety, economic need, the desire to gain status, or all of these motivations together. Numerous women, therefore, found it desirable to spend their lives in a convent or in a conventlike institution, voluntarily choosing to profess or to retreat.[16]

Within convents, women had a special world of their own, with inspiring models, such as the Virgin Mary and the female saints. They also had a certain degree of personal independence and security, as well as the respect and status granted to them as the chosen brides of Christ. Conventual life was not easy, though, as it stressed self-sacrifice before the final reward. Many of those who professed experienced great difficulties in achieving the much desired state of perfection, and, in their struggle to reach it, they left for posterity some of the few available samples of feminine writing and spirituality.

Many of the best examples of feminine colonial literature were produced within the cloisters. In the convents, women had access to education as a legitimate and even necessary means of expression for their inner lives. This was not the situation outside, especially in the seventeenth century, when feminine education suffered a setback from the meager gains of the previous century.[17] This religious literature has a confessional character, as it was mostly written under the suggestion of the nun's confessor. As a sign of humility, most nuns were reluctant to see their works published or known outside the convent.[18] Few raised any questions about this situation, but some did with varying degrees of restraint and conviction. Sor Catalina de Jesús Herrera was ironic, but subdued, when she asked why women's writings were objected to (Document 6).[19] Mariana de Santa Pazis had an intuitive sense of the historical relevance of her convent's history and the need to preserve it by printing the work of the nun who recorded it (Document 7).[20]

The powerful voice of Sor Juana Inés de la Cruz (1648–1695), however, went beyond confessional boundaries. Compelled by strong intellectual necessity, she never hid her own personality, but wrote as the truly exceptional woman that she was. Acclaimed in her own life as the Tenth Muse, she received constant attention, praise, and even adulation, from the time she was introduced in the Mexican Viceregal Court as a young girl, hardly beyond her puberty. Having professed as an alternative to marriage, she probably had only a limited vocation for either state. But, as she could not restrain her literary impulses, it was easier to find an outlet for them in the convent than in the home as a married woman. Her prolific pen produced works ranging from love poems, written prior to profession, to the more usual religious songs, as well as plays, symbolic poetry, and theological-philosophical works.[21] She justly outranked all women—lay or religious—in colonial Spanish America. This fame was not due only to the quality of her versatile work, but also to the indomitable freedom of her mind, which refused to accept the boundaries imposed by society and church on members of her sex (Document 8).[22]

Mysticism predominates in the literary production of the majority of nuns, although some penned books of spiritual exercises. Most of these works have remained unknown for centuries, with only a few receiving attention in the twentieth century. Poetry was often used to express the intimate dialogue of the soul with God (Document 9).[23] Plays were composed by some nuns for the profession of other sisters or the celebrations of a feast. However, mystical prose was the most used form of expression.[24] Sor Josefa de la Concepción de Castillo (1671–1742), who professed in the convent of Santa Clara in Tunja, New Granada (Colombia), is probably the best exponent of this genre. Although she was not well educated or well read, the spirituality characteristic of her time shines in her work (Document 10).[25]

The emphasis in religious life was a personal salvation through works and faith, and this continued to be the norm until the end of the colonial period. However, a new element was introduced in the set of conventual life values when women's education became desirable, reflecting the first winds of influence of the Enlightenment. Since the sixteenth century, girls had been received in convents for their education, but these efforts to educate women were neither systematic nor socially broad enough to make an appreciable impact on the total female population. By the 1730s, however, both lay and ecclesiastical members of the society had become increasingly receptive to the idea of female education, and, by the end of the century, members of the bureaucracy and the social elite—including women—were among the many supporters of the foundation of schools. The order of Mary, first introduced in Mexico in 1754, as well as several other convents in Spanish America, combined religion and education (Document 11).[20] These convents trained the nuns to teach, took boarders, and developed an educational curriculum. They also opened public schools for girls of all social classes. For the first time, cloistered nuns engaged in a socially significant activity.

There were many aspects of conventual life which put nuns in close touch with the world, despite the avowed spiritual aims of their chosen way of life. As an integral part of the cities in which they flourished, convents established many ties with these cities' inhabitants and institutions, ties that went beyond the expected relations with the families of the nuns. Nunneries required a substantial economic base for their survival, which had to be developed and preserved by means of careful administration. Donations were invested in land or houses. Accumulated capital was lent at 5 percent interest. Nunneries, thus, found themselves in the position of property owners, holders of mortgages, leasers of land, litigants in court to collect rents, or even as plaintiffs against their administrators.[27] These material pursuits helped to create worldly ties with the community and to engage nuns in administrative activities not commonly experienced by lay women (Document 12).[28]

Other worldly affairs were reflected in the convents, especially those not following the stricter rules. The discalced (meaning "shoeless" or sandaled) branches of the regular orders took stricter vows of poverty and lived an austere life; these branches forbade servants or slaves in the cloisters and received alms for many of their sustaining needs. But convents that did not follow these rules allowed a large number of protegées, servants, slaves, and school-age girls within their walls. The gossip of the city and of their own families penetrated the conventual microcosm, as well as fashion, political, and social news. Social events, such as musical entertainment, were allowed in many convents in the seventeenth century, and the professions of nuns were celebrated with great displays of wealth amidst throngs of relatives and curious bystanders.[29] Some nunneries allowed the sale of goods, such as earthenware and sweets, to raise funds for the community or for individual nuns.

Within the convent, personal enmities developed, and the elections of conventual officers could be become riddled by factionalism and animosity. Confrontations between nuns and their religious superiors were not unheard of. Some strict bishops and archbishops, concerned over the worldly activities of certain convents, introduced reforms to eradicate what they regarded as transgressions of the true religious goals of the communities and thus antagonized their flocks, who resorted to legal challenges in the courts.[30] There are also instances of convents that wished to change their allegiance from the regular orders to the diocesan authorities as a response to unwanted regulations.[31] Some convents suffered years of internal struggle as a result of such incidents.

Challenges to ecclesiastical authorities were, however, the exception, not the rule. The ties between women and the church were strong, and most women grew up accustomed to regarding the church and its ministration as a source of special material and spiritual power which could affect them positively or negatively, and, therefore, should be treated with great respect. Because of the closeness of the state-church relationship in the Spanish colonial system, the church had total control over the individual's religious and moral behavior. The church had its own attorneys, judges, and trials. It could excommunicate, prosecute, and imprison individuals for transgressions against the sacraments or the faith. Although the crown had started to restrict the power of the church in the economic and judicial spheres, by the mid-eighteenth century, this curtailment was more a matter of degree than of essence in those areas in which the clerical jurisdiction affected women directly.[32]

The Inquisition, introduced in Lima in 1570 and in Mexico in 1571, was only one of the mechanisms used by the church to survey the personal behavior of women and men. It dealt with matters of faith and certain social-sacramental transgressions, such as bigamy.[33] Witchcraft in Spanish America did not achieve the level of intensity and complexity that it reached in Europe. Mostly, it consisted of popular pre-Columbian and Iberian practices to gain personal favors or to avenge individual grievances.[34] Women, naturally, were the frequent subject of inquisitorial investigations, and a broad range of them appears in those records

(Document 13).[35] There is no evidence, however, that they were specially targeted for harsher persecution than men. Burning was infrequent in Spanish America, and most instances took place before the mid-seventeenth century, when the Inquisition was dealing with cases of covert practice of Judaism.

A matter historically less colorful, but one that certainly affected women more thoroughly than the Inquisition, was the church's right to review all issues relating to marriage. Decisions concerning disagreement over the choice of marital partners, determination of the permissible degree of consanguinity between bride and groom, prosecution of incest, rape, and premarital and extramarital relations, as well as marital abandonment and divorce, were all under the jurisdiction of the church. In view of the church's broad jurisdiction in matters of personal behavior, it is easy to understand why women resorted to ecclesiastical authorities to help them solve their personal problems—a clear indication of the blind trust many of them had in the paternal figures of the men of the cloth and in the church as a source of protection and justice (Document 14).[36]

The many nuances and complexities of the relationship between the church and women stand out as significant features of the social history of Spanish America prior to independence. This relationship involved both women professed in the church and lay women, who were directly, although differently, influenced by it. Of these two groups, the former is better understood than the latter because the historical issues are more clearly defined and easier to grasp and analyze.

From the time of their arrival in Spanish America through the end of the eighteenth century, the role of nuns was largely passive. Evangelization, charity, and hospital work were tasks reserved for friars and priests. Only in the field of education did nuns make a contribution, again, mostly of a personal character, until the foundation of teaching orders. On the other hand, nuns formed the only clearly identifiable female group in colonial society. The larger body of the church lent them an inner cohesiveness and an institutional framework that gave nunneries a measure of social status, and even power, in such areas as the economy. The intellectual productions of a number of nuns point to yet another area in which institutional religion helped to set these women apart from other members of their sex.

The relationship of nunneries with the male clerical hierarchy was essentially similar to that of women and men in lay society. There was a certain margin of autonomy within the system, but not total independence. Thus, while the nunneries had internal governments of their own, they still remained supervised by their prelates and were ultimately dependent upon them in the most impregnable of all relationships: the spiritual one.

In a society with a state religion, in which the moral and spiritual powers of the church were backed by the strength of the law, the impact of this institution on lay women was just as rich in historical meaning as its impact on women within the ecclesiastical establishment. Having the power to create and enforce models of social behavior made the church the arbiter of many social issues involving the female sex. For example, the church changed the course of Indian women's lives after the conquest by imposing monogamy in those groups that had previously practiced polygamy and by introducing Western values of male-female relationships.

The Spanish American society was corporative and patriarchal in character. The assumption that there was a specific position for women in this type of society entailed a "contract" of deference, submission, or acquiescence from women themselves, in exchange for the protection of their roles and functions as women in matters of personal justice and family rights. The church, as one of the highest sources of power in society, spoke on behalf of family values across all social groups and recognized women's contributions to family life as mothers and wives. However, at a personal level, it supported the superior position of the male, upheld the indissolubility of the conjugal bonds, and maintained a close supervision over women's behavior, imposing stronger moral sanctions on them than on men. For three centuries, the church influenced women's personal lives and controlled their spiritual activities. The full impact of this historical heritage is only now beginning to be appreciated.

A nun kneeling in obedience before an abbess, sixteenth-century Peru. Drawing by Felipe Guamán Poma de Ayala. [From F. Guamán Poma de Ayala, *Nueva Crónica y Buen Gobierno* (Paris: Institut d' Ethnologie, 1936), p. 482.]

Sor Juana Inés de la Cruz (1651–1695), poet, scholar, and humanist of seventeenth-century Mexico. Portrait by Juan de Miranda, circa 1713. [Courtesy Private Collection, Mexico City.]

Sor María Ignacia de la Sangre de Christo, daughter of Manuel de Uribe y Sandoval and María Josefa Valcárcel Velazco. Professed as a nun in the convent of Santa Clara (Saint Clare) in Mexico in 1777, at the age of twenty-two. [From Jesús Romero Flores, *Iconografía Colonial* (Mexico: INAH, 1940), p. 135.]

Lay woman bringing alms to a nun, sixteenth-century Peru. Drawing by Felipe Guamán Poma de Ayala. [From F. Guamán Poma de Ayala, *Nueva Crónica y Buen Gobierno* (Paris: Institut d' Ethnologie, 1936), p. 633.]

Sister of Charity, María Antonia Matea Frajela, Beata of the Order of Saint Francis. [From Edward W. Mark, *Acuarelas de Nueva Granada, 1843–56* (Bogotá: Banco de la República, 1963), p. 296.]

Peruvian Nun, Lima, Peru, by Johan Moritz Rugendas. [From Juan Flores Araoz, ed., *José Mauricio Rugendas: El Perú Romántico del Siglo XIX* (Lima: Carlos Milla Batres, 1975), p. 212.]

Sister of the Order of Saint Clare, Lima, Peru, by Johan Moritz Rugendas. [From Juan Flores Araoz, ed., *José Mauricio Rugendas: El Perú Romántico del Siglo XIX* (Lima: Carlos Milla Batres, 1975). p. 211.]

Documents: Women and Religion in Spanish America

1. ***The Foundation of a Convent***
2. ***The Education and Vocation of an Indian Nun***
3. ***A New Convent for Indian Women***
4. ***The Experience of Religion for a Mulatto Woman***
5. ***Membership in a Third Order***
6. ***A Subdued Defense of Women's Writings***
7. ***Preserving the Memory of a Foundress***
8. ***A Poet, Writer, and Nun Speaks on Learned Women and the Church***
9. ***Poetry in the Cloisters***
10. ***The Writings of a Mystic***
11. ***A Teaching Order for the Education of Women***
12. ***The Administration of a Convent***
13. ***An Inquisitorial Investigation***
14. ***Letters of Appeal to the Church from Lay Women***

Document 1: The Foundation of a Convent (Royal Decree for the Foundation of a Convent in Guatemala)

The foundation of convents was carefully regulated by laws and, by the eighteenth century, followed a precise and well-established procedure. The following royal decree illustrates the complexities of the process, which required the coordinated effort of many lay and ecclesiastical persons, the consent of the community at large, and the approval of the highest authorities in the colonial bureaucracy. Previous royal decrees mentioned in this excerpt, which forbid new foundations, were ineffective attempts made in the sixteenth and seventeenth centuries to prevent the proliferation of convents that might become financial burdens to their communities.[37]

I, the King, inasmuch as by a dispatch of 17 November 1720 it was my will to order the President of my royal Audiencia of the city of Guatemala, and to ask the Reverend in Christ, the Father Bishop of its Cathedral Church, that in conformity with the laws that rule the foundation of convents, they inform me with the greatest length and clarity, of the need and just causes for the transfer of the Capuchine nuns of this Court to found a convent of their Order in that city; which request they satisfied in letters of 24 and 25 November 1723, the aforementioned Bishop stating the opinion of the City Council on the site of the convent . . . and asking that the number of religious for this Capuchine convent be set at twenty-five, twenty black veil nuns and five lay sisters. The President, in the aforementioned letter, informed me that the best site for the foundation of the Capuchine convent was where there is already a church under the advocacy of Our Lady of Carmel, built by a priest of that city, which is not subject to any patronage or any other impediment, and located in an appropriate and healthy place, in the best part of the city; and with the approval of the [Audiencia's] Attorney, the President accepted in my name the donation of everything pertinent to my royal patronage, expressing how useful the foundation of this convent would be to the city, by serving to remedy the needs of many noble maidens, inclined to religion, but who due to their poverty cannot profess, and stating that Don Juan de Barreneche, a citizen of that city, out of devotion and charity, has offered to pay the expenses of the trip of the religious from this Court to the city of Veracruz, and that the expenses of traveling from that port to the city of Guatemala would be met by another citizen. At the same time, the aforesaid city of Guatemala, in a letter of 25 November of the same year of 1723, expressed the joy with which the news of the Capuchine foundation had been received, and how acceptable it would be to all, expressing that without burdening the Royal Exchequer, they had secured all the means for transporting the founders from this Court to that city, as it had been promised and assumed by Don Juan de Barreneche, resident of that city, and by the sergeant major and city counselor, Don Francisco Marcelino Falla . . . expressing that all the residents of that city begged me to grant my licence for the aforesaid foundation. The aforementioned letters . . . having been seen by my Council of the Indies, and having taken into consideration the Attorney's statements, and knowing that the place named Our Lady of Carmel is the most appropriate and convenient for this foundation, and being aware of the sentiments expressed in the aforementioned reports, I have resolved, after request from my referred Council of the Indies dated 11 December 1724, to grant, as I presently grant, to the Capuchine religious of this Court, the licence they solicit to found a convent of their Order in the city of Guatemala. . . . Therefore, I order the President and members of the royal Audiencia of Guatemala, and any other judges and justices, and request from the Reverend in Christ, the Father Bishop of the Cathedral Church of that city, and the ecclesiastic communities of the city and the bishopric, that they do not put any impediment to this foundation, so that it takes place in conformity to that which I have expressed . . . for which foundation I abrogate with this royal decree, those of 19 March 1593, 3 April 1605, 14 July 1643, 4 March 1704, and 5 May 1717, which forbid the foundation of convents, and any other which may counter this foundation; but leaving them in force for any other, that being my will. Given in Aranjuez, 5 May 1725, I, the King. By order of the King, Our Lord, Don Andrés del Coro Barrutia y Zupide.

Document 2: The Education and Vocation of an Indian Nun

Prior to the eighteenth century, Indian women throughout Spanish America were only exceptionally admitted into convents to profess as nuns, even though the elite among them were educated in these institutions. The foundation of the first convent specifically designed for Indians did not take place until 1724, when a Mexican viceroy obtained the approval for the convent of Corpus Christi, in Mexico City, for cacique or noble Indians. The biography of one of the first women to take the veil in Corpus Christi tells of her early education and her accomplishments as a nun. This work resembles others written about white nuns, extolling the same virtues and portraying the same devoted practices.

Life of the Venerable Mother Magdalena de Jesús, Cacique Indian.

The venerable mother, Sor Maria Magdalena de Jesús, cacique Indian and professed nun in the convent of Corpus Christi, was born in the town of Tlajomulco, in the diocesis of Guadalajara. . . .

The Divine Providence favored her with good and Christian parents, who could afford to give her a good education, the foundation of the sanctity for which she was destined. Her parents were addressed as Don and Doña both were cacique and principal Indians of that town. Well aware of their duties, they carefully looked after the education of their children. The father's wishes that this education would be fruitful made him think of the best means to achieve it. Thus, considering the difficulties of obtaining it at home, he decided that Maria Magdalena, even though she was still in her tenderest years, would enter with two small sisters in the convent of Santa Maria de Gracia, in the city of Guadalajara. The father showed much maturity and discretion not only in determining that the education of his daughters be carried out in a sheltered place, but also in choosing the nun to whom he would deliver them. She was the Reverend Mother Sor Isabel Cierva, a virtuous nun of well-known fame in the city. . . . She received the girls, consoling the good Indian with the promise of a careful instruction. . . . Above everything, she put her solicitous diligence in instructing them in the mysteries of our holy faith. . . . She also exercised them in devotion and piety. . . . She did not forget, however, to teach them how to read and write, and those other activities appropriate for the female sex, which they would later use profitably in serving their families.

Even though each of the little sisters took advantage of her teachings, thus reciprocating the vigilant care of the venerable nun, the latter specialized from the very beginning on Magdalena, in whom she recognized an amiable disposition, accompanied by natural sincerety, accomodation to virtue and a clear ability for everything. She was naturally inclined to retirement in life and to devotional exercises, and thus, her venerable teacher hardly had any trouble on making her devout. . . .

Living such a devout life, Magdalena's spirit developed a horror for the world. She knew the obstacles it offered for achieving goodness, and the thought of having to return to it frightened and saddened her. . . .

Regardless of how much progress Magdalena had made in the acquisition of saintly virtues, she felt a growing need to achieve the most perfection. These sentiments were derived from the gains that the love of God had made in heart, and from the saintly emulation of her teacher. . . . It was God's will to give her the greatest consolation she could desire . . . for the news reached her of the new convent for cacique Indians founded in Mexico, at the expense of the pious and excellent Viceroy, Marquis of Valero.

It was natural that, immediately after learning about the new foundation, she took an absolute, firm, and definitive decision to become a nun. She communicated it to Mother Cierva, who, having no doubts that her vocation was legitimate and sincere, approved of her saintly decision and, without any waste of time, took steps to achieve it. The distance and the large number of applicants from Mexico and its surroundings could have impeded or set back Magdalena's application, but it was God's wish that she should honor with her virtues the beginnings of the new monastery. . . . She was admitted and, after fulfilling all the admission procedures, her move to that city [Mexico] was arranged. Magdalena's father was very agreeable to his daughter's decision, which he regarded as useful to her and honorable to him. The novelty of achieving the religious state for Indians was celebrated by her relatives and by others in the city, who were all happy that an Indian girl of that region could attain it so early in its beginnings. As her father was well endowed in worldly riches, he wished that his daughter should be carried to Mexico with all the security and magnificence fitting his nobility and wealth. He hired a retinue of pacified Chichimeca Indians, who armed with bows and arrows escorted her for defense, but at the same time calling attention to the reason for such a strange accompaniment, which while appearing to be protective also had the luster of triumph. . . .

Document 3: A New Convent for Indian Women

After the foundation of Corpus Christi, two other convents for cacique Indian women were founded in Mexico: Our Lady of Cosamaloapán, in Patzcuaro (1737), and Santa María de Los Angeles, in Oaxaca (1775). This last foundation for Indian women belonged to the teaching Order of Mary, which accepted noncacique Indians for profession. Having emerged from a well-established, Jesuit-sponsored lay school for Indian women, the conversion of noncacique women into a cloistered convent was a reaffirmation of the appropriatedness of religious life for Indian women.[39] *In the following document, the students from the Royal School for Indians of Our Lady of Guadalupe (Mexico) request the foundation of a convent of La Enseñanza in the school, 1806.*

The undersigned, all members of the Royal School for Indians of Our Lady of Guadalupe, and maidens of this city [Mexico] state that: Of our own spontaneous will, we desire, consent to, and beg our director, the Marquis of Castañiza, to promote in all possible manners, and in accordance to the laws of this Kingdom, the foundation in this school of a convent of the Company of Mary, known as La Enseñanza, for Indian maidens of all the Americas; and that he direct his petition to our Catholic Monarch, who, in consonance with the love which he has always professed our race, is begged to condescend in his piety to grant this favor, in return for which, we will pray constantly to God for the happiness of his royal person and his family, and that of all his estates and dominions. And so that it may be recorded, we sign [this petition] today, the 21st of February of 1806, in the said royal school.*

Document 4: The Experience of Religion for a Mulatto Woman

*Black or mixed blood women had little access to institutionalized religion, and only on very rare occasions could they profess as lay sisters (*donadas*). Mostly, they lived as servants or slaves within the convents. However, these women could excel in spiritual virtues, and when they did, they received social and religious recognition, as the following excerpt illustrates. Sister Estefanía de San José was a mulatto from Cuzco, who lived most of her life in Lima, where she received the esteem of religious authorities and the veneration of the humble people for her life of devotion and selfless piety. Her life was considered edifying enough to be included in a seventeenth-century Chronicle of the Order of Saint Francis.*[40]

In the heavenly court, where only merits count, all are equally rewarded when their deeds deserve it: the noble and he who is not; the rich and the poor; the black and the white, because, as Saint Paul stated when writing to the Romans (Romans X), God does not make any exceptions, He does not exclude anybody; He calls all to His mansion and to His wedding. . . . This was verified in the case of Sister Estefanía de San José, who being of tawny color, daughter of a slave woman, dressed in rags and often disdained, offered herself to God, endeavored to observe His holy law, loved Him with all her might, and the Lord gave her, while still living, a certain lustre and splendor . . . enriching her with celestial blessings, guiding her to such a holy life, that even in life, she seemed like a Seraphim, burning in the love of God. So much did her exercises spiritualize her. . . .

Relation of her Life by Canon Avila. Sister Estefanía de San Joseph was a native of Cuzco, daughter of a black woman called Isabel the Portuguese (because she was born in Portugal), slave of Captain Maldonado, the rich. After his death, as he had set her free, she entered the convent of Saint Clare of that city as a *donada* (lay sister). There I met her and talked to her many times. She professed and died with a saintly reputation around 1580. This was, then, her mother. Her father was a Spaniard. Estefanía remained in the house and with the family of her master. She was a good looking girl, and in his last will her master set her free. However, his heirs tried to retain her as a slave, which obliged her to flee Cuzco for Lima to defend legally the cause of her freedom. And God was served that she succeeded in gaining it from the Royal Audiencia. Our Lord was thus disposed that

---

*The rector and nineteen students signed. Seven more could not sign, but their will was recorded.

she should achieve her salvation, and free her soul, as He had freed her body. . . .

She was very compassionate, and out of charity she raised four poor Spanish children, two boys and two girls, who, with such good breeding, indoctrination and example, became members of the Church. One boy became a priest and the other a Jesuit. The girls went to the cloisters to serve God as nuns. One professed in the monastery of La Encarnación, of Augustinian nuns, and the other in the Dominican convent of Saint Catherine.

She was very devoted to the Seraphic Father Saint Francis. She professed in his Third Order, and was among those who fulfilled her obligations with the greatest fervor and observance. She helped the abbesses in the administration; collected alms for masses and the saints' feasts. She lived from the work of her hands, making mattresses for four reales,* and with this and some alms, she sustained herself in her poverty.

Very Charitable with the Sick. She visited the sick, especially those of her Order, and with great charity cared for them, giving them the remedies they required. She collected old linen rags, and after having them washed clean, she made bandages. These she took to the hospitals, to minister to the sick, whom she continuously visited with the greatest charity.

Exercised Her Weakened Body in Penitence. She exercised herself in all kinds of penitences and asperities, *cilicios,*† and disciplines. She fasted on Mondays, Wednesdays, Fridays and Saturdays of every week with rigor and abstinence, and especially on Advent and Lent. She showed no anger for any offense. She was always peaceful and patient.

Very Fervent on the Churches which She Continuously Visited. She visited all churches, and attended all sermons and feasts, jubilees and religious celebrations with such fervor and spiritual joy that she edified all who saw her. . . .

And as this blessed woman loved and feared God so much, she strove by all means feasible to her person and humbleness to attract all whom she could, to the exercise of virtues. She was happy, affable, humble, gracious, and these qualities paved her way into the homes of the principal and richest ladies of the city. . . .

She had several grave diseases, and the last, which was very grievous, with fever and acute pains, she endured with much patience and good example. She asked to be taken to the Hospital of Charity, a very well served women's hospital. . . .

One day, when the Most Excellent Don Pedro Toledo, Marquis of

*One half of a silver peso. Three hundred pesos a year was considered a good living in the seventeenth century.

†Metal instrument with points or bristles worn as an act of penitence.

Mancera, Viceroy of these kingdoms, was visiting the sick of the hospital with My Lady the Marchioness, as they often did, they both came to Estefanía's bed, and talked to her with great love, and asked her to commend them to God, Estefanía, who was already very weak, became animated and answered: "My Lord, is not Your Excellency the Viceroy? Why are you visiting a poor mulatto, as myself?" She made them pray a prayer on their knees, and asked them to give alms to the poor, and bid them good-by, begging God to confer His grace on them. The Marquis asked for her hand, and she stretched it, and they both kissed it, and asked her for blessing. And the poor woman gave it to them, making the sign of the cross over their Excellencies. All those present, and I among them, were very edified by the strength of the virtue which made possible such actions: giving valor to a humble woman, a former slave, to talk to such high persons, who, recognizing the sanctity of the sick woman, would kiss her hand and ask for her blessing. . . .

Of Her Blessed Death. On the following day, having received the Extreme Unction, she gave her soul to God at three o'clock in the morning of 9 May, 1645, at age 84. . . . The following day she was given solemn burial in the convent of our Father Saint Francis, which all religious communities attended, as well as the clergy of the Cathedral and many priests . . . the brothers of the Third Order, and a great multitude of people, who accompanied her body . . . with the veneration owed to a saintly woman. . . .

Document 5: Membership in a Third Order (The Life and Religious Experiences of a Woman Member of the Third Franciscan Order)

Women who joined the Third Orders could become directly involved in social welfare activities and charitable works, and, at the same time, carry out an intense religious life without taking formal religious vows. The biography of Doña Isabel de Porras, written by a member of the Franciscan Order in the mid-seventeenth century, is characteristic of that period's spirituality and hagiography. The former stressed the inner and most personal aspects of religious experiences, while the latter, as an expression of popular religiosity, uncritically accepted supernatural deeds as evidence of grace. Although Porras does not represent the typical member of the Third Order or the colonial beata, *she does illustrate, in her dedication to women's institutions, the possibilities for social service open to women of the period. In the 1630s, a process for her beatification was started in Rome, but it was unsuccessful.*[41]

Doña Isabel de Porras Marmolejo, native of the most noble city of Seville, in the kingdom of Spain, came to the world to illuminate it with the light of her example and her life. She was the legitimate daughter of Hernando de Alfaro Marmolejo and Doña Isabel de Archuleta, both noble and of noted ancestry. She was married to Juan Bautista Montes de Heredia, from Madrid, of well-known nobility. After she became a widow, and with the special intent of becoming a nun, she left her motherland and went to Peru, the city of the Kings, Lima, where she lived for nearly forty years as a singular example of virtue and sanctity, wearing the habit of the Third Order of Penitence of Our Father Saint Francis . . . being among the first ones who wore it, and observing faithfully its rules and obligations. For this reason, she was chosen as Abbess of the retreat for divorced women in that city, which she governed for eight years. Having straightened the affairs of that retreat, she was appointed as Abbess of the retreat and Hospital of Mercy, assigned to receive all women desiring seclusion and virtue, as well as to the cure of the sick. And, as in the exercise of these ministries her good name and credit for saintliness increased . . . she was named founder of the school of Santa Teresa de Jesús, for the good education and the teaching of maidens while they waited "taking state." She was the Abbess of this house for eighteen years, until her death. . . .

But, who could justly refer here to the harmony and consonance of the admirable virtues of this servant of God? Who could describe the treasures of heavenly gifts with which God endowed her? . . .

Fasts. All year long was a perpetual fast for her. Most of the days she ate only two mouthfuls of bread in the evening, and the three days of the week in which she took communion (Sunday, Wednesday and Friday), she did not eat, and if entreated to take some sustenance, she took a few herbs and nothing else. It looked as if she entertained death rather than conserved life. . . . Her bed was a hard piece of wood, pushed against the wall, covered with a sackcloth, and a cross serving as bedstead. She spent her nights in vigil and prayer, always wearing her iron *cilicios.* She undertook rigorous discipline daily, not counting others which she added on other days of her devotion. . . .

This servant of God was like a lighted torch, shedding such a light that she illuminated not only her school, but shone with splendor on the whole city, attracting persons of all walks of life: some seeking advice, others counsel; and all seeking remedy for their needs. And the school was like a sacred public asylum, all persons finding there what they were searching for. The Viceroys Marquis of Montesclaro, the Prince of Esquilache, and the Marquis of Guadalcázar, commended themselves to her prayers and used her advice. The Vicereines visited her and held her virtue in great esteem. God granted her the gift of curing, and with the touch of her hands and her prayers, many sick persons were cured miraculously of their diseases and sores. . . .

Juana de Cea, thirty years ago, having already taken the sacraments in preparation for having a tumor removed from her left breast, was cured in the presence of many witnesses and has remained well since, as the blessed Abbess made the sign of the cross with her hand, and applied saliva from her mouth to the breast. . . .

She Had the Gift of Prophecy. God also gave her the gift of prohecy and a sovereign light, which clarified her soul and allowed her to see past events, and those that would take place, as if they had already happened. This was verified and proved on many occasions. . . .

One morning, after communion, as she was wrapped up in prayer, a married woman came to visit her, and after having waited for her, the blessed Abbess came out and told her: "Thank God, for He has saved your husband from the danger of death." When the woman returned to her home that morning, her husband told her that three men had attacked him with their swords, but that God had miraculously saved his life. . . .

She Had Bodily Elevations in the Air. On several occasions, in the presence of many persons who have sworn to it, she was publicly seen with her body lifted half a *vara** above the ground, when she was experiencing ecstasy.

Once, as the Most Blessed Sacrament was being carried through the streets, she knelt at the door way to adore it, and thus kneeling, she went into rapture, lifting herself half a *vara* above the ground.

On two occasions, she was in rapture and suspended in the air, they took the measure of the height, and it was found to be half a *vara*. On some occasions, she was in the air for an hour. . . .

A Day of Communion the Lord Visits Her. She was very devout toward the Most Holy Sacrament, from which she received most singular gifts. Among them was one experienced by her on a confession day. Her confessor asked her how she had fared, and she answered: "Today has been a glorious day. From . . . the grill of the choir, where I was, it appeared as if a thousand suns in their splendor were not as luminous and strong, as the light that reached me, and innumerable angels feasted the Lord, blessing and praising Him incessantly. And when I returned from my ecstasy, I felt as though I were in darkness, even though it was midday."

Many Angels Kept Her Company. Ordinarily, the Abbess saw many angels, who kept her company, and in her last sickness, she enjoyed seeing them entering her room in a procession, naming them by their names. . . .

In this sickness the Queen of Heavens appeared to her, dressed in all her glory, and consoled her. Saint Joseph also visited her; and Saint Ursula and the Eleven Thousand Virgins were around her bed; even more, the Most Holy Trinity appeared to her in its immense glory. . . .

By the Authority of the Most Illustrious Archbishop, a Report of Her Life

---

*The *vara* is equivalent to thirty-three inches.

and Marvels has been made. The opinion of sanctity and the prodigious life of this servant of God, was extolled in this city for its great excellence. And in order that the example of so many enlightened virtues could be of edification to the faithful, the Most Illustrious Archbishop of this city of the Kings, Don Fernando Arias Ugarte, of blessed memory, on 30 August 1633, named the licenciate Bartolome Menacho, Canon of this Holy Church of Lima, to make a report, as the Sacred Canons demand, of her life and marvels. . . . This process, with letters of the City and Clerical councils, and the religious communities of the city addressed to the Pope Urbane VIII, were sent to the Roman Curia in 1634, begging His Holiness to open a process in the Sacred Rota . . . and to start proceedings toward her beatification, for the glory of God. . . .

Document 6: A Subdued Defense of Women's Writings

Sor Catalina de Jesús Herrera (1717–1795) was a native of the city of Guayaquil (contemporary Ecuador) and professed in the Dominican convent of Santa Catalina, where she eventually became Abbess and a teacher of novices. As many other nuns, on the advise of her confessor she wrote a full-length work that described her spiritual experiences. This work remained unknown until 1950, when it was published under the title of Secrets between the Soul and God (Secretos entre el alma y Dios). *Although most of the work consists of a dialogue between the soul and Christ—or God—the passage below is an ironic comment, under the guise of humility, on the studied contempt in which many educated men held women's writings, and a statement of her belief that women with creative, God-given writing abilities should use them.*[42]

1. Now I render account to you, my Reverend, of the state of my soul at this time, which is the main goal of this work.

2. For the rest, there are plenty of books, and everything has already been written for the benefit of all souls.

3. There is nothing new to add, let alone from a woman's hand, and a woman such as I, since it may give cause for laughter. I have seen women's writings being objected to, and regarded as things of lesser value.

4. And those thus treated were such women that they could have been called men endowed by the Holy Spirit, since they could not have written such grandiose words with a lesser aid.

5. They [men] are embarrassed to repeat even a saying from these great saints and servants of God in sermons and pulpits, and even in their conversation.

6. Poor I, my Father, a sinful and unlettered woman lacking the virtues that might appeal to the Divine Spirit. Only the grace of God allows me to put together these poor lines to account for my soul, but

not to become a source of offenses against God, or of gossiping and teasing laughter.

7. Thus, I would be grateful that, after Your Reverend has read what I have here written for the better governance of my soul, you throw these papers into the fire.

8. [However] I subject myself to holy obedience in all. Your Most Reverend, as my true Prelate, will do what you wish with these writings, even though this may mean that I suffer the laughter of the learned after my death.

9. But, if they should have some merit, I will be pleased. May the Lord be praised.

10. Women, it seems to me, are more impressed by the writings of their fellow creatures because they are closer to simplicity and sincerity in reasoning.

11. And for this reason, mainly, it seems to me that it was God's will that women also write.

12. And also, for the humiliation of the learned men of the world, as His Divine Majesty has communicated it to His women servants.

13. Men do not wish to be humiliated; they wish to mock women. This does not apply to truly spiritual men, but to the presumptious erudites, who have not learned in the school of the Holy Spirit, but in the school of merely human cleverness.

14. The Lord may grant us humility. Without this gift from on High, we would have a wretched death.

15. May you, Lord, concede humility to us in Your great mercy. Amen.

Document 7: Preserving the Memory of a Foundress

The most common fate of works written by religious women was either oblivion in the archives of their convents or their use by male authors for writing the histories of these institutions or the biographies of the nuns themselves. The uncommon historical awareness of Sor Mariana Santa Pazis, prioress of the convent of Señor San Joaquín in Lima, is evident in this pastoral letter to her sisters, written as a prologue to the biography of the founder of her order and published at her urging in 1793. The historical element retains devotional connotations, but the emphasis on preserving the memory of the past gives this document its distinctive character.[43]

It is unjust, dear Sisters, that the memory of our illustrious founder, the Venerable Mother Antonia Lucía del Espíritu Santo, who the Divine Providence chose to inspire with the plans for the foundation of our sacred Nazarene order should perish. The foolish vanity of the people in the outside world leads them to boast of the deeds of their forefathers by carving their actions in marble to perpetuate their memory and to stimulate the imitation of their deeds in their followers. Should we allow to be buried in oblivion the glorious memory of a heroine who is the noble trunk of the Nazarene religion, the mother and the foundation of such glorious undertaking as this new order of virgins consecrated to the Lord to make of themselves spirited images of the Divine Nazarene? Such ugly ingratitude is far from us. I have no doubts that each one of us has ingrained in her breast the tender and sweet memory of the virtues and great deeds of our Venerable Mother, not only through the tradition of our elder sisters, but also through the manuscript account of her life, left by her daughter and successor in the government of this house, Mother Josefa de la Providencia. [However, the latter] is not a sufficient monument for posterity or for the perpetuation of her memory. As a work of the pen, and there being only one copy, it is exposed to the inconstancy of time if it is not preserved in a printed form, with multiple copies that may keep the strength [of her memory] and disseminate it.

These reflections inspired me to solicit the printing of this booklet, found by fortune in the archives of our monastery. It is the original of the sincere account written by Mother Providence, eldest daughter of our Venerable Mother Antonia, under obedience of her spiritual director, the Most Illustrious Lord, Don Mateo Amusquibar.... Mother Providencia was a witness to the heroic deeds, and was an intimate confidante of the secrets of [Mother Antonia's] soul.

It might be that severe critics may miss in this history the pomp and eloquence, the harmony in the events, the methodology of works of this genre, and all those ornaments with which the art of rhetoric dresses up its discourses. However, such a censure would be unjust if it does not take into consideration the motives which moved the author of this account, and the weakness of a feminine hand, which cannot compete with [those of] lettered men, and has to be contented with the simplicity of truth, and the bareness and lack of ornaments [the presence of] which might embarrass its modesty.

The motives moving Mother Providencia to put together this small volume, besides obedience to her spiritual director, was the one which she herself expresses at the end of this work: the greatest honor and glory of God, so that He may be praised for the greatness of his works, and for the edification of the Nazarene religious. It places before us the domestic example of the life of the heroine who raised the flag of this sacred order, and it will encourage us, through the example of her virtues, to become excellent and fervent disciples of the Divine Nazarene Teacher....

Document 8: A Poet, Writer, and Nun Speaks on Learned Women and the Church

Sor Juana Inés de la Cruz (1648–1695) has become the epitome of the intellectual woman born ahead of her times. Having an extraor-

dinary passion for intellectual learning and unusual abilities as a writer, she enjoyed great popularity and success in the viceregal court of New Spain. Her profession as a nun is still the subject of historical controversy, since some researchers cannot accept her plain explanation of having a great aversion towards matrimony. She lived most of her life as a professed nun in the Hieronimite convent of San Gerónimo, in Mexico City, and despite the fact that she reached her prime as a writer within the orthodox confines of this institution, she encountered much opposition to her activities from within the church itself. In one of her most famous works, the "Response to Sor Filotea de la Cruz," the latter being the Bishop of Puebla's pen name, she rebutted not only some of his criticisms of one of her previous works, but his view of her whole life as a writer. She defended the right of all women to use their intellect, since nothing in the Catholic Church, she argued, expressly forbade them to do so. This work has been a tour de force *for all those who have identified Sor Juana as one of the earliest advocates of women's rights.*[44]

I give thanks to God, Who willed that such an ungovernable force be turned toward letters and not to some other vice. From this it may also be inferred how obdurately against the current my poor studies have sailed (more accurately, have foundered). For still to be related is the most arduous of my difficulties . . . and still unreported the more directly aimed slings and arrows that have acted to impede and prevent the exercise of my study. Who would have doubted, having witnessed such general approbation, that I sailed before the wind across calm seas, amid the laurels of widespread acclaim. But our Lord God knows that it has not been so; He knows how from amongst the blossoms of this very acclaim emerged such a number of aroused vipers, hissing their emulation and their persecution, that one could not count them. But the most noxious, those who most deeply wounded me, have not been those who persecuted me with open loathing and malice, but rather those who in loving me and desiring my well-being . . . have mortified and tormented me more than those others with their abhorrence. "Such studies are not in conformity with sacred innocence; surely she will be lost; surely she will, by cause of her very perspicacity and acuity, grow heady at such exalted heights." How was I to endure? An uncommon sort of martyrdom in which I was both martyr and executioner. And for my (in me, twice hapless) facility in making verses, even though they be sacred verses, what sorrows have I not suffered? . . .

I confess, too, that though it is true, as I have stated, that I had no need of books, it is nonetheless true that they have been no little inspiration, in divine as in human letters. . . . Without mentioning an infinity of other women whose names fill books, for example, I find the Egyptian Catherine, studying and influencing the wisdom of all the wise men of Egypt, I see a Gertrudis studying, writing and teaching. And not to overlook the examples close to home, I see my most holy mother Paula, learned in Hebrew, Greek, and Latin, and most able in interpreting the Scriptures. . . .

The venerable Doctor Arce . . . in his scholarly *Bibliorum* raises this question: Is it permissible for women to dedicate themselves to the study of the Holy Scriptures, and to their interpretation? and he offers as negative arguments the opinions of many Saints, especially that of the Apostle: Let women keep silence in the churches; for it is not permitted them to speak, etc. He later cites other opinions and, from the same Apostle, verses from his letter to Titus: *The aged women in like manner, in holy attire . . . teaching well,* with interpretations by the Holy Fathers. Finally, he resolves, with all prudence, that teaching publicly from a University chair, or preaching from the pulpit, is not permissible for women; but that to study, write and teach privately not only is permissible, but most advantageous and useful. It is evident that this is not to be the case with all women, but with those to whom God may have granted special virtue and prudence, and who may be well advanced in learning, and having the essential talent and requisites for such a sacred calling. This view is indeed just, so much so that not only women, who are held to be so inept, but also men, who merely for being men believe they are wise, should be prohibited from interpreting the Sacred Word if they are not learned and virtuous and of gentle and well-inclined natures; that this is not so has been, I believe, at the root of so much sectarianism and so many heresies. For there are many who study but are ignorant, especially those who are in spirit arrogant, troubled, and proud, so eager for new interpretations of the Word (which itself rejects new interpretations) that merely for the sake of saying what no one else has said they speak a heresy, and even then are not content. . . .

For such as these, I reiterate, study is harmful, because it is as if to place a sword in the hands of a madman. . . . To these men, wisdom was harmful, although it is the greatest nourishment and the life of the soul; in the same way that in a stomach of sickly constitution and adulterated complexion, the finer the nourishment it receives, the more arid, fermented, and perverse are the humors it produces; thus these evil men: the more they study, the worse the opinions they engender. . . . Of which the Apostle says: *For I say, by the grace that is given me, to all that are among you, not to be more wise than it behoveth to be wise, but to be wise unto sobriety, and according as God hath divided to every one the measure of faith.* And in truth, the Apostle did not direct these words to women, but to men; and that *keep silence* is intended not only for women, but for *all* incompetents. . . .

All this demands more investigation than some believe, who strictly as grammarians, or, at the most, employing the four principles of applied logic, attempt to interpret the Scriptures while clinging to that *Let the women keep silence in the church,* not knowing how it is to be interpreted. As well as that other verse, *Let the women learn in silence.* For this latter scripture works more to women's favor than their disfavor, as it commands them to learn; and it is only natural that they must maintain silence while they learn. . . . I would want these interpreters and expositors of Saint Paul to explain to me how they interpret that scripture, *Let the women keep silence in the church.* For either they must understand it to refer to the material church, that is the church of pulpits and cathedras, or to the spiritual, the community of the faithful, which is the Church. If they understand it to be the former, which, in my opinion, is its true interpretation, then we see that if in fact it is not permitted of women to read publicly in church, nor preach, why do they censure those who study privately? And if they understand the latter, and wish that the prohibition of the Apostle be applied transcendentally—that not even in private are women to be permitted to write or study—how are we to view the fact that the Church permitted a Gertrudis, a Santa Teresa, a Saint Birgitta, the Nun of Agreda, and so many others, to write? And if they say to me that these women were saints, they speak the truth; but this poses no obstacle to my argument. First, because Saint Paul's proposition is absolute, and encompasses all women not excepting saints, as Martha and Mary, Marcella, Mary, mother of Jacob and Salome, all were in their time, and many other zealous women of the early church. But we see, too, that the Church allows women who are not saints to write, for the Nun of Agreda and Sor María de la Antigua are not canonized, yet their writings are circulated. In which case, Saint Paul's prohibition was directed solely to the public office of the pulpit, for if the Apostle had forbidden women to write, the Church would not have allowed it. . . .

Document 9: Poetry in the Cloisters

Relatively little is known about the many women poets who flourished in Spanish American nunneries. Sor Paula de Jesús Nazareno (1687–1754) is a good example. She was born into an elite Lima family, the daughter of a Knight of Alcántara, Don Pedro Vallejo y Carriego, and a Peruvian mother, Doña María Magdalena de la Canal. She had a twin sister, who apparently did not profess, and a brother, who returned to Spain as a member of the royal army. Sor Paula professed in the convent of Nuestra Sra. de las Mercedes in 1719. Under her confessor's orders, she wrote her biography and several poems. While that biography remains in the conventual archive, some of her poetry was published for the first time in 1955—201 years after her death.[45]

DIALOGUES WITH GOD (VI)

Let us go to the fountain
Oh, my beloved,
Where I shall live by thy side
Bending my will to thine.
Let death come,
As I so dearly desire,
And Deliver my soul
From this vile Body.
For if, while I live,
I might lose thee,
Then, would I be secure
From such dread peril.
Though death to all others is terrible;
To me it is but
Merciful, for it releases us
From captivity.
Let us go to thy palaces,
Thy courts and thy towns,
Where praise of thee
Shall be my sole endeavor.
Set me free from my imprisonment.
Let us go now
To where I can rejoice in thee
For all of eternity.

Document 10: The Writings of a Mystic (Mother Francisca Josefa de Castillo's Mystical Writings)

Mother Francisca Josefa de la Concepción de Castillo (1671–1742), a nun in the convent of Saint Clare in the city of Tunja, New Granada (contemporary Colombia) wrote a biography, several poems, and a collection of mystical pieces in prose which she entitled My Affections. *Her autobiography was a task she undertook and fulfilled as an act of obedience but without much inspiration. In contrast, the* Affections, *written throughout her life, reflect deeply felt spiritual emotions. The search for the mystical union of the soul and God served her as a refuge from her trying life as a nun. Long-known among literary circles, the* Affections *have been regarded as one of the best examples of mystical prose in colonial Spanish American literature.*[46]

Affection 15, First Part.

At night, as I retired to give my body some rest . . . I felt His presence . . . with ineffable benignity, majesty and love. The soul heard His words, as soft, sweet and amorous as those of a loving husband, and as His presence made the soul burn, it broke into a thousand endearments, forgetting all fears. Among many other things, it seemed to the soul that He said: "Take me, I am your sustenance." Entering into the soul and the heart, He said: "Your heart must burn since it is united with mine, which is all fire." He infused such purity and a desire for even more, into the soul, that I remembered the blessed Saint Agnes when she said: "Reaching Him I will be purer; touching Him I will be more chaste." . . . But beware, my soul, that you always walk towards your God, and that only in the love of the Husband you find rest, and that His praise is always in your lips. . . . Do you know that this is a mutual correspondence and a tight knot, whereby to love is to be loved, and to give is to receive? . . . Does not the lover hide burning coals in His chest* casting them on the head of His beloved when they give themselves to each other? What should the soul give to God but the heart, receiving in it the fire with which it is stolen, and returning what it has received? . . .

Affection 128, First Part.

Having received our Lord [in the sacrament] I knew that like a crystal, or like the purest and clearest mirror, all encompassing, He surrounded my soul; and in that immense and purest of lights, better than under the light of the sun, even the most minimal atoms, as well as the smallest imperfections of the soul are visible. Your eyes saw my imperfections; in Your book all is written. Thus, the soul has no other words than those for praying and asking for your mercy, my God. . . .

You, my Lord, tested me with the waters of contradiction, and learned how far are my thoughts from the imitation of your Son. . . . You carefully examined the mixture of the twisted path of self-esteem and vain acceptance of the world [in me], and you probed my heart, since you wished it to be of the gold of your approval. You put it in the oven of tribulations, anguish, contradictions and despisement of men. Oh! How good it was for me, my Lord, to be humiliated, so that I learn about my imperfections, and know them as well as you do, and feeling them, I humble myself. . . .

Affection 155. Second Part.

I felt in the most intimate of my soul the strong voice of the Lord, powerful and majestic. . . . God in His majesty makes His voice sound over many waters. . . . When the Lord speaks all become silent, or so muted that it is as if they became silent. . . . How confident is the soul of the powerful voice of God in His majesty. Neither the showers of tribulation, nor the avenues of rivers and seas make a sound when the Lord speaks. . . . Only His voice is heard all over the earth in its greatness and magnificence. His voice is powerful enough to break down the cedars of Lebanon. His voice grants swiftness to the deer climbing the mountains. God's voice can destroy the arrogant and break down the proud. It can give swiftness to those climbing the

*Proverbs 25:22. "For thou shalt heap coals of fire upon his head."

heights of perfection, preparing them, carrying them over and helping them to ascend and to aspire and wish for the best, the cleanest, the most sacred. . . .

This voice of the Lord in His majesty is chaste, pure, and clean in its speech . . . one hundred times washed of all earthly traces; and as silver coming out of the fire, pure and resplendent, it leads to purity. . . . And revealing what is hidden from the eyes of the flesh, it shows the ugliness of sins and the beauty of virtue, the end and deceit of vanity . . . the immensity and loveliness of the Creator, the end of all time, the center of the soul, and the happy and highest goal of His path.

Affection 191. Second Part.

Oh, my soul, the Lord will speak on your behalf and all your enemies will be silenced, all evil tongues will be cast away. Be silent now and suffer, since the Lord is silent. Remain silent, lying at His feet and contemplating His divine countenance. Listen only to His life-giving words. He will will speak on your behalf, and a day will come when He will call the earth to its rest. Oh, that you would be clean earth, without the seeds of corruption sowed in your flesh! Try to burn more and more, every day, every hour, in the fire of love and pain, so that the offenses which you have committed shall die in you; let the fire burn and renew itself every instant in His divine presence.

Document 11: A Teaching Order for the Education of Women

The following document is a petition to the king requesting royal licence for the foundation of a teaching convent of the Order of Mary in Mexico City. The teaching Order of Mary was founded by Joanne de Lestonnac (1556–1640) in seventeenth-century France. This order was first introduced in the New World in Mexico by the titled heiress of a substantial fortune, who professed as a nun in Spain and who succeeded in overcoming several obstacles raised against the transplant of the order overseas. The Order of Mary allowed the cloistered nuns of Spanish America to engage in the methodic education of a substantial number of girls from all social classes. The foundation of convents of this order in several cities throughout the continent was supported by members of the social elite, who in the eighteenth century became concerned about the haphazard character of female education.[47]

In the convent of Our Lady of La Enseñanza, in the city of Tudela . . . on the 23rd of December of 1744 . . . the most illustrious lady, Sister María Ignacia de Azlor, novice in this holy convent, from the city of Mexico in New Spain, legitimate daughter of the most illustrious Don Joseph de Azlor and Doña Ignacia Xaviera de Echeverz, marquis and marchioness of San Miguel de Aguayo and Santa Olalla. . . .

Sir: Sister María Ignacia de Azlor y Echevers . . . at the feet of Y.H. [Your Highness], with the greatest obeissance, I represent that, having determined to follow Christ in the most secure path of religion, and feeling especially called from heaven to embrace [the Order of] La Enseñanza, originated in France, where it is perceived as of the highest public utility, as the goal of this sacred Order is to employ its religious, without any stipend, in the education of girls . . . I came to this Kingdom from New Spain, with the intention of soliciting my admission in a convent of this Order. I desire to transplant, afterwards, such a necessary and plentiful spring of goodness to that remote land, where for lack of instruction, the delicate sensitivity of the girls suffers a lamentable aridity, lacking the most precious waters of education, and even worse, remaining in total ignorance. With such bad beginnings, the most painful and irremediable consequences result, being such a populous Kingdom, and kindled by a lack of restraint alien to that prescribed by our holy law. This sad situation cannot be regarded without concern by those who are pained by the loss of so many souls. Thus, having been admitted with the greatest good will into this convent of La Enseñanza of Tudela, this supplicant only needs the means to help those of her remote and beloved motherland, the main city of New Spain (which is Mexico) to share the happiness of having one of these convents. I intend to facilitate it [the foundation] with the renunciation of all my worldly possessions and with the generous alms that I expect from the inhabitants of that land. Therefore, I beg and entreat Y.M. [Your Majesty] to grant the necessary licences so that in the said city I may found this convent, taking from here, when the time comes, several religious for that purpose. With this, that kingdom will receive the most special mercy of the piety of Y.M. [Your Majesty]. . . .

Document 12: The Administration of a Convent (Instruction of a Bishop on the Economic Administration of a Convent)

During the last quarter of the sixteenth century and much of the seventeenth century, most convents in Spanish America were poor, as the original donations accumulated for their foundation were used in the building of their living headquarters and their churches. Maladministration of their funds was also common. However, by the end of the eighteenth century, especially in the larger urban areas, some women's convents achieved outstanding economic well-being, owning both urban and rural properties, and having enough liquid assets to lend money to property owners. Vigilance in the administration of conventual funds was essential for economic stability and growth, as the following document to an Abbess from the Bishop of Guadalajara, Mexico, carefully stresses. Even though the collection of rent and dealings with the outer world were carried out by a major-

domo, the nuns had a share in the administration and management of the convent's assets.[48]

In the city of Guadalajara, on the 15th of November, 1738. His Most Illustrious Lordship, Doctor Don Juan Gómez de Parada, Bishop of Guadalajara in the Kingdom of New Galicia and León, ordered the following rules to be observed for the better government of the convent of the Augustinian Discalced of Santa Mónica. . . .

The Third. Insofar as the excessive expenses which the nuns incur when they profess, such as musicians and chocolate at the parlor of the convent, and worse, fireworks and noise, are very prejudicial for the family and parents of the nuns, and of no utility whatsoever, His Illustrious Lordship orders the Abbess that from now on these practices should stop, and if they continue, either at the entrance or at the final profession of any nun, he should be notified, in order to deny the habit of profession to the aspirant. Thus, it will not be so onerous for parents to have a daughter become a religious, and poor girls who cannot afford the expenses may profess without incurring them. Those who are professing humility and poverty should not give the bad example of vanity and pride themselves.

The Fourth. Aspirants should not take the veil without having made a will, under which dispositions they should profess. This will should be kept, along with others, separate from other papers in the monastery's archive, so that the convent knows at all times what might come to it, to its church or its chaplain, in order to be able to claim it.

The Fifth. That all the legal deeds of any income belonging to the convent, or its endowed chaplain, or its feasts and pious deeds, be kept in the conventual secretariat, in a double-key coffer, one key for the Prelate and the other for the Abbess. Legal deeds are as important as possession of money itself. . . . Conventual funds should be spent only on its sustenance, not in feasts, masses or pious deeds (excepting those of chantries, which the chaplain should collect himself). . . . The majordomo should have a list of, and officially account for all the legal deeds, and he should supply the Abbess with the money to be spent for specific purposes.

The Sixth. The great losses of capital and interest experienced in other convents have been due to the great licence granted to the majordomos, and to the fact that they have been allowed to retain funds and to use them as their own in their businesses. These bad practices moved my predecessor to adopt the practice carried out in Guatemala, of entrusting the funds of new dowries or redeemed capital to the Abbess, with the assent of the Prelate or his Provisor, and in the presence of the Prelate's secretary. The money is kept in a three-key coffer, and all involved in any transaction sign a receipt book. No money will be deposited or withdrawn from the convent unless it is allowed by these three persons, and all legal deeds should be given to the Mother-secretary, following this procedure. We order that in our time these practices be observed, and request for the sake of God's love, that our successor follow them, for the benefit of the convent. There is no reason for the majordomo to retain any conventual money, and this practice is against all reason and justice. We also request our succesors, and advise the nuns, that they never grant to any person a general power of attorney in any amount, or transfer liens, or make any contract to give and receive any capital, or sign any obligation or redemptions, except for the collection of interest, and give a receipt for such collection. The convent may not spend over 20 pesos in house repairs or legal suits without the Prelate's licence.... Without such licence anything the majordomo may do to carry out any business transaction is invalid. The majordomo must render his accounts yearly, exhibiting all necessary receipts of whatever has been paid to and by the convent. These practices will prevent entanglements and injury to the convent. The practice of giving the convent all its money should be observed, especially whenever an intelligent nun is in charge of its government and management....

Document 13: An Inquisitorial Investigation (The Inquisitor Attorney of the Holy Office vs. Anna María, mulatto spinster, for witchcraft, Guanajuato, 1768)

In the eighteenth century, many of the cases brought to the attention of the Inquisition dealt with bigamy, blasphemy, and the practice of the so-called arts of witchcraft, such as the use of powders, amulets, and similar paraphernalia, for obtaining personal favors from other persons, often lovers. Many of the women involved in inquisitorial inquiries in the countryside were either Indians or persons of mixed blood, even though Indians were officially beyond the Inquisition's jurisdiction. However, white women also appear to have been involved in similar cases. The following excerpt is taken from a suit brought against a woman accused of engaging in witchcraft practices to promote correspondence in a love affair. The charges, apparently disproportionate to the offense, follow the usual verbal phrasing of the period. Anna María, the woman accused in this suit, died before she could be taken to Mexico for trial.[49]

Guanajuato, 3 December 1769. The Inquisitor Attorney of this Holy Office.... As a result of the denunciation and other inquiries practiced against Anna María, mulatto spinster of this city of Guanajuato, it has been sustained that the aforesaid has incurred in transgressions of superstition, witchcraft and others ... and is suspect of heresy, as I make evident in the sworn revision of her cause, which I hereby present. And since as a result she has become liable to be jailed to receive due punishment from this Holy Tribunal, I request

Your Most Illustrious Lordship, to order her imprisonment and the seizure of all her possessions, so that she be maintained with all necessary security in the secret jail of this Holy Office and charges be brought against her. . . .

[Among Anna María's denouncers was another mulatto woman, María Manuela, who also involved another accomplice, the Indian Phelipa. Her declaration, given on July 10, 1768, supplies details on Anna María's practices.]

Sir: On the tenth of this month a woman called María Manuela Martínez, of about 35 to 40 years of age, married to Felix Montero, both mulattoes, and residents in this city, appeared before her confessor for discharging her conscience, and denounced that: In the month of August of the year 1756, while she was living in this city, in the place known as Escalones of Cortés, and being the widow of Joseph Mathias Valenzuela, she was carrying an illicit friendship with the aforesaid Felix, who is today her husband, and was experiencing much lack of attention from him, which hurt her feelings very much. Being in that situation, one day, coming from the mine of Rayas, she came to the door of the house of the Indian Phelipa, married to Pedro the cobbler, who was then by herself, and who asked her what she was doing. And she answered that she had come to Guanajuato to see Felix. Phelipa asked her if Felix had not shown up, and having answered in the negative, Phelipa asked her: "Do you wish to see a Devil I have?" María answered that she did, and followed Phelipa, who said: "You will see how Felix will never leave you." The denouncer assented to everything, and Phelipa called for Anna María, a mulatto spinster, who today lives behind the place called Mellado, and she came, and Phelipa told her: "Here is a friend of mine who has some problems in her hands." And Anna asked the denouncer if she had any animosity against Felix, and she answered that she did not, but rather sadness that he did not want to be with her. And to this Anna replied that she should not worry because she would help her. She asked for one *real* for candles, and breaking them into many small pieces she lighted them all, and putting two of the most alike together, she said: "These are you and Felix." And leaving them lighted, they bid each other good-by. On the following day, near noon, Anna went to María Manuela's house, and put several cotton seeds and rosemary flowers in a pail of water, and then she took two flowers and two seeds out of the water, telling her that she should always carry them in the hem of her skirt. She also gave her a dead person's bone, telling her that with those things Felix would never leave her. She also gave her a print of the Devil in the shape of a man with yellow wings and black body. She insisted very much that María Manuela should keep those things hidden from Felix and everybody else. She returned the same week and asked María about her affair, and María answered that everything was all right. Then Anna asked her for two *reales* for candles, and for a small pot of blessed water. She gave her what she requested, and Anna took it all with her to her home. Although the denouncer did not know what the other woman did with the blessed water or the candles, she experienced a great love from Felix, who at that time was still married to María Castora, mestiza. . . . And although María has not consented in further witchcraft practices, she is persuaded that Anna continues practicing them, since she has no known occupation and has enough to spend and decent clothing. . . .

[After examination of the case and the witnesses, the inquisitors reached the following decision]: We have seen the enclosed facts and declarations on crimes in which we note two accomplices: one *in recto,* and thus in greater malice, for having induced the practice of superstition, and the other *in obliquo,* with less malice. The latter is she, who moved by her jealousy and sentiments for her lover complained to the former, who said that she would take care of everything. . . . And thus, proceeding to judge, it is our opinion that the facts and testimonies mark them both as superstitious, love sorcerers, diviners, pyromantics and necromants, with explicit pact with the devil, and thus suspect of heresy. . . .

Document 14: Letters of Appeal to the Church from Lay Women

The church was viewed as a source of protection and justice for lay women and many of them turned to it for the solutions to their personal problems. They appealed to the bishops and archbishops as the ultimate spiritual authorities within the ecclesiastical hierarchy, requesting protection and justice, even in cases that fell outside the jurisdiction of these men or that of any religious authority. The variety of situations presented to the bishops and other members of the church, by a diverse spectrum of colonial society, speaks of the blind confidence which such religious authorities inspired among the humble and uneducated. The letters that follow represent women of several walks of life: a slave, a mother requesting help for her children, a pauper, and a penniless novice. Only in the last instance may the petitioner be clearly identified as literate. The other petitioners probably dictated their requests to a scribe, who put them into a more formal language. Although none of the requests involve spiritual issues, all were inspired by a naive faith in the power of the church. These letters were addressed to two Bishops of Michoacán and to the Canon of the Cathedral Church of Mexico City in the first half of the eighteenth century.[50]

I, Felipa de Santiago, slave of Doña Francisca de Oropesa, resident of this congregation, lying at the feet of Your Most Illustrious Lordship, state that Agustín García, resident of this congregation, under promise of marriage, violated my daughter and made use of her under this understanding as long as he wished until she became pregnant. From this have followed not only great expenses to me, but the fact that my daughter and all my posterity will remain slaves, because my mistress had promised her her freedom only under the condition that she married anyone she wished, as she has done with my other daughters who have married. Because of this, and the fact that García has left for the town of San Francisco, fearing punishment for his transgression by the Ecclesiastical Judge. I wish that a suit be followed, and that due to our poverty, neither I nor my daughter be left without a defense. I beg from Your Most Illustrious Lordship to issue a sovereign decree so that the aforesaid Judge make him [Garc ía] appear in his court, and that you order as well that, due to my poverty I receive some aid, as a pauper, or that the costs be paid by the referred García, as is only just. Therefore, I ask and beg Your Most Illustrious Lordship that you so order, and I implore justice.

I do not know how to sign.

Doña Anna María Cabezas, resident of the city of Valladolid, widow of Don Joseph Bustillos, with much reverence I appear before the greatness of Your Most Illustrious Lordship, to state that from my said husband I have two daughters, named Doña Rosalía and Doña María Guadalupe. My extreme necessity and the lack of a protector, the nakedness of my daughters, and the risks they were exposed to, being obvious to several persons, they offered to contribute the required fee to maintain them in the girls' school of Santa Rosa of this city, where they have remained for one year. They are now in the contingency to leave, because some of their protectors cannot continue to furnish the promised contribution, having arrears in their income. Since the orphanage and poverty of my daughters is so evident, may the piety of Your Most Illustrious Lordship be exerted by relieving one of them from the payment of the aforesaid fee, and order the school to retain her as a pauper.

Therefore, I beg most humbly Your Most Illustrious Lordship to issue this order, from which I will receive much benefit and mercy.

Doña Anna María Cabezas (not her signature)

Sr. D. Martin Elizacochea.

Most Illustrious Lord. This poor old maiden is at the door of your charity begging for alms to make a gown. Lacking one I cannot humanly provide for one by my own wits, due to my old age and the absence of a protector. Having lost my master, the curate Saiz, I have experienced many privations, the present one of lacking a gown being one of them. Thus, I beg it from Your Most Illustrious Lordship, for the love of Jesus, Mary and Joseph, who, being my godparents, I hope will entreat your liberal hand.

I most humbly kiss the hand of your Most Illustrious Lordship.

Josepha Ramos (not her signature)

Most Illustrious Sir: Venerable Dean, and Chapter.

Sor María Micaela de la Santisima Trinidad, novice in the sacred convent of Mary and my Father Saint Bernard, lying at your feet, I present to you the grave need in which I find myself. I am detained at the novitiate for not having the entire dowry for my profession. For this reason I request your patronage in awarding of one of the existing dowries for novices detained for the lack of one. I hope that the piety of Your Lordship will favor me. I will remain most grateful and will be obliged to you in my prayers.

Your lesser subject,
María Micaela de la Trinidad

Women in Colonial French America

CHRISTINE ALLEN

The seventeenth and eighteenth centuries witnessed an extraordinary transformation in western history. While Europe reverberated from the Protestant Reformation, France became the focal point for the Roman Catholic Counter-Reformation.[1] Hundreds of missionaries left the country with the hope of beginning a renewed form of Christian life, modeled on the examples of the Christians of the first century.

These missionaries left behind a country that was weakened from years of war with the Spaniards, Dutch, and English, and living in the shadow of a civil war. In this violent context, France produced some of the most important intellectual achievements of its history. The crumbling medieval outlook on the world painfully gave way to modernity in Europe through the contributions of Harvey, Galileo, Kepler, Newton, Descartes, Pascal, Voltaire, and Rousseau.

The situation of women in France was also changing dramatically. At the end of the sixteenth century, peasant women were still being haunted by the specter of witchcraft.[2] In addition, female mystics from the upper classes were in danger of being accused of diabolical possession.[3] Yet, within this environment of fear, women were slowly developing a new intellectual base in "polite society" through the introduction of the salon.[4] And from this foundation, women began to write books in which they argued for the equality of woman and man.[5] This movement was derided by some French writers, while others attempted to produce deeper philosophical arguments for equality.[6] All of this debate created an atmosphere of questioning about the proper identity of the sexes. The controversy focused first on the right of equal access to institutionalized education, but expanded eventually to include equal rights to participate in society at large.[7]

The Counter-Reformation offered women an opportunity for equality through the practice of a new kind of life of Christian perfection. Equality between women and men in the past had been found primarily in martyrdom or within the double monasteries of the Benedictine congregation, where aristocratic individuals of both sexes were educated from A.D. 800 to 1200.[8] In the thirteenth century, with the founding of the mendicant orders such as the Dominicans and the Franciscans, women religious became strictly cloistered. The further removal of higher education from the Benedictines by the secular bishops and mendicant orders who established the University of Paris undermined any previous equality of the sexes. Women were excluded from centers of learning, and the opportunity to affect society through the practice of law or medicine was withheld from them. However, in the seventeenth century, the Counter-Reformation enabled ordinary women to enter into the mainstream of social change. The new Catholics were determined to establish a world order that would overcome all limitations of class, sex, and race.

NEW OPPORTUNITIES IN NORTH AMERICA

The missions of the New World offered the Catholic women of France an opportunity to live, side by side with men, with the common goal of building a better world. This chapter describes six women who, between 1600 and 1800, seemed to exemplify the best kind of Christian vocations in New France:[9] Marie of the Incarnation (1599–1672); Jeanne Mance (1606–1673); Marguerite Bourgeoys (1630–1700); Kateri Tekakwitha (1656–1680); Jeanne le Ber (1662–1714); and Marguerite D'Youville (1701–1771). The chapter covers the period from the arrival of the first French settlers in 1608 to the conquest of New France by the English in 1763.[10] Each of these women was affected differently by the challenges of the New World, although they all lived their vocations with intensity and persistence. Indeed, a study of their lives reveals a power and creativity as each one gave her own example of women's options in the world.

The first three of these women were born in France and came to North America as part of the dynamic missionary activity of the Counter-Reformation. Marie of the Incarnation left a cloistered Ursuline convent in Tours, France, for Quebec City in 1639, as the first woman missionary from that country. Her primary aim was to convert the Indians to Christianity, and, with that goal in mind, she opened the first school in Quebec City for girls of all classes and races. Jeanne Mance co-founded the city of Montreal (Ville Marie) in 1642 and was one of the first lay women missionaries to the New World.[11] She also established the first hospital in that settlement, L'Hôtel Dieu, and served as treasurer of the colony. In 1657, Marguerite Bourgeoys opened the first schools in Montreal and founded the first noncloistered religious community for women in the New World, the Congregation of Notre Dame.[12]

All three of these women were from the class of skilled commoners:

from the families of a master baker, an attorney, and a candle maker, respectively.[13] From separate areas of France—Tours, Langres, and Troyes—they responded to the challenges of New France described in the *Jesuit Relations* of 1634.[14] Marie of the Incarnation secured the public patronage of Madame de la Peltrie, and Jeanne Mance was supported secretly by a French society woman named Madame de Bullion. Marguerite Bourgeoys, on the other hand, chose to come to the New World with no financial backing at all in order to practice strict poverty.

The last three women included in this chapter were all born in North America. Kateri Tekakwitha was the daughter of an Iroquois chieftain and an Algonquin Christian mother who had been kidnapped from Three Rivers. After converting to Christianity and escaping to Caughnawaga near Montreal in 1679, she became the first Indian to make a Christian vow of virginity and to live a life of penitential spirituality. Jeanne le Ber, the daughter of one of the wealthiest merchants in Montreal, entered a cell in 1695, where she remained as a consecrated recluse for the next nineteen years. Marguerite D'Youville, the daughter of a military leader in New France, took over the General Hospital of Montreal, after becoming a widow in 1747, and opened it to all the destitute of society: the elderly, orphans, and prostitutes, as well as wounded soldiers. She had separate areas for soldiers from all of the conflicting sides of the battles waged near Montreal, and she hid anyone caught behind the constantly changing enemy lines in the basement of the hospital. Her path of universal charity became incorporated into a new order of Grey Nuns, the first religious order to be established by a native of New France.

Among the most striking characteristics of these six women are the diverse ways in which they felt called to follow Christ. As mystic, teacher, intellectual, nurse, businesswoman, contemplative, artist, penitent, and servant of the poor, each led a life of traditional Christian witness in the new context of North America. While the first three women followed the apostolic, and the last three followed the penitential Catholic tradition of spirituality, their times and situations demanded different responses to the specific challenges of New France.

In spite of their great differences in background and vocation, these six women shared a common religious piety. First, the Virgin Mary played a central role in all of their lives. Marie of the Incarnation reported having a vision of Mary, which she interpreted as a call to New France (Document 1). Marguerite Bourgeoys described a message from Mary that confirmed her decision to come to Montreal (Document 12). She also defended her decision to found an uncloistered order by arguing that the Blessed Virgin was not cloistered (Document 16). Kateri Tekakwitha made her vow of virginity on a feast of the Blessed Virgin (Document 18). In 1711, Jeanne le Ber made a banner with the image of the Immaculate Conception for the French to carry in their defense against the English (Documents 21, 22). Marguerite D'Youville's first religious vows were made before a statue of the Blessed Virgin (Document 24). Their faith in the power of the Virgin Mary appears to have liberated and strengthened, rather than repressed, these women.

Another common feature in the lives of these women was their heroic response to the difficult living conditions of the New World. While each one may have begun her Christian life with high ideals, the situation in New France constantly challenged her in real ways. The climate, poverty, and frequent, destructive fires required continually renewed efforts to rebuild and go on with the original work (Documents 3, 10, 17, 25). The fear of English conquest or of meeting violent death at the hands of the Iroquois was countered by repeated decisions to carry on with missionary activity (Documents 4, 5, 6).

PAINFUL CONTRADICTIONS OF NEW FRANCE

From a contemporary perspective, the ideal of the early Christian settlers of New France was not realized. The Indians did not immediately convert *en masse* to Christianity, and New France did not establish a society that reflected the quality of life of the early Christians. The search to discover "What went wrong?" touches on many of the basic contradictions of the colonialist movement in the seventeenth and eighteenth centuries.

French-Indian Interactions

From the very beginning, French and Indian relations were violent. In 1534, Jacques Cartier kidnapped two Indians from the East Coast to take back to France.[15] In 1570, the Mohawks, Oneidas, Onondagas, Cayugas, and Senecas formed themselves into an Iroquois-speaking nation of approximately sixteen thousand members.[16] Then, in 1609, Samuel de Champlain, caught with Algonquin Indians in an ambush by the Iroquois, fired the first shots against the native people who would become the most feared enemy of the French. In the midst of this violence, the missionaries attempted their work of conversion; it is no wonder that many were martyred.

The turbulent relationship between the Iroquois and the French is detailed in this chapter through the correspondence of Marie of the Incarnation, in the *Annals* of Sr. Marie Morin, in fragments from the writings of Marguerite Bourgeoys, and in the eye-witness account of the life of Kateri Tekakwitha by the Jesuit Father Cholenec. These sources reveal the slow shift from hope for the conversion of the Iroquois, to horror at the Iroquois' brutal torturing and killing of their enemies, to relief with King Louis XIV's final decision to send an army to destroy the Iroquois threat once and for all. The French missionaries came to believe that the Iroquois were possessed by the devil and that, if conversion was impossible, their dispersion was inevitable and necessary to the Christianization of the New World.

It was often difficult for the French to distinguish the Christianization from the Francofication of the native peoples. Marie of the Incarnation made this distinction in some of her letters (Document 3). However, she frequently revealed her preference for French culture and was surprised at the free life-styles of the Indian girls, who reacted against strict French discipline by simply running off into the woods. In spite of this cultural bias, however, Marie of the Incarnation appears to have had a very genuine interest in the variety and characters of the different Indian tribes and peoples. Her detailed descriptions of the thoughts and life-styles of the Indians, as well as her success in writing the first dictionaries in the Algonquin, Montagnais, Huron, and Iroquois languages, attest to this (Documents 2, 8).

In addition to war and cultural bias, another painful contradiction in the relationship between the French and Indians involved the death of native peoples through infectious diseases. It is believed that, before European colonization, the Indians had been relatively free from disease. The Europeans brought typhus, smallpox, measles, whooping cough, influenza, diptheria, scarlet fever, tuberculosis, and the remnants of bubonic plague to the New World. Marie of the Incarnation's letters reveal that the Iroquois thought that the French *intended* to kill them through disease (Document 4), Marguerite Bourgeoys describes one of her trips to New France on a ship that had been contaminated (Document 14), and Fr. Cholenec states that Kateri Tekakwitha's mother, father, and brother were killed by smallpox, a disease which also left her severely scarred and partially blind (Document 18). It is estimated that the Micmac Indians (presettlement population of 4,880), the Hurons (presettlement population of between 18,000 and 30,000), and the Montagnais (presettlement population of 5,500) were reduced to approximately one-third of their original numbers by disease during their first hundred years of contact with the Europeans.[17] The French missionaries had to accept the painful fact that they were destroying through disease the very Indians who had welcomed them as friends.

Indian-Indian Interaction

When the first settlers arrived in the New World, they found various Indian nations engaged in tribal warfare. Inevitably, perhaps, since the French were welcomed by the Algonquin, Huron, and Montagnais nations, they would become enemies of the Iroquois who had been raiding, killing, and kidnapping their nothern neighbors. However, when the Dutch and English befriended the Iroquois, the hostilities took on a new dimension. The native people were encouraged by the Europeans to steal skins from their enemies in order to increase trade. The Indians were given, in exchange, metal tools, guns, and horses, which escalated the violence in their wars. Therefore, although entrenched hostilities certainly existed at the time of the European settlement, they increased in intensity as a result of the presence and the demands of the settlers. And with the subsequent war between the English and French, the divisions between the various Indian peoples were exploited even further. By the end of the eighteenth century, mere tribal rivalries had evolved toward wholesale destruction that bordered on the genocide of the various nations of the native peoples, and many Indians who had escaped death from disease fell instead in battle.

Some Indians chose to assimilate with the French. Those Iroquois, for example, who converted to Christianity moved to a reservation near Montreal. The French sought to establish different communities of Christian Indians, protected by a fort and doing agricultural work.[18] This was a difficult venture, because so many Indian nations were migratory and preferred hunting to farming. However, the French did establish some stable communities of Christian Indians. These Indians, in turn, were detested by those who remained non-Christian. The life of Kateri Tekakwitha reveals the price that, as a Christian Iroquois, she had to pay when recaptured by her hostile nation (Document 18).

Many Indians melded into the French culture by marriage. However, it seemed eventually that assimilation was working in the "wrong" direction—that is, French soldiers who married Indian women began to adopt the freer life-style of the native people. Therefore, between 1646 and 1715, the French sent over several young women to marry and settle in New France. These women, "Les Filles du Roi," were cared for and matched to prospective husbands by Marguerite Bourgeoys and her sisters.[19]

French-French Interaction

The New World also saw conflicts among the French themselves. From the outset, the colony was settled by people with two different aims. The missionaries sought to convert the Indians and to establish a society based on Christian principles; the merchants wanted to make money. It did not take long before this contradiction between the religious and commercial interests became evident. The *Correspondence* of Marie of the Incarnation reveals how the merchants undermined the work of the missionaries (Document 7). The most serious problem was the sale of alcohol, which damaged the Indians who had not been previously exposed to the grave effects of liquor. The church appealed to the governor to stop this practice, but the government sided with the merchants. The church became isolated and driven to employing moral exhortation and excommunication. The fact that the church continued to fight against the exploitation of the Indians through alcohol is revealed in the life of Marguerite D'Youville, whose husband was involved in this illicit trade (Document 23).

In addition to the tension between the French missionaries and the French merchants, there was also conflict between the aims of the French from the Old World and the French of the New World. While the colony was being supported by wealthy benefactors from Europe, who established hospitals, schools, and even paid for the army in emergency situations, King Louis XIII and King Louis XIV believed that New France had little to offer, and so they gave it as little as possible. When France finally did come to the rescue, it was too late. After the English conquest, the king completely withdrew his support. The French military elite in New France returned to their motherland, and debts were left unpaid. The letters of Marguerite D'Youville reveal how this abandonment of the colony by the French left the remaining settlers precariously dependent upon the English (Document 29).

French-English Interaction

When the French and English first settled in the New World in 1607 and 1608, there was very little difference in the size of their respective populations.[20] However, by the end of the seventeenth century, an imbalance in numbers was apparent: there were ten thousand French settlers in comparison to two hundred thousand English settlers. By the time of the English conquest in 1763, there were fifty-five thousand French settlers and a million and a half English settlers.

For the Roman Catholic French, the English were apostates who had rejected true Christianity. Although New France had been briefly conquered by the English in 1629, it was returned to the French in 1631, as part of an agreement in connection with the wars in Europe. Many settlers of New France moved out from their northern base and traveled down the Mississippi around 1685, and, in 1711, the English tried unsuccessfully to reconquer New France. It was in this battle that the recluse Jeanne le Ber played a miraculous role for the French (Documents 21, 22). In 1755, over six thousand French settlers in Acadia were deported and dispersed by the English to become the "Cajuns" of the Mississippi Valley. The English conquered Quebec City in 1759 and Montreal the following year, and in 1763, the Treaty of Paris was signed. A Province of Quebec, within an English country, was officially established in 1764. Marguerite D'Youville's letter to the Governor General of Canada in 1771 demonstrates the shift in relationship between the English, French, and Indians from the military battlefield to the level of government and the courts, where it remains today (Document 25).

CONCLUSION

Twentieth-century Quebec and Canada are still involved in a conflict between the "two solitudes" of the English- and French-speaking populations.[21] This conflict, in turn, goes on with a background of the "third solitude" of the native peoples. The fact that most of the sources used for this study are generally inaccessible to English-speaking North America demonstrates the entrenchment of this situation. Hopefully this chapter, which provides original writings and eye-witness accounts of some of the early women in New France, will help bridge the differences between the three cultures.[22]

The women of these documents represent, for the most part, forms of Counter-Reformation Catholic spirituality that have become foreign to modern Christians, including many Roman Catholics. Their ascetic practices focused on the intense personal mortification of the body and the will. Following a process similar to that of learning to read a foreign language, one must try to discipher the actual meaning of this spirituality in these women's lives and to discern how such practices expressed their inward power and resolve, providing them with an unassailable sense of identity and purpose in the context of their culture.[23]

Marie of the Incarnation, the first French woman missionary to come to the New World, founded an Ursuline convent in New France in 1639. She wrote dictionaries in the Algonquin, Huron, and Iroquois languages and dedicated her life to the conversion of the Indians to Christianity. [Courtesy Les Ursulines de Québec.]

By 1640, the Ursuline Convent in Quebec City was the largest building in New France. It was funded by Madame de la Peltrie, whose home is pictured below the convent. [Courtesy Les Ursulines de Québec.]

Jeanne Mance, one of the first lay women missionaries in North America, founded and directed the hospital L'Hôtel Dieu and co-founded the city of Montreal in 1642. [Courtesy Religieuses Hospitalières de St. Joseph, L'Hôtel Dieu, Montreal.]

Marguerite Bourgeoys arrived in Montreal in 1653 to set up schools to teach Indian and French children of the colony. [Courtesy Cathedral, Marie Reine du Monde, Montreal.]

In 1659, the first Hospital Sisters (Religious Hospitallers) of St. Joseph were welcomed by the settlers of Montreal. They came from France to help run L'Hôtel Dieu after Jeanne Mance became temporarily incapacitated by a broken arm. [Courtesy Religieuses Hospitalières de St. Joseph, L'Hôtel Dieu, Montreal.]

The only authentic portrait of Marguerite Bourgeoys was painted by Pierre le Ber, the brother of Jeanne le Ber, shortly after her death in 1700. [Courtesy La Congrégation de Notre-Dame, Montreal.]

Kateri Tekakwitha, from the Mohawks of the Iroquois Nation, became the first Indian to consecrate herself to perpetual virginity in 1679. [Courtesy Ellen Walworth.]

The only authentic portrait made of Kateri Tekakwitha was made by the Jesuit Father Chauchetière, who knew her personally after she escaped to Caughnawaga, a community of Christian Iroquois near Montreal. [Courtesy Georges Vanier Library, Loyola Campus, Concordia University, Montreal.]

While in her cell, Jeanne le Ber lived a life of contemplative prayer in the context of the artistic work of embroidering altar cloths and church vestments. [Courtesy La Congrégation de Notre-Dame, Montreal.]

Marguerite D'Youville was born in Varennes, Quebec, in 1701. After becoming a widow, she devoted herself to works of charity and founded the Grey Nuns. [Courtesy Les Soeurs Grises, Montreal.]

Documents: Women in Colonial French America

MARIE OF THE INCARNATION: THE THERESA OF THE NEW WORLD

1. *The Call to New France*
2. *The First Indian Converts*
3. *Life in Early New France*
4. *Disease and the Death of Fr. Issac Jogues*
5. *Renewed Missionary Activity*
6. *The Study of the Native Languages*
7. *The Indians Exploited by Alcohol*
8. *Beliefs and Practices of the Native People*
9. *Mystical Life of Marie of the Incarnation*

JEANNE MANCE: CO-FOUNDER OF MONTREAL AND FOUNDER OF L'HOTEL DIEU

10. *The Call to New France*
11. *The First Settlers in Montreal*

MARGUERITE BOURGEOYS: FOUNDER OF THE CONGREGATION OF NOTRE DAME

12. *The Call to New France*
13. *Traveling in France*
14. *Contaminated Ships*
15. *The Work of Poverty and Teaching*
16. *Freedom from the Cloister*
17. *Reaffirmation of the Spirit of Poverty*

KATERI TEKAKWITHA: THE LILY OF THE MOHAWKS

18. *The Life of Kateri Tekakwitha*

JEANNE LE BER: CONSECRATED RECLUSE

19. *Jeanne le Ber Described by Marguerite Bourgeoys*
20. *Jeanne le Ber Described in Annals* of Sr. Marie Morin
21. *Jean le Ber's Prayer to the Mother of Christ*

22. Jeanne le Ber's Description of the Banner of the Immaculate Conception

MARGUERITE D'YOUVILLE: FOUNDER OF THE GREY NUNS AND MOTHER OF UNIVERSAL CHARITY

23. Petition of Nipissing Indians Against M. D'Youville
24. The Life of Marguerite D'Youville
25. After the English Conquest

MARIE OF THE INCARNATION: THE THERESA OF THE NEW WORLD

Marie Guyart was born in Tours, France, in 1599. Her father was a skilled commoner and her mother was of noble lineage. In 1616, she married, only to be widowed two years later and left with an infant son. For the next ten years, she worked in the trading company of her brother-in-law. Then, in 1631, she left her son Claude and joined the Ursulines, a cloistered order of nuns in Tours. Her son reacted by repeatedly assailing the convent with sticks and stones, crying: "I want my mother back!"

In 1633, Marie of the Incarnation felt a "call" to New France and, seven years later, arrived in Quebec City as the first French woman missionary to the New World. She worked indefatigably during the next forty years to convert the native people to Christianity. Her more than thirteen thousand letters to her homeland are a legacy of valuable information about life in early New France and about the mentality of the missionaries. Many of these letters were written to her son who became an abbot of a Benedictine monastery in France.

In the following documents (1–9), we see suggestions of Marie of the Incarnation's extraordinary skill at observation, her dedication to learning the language and thought of the various Indian nations in America, and her powerful mystical experiences. These documents also provide an important historical record of the extremely difficult circumstances that faced the first settlers in New France.[24]

Document 1: The Call to New France[25]

From Tours, to Dom Raymond de S. Bernard, 3 May, 1635 (?)

My very Reverend Father. Since I cannot hide anything from you of the graces that our Lord sends me with His goodness, I shall tell you with my usual simplicity that one year ago at Christmas time, five or six days before my Mother Ursule and I entered the Noviciate to take up its direction, I felt very strongly united to God. Then after I fell asleep, it seemed to me that a friend and I, holding hands, were walking in a very difficult place. We could not see the obstacles which stopped us, we only felt them. However, we had so much courage that we surmounted all these difficulties and we arrived in a place called the tannery, where skins are left to dry out for two years before using them for different things. We had to go this way to get to our lodging. At the end of our path, we found a solitary man, who let us in a large and spacious place, with no other roof than the sky: the paved floor was as white as alabaster, spotless, but bordered with vermillion. There was an admirable silence. This man indicated with his hand the direction we had to turn, because he was as silent as he was solitary, saying only what was absolutely necessary. We saw in a corner of this place a little hospice or house made of white marble and made in the antique way with admirable architecture. There was on the roof an opening in the shape of a seat on which was sitting the Virgin Mary holding the baby Jesus in her arms. I was the first to move quickly towards her and spread my arms which extended to both sides of the place where she was sitting. My friend remained stationary in a place beside, from where she could easily still see the Blessed Virgin and her baby Jesus. This house was facing the east. It was built on a high place below which were large spaces, in which was situated a Church surrounded by such a thick mist that we could only see the top of the roof which was in clearer air. There was a path to go down from this large and spacious place, which was very dangerous with horrible rocks on one side and frightening precipices without openings, on the other side. In addition, it was so steep and so narrow that it was terrifying even to look at it. The Blessed Virgin was looking toward this very afflicted place, while I was burning from the desire to see the face of this "Mother of beautiful, tender love" because I could only see her back. As I was having these thoughts, she turned her head towards me, and showing me her face with a ravishing smile, she gave me a kiss. She turned also towards her baby Jesus, talking to him in secret, as if she had some designs on me. She did the same thing three times. My friend who had already started going down the path did not have any part in the caresses of the Blessed Virgin, she only had the consolation of seeing her from where she was.

The pleasure I felt from such an agreeable event can not be expressed. I awakened then, still feeling the kindness I experienced, and this lasted for many days. However, then I kept wondering what such an extraordinary thing could mean whose execution had to remain very secret: for in the vision that was shown to me, everything happened so secretly that only the man I talked about knew about it and said a few words.

At the beginning of this year, as I was in prayer, all that was brought back into my mind with the thought that this so afflicted place I saw was New France. I felt a very interior attraction to found there a House for Jesus and Mary. I was then so strongly taken by this thought that I gave my consent to the Lord and promised Him to obey Him if He would give me the means. The command of Our Lord and the promise I made to obey Him are so imprinted on my mind, on top of the feelings already communicated to you, that even if I had a million lives I would have no fear about risking them. And really, the vision and the strong faith that I feel will condemn me on the day of Judgement if I do not act according to what the Divine Majesty asks of me. Think about that a little, I beg you. These things happened in the simplicity I just described to you, and I felt obliged to tell you, and then to abandon them to the Providence of our Divine Spouse.

Document 2: The First Indian Converts[26]

From Quebec City to a Woman of Quality [Marguerite Therisault?], 3, September, 1640

Madame . . .

The name of the first Indian who was given to us as a student was Marie Negabmat; she was so used to running in the woods that we were losing all hope of retaining her in the school. Father Le Jeune, who had persuaded her father to give her to us, sent two older Christian Indian girls with her, to stay with her and try to calm her, but in vain because four days later she fled into the woods, having torn a dress we gave her to pieces. Her father, who is an excellent Christian and lives like a saint, ordered her to come back to the school, which she did. She had not been there two days when an admirable change occurred in her. She did not seem to be herself any more because she was so inclined to prayer and practices of Christian piety; today she is an example for the girls of Quebec, although they are all very well raised.

At the same time we were given an older girl, seventeen years old, called Marie Amiskvian. It is impossible to see anyone more supple or innocent; or more honest, because we have not once caught her lying, which is a great virtue when it is a question of Indians. If her friends accuse her, she never defends herself: she is so ardent in her prayer that it is never necessary to remind her about it; she even encourages the others to pray and she seems like their mother, because she shows so much charity towards them. She is very intelligent, and remembers everything she is told, particularly concerning the mysteries of our holy faith; which makes us hope that she will do a lot of good when she will be back among the Indians. Oh, may God grant the grace of someone in France to help her build a little house! She would certainly accomplish work of great merit. This girl helped us very much with the study of the language because she speaks French well. In a word, this girl touches the sensibilities of everyone with her gentleness and her beautiful qualities.

Your god-daughter Marie Magdelaine Abatenau was given us covered with small pox and only six years old. At this age she had helped her father and mother during this disease from which they died, with such an ability that all of those who saw her were filled with admiration. It is impossible to see anyone more obedient than this child: she even anticipates obedience because she has the talent of putting herself in places where she sees beforehand that she might be needed: and she does what she is told with so much good will and with such grace that she could be taken for a "girl of quality". Well, she is your god-daughter, I would even say your daughter in Christ. I shall add for your consolation that she knows by heart her catechism and the Christian prayers which she recites with such a devotion that she inspires people who see her. . . .

It would take too long to talk separately of each one of them but in general I will tell you that these young girls love us more than their own parents, showing no signs of wanting to return to them, which is quite extraordinary among Indians. They learn from us as much as their age and condition allows. When we are doing our spiritual exercises they kept a profound silence; they did not even dare to look up, or watch us, thinking that they would interrupt us. But it is impossible to describe their caresses which they never give to their natural mothers, when we were finished. Four of them made their First Communion at Easter; they acted with such purity that the least shadow of sin frightened them and with such an ardor and wish to unite themselves to Our Lord, that while waiting to receive Him they could not help crying out: "Ah, when will Jesus at last come and kiss our heart." The R. Father Pijart, who had baptized and instructed them for Communion, seeing such an angelic attitude, could not restrain his tears. We received eighteen of them, not counting the women and Indian girls who are allowed to come to the place reserved for the instruction of the French and Indian girls. After the instruction and the prayers we prepare a festive meal according to their habits. Their hunger is the clock which lets them know the hour of the meal; so after having set the table for our students, we must also think of those others who may come. This is done especially in winter, when old people can not follow the hunt, and if we did not take care of them at this time they would die of hunger in their huts. God gave us this grace to allow us to help them until spring so that they have partaken of good company, and it will be for us a real consolation to be able to continue helping them with the aid of the charitable people of France, without whom this would be completely impossible; our little school cannot meet the large expenses which are necessary for the upkeep of the students and help the other Indians by itself. I assure you, Madam, these expenses are incredible. We had brought clothes for two years; everything has been used this year, and we now have to clothe them with part of our own clothes. All the clothes (and linens) that Marie our Foundress gave us for our own uses, and part of what our Mothers of France sent us, have been employed also to clothe them. It is a special consolation for us to deprive ourselves of necessities, to win souls for Jesus Christ, and we would rather lack everything than leave our daughters to the unbearable dirt which they bring from their huts. When they are given to us they are as naked as worms and we must wash them from head to toe, because of the grease their parents cover their body with: and in spite of our diligence and in spite of the fact we often change their clothes, it takes a long time to get rid of the vermine (lice) caused by all of this grease.

One of the Sisters spends part of the day doing that. It is a work everybody looks forward to; the one who is chosen judges herself rich in happiness; the others judge themselves unworthy of this chore and remain humble. Madame our Foundress (Madame de la Peltrie) did it almost all year long; now it is Mère Marie of St. Joseph who benefits from this happiness. . . .

Document 3: Life in Early New France[27]

From Quebec, to her son, 26 August, 1644

Jesus, Mary, Joseph

My very dear and well-loved Son . . .

To answer your questions about the country, I will tell you, my dearest son, that there are houses made of stone, wood, and bark. Ours is all stone; it is ninety-two feet long and twenty-eight feet wide: it is the most beautiful and the largest one in Canada. This includes the church whose length is the width of the house, seventeen feet wide. You may think that this is small but the intense cold does not allow for a vast place. At times the priests are in danger of having frostbitten hands or ears. Our choir, the school, and our lodging are, as I said, included in ninety-two feet of length and twenty of width. The fort is made out of stones as are the houses under its protection. Those of the R. PP, of Madame our Foundress, of the Mères hospitalières, and of the sedentary Indians are made of stone. Those of the inhabitants, of masoned wood construction; of which two or three are made of real stones. Some of the Indians have their movable houses made of birch bark, which they put up very nicely with long wooden supports. At the beginning we had one like that for our school. Do not imagine that our houses are made out of cut stones; no, just the corners. We use a special kind of stone, which resembles a black marble, and which cuts very well, better than that of central France. The corners are very beautiful but very expensive to cut because of their hardness. One worker costs thirty sols a day and we feed him on Feast days, Sundays, and during bad weather. We have our workers come from France and we rent them for three years or more. We have ten of them who do all our work, but the settlers provide us with the oxide of calcium, sand, and brick. Our house has three floors. Our cells are in the middle one, made just like those in France. Our fireplace is at the end of the dormitory to warm up the corridor and the cells are only separated by pinewood. We could not heat them otherwise, and I do not think one could stay very long in one's cell in winter without heat. To say one hour would be a gross exaggeration; even then one must have the hands protected and be well clothed. Outside of the Observance of the Office, by necessity, the usual place to read, write, and study is near the fire which is inconvenient, and an extreme imposition particularly for me, who never needed heat in France. Our beds are made of wood and close up like closets and, although they are covered with blankets, we can hardly warm up in them. In winter our Indians leave their stone houses and go build huts in the woods where it is not as cold. We put on five or six logs at a time, for one can only burn large wood, and in spite of that, one side gets warmed up, but the other one freezes. With four fireplaces, we burn during the year, six months of which are winter, one hundred and seventy five cords of wood. Despite the intense cold, we keep the choir open all winter long, but there one is only slightly uncomfortable. . . .

The Indians have clothes. In summer they wear a big moose skin, square, like a blanket, and a large cow skin, that they put on their shoulders. They attach it with little cords, so as to leave their arms naked on both sides. That is all they wear besides an underskin; their feet and their heads remain naked. Alone, in the country, or when they are fighting their enemies, they are as naked as the hand, except for a piece of skin which covers them modestly enough; their skin is almost invisible because of the sun and the greases with which they cover themselves, and their face is painted with red and blue lines. In winter they use blankets for dresses, fixed as described above, with sleeves and leather shoes, or old blankets which reach to the belt. They wear a furry beaver skin for a coat. Those who cover their head buy red night caps at the store. They also have capes or wide brimmed hats which the Fathers abandon, and we give to them. That holds for those who are well clothed; but some are nearly naked summer or winter because of their poverty. As far as the women are concerned, they are very modestly clothed; they always wear belts (the men almost never do and their dresses fly in the wind); their dresses go to knee length from the top of the neck; their arms and head are almost always covered with a red night cap, or a wide brimmed hat or cape, their hair falling down at the front and attached in back. They are very modest and chaste. We are making little long dresses for our students, and cutting their hair in French styles. It would be hard to distinguish a man from a woman if it were not for the belt, because their faces look the same. Their shoes are made of the moose's skin, a sort of buffalo. They sew this in front; there is a square piece for the heel. They pass a little string through, as on a purse, and these are their shoes. The French do not wear anything else in winter, because it is impossible to go out without snowshoes to walk on the snow and so French shoes are useless. There, that is what you wanted to know on that point.

Is our community large? Just enough for the time being. We are eight choir sisters and one domestic sister, four come from our house in Tours and four from the Paris Congregation; the domestic sister is from Dieppe. I shall write further of all that. The Mothers of the hospital have only five in the choir and one domestic sister.

Are our Indians as perfect as I have told you? As far as their natural ways are concerned they do not display French "politesse": I mean if one means French comportment as a norm. We have not put our efforts there, but rather in teaching them the commandments of God and of the Church, all the points of our faith, all the prayers, to do their examination of conscience well, and all other religious actions. An Indian goes to confession as well as a male or female religious; they are very innocent and attach importance to the smallest things, and when they commit a sin, they do public penances with great humility. . . .

Document 4: Disease and the Death of Fr. Issac Jogues[28]

From Quebec to her son, summer 1647

My very dear and well-loved son.

Since every year I tell you of the graces and blessings that God pours on this new Church, I should also let you know about the afflictions He also allows. Sometimes He consoles us like a loving father, and at other times he punishes like a severe judge, and particularly me who, more than anyone else, provokes his anger with my continual infidelities. This year He made us all feel the heaviness of his hand through a sadness particularly bitter for those concerned with the salvation of souls. It is the story of the treacherous Iroquois breaking the peace and killing many Frenchmen and Christian Indians, and particularly Father Jogues.

The hatred for our faith and prayer, that some Huron captives gave them, impelled the barbarians to shatter what we thought was a well-established peace. They pretended that it was the cause of all sorts of trouble for their nation, and that it helped infect them with contagious sickness, and made their hunting and fishing expeditions less successful than when they were following their ancient customs. At almost the same time death touched their nation; it spread in their villages, and took many people in a very short time. The evil wind produced some kind of worm in their blood which nearly drove them all mad. These unfortunate happenings easily convinced them that what the captive Hurons told them was true. Father Jogues, who had visited them as representative of the Governor and all Christians, French as well as Indians, to confirm the peace, had left his hosts, as a guarantee of his return, a small valise with some books and some religious items; they thought these things that he left among them demonic, the cause of their misfortunes. All these reasons, together with their infidelity (for they do not know what it means to keep one's word), plus the loss of the spoils they used to acquire from their victories over their enemies, made them ignore all the promises they had made to us and to vow the destruction of their old adversaries. At the same time, they sent presents to the leaders of the Iroquois Nations, that is the Onondageronous (Senecas) and others, to seduce them to their conspiracy, which they quickly joined.

In the meantime the Governor, who did not know anything about this change, prepared some Frenchmen and some Hurons to go to visit them. Father Jogues, who had already begun to shed his blood in this ungrateful country, joined them to give them advice and help during the trip. They left Three Rivers on September 24, 1646 and arrived at the Iroquois Ageneronons (Mohawks), after much hardship on October 17 of the same year. As soon as they arrived they were treated in a way they were not expecting. They did not even have time to get inside the cabins before they were mistreated. First, their clothes were pulled off, then they were met with blows from sticks and fists, and with these words: "Do not be surprised by this kind of treatment, because tomorrow you will die. But console yourselves you will not be burned; you will be chopped up by axes and your heads will be put on the fences around our village, so that your brothers will see you when they are captured." They knew from this reception that the others were so cruelly turned against them that there was no hope; so they prepared themselves for death in the short time that was left to them. But the following day was quiet and this led them to think that these barbarians were softening. But in the evening an Indian of the Bear Nation took Fr. Jogues into his cabin for supper; another was hidden behind the door, waiting for him; he hit him with an axe and he fell on the ground, dead. He did the same to a young Frenchman, named Jean de la Lande, from Dieppe, an aide to Father J. A barbarian cut off their heads and put them up as trophies on the fence, and threw their bodies into the river. This is how this great servant of God consummated his sacrifice. We honour him as a Martyr since he was massacred out of hatred for our Holy Faith and for the prayers that these infidels take as sorcery and enchantments.

Document 5: Renewed Missionary Activity [29]

From Quebec, to her son, 24 September, 1654

My very dear son. Jesus be our life and our all for Eternity.

I cannot let the ships leave without telling you something of what happened in this new Church since last year. I told you about the captivity of Father Poncet, and how he returned to God after the Iroquois had made him suffer many things. (These events seemed to tell us that God's pleasure was that this good Father be offered to die as a sacrifice, to praise Him, and thus to give peace to the whole country by his death.) Since then the Iroquois have not ceased coming and asking for peace. And what is most marvelous is that those from the neighboring Nations, who were not familiar with what was happening among the other Nations, also came to the same time to talk with us. To show that they were sincerely desiring peace, they brought back at their own expense, and sent him back to his home, a young man from Montreal, who was the surgeon of the French Colony, having heard that a barbarous Nation had taken him as prisoner. They offered important gifts to the French to persuade them to spend the winter with them and to serve as a witness the faith. We gave them two priest volunteers. During all the time they lived there, they were cherished and loved in an extraordinary way, and finally brought them back in the spring, carrying letters with them from the Dutch, testifying of the good faith of the Iroquois asking for peace.

All year long the French, the Hurons, the Algonquins, and the Montagnais lived together like brothers. We worship, farm, and trade with total liberty; still the poor Indians do not dare in general, to have full confidence in the Iroquois, having suffered so many times from their faithlessness. They keep saying to our Frenchmen that the Iroquois are frauds, that all their peace talks are only ploys to destroy us. They also say that to the Iroquois themselves, which we thought would spoil and end the whole enterprise. But the Iroquois carried on with such insistence that we gave in to their prayers. It is edifying to hear them talk about peace; they only employed the most sensitive among them to be their Ambassadors for this treaty, and those who are known to be very intelligent and to know how to comport themselves. . . .

If this peace lasts, and there is reason to hope, this country will be very good, and amenable for colonization by the French, who become more numerous, and who fairly well cultivate the fields that are quite fertile now that the large and forbidding forests have been felled. After three or four years of ploughing the earth is as good as, and in some places better than, in France. We raise cattle for the meat and the milk products. This peace increases the trade, particularly in beaver, of which there are many this year because we could go hunting everywhere without being afraid. However, the traffic of souls is the joy of those who crossed the seas to find them, and win them to Jesus Christ.

Document 6: The Study of the Native Languages[30]

From Quebec, to her son, 10 August, 1662

My very dear Son . . .

Despite their lovely talks of peace, the Iroquois began murdering again, near Montreal, at the beginning of Fall. Those who kill are Agneronons (Mohawks), and those who ask for peace are the Onnontageronons (Senecas) and the Oiogueronons (Oneidas); but confidence in either one is groundless.

We do not yet know what happened to Father le Moine nor to our

French prisoners, nor to Father Mesnard who is staying with the Outaouok (Ottawas), with whom he was supposed to go this year and where he should already have arrived. The Iroquois, who heard about it, hid along the trails to take them prisoner and to steal all their skins. There were about three or four hundred. If they complete the journey successfully, the French merchants who come here to trade will gain a great deal; but if they are destroyed, our merchants will have made the trip for nothing. One of them told me today that he would lose, himself, more than twenty thousand pounds. But alas! All things considered, what is most deplorable is what happens to the souls of these people, most of whom are not yet Christians. If they had been able to come here they would have spent the winter here and we would have had time and opportunity to teach and baptise them. Everyone gravitates to what he likes: the merchants to money, the Fathers and us to souls. This last motive can be a strong spear, to pierce and inspire the heart. Last winter I had three or four young sisters staying near me hoping to learn what I know about the languages of the country. Their strong and fervent desire gave me the ardor and requisite strength to instruct them orally and in writing all that was necessary. From Advent to the end of February I wrote a Huron Catechism, three Algonquin Catechisms, all the Christian prayers in that language, and a big Algonquin dictionary for them. I became extremely tired, I assure you, but it was necessary to satisfy these hearts wishing to serve God in the functions our Institution demands. Pray to the Divine Goodness that all be for His great glory. . . .

Pray for us, I beg you, because we suffer another cross, much heavier than the Iroquois, because it tends to destroy Christianity. I shall talk about it in another letter, since the ship which is leaving obliges me to finish this letter.

Document 7: The Indians Exploited by Alcohol[31]

From Quebec, to her son, 10 August, 1662

My very dear son.

I mentioned to you in another letter a cross which I told you was more painful to me than all the hostilities of the Iroquois. Here is what it is. There are some Frenchmen in this country so low and without fear of God, that they lose all our new Christians by giving them strong drinks like wine and 'eau de vie' to get beaverskins. These drinks destroy all these unfortunate people, men, women, boys, and even girls; because everyone is master in the cabin when it is a question of eating and drinking; they are caught right away and become wild. They run naked with swords and other arms and frighten everyone, day or night, across Quebec City and no one can stop them. They then commit murders, violent ones, and awful, and incredible brutalities. The Fathers did their utmost to destroy this evil both on the French side as on that of the Indians; all their efforts were in vain. When we tried to show to our Indian daughters who come from outside to our classes, the evil they cause by following their parents example, they did not set foot here anymore. The nature of the Indians is like that: they do whatever they see those of their Nation do as far as habits are concerned, unless they are well formed in Chritian morality. An Algonquin chief, an excellent Christian and the first to be baptised in Canada, complained while visiting us, saying: "Onontio," that is the Governor, "kills us by allowing alcohol to be given to us." We answered, "Tell him to forbid it." "I already told him twice," he said, "and he does not do anything; but beg him yourself to forbid it, maybe he will listen to you."

Document 8: Beliefs and Practices of the Native People[32]

From Quebec, to her son, 1670

My very dear Son,

By this letter I answer precisely the questions you ask concerning our Indians. What I forgot was answered by a good Father, and you can be sure that everything is true. You will see the absurdities of men who neither have faith nor natural insights because of the corrupted nature all powerful in them before baptism. You ask:

1. If the Indians, before seeing the Europeans had any knowledge of the true God, and what kind of knowledge they had?

I answer that they did not have any. Only some of them, reflecting on the movements of the sky, the disposition of the stars, and the constant order of the seasons, knew by natural reasoning that there was some powerful genius, who having created all these things ruled them with such wisdom. I knew some who, filled with admiration in view of the harmony of things which are in Nature, were meditating on these and saying: "Certainly there exists an Author of all the things we see in the world because all that can not have been done by itself." In this way, they were praying to the one who made everything, and those who became Christians kept this way of praying so that when they went to pray to God they say: "You who made everything, etc." These, convinced by their reason, spoke as I explained, and offered Him gifts like cornflour and tobacco which are the most precious things they have. Two Algonquin captains who were among them, after hearing Father le Jeune, believed right away and embraced our faith. They were the first two Christians and both of them gave us their daughters the day after we arrived in this country. There are many examples of that which show the admirable goodness of God.

2. If they were worshipping some Divinity and what kind of cult they were honouring it with?

Some were worshipping the Sun and offering it sacrifices, throwing bear fat, or moose fat, or fat of other animals in the fire, or burning tobacco or corn flour. Some believed in a certain Messou, who redeemed the world. This belief is beautiful, and is well in agreement with the coming of the Messiah, who was the Redeemer of the world. However, the blindness of infidelity stained this beautiful light by the most ridiculous story: the Hurons who had this belief pretended that this Messou redeemed the world with the help of some muskrats. Some others believed in a certain genius whom they said ruled over the waters, the woods, mountains, valleys and in other places. But all of them were obeying their dreams like a divinity, doing exactly what they saw in their sleep. If a man had dreamt that he was killing another man, as soon as he woke up he went to look for him, surprised him, and killed him. Those who did not receive the Faith are still doing that, because they feel obliged to obey their dreams; and this evil is one of the main obstacles to the Faith. I just learned two stories which confirm what I just told you and which can move the hearts of those born into Chrisitianity to thank the Divine Goodness for such a precious destiny, so pure, so remote from error. An Indian who was far within the Iroquois territory, having dreamt that he had to kill his wife, who was then in Montreal in a village of Indians, most of them Iroquois, got up quickly and came to this village, which is more than 100 leagues (four hundred kilometers) from his country to kill this woman who is Christian. The Fathers, having heard about the madness of this man, hid her in a closed cabin. This furious man entered anyway, with dogs biting the woman, since they are raised for that. She ran to the attic, the dogs following her. Finally she jumped outside, fled, and the Indians caught her. You can see the blindness of these infidels who can walk more than one hundred leagues to obey a dream. Another one dreamt that he had to kidnap a girl and he walked as far as the first one to obey his dream. She fled to the Fathers who hid her; the other one, as furious as ever, threatened to kill everyone if this girl was not given to him. While a Father was talking to him to keep him busy, the girl was put in a canoe to escape; the other one runs after her. She was taken to Chambly which is one of the Forts on the Iroquois paths; he still pursues her. She was hidden in different places; but he did not give up his search. Finally, he caught her and kidnapped her. Isn't that a strange barbarity? What makes it worse are the drinks that the French give to the Indians; because when these have drunk 'eau de vie' they not only idolize their dream, but also their drunkenness, and when these two things are joined together one cannot see anything more ferocious: for they kill each other, they cut off each others' noses and ears and we can see a great number of them mutilated. But let us go back to our questions.

3. Did they believe in the immortality of the soul and if they did what happened to the soul after death?

They believed in the immortality of the soul and the honour which they bestowed on the body is a proof of that. They thought that the souls separated from the bodies were going beyond the sea where they remained in peace. To make this trip they gave them some provisions, burning some animal fat near the grave of the dead. They even gave them some arms and other necessary things for the trip. Generally speaking, all the people of America think that the soul is immortal, and that after death it goes where the sun sets and never rises. They were so immersed in that thought, before they met the Europeans, that when we were teaching them catechism and talking about Heaven, they said they did not want to go there, but to the country of the souls where their parents were going. They thought the souls were living there off beaver's, moose's, or other animals souls whose bodies they ate during their life. This belief in the immortality of souls helps them a lot for their conversion.

4. If they had some kind of police for peace, for war, for government?

Yes, they did. They send Ambassadors to each other for peace talks, but they often unfairly kill the Ambassadors. They make war by taking each other by surprise. They sometimes attack the villages, and take them; sometimes they lift the siege. They do not fight too often because their government is not all powerful. The chiefs direct the young the way they want with simple remarks, but they need much eloquence and persuasion to win them.

5. Did they have any knowledge about the creation of the world, the flood, or some writing close to the Gospel?

No, not of the first one, except that through reasoning they concluded from the harmony of the world that there was some great genius who created it, and who kept it in such good and precise order, as I already mentioned. For the second point their fables have something in common with what Scripture says about the flood. The Abnakiouois (Abenaki's) who are a people from the south talk about a Virgin who gave birth to a big Nan. These people had less contact with the Europeans than with the other Nations of America, so this knowledge of the Virgin Mother is extraordinary and amazing. The same goes for this big Nan whose Mother she is, because it is this Messou I spoke about whom the Hurons pretend redeemed the world with muskrats.

6. How did they keep the traditions of their past and of what happened in the past; did they have some alphabet to do so?

They kept the traditions of their past by the stories that fathers told their children, and the elders to the young; they do not use writing or any other character. This lack of writing is the reason that their traditions are mixed with a lot of fables and falseties, which get exaggerated with time. They can not understand how, by letters, we are able to know what is happening in France and other places. Their faith becomes stronger when we tell them that writing teaches us our Mysteries. If they are three or four hundred leagues away, and when their people who come here for the fur trade, go back carrying letters to the Fathers who look after them, they are amazed that these Fathers tell them all they did and said in Quebec. They can not understand how this letter they carried could say such amazing truths without ever making an error. That is why they think of the Fathers as "Manitoux", from whom nothing can be hidden and for whom nothing is impossible, and this helps a lot in their Faith.

7. What arms are they using for war, and how did they make them?

They use wooden hatchets, bows and arrows whose point was made of moose or caribou bone, or of stones which they sharpened. They carried a quiver on their backs when they went to war.

8. How did they live, having no kitchen tools, nor the use of fire; or if they did not know how to keep it?

They used very well made bark dishes. Before they met the Europeans they could make fire with stones, of which they had many. And to cook meat, either they roasted it over the fire or they boiled it in large dishes made of bark which they filled with water; then they heated a good number of stones until they became red and put them in the water to heat it and boil it until the meat was cooked. . . . I showed what I just wrote to one of our Fathers who is very knowledgeable in these matters, so as not to tell you anything not fully true. I send it to you with his approbation.

Document 9: Mystical Life of Marie of the Incarnation [33]

From Quebec, to her son, summer 1647

My very dear and well-beloved Son, the peace of our most lovable and most adorable Jesus be with you.

I received your letter and everything in the package when I was not expecting it anymore. . . . You reproach me for a lack of affection which I can not bear to leave without response, since I am still alive as is God's will. You have some ground to complain about my leaving you. And for myself, I would gladly complain, if I had permission from the one who brought the sword on the earth to make such strange separations. It is true that despite the fact that you were the only thing in the world left for me to which my heart was attached, He still wanted to separate us when you still were at the breast, and I fought almost twelve years more to keep you before it was necessary to part from one another. At last it was necessary to submit to the strength of Divine love and accept this wound of separation, more painful than I can describe to you; this did not stop me from reproaching myself a thousand times for being the cruelest of mothers. I ask your forgiveness my dearest son; you suffered a great deal because of me. However, let us console ourselves in the fact that life is short and that we shall have, thanks to the mercy of Him who separated us in the world, the whole eternity to see each other and to rejoice in Him. . . .

You wish to know how God works in me. I would be happy to tell you so that you can bless this eneffable goodness which so lovingly calls us into its service. However, you know that there is so much danger that these letters might fall into other hands, that the fear that this may happen prevents me. However, I assure you that in the following I will not hide anything of my present state of mind from you: at least I shall describe it so clearly that you will be able to know of it. To tell the truth I feel I owe that to a son who consecrated his life to the service of my divine master and with whom I share the same spirit. Here is a record which will show you in what disposition of mind I was when I recovered from my sickness almost two years ago. Not that I indulge in recording my feelings if it is not necessary; but at that time a sentence of Holy Scripture so drew my mind that, because of my weakness, incapable of sustaining this excitement, I was forced to calm myself by taking my pen and writing these few words, which will let you know the path through which this infinite Goodness leads me. . . .

Since my sickness my interior disposition has been characterized by a very particular detachment from all things, so that all exterior things are a cross to me. They do not trouble me, though, for I suffer them by accepting God's orders which put me in a state of obedience in which nothing can happen to me except from Him. I feel in me something which gives me a steady inclination to follow and embrace what I know to be best for the glory of God and what seems most perfect in the maxims of the Gospel, conforming to my situation, everything under the direction of my Superior. I make endless mistakes which extremely humiliate me.

For almost three years I have been thinking of death all of the time; however, I do not want, and can not want, either life or death, but only Him who is the Master of life and death, according to whose adorable judgement I commit myself to doing whatever He in eternity arranged for me. These feelings give my soul and my body a fundamental peace and a spiritual food which helps me to survive and support all kinds of accidents and all the things, general or particular, which happen to others or to me with a balanced mind—in this part of the world, where it is easy to find occasion to practice patience and other virtues that I do not have.

Anyway, do not rejoice, as you say, at the fact that you have a mother who serves God with purity and fidelity; but after having given thanks to this ineffable Goodness for the favours I am filled with, ask Him forgiveness for my infidelities and spiritual impurities;

I ask you not to forget that, and to ask for the opposite virtues. Here then is this record I described; I copy it because it is only a rough copy composed without any purpose and only to comfort a weak head. After reading these words of the Prophet: *Speciosus forma proe filiis hominum* (You are the most beautiful of the children of man. Ps. 44, 3), a light filled my mind with the double beauty of the Son of God, and I had to clarify my mind with my pen, but without thinking, because the spirit did not allow it. Since it was to the second person of the Holy Trinity that my soul had access, it was to Him that my aspirations were directed, following the ways of the spirit. Everything is ineffable at its foundation, but this is what can be expressed:

You are the most beautiful of all the children of man, O my Beloved! You are beautiful, my dear Love, in both your divine and human beauty.

You are beautiful, my dear Love, and you transport my mind in an interior vision of what you are in your Father and of what your Father is in You. But how could I stand before your splendours, unless you ravished my heart and mind. In this ravishing you brought it to yourself allowing it to be one with you. So even though I see you as God of God, Light of Light and True God of True God, still I kiss you as being my Love and all my goal.

O my Divine Spouse! How is this? I see you belonging to your Father and you belong to me: your Father and you belong to me; your Father also belongs to me and I do not know how this came about.

I see myself in the One in Whom I do that which I desire by the power that this One gives to me, who is my Love and my Life.

O my dear Beloved: In this familiarity which entices my soul I feel I am losing myself in a bottomless abyss. You are this profound abyss, You who hold me with Your power; and then, oh Father, at the same time You inspire me in such a way that I talk to you as if I had power over You.

Forgive my liberty, of which You are Yourself the cause, because in this state you consume me.

This opening you made in my heart, which is continually inhaling, breathing, and sighing, is a mouth which tells you words which would kill the body, if it had to go through the senses, since everything comes to saying that I see You to be essentially Love! Love! Having made me sing this canticle which makes me find myself in You again and again, You render me mute.

I am powerless by a consumption of love in You that I can not express: I can see aspects of your greatness and of your loving actions, O Uncreated Word, they destroy my thoughts in a deep abyss where they become lost.

You know, my dear Spouse, what occurred in my heart at the words my spiritual Father told me after having received my confession: that even if I should die alone and away from him, because of the channel you provide to my soul, I should not be afraid, otherwise I would not treat You like a spouse in whom I must have confidence. My spirit is still touched by these words: to not see you as a Spouse, that is unbearable; that is why, after that, I did not worry about anything anymore.

My beloved, I used to tell You, You know all my affairs; take care of them for me, You know how many souls I am responsible for, presenting them every day to Your Father or Your divine heart; today I am so sick and so weak, that I could not do it any more. I abandon myself to Your will.

After that I felt discharged of all my worries, and my heart aspiring towards You, I spoke with You from time to time, as if abandoned in You: my beloved, you are taking care of my affairs, my dear Love, You took on the responsibility.

I felt annoyed when my Father commanded me to ask You what place You would give me if you called me near You. Because, my dear Love, I so much abandoned myself to Your desires that I barely considered what would become of me.

I asked you, anyway, what obedience wanted me to; but while asking You I felt transported in this abandonment: put me where You want, everywhere You will be my Love. I hope I shall see You in Your double divine beauty—human among the splendour of the saints on the day of Your victory. You, my Beloved, Who, for the love of men became man and visible to make men divine through participation.

I joyfully await your final coming, so that my soul, seeing you triumph over your enemies, may sing Your Victories with You.

What I find incomprehensible to me here, is the degree of possession that your beloved will accept from You.

If my heart follows its bent, only You know the channel it has to Your divine heart.

Ah! I must finish here my dear Love, my pledge, my caution, and my life. You are all to me, and I find I belong to You in spite of my corruption and my weaknesses.

Enough of these matters, my beloved son, for this year. I am so deeply worried by external affairs, that I may only write to you during the brief moments I steal away. I also have to answer more than twenty-six letters and send the other writings to the Community in France. This is how we must spend this life, while waiting for Eternity, which does not pass away. You comforted me by informing me of the news of your holy Congregation and the happy success of its projects. For you finally only know God; remain hidden from all talk except that in which God will be glorified: otherwise remain hidden in our very adorable Jesus, our only Good, our Life, and our Totality.

JEANNE MANCE: CO-FOUNDER OF MONTREAL AND FOUNDER OF L'HÔTEL DIEU

Jeanne Mance was born in 1606 at Langres, one of the frontier towns caught in the throes of the Thirty Year's War, and was a nurse at one of the many hospitals for the wounded. In 1640, she learned that women too had made the trip to New France, and she decided to follow along. Two years later, after securing funds from the wealthy Madame de Bullion, she co-founded Ville Marie de Montréal. Soon afterwards, she built L'Hôtel Dieu, the first hospital of the settlement.

During the next thirty years, Jeanne Mance directed the hospital, served as treasurer of the settlement, and helped develop a community of lay Christian women and men—an innovation in Roman Catholic spirituality, which had placed so much emphasis on clerical communities. Jeanne Mance saved Montreal three times by procuring necessary funds either through trips to France or through transferring funds given for the hospital into finances for arms.

Since L'Hôtel Dieu burned three times, the original writings of Jeanne Mance have been lost. However, an eye-witness account of her life has been preserved in the Annals *of Sr. Marie Morin, the first North American-born religious who entered the Religious Hospitallers of St. Joseph in Montreal in 1662. Sr. Morin is also considered to be the first historian of Ville Marie de Montréal. In the following documents (10–11), Sr. Morin described the life of the first settlers in Montreal and Jeanne Mance's role in this lay community.*[34]

Document 10: The Call to New France[35]

The island of Montreal is situated near the middle of Canada on the southern side as compared with Quebec which is more toward the north; it is said to be thirty leagues long. In the middle is the mountain called Mount Royal, which gave its name to the whole island, though it is singly called today Ville-Marie. M. de la Dauversière to whom it belonged, gave it this beautiful name, then he gave it as a present to the Priests of St. Sulpice of the Seminary of Paris who are now the Seigneurs. Since they profess a special respect and love for the Holy Virgin and are very anxious to have her honoured, they appreciated very much this beautiful name and contributed to the settlement. Ville Marie is thought to be the most advantageous outpost of New France, at least by the people who know it, for two reasons. First because of the commerce; this place is the meeting point for all the Indian tribes who come from everywhere to bring beaver pelts and other skins they find in their countries. The French merchants covet these and they have much business with Old France and other kingdoms in times of peace.

If Ville Marie has these advantages compared with many other cities and seigneuries, it is also exposed to a very special suffering: it is the city the most exposed to our enemies, the Iroquois and the English. Being close by they war on us more easily, which is very costly for the settlers. Many of them were killed by the Indians, or taken into captivity to their lands, and burnt alive with great cruelty. . . .

The Holy Providence which took such good care of the affairs of the Colony of Montreal knew well that it needed a hospital to care for the sick, the French as well as the Indians. . . . The Holy Spirit first spoke to the heart of Mlle. Mance, and then of Madame de Bullion. Here is how it happened. This young woman was from the city of Langres; she consecrated herself to God with a vow of chastity at the age of six or seven, as she told me herself many times. She lived very devotedly in her father's house, who never opposed her vocation because he loved his daughter dearly and indulged her. She never gave him any reason for sorrow with her ascetical life which she always adjusted to his desires. This good father died and left his daughter an orphan, since her mother had died many years before. She was then her own master, free to follow the directions of grace. Mlle. Mance decided to give herself completely to God, and to try to be more worthy of Jesus Christ whom she had chosen for her spouse since childhood. Among her different reveries there was the one of going to Canada. She thought it might help her to win the good favour of the only One whom she tried to please. After this dream, her desire became so strong that she decided to go to Paris to discover how to go to Canada. She talked about it with her friends who either took her seriously—or else thought that this was a pretext to go to the big city to show off as many others were doing at the time. Her confessor who could not make her forget this dream, one day told her: "Go, Miss, go to Canada, I give you permission." She left Langres for Paris to find her way to Canada, though everybody thought it was a joke. . . . She met many people, and became friendly with those who knew about the projected new colony of Montreal. It gave her much joy and consolation to find such a beautiful opportunity to fulfill her ideal. . . .

As soon as the groundwork concerning the foundation of the hospital of Ville Marie were arranged in Paris, Mlle. Mance began getting ready to leave France to go to Canada, towards which grace was pulling her with so much force and insistance. She wrote to M. de la Dauversière whom she knew to be the head of this project. He answered her to hurry to meet him at La Rochelle on a certain date, when they would have time to talk freely. They arrived there almost at the same time, and pushed by the same enthusiasm to work for, and give themselves to God, they opened their hearts to one another, both of them afire with divine Love. Mlle. Mance talked of these matters like an angel, . . . and much better than many doctors could. . . . She told him everything that had happened in relation to the new colony, of the foundation of her hospital, and her vocation to live in Canada, particularly Ville Marie which she already saw as the place she was destined to work in the Lord's vineyard and to consummate her sacrifice by serving the poor, sick Indians and the French people of the colony.

Document 11: The First Settlers in Montreal [36]

They [Mille Mance, M. de Chomedey, and their party] left Quebec, one thinks, at the beginning of May since they arrived at the island of Ville Marie, the country of their promises and hopes, on the seventeenth of that month. As soon as they saw this dear, this future city in the plans of God, which was still only deep woods, they sung Canticles of joy and thanksgiving to God for having taken them so happily to the end of their journey, like the Israelites in other times.

They set foot on the earth where the city now stands. Mlle. Mance told me many times that along the riverside for more than half a league you could see only charmingly, beautiful woods covered with wild flowers of all colours! M. de Chomedey, as soon as he set foot on the bank, fell to his knees to adore God in this wild land, and all the others with him rendered praise together to the Holy Majesty of God, Who had never yet been offered this barbarous place, inhabited by those people who have up to now been at war with us. . . .

M. de Chomedey . . . organized a fraternity of five brothers and five sisters. He was the first of the brothers with M. Lambert Closse, M. Lucan, M. Minime Barbier, M. Prudhomme. The sisters were Madame Dailleboust, Madame de la Peltrie, Mlle. Mance, Mlle. de Boulogne, and the maid who as I mentioned served Madame de la Peltrie. They called each other brothers and sisters, pledged to help one another, and serve the others where they needed their help, to attend to the sick, etc. They made many novenas and pilgrimages to the mountain, on foot, and risking their life because the Iroquois who could easily hide on the paths and wait for them. It was not yet cleared and was all covered with thick woods. This did not stop the women's devotion and they persevered going up this steep and treacherous mountain nine days in a row (today the most robust people still suffer and sweat going up there even though the trails are all laid). . . . Meanwhile the men were working to protect Our Lord from the rain. A small chapel of nine or ten square feet was built neatly near the house of Mlle. Mance. Here the Blessed Sacrament was kept. However, since our "Israelites" did not have enough oil to keep a light burning day and night in front of the altar, they decided to put in a jar of fine glass filled with insects called fire-flies who live only during the summer. The glass seemed as bright and shiny during the night as if there were many little candles inside. . . .

By the orders of M. de Chomedey everyone worked together to cut down trees, and trim them to build houses. They started with the fort which was big enough to contain the colony of Montreal, which actually remained inside of it long enough as was necessary to serve as a defense against the Iroquois. For safety they placed guards or sentinals day and night. However, with all of this, they would not have escaped the Iroquois had the Lord not watched over their defence and salvation.

MARGUERITE BOURGEOYS: FOUNDER OF THE CONGREGATION OF NOTRE DAME

Marguerite Bourgeoys was born in Troyes, France, in 1620, of an affluent but not aristocratic family. She was orphaned at the age of nineteen and soon joined a noncloistered wing of the Congregation of Notre Dame. The director of this group was the sister of Paul de Chomedey de Maisonneuve, and through her, Marguerite Bourgeoys learned about his plans to settle Ville Marie de Montreal.

In 1653, Mademoiselle Bourgeoys arrived in Montreal. At first children were thought not able to survive the severe climate, so she could not open a school until 1658. Twelve years later, she founded the first noncloistered teaching order in North America, the Congregation of Notre Dame. She overcame the reticence of bishops and clergy toward the noncloistered character of her congregation, and in 1689, at the age of sixty-nine, she walked the 180 miles to Quebec City to found a second community of noncloistered teachers there.

Some writings of Marguerite Bourgeoys remain in spite of two major fires. In these documents (12–17) we see her adventursome spirit, the extreme difficulty of life in early Montreal, and her dedication to poverty.[37]

Document 12: The Call to New France[38]

I stayed with Mlle. de Chully, a sister of M. de Maisonneuve, who had gone to Montreal as governor in 1640 as I was able to learn later. When he was leaving, his sister, who was a religious of the Congregation, pleaded with him very strongly to take three or four nuns with him to make a foundation in Montreal. She had given him a picture of the Blessed Virgin on which was written: "Holy Mother of God, pure Virgin with a faithful heart, keep for us a place in your Montreal." When M. de Maisonneuve returned to France, these nuns urged him and begged him to take them back with him, but he said that it would be impossible at that time. He was going back and these good women asked me if I would be one of the company when they would go to Montreal. I promised them that I would.

He returned to France in 1652 and he confirmed that he could not bring nuns back with him. I offered to go and he accepted me; but I would have to go along. After he spoke to Father [Jandret], he went away. . . . I spoke to this good Father and asked him how this could be done . . . to go to Canada alone without any other escort than that of M. de Maisonneuve. His answer was: "Place yourself under this man's protection as though you were in the hands of one of the Just Knights of the Chamber of the Queen of Angels." . . . The Bishop was away, otherwise I would have asked his opinion also. . . .

One morning, which I was fully awake, a tall woman dressed in a robe of white serge, said to me very clearly: "Go, I will never forsake you." I knew that it was the Blessed Virgin. This gave me great courage and I found nothing difficult, even though I feared illusions. This made me believe that if this was of God, I did not have to make any preparations for it; consequently I did not bring a penny for the voyage.

Document 13: Traveling in France [39]

On the trip from Troyes to Paris, it was Sunday and the bells were ringing for Mass. We asked the coach driver to allow us to hear Mass, but we could not obtain our request. Around noon, one of his wheels broke into two pieces. We were fifteen or sixteen. It was necessary to go to Paris for another wheel. Those who could not go on foot remained there. After dinner, a little bell rang, and a priest who appeared totally debilitated chanted Vespers with five or six sickly men. This priest told us about all the calamities of the war in this place: all the houses ruined, a large number of dead horses, and even [the corpses] of some men and women. We tried to cover them over with a little earth.

On the trip to Orleans in an inn where there were only men staying, a very old woman refused to give me lodging. I could not leave the coach; all these men said many disagreeable things to me. But there was a gentleman dressed in black who took my part and the woman permitted me to spend the night lying fully dressed on her bed. In another inn they also refused to give me lodging even though there were still several rooms where there were three beds for persons who could pay. I offered to pay them and to spend the night in front of the fire. My request was not granted. One of the drivers said that he was from my part of the country; he asked them to give me lodging, saying that he would pay for everything. I was led to a room that was very far away. I closed the door and barricaded it with everything I could find. I lay down on the bed fully dressed. After some time, there was a knock on the door. Someone tried to open it.

Someone called out: "Countrywoman, open the door for me." After all these persistent demands, I went to the door to see whether it was really he, and I spoke to him as if I were a person of great importance; I said that I would bring charges against him and that I would know quite well how to have him found. Finally he went away. I heard a great deal of noise around that room. Next morning, I lifted one of the hangings and there was an open door and there was a whole crew of men, lying there asleep after having spent the night carousing. It was said that since the war all those people were still aroused and fierce.

Document 14: Contaminated Ships [40]

We had a ship which had served as a hospital during the war. . . . Disease broke out on the ship and eight or more persons died. M. Le Maistre buried them. Some had the plague. These he took with their blankets in which he wrapped them before lowering them into the sea. The Thibaudeau family were all near death, except a little girl who was still nursing at the breast. I asked for her against the advice of our entire group who were all ill. But I had heard them speaking of throwing her into the sea and that was too pitiful for me.

When we had arrived in Quebec, we were housed in the storehouse of the Montreal settlement. I asked the Thibaudeaus, who were better, to keep their daughter until our departure for Montreal in order to give our young women some relief from the child's crying. But they built a large fire and put the sleeping baby too close to it and her back was burned. She was suffering a great deal and I had no ointment to dress her burns. This troubled me a great deal during the whole trip. Once we were back in Montreal, she was better. I gave her to a nurse and she died shortly afterwards. They said that putting her back at the breast had caused her death.

Document 15: The Work of Poverty and Teaching [41]

I must acknowledge that God has sustained this house in a marvelous way, for when I came alone to Canada for the first time, I did not bring a cent with me. Nevertheless, I undertook the building of a chapel to the Blessed Virgin and in order to succeed I urged a few people who were here at the time to gather stone. I used to do sewing and in payment, I would ask for a day's work. I collected alms to pay for the masons' work. M. de Maisonneuve had the necessary timber squared. Others prepared the lime, the sand and the boards and soon I had found enough [material] to build it and roof it.

. . . [Teaching] is the work [most] suited to draw down the graces of God if it is done with purity of intention, without distinction between the poor and the rich, between relatives and friends and strangers, between the pretty and the ugly, the gentle and the grumblers, looking upon them all as drops of Our Lord's blood. When we must correct, we must be very moderate and act in the presence of God.

Document 16: Freedom from the Cloister[42]

We are asked why we prefer to be "wanderers" rather than cloistered, the cloister being a protection for persons of our sex.

Why do we not make solemn vows which are condusive to great perfection and which draw women to religious life? . . .

Why do we prefer to be women of the parish rather than to live in our own institution and not have to submit outselves to the parish?

Why do we go on missions which put us in danger of suffering greatly and even of being captured, killed or burned by the Indians? . . .

Here are some reasons:

There are signs that the Blessed Virgin has been pleased that there is a company of women to honour the life she led in the world and that this company be formed in Montreal, and that afterwards there be a seminary under her protection; that a church under her patronage be built, and that the city built there have as its name Ville-Marie.

Further, the Blessed Virgin was never cloistered. . . .

Document 17: Reaffirmation of the Spirit of Poverty[43]

Our food, our dress, and all the other necessities of life ought to appear poor and simple because [with the Blessed Virgin] food, drink, clothing and all the other necessities were always poor; all that was not necessary was curtailed. We ought to love the contempt which is ordinarily the consequence of poverty. . . .

Littleness and humility ought to be the characteristics of this community. Just as we put the mark of the Congregation on all utensils and clothing, the marks of poverty must also appear in all our posts and occupations. We must never seek after any renown or marks of eminence. . . .

I notice that there are sisters who show more esteem for a girl who has social rank than for one who might be more virtuous. Some also are harsh with the poor, both in allowing them pleasure or in lending to them even when this can be done without inconveniencing themselves. . . .

When Bishop Laval made his first visit to this house, he inspected all our beds and was very pleased to find there only straw mattresses and blankets. At present, that is not enough for us. Whatever sheets we could get, were for lending to poor women in their need. This must no longer be done; this necessity no longer exists. . . .

I believe that our failure in this house comes from having too much. And it seems to me that this simple life of ours will last only while we are waiting for better, for it is very difficult to take back from our nature whatever we have given it, over and beyond its needs.

For a long time now, we have been baking bread like that which is sold in bakeries; we have brown bread for the servants and white bread for the community. Formerly, all the bread was the same.

In the infirmary, everything is very fine and people are treated better than they ought to be. Everything used there must be elegant; the linens fine. In short, no one wishes any poverty to be found there.

Pointe Saint Charles burned in 1693, about three months before election and we never knew how the accident happened. Several people have told me that it was the good God who wished to give us a providential cross to enable us to return to our first simple mode of life which is more in conformity with the life of the Blessed Virgin. In the beginnings, the missions were on this footing, when we were to imitate the apostles and work so that we would be a burden to no one, and this succeeded. Now, we must have mattresses, sheets and all sorts of utensils; we want to live in a different fashion from simple people. We want to have all the comforts that the settlers do not have.

KATERI TEKAKWITHA: THE LILY OF THE MOHAWKS

Kateri Tekakwitha was born in 1656, in a Mohawk village near what is now Auriesville, New York. Her mother, an Algonquian Christian, has been kidnapped and assimilated into the Iroquois, of which her father was chief. It is possible that, just ten years earlier, Father Issac Jogues had been martyred in her village. In the Iroquois nation, the women decided whether prisoners would be tortured, killed, or integrated into the tribe. Kateri grew up in a world in which brave tolerance to physical pain was very much admired.

Kateri Tekakwitha eventually converted to Christianity and escaped from her childhood home with the aid of an Oneida Christian brave named "Hot Ashes." She arrived in Caugnawaga, near Montreal, in 1677, and there she lived an extremely ascetic life until her death three years later. She was the first Indian to take the vow of consecrated virginity, and she accepted her own martyrdom as a sacrifice in reparation for the sins of her people.

Although Kateri Tekakwitha mastered several Indian dialects, she never learned to read or write. Information about her life, therefore, comes from the Jesuit Fathers Cholenec and Chauchetière who knew her at Caugnawaga. The following document (18) describes her life among the Iroquois and her extraordinary spiritual intensity.

Perhaps even more remarkable than her life is the spectacular influence she had on America after her death. Beginning in 1681, Kateri Tekakwitha is said to have miraculously helped hundreds of people from her own reservation as well as from nearby Lachine and Laprarie. By 1695, her miracles were said to affect people from Quebec City to Auriesville. She not only cured the Indians and poor

French farmers who visited her tomb or touched the ashes from her clothes and earth from her grave, she also cured the elite of New France. M. de Champigny, the Commandant of Quebec City, M. de la Columbière, Canon of the Cathedral of Quebec, and M. du Luth, the Commandant at Fort Frontenac, all claimed to have been cured by Kateri. Of all the women in New France, Kateri Tekakwitha was the only one to call forth such widespread posthumous veneration.

Document 18: The Life of Kateri Tekakwitha[44]

Tegahkouita (which is the name of the sainted young woman about whom I am going to inform you), was born in the year 1656, at Gandaouagué, one of the settlements of the lower Iroquois, who are called Agniez (Mohawk). Her father was an Iroquois and a heathen; her mother, who was a Christian, was an Algonquin, and had been baptized at the village of Three Rivers, where she was brought up among the French. During the time that we were at war with the Iroquois, she was taken prisoner by these Indians and remained a captive in their country. . . . By her marriage she had two children, one son and one daughter. . . . In a few days the smallpox which ravages the Iroquois country, removed her husband, her son and herself. Tegahkouita was also attacked with the others, but she did not sink as they did under the violence of the disease. Thus, at the age of four years she found herself an orphan, under the care of her aunts, and in the power of an uncle who was the leading man in the settlement. . . .

M. de Tracy, having been sent by the government to bring to reason the Iroquois nations who laid waste our colonies, carried the war into their country and burned three villages of the Agniez. This expedition spread terror among the Indians, and they acceded to the terms of peace which were offered them. Their deputies were well received by the French, and a peace concluded with the advantage of both nations.

We availed ourselves of this occasion, which seemed a favourable one, to send missionaries to the Iroquois. . . . They happened to arrive there at a time when these people are accustomed to plunge into all kinds of debauchery, and found no one therefore in a fit state to receive them. This unseasonable period, however, procured for the young Tegahkouita the advantages of making early acquaintance with those of whom God wished to make use to conduct her to the highest degree of perfection. She was charged with the task of lodging the missionaries and attending to their wants. . . .

At length Tagahkouita became of marriagable age, and her relations were anxious to find a husband for her, because, according to the custom of the country, the game which the husband kills, is appropriated to the benefit of his wife and the other members of her family. But the young Iroquois had inclinations very much opposed to the designs of her family. . . . They cast their eyes upon a young man whose alliance appeared desirable, and made the proposition both to him and to the members of his family. The matter being settled on both sides, in the evening the young man entered the cabin which was destined for him, and seated himself near her. . . . Tegahkouita appeared utterly disconcerted when she saw the young man seated by her side. She first blushed, and then rising abruptly, went forth indignantly from the cabin; nor would she re-enter until the young man left it.

Artifice having proved unsuccessful, they had recourse to violence. They now treated her as a slave, obliging her to do everything most painful and repulsive, and maliciously interpreting all of her actions, even the most innocent. They reproached her without ceasing for the want of attachment to her relatives, her uncouth manner and her stupidity, for it was thus that they termed the dislike she felt for marriage. They attribued it to a secret hatred of the Iroquois nation, because she herself was of the Algonquin race. . . .

At this very time Father James de Lamberville was conducted by Providence to the village of our young Iroquois. . . . He entered [the cabin] of Tegahkouita. This good girl on seeing him was not able to restrain her joy. She at once began to open her heart to him, even in the presence of her companions, on the earnest desire she had to be admitted into the fold of the Christians. . . . He therefore applied himself particularly to instruct her in the truths of Christianity, but did not think he ought to yield so soon to her entreaties, for the grace of Baptism should not be accorded to adults, and particularly in this country, except with great care and after long probation. All winter, therefore, was employed in her instruction. . . . And so he hesitated no longer to grant her Holy Baptism, for which she asked with so much godly earnestness. She received it on Easter Sunday, 1676, and was named Katharine. . . .

Whenever she went to the chapel they caused her to be followed with showers of stones cast by drunken people, or those who feigned to be so, so that, to avoid their insults she was often obliged to take the most circuitous paths. This extended even to the children, who pointed their fingers at her, hooted after her, and in derision called her "The Christian".

On the very day that Katharine received Baptism, one of the most powerful of the Agniez (the Oneida chief "Hot Ashes") returned to the mission in company with thirty of the Iroquois of that tribe whom he had gained to Jesus Christ. This neophyte would very willingly have followed him, but she depended, as I have said before, on her uncle who would only look with sorrow on the depopulation of his village, and who openly declared himself the enemy of those who thought of going to live among the French. It was not until the following year that she obtained the desired opportunity for the execution of her design. . . . [She] arrived at the Mission of the Sault at the end of autumn, 1677.

Thenceforth the church became her whole delight. There she went at four o'clock in the morning, attended Mass at the dawn of day, and afterwards assisted at that of the Indians, which was said at sunrise. From time to time during the course of the day she broke off her work to go and hold communion with Jesus Christ at the foot of the altar. In the evening she returned again to the church and did not leave until the night was far advanced. To those inclinations for prayer, she joined an almost unceasing application to labor. . . .

Interested views inspired her sister [aunt] with the design of marrying her. She supposed there was not a young man in the Mission of the Sault, who would not be ambitious of the honour of being united with so virtuous a woman, and that thus having the whole village from which to make her choice, she would be able to select for her brother-in-law some able hunter who would bring abundance to the cabin. . . . She immediately came to seek me, to complain bitterly of this importunate solicitations of her sister. As I did not want to appear to accede entirely to her reasoning and, for the purpose of proving her, dwelt on the considerations which ought to incline her to marriage, she said: "Ah, Father, I am not any longer my own. I have given myself entirely to Jesus Christ, and it is not possible to change masters. The poverty with which I am threatened give me no uneasiness. So little is needed to supply the necessities of this wretched life, that my labor can furnish it, and I can always find some miserable rags to cover me." I sent her away saying that she should think well on the matter, for it was one which merited her most serious attention. . . .

It was then the end of autumn, when the Indians are accustomed to form their parties to go out to hunt during the winter in the forests. The sojourn which Katherine had already made there, and the pain she had suffered at being deprived of the religious privileges she possessed in the village, had induced her to form the resolution, . . . that she would never during her life return there . . . and so she remained in the village during the winter, where she lived only on Indian corn, and was subjected indeed to much suffering. But not content with allowing her body only this insipid food, which could scarcely sustain it, she subjected it to austerities and excessive penances, without taking counsel of any one, persuading herself that so long as the object was self-mortification, she was right in giving herself up to everything which could increase her fervour. She was incited to these holy exercises by the noble example of self-mortification which she always had before her eyes. The spirit of penance reigned among the Christians of the Sault. Fastings, discipline carried even unto blood, belts lined with points of iron—these were the most common austerities. And some of them, by these voluntary macerations, prepared themselves, when the time came, to suffer the most fearful torments.

The war was once more rekindled between the French and the Iroquois, and the latter invited their countrymen who were at the Mission of the Sault to return to their own country, where they promised them entire liberty in the exercise of their religion. The refusal with which these offers were met threw them into such a rage, that the Christian Indians, who remained at the Sault were immediately declared enemies of their nation. A party of Iroquois surprised some of them while hunting, and carried them away to their country, where they were burned by a slow fire. But these noble and faithful men, even in the midst of the most excruciating torments, preached Jesus Christ to those who were torturing them so cruelly. . . .

The women were not behind their husbands in the ardor they showed for a life of penance. They even went to such extremes that when it came to our knowledge we were obliged to moderate their zeal. . . . Although those who inflicted these mortifications on themselves were particular to conceal them from the knowledge of the public, yet Katharine, who had a quick and penetrating mind, did not fail from various appearances to guess the secret, and as she studied every means to testify more and more her love for Jesus Christ, she applied herself to examine everything that was done pleasing to the Lord, that she might herself immediately put it in practice. It was for this reason that while passing some days in Montreal, where for the first time she saw the nuns, she was so charmed with their modesty and devotion, that she informed herself most thoroughly with regard to the manner in which these holy sisters lived, and the virtues which they practiced. On learning that they were Christian virgins consecrated to God by a vow of perpetual chastity, she gave me no peace until I had granted her permission to make the same sacrifice herself, not by a simple resolution to guard her virginity, such as she had already made, but by an irrevocable pledge which would oblige her to belong to God beyond recall. . . . For this great event she chose the day on which we celebrate the festival of the Annunciation of the Most Holy Virgin.

To keep alive her devotion for the mystery of Our Saviour's Passion, and to have it always present in her mind, she carried on her breast a little crucifix which I had given her. . . . One day . . . she made a perpetual oblation of her soul to Jesus in the Eucharist, and of her body to Jesus attached to the cross; and thenceforth, she was ingenious ever to invent new ways of afflicting and of crucifying her flesh. . . . During the winter while she was in the forest with her companions, she would follow them at a distance, taking off her shoes and walking with her naked feet over the ice and snow. . . . At another time she strewed the poor mat on which she slept with large thorns, . . . she rolled herself for three nights in succession on these thorns, which caused her the most intense pain. In consequence of these things her countenance was entirely wasted and pale, which those around her attributed to illness. . . .

In the midst of her continual infirmities, she always preserved a peace and serenity of spirit which charmed us. She never forgot herself either to utter a complaint or give the slightest sign of impatience. During the last two months of her life her sufferings were extraordinary. . . . Her countenance, which had been extremely attenuated by her sickness and constant austerities, appeared so changed and pleasant some moments after her death that the Indians who were present were not able to restrain the expression of their astonishment. . . . God did not delay to honor the memory of this virtuous girl by an infinite number of miraculous cures, which took place after her death, and which continue to take place daily through her intercession. This is a fact well known, not only to the Indians, but also to the French at Quebec and Montreal, who often make pilgrimages to her tomb.

JEANNE LE BER: CONSECRATED RECLUSE

Jeanne le Ber was born in 1662, five years after her father, a merchant and seigneur, moved from Rouen to Montreal. Jacques le Ber, who was ennobled in 1696, became a very successful businessman in the New World. He amassed a fortune through fur trade, cod fisheries, the exportation of sheathing to France, and the importation of European fruit trees. Thus it surprised Montrealers that the wealthy Jeanne le Ber shunned marriage and the public life. For several years, she lived a recluse in her own home, even refusing to leave her room to attend her dying mother.

After Marguerite Bourgeoy's convent was destroyed by fire, Jeanne le Ber offered to pay for its reconstruction if she could live as a consecrated recluse in a small floored cell behind the altar. In 1695, after a formal procession through the streets of Montreal, Jeanne le Ber entered her cell and lived the remaining ninteen years of her life in contemplative prayer, adoration of the Eucharist, and artistic endeavors.

Jeanne le Ber became important despite her self-effacing life. Montrealers began to seek her counsel. When, in 1711, the English threatened to invade Quebec City, she told M. de Belmot, the commander of the defense of Montreal: "The very holy Virgin will guard the country; she is the guardian of Ville-Marie, we have nothing to fear." She composed a prayer for the sisters of the Congregation of

Notre Dame and crafted a banner of the Immaculate Conception for the army to carry into battle. As the English approached Quebec City, a violent gale dashed their ships against the rocks. Jeanne le Ber's invocation of the protection of the Mother of Christ was credited with saving the French.

Document 19: Jeanne le Ber Described by Marguerite Bourgeoys[45]

The day Mademoiselle Le Ber entered this house as a recluse, I was very happy. It was Friday, the fifth of August, 1695, at about five o'clock in the afternoon. While the litanies of the Blessed Virgin were being sung, M. Dollier, Vicar General of the diocese and Superior of the Seminary, conducted her to the room built for this purpose, in the chapel but outside the main part of the house. He spoke to her, exhorting her to perseverance. Like St. Madeleine in her grotto, she never went out and she spoke to no one. Her meals were carried there through an outside door and given to her through a little opening. She had a small grill in her room through which she could see the Blessed Sacrament and receive Holy Communion.

Document 20: Jeanne le Ber Described in Annals *of Sr. Marie Morin*[46]

Sr. Bourgeoys, daughter without inheritance and wealth, inspired by the love of God and concern for his glory, still lives today in the odour of sanctity, so humble and so modest that she inspires a love for humility by only observing her. She is always present at the divine service of the parish although there is a church in her convent that Miss Jeanne Leber had built for them. She is a rich young woman with one hundred thousand pounds who gave herself to them as a recluse and who closed herself in a room which she had built in back of the altar of the church. She does not see or talk to anyone except her director, who is now also ours. There she does night and day on earth what the angels do in heaven. She only works at the decoration of the altars, and does not do any other kind of work. Thus Sr. Bourgeoys can say that the prediction of her director came true: this woman honours the contemplative and secluded life of the very Holy Virgin, while the other women emulate the Virgin's teaching life to win souls to God, and ourselves her working life by helping the sick.

Document 21: Jeanne le Ber's Prayer to the Mother of Christ[47]

Queen of Angels, our sovereign and very good Mother, your daughters of the Congregation completely confide their houses and their possessions to your care. We place in you all our confidence, hoping that in your goodness you will not allow our enemies to touch what was given to those who are under your protection.

Document 22: Jeanne le Ber's Description of the Banner of the Immaculate Conception [48]

Our enemies place all their confidence in their arms, but we place ours in the name of the Queen of Angels whom we invoke. She is more terrible than an army prepared for battle; under her protection we hope to conquer our enemies.

MARGUERITE D'YOUVILLE: FOUNDER OF THE GREY NUNS AND MOTHER OF UNIVERSAL CHARITY

Marguerite la Jammerais was born in Varennes, Quebec, in 1701, daughter of a high-ranking military officer. Educated by the Ursulines in Quebec City, she moved to Montreal after her widowed mother remarried an Irish physician. In 1722, Marguerite married Francois D'Youville, a merchant secretly involved in the trading of alcohol with the Indians. During the next eight years, she bore six children, of whom two survived. Her husband's premature death in 1730 left Marguerite destitute. She earned money sewing, everything from army tents to ball gowns, and practiced acts of charity to her neighbors.

After gathering together similarly minded women, Marguerite D'Youville began to direct her small community to works of charity. The tales of her husband's misadventures followed her as this community became known as Les Soeurs Grises, meaning "the drunken sisters." Later, when the community became recognized, Marguerite D'Youville profited from the double meaning of the word grise and called her sisters Les Soeurs Grises, meaning "The Grey Nuns."

Marguerite D'Youville lived through the English Conquest of New France. In the biography written by her youngest son (Document 24), we see the grandeur of her ideal of "universal charity." Then in the letters written around the time of the destructive fire of 1765 (Document 25), we see her defend her work with the poor and describe the unfortunate results of the English Conquest for the settlers of Montreal.

An interesting dimension of Marguerite D'Youville's life was her remarkable openness to combatants on all sides of the conflicts in New France. In one famous incident, she hid an English soldier named Southworth, who was being chased by an Indian ally of the French, under a tent she was mending. She then led the Indian toward the exit of the convent. Later this same Englishman saved the General Hospital from bombardment by the English during the final stages of the conquest. She cared for wounded of the French, English, and various Indian nations in separate wings of the Hospital. Finally, she hid anyone who got caught behind enemy lines in the hospital's basement. Thus, she became known as the "mother of universal charity."

Document 23: Petition of Nipissing Indians Against M. D'Youville [49]

O Father, we come to tell you that we cannot pray to God because Youville, who has set up trade on the island of Tourtes, gets us drunk every day, and makes us drink up the value of all our furs, so that we are miserable and naked, without even shirts or clothes of any kind to cover us, or firearms to hunt with. Every morning he comes into our cabins with wine and brandy, saying with reference to the Marquis de Vaudreuil, "You have a good father; he wants you to drink his milk," and he always gets us drunk to the full value of the pelts, so that the good missionary, who makes us pray to God, always finding us thus senseless, told us that he would not teach us any more. So we make this strong appeal to you, O father, to tell you that we want to pray to God, and that if you do not send Youville away from the island of Tourtes, we do not want to go there any more.

Document 24: The Life of Marguerite D'Youville [50]

Madame D'Youville's nobility of soul, her universal charity which impelled her to seek out and joyfully seize upon every occasion for helping her neighbour; this rare capacity which helped her provide for her poor in the most desperate circumstances, the deep peace of her soul which was reflected in her face in even the most difficult adversities, this blind confidence in divine Providence, which was her principal characteristic . . . ; all these rare qualities led many respectable persons, not only from the clergy, but also from the government, to refer to her often as the strong woman who was mentioned in the book of *Wisdom*. . . .

Madame D'Youville was only about twenty-one years old when, more by reason than inclination, she married Mr. Francois D'Youville, who was one of the handsome young men of her time, and who could have made her very happy if he had lived up to his family responsibilities. Up until her marriage she lived in Varennes with her mother, but after her marriage she was obliged to go to Montreal to live with an old mother-in-law who was very stingy and made life difficult for her. . . .

The goodness of her heart was such that all the indifference and hardness of her husband for her did not prevent her from being extremely afflicted by his death. She mourned him sincerely and cried for a long time. After her husband's death, being without any money or protection, she decided to start a little business to sustain herself and her two children.

From the beginning of her widowhood she was full of charity for her neighbour; she considered it a duty and an honour to visit the poor, the sick, and the prisoners taking from her own means enough to sooth the suffering limbs of the Saviour; she was seen setting a good example of begging door to door for money to bury the dead. Her charity was not satisfied by helping only the poor of the city, she also visited the poor of the General Hospital, called then the House of the Brothers Charon. . . .

In 1738 Madame D'Youville rented a house in Montreal, closed to the Recollects (Reformed Franciscans), which belonged to Madame le Verrier. She entered this place the day before All Saints Day, accompanied by Sister Thammar, Sister Demers, and Sister Cusson. . . . As soon as they entered, they knelt down in front of a statue of the Holy Virgin, given to them by a priest, then Madame D'Youville, speaking firmly, with an intense gaze, inspired by confidence in the Mother of God, begged her to take their small community under her protection, insisting that their only goal was to serve the poor. . . .

No sooner was this little society installed in Madame le Verrier's house than the public rose up against her, and actively persecuted her; even her own parents were among her tormentors. The day after their arrival, as they were going to the parish mass, people threw stones at them accompanied with obscenities. They were even accused of selling alcohol to the Indians and getting them drunk. This rumour even reached the ears of M. de Beauharnois, the Governor General. The priests of the Seminary of Montreal were also charged with the same calumny and accused of furnishing the Grey Nuns (the name the public gave them from the very first day of their installation to riducule them) with alcohol which they in turn sold to the Indians. The calumny was pushed to the point of accusing them of getting drunk themselves which led them, said their libellous enemies, to furious disputes between themselves and even fistfights! . . . Who could have imagined such persecution? This newborn community found persecutors even in the clergy, secular or regular. Some priests went so far as to publicly refuse them communion. . . .

In 1745 God afflicted them with a fire which happened during the coldest time of the year, since it was the last day of January. About one hour after midnight the fire started inside their house and it spread so quickly that they lost almost everything that they owned; a retarded girl also died in the flames. She had been taken out of the house, but she went back in to get her socks and was caught in the flames. It was a very sad spectacle to see the Sisters and the poor on the snow, in the bitter cold, half clothed, and even many of them barefoot. . . . "What will happen to us, Madame," cried these unfortunate members of the Saviour; "what will happen to us if you abandon us? We will be without help or protection!" This true mother of the poor, full of confidence in divine Providence, consoled them and gave them assurance that she would not abandon them. . . . The public looked at this fire as a just punishment from the heavens: it was a vengeance for the crime they had committed, they said, by selling alcohol to the Indians. . . .

Mr. Charon, a citizen of Montreal, thought he could not make any better use of the wealth God gave him than by using it for the care of the poor and he decided to found in Montreal a general hospital. In 1747 Madame D'Youville took possession of this hospital. . . . There were living there at that time only two poor men and two religious brothers, one of them senile. In addition, the hospital was in debt more than 48,000 pounds and only received 700 pounds from the city government. . . .

. . . Our sisters had then ten or twelve poor pensioners. No sooner were they in this new house than they received many poor of both sexes, as many as the rooms could contain. . . .

In addition to the poor, the sisters had a very large room at the top of their house, that the public called "the Jericho", where they charitably took in insane women and prostitutes. A soldier, one day in despair, because his mistress had been locked in this Jericho, came with a pistol to the door of the community with the intention of assassinating Madame D'Youville. She, having learned of the danger she was threatened with, not only was not frightened, but she even came quietly and told this man to leave. . . .

It was in 1760 that our sisters first took charge of abandoned children. When Montreal surrendered to the British Empire, these children who used to be under the protection of the King of France were suddenly without any support. Madame D'Youville, hearing one day that two of these children were found drowned in the little stream which runs in front of the city, and on another day finding on her path one of these little unfortunate infants half buried, became so moved that she resolved to assume the care of these children. Although she knew it would be a big expense for her community she accepted it, and after her death her friends continued the same good work, in spite of their lack of money. . . .

In 1765, the 18th of May, the City of Montreal was afflicted by a fire which destroyed a large number of houses. Our sisters believing that their community was safe, since it was far away, went quickly into town, almost all of them, to help the victims. However, Divine Providence, wanting once more to teach them something, allowed the fire to reach their home, and it moved so fast that they could only save a very few things, and even some of the little they saved was stolen. Madame D'Youville, in this adversity filled with the same feelings as the holy man Job, and wanting to give her companions an example of resignation, knelt down, exhorting her sisters to do the same, and join her in singing the *Te Deum.*

Document 25: After the English Conquest[51]

To Mr. Débarasse, 1764, 7bre 16

Sir, I received your letter of April 2nd via Mr. Mongolfier. I realized after the bill was sent that I took out 33 pounds and 55 shillings more than necessary, but it is done; we will pay the surplus with our prayers. Tomorrow we will say mass for the healing of your leg; I think that it is cured already, but with God nothing is lost, and it will be used for some other future need. How are we keeping now that we live with the English? They have neither done us any good nor bad until now. We have a hard time providing for ourselves; money is very scarce and there is no work. These people do not provide work and their King even less. The worst is that this poor country is so isolated. All the good citizens leave; we suffer the pain of seeing our relatives, our friends, our benefactors leave knowing that we will never see them again. Nothing could be more sad. Every day, new sacrifices. . . .

To Mr. Savarie, 22 July, 1765

Sir, you will probably have heard about the accident which happened to us on the 18th of May. It was the will of God to send us a fire which not only took away our building but also almost all of our furniture, clothes, linens, beds. We are trying though to rebuild. In this connection we would appreciate learning in which way the King of France arranged for the payment of our papers. If he was generous we would borrow to reestablish ourselves; if he is not we will be satisfied with very little, not to place ourselves in debt; but in not knowing anything we are placed in the worst kind of embarrassment. We did not receive any of your letters or of M. de L'Isle-Dieu, and I am afraid you will give them to M. Briand who will come perhaps only this winter or even next year. I beg you, Sir, if this letter reaches you to give me an answer as soon as possible. It is the grace that I ask of you.

To M. Saint-Ange Charli, 1765

Sir, I have the honour to write to you to assure you of my respect and tell you that I bought the Seigneury of Châteauguay some time before the urban conflagration burnt our house and all the adjacent buildings in one of the greatest fires, when we were least expecting it, since we were so far from the flames. You can imagine the misery to which this accident has brought us and how it has made us incapable of paying what we owe you for the Seigneury. I dare hope you will have the goodness to wait a few years, or even the charity of remitting a part of the back rent.

To Mr. Savarie, 17 August, 1766

Sir, I had the honour of receiving your letter of April 18th. . . . I can not believe that the King will not compensate the communities of this country for the injustice he does them, especially ours to whom he never gave any annual payment since it was started 29 years ago. We always did work for the stores of the King, especially for the last 12 years when the storekeepers realized how profitable it was for the King to have us work for him, and we have not been paid more in 1760 than we were in 1728, even less. . . .

I am much obliged to you for the role you took in the accident which happened to us. After much hardship and worries, we reentered a part of our house in December: our community, the poor men and women, the abandoned children, and our women pensionnaires all of the segments of his hospital.

To Mr. Héry, 1770, 7bre 24

. . . You know all that we lost through the King of France. Here nobody does anything, there is no work like there used to be. There are more poor; we would like to help them, but we lack everything. If we had not been helped by the charities of London like we have been (we received in 3 years more than 18,000 pounds) we would never have been able to recover after the fire. We are now as well constructed as before. . . .

To Mr. Carleton [Sir Guy Carleton, Governor of Canada], 1771, 7bre 23

Sir, your absence and the fear of losing you render the news of your return even more agreeable. I hope the same benevolence which you showed the Canadiens will still be there when you return; I request it from you, Sir, for our house and particularly for the abandoned children we find since we are under the English sovereignty, I ask the honour of your protection under His Majesty of Britain, to obtain some kind of help for these unfortunate children. I am afraid to have to abandon this good work for lack of means to sustain it. You can imagine, Sir, how much suffering this would give to people who would like to hide their shame over their children. This consideration is enough to impress a compassionate and charitable heart. I hope you will not refuse me this grace. I dare too to ask you to take an interest in helping us, if it is possible, to bring the following objects over here; they are still in the hands of M. Joubert, the director and treasurer of the Seminary of St. Sulpice in Paris. M. le Normand, Vicar General and Superior of the Seminary of St. Sulpice of Montreal and our Founder, deceased (1759) gave them to us. They are a chalice with its silver paten, the two burettes with the silver plate, the golden-silver monstrance, included with a gold incense burner, six candle holders with the silver cross, and two candle holders for the acolytes.

I hope, Sir, that you will not spend your time in vain, but whether you succeed or not, as I am certain that it will not depend entirely on you. I assure you in advance of all my gratitude.

I must still mention to you, Sir, an affair you already know about. It is about the Indians of Sault St. Louis and their poorly founded claim to the grounds of the Seigneurie of Châteauguay. I would be delighted if this matter could be settled and the poor could be freed from their importunities.

New England Women: Ideology and Experience in First-Generation Puritanism (1630–1650)

ROSEMARY SKINNER KELLER

Two contradictory views of the nature of woman were ingrained in the minds of first-generation Puritans in the New England colonies. William Perkins, the distinguished English divine and "high priest" of Puritanism, pronounced those views categorically on the eve of the English migration.

When Perkins described the nature of the family in his *Christian Oeconomie,* first published in 1590, he expressed high regard for woman and her relationship with man: "The duty of the husband is to honor his wife: 1 Peter 3:7 . . . as his companion, or yoke-fellow. For this cause, the woman, when she was created, was not taken out of man's head, because she was not to rule over him; nor out of his feet, because God did not make her subject to him as a servant, but out of his side, to the end that man should take her as his mate."[1]

However, in *A Discourse of the Damned Art of Witchcraft,* which Perkins wrote six years later, he stated: "In all ages it is found true by experience that the devil hath more easily and oftener prevailed with women than with men. Hence it was that the Hebrews of ancient times used it for a proverb: the more women, the more witches."[2]

At first glance, it may be difficult to conceive of one person espousing two such contradictory views of the nature of woman. For the Puritan, however, there was no such neat separation of ideas. The inheritance of "the bad woman" and "the good woman" formed two sides of one complex reality in the minds and experience of seventeenth-century Puritans. The wife remained the good woman as long as she maintained her dutiful helpmate function within the domestic sphere and was subordinate to man. When she stepped out of that circumscribed sphere, seeking to think and act independently without the proper sanction of male authorities in the family, the church, or the state, the Puritans branded her an instrument of the devil.

The testing ground of this ideology was New England colonial soil in the first generation of Puritan settlement in America, between 1630 and 1650. This chapter seeks, first, to determine the lineage of the Puritan view of woman, which grew out of two strands of Medieval and Reformation ideology. The Puritan conception of the nature of woman was formed in England. Therefore, to understand it, one must trace its European and English roots. Second, this chapter analyzes the myth upon which Puritan society in New England was founded and its essential dependence on a good woman who sought to serve God through her prescribed station in the social order. The third section of this chapter examines the trials and personal fate of first-generation Puritan women who chose to think independently and to advance a claim of equality with men in the name of Christ. Finally, the chapter evaluates the significance of the activism of first-generation Puritan women in the church and the reaction of established authorities in light of the Puritan legacy and women's experience within it.

I

The Puritan view of women arose from two movements that swept across Europe at the beginning of the sixteenth century: the witchcraft craze and the Protestant Reformation. Witchcraft persecutions spanned a five-hundred-year history, and estimates of the death toll range from fifty thousand to one million persons. Originating on the European continent in the thirteenth century, the persecutions extended to England and the American colonies, and did not die out until the end of the seventeenth century and the beginning of the eighteenth century. They were directed primarily toward women—as evidenced by the disproportionate ratio of women to men accused of being witches—and resulted in the annihilation of nearly all the women in some villages of Europe.[3]

The justification for witchcraft persecution and for its focus on women was pronounced in the *Malleus Maleficarum,* or *Hammer Against Witches,* written in 1486 as a handbook for inquisitors in the crusade against witches. The primary argument of the *Malleus* was that women were more likely than men to be witches because they were feebler both in mind and body. All witchcraft originated from carnal lust, described as insatiable in women. The female sex always followed the example of the first woman, Eve, who succumbed to the devil's temptation through the serpent. Women left men with this lesson: "A woman is beautiful to look upon, contamination to the touch, and deadly to keep."[4]

Equally significant in the development of the Puritan view of women was the heritage of the Protestant Reformation, which challenged the exaltation of celibacy as the higher order for religious life by the Roman Catholic Church in the Middle Ages. Growing out of the teaching of Augustine that sexuality was disordered through original sin and hence even marital sexuality was venially sinful, the predominant view of the Middle Ages was that marriage was nothing more than a "necessary evil."[5]

Martin Luther took the decisive step toward a more positive concept of marriage and sexuality, preparing the way for the Protestant conception of marriage for generations to come. Marriage became an honorable estate for the Christian life, and sexual intercourse within marriage, primarily for procreation, was ordained by God. In the garden, woman had been free, an equal partner with man in ruling the created order. But because she had yielded to the serpent, woman was now compelled to stay at home and to be governed, though benevolently, by man. Now woman was "necessary" to keep the household for her husband and family, to enable men to avoid sexual sins, and to bear children. Procreation was a "gladsome punishment," however, because it carried with it the honor of being a mother of all living things and the promise of eternal life. Reformers introduced the "subordinate but equal" dilemma which henceforth characterized Protestant thought. Though woman was to be governed by man, both were given callings by God. Her place was confined to the domestic sphere, while his was to be out and about, immersed in the affairs of the world.[6]

Views of the Church of England and the English Reformation were a third and even more direct influence on the ideology of women in New England Puritanism. Diverse understandings of marriage and sexuality in the first two editions of the *Book of Homilies,* a collection of sermons to be read on consecutive Sundays in all parishes of the kingdom, illustrate the changing ideas of women in the Church of England. The first edition, published in 1547, contained no sermon on marriage. One homily, entitled "Against Whoredom and Uncleanness," advanced a negative view of sexuality: that celibacy was the "higher way," but laity may marry, if they must, to avoid fornication. However, when the *Book of Homilies* was reissued in 1563, praise of celibacy was replaced by advocacy of the "friendly fellowship" of marriage, a position undoubtedly influenced by the church's sanction of clergy marriage in 1549, after four centuries of enforced celibacy.[7]

"An Homily of the State of Matrimony," which appeared in the 1563 collection of sermons, defined marriage as a sacred state ordained by God (Document 1). The two prime purposes of marriage in Luther's view—for women to bear children and for men to avoid unlawful lust—were reaffirmed. Further, the clear delineations of man as the head and woman as the subordinate were maintained, in order that the "perpetual

Friendship" of marriage might grow. At the same time, however, this homily moved beyond its Reformation heritage by introducing the spiritual state of marriage rooted in family prayers and resulting in a state of companionship, though of unequal partners, between husband and wife. Yet fear of the devil's active presence weighed heavily on the ears of those who heard the sermon, for "we see how wonderfully the Devil deludeth and scorneth this State," constantly injecting "Chidings, Brawlings, Tauntings, Repentings, bitter Cursings and Fightings" between husband and wife. Signs of a wife's discontent with her prescribed role were a clear indication that the devil was close at hand. And the woman, such a "frail Vessel," might so easily succumb.

When William Perkins delivered his pronouncements on the Christian family in 1590 and on witchcraft in 1596, his primary influences were the view of marriage that had been formulated by the Protestant Reformation and the Anglican Church and the witch hunts in England and on the European continent. At that time, England has been wrenched by the witch craze for over fifty years. A series of parliamentary statutes, the first passed in 1542, declared all witch practices illegal. Many thousands of persons were brought before the courts on witchcraft charges during two centuries from 1542 to 1736. Nearly one thousand were executed from 1563 until 1685.[8]

In *A Discourse of the Damned Art of Witchcraft,* Perkins posited two kingdoms, one ruled by God and the other by the devil. Satan was "the prince of darkness, the god of this world ruling and effectively working in the hearts of the children of disobedience" (Document 2). Among all the devil's ordinances to keep his subjects in disobedience, the precepts of witchcraft were to be feared the most. Though men as well as women might be witches, Moses had used the feminine gender to define the witch. This was done to remind us, first, that women are the weaker sex and "sooner entangled by the devil's illusions with this damnable art" than are men. Second, the feminine gender was used to make it clear that weakness in this case lessened neither the crime nor the punishment. For Exodus 22:18 states, "Thou shalt not suffer a witch to live."

A close look at two well-read pieces of Puritan advice literature for families helps clarify the relationship between the woman as witch and the place of the woman within marriage. William Perkins's *Christian Oeconomie* (1590) and William Gouge's *Of Domesticall Duties* (1622) both affirm the sanctity of the family as ordained by God to be the foundation of society, the "Seminarie of all other Societies," the training ground for church and state (Documents 3, 4).

Perkins presents a model Puritan definition of the relationship of the good wife to the good husband within marriage: "A couple, is that whereby two persons standing in mutuall relation to each other, are combined together as it were in one. And of those two, the one is alwaies higher, and beareth rule, the other is lower, and yeeldeth subjection."

The good man was to treat his wife as his companion, or yoke-fellow. And the good woman was always to hold her husband in reverence "as her head in all things." She was never to succumb to the mischief of the devil, "the sins of wives: To be proud, to be unwilling to beare the authority of their husbands; to chide and braule with bitterness; to forsake their houses."

Underlying Perkins's *Christian Oeconomie* was a tension between, on the one hand, a "mutuality" that affirmed the interdependence and equality of man and woman in marriage and, on the other hand, the traditional hierarchical relationship of male and female. It was a precarious and short-lived balance, however, and when it shattered, the result was a consequential addition to the Puritan ideology of woman.

In the opening pages from *Of Domesticall Duties,* William Gouge addressed a condition of at least mild insurrection by the women of his congregation. He stated, in his introduction, that much exception was taken by women of the church when he first delivered the *Duties* from the pulpit. The women objected because he opposed a wife's disposition of property held in common with her husband without or against his consent.

With this backdrop of a potentially explosive situation in his church, Gouge's treatises became a practical defense against women's protests of their prescribed subjection. Gouge then drew the distinctions, which would become a bone of contention for Puritan women in the American colonies, between the covenant of grace, the relationship of God to human beings in Jesus Christ, and the social covenant. Through the covenant of grace, all are equal, one, and free in Jesus Christ. However, such a condition was to be realized only in eternal life, according to Gouge's interpretation of the Scriptures. Women were not to resist their assigned submission to men in the social order because *all* persons are bound to submit to their places in a variety of social structures: "Magistrate and subject, Minister and people, husband and wife, parent and childe, master and servant, neighbours and fellowes." Further, Gouge urged that a husband treat his wife with benevolent paternalism, that he might make his wife's yoke "light and easie," so the "wife will be no more pinched therewith then the husband." But Gouge did not go so far as to suggest that Christian duty ever required superiors to submit themselves mutually to those classified as inferiors.

II

Those early Puritans who migrated to the Massachusetts Bay colony and to the Pilgrim colony just south in Plymouth probably assumed that they had left behind in England the "bad" woman, who bore any serious semblance to the witchlike character. As God's chosen people, sifted like fine grains of sand from all creation, their purpose was to establish a model community, "a city set upon a hill" that all the world might see their light and emulate it.[9]

The community, as John Winthrop described it to the first settlers while they were still at sea on the Arabella, was to be an organic society in which all would "be knitt together in this worke as one man"—a world without conflict, dissension, or strife. They were to "enjoy the liberties of the gospel in purity with peace." The word *liberty* did not imply freedom of conscience in religious belief, however, but freedom to obey the will of God and to restore God's order in a chaotic world. Such a vision depended upon a highly structured hierarchical society in which all people knew their places and voluntarily chose to stay in them.[10]

At the same time, both the laity and the family gained at the expense of the hierarchy. English Puritanism was primarily a movement of active lay men and women to abolish religious ritual and to undermine the power of the Anglican hierarchy. The family as the foundation of social institutions took on new dimensions in Puritan homes of England, and its significance increased in the American colonies.[11]

Carol Karlsen has interpreted the increased worth and dignity of women in the home in relationship to two factors: first, the elevation of heads of households to a Godlike position in the family, and, second, the function of the family in ensuring a well-ordered hierarchical society:

> Puritan ministers were not so much interested in a new evaluation of the female sex as they were in serving the needs of the men they counted on to bring order out of chaos—godly men, like themselves, who would pursue their callings with diligence, who could be entrusted with responsibility, and who would control their own moral impulses for the sake of their salvation and the good of society. Such men needed helpmeets, not hindrances; companions, not competitors, alter egos, not autonomous mates. They needed wives who were faithful and loyal: who assisted them in their piety, in their vocations, and in the government of their families; who reverenced them and acknowledged them as "Lord."[12]

There could be no place in such a belief system for the woman who was incapable of fulfilling the helpmate role—or the woman who chose not to abide by it. It was essential, therefore, to create a "new conception of woman," one that simultaneously denied her special proclivity for evil and enjoined "voluntary subjection . . . for conscience sake." Further, such an understanding gave women their religious as well as their sexual role. "Women who failed to serve men, failed to serve God. The only women who would be numbered among God's elect were those who acknowledged this service as their sole calling and *believed* that they were created for this purpose."[13]

The words of John Robinson, the "Pastor of the Pilgrim Fathers," illustrate the way in which first-generation Puritans in New England both incorporated and cast aside parts of their European and English heritage (Document 5). Fundamentally, Robinson saw woman as a "necessary good" rather than a necessary evil, for "if woman be a necessary evil, how evil is man, for whom she is necessary!" The good woman within marriage was to maintain a "reverend subjection" of the "weaker vessel" in relationship to her husband. Robinson placed greater emphasis on affection, love, and companionship in the Puritan image of marriage than had his Reformation forebears. Further, his concept of the spiritualization of the household was central to the relationship of parents to children. Religious nurture was at the heart of all education and rearing because the parents' primary responsibility to their children was to raise them to be "godly" human beings. While the parents bore an "equal yoke" in childcare, the father's responsibility would be greater than the mother's as the child grew older because he would guide in development of the child's mind in both religious and secular education. The mother, on the other hand, was more fit to care for her children's emotional needs and to develop their values in early years.[14]

John Winthrop, the first governor of the Massachusetts Bay Colony, and his third wife, Margaret, provide a fitting example of the prescribed relationship of the Puritan couple and the wife's purpose in serving her husband's and her family's needs (Document 6). The "yoke-fellow" relationship consigned them to distinct and separate spheres—her sphere within the home, caring for the baby and an aging mother, and his on journeys that took him from Boston to tend the affairs of government and church. They shared a "love of each other as the chief of all earthly comfort" in which their first and ultimate commitment was to God. Much of her role in their correspondence was gracious acknowledgment of his letters, and the sermonlike nature of many of her letters was to give him support in his religious devotion and to cleanse and purify herself.[15]

The spiritualization of the Puritan household, as exemplified in the relationship of John and Margaret Winthrop, must have played a major part in energizing an aggressive lay piety in the American colonies. Membership in New England churches increased rapidly throughout the 1630s and early 1640s, with 70 and 80 percent of both male and female inhabitants joining churches in some Massachusetts and Connecticut towns. By the 1650s, however, more women than men had become members of New England churches. Even before this time, women were joining churches in numbers that were greater than their actual proportion of the total population. And the proportion of female members would continue to grow in the later years of the seventeenth century and increase at an even faster rate in the eighteenth and nineteenth centuries.[16]

Although women did not take active parts in church government or hold leadership positions in religious institutions, increased female membership did have two significant long-range implications. First, women began to assume a larger role than men in the religious training of children in the home. Second, wives began to act as their husbands' spiritual guides, rather than as simply their spiritual supporters. This mounting trend would result in a general cultural shift by the nineteenth century toward spiritual leadership of women rather than men within the home, described as the feminization of American culture and religion.[17]

Damage to the Puritan order could result if the expanding numbers of women entering churches led to their increased study and participation in public activities, according to John Winthrop. One likely fate struck Mrs. Hopkins, wife of the governor of Connecticut. Winthrop described her as going insane from "giving herself wholly to reading and writing." Mrs. Hopkins had committed what the Puritan world view regarded as the primary sin of women. She had sought to cast aside her God-given place in society. Winthrop wrote of Mrs. Hopkins: "If she had attended her household affairs, and such things as belong to women, and not gone out of her way to meddle in such things as are proper for men, whose minds are stronger, etc., she had kept her wits, and might have improved them usefully and honorably in the place God has set her."[18]

III

Keeping women in their socially prescribed place was essential to the maintenance of the Puritan order, and most women probably accepted their subordination without question. Yet the social order was strained even during the first generation of Puritan settlement because a considerable number of women applied the implications of radical spiritual equality in St. Paul to themselves. Their primary text, and one to which William Gouge referred, was Galatians 3:28: "There is neither Jew nor Greek, bond nor free, male nor female: for you are all one in Christ Jesus." They also gained the biblical support of Paul from Titus 2:3–4, which sanctioned older women to teach younger women: if they be "teachers of honest things, they may instruct the young women to be sober minded, that they love their husbands, that they love their children." Further, the ambiguity in interpreting woman's role in 1 Corinthians 11:3–5 offered some liberating possibilities for women. The text states that Christ is the head of man and man the head of woman; therefore, any woman who prays or prophesies bareheaded dishonors her head. "The implications of inferiority is clear; but so is the possiblity of speaking in the church, and the ancient biblical tradition of women prophets receives recognition."[19]

The most well-known case of female insubordination was Anne Hutchinson's classic conflict with authorities of church and state in Massachusetts Bay as early as 1637 (Document 7). Hutchinson rejected a primary teaching of the Massachusetts Bay clergy that salvation depended primarily on observance of the covenant of works, that outward behavior was a sign of justification and redemption. Salvation was given through the covenant of grace, Hutchinson insisted, meaning that redemption was a spiritual gift of grace given individually and personally to whomever God chose to give it—and a person's status in the social order had nothing to do with God's choice. She further testified at her trial for heresy that she had received a direct revelation from God that the clergy of Massachusetts Bay were not able ministers. Even more, Hutchinson held meetings, which she considered private not public, in her home for the purpose of teaching her beliefs to men and women of the Boston church. Hutchinson's contention that grace came to individuals directly from God and that the New England clergy were not fit ministers was a direct challenge to the theological base and the political power structure of the Puritan order. Because she was acquiring a large and influential following, she became a concrete threat to the established authorities of the colony. Anne Hutchinson's bold and radical proposition that spiritual equality before God sanctioned social equality of men and women on earth led her inquisitors to respond that her behavior was neither "tolerable nor comely in the sight of God nor fitting for your sex." The only recourse that the Massachusetts Bay authorities saw to such religious and sexual insubordination was banishment from the colony.[20]

Anne Hutchinson was the most notorious of a large number of women who were charged with heresy, and even witchcraft, because of their dual insubordination to God and men. In most cases, the women were tried simply for heresy, since authorities undoubtedly realized that there would be little basis for charges of witchcraft in these cases. They also realized, however, that the women would be more greatly discredited in the eyes of the public by implications that they were in league with the devil.[21]

John Winthrop was aware of that purpose in identifying Hutchinson and two of her followers, Mary Dyer and Jane Hawkins, as witches. Winthrop claimed that Hawkins's reputation as a witch originated with her medical practice, particularly with her dispensing of fertility potions to barren women and her insistence that her patients must "believe" if her cures were to be effective. But Winthrop did not specify in whom or what Hawkins insisted her patients must believe and trust. Anne Hutchinson served as midwife, along with Jane Hawkins, during Mary Dyer's labor in which she was delivered of a deformed, stillborn child. Winthrop described the decaying corpse as a monster with horns, claws, and scales, and he stated that the bed shook when it died in its mother's body two hours before its birth. He implied that the shaking bed indicated that the fetus itself was a devil and that the participation of these three women—Hutchinson, Dyer, and Hawkins—meant that they all were witches. Hawkins was banished from the colony in 1640, three years after Hutchinson's expulsion, because of her medical practice and her persistent defiance of religious and secular authority.[22]

During the late 1630s and 1640s, several other female rebels were prosecuted by the Massachusetts ministers and magistrates for doctrinal errors and for failure to comply with the authority of their husbands or church officials. Tried on both counts was Katherine Finch, who in 1638 was ordered to be whipped for "speaking against the magistrates, against the churches, and against the elders." A year later, she was brought forward again for not carrying herself "dutifully to her husband," but she was released on promise of reformation.[23]

In 1639, Philip[a] Hammond, a widow who had assumed her maiden name after her husband's death and who operated a business in Boston, was excommunicated from the Boston church (Document 8). She was charged "as a slaunderer and revyler both of the Church and Common Weale," for speaking evil of "Authority both in Church and Commonweale" and for declaring in court that Mrs. Hutchinson did not deserve excommunication from the church and banishment from the state.[24]

The church trial of Ann Hibbens, which took place in Boston in 1640, provides a notable comparison to the case of Anne Hutchinson (Document 9). Hibbens's case involved secular issues: her dispute was with town carpenters over work that she had contracted but which, she contended, was poorly done and overcharged. The case was brought before the church on grounds that she had made false accusations and behaved contentiously. However, the trial became focused on the issue of her alleged transgression of male authority—in this case, her husband's. As in the Hutchinson trial, there was no question what decision the court would make. Ann Hibbens was excommunicated in 1640, and sixteen years later, two years after her husband's death, she was convicted of witchcraft and executed.[25]

Further convictions by the Boston church and secular court were based on accusations similar to those raised against Anne Hutchinson—speaking in public church meetings and acting on authority claimed directly from Christ. Such cases included that of Sarah Keayne in 1646, who was declared guilty of "irregular prophesying in mixed assemblies." And nine years later, Joan Hogg was punished "for her disorderly singing and her idleness," and for "saying she was commanded of Christ so to do."[26]

This pattern established in Boston was duplicated in both Salem and New Haven. Richard Gildrie's study of Salem reveals that the community was relatively calm in the 1630s and 1640s, where its institutions served primarily to foster peace and unity and to maintain a stable hierarchical authority in the home, the church, and the community at large. Yet dissenters in its midst placed strains on the town's basic sense of unanimity. Of the nine dissenters described by Gildrie, five were women. And almost all of the cases that involved women were concerned with controversy over serious doctrinal issues, whereas only one man was tried on doctrinal points.[27]

The earliest case was that of Mary Oliver, whom Winthrop described as having been an even "fitter instrument to have done hurt" than Mrs.

Hutchinson because of her ability of speech, her zeal, and her devotion. Yet she posed less danger to society because she was poor and had little influence (Document 10). Though Winthrop did not accuse her of witchcraft, his implication was plain enough when he said, "The devil would never cease to disturb our peace, and to raise up instruments one after another." For Oliver mounted a sustained attack against root issues of church authority and governance. She took offense that she was not allowed to receive communion without testifying to her conversion experience before the church. She argued that all townspeople who wished to join the church should be admitted, not just those who had had a conversion experience. And she believed that both secular and church authorities, magistrates and ministers, should jointly hold power to ordain ministers. For these views, Mary Oliver was punished severely in public, and in 1651, she was ordered to return to England, where she died shortly thereafter.[28]

Women of higher social standing, such as Lady Deborah Moody, sometimes proved equally contentious toward the established authorities of Salem. The wealthy Lady Moody was ordered to appear in court in 1644 on charges of anabaptism. Instead of appearing, she moved to Long Island and continued to press her ideas on Massachusetts leaders and their wives through correspondence. Her separatist assumption was a direct challenge to the Puritan belief that infant baptism was the seal of a child's provisional membership among the "chosen people."[29]

Another account from the Salem community, the case of Dorothy Talby, reveals what terrifying ramifications the Puritan doctrine could have for those who tried but failed to fulfill it. Talby was hanged in Boston in 1638 for killing her three-year-old daughter named Difficult. Though she and her husband were both church members, they had been unable to create a family that personified Puritan ideals. The failure drove her insane, and at various times she attempted to kill her husband and her children, as well as herself, claiming that she had been acting upon revelation.[30]

Just as a circle of female supporters had formed around Anne Hutchinson in Boston, so a similar network developed around Anne Eaton, a heretic of high status in New Haven. The daughter of an English bishop and the unhappy wife of Governor Theophilus Eaton, she was tried and excommunicated in 1644.[31] Mrs. Eaton had denounced infant baptism and then proceeded to walk out of church services before the Lord's supper and baptism were administered, judging herself not to have been baptized. Like her sister heretics, Mrs. Eaton had failed to seek help from her husband, her pastor (John Davenport), or the members of the church.

The "party" that formed around Mrs. Eaton included a Mrs. Brewster, a Mrs. Moore, and a Mrs. Leach. These three women were brought before the court at New Haven in June 1646 (Document 11). The spirit of independent judgment among these women ran as high as that among Anne Hutchinson's followers. Mrs. Brewster was charged with claiming that Pastor Davenport identified church membership with salvation in Christ. It was further alledged that Mrs. Brewster declared herself "sermon sick" of his preaching and that she had her son "make waste paper" of the notes from Davenport's sermon after Sunday church service. Though she denied all charges, they are perhaps too colorful to have been fabricated.[32]

Mrs. Moore, too, was charged with high heresy for declaring that "pastors and teachers are but inventions of men" and that no one in the congregation could be turned to the Lord "until the veil before the eyes of the minister and the people in this place be taken away." Mrs. Moore denied the allegation. However, her daughter, Mrs. Leach, readily accepted the charge against her: she had formerly "had a mind to join the church, but now declined it, because she found so many untruths among them."[33]

These three women confounded the magistrates and deputies, who drew back from censuring them because of the nature and weight of their offenses. Their cases were referred to the higher court of magistrates of the jurisdiction.

IV

Before the end of the first generation of English settlement in New England, the Puritan model of the "good woman," who voluntarily subjected herself to man and to God for conscience' sake, had been challenged and found less than fulfilling. Until recently, the "Anne Hutchinson Affair" has been held up as an anomoly, an example of a single rebellious woman who stood out strikingly against a background of general conformity by New England women. More recent investigation and analysis of sources, however, point to a need for a revised interpretation which allows the significant impact of the notorious Jezebel.

Most Puritan women continued to fulfill the role that merited the title of "Goody" before their last names: yet, female dissent was a widespread phenomenon of the late 1630s and 1640s. Anne Hutchinson was simply the symbol, and probably the impetus, for a large number of women and of female circles who challenged religious and sexual subordination. Their activism was a direct affront to the utopian vision of an organic society which provided no room for independent judgment and pluralistic religious views. When the religious challenge was made by the subordinate sex, Puritans had to acknowledge the reality and presence of the "bad woman"—and to effectively dispose of her!

Several implications of women's dissent contributed to a changing world of women and religion in New England. Most immediate was the reaction of civil and religious officials towards women's activism. Though many women were deemed in collusion with the devil, only one New England woman was punished for being a witch before 1647. She was Jane Hawkins, Anne Hutchinson's associate, and her trial took place in 1638. After 1647, however, women's activism was abruptly halted as authorities began to try women as witches. After witch trials had become a regular part of the New England scene, the Quakers were the only female religious activists who continued to maintain spiritual independence.[34]

Second, the introduction of the bad woman as an instrument of the devil, and the brand of witchcraft placed on subsequent activity throughout the century, points to a revised interpretation of the Salem witch hunts in 1692. No longer do they stand out as a stark and singular phenomenon. Rather, they can be considered the culmination of witchcraft beliefs that had been festering since the early days of New England settlement. The end of the "world of witchcraft" in the colonies after the Salem outbreak marked the shattering of an ideology that had been five centuries in the making.

Third, the case of Anne Hutchinson became a symbol of wider dissent by women who were calling for greater strictures of woman's role in the church. When, in 1645, John Brinsley held up "A Looking Glass for Good Women" to his congregation in Yarmouth, England, his one explicit reference to the outbreak of female activism spreading across England as well as the colonies was to "the notorious Mastris Hutchinson" (Document 12). "Henceforth then no more Women Preachers," he admonished. However, Brinsley identified the new women of faith, modeled after the women on the scene of Jesus' resurrection, as those who were now called to "undeceive man"—just as Eve had originally been the devil's instrument for Adam's deception.[35]

Finally, what was the positive role that women were to play in wiping away the deception they had brought upon the opposite sex? "Singing of Psalms a Gospel-Ordinance, 1650," a sermon by John Cotton, teacher of the Boston church that included Anne Hutchinson and a host of other female dissidents, provides an appropriate bridge to the new role of women (Document 13). Cotton gave two reasons why women may speak in church: first, "in way of subjection when she is to give account of her offence," and second, in "singing forth the praises of the Lord together with the rest of the Congregation." So women's religious voice was not to be silenced, at home or in public. But it was to sound a note of righteousness, not dissidence, to bring their husbands and sons to Christ. The passing of the Salem witch hunts brought the demise of the bad woman, the figure in need of regeneration. And in her place rose the woman of the Great Awakening, the instrument of regeneration.[36]

Anne Hutchinson preaching to a religious gathering in her home. New York Public Library. [From June Sochen, *Herstory: A Woman's View of American History* (New York: Alfred Publishing Co., 1974), p. 51.]

Mary Dyer, Quaker missionary, being led forth to be hanged on Boston Common, 1660. Dyer had been expelled from Boston in 1635 for supporting Anne Hutchinson in the antinomian controversy. [Painting reproduced courtesy the Friends Historical Library, Swarthmore College, Swarthmore, Pennsylvania.]

A Quaker woman preaching in a Friend's meeting. Drawn by a hostile artist who portrays the Quakers as witches. Library of Congress. [From James I. Clark and Robert V. Remini, *We the People: A History of the United States* (Beverly Hills, CA.: Glencoe Press, 1975), p. 81.]

Bridget Bishop, convicted of witchcraft and hanged at Salem, Massachusetts, 1692. [From June Sochen, *Herstory: A Woman's View of American History* (New York: Alfred Publishing Co., 1974), p. 47.]

Documents: New England Women: Ideology and Experience in First-Generation Puritanism (1630–1650)

IDEOLOGY: THE PLANTING

ENGLISH ROOTS

1. ***Resisting the Devil's Intrusions in the "Perpetual Friendship" of Marriage***
2. ***"The More Women, the More Witches"***
3. ***The "Tender Mutuality" in which One "Beareth Rule" and the Other "Yeeldeth Subjection"***
4. ***"Many Have Done Vertuously, but Ye Excell Them All"***

NEW ENGLAND BRANCHES

5. ***If Woman "Be a Necessary Evil, How Evil Is the Man, for Whom She Is Necessary!"***
6. ***"The Love of Each Other as the Chief of All Earthly Comfort"***

EXPERIENCE: THE FRUITS

SEPARATING THE BITTER FROM THE SWEET

7. ***"Say No More, the Court Knows Wherefore and Is Satisfied"***
8. ***"Cast Out . . . as a Slaunderer and Revyler Both of the Church and Common Weale"***
9. ***"In All This I Have But Only Desired to Find Out the Truth . . . and to Do Them Good"***
10. ***"The Devil Would Never Cease to Disturb Our Peace"***
11. ***"Pastors and Teachers Are But the Inventions of Men"***

IDEOLOGY: THE PLANTING

English Roots

Document 1: Resisting the Devil's Intrusions in the "Perpetual Friendship" of Marriage

Views formulated by the Church of England were the most direct influence on the Puritan understanding of women before the colonization of America. Ideas that the church wanted to impress on its members were developed in sermons to be read consecutively on each Sunday of the year in all churches.

The first sermon on marriage, "An Homily of the State of Matrimony," was contained in the 1563 collection of Certain Sermons or Homilies Appointed to be Read in Churches. *While it affirmed marriage as ordained by God, the sermon also warned of the devil's active intervention in stirring women to challenge their subjection to husbands.*[37]

The Word of Almighty God doth testify and declare whence the Original Beginning of Matrimony cometh, and why it is ordained. It is instituted of God, to the intent that Man and Woman should live lawfully in a perpetual Friendship, to bring forth Fruit, and to avoid Fornication; by which Mean a good Conscience might be preserved on both Parties, in bridling the corrupt inclinations of the Flesh within the limits of Honesty; for God hath straitly forbidden all Whoredom and Uncleanness, and hath from time to time taken grievous punishment of this inordinate Lust. . . . St. Paul describeth it to them, saying, "Neither Whoremongers, neither Adulterers shall inherit the Kingdom of God. (I Cor. 6). This horrible Judgment of God ye be escaped through his mercy, if so be that ye live inseparatly, according to Gods Ordinance. But yet I would not have you careless without watching; for the Devil will assay to attempt all things to interrupt and hinder your Hearts and godly Purpose, if ye will give him any entry. For he will either labor to break this godly knot once begun betwixt you, or else at the least he will labor to incumber it with divers griefs and displeasures.

And this is the principal craft to work dissension of Hearts of the one from the other; that whereas now there is pleasant and sweet Love betwixt you, he will in the stead thereof bring in most bitter and unpleasant discord; . . . Wherefore married Persons must apply their minds in most earnest wise to Concord, and must crave continually of God the help of his Holy Spirit, so to rule their Hearts and to knit their Minds together, that they be not dissevered by any Division or Discord. This necessity of Prayer must be oft in practice and using of married Persons, that oft times the one should pray for the other, lest hate and debate do arise betwixt them. And because few do consider this thing, but more few do perform it, (I say, to pray diligently) we see how wonderfully the Devil deludeth and scorneth this State; how few Matrimonies there be without Chidings, Brawlings, Taunting, Repentings, bitter Cursings and Fightings. . . . Learn thou therefore if thou desireth to be void of all these miseries, if thou desirest to live peaceably and comfortably in Wedlock, how to make thy earnest Prayer to God, that he would govern both your Hearts by the Holy Spirit, to restrain the Devils power, whereby your Concord may remain perpetually. But to this Prayer must be joyned a singular diligence, whereof St. Peter giveth this precept, saying, "You Husbands, deal with our Wives according to knowledge, giving honor to the Wife as unto the weaker Vessel, and as unto them that are Heirs also of the grace of Life, that your Prayers be not hindered." This precept doth particularly pertain to the Husband, for he ought to be the Leader and Author of Love, in cherishing and increasing Concord, which then shall take place if he will use Moderation and not Tyranny, and if he yield something to the Woman: For the Woman is a weak Creature, not indued with like strength and constancy of Mind, therefore they be the sooner disquieted; and they be the more prone to all weak affections and dispositions of Mind more than Men be, and lighter they be, and more vain in their Fantasies and Opinions. These things must be considered of the Man, that he be not too stiff, so that he ought to wink at some things, and must gently expound all things, and to forbear. . . .

Now as concerning the Wives Duty, What shall become her? Shall she abuse the gentleness and humanity of her Husband, and at her pleasure turn all things upside down? No surely, for that is far repugnant against God's Commandment; for thus doth St. Peter preach to them, "To Wives, be ye in subjection to obey your own Husbands." To obey is another thing than to controle or command, which yet they may do to their Children and to their Family. But as for their Husbands, them must they obey, and cease from commanding, and perform subjection, for this surely doth nourish Concerd very much, when the Wife is ready at hand at her Husbands commandment, when she will apply herself to his Will, when she endeavoreth her self to seek his contentation, and to do him pleasure, when she will eschew all things that might offend him. . . .

Here you understand that God hath commanded that ye should acknowledge the Authority of the Husband, and refer to him the honor of Obedience. And St. Peter saith in that place before rehearsed, that holy Matrons did in former time deck themselves, not with Gold and Silver, but in putting their whole hope in God, and in obeying their Husbands, as Sarah obeyed Abraham, calling him Lord, "Whose Daughters ye be (saith he) if ye follow her Example." This

Sentence is very meet for Women to print in their remembrance. Truth it is, that they must specially feel the grief and pains of their Matrimony, in that they relinquish the Liberty of their own Rule, in the pain of their Travelling, in the bringing up of their Children. In which Offices they be in great Perils, and be grieved with great Afflictions, which they might be without if they lived out of Matrimony. But St. Peter saith, "That this is the chief Ornament of holy Matrons, in that they set their hope and trust in God;" that is to say, in that they refused not from Marriage for the business thereof, for the gifts and perils thereof, but committed all such Adventures to God, in most sure trust of help, after that they have called upon his aid. O Woman! do thou the like, and so shalt thou be most excellently beautified before God and all his Angels and Saints, and thou needest not to seek further for doing any better works; for, obey thy Husband, take regard of his Requests, and give heed unto him to perceive what he requireth of thee, and so shalt thou honor God, and live peaceably in thy House. And beyond all this, God shall follow thee with his Benediction, that all things shall well prosper both to thee and to thy Husband, as the Psalm saith, "Blessed is the Man which feareth God, and walketh in his ways, thou shalt have the Fruit of thine own hands, happy shalt thou be, and well it shall go with thee. Thy Wife shall be as a Vine, plentifully spreading about thy House. Thy Children shall be as the young Springs of the Olives about thy Table. Lo, thus shall that Man be blessed (saith David) that feareth the Lord." . . .

Document 2: "The More Women, the More Witches"

English divine William Perkins's treatise, A Discourse of the Damned Art of Witchcraft, *written in 1592, grew out of the strong influence of the witchcraft craze in Europe and England on Puritan ideas of women. He understood two kingdoms of good and evil, ruled by God and the devil, to be in mortal combat, with woman as the primary subject of the devil's wiles. Only by positing a formidable duality within the nature of woman could Puritans regard her as possessing such potentiality for good or evil, as a wife or as a witch.*[38]

Exod. 22.18. *Thou shalt not suffer a witch to live.*

This text containeth one of the judicial laws of Moses touching the punishment of witchcraft; which argument I have chosen to entreat of for these causes.

First, because witchcraft is a rife and common sin in these our days and very many are entangled with it, being either practitioners thereof in their own persons or, at the least, yielding to seek for help and counsel of such as practise it. Again, there be sundry men who receive it for a truth that witchcraft is nothing else but a mere illusion and witches nothing but persons deluded by the devil: and this opinion takes place not only with the ignorant, but is holden and maintained by such as are learned, who do avouch it by word and writing that there be no witches, but as I said before.

Upon these and suchlike considerations, I have been moved to undertake the interpretation of this judicial law, as a sufficient ground of the doctrine which shall be delivered; in handling whereof two things are distinctly to be considered: the first, what is a witch; the second, what is her due and deserved punishment. And both these being opened and handled, the whole meaning of the law will the better appear. . . .

Of the nature of witchcraft

To begin with the first: according to the true meaning of all the places of holy scripture which treat of this point it may be thus described. Witchcraft is a wicked art serving for the working of wonders by the assistance of the devil, so far forth as God shall in justice permit. . . .

For manifestation whereof it is to be considered that God is not only in general a sovereign lord and king over all his creatures, whether in heaven or earth (none excepted, no not the devils themselves), but that he exerciseth also a special kingdom, partly of grace in the church militant upon earth and partly of glory over the saints and angels, members of the church triumphant in heaven. Now in like manner the devil hath a kingdom called in scripture the kingdom of darkness, whereof himself is the head and governor; for which cause he is termed the prince of darkness, the god of this world ruling and effectually working in the hearts of the children of disobedience (Eph. 6. 12; 2 Cor. 4.4).

Again, as God hath enacted laws whereby his kingdom is governed, so hath the devil his ordinances whereby he keepeth his subjects in awe and obedience, which generally and for substance are nothing else but transgressions of the law of God. And amongst them all, the precepts of witchcraft are the very chief and most notorious, for by them especially he holds up his kingdom and therefore more esteems the obedience of them than of other. Neither doth he deliver them indifferently to every man, but to his own subjects the wicked, and not to them all, but to some special and tried ones whom he most betrusteth with his secrets as being the fittest to serve turn, both in respct of their willingness to learn and practise, as also for their ability to become instruments of the mischief which he intendeth to others. . . .

What witches be and of how many sorts

Having in the former part of this treatise opened the nature of witchcraft and thereby made way for the better understanding of this judicial law of Moses, I come now to show who is the practiser hereof whom the text principally aimeth at, namely the witch, whether man or woman. A witch is a magician who, either by open or secret league, wittingly and willingly consenteth to use the aid and assistance of the devil in the working of wonders. . . . I comprehend both sexes or kinds of persons, men and women, excluding neither from being witches, a point the rather to be remembered because Moses in this place, setting down a judicial law against witches, useth a word of the feminine gender (*mecashepah*) which in English properly signifieth a woman witch, whereupon some might gather that women only were witches. Howbeit Moses in this word exempteth not the male, but only useth a notion referring to the female for good causes, principally for these two.

First, to give us to understand that the woman being the weaker sex is sooner entangled by the devil's illusions with this damnable art than the man. And in all ages it is found true by experience that the devil hath more easily and oftener prevailed with women than with men. Hence it was that the Hebrews of ancient times used it for a proverb. The more women, the more witches. His first temptation, in the beginning, was with Eve a woman and since he pursueth his practice accordingly, as making most for his advantage. For where he findeth easiest entrance and best entertainment, thither will he oftenest resort.

Secondly, to take away all exception of punishment from any party that shall practise this trade and to show that weakness cannot exempt the witch from death. For in all reason, if any might allege infirmity and plead for favour it were the woman, who is weaker than the man. But the Lord saith if any person of either sex among his people be found to have entered covenant with Satan and become a practiser of sorcery, though it be a woman and the weaker vessel she shall not escape, she shall not be suffered to live, she must die the death. And though weakness in other cases may lessen both the crime and the punishment, yet in this it shall take to place.

Document 3: The "Tender Mutuality" in which One "Beareth Rule" and the Other "Yeeldeth Subjection"

William Perkins was one of the first Puritan preachers to write lengthy treatises of family advice literature categorically spelling out the "complementary" roles of men and women in marriage. The strong sense of order in Puritanism pervades Perkins's Christian Oeconomie. *While husbands are admonished to rule over their wives with gentleness, women are to revere their husbands as the living image of God. Accusations of insubordination were signs of the devil's effective workings.*[39]

Right Honorable, Among all the Societies & States, whereof the whole world of mankinde from the first calling of *Adam* in Paradise, unto this day, hath consisted, the first and most ancient is the Familie. . . .

the ground of all the rest. Some againe have compared it to the Bee-hive, which we call the Stock, wherein are bred many swarmes, which thence doe flie abroad into the world, to the raising and maintaining of other States. . . .

Upon this condition of the Familie, being the Seminarie of all other Societies, it followeth, that the holie and righteous government thereof, is a direct meane for the good ordering, both of Church and Common-wealth; yea that the laws thereof being rightly informed and religiously observed, are available to prepare and dispose men to the keeping of order in other governments. . . .

Christian Oeconomie, is a doctrine of the right ordering of a Familie. The only rule of ordering the Family, is the written word of God. . . .

A couple, is that whereby two persons standing in mutuall relation to each other, are combined together as it were in one. And of these two, the one is alwaies higher, and beareth rule, the other is lower, and yeeldeth subjection. . . . Marriage of it selfe is a thing indifferent, and the kingdome of God stands no more in it, than in meats and drinks; and yet it is a state in it selfe, farre more excellent, then the condition of single life. For first, it was ordained by God in Paradise, above and before all other states of life, in *Adams* innocencie before the fall. . . .

Neverthelesse, since the fall, to some men who have the gift of continencie, it is in many respects farre better then marriage, yet not simplie, but only by accident, in regard of sundrie calamities which came into the world by sin. For, first it freeth a man from many and great cares of houshold affaires. Againe, it maketh him much more fit & disposed to meditate of heavenly things, without distraction of mind. Besides that, when dangers are either present, or immenent, in matters belonging to this life, the single person is in this case happie, because he and his are more secure and safe, then others be who are in maried state. . . .

The good man or master of the familie, is a person, in whom resteth the private and proper government of the whole household, and he comes not unto it by election, as it falleth out in other states, but by the ordinance of God, selted even in the order of nature. The husband indeed naturally beares rule over the wife; . . .

[The duty of the husband] To honor his wife: I. Pet. 3:7 *Giving honor to the woman.*

This honor stands in three things: First, in making account of her, as his companion, or yoke-fellow. For this cause, the woman, when she was created, was not taken out of the mans head, because she was not made to rule over him; nor out of his feet, because God did not make her subject to him as a servant, but out of his side, to the end that man should take her as his mate. Secondly, in a wise & patient bearing or covering of her infirmities, as anger, waywardness and such like, in respect of the weakness of her sex, I. Pet. 3:7 . . . Thirdly, by suffering himselfe sometimes to be admonished or advised by her . . . and consequently, that he ought not in modestie to challenge the privilege of prescribing and advertising his wife in all matters domesticall, but in some to leave her, to her owne will and judgement.

Heere question is moved, whether the husband may correct the wife?

Answ.: Though the husband be the wives head, yet it seemeth he hath no power nor libertie granted him in this regard. For we reade not in the Scriptures, any precept or example to warrant such practice of his authorities. He may reprove & admonished her in word only, if he seeth her in fault. . . . But hee may not chastise her either with stripes, or stroke. The reason is plaine; Wives are their husbands mates; and they two be one flesh. And no man will hate, much less beat his owne flesh, but nourisheth and cherisheth it, Ephes. 5:29. . . .

The wife is the other married person, who being subject to her husband, yeeldeth obedience unto him. . . .

Now the duties of the wife, are principally two.

The first is, to submit her selfe to her husband; and to acknowledge and reverence him as her head in all things. . . . For of ancient times, the wife was covered with a vaile in the presence of her husband, in token of subjection to him. . . . The reason hereof is good. For the wife enoieth the priviledges of her husband, and is graced by his honor and estimation amongst men. His Nobilitie maketh her noble, though otherwise shee is base and meane; as contrariwise, his basenesse and low degree, causeth her, though shee bee by birth noble and honorable, to bee by estate base and meane.

The second dutie is, to be obedient unto her husband in all things; that is, wholly to depend upon him, both in judgement and will. For looke as the Church yeelds obedience to Christ her head, and heelds her selfe to be commanded, governed, and directed by him, so ought the woman to the man. . . . Contrary to these duties, are the sins of wives; To be proud, to be unwilling to beare the authority of their husbands; to chide and braule with bitterness; to forsake their houses. . . .

The Goodwife or Mistresse of the house, is a person which yeeldeth helpe and assistance in governmet to the Master of the familie. For he is, as it were, the prince and choece ruler; she is the associate, not only in office and authoritie, but also in advise and counsell unto him.

Document 4: "Many Have Done Vertuously, but Ye Excell Them All"

Puritan minister William Gouge wrote his massive work, Of Domesticall Duties: Eight Treatises, *in 1622, just eight years before*

John Winthrop's first migration of Puritans to New England. Its opening pages attest that even then women were not accepting the unqualified authority of husbands over their lives, here in reference to disposal of property.[40]

The following excerpt demonstrates Gouge's efforts to qualify the authority of husbands and to justify the positions of superiority and subordination of man and woman with all orders of society. Though he only alludes to it briefly, Gouge recognizes the equality of all persons in Christ, a concept that would become the primary defense against insubordination by a notable number of American colonial women.

. . . when these *Domesticall Duties* were first uttered out of the pulpit, much exception was taken against the application of a wives subjection to the restraining of her from disposing the common goods of the family without, or against her husbands consent. . . . But when I came to deliver husbands duties, I shewed, that he ought to make her a joynt Governour of the family with himselfe. . . . In a word, I so set downe an husbands duties, as if he be wise and conscionable in observing them, his wife can have no just cause to complaine of her subjection. That which maketh a wives yoake heavy and hard, is an husbands abuse of his authority: and more pressing his wives dutie, then performing his owne: which is directly contrary to the Apostles rules . . . so on the one side it may appeare, that if both of them be conscionable and careful to performe their owne duty, the matrimoniall yoke will so equally lie on both their necks, as the wife will be no more pinched therewith then the husband, but that it will be like Christs spirituall yoke, light and easie: and that on the other side it may be manifest that there is commonly as much failing by husbands in their duties, as by wives in theirs. . . .

Because there is not one word to comprise under it both masters and mistresses, as fathers and mothers are comprised under Parents, and sonnes and daughters under Children, I have according to the Scripture phrase comprised Mistresses under Masters: so as the duties enjoyed to them belong to these, so farre as may stand with the sex. . . .

. . . As God is carefull to instruct us how to carrie our selves both to his owne Majestie, and also one to another, so let us in both approve our selves to him: remembring what Christ said to the Pharisies, These ought ye to have done, and not to leave the other undone. The same Lord that requireth praise to his owne Majestie, injoyneth mutuall service one to another; the neglect of this, as well as of that, sheweth too light respect of his will and pleasure: What therefore God hath joyned together, let not man put asunder. . . .

3. Of every ones submitting himselfe to another.

Be not high minded, nor swell one against another. Though in outward estate some may be higher than other, yet "in Christ all are one whether bond or free": all "members of one and the same body." Now consider the mutuall affection (as I may so speake) of the members of a naturall body one towards another: not any one of them will puffe it selfe up, and rise against the other: the head which is the highest and of greatest honour will submit it selfe to the feet in performing the dutie of an head, as well as the feet to the head in performing their dutie, so all other parts. Neither is it hereby implied that they which are in place of dignitie and authoritie should forget or relinquish their place, dignitie, or authoritie, and become as inferiours under authoritie, no more than the head doth: for the head in submitting it selfe doth not goe upon the ground and beare the body, as the feet; but it submitteth it selfe by directing and governing the other parts, and that with all the humilitie, meeknesse, and gentlenesse that it can. So must all superiours; much more must equals and inferiours learne with humilitie, and meeknesse, without scorne or disdaine, to performe their dutie: this is that which was before by the Apostle expressly mentioned, and is here againe intimated; none are exempted and privileged from it. We know that it is unnaturall, and unbeseeming the head to scorne the feet, and to swell against them, but more than monstrous for one hand to scorn another: what shall we then say if the feet swell against the head? Surely such scorne and disdaine among the members, would cause not only great disturbance, but also utter ruine to the body. And can it be otherwise in a politique body? But on the contrarie, when all of all sorts shall (as hath been before shewed) willingly submit themselves one to another, the whole body, and every member thereof will reape good thereby: yea, by this mutuall submission, as we doe good, so we shall receive good. . . .

Question. Why among other inferiours are wives first brought into the schoole of Christ to learne their duty?

Answer. Many good reasons may be given of the Apostles order even in this point.

First, of all other inferiours in a family, wives are farre the most excellent, and therefore to be placed in the first ranke.

Secondly, wives were the first to whom subjection was injoyned; before there was childe or servant in the world, it was said to her, "thy desire shall be subject to thine husband."

Thirdly, wives are the fountaine from whence all other degrees spring: and therefore ought first to be cleansed.

Fourthly, this subjection is a good patterne unto children and servants: and a great means to move them to be subject.

Fifly, I may further adde as a truth, which is too manifest by experience in all places, that among all other parties, of whom the Holy Ghost requireth subjection, wives for the most part are most backward in yeelding subjection to their husbands. But yee wives that feare God, be carefull of your duty: and though it may seeme somewhat contrary to the common course and practise of wives, yet "follow not a multitude to doe evill. Though it be harsh to corrupt nature, yet beat downe that corruption: yea though your husbands be backward in their duties, yet be ye forward, and strive to goe before them in yours: remembring what the Lord saith (Mat. 5. 46, 47.) "If you love them which love you, what singular thing doe ye?" Yes remembring also what the Apostle saith, (I Tim. 2. 14). "The woman was first in the transgression," and first had her duty given unto her, and "was made for the man, and not man for the woman."

Thus shall ye deserve that commendation of good wives, "Many have done vertuously, but ye excell them all." . . .

New England Branches

Document 5: If Woman "Be a Necessary Evil, How Evil Is the Man, for Whom She Is Necessary!"

These words of John Robinson, pastor of the Pilgrim settlers in Plymouth, Massachusetts, illustrate the way in which the Puritans sought to give greater dignity to woman's role in marriage while still maintaining her subjection. Through spiritualization of the household, greater emphasis was placed on mutual love and the companionship of women and men in marriage. The home became the primary locale for the education of children, with religious training central to this education in a society defined by its sacred character. Though the father was designated the educator, the mother bore equal responsibility in the actual training. Both the meaning of the home and the parents' roles would change radically during the revolutionary war era.[41]

Of Marriage

God hath ordained marriage, amongst other good means, for the benefit of man's natural and spiritual life, in an individual society, as the lawyers speak, between one man and one woman: and hath blessed it alone with this prerogative, that by it, in lawful order, our kind should be preserved, and posterity propagated. . . .

Not only heathen poets, which were more tolerable, but also wanton Christians, have nick-named women, necessary evils; but with as much shame to men, as wrong to women, and to God's singular ordinance withal. When the Lord amongst all the good creatures which he had made, could find none fit and good enough for the man; he made the woman of a rib of him, and for a help unto him, Gen. ii, 20, 21; neither is she, since the creation, more degenerated than he, from the primitive goodness. Besides, if the woman be a necessary evil, how evil is the man, for whom she is necessary!

Some have said, and that, in their own and others' judgment, both wittily and devoutly, that marriage fills the earth, and virginity heaven: but others have better answered, How should heaven be full, if the earth were empty? I add, that, because Christ hath said, that the children of the regeneration neither marry wives, nor are married, but are like the angels in heaven, Matt. xxii, 3; many, whilst they would, by preposterous imitation, become like the angels in heaven, have in truth become like the devils in hell: for they also neither marry wives, nor are married. But this is, indeed, the very dregs of Popery, to place special piety in things either evil, or indifferent, at the best; as is abstinence from marriage, and the marriage bed; which is no more a virtue, than abstinence from wine, or other pleasing natural things. Both marriage and wine are of God, and good in themselves; either of them may in their abuse, prejudice the natural or spiritual life: neither of them is unlawful, no not for them which simply need them not: which also not to need, argues bodily strength in the one, but a kind of weakness in the other. . . .

The virtue of the wife is the husband's ornament, so is the husband's the wife's, much more. And therefore Philon's wife, being demanded why she alone went so plainly apparelled, made answer, that her husband's virtues were ornament sufficient for her. If her practice were a rule, and that husbands' virtues were to be measured by their wives' homeliness in attire: either fewer husbands would be thought virtuous than are, or more wives found soberly apparelled than are.

After goodness, fitness in marriage is most to be regarded: and that so much that as for a pair of gloves or yoke of oxen, two alike, though meaner, both of them are fitter and better for use, than if the one were more excellent; so in this marriage pair and yoke, the woman best qualified is not always the best wife for every man; nor every man the best qualified, the fittest husband for every woman: but two more alike, though both meaner, sort better usually. And according to this, Pittacus, being demanded by a friend what kind of wife he should marry, answered: one fit for him. Fitness of years is requisite, that an old head be not set upon young shoulders; nor the contrary, which is worse: fitness in estate, lest the excelling person despise the other, or draw him to a course above his reach: fitness for course of life and disposition unto it, the dislike whereof, in either by other, breeds many discontentments. Lastly, agreement of affection and inclination, what may be, to all good persons and things. Only, it is good, if the one be too fiery hot and suddenly moved, that the other can cast on the more cold water of forbearance. But now, seeing there is seldom or never found such conformity between man and wife, but that differences will arise and be seen, and so the one must give way, and apply unto the other; this, God and nature layeth upon the woman, rather than upon the man; although the man should not too much look for it, nor use all his authority, ordinarily at least, which none but fools will do.

Many common graces and good things are requisite both for husband and wife: but more especially the Lord requires in the man love and wisdom; and in the woman subjection. Eph. v. 22–25. The love of the husband to his wife must be like Christ's to his church; holy for quality, and great for quantity, both intensively and extensively. Her person, and whatsoever is good in her he must love fervently; mending or bearing, if not intolerable, what is amiss: by the former of which two he makes her the better, and himself by the latter. And if her failings and faults be great, he by being inured to bear them patiently, is the fitter to converse quietly and patiently with other perverse persons abroad; as Socrates said, he was, by bearing the daily home-brawlings of Xanthippe. Neither sufficeth it, that the husband walk with his wife as a man of love, but before her also as a man of understanding. I Pet. iii. 7; which God hath therefore afforded him, and means of obtaining it, above the woman, that he might guide and go before her, as a fellow heir of eternal life with him. It is monstrous, if the head stand where the feet should be: and double pity, when a Nabal and Abigail are matched together. Yea, experience teacheth how inconvenient it is, if the woman have but a little more understanding, (though he be not wholly without,) than her husband hath.

In the wife is specially required a reverend subjection in all lawful things to her husband. Eph. v. 22, 7c. Lawful, I mean, for her to obey in, yea though not lawful for him to require of her. He ought to give honour to the wife as to the weaker vessel, I Pet. iii. 7: but now, if he pass the bounds of wisdom and kindness; yet must not she shake off the bond of submission, but must bear patiently the burden, which God hath laid upon the daughters of Eve. The woman in innocency was to be subject to the man: but this should have been without all wrong on his part, or grief on hers. But she being first in transgression, I Tim. ii. 14, hath brought herself under another subjection, and the same to her, grievous; and in regard to her husband, often unjust; but in regard of God, always most just; who hath ordained that her desire should be subject to her husband, Gen. iii. 16, who by her seduction became subject to sin. . . .

As marriage is a medicine against uncleanness; so adultery is the disease of marriage, and divorce the medicine of adultery; though not properly for the curing of the guilty, but for the easing of the innocent: which remedy he may, but is not simply bound to use, as some are the former. Some have said, that he who conceals the faults of his wife this way, becomes a patron of her filthiness: but this is rightly restrained by others to certain cases. . . .

As a man may surfeit at his own table or be drunken with his own drink; so may he play the adulterer with his own wife, both by inordinate affection and action. For howsoever the marriage bed cover much inordinateness this way: yet must modesty be observed by the married, lest the bed which is honourable, and undefiled, Heb. xiii. 4, in its right use, become by abuse hateful, and filthy in God's sight. It hath been by some well observed, that divers of the patriarchs conversed with many wives, whom they took out of a singular desire of a plentiful progeny, more chastely, than many others did and do with their one.

Of Children and Their Education

Children, in their first days, have the greater benefit of good mothers, not only because they suck their milk, but in a sort, their manners also, by being continually with them, and receiving their first impressions from them. But afterwards, when they come to riper years, good fathers are more behoveful for their forming in virtue and good manners, by their greater wisdom and authority: and oftentimes also, by correcting the fruits of their mother's indulgence, by their severity.

They are a blessing great, but dangerous. They come into the world at first with danger, both in respect of themselves, as passing sometimes, from the womb to the grave; sometimes, being born deformed in body; sometimes, incapable of understanding: as also in regard of the mother, the first day of their being in the world, being often her last in it. After their coming into the world through so many dangers, they come into a world of dangers. In their infancy, how soon is the tender bud nipped, or bruised by sickness or otherwise! In their venturesome days, into how many needless dangers do they throw themselves, in which many perish, besides those into which God brings them, and that all their life long! Above all other, how great and many are their spiritual dangers, both for nourishing and increasing the corruption which they bring into the world with them; and for diverting them from all goodness, which God's grace, and men's endeavour might work in them! . . .

. . . And surely there is in all children, though not alike, a stubbornness, and stoutness of mind arising from natural pride, which must, in the first place, be broken and beaten down; that so the foundation of their education being laid in humility and tractableness, other virtues may, in their time, be built thereon. This fruit of natural corruption and root of actual rebellion both against God and man must be destroyed, and no manner of way nourished, except we will plant a nursery of contempt of all good persons and things, and of obstinacy therein. It is commendable in a horse, that he be stout and stomachful, being never to be left to his own government, but always to have his rider on his back, and the bit in his mouth. But who would have his child like his horn in his brutishness? Indeed such as are of great stomach, being thoroughly broken, and informed, become very serviceable, for great designs: else, of horses they become asses, or worse: as Themisctocles' master told him, when he was a child, that either he would bring some great good, or some great hurt to the commonwealth.

Document 6: "The Love of Each Other as the Chief of All Earthly Comfort"

The letters of John Winthrop to his wife illustrate the benevolent and protective love that Puritan men were meant to feel toward their wives. Margaret's letter in this section reveals her own deep religious spirit and her belief that their earthly love must take second place to God's will for them. Taken together, their relatively large preserved correspondence conveys the intended meaning of the spiritual relationship between man and woman in Puritan marriage: warmth and concern for one another in Christ's name, while both maintained distinct spheres and hierarchical relationships within the social order.[42]

John Winthrop to his Wife

To my loving friend Mrs. Winthrop at Chelmsly House in Great Maplested, Exxes.

My Dear Wife,—I beseech the Lord of good God to bless thee and thy little babe with all spiritual blessings in heavenly things, and with a comfortable supply of all things needful for this present life, with such a portion of the true wisdom as may cause us allways to discern of the worth & excellency of Christ Jesus, to take him as our onely portion, & to love him with all our heart, as our best thank offering for his unspeakable love & mercy in redeeming us from our sins by his own death, & adopting us into the right of the inheritance of his father's Kingdom. To him be glory & praise for ever, Amen.

Albeit I cannot conveniently come to thee yet, I could not but send to know how thou doest, & in what state thy good mother continueth, with the rest of our friends: That which we now forsee & fear in her, we must look to come to ourselves, & then neither friends nor goods, pleasure nor honor, will stand us in any stead, onely a good conscience sprinkled with the blood of Christ shall give us peace with God & our own souls.

We are all here in good health (I praise God) yet not well contented until thou returnest to Groton, but I will not hasten to abridge thy dear mother of that comfort which she may receive in thy company. My sweet spouse, let us delight in the love of each other as the chief of all earthly comfort: & labor to increase therein by the constant experience of each other's faithfulness & sincerity of affection, formed into the similitude of the Love of Christ and his Church. Look for me on Thursday or Friday (if God will) & remember me to thy good mother & all the rest, as thou knowest my duty & desires, etc. My parents salute thee; many kisses of Love I send thee: farewell.

[John Winthrop]

July 12, 1620
[Groton]

John Winthrop to his Wife

Most dear & loving Wife,—I wrote unto thee by our neighbor Cole, being then uncertain of my return, yet I hoped to have been with thee on Saturday but it so falleth out, that I am enforced to stay except I should leave my sister Goldings destitute, & the business I came for without effect, which I cannot now fail with comfort & good report. Therefore I must entreat thy gentle patients until this business be dispatched, which I hope will be by the next week. In the mean time thou art well persuaded that my heart is with thee, as (I know) thine is with him to whom thou has given thyself, a faithful & loving yokefellow: who truly prizing this gift as the greatest earthly blessing, provokes thy Love to abound in those fruits of mutual kindness, etc., that may add a daily increase of comfort & sweet content in this happiness. I would willingly offer a request unto thee, which yet I will not urge (not knowing what inconveniences may lie in the way), but it would be very grateful to me to meet thee at Maplested on Wednesday next, but be it as God shall guide thy heart & the opportunity. It is now near XI of the clock & time to sleep, therefore I must end. The Lord of heavenly father bless & keep thee & all ours, & let this salutation serve for all, for I know not how safe a messenger I shall have for these. Remember my duty & Love as thou knowest how to bestow them. Farewell,

Thine John Winthrop.

I send thee divers things by Wells in a trusse.
May 10: 1621
[London]

Margaret Winthrop to her Husband

Dear in my thoughts,—I blush to think how much I have neglected the opportunity of presenting my love to you. Sad thoughts possess my spirits, and I cannot repulse them; which makes me unfit for any thing, wondering what the Lord means by all these troubles among us. Sure I am, that all shall work to the best of them that love God, or rather are loved of him. I know he will bring light out of obscurity, and make his righteousness shine forth as clear as the noon day. Yet I find in myself an adverse spirit, and a trembling heart, not so willing to submit to the will of God as I desire. There is a time to plant, and a time to pull up that which is planted, which I could desire might not be yet. But the Lord knoweth what is best, and his will be done. But I will write no more. Hoping to see thee to-morrow, my best affections being commended to yourself, [and] the rest of our friends at Newton, I commit thee to God.

Your loving wife,
Margaret Winthrop.

Sad Boston, 1637

John Winthrop to his Wife [In response to the above]

For Mrs. Winthrop at Boston.

Dear [torn],—I am still detained from thee, but it is by the Lord, who hath a greater interest in me than thyself. When his work is done he will restore me to thee again to our mutual comfort: Amen. I thank thee for the sweet Letter: my heart was with thee to have written to thee every day, but business would not permit me. I suppose thou hearest much news from hence: it may be, some grievous to thee: but be not troubled, I assure thee things go well, & they must needs do so, for God is with us & thou shalt see a happy issue. I hope to be with thee tomorrow & a friend or 2, I suppose. So I kiss my sweet wife & rest

Thine Jo: Winthrop.

This 6: day

EXPERIENCE: THE FRUITS

Separating the Bitter from the Sweet

Document 7: "Say No More, the Court Knows Wherefore and Is Satisfied"

The trial and excommunication of Anne Hutchinson by civil and church officials in 1637 remains the most notorious case involving a woman's sexual and religious freedom in colonial New England's history. The excerpts from the trial printed here reveal that the decisions regarding her guilt and excommunication were reached before the trial had even begun. Today the case of Anne Hutchinson cannot be considered an isolated bizarre happening but represents the fate of a large number of New England women of her generation who received similar judgments before the law.[43]

November 1637

The Examination of Mrs. Anne Hutchinson at the court at Newton.

Mr. Winthrop, governor. Mrs. Hutchinson, you are called here as one of those that have troubled the peace of the commonwealth and the churches here; you are known to be a woman that hath had a great share in the promoting and divulging of those opinions that are causes of this trouble, and to be nearly joined not only in affinity and affection with some of those the court had taken notice of and passed censure upon, but you have spoken divers things as we have been informed very prejudicial to the honour of the churches and ministers thereof, and you have maintained a meeting and an assembly in your house that hath been condemned by the general assembly as a thing not toberable nor comely in the sight of God nor fitting for your sex, and notwithstanding that was cried down you have continued the same, therefore we have thought good to send for you to understand how things are, that if you be in an erroneous way we may reduce you that so you may become a profitable member here among us, otherwise if you be obstinate in your course that then the court may take such course that you may trouble us no further, therefore I would intreat you to express whether you do not hold and assent in practice to those opinions and factions that have been handled in court already, that is to say, whether you do not justify Mr. Wheelwright's sermon and the petition.

Mrs. Hutchinson. I am called here to answer before you but I hear no things laid to my charge. . . .

Gov. Why do you keep such a meeting at your house as you do every week upon a set day?

Mrs. H. It is lawful for me so to do, as it is all your practices and can you find a warrant for yourself and condemn me for the same thing? . . .

Gov. For this, that you appeal to our practice you need no confutation. If your meeting had answered to the former it had not been offensive, but I will say that there was no meeting of women alone, but your meeting is of another sort for there are sometimes men among you.

Mrs. H. There was never any man with us.

Gov. Well, admit there was no man at your meeting and that you was sorry for it, there is no warrant for your doings, and by what warrant do you continue such a course?

Mrs. H. I conceive there lyes a clear rule in Titus, that the elder women should instruct the younger [Titus 2:3–5] and then I must have a time wherein I must do it.

Gov. All this I grant you, I grant you a time for it, but what is this to the purpose that you Mrs. Hutchinson must call a company together from their callings to come to be taught by you?

Mrs. H. Will it please you to answer me this and to give me a rule for then I will willingly submit to any truth. If any come to my house to be instructed in the ways of God what rule have I to put them away?

Gov. But suppose that a hundred men come unto you to be instructed will you forbear to instruct them?

Mrs. H. As far as I conceive I cross a rule in it.

Gov. Very well and do you not so here?

Mrs. H. No Sir for my ground is they are men.

Gov. Men and women all is one for that, but suppose that a man should come and say Mrs. Hutchinson I hear that you are a woman that God hath given his grace unto and you have knowledge in the word of God I pray instruct me a little, ought you not to instruct this man?

Mrs. H. I think I may.—Do you think it not lawful for me to teach women and why do you call me to teach the court?

Gov. We do not call you to teach the court but to lay open yourself.

Mrs. H. I desire you that you would then set me down a rule by which I may put them away that come unto me and so have peace in so doing. . . .

Mr. Bradstreet. I am not against all women's meetings but do think them to be lawful.

Mr. Dudley, dep. gov. Here hath been much spoken concerning Mrs. Hutchinson's meetings and among other answers she saith that men come not there, I would ask you this one question then, whether never any man was at your meeting?

Gov. There are two meetings kept at their house.

Dep. gov. How; is there two meetings?

Mrs. H. Ey Sir, I shall not equivocate, there is a meeting of men and women and there is a meeting only for women.

Dep. gov. Are they both constant?

Mrs. H. No. but upon occasions they are deferred.

Mr. Endicott. Who teaches in the men's meetings none but men, do not women sometimes?

Mrs. H. Never as I heard, not one.

Dep. gov. I would go a little higher with Mrs. Hutchinson. About three years ago we were all in peace. Mrs. Hutchinson from that time she came hath made a disturbance, and some that came over with her in the ship did inform me what she was as soon as she was landed. I being then in place dealt with the pastor and teacher of Boston and desired them to enquire of her, and then I was satisfied that she held nothing different from us, but within half a year after, she had vented divers of her strange opinions and had made parties of the country, and at length in comes that Mr. Cotton and Mr. Vane were of her judgment, but Mr. Cotton hath cleared himself that he was not of that mind, but now it appears by this woman's meeting that Mrs. Hutchinson hath so forestalled the minds of many by their resort to her meeting that now she hath a potent party in the country. How if all these things have endangered us as from that foundation and if she in particular hath disparaged all our ministers in the land that they have preached a covenant of works, and only Mr. Cotton a covenant of grace, why this is not to be suffered, and therefore being driven to the foundation and it being found that Mrs. Hutchinson is she that hath depraved all the ministers and hath been the cause of what is fallen out, why we must take away the foundation and the building will fall.

Mrs. H. I pray Sir prove it that I said they preached nothing but a covenant of works.

Dep. Gov. Nothing but a covenant of works, why a Jesuit may preach truth sometimes.

Mrs. H. Did I ever say they preached a covenant of works then?

Dep. Gov. If they do not preach a covenant of grace clearly, then they preach a covenant of works.

Mrs. H. No Sir, one may preach a covenant of grace more clearly than another, so I said. . . .

D. Gov. When they do preach a covenant of works do they preach truth?

Mrs. H. Yes Sir, but when they preach a covenant of works for salvation, that is not truth.

D. Gov. I do ask you this, when the ministers do preach a covenant of works do they preach a way of salvation?

Mrs. H. I did not come hither to answer to questions of that sort.

D. Gov. Because you will deny the thing.

Mrs. H. Ey, but that is to be proved first.

D. Gov. I will make it plain that you did say that the ministers did preach a covenant of works.

Mrs. H. I deny that.

D. Gov. And that you said they were not able ministers of the new testament, but Mr. Cotton only.

Mrs. H. If ever I spake that I proved it by God's word. . . .

[Extended questioning follows regarding Mrs. Hutchinson's position on the covenant of works and the covenant of grace and her attribution of these views to the Massachusetts clergy.]

Gov. Mrs. Hutchinson, the court you see hath laboured to bring you to acknowledge the error of your way that so you might be reduced, the time now grows late, we shall therefore give you a little more time to consider of it and therefore desire that you attend the court again in the morning.

[The next morning.]

Gov. We proceeded the last night as far as we could in hearing on this cause of Mrs. Hutchinson. There were divers things laid to her charge, her ordinary meetings about religious exercises, her speeches in derogation of the ministers among us, and the weakening of the hands and hearts of the people towards them. Here was sufficient proof made of that which she was accused of in that point concerning the ministers and their ministry, as that they did preach a covenant of works when others did preach a covenant of grace, and that they were not able ministers of the new testament, and that they had not the seal of the spirit, and this was spoken not as was pretended out of private conference, but out of conscience and warrant from scripture alledged the fear of man is a snare and seeing God had given her a calling to it she would freely speak. Some other speeches she used, as that the letter of the scripture held forth a covenant of works; and this is offered to be proved by probable grounds. If there be any thing else that the court hath to say they may speak.

Mrs. H. The ministers come in their own cause. Now the Lord hath said that an oath is the end of all controversy; though there be a sufficient number of witnesses yet they are not according to the word, therefore I desire they may speak upon oath.

Gov. Well, it is in the liberty of the court whether they will have an oath or no and it is not in this case as in case of a jury. If they be satisfied they have sufficient matter to proceed. . . .

Mrs. H. But it being the Lord's ordinance that an oath should be the end of all strife, therefore they are to deliver what they do upon oath.

Mr. Bradstreet. Mrs. Hutchinson, these are but circumstances and adjuncts to the cause, admit they should mistake you in your speeches you would make them to sin if you urge them to swear.

Mrs. H. That is not the thing. If they accuse me I desire it may be upon oath.

Gov. If the court be not satisfied they may have an oath.

Mr. Nowel. I should think it convenient that the country also should be satisfied because that I do hear is affirmed, that things which were spoken in private are carried abroad to the publick and thereupon they do undervalue the ministers of congregations.

Mr. Brown. I desire to speak. If I mistake not an oath is of a high nature, and it is not to be taken but in a controversy, and for my part I am afraid of an oath and fear that we shall take God's name in vain, for we may take the witness of these men without an oath.

Mr. Endicot. I think the ministers are so well known unto us, that we need not take an oath of them, but indeed an oath is the end of all strife. . . .

Gov. Let those that are not satisfied in the court speak.

Many say.—We are not satisfied.

Gov. I would speak this to Mrs. Hutchinson. If the ministers shall take an oath will you sit down satisfied?

Mrs. H. I can't be not withstanding oaths satisfied against my own conscience.

Mr. Stoughton. I am fully satisfied with this that the ministers do speak the truth but now in regard of censure I dare not hold up my hand to that, because it is a course of justice, and I cannot satisfy myself to proceed so far in a way of justice, and therefore I should desire an oath in this as in all other things. I do but speak to prevent offence if I should not hold up my hand at the censure unless there be an oath given.

Mr. Peters. We are ready to swear if we see a way of God in it. . . .

Mr. Endicot. If they will not be satisfied with a testimony an oath will be in vain. . . .

Mr. Shepard. I know no reason of the oath but the importunity of this gentlewoman. . . .

Mrs. H. They say I said the fear of man is a snare, why should I be afraid. When I came unto them, they urging many things unto me and I being backward to answer at first, at length this scripture came into my mind 29 Prov. 15. The fear of man bringeth a snare, but whoso putteth his trust in the Lord shall be safe. . . .

Gov. The elders do know what an oath is and as it is an ordinance of God so it should be used. . . .

Mr. Eliot, Mr. Shepard. We desire to see light why we should take an oath.

Mr. Stoughton. Why it is an end of all strife and I think you ought to swear and put an end to the matter.

Mr. Peters. Our oath is not to satisfy Mrs. Hutchinson but the court.

Mr. Endicot. The assembly will be satisfied by it.

Dep. Gov. If the country will not be satisfied you must swear.

Mr. Shepard. I conceive the country doth not require it.

Dep. Gov. Let her witnesses be called.

Gov. Who be they?

Mrs. H. Mr. Leveret and our teacher and Mr. Coggeshall. . . .

Gov. Will you Mr. Coggeshall say that she did not say so?

Mr. Coggeshall. Yes I dare say that she did not say all that which they lay against her.

Mr. Peters. How dare you look into the court to say such a word?

Mr. Coggeshall. Mr. Peters takes upon him to forbid me. I shall be silent. . . .

Gov. Well, Mr. Leveret, what were the words? I pray speak.

Mr. Leveret. To my best remembrance when the elders did send for her, Mr. Peters did with much vehemency and intreaty urge her to tell what difference there was between Mr. Cotton and them, and upon his urging of her she said. The fear of man is a snare, but they that trust upon the Lord shall be safe. And being asked wherein the difference was, she answered that they did not preach a covenant of grace so clearly as Mr. Cotton did, and she gave this reason of it because that as the apostles were for a time without the spirit so until they had received the witness of the spirit they could not preach a covenant of grace so clearly. . . .

Gov. Mr. Cotton, the court desires that you declare what you do remember of the conference which was at that time and is now in question.

Mr. Cotton. . . . the greatest passage that took impression upon me was to this purpose. The elders spoke that they had heard that she had spoken some condemning words of their ministry, and among other things they did first pray her to answer wherein she thought their ministry did differ from mine, how the comparison sprang I am ignorant, but sorry I was that any comparison should be between me and my brethren and uncomfortable it was, she told them to this purpose that they did not hold forth a covenant of grace as I did, but wherein did we differ? why she said that they did not hold forth the seal of the spirit as she doth. . . . You preach of the seal of the spirit upon a work and he upon free grace without a work or without respect to a work, he preaches the seal of the spirit upon free grace and you upon a work. I told her I was very sorry that she put comparisons between my ministry and their's for she had said more than I could myself, and rather I had that she had put us in fellowship with them and not have made that discrepancy . . . this was the sum of the difference, nor did it seem to be so ill taken as it is and our brethren did say also that they would not so easily believe reports as they had done and withall mentioned that they would speak no more of it, some of them did; and afterwards some of them did say they were less satisfied than before. And I must say that I did not find her saying they were under a covenant of works, nor that she said they did preach a covenant of works. . . .

Dep. Gov. They affirm that Mrs. Hutchinson did say they were not able ministers of the new testament.

Mr. Cotton. I do not remember it.

Mrs. H. If you please to give me leave I shall give you the ground of what I know to be true. Being much trouble to see the falseness of the constitution of the church of England, I had like to have turned separatist; whereupon I kept a day of solemn humiliation and pondering of the thing; this scripture was brought unto me—he that denies Jesus Christ to be come in the flesh in antichrist—this I considered of and in considering found that the papists did not deny him to be come in the flesh, nor we did not deny him—who then was antichrist? Was the Turk antichrist only? The Lord knows that I could not open scripture; he must by his prophetical office open it unto me. So after that being unsatisfied in the thing, the Lord was pleased to bring this scripture out of the Hebrews. He that denied the testament denied the testator, and in this did open unto me and give me to see that those which did not teach the new covenant had the spirit of antichrist, and upon this he did discover the ministry unto me and ever since, I bless the Lord, he hath let me see which was the clear ministry and which the wrong. Since that time I confess I have been more choice and he hath let me to distinguish between the voice of my beloved and the voice of Moses, the voice of John Baptist and the voice of antichrist, for all those voices are spoken of in scripture. Now if you do condemn me for speaking what in my conscience I know to be truth I must commit myself unto the Lord.

Mr. Nowell. How do you know that that was the spirit?

Mrs. H. How did Abraham know that it was God that bid him offer his son, being a breach of the sixth commandment?

Dep. Gov. By an immediate voice.

Mrs. H. So to me by an immediate revelation.

Dep. Gov. How! an immediate revelation.

Mrs. H. By the voice of his own spirit to my soul. I will give you another scripture . . . out of Daniel chap. 7. and he and for us all, wherein he shewed me the sitting of the judgment and the standing of all high and low before the Lord and how thrones and kingdoms were cast down before him. When our teachers came to New England it was a great trouble unto me, my brother Wheelwright being put by also. I was then much troubled concerning the ministry under which I lived, and then that place in the 30th of Isaiah was brought to my mind. Though the Lord give thee bread of adversity and water of affliction yet shall not thy teachers be removed into corners any more, but thine eyes shall see thy teachers . . . this place in Daniel was brought unto me and did shew me that though I should meet with affliction yet I am the same God that delivered Daniel out of the lion's den, I will also deliver thee.—Therefore, I desire you to look to it, for you see this scripture fulfilled this day and therefore I desire you that as you tender the Lord and the church and commonwealth to consider and look what you do. You have power over my body but the Lord Jesus hath power over my body and soul, and assure yourselves thus much, you do as much as in you lies to put the Lord Jesus Christ from you, and if you go on in this course you begin you will bring a curse upon you and your posterity, and the mouth of the Lord hath spoken it. . . .

Dep. Gov. I desire Mr. Cotton to tell us whether you do approve of Mrs. Hutchinson's revelation as she hath laid them down.

Mr. Cotton. I know not whether I do understand her, but this I say, if she doth expect a deliverance in a way of providence—then I cannot deny it.

Dep. Gov. No Sir we did not speak of that.

Mr. Cotton. If it be by way of miracle then I would suspect it.

Dep. Gov. Do you believe that her revelations are true?

Mr. Cotton. That she may have some special providence of God to help her is a thing that I cannot bear witness against. . . .

Mrs. H. By a providence of God I say I expect to be delivered from some calamity that shall come to me.

Gover. The case is altered and will not stand with us now, but I see a marvellous providence of God to bring things to this pass that they are. We have been hearkening about the trial of this thing and now the mercy of God by a providence hath answered our desires and made her to lay open her self and the ground of all those disturbances to be by revelations . . . but all this while there is no use of the ministry of the word nor of any clear call of God by his word, but the ground work of her revelations is the immediate revelation of the spirit and not by the ministry of the word, and that is the means by which she hath very much abused the country that they shall look for revelations and are not bound to the ministry of the word, but God will teach them by immediate revelations and this hath been the ground of all these tumults and troubles, and I would that those were all cut off from us that trouble us, for this is the thing that hath been the root of all the mischief. . . .

Mr. Endicot. I speak in reference to Mr. Cotton . . . Whether do you witness for her or against her, Mr. Cotton.

Mr. Cotton. This is that I said Sir, and my answer is plain that if she doth look for deliverance from the hand of God by his providence, and the revelation be in a word or according to a word, that I cannot deny.

Mr. Endicot. You give me satisfaction.

Dep. Gov. No, no, he gives me none at all.

Mr. Cotton. But if it be in a way of miracle or a revelation without the word that I do not assent to, but look at it as a delusion, and I think so doth she too as I understand her.

Dep. Gov. Sir, you weary me and do not satisfy me.

Mr. Cotton. I pray Sir give me leave to express myself. In that sense that she speaks I dare not bear witness against it.

Mr. Nowell. I think it is a devilish delusion.

Gover. Of all the revelations that ever I read of I never read the like ground laid as is for this. The Enthusiasts and Anabaptists had never the like. . . .

Dep. Gov. I never saw such revelations as these among the Anabaptists, therefore am sorry that Mr. Cotton should stand to justify her. . . . I am fully persuaded that Mrs. Hutchinson is deluded by the devil, because the spirit of God speaks truth in all his servants.

Gov. I am persuaded that the revelation she brings forth is delusion.

All the court but some two or three ministers cry out, we all believe it—we all believe it. . . .

Gov. Seeing the court hath thus declared itself and hearing what hath been laid to the charge of Mrs. Hutchinson and especially what she by the providence of God hath declared freely without being asked, if therefore it be the mind of the court, looking at her as the principal cause of all our trouble, that they would now consider what is to be done to her.— . . .

Mr. Coddington. . . . I do not speak to disparage our elders and their callings, but I do not see any thing that they accuse her of witnessed against her, and therefore I do not see how she should be censured for that. . . . I do not for my own part see any equity in the court in all your proceedings. Here is no law of God that she hath broken nor any law of the country that she hath broke, and therefore deserves no censure, and if she say that the elders preach as the apostles did, why they preached a covenant of grace and what wrong is that to them, for it is without question that the apostles did preach a covenant of grace, though not with that power, till they received the manifestation of the spirit, therefore I pray consider what you do, for here is no law of God or man broken. . . .

Mr. Colburn. I dissent from censure of banishment.

Mr. Stoughton. The censure which the court is about to pass in my conscience is as much as she deserves, but because she desires witness and there is none in way of witness therefore I shall desire that no offence be taken if I do not formally condemn her because she hath not been formally convicted as others are by witnesses upon oath.

Mr. Coddington. That is a scruple to me also, because Solomon saith, every man is partial in his own cause, and here is none that accuses her but the elders, and she spake nothing to them but in private, and I do not know what rule they had to make the thing publick, secret things ought to be spoken in secret and publick things in publick, therefore I think they have broken the rules of God's word. . . .

Gov. We'll give them their oaths. You shall swear to the truth and nothing but the truth as far as you know. So help you God. What you do remember for her speak, pray speak.

Mr. Eliot. I do remember and I have it written, that which she spake first was, the fear of men is a snare, why should she be afraid but would speak freely. The question being asked whether there was a difference between Mr. Cotton and us, she said there was a broad difference. I would not stick upon words—the thing she said—and that Mr. Cotton did preach a covenant of grace and we of works and she gave this reason—to put a work in point of evidence is a revealing upon a work. We did labour then to convince her that our doctrine was the same with Mr. Cotton's: She said no, for we were not sealed. That is all I shall say.

Gov. What say you Mr. Weld?

Mr. Weld. I will speak to the things themselves—these two things

I am fully clear in—she did make a difference in three things, the first I was not so clear in, but that she said this I am fully sure of, that we were not able ministers of the new testament and that we were not clear in our experience because we were not sealed.

Mr. Eliot. I do further remember this also, that she said we were not able ministers of the gospel because we were but like the apostles before the ascension. . . .

Mr. Coddington. What wrong was that to say that you were not able ministers of the new testament or that you were like the apostles—me thinks the comparison is very good.

Gov. Well, you remember that she said but now that she should be delivered from this calamity. . . . The court hath already declared themselves satisfied concerning the things you hear, and concerning the troublesomness of her spirit and the danger of her course among us, which is not to be suffered. Therefore if it be the mind of the court that Mrs. Hutchinson for these things that appear before us is unfit for our society, and if it be the mind of the court that she shall be banished out of our liberties and imprisoned till she be sent away, let them hold up their hands.

All but three.

Those that are contrary minded hold up yours.

Mr. Coddington and Mr. Colborn, only.

Mr. Jennison. I cannot hold up my hand one way or the other, and I shall give my reason if the court require it.

Gov. Mrs. Hutchinson, the sentence of the court you hear is that you are banished from out of our jurisdiction as being a woman not fit for our society, and are to be imprisoned till the court shall send you away.

Mrs. H. I desire to know wherefore I am banished?

Gov. Say no more, the court knows wherefore and is satisfied.

Document 8: "Cast Out . . . as a Slaunderer and Revyler Both of the Church and Common Weale."

The trial of widow Philip[a] Hammond before the First Church in Boston resulted in her excommunication two years after a similar verdict had been laid upon Anne Hutchinson. The record of the Hammond case, as reprinted here, indicates that charges against her were based on her close ties and continued defense of Anne Hutchinson's right to remain in the church and the Massachusetts commonwealth despite her open criticism of church authorities.[44]

The 1st of the 7 Monthe 1639.

Philip the wife of our brother Robert Harding admitted by the name of Philip Hammond widdow was Excommunicated for speaking evill of Authority both in Church and Common weale: For having said in open Court that Mrs. Hutchinson neyther deserved the Censure which was putt upon her in the Church, nor in the Common Weale; It was proved against her in the Church by the witness of our brother Richard Truesdale and our brother Samuell Cole that she had also spoken the like words of Defamation both in her shopp and other meetings, whereof not being able to give any account from Scripture, she was finally Cast out of the Church as a slaunderer and revyler both of the Church and Common Weale, after the example of Miriam, Numbers 12.1, to 15th and according to the Rule of the Apostle 1. Cor. 5. 11.

Document 9: "In All This I Have But Only Desired to Find Out the Truth . . . and to Do Them Good"

Like Anne Hutchinson, Ann Hibbens was tried before a church court. However, Hibbens was brought before the First Church of Boston in 1640 for insubordination to men in regard to totally secular issues: contention with town carpenters over work she had contracted with them and alleged disobedience of her husband's authority. While this trial resulted in her excommunication from the church, she was executed for witchcraft in 1656, two years after her husband's death.[45]

Church Trial of Mistress Ann Hibbens

. . . *Pastor:* All this that you now relate is only to excuse yourself and lessen your own fault and lay blame upon others; and therefore you have in an unsatified way sent from workman to workman, and from one to another, to view the work and to [ap]praise it; and when the elders and others that met at your own house about this did see reason that you should be satisfied, yet you have been so suspicious and used such speeches to accuse our Brother Davis and other workmen, when they would not speak as you do. Yet you have continued still to be so unsatisfied, that you have caused more expense of time than all your work is worth. And when our Teacher and the elders and myself, upon due search and examination of the matter, we did not find that there was any great wrong done to you.—or if it were a wrong yet we thought you ought to have been satisfied and to stir no more in it—but such has been the unquiet frame of your spirit, that you would take no warning, nor hearken to our counsel and exhortation, but have still been stirring, to the offense of many of the congregation whose names and credits you have defamed, and we are unsatisfied also. Therefore consider what whether this has been according to the rule of Christian love; and therefore if you cannot give a better answer, you must expect the further proceedings of the church against you, as shall be most wholesome for your soul.

Elder Oliver: Sister, methinks [this]: the last meeting we had about this business when there was ten of us together, (five for you and five for our Brother Davis), and many witnesses examined, and the joiners professing as in the presence of God that they had rated it as low as ever as they could, and so low as we can get no other joiners in this town to do the like—and they brought it to ten pounds or thereabout—and therefore methinks you should be satisfied and speak no more.

Mrs. Hibbens: There was a joiner from Salem and some others that saw it that did not reckon it above half the price of what he took for it.

Brother Penn: All that our Sister hath spoken tends not to any measure of repentance or sorrow for her sin, but to her further justification and excusing of herself, and casting blame upon others, which savors of great pride of spirit and a heart altogether untouched by any of those means that hath been used with her.

Sgt. Savage: I think if all other offenses were passed by, that hath been mentioned, yet she hath shed forth one sin in the face of the congregation worthy of reproof: and that is transgressing the rule of the apostle in usurping authority over him whom God hath made her head and husband, and in taking the power and authority which God hath given to him out of his hands; and when he was satisfied and sits down contented she is unsatisfied, and will not be content, but will stir in it, as if she were able to manage it better than her husband, which is a plain breach of the rule of Christ.

Pastor: That indeed is observed in her by diverse [people] as a great aggravation of her sin; in so much that some do think she doth but make a wisp of her husband. Yet this she alleged for herself: that her husband did give her leave to order and carry on this business to her own satisfaction.

Brother Corser: It is thought by many that it is an untruth which she speaks and yet it will be proved on oath that her husband would have her contented and rest satisfied—and she would not.

Brother Hibbens: At the first I did give my wife leave to agree with the joiner, and to order the business with him as she thought good. Yet I must needs say in faithfulness to the church that when difference did arise about the work, my wife told me she had agreed with him to do it for forty s[hillings]—which I cannot affirm, having no witness but my wife's own affirmation, which he denied from the first. And therefore conceiving that the work was too much for the price, I told him [that] when it was done, what it came to more, I would give him, as two men should judge it worth. And I chose my Brother Davis, of whose faithfulness I am well satisfied, and was very willing to stand to that agreement he made, and did persuade my wife, and could have wished with all my heart she had been willing to have done the same. And I have had some exercise of spirit with her, that she hath not done so. . . .

Mrs. Hibbens: The Lord knoweth that in all this I have but only desired to find out the truth of a thing and to do them good with whom I had to deal. For there being a general complaint of oppression in work and workmen, and I finding this to exceed all reason—in so much as some cried out of the excess of it, and advised me to complain of it in the Court—and because the truth of it would hardly be found out by the joiners of this town, I was counseled to seek out to others in some other town, that would speak the truth, and when they had spoken it, would not be afraid to stand to it; which I did. And because I feared that some such things might be objected, that I did it for lucre of gain, while I might lawfully take that it is my own, yet to prevent that objection, though I found he had taken more by half than the work was worth yet I resolved not to purse one penny of it, but to dispose it to some other use.

Pastor: It is now late and we must draw to a conclusion. And therefore the church is to express themselves, whether we shall proceed to pass some censure upon her, as that of Admonition—for the further melting and humbling of her soul, if God so please; or if He leave her to obstinacy and impenitence, it may make way to the more speedy and finally cutting of her off by that great censure of Excommunication. . . .

[The church then proceeded to approve and deliver the censure of admonition against Mrs. Hibbens.]

Mrs. Hibbens, her next examination by the church, after her former Admonition: upon a second day of the week, appointed on purpose only for her business, to see how her former Admonition had wrought upon her, and also to give account to Elders of other churches, or any strangers that should come, of the grounds of the church's former proceedings against her; because she conceived and had informed others as if the church had not dealt righteously with her. Therefore this meeting was not on the Lord's day, but appointed on purpose to be on a second day of the week, being the first day of the 12th month, 1640, that strangers might come. . . .

Capt. Gibbens: As this Sister hath made my heart sad, amongst diverse other Brethren, so I would be glad to hear some such expressions from her as may cause myself, with others, to rejoice. Therefore I desire she may not answer things in expressions and terms of will, but let her answer plainly, whether she did indeed accuse our Brethren that they did wickedly, and did sin against the conscience, or no.

Sister Hibbens: I do not remember that I did use any such words, but because two witnesses say so, I am willing to suspect my own self that I might do so.

Mr. Cotton: But if you did so, have you not cause, think you, to judge yourself for it as a Sin?

Mrs. Hibbens: I can say no more than what I have. I do not remember that I spake the words.

Teacher: But that is not the thing you are called to give answer to. Therefore speak plainly to the point. And to help you a little in it before, the thing is this: whether if these Brethren do testify as in the sight and presence of God, that they have done justly and according to a good conscience, then whether you are not bound to believe them, and to acknowledge that you were uncharitable in thinking and speaking so of your Brethren.

Mrs. Hibbens: Yes, I think I ought to believe them, and am to judge myself for it, and lay after such thoughts.

Sgt. Oliver: The answer she makes doth not reach the thing expected from her. Her answer expresseth no more than what any man say in the point of judgment; but that which now is expected from our Sister is penitency and brokenness of spirit for that wrong she hath done them, and those evil thoughts she hath taken up against them.

Pastor: Therefore speak punctually: are you indeed convinced in your conscience that you have wronged them, and do sit as God in the consciences of your Brethren to judge their conscience, which belongs only to God?

Mrs. Hibbens: I can say no more than what I have. I leave that to their own conscience to judge.

Elder Oliver: I desire to speak one word to our Sister, because she hath often affirmed that she doth not remember that she accused our Brethren of wicked and unconscionable dealing. Now I would ask you whether you do not remember such an expression as this, that if you should hold your tongue, the very beams of your house would cry to God for vengeance against them.

Mrs. Hibbens: Yes, I do remember I did so say, and I do think so still.

Elder Oliver: If you can remember those words, it doth plainly argue that you used the former then. So, I marvel you should remember this and still justify it, and not the other.

Brother Penn: The answer of our Sister seems to be strange and intolerable. . . .

Mr. Wells (probably from Roxbury): I do bless God with my heart and soul to see the patience and lenity of this church, and the wise dealing of the church in laboring to convince her and to bring so many witnesses to prove things. Therefore I do not marvel at the hardness of the heart of this Sister and her uncharitableness of these brethren [more] than I do at the lenity and wisdom and patience of the church in dealing with her. Neither did I come this day with any prejudice against the church in their proceedings with this Sister, so much as to see and hear what may be of use and profitable to ourselves and our church in any such proceedings. Only I think by what I have heard there is just cause in this church, or any other, to have proceeded to Admonition against any member for so many plain breaches of rule. Therefore I must needs justify and join with the church in what they have done, for I have observed all this day, that notwithstanding all the pains that hath been taken with her, yet her acknowledgements hath rather been forced, than voluntary; and that they have been very lean, and thin, and poor, and sparing, without any sign of sorrow and brokenness of spirit, for such great offenses laid to your charge. . . .

Brother Penn: It seems to me our Sister hath an incorrigible spirit, for when she is called to acknowledge for the sin and offense she hath given, she seeks to hide her sin by laying the cause of this carriage of hers [upon others]. . . .

Brother Eliot: I think this should farther be pressed upon her spirit: her want of wifelike subjection to her husband, and in following his advice and not to do things contrary to it.

Mrs. Hibbens: You may remember, sir, that you have delivered it as an ordinance of God, that a man should hearken to the counsel of his wife—from that speech of God to Abraham, hearken to thy wife in all that she shall say to thee.

Mr. Cotton: Did you hear me say so, or deliver any such point?

Mrs. Hibbens: I was told you did deliver it before I came.

Mr. Cotton: If any told you so, they told you an untruth, for I dare confidently affirm that I never delivered any such thing.

Capt. Gibbens: I desire that our Sister would express who that was, which should tell her so; for myself sometimes dealing with her about her doing things contrary to the advice of her husband, she answered me thus: whether it it better to obey God or man, that judge you. By which she intimated to me that disobedience to the counsel of her godly husband was her obedience to God, and that God would have her to do what she did. So that it argues, she takes it for a principle that the husband must hearken to his wife in the counsel she shall give, and not the wife to the husband. And so she makes a cipher of her husband and his authority, which she should have in great respect.

Brother Fairbank: I conceive she is settled in that opinion, for myself having occasion to speak with her at our Pastor's house about the obedience of wives to husbands, she answered me from that speech of God to Abraham—hearken to thy wife, in all that she shall say to thee.

Mr. Cotton: That is to be understood when a wife speak as the oracles of God, according to the mind and will of God—as indeed then the speech of godly women were as oracles, and did declare the mind and counsel of God to their husbands, and then they were to hearken to them as to God. But that wives *now* should be always God's oracles to their husband, and that the husband should obey his wife, and not the wife the husband, that is a false principle. For God hath put another law upon woman: wives, be subject to your husbands in all things. Except they should require something of you that is a plain sin, or a direct breach of rule, you ought to obey them and be subject to them in all things. Are you convinced therefore that you ought to hearken to the counsel of your husband, and that it is a sin in you at any time to transgress the will and appointment of your husband?

Mrs. Hibbens: Yes sir, I do think that I am bound to obey my husband in all lawful things, and that it is a sin to do the contrary.

Pastor: And are you also convinced that it was a sin in you not to obey your husband in being satisfied with that appraisement of brethren, without further agitation?

Mrs. Hibbens: I have said that my husband gave me leave to wade farther, to find out the sin in this business.

Brother Fairbank: I desire it may be put to our Sister again, to declare who it was that told her that our Teacher did declare such a doctrine as she hath expressed.

Elder Oliver: I pray, Sister, satisfy the brethren in what they desire.

Mrs. Hibbens: It was my Sister Bellingham, that told me so, that you delivered such a thing at our Elder Leveret's daughter's marriage.

Mr. Bellingham: This I can testify, that it was neither the opinion nor practice of my wife—but if she had at any time given offense in any such way, she would speedily come in with submission and much melting of spirit.

Mr. Cotton: I know she was of another mind and therefore I doubt our Sister Hibbens did mistake our Sister Bellingham which is now dead. It was with some other expression that did alter that sense which you took it up in.

Pastor: I would have you, Sister, consider [what] the Lord [means], by all this accusation of the brethren, which makes them so jealous of the frame of your spirit and carriage toward your husband; and whether there is not much sin this way in your carriage to your husband, and therefore God leaves you in so great jealousy in the hearts of brethren in this thing, that though you may not be guilty at this time, yet in some such carriages formerly. . . .

[The final questioning of Mrs. Hibbens by Mr. Cotton then took place.]

Mr. Cotton: . . . [Now] for your uncharitable censurings, and judgments of your brethren: they have by oath cleared themselves of your prejudice; therefore you are bound to believe them. If you do not, you take upon you to judge their consciences, and so you thrust yourself into God's throne and seat, to know the hearts of men, which is God's peculiar prerogative which he will give to no other. Do you not think it is a sin for you to sit in God's throne? I pray speak.

Mrs. Hibbens: Yes, if I should do so, it were a great sin.

Mr. Cotton: Why, you do so, if after their clearing by oath you do not clear them in your conscience—if you do not believe them, but retain your uncharitable opinion of them still. Therefore, I pray, give

God the glory. Do you believe now that they have spoken the truth, and that you have done them wrong, to entertain such thoughts of them as you have done?

Mrs. Hibbens: I dare not clear them, but I leave them on their consciences to God.

Mr. Cotton: I am sorry to hear you say so, and that your heart is so prejudiced against your brethren. The next, then, you are to consider of, is those lies and untruths that you are accused of in speaking about the work. I hope you will acknowledge that all lies or untruths are sins against God.

Mrs. Hibbens: I do not remember that I spake as they accuse me, or with that meaning as they gather, but if they say so, I must submit to it, because I cannot dispute them.

Mr. Cotton: Another offense you are to consider and to give satisfaction for, is your usurping authority over such a head and husband which God hath given to you, who is able to guide and direct you according to God. Now, do you think it is a breach of rule in a wife to transgress the will of her husband, when he requires that which is according to God?

Mrs. Hibbens: My husband did give me leave to search further into the foulness of this business, . . .

Pastor: We see the Lord hath not yet broken her spirit, nor there is nothing comes from her that tends to satisfactions. Therefore we must propound it to the church, what is farther to be done. . . .

[Several men then spoke of their approval of the censure of excommunication.]

Capt. Gibbens: This Sister of ours hath held forth many sins this day in the face of the congregation, the least whereof deserves a sharp censure. She hath accused diverse of the brethren falsely, when no such things appear, and so hath borne false witness against the rule of the Word. She hath taken away their names and credits, what in her lies, which is as precious as life itself. She hath accused others to justify herself. She hath sat in the throne of God himself, as hath been shown her, in judging the consciences and hearts of her brethren. She hath usurped authority over her guide and head, whom she should have obeyed, and unto whom God hath put her in subjection, yet she hath exalted her own wit and will and way above his, to the great dishonor of God and of him. She hath committed one of those seven sins which Solomon saith God hates, that is to sow sedition and strife among brethren. And she has been eminent this way and not only amongst brethren, but she hath done her endeavor to sow discord between churches, and to set them at variance, and to hatch jealousies between them. And indeed I do not know what sin she is not guilty of. And all these are accompanied with impenitency and obstinacy, and therefore I think the church should be unfaithful to her soul if they should not proceed to a farther and sharper censure, and to cast her out from that society which she hath so slight an esteem for. . . .

Sgt. Oliver: For my own part, I look at the case of this Sister of ours to be somewhat like that of Miriam, which rose up against Moses and Aaron, whose leprosy appeared in the face of the Congregation—and there was a law for lepers, that the priest should search and view them, and if upon the search, they found leprosy appearing, the priest was to pronounce them leprous, and then they were to be thrust out for a time, till they were healed of that disease, from the congregation and the society of God's people. As this sister hath been diligently searched and viewed, and upon the search she is found leprous, and diverse spots are risen, and do manifestly appear to the congregation; therefore according to the law of God I think she ought to be pronounced unclean, and as a leprous person, to be put out from amongst us. And it appearing so plainly, I know not how with safety, or without danger of infecting others, we may keep her one week longer amongst us. It hath been too long forborne already, and there is danger that many hath been infected by the church's delay. . . . Therefore I think the censure ought speedily to be applied and to cast her out of the church as leprous.

Mr. Hibbens: I humbly crave leave for a word or two of the congregation, in regard of that relation that is between us. I am sorry that I should have any occasion to speak, yet is is not to hinder the church in their proceedings. But what they shall conclude of, I shall sit down contented with. Only I would humbly propose one place, to your wise consideration, if it may be of any use to your direction; and to crave a little more patience and lenity that the Lord may sanctify that to my dear wife. . . . If church would show their bowels of pity in sparing or respiting her censure for a time, that Lord may so bow the heart of my wife, that she may give the church full satisfaction, which would be the rising of my soul. I shall wholly leave it with you.

[The church members then proceeded to assent to the excommunication of Mrs. Hibbens. The pastor delivered the sentence of excommunication.]

Document 10: "The Devil Would Never Cease to Disturb Our Peace"

Throughout the colonies, circles of women met together to read and to interpret the Bible. Others besides the Boston group led by Anne Hutchinson seriously questioned the prescribed authority of the church and state. The problem in Salem, as in Boston, was that the study of the Bible led women to think for themselves and to raise serious doctrinal issues. The poor but highly articulate Mary Oliver sought a leveling influence in the church, as had Anne Hutchinson, by arguing that membership qualifications should be broadened and church governing power should be distributed more widely—even to allow secular as well as sacred officals the power to ordain ministers! For these doctrinal errors, she was tried and punished in 1638. John Winthrop included his view of the case in his journal.[46]

The devil would never cease to disturb our peace, and to raise up instruments one after another. Amongst the rest, there was a woman in Salem, one Oliver his wife, who had suffered somewhat in England for refusing to bow at the name of Jesus, though otherwise she was conformable to all their orders. She was (for ability of speech, and appearance of zeal and devotion) far before Mrs. Hutchinson, and so the fitter instrument to have done hurt, but that she was poor and had little acquaintance. She took offence at this, that she might not be admitted to the Lord's supper without giving public satisfaction to the church of her faith, etc., and covenanting or professing to walk with them according to the rule of the gospel; so as, upon the sacrament day, she openly called for it, and stood to plead her right, though she were denied; and would not forbear, before the magistrate, Mr. Endecott, did threaten to send the constable to put her forth. This woman was brought to the court for disturbing the peace in the church, etc., and there she gave such peremptory answers, as she was committed till she should find sureties for her good behavior. After she had been in prison three or four days, she made means to the governor, and submitted herself, and acknowledged her fault in disturbing the church; whereupon he took her husband's bond for her good behavior, and discharged her out of prison. But he found, after, that she still held her former opinions, which were very dangerous, as, 1. That the church is the heads of the people, both magistrates and ministers, met together, and that these have power to ordain ministers, etc. 2. That all that dwell in the same town, and will profess their faith in Christ Jesus, ought to be received to the sacraments there; and that she was persuaded, that, if Paul were at Salem, he would call all the inhabitants there saints. 3. That excommunication is no other but when Christians withdraw private communion from one that hath offended.

About five years after, this woman was adjudged to be whipped for reproaching the magistrates. She stood without tying, and bore her punishment with a masculine spirit, glorying in her suffering. But after (when she came to consider the reproach, which would stick by her, etc.) she was much dejected about it. [She had a cleft stick put on her tongue half an hour, for reproaching the elders.]

Document 11: "Pastors and Teachers Are But the Inventions of Men"

The spirit of independent judgment spread throughout the circle of women who gathered around Anne Eaton in New Haven, as is apparent in the trials of Mrs. Brewster, Mrs. Moore, and Mrs. Leach in 1646. Their own study of biblical texts led them to question the interpretation and the final authority of the New Haven clergy. Like Anne Hutchinson, the New Haven women believed that God gave all followers, clergy and laity, men and women, the power and authority of discernment for themselves.[47]

At the Court Held at New Haven this 2nd June, 1646:

Mrs. Brewster, Mrs. Moore & Mrs. Leach being warned about several miscarriages of a public nature, appeared and were charged severally as followeth,

Elizabeth Smith late servant to Mrs. Leach, said that hearing Mrs. Brewster loud in conference with Mrs. Eaton, Mrs. Moore & her Mrs. as she sat at work in the next room, she called Job Hall, her fellow servant to hear also, who could better remember the particulars of such a conference than herself.

Job and Elizabeth both affirm that Mrs. Brewster repeating something of Mr. Davenport's prayer to this purpose, "Lord add to the church such as shall be saved and build up to perfection those whom thou has added;" and speaking of his sermon said, "Mr. Davenport makes the people believe that to come into the church is as much as the receiving of Christ." Job said she added, "Mr. Davenport carrieth it as if they could not have salvation without coming into the church." What concerneth Job in this part of his testimony he gave in writing, and affirmed before the magistrates, yet now in court was somewhat doubtful whether he heard the words from Mrs. Brewster herself, or only heard Elizabeth repeat them from Mrs. Brewster. His best light, [he said,] serveth for the former, yet he was loath to give oath therein. The court blamed him that he had not better considered this before, yet wished him to deliver nothing upon oath but what he was clear about.

Mrs. Brewster as before the Governor & Mr. Goodyeare formerly, so now in court denied the charge.

2ndly, Job & Elizabeth affirm that Mrs. Brewster speaking of something Mr. Davenport had delivered upon Ephes. 4. 12, concerning personal faith, that "if a man lived where he might join to the church & did not, it would prove a delusion to him." Job affirmed that Mrs. Brewster said, "when she heard it her stomach rumbled as when she bred child," & spake it twice or thrice if not oftener in reference to the sermon. Elizabeth said, that twice or thrice she spake to that purpose, that she was sermon sick, and that proceeding in conference she presently said that when she came home she bad her son make waste paper of it, which she then said Elizabeth's conceiveth was spoken in reference to the notes of Dr. Davenport's sermon.

Mrs. Brewster denied these words, sermon sick, or that it was in reference to the sermon, & those words of making waste paper &c, but confessed she said her stomach wrought, smelling an ill savor in the seat, wherein she gave no satisfaction to the court.

3rdly, Job & Elizabeth affirm that Mrs. Brewster (in conference speaking of scandalous persons), asked Mrs. Moore whether she had not heard for what Mrs. Eaton was cast out of the the church. Mrs. Moore asked Mrs. Eaton why she did not confess her sin. Mrs. Eaton answered she had done it, but not to the church's satisfaction. Mrs. Brewster said "if Mrs. Eaton had seen her light before she came into the church, she would not have come in."

Mrs. Brewster confessing the former part, said she remembers not that she spake those words, "if Mrs. Eaton had seen her light &c;" she hath heard that Mrs. Eaton came into the church in a hurry, and went out in a hurry. . . .

[The proceedings continued through twelve such charges brought before the court regarding Mrs. Brewster.]

Job Hall, servant to Mr. Leach saith, that Mrs. Moore in prayer with Mr. Leach's family saith, . . . "when Christ ascended, he gave gifts to men, some to be apostles, some prophets, some evangelists, some pastors, some teachers, but they are gone through the world & are now ascended into heaven." That in opposition, as he conceiveth to Mr. Davenport's sermon upon Ephesians 4,11 verse, she added that night in prayer, that "now pastors & teachers are but the inventions of men." That in conference with Mrs. Brewster, she said, "a veil is before the eyes of ministers and people in this place, & til that be taken away, they cannot be turned to the Lord." He saith further, that Mrs. Moore "used to express content & satisfaction when Mr. Davenport holdeth forth the excellency of Christ in his ministry, but she saith she loveth not to hear him preach for practice." . . .

Mrs. Moore again denied the charge, & particularly that ever she said, pastors & teachers were the inventions of men. She affirmed herself to be a member of a church. She was asked of what church, but made no reply. She was told that by three witnesses it is affirmed she had upon several times & upon several occasions said, that pastors & teachers are the inventions of men. . . .

Mrs. Moore was told that the evidence was full & particular, & sufficient to convince her. Yet since she seemeth not satisfied, the court, (as in such cases,) would require oath. And accordingly Lieut. Joseph Godfrey, Thomas Kinberly, Job Hall & Elizabeth Smith, upon oath, testified what they had severally affirmed.

Mrs. Moore's daughter, Mrs. Leach, being charged that, upon a question or conference about joining with this church, she had said to Mrs. Brewster, (as formerly to Mrs. Wackman or some others of the church,) that she sometime had a mind to join, but now declined it, because she found so many untruths among them.

The Governor asked what she said to the charge. She readily owned it, confessing she had said so. Being demanded what moved her to lay such a slanderous reproach upon a church of Christ, desiring to walk uprightly, & to go from one to another with such a slander, she boldly answered. She was told it was a clear evidence of the church's integrity that they could not bear with them that are evil. That as they are able, they keep their watch, exhort & censure according to rule, that upon such a ground any might have declined Christ's family, because there was a thief, a devil, in it & might have reproached that primitive pure church at Jerusalem because Ananias & Saphira were found out & punished for lying. Such discoveries & censures did & ought to restrain the presumption of hypocrits, but believers were the more added, and the people saw cause to magnify such a church. Acts 5:13, 14.

Mrs. Leach neither excused nor replied, but as guilty seemed to take the weight of the charge upon herself. Continuing in Court, she spake uncomely for her sex & age, and once falsely charged the witnesses with contradiction, when there was no appearance or disagreement between them, so that her carriage offended the whole court.

These 3 cases being thus opened, & proof thus made, were all ready for censure. But upon consideration of the nature & weight of the offences, the magistrates & deputies conceived they were all proper for a higher court. By order, therefore, sentence was respited & referred to the court of magistrates for the jurisdiction.

Pruning for the Future Harvest

Document 12: "That Notorious Mastris Hutchinson of New-England . . . Henceforth Then No More Women Preachers"

By 1645, Anne Hutchinson had become a symbol, both in Old and New England, of women who challenged the established authority of the church by their independent judgment and public preaching. The following sermon, which was preached by John Brinsley, a minister in Yarmouth, England, was addressed to women of his own congregation and vicinity who had been infected by Satan with a discontented spirit that caused them to question their subjected state within the home and church. Brinsley, however, did not mention those women he considered guilty of contentious conduct in his own England, but only pointed to the "notorious Mastris Hutchinson"—whose name had obviously become a "scare word" throughout the entire kingdom by that time.

To all the well affected, but ill advised of the weaker Sex, who are either turned, or turning from the way of the Church of Christ in Old

England, to the refined Error of separation, Specially those in the Town of Great Yarmouth.

Daughters of Jerusalem,

To you is this Glasse presented, with a Requests, That you will vouchsafe to look into it, and that with an Eye not prejudiced against it. Possibly you may here see more of Satan, and your selves, his wiles, your weaknesse, then before you were aware of. If any shall herein espy some spots and blemishes discovered, not becoming the face of profession, let them not blame the Glasse, which represents things as they are, but themselves, or others, who have given the ground to these reflections. . . .

A discontented spirit is a forge and Anvile fit for Satan to forge and hammer anything upon that is evil: In the fear of God would you not be deceived as your Mother was; take heed of such a spirit: Beware how you entertain groundlesse and causeless dislikes, which should make you discontented with your present personall state, or the state of the Church of God wherein you live. . . .

O Brethren and Sisters (for to you I am now principally speaking) take we heed all of us of such dangerous, and pernicious discontents as these, the very Spawne, and first borne of Satan. So they were in the first woman; The first product and issue of Satans temptations in her, was a secret dislike of, and discontentednesse with her present condition, the condition wherein God himself had set her; and that letteth in a Sea of Temptations upon her, so making way from her seduction. . . .

Now herein God be mercifull to us, and to his Churches: Was it not such an other thing that undid the world at first: viz. The inordinate affectation of Independency: Our first parents would be absolute: Me thinks the remembrance hereof, should make us for ever jealous both of the name and thing. . . .

The woman being discontented with her present state, she is inordinately desirous to better it by what ever way or means should be propounded to her. I, be it to touch, and taste the Apple, though a prohibited fruit, yet so there may be but hopes of abetting her condition, she will adventure upon it. And is it not so (beloved) with some amongst us (as it is with many in some parts of the Kingdom?) who being discontented with their present condition, they will adventure upon any way or means that shall be reached forth unto them by what hand so ever, with hopes of bettering it; It matters not though prohibited by the Laws of men, and for ought they know, may be so by the Laws of God, yet they will try it. . . .

To this let the Apostle himselfe return the answer. I presume you will not take it amisse from his hands, the remembrance hereof (as he applieth it) should teach those of that Sex a double lesson; 1. Of Silence, 2. Of Subjection. Silence, not to take upon them to preach, or teach, or speak in the publike. Subjection, not to usurpe Authority over their Husbands, but to be subject to them. . . .

1. In the first place, women must be silent, viz. In the publick Congregations: where they must hear, and learn in silence, not taking upon them the exercise of any office, or gift in publick. So are we to understand the Apostles injunction, and inhibition.

Not as if women were hereby interdicted, and prohibited either to read the Scriptures, or to confer of them . . . so it be done with modesty, and sobriety, with a desire to benefit themselves or others, is not only lawfull, but commendable. . . .

This women may do: Read the Scriptures, and confer of them. And more then this. They may, and ought to teach, and instruct their families, to Catechise children and servants, I, and to performe other Family-duties with them; in case the husband be absent, or not able, or not willing to discharge them. . . . And thus indeed women may teach and instruct others, both Women, and men, communicating the knowledge which God hath given them, in a private way. . . .

But to teach publickly, or to exercise any publick Administration in the Church, this they may not do. This (as it seemeth) some in Saint Pauls time began to do. Some being induced with extraordinary gifts, as of Prophesie, &c. (as we read of Philip the Evangelists four daughters, all Prophetesses) they took upon them to speak in the publick Congregations: And herein (as Estius conjectures) they might possibly be imitated and followed by some others. A like practise whereunto hath been taken up by some of that Sex in after Ages. . . .

And I shall not need to tell it you, how the former hath been of late time practiced by some of that Sex. Instance in that notorious Mastris Hutchinson of New-England, who under a colourable pretext of repeating of Sermons, held a weekly Exercise, whereby in a little time she had impoysoned a considerable part of that Plantation with most dangerous and detestable, desperate and damnable, Errors and Heresies.

Henceforth then no more Women Preachers. . . .

Sure we are that in an ordinary course the Apostles prohibition is expressed, Women may not teach in publick. And were there no other Reason for it, this alone might be sufficient to silent them. The woman by her taking upon her to teach at the first, became the Instrument of Seduction, and Author of Transgression to her husband, and consequently of ruine to him and all his posterity. Henceforth then no more Women-Preachers. A point wherein Master Calvin seemeth to be very zealous, and earnest, averring this, for women to take upon them the office of Teaching, to be no lesse then a mingling of Heaven and earth together, an inversion of the course and order of nature. . . .

. . . True, the woman was deceived at the first, and by her counsell was a means to deceive her Husband. That first Counsell succeeded ill, & proved Destructive to him that hearkened to it. But what then? Must her Counsell therefore no more be hearkened to? Not so. Let not this first miscarriage be remembered in such a way, or yet in any way that may be to the prejudice or disparagement of the Sex.

No reason for it. In as much as Christ himself hath sufficiently repaired and restored that Sex in point of Honour. This he did in the dayes of his flesh, in shewing many tokens of speciall grace and favour to some of that Sex. But more fully after his Resurrection, in appearing first unto them. Therein did he apply a Salve to this first Soar, and that a very proper one, salving, and taking of the fear and blemish of that first infirmity, as may appear in some particulars. 1. Did Satan appear and speak, first to the Woman? So did Christ after his Resurrection first appear, and reveal himself to the Woman. 2. Was the Woman first deceived by Satans suggestions? So was the Woman here first undeceived, as touching the mysteries of Christs Resurrection, and that by his own Instructions. 3. Was the Woman made the Instrument to deceive the man?

Lo here the woman made an Instrument to undeceive the man, to undeceive even the Apostles themselves, who (as it seemeth) were in a great measure mistaken about the Mystery of the Resurrection, until such time as they had received it from the Women, who had been eye and ear Witnesses of it. Such honour did Christ himself put upon this Sex; making those women (as Jerome saith elegantly) Apostlelorum Apostolas, Apostelesses to the very Apostles themselves. Let not then this old sore, which is so fairly and thorowly heale be ever rubbed upon again in any such a way to the contumelious disparagement of the Sex. This being promised by way of Caution; Let me now shew you what use men may, and ought to make of this infirmity in that Sex. . . .

Document 13: "Ground Sufficient" for Women to Sing "Forth the Praises of the Lord Together with the Rest of the Congregation"

Of all the authoritative spokesmen of first-generation Puritanism, no man was more a part of the story of dissenting women than John Cotton, the teacher of the Boston church who gave testimony at the trials of both Anne Hutchinson and Ann Hibbens. It is fitting that Cotton's pronouncement, "Singing of Psalms a Gospel-Ordinance. 1650.," should mark the transition of this period—from the clash of separatist-minded women with established authorities to the sanction of women's emerging role in singing the praises of the Lord along with men in church. In this role, women would one day be designated the bearers of religious piety within the home and take a lead as evangelists throughout the churches.[49]

Concerning the Singers: Whether Women, Pagans, and Profane and Carnal Persons.

The third question about singing of Psalms concerneth the Singers. For though vocal singing be approved and also the singing of David's Psalms, yet still it remaineth to some a question who must sing them. And here a threefold scruple ariseth. 1. Whether one be to sing for all the rest, the rest joining only in spirit and saying Amen; or the whole Congregation? 2. Whether women as well as men; or men alone? 3. Whether carnal men and Pagans may be permitted to sing with us or Christians alone and Church-Members? . . .

The second scruple about Singers is Whether women may sing as well as men." For in this point there be some that deal with us as Pharaoh dealt with the Israelites, who though he was at first utterly unwilling that any of them should go to sacrifice to the Lord in the Wilderness yet being at length convinced that they must go, then he was content the Men should go but not the Women. So here, some that were altogether against singing of Psalms at all with a lively voice, yet being convinced that it is a moral worship of God warranted in Scripture, then if there must be a Singing one alone must sing, not all (or if all) the Men only and not the Women.

And their reason is. "Because it is not permitted to a woman to speak in the Church (I. Cor. xiii. 34.) How then shall they sing? 2. Much less it is permitted to then to prophesy in the Church (I. Tim. ii. 11, 12.) And singing of Psalms is a kind of prephesying."

One answer may at once remove both these scruples and withal clear the truth. It is apparent by the scope and context of both those Scriptures that a woman is not permitted to speak in the Church in two cases: 1. By way of teaching, whether in expounding or applying Scripture. For this the Apostle accounteth an act of authority which is unlawful for a woman to usurp over the man, II. Tim. ii, 13. And besides the woman is more subject to error than a man, ver. 14. and therefore might soon prove a seducer if she became a teacher.

2. It is not permitted to a woman to speak in the Church by way of propounding questions though under pretence of desire to learn, for her own satisfaction; but rather it is required she should ask her husband at home.

For under pretense of questioning for learning sake, she might so propound her question as to teach her teachers; or if not so, yet to open a door to some of her own weak and erroneous apprehensions, or at least soon exceed the bounds of womanly modesty.

Nevertheless in two other cases, it is clear a woman is allowed to speak in the Church: 1. In way of subjection when she is to give account of her offence. 2. In way of singing forth the praises of the Lord together with the rest of the Congregation. For it is evident the Apostle layeth no greater restraint upon the women for silence in the

Church than the Law had put upon them before. For so himself speaketh in the place alleged: "It is not permitted to the women to speak, but to be under subjection as also saith the Law." The Apostle then requireth the same subjection in the woman which the Law had put upon them.—no more. Now it is certain the Law, yea, the Lawgiver Moses, did permit Miriam and the women that went out after her to sing forth the praises of the Lord, as well as the men, and to answer the men in their song of thanksgiving: "Sing ye to the Lord for he hath triumphed gloriously: the horse and his rider hath he thrown into the Sea." Which may be a ground sufficient to justify the lawful practice of women in singing together with men the praises of the Lord.

The Religious Experience of Southern Women

ALICE E. MATHEWS

The Virginia Company of London recognized the importance of both women and religion in constructing and maintaining society in the first permanent English colony. Not only were company members interested in converting the heathen—an often-mentioned religious motive for colonization—but they also believed that sermons, prayers, communion, and fasting helped provide discipline and order for those Englishmen living in the Virginia settlements and might, incidentally, invoke God's blessings on the colony. Just as the church could promote the social order, young women could also provide stability and permanence. In 1619, Sir Edwin Sandys noted the need for one hundred "maids, young and uncorrupt, to make wives to the Inhabitants" so that the men there would be "more setled [sic] and lesse moveable." Two years later, the board of governors assured officials in the colony that more women were being sent because Virginia could "never flourish till families be planted, and the respect of wives and Children fix the people on the Soyle."[1]

This chapter is intended to demonstrate the relationship between women and religion in the southern colonies. It is primarily concerned with women in the principal denominations, especially the Church of England, rather than those females in the pietistic sects such as Quaker and Moravian, who enjoyed a unique status, but who were not especially representative of the developing culture found in the southern societies. It will suggest that religion was a positive force, which provided women with a more secure identity and a greater awareness of themselves as individuals.

Unlike in the Massachusetts Bay Colony, social stability was hard to achieve in seventeenth-century Virginia and Maryland. The few women in both colonies, the large number of bachelors, and, hence, the lack of settled families, contributed to a social uncertainty, which was heightened by high mortality rates. Nor was there the religious zeal, the belief that they were on a mission for the Lord to set up a purified church to offer encouragement and to bind residents of the early Chesapeake colonies together. Nevertheless, local leaders realized the importance of religious institutions and desired to promote the spiritual and moral welfare of their communities. Those women who made seventeenth-century Virginia and Maryland their home, whether Anglican, Roman Catholic, or Dissenter, particularly those who were literate, also viewed their role in society as one of helping to maintain civilization. The majority of women were undoubtedly Anglican. But in Maryland, especially among the wealthier settlers, there were a substantial number of Catholics since the colony had been founded as a refuge for them. However, as immigration continued and because of Lord Baltimore's policy of religious toleration, dissenters, including Quakers, quickly grew in numbers. Within these various denominations, only Quaker women had a voice in the affairs of the meeting house or could preach openly the word of God. Although other women did not have this degree of freedom in church government, they could still participate in church services, could thus give moral support to religious institutions, and could share responsibility for the religious instruction of their families. They could also admonish their husbands or other menfolk in a "mild and sweet manner" when they believed that the Gospel was not always being followed.

Next to the Bible, one of the books most often listed in seventeenth-century Virginia estate records was *The Whole Duty of Man,* attributed to the Reverend Richard Allestree, a Church of England clergyman. One of the sermons in that volume, concerned with the relationships between husbands, wives, parents, and children, described well the role of women within the family, a view that both the clergy and their female audience found prescribed by the Scriptures. The meditation directed that women owed their husbands obedience, fidelity, and love. Nor would any faults or provocations—even religious infractions—of the husbands justify any overt wifely criticism. "The worse the Husband is, the more Need there is for the Wife to carry herself with that Gentleness and Sweetness that may be most likely to win him." The writer noted that women's good behavior in the days of Paul had been "thought a powerful means to win Men from Heathenism to Christianity." It might now bind them to their families and discourage them from "Company-keeping" (Document 1). This definition of the wife's role in the family shaped the attitude of many colonial women in their view of themselves in relation to society and their religious function. Their life evolved around the home; it was clearly a secondary position that had been commanded by God, in part due to Eve's transgressions. On the other hand, since religious instruction was an obligation, they could find an outlet that occasionally led them outside the family. For example, the records for Northampton County, Virginia, noted, in 1684, Elizabeth Daniell's occasional purchase and distribution of Bibles (Document 2). And at about the same time, Mary Taney, the wife of the sheriff of Calvert County, Maryland, was asking the Archbishop of Canterbury for a church and a minister, since such a settlement would prove "a nursery of religion and loyalty through the whole Province" (Document 3).

Not only Anglicans served the Lord and their church in a fashion befitting their sex, but also Catholic women demonstrated their devotion. The Jesuit Annual Letter from Maryland for 1638 reported that the attendance of Catholics "on the sacraments here is so large, that it is not greater among the faithful in Europe, in proportion to their respective numbers." No doubt many of these individuals were happy to be free to follow their religious persuasion without fear of persecution. In the same letter, the priest wrote of the death of "a noble matron," who had accompanied the first settlers and who had borne "all her difficulties and inconveniences with more than a woman's courage." In continuing to describe this individual, the letter noted that

> She was much given to prayer and most anxious for the salvation of her neighbours, setting them a perfect example both in her own person and in her domestic concerns. She was fond of our Society when living, and a benefactor to it when dying, and was held in blessed memory by all for the edification which she gave in her charity to the sick, as well as in other virtues.[2]

Over twenty years later, William Bretton, "with the hearty good likeing of my dearly beloved wife Temperance Bretton," gave land to the inhabitants of New Towne and St. Clement's Bay for a Roman Catholic chapel.[3]

But Catholic women could also find themselves in a precarious position because of their religious faith. As a result of the tension between Catholic and Protestant settlers in Maryland, which erupted periodically in political confrontations and civil war, the assembly, while under royal government, in 1691 established the Church of England. In 1715, it passed an act which provided that children whose Protestant father had died and whose mother had married a Catholic or was a Catholic could be removed so that they might "be Securely Educated in the protestant religion."[4] A woman's religious faith could offer her comfort, but because of it, she could also lose her children in Maryland.

Not many women who lived in the southern colonies had the opportunity to leave a testimony to their faith, since perhaps as many as 75 percent were illiterate in the seventeenth century and 50 percent in the eighteenth century.[5] But it can be assumed that, first, for most of them, the model provided in *The Whole Duty of Man* was the example to follow and, second, religion offered them a comfort or a solace during the many hardships that they endured. Religious faith clearly provided meaning and order for their lives. And for some individuals, it could also secure their freedom. At least one black woman, Elizabeth Key, whose mother had been a slave, was able to gain her liberty in the 1650s on the basis of common law—because her father was English and she was a Christian. Key had not only been baptized with a godfather present, but also "by report shee is able to give a very good account of her fayth" (Document 4).

Only in Maryland and Virginia was the Church of England firmly established in the eighteenth century. And a majority of the people were Anglican in only those colonies and South Carolina. As population increased, especially in the Carolinas and Georgia, the number of dissenters grew. The Scots and Scotch-Irish settlements meant the growth of Presbyterianism. And after the Great Awakening began to attract an audience in southern communities, not only New Light Presbyterians but also Baptists and later Methodists grew and gained converts, especially among the lower classes. There were Quakers in all of the southern colonies and Moravians settled in the North Carolina piedmont. Other German Protestants and French Huguenots also found homes in the South. As toleration became more a reality, not only dissenters migrated to these colonies but also Catholics and Jews. By the time of the Revolution, Charles Town could boast among its churches, in addition to the Anglican St. Philip's and St. Michael's, Presbyterian, Independent, French Huguenot, Baptist, and Catholic, as well as a Jewish synagogue. Eliza Lucas noted on her arrival that St. Philip's was a very elegant church "and much frequented." She continued that "there are several more places of publick worship in this town and the generality of people [are] of a religious turn of mind."[6] The various denominations resulted in part from the government's early policy of encouraging white, foreign Protestants to settle in Carolina. In addition, both the Great Awakening doctrine and Enlightenment idealism encouraged diverse religious views, which fostered religious toleration and in some circles led to a demand for more religious freedom—a goal that was gaining widespread support in several southern communities by the time of the revolution.

The Jewish immigrants who settled in the southern colonies illustrate well this atmosphere of toleration, which found elegant expression in the letters of a young Jewish woman, Rachel Mordecai, to Maria Edgeworth, the British novelist. Mordecai, the eldest daughter of Jacob Mordecai, helped her father operate a highly successful academy for young women in Warrenton, North Carolina, at the beginning of the nineteenth century. She was a devotee of Edgeworth's writings and in *The Absentee* discovered a villain by the name of Mordecai. With some trepidation, she felt obligated to write the novelist and ask how, as enlightened as Edgeworth was, she could share age-old prejudices against Jews. Mordecai further noted that in the United States, particularly in the South, "religious distinctions are scarcely known" (Document 5). The Mordecai family, while the only Jewish family in Warrenton, was not the only southern Jewish family. Jews had very early come to Charles Town and Savannah. A group of Sephardic and Ashkenazic Jews, composed not only of families but also single men and women, came to Savannah in the first year of its settlement, 1733, and although many of the first immigrants moved elsewhere, the remnants of the community remained with familial connections in both Charles Town and the West Indies.[7] One can especially imagine the pleasure of the Savannah women when the community constructed a *mikveh* (a ritual bath) for them in 1738. The Jewish women of early Charles Town and Savannah, like their Anglican sisters, were in a secondary status in religious matters, and although they too had a special role in the family, they were even more excluded from religious services than their Christian peers.

The established church was a part of the public realm; men dominated its government and ceremonies. Women had no public voice in its activities. For many individuals, the church was as much or more a social institution in the eighteenth century as it was one to provide for spiritual needs. The Church of England in the southern colonies was not aggressive in making converts; it seemed to enjoy its privileged status and to reflect the accepted order in society rather than to encourage any social or political change. Most of its members were opposed to the doctrines of the Great Awakening. Despite the fact that many Anglicans did not take their profession of faith seriously, there were also many who were devout. For most communicants, it was a rational piety that stressed moderation, repentance, and salvation.[8] The letters of Eliza Lucas Pinckney demonstrate as well as any source the religious beliefs of Anglicans generally, and Anglican women more specifically, especially with respect to their tone of moderation. When her brother entered the army, Eliza Lucas wrote him several letters, in part to remind him of his spiritual welfare, "to be particularly careful of his duty to his Creator, for nothing but an early piety and steady Virtue" could "make him happy." A few months later, she reminded him that "God is Truth" and that "the Christian religion is what the wisest men in all ages have assented too." Eliza Lucas, in her references to religion or her sometime gravity, did not want to be thought "religiously mad," but rather stressed in her correspondence that in no way did Christianity counter reason (Document 6).

In expressing her sentiments privately to friends and relatives, Lucas indicated one way that women could exercise some thought and influence, which could furnish a source of identity and an emotional outlet. She, of course, enjoyed a tremendous amount of freedom as a young, single woman who was allowed to supervise her father's plantations, and after her marriage to Charles Pinckney, she not only continued those tasks but also managed her husband's holdings. Not many women had the same opportunities or ambitions, but they could appreciate, as she did, the importance of the family and its role in providing religious instruction for children and, in some cases, for slaves (Document 7). Advice literature, such as *The Whole Duty of Man* and later Dr. James Fordyce's *Sermons to Young Women,* prepared these women for their future status (Document 8). Young ladies began their religious training early; some girls did not receive much instruction other than learning to read the Bible and religious tracts. In most cases, their mothers or other female relatives were their teachers, not only in reading but in housewifely tasks. Social scientists have argued that female personalities form earlier than male, since girls mature faster and generally identify with older individuals such as their mothers, aunts, or grandmothers for role models. They naturally become women whereas boys have to learn to be men. Consequently, they may not have as great a sense of accomplishment or, hence, self-esteem, since they associate themselves more with a gender group than with their own individuality.[9] This situation aptly describes the young women who grew up on southern farms and plantations in the eighteenth century. Their major goal or accomplishment was marriage, followed by children. Once housekeeping was begun, they no longer needed to think of the future—except with respect to their souls and the spiritual well-being of their families. By the eighteenth century, women were clearly thought to have a more religious nature than men, and this aspect of their personalities, tied to their low self-esteem and underscored by Eve's legacy, and their domestic activities defined their lives. On the other hand, religion offered them a way to find a more secure identity—to cultivate their individuality. It encouraged them to have private devotions, to write out religious exercises, to develop their own prayers. A diary could become an expression of religious sentiment and an awakening of the self.

Martha Laurens Ramsay, a member of the Independent Congregation in Charles Town after she married Dr. David Ramsay, was raised an Anglican and very early began to write religious exercises (Document 9). Betsy Foote Washington, an Episcopalian, continually set down rules for her personal conduct in addition to writing prayers and daily devotions (Document 10). Both Ramsay and Washington were born a generation later than Eliza Lucas Pinckney, both grew up during the war years, and both experienced the evangelicalism of the last quarter of the eighteenth century. Both women were deeply religious and devout, despite different denominational affiliations. Although the younger women demonstrated more evangelical fervor, characteristic of the era, all three women sincerely followed the dictates of religious pamphlets that advised women of their secondary status and the respect that they should pay their husbands. All three also provided instruction for their slaves, and Pinckney and Ramsay both supervised the religious and secular education of their children. There is a great deal of similarity between the religious sentiments of Ramsay and Washington. Both were aware of human frailty, the need for repentance, and the goal of salvation. Religion obviously offered them much solace and hope. It also provided them with an identity and a reason for being.

Shortly before her marriage, Betsy Foote Washington began a diary that opened with a desire to please her future husband and to be "a dutyful obedient wife." She had prepared herself for the worst—that her marriage might be unhappy (which she would accept as the will of God)—but she hoped for the best: for happiness and a husband who would "never be against my being as religious as my inclination may lead me." Foote's marriage to Lund Washington, a cousin to George Washington and manager of Mt. Vernon during the war years, proved happy, but none of her children survived infancy. She had especially wanted a daughter, and after the death of her second daughter, Lucinda, who was about a year old, she prayed: "My gracious God—thou hast confer'd great honour on me—that thou shouldest think me worthy to bring children who thou has thought was only fit to live with thee."[10] At the time that Lucinda had been born, she had written, "let me tell my dear child—that there is no real happiness without religion." Her longing for a daughter might have secured her feelings of self-worth, but when she was denied that possibility, she turned to her larger family, her servants or slaves, and found comfort in her religion. Unfortunately, her slaves were also a disappointment since they became Baptists and refused to attend her devotions and to pray with her. Whether she ever accepted this religious rebelliousness is not known, but after her husband's death in 1796, and in keeping with his wishes and her own feelings, she emancipated them. Betsy Foote Washington experienced a piety or a religious intensity that one would expect from one of the evangelical sects; but it was also a romantic piety that was then being praised by orthodox clergymen. It not only reflected the change in religious thought in the developing southern culture, but also the model desired by ministers for women to follow.

Eliza Lucas Pinckney, Martha Laurens Ramsay, and Betsy Foote Washington represented Protestant models of piety, but non-Protestants—Roman Catholics and Jews—could experience the same kind of religious intensity. They could also feel—perhaps even more strongly—the obligation to instruct their children in religious principles that were not held by the majority of eighteenth-century southerners. Margaret Sharpe Gaston, a devout English Roman Catholic, who had been educated in a convent, married Dr. Alexander Gaston, a Protestant physician who had settled in North Carolina in 1765. In 1781, six years after they had married, Tory raiders killed Gaston. Margaret then had the full responsibility of raising her two young children, William and Jane, and her religious faith provided her with much support. Although she left no diary or religious exercises that expressed her private thoughts, she served as a model of Christian and Catholic motherhood to her two children and the Catholic priests in Philadelphia and Georgetown who looked after twelve-year-old William when he was sent there to school (Document 11). William's letters to his mother, while he was at Georgetown, gave ample proof of her piety and the success of her religious instruction. He was also aware of how difficult it was to be a Catholic in a town like New Bern, where there was neither priest nor church. Margaret, on the other hand, after William's decision to attend Princeton for his higher education, was well aware of how easy it might be for William to give up his Catholic faith. She did not need to worry. As William wrote, he could "never forget the many virtuous lessons which I had been taught by your maternal care."[11]

Although teaching catechism and prayers to their children was a primary function, many southern women also instructed their slaves in Christian principles. If many white women were illiterate, black women had an even more difficult time in obtaining any reading and writing unless they had a mistress like Washington, Ramsay, or Pinckney. Both the Society for the Propagation of the Gospel and Dr. Bray's Associates were interested in the conversion of black slaves, and Dr. Bray's Associates attempted to set up schools for black children in several communities. One of their most successful enterprises was in Williamsburg, Virginia, where in 1761 they began a finishing school, which was placed under the supervision of William Hunter first, and later Robert Carter Nicholas. Hunter hired Mrs. Anne Wager as teacher, and with a great deal of dedication, she undertook the religious instruction of the young Negroes. During the years that the school was in operation, the difficulties with convincing owners to allow black children to attend are often mentioned. The young scholars generally exceeded the expectations of the visitors, and Mrs. Wager's efforts were praised. At the time of her death, in 1774, Nicholas advised the associates that he had discontinued the school, apparently because he could not find another person like Mrs. Wager to continue instruction (Document 12). With the exception of those Quaker preachers who were women, there is not much evidence of southern, colonial women being actively engaged in a Christian charity. Anne Wager, however, was obviously so motivated and had the opportunity to influence some of the young blacks of Williamsburg. How many of her students were girls is not known, but no doubt some black women learned to read the Bible because of her efforts.

The fact that the Washington slaves turned Baptists was not unusual in the 1780s and 1790s. In the Great Awakening, ministers preached the very appealing message of spiritual equality. Not only blacks, but many women in general found that doctrine attractive, and by 1800, a number of women, sometimes despite their husbands' objections, were participating in the revivals and joining the Baptists and Methodists. Historians have recently called attention to the numbers of women who joined the evangelical denominations in the early nineteenth century—however, this move was already beginning in the South during the revolutionary era.[12] In revivals and evangelical church services, women no longer played a secondary role, but were given an equal footing with men. Robert Semple noted the objection of one Regular Baptist preacher to the ordination of Daniel Marshall: "that he believed them [Separate Baptists] to be a disorderly sect: suffering women to pray in public, and permitting every ignorant man to preach that chose: that they encouraged noise and confusion in their meetings." Marshall's wife (the sister of revivalist Shubal Stearns) also preached, which must have both amazed and irritated the Regular Baptists even more. Semple thought her, however, "a lady of good sense, singular piety, and surprising elocution." On countless occasions, she had "melted a whole concourse into tears, by prayers and exhortations."[13] The evangelical denominations could offer women an emotional outlet and identity that was not available through other groups. They could also bring black and white women together. A Presbyterian minister described one revival in North Carolina where he walked near "a black-woman grasping her mistress' hand and crying 'O Mistress you prayed for me when I wanted a heart to pray for myself. Now thank God he had given me a heart to pray for you and every body else' " (Document 13).

By the end of the revolutionary era, a recognizable southern culture was gradually emerging. With respect to religion, there was no longer a church establishment, and southerners, even in the upper classes, were beginning to replace their rational piety of the Enlightenment with the evangelical zeal and religious diversity of the antebellum period. It is quite possible that as the church became separated from the public realm (the world of men) and more identified with the domestic sphere (the world of women), it was feminized, and women had a larger voice in church government. Before 1800, however, women who lived in the southern colonies, and later the new states, although they were placed in a secondary role in society, could find happiness in their religious faith—could find identity and purpose for themselves in raising their children properly and, especially with respect to those who owned slaves, in providing their households with religious instruction. Religion gave meaning and order to the lives of these women; it could also bind them together as sisters, even with their slaves. If it did not provide civil identity, at least religion provided spiritual liberation.

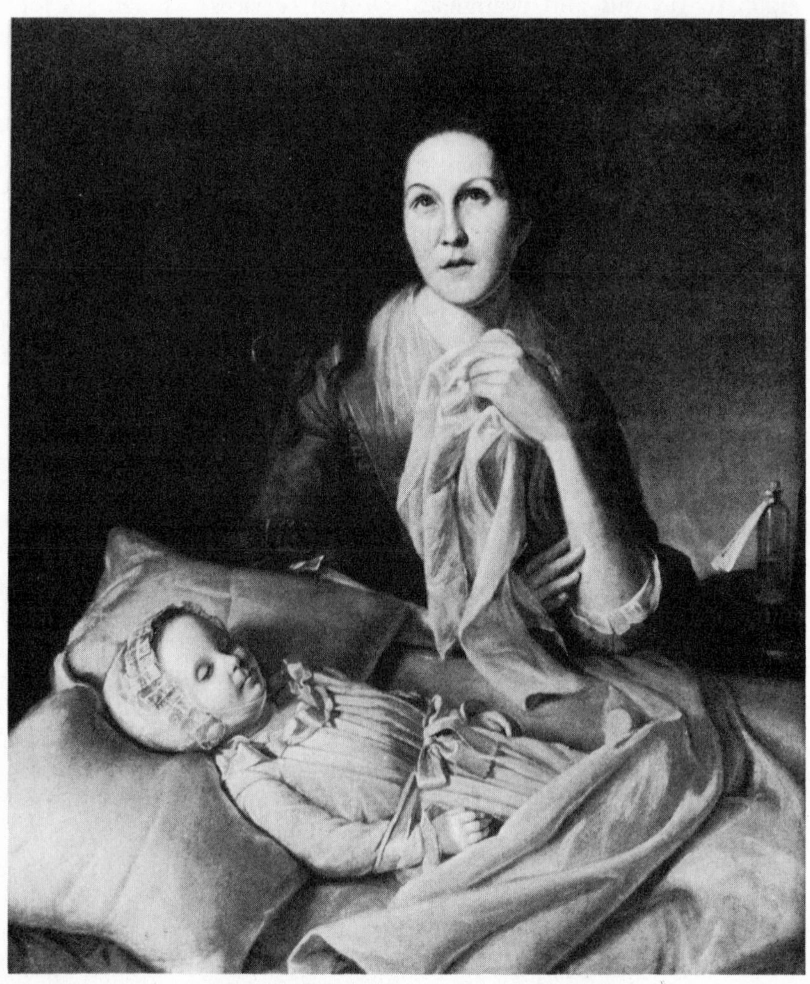

Rachel Weeping, by Charles Willson Peale. A portrait of his wife grieving over the body of their infant daughter, Margaret, who died during the smallpox epidemic in Annapolis, 1772. Courtesy the Philadelphia Museum of Art, Philadelphia.

Martha Laurens Ramsay (1759–1811), daughter of a wealthy Charleston merchant. Her *Memoirs* are a prime example of eighteenth-century advice literature. Portrait by John Wollaston, circa 1767. [From George C. Rogers, ed., *Papers of Henry Laurens,* (Columbia: University of South Carolina Press, 1974), vol. 4, frontispiece.]

George Whitefield preaching. Portrait by John Wollaston, 1742. [Courtesy of the National Portrait Gallery, London.]

A graphic entitled *Keep within Compass,* which illustrates the path of virtue for the good woman and the dangers to be avoided, 1785–1805. [Reproduced by permission of the Henry Francis dePont Winterthur Museum, Winterthur, Delaware.]

Documents: The Religious Experience of Southern Women

1. ***An Obedient, Faithful, Loving Wife: "The Special End of Woman's Creation"***
2. ***Elizabeth Daniell: The Distribution of Bibles to the Deserving***
3. ***Mary Taney: A Request for an Anglican Priest***
4. ***Elizabeth Key: "By Report Shee Is Able to Give a Very Good Account of Her Fayth"***
5. ***Rachel Mordecai: "We Find the Jews to Form a Respectable Part of the Community"***
6. ***Eliza Lucas Pinckney: A Rational Piety***
7. ***Religious Instruction in the Home: Devereux Jarratt Discovers True Religion***
8. ***"Virtuous Women are the Sweetness, the Charm of Human Life"***
9. ***Martha Laurens Ramsay: "A Life of Prayer"***
10. ***Elizabeth Foote Washington: "A Dutiful, Obedient Wife"***
11. ***Margaret Sharpe Gaston: A Model for Catholic Motherhood***
12. ***Mrs. Anne Wager, Williamsburg Schoolmistress for Young Blacks***
13. ***A Revival in North Carolina: A Black Woman and Her White Mistress Pray Together***

Document 1: An Obedient, Faithful, Loving Wife: "The Special End of Woman's Creation"

The Whole Duty of Man *is attributed to the Reverend Richard Allestree (1619–1681), a Church of England clergyman. Written in the form of sermons and directed toward helping its readers to live moral lives, it was widely read in both the seventeenth and eighteenth centuries. Attitudes toward its usefulness may well have changed by 1775, however, when Richard Sheridan wrote* The Rivals. *His heroine, Miss Lydia Languish, hid* The Innocent Adultery *within its covers and her maid used it to press lace.*[14]

8. The third Relation is that between Husband and Wife: This is yet much nearer than either of the former, as appears by that Text, *Ephes.* v. 31. *A Man shall leave his Father and Mother, and shall be joined unto his Wife, and they two shall be one Flesh.* Several Duties there are owing from one of these Persons to the other, and first for the Wife, she owes Obedience: This is commanded by the Apostle, *Col.* iii.18. *Wives, submit yourselves unto your own Husbands, as it is fit in the Lord:* They are to render Obedience to their Husbands in the Lord, that is, in all lawful Commands; for otherwise it is here as in the Case of all other Superiors, God must be obeyed rather than Man, and the Wife must not, upon her Husband's Command, do any Thing which is forbidden by God: But in all Things which do not cross some Command of God's, this Precept is of Force, and will serve to condemn the peevish Stubbornness of many Wives who resist the lawful Commands of their Husbands, only because they are impatient of this Duty of Subjection which God himself requires of them. But here it may be asked, what if the Husband command something, which, though it be not unlawful, is yet very inconvenient and imprudent, must the wife submit to such a Command? To this I answer, That it will be no Disobedience in her, but Duty, calmly and mildly to shew him the inconvenience thereof, and to persuade him to retract that Command; but in case she cannot win him to it by fair Intreaties, she must neither try sharp Language, nor yet finally refuse to obey, nothing but the Unlawfulness of the command being sufficient Warrant for that.

9. Secondly, The Wife owes Fidelity to the Husband, and that of two sorts; first, That of the Bed; she must keep herself pure and chaste from all strange Embraces, and therefore must not so much as give an Ear to any that would allure her, but with the greatest Abhorrence reject all Motions of that Sort, and never give any Man, that has once made such a Motion to her, the least Opportunity to make a second. Secondly, She owes him likewise Fidelity in the managing those worldly Affairs he commits to her; she must order them so, as may be most to her Husband's Advantage, and not, by deceiving . . . him, employ his Goods to such Uses as he allows not of.

10. Thirdly, She owes him Love; and, together with that, all Friendliness and Kindness of Conversation: She is to endeavour to bring him as much Assistance and Comfort of Life as is possible, that so she may answer that special End of the Woman's Creation, that of being a *Help to her Husband, Gen.* ii.18: and this is all Conditions, whether Health or Sickness, Wealth or Poverty, whatsoever Estate God by his Providence shall cast him into, she must be as much of Comfort and Support to him as she can. To this all Sullenness and Harshness, all Brawling and Unquietness is directly contrary, for that makes the Wife the Burden and Plague of the Man, instead of a Help and Comfort! And sure if it be a Fault to behave one's self so to any Person, as hath been already shewed, how great must it be to do so to him to whom the greatest Kindness and Affection is owing?

11. Nor let such Wives think, that any Faults or Provocations of the Husband can justify their Forwardness, for they will not either in respect of Religion or Discretion; not in Religion, for where God has absolutely commanded a Duty to be paid, it is not any Unworthiness of the Person can excuse from it; nor Indiscretion, for the worse the Husband is, the more Need there is for the Wife to carry herself with that Gentleness and Sweetness that may be most likely to win him. . . . [I]t seems the good Behaviour of the Wives was thought a powerful Means to win Men from Heathenism to Christianity; and sure it might now-a-days have some good Effects if Women would have but the Patience to try it; at the least it would have this, that it would keep some tolerable Quiet in Families; whereas on the other Side, all ill Fruits of the Wives Unquietness are so notorious, that there are few Neighbourhoods but can give some Instance of it. How many Men are there, that, to avoid the Noise of a froward Wife, have fal'n to Company-Keeping. . . . [W]henever there happens any Thing, which, in Kindness to her Husband, she is to admonish him of, let it be with that Softness and Mildness, that it may appear it is Love, and not Anger, makes her speak.

Document 2: Elizabeth Daniell: The Distribution of Bibles to the Deserving

Elizabeth Daniell believed that Virginian men needed more religion, and she decided to help them improve their spiritual condition by giving them Bibles to read. She did not like the attitude of Richard Shepard, one of her chosen recipients, however, and asked him to give back the Bible right there in the store. Shepard refused and was therefore tried in the Northampton County Court in 1684 on a charge of theft.[15]

The Deposition of John Wescott aged 25 years or thereabouts saith that the depont. heard John Daniells wife that shee called for a bible and did prefer to give it to Richard Shepard upon the condition that hee would goe downe upon his knees and say his prayers, and he Answered that hee had prayed her into hell. And the Devil, pray her out againe. And she holding the bible in her hand towards him hee tooke it out of her hand she asking him say his prayers he refused it she demanding ye bible againe he answered nothing was freer than [a] gift Shee then bidding ye merchant looke after his goods and further saith not.

The Deposition of Michael Dickson aged 30 years or thereabouts Saith that on Saturday being ye 15th day of this instant November at ye house of Mr. Nath[anie]l Wilkins in the County of Northampton yor. depont. was with one Richard Shepard a sawyer in Mr. Jacksons store where yor. said depont. laid out some Tobacco to give ye said sawyer—Credit for a parcell of Tobacco due to him. And in ye said time of yor. depont. & the said sawyers stay there Elizabeth the wife of John Daniell came into the said store and after some words betweene ye said sawyer & Elizabeth Daniell the said Eliz. Daniell called to ye said mercht. Jackson for one of his Bibles And hee handed her one. . . . And shee bid ye said Jacksons Assistant that was booking what goods hee delivered books her for the said Bible. And as shee had the bible in her hand shee said to the said Richard Shepard now if you will downe of your knees I will give you this Bible which hee promised her to due & on that shee gave him ye Bible & hee putt it in his pockett but whither hee performed ye ceremony—Enjoyned yor depont. cannot certainly tell: tho said mercht afterwards saying that was ye ninth bible ye said Elizabeth Daniell had had of him w[hi]ch said Bible ye said mercht. would afterwards have had from ye said sawyer Againe. But hee would not deliver it on which ye mercht taxed him for stealing of it out of his store.

Document 3: Mary Taney: A Request for an Anglican Priest

Maryland experienced a great deal of political and religious turmoil in the seventeenth century. The colony's officials were primarily Catholic and were, in many cases, related to the Calvert family. However, the majority of the inhabitants were Protestant, who were divided in their loyalty to the proprietor, Lord Baltimore. Despite the number of Anglican residents, there were few Church of England clergymen in the colony. As a result, Mary Taney made her request for a minister, and the Reverend Paul Bertrand subsequently arrived in 1689. Mary's husband, Michael Taney, even though he was the sheriff of Calvert County under proprietary rule, was the same year described as a "very good Protestant." Mary appears equally so.[16]

May it please your Grace, I am now to repeat, my request to your Grace for a church, in the place of Maryland where I live. Our want of a minister and the many blessings our Saviour designed us by them is a misery which I and a numerous family and many others in Maryland have groaned under. We do not question God's care of us, but think your Grace and the Right Rev. your Bishops, the proper instrument of so great a blessing to us. We are not, I hope, so foreign to your jurisdiction but we may be owned your stray flock, however the Commission to 'Go and baptise all nations' is large enough. But I am sure we are, by a late custom on tobacco, sufficiently acknowledged subjects of the King of England and therefore, by his protection, not only our persons and estates, but of what is far more dear to us, our religion. I question not but that your Grace is sensible that without a temple it will be impracticable. Neither can we expect a minister to hold out, to ride ten miles in a morning and before he can dine ten more—and from house to house in hot weather, will dishearten a minister, if not kill him.

Your Grace is so sensible of our sad condition and for your place and piety's sake have so great an influence on our most Religious and Gracious King that if I had not your Grace's promise to depend on, I could not question your Grace's intercession. 500 or 600 L for a church with some small encouragement for a minister—will be extremely less charge than honor to His Majesty. Our church settled according to the Church of England, which is the sum of our request, will prove a nursery of religion and loyalty through the whole Province. But your Grace needs no argument from me, but only this: it is in your power to give us many opportunities to praise God for this and innumerable mercies, and to importune His goodness to bless His Majesty with a long and prosperous reign over us, and long continue to your Grace the great blessing of being an instrument of good to His Church—and now, that I may be no more troublesome I humbly entreat your pardon to the well meant zeal of your Grace's most obedient servant.

Mary Taney.

Document 4: Elizabeth Key: "By Report Shee Is Able to Give a Very Good Account of Her Fayth"

Elizabeth Key was the daughter of an Englishman, Thomas Key, and an unknown slave woman in early Virginia. When Elizabeth was a child, her father had her bound out for nine years, and after her master had died, the overseer of the estate questioned her status. In 1756, she brought suit in the Northumberland County Court for her freedom on the basis that her father was a free man, that she had been baptized a Christian, and that she had been sold for a definite period of time. If the case had occurred five years later, there would have been no question about her status; she would have taken the condition of her mother. In this instance, however, Elizabeth's Christian faith helped to determine her freedom. She won her case and later married her attorney.[17]

A Report of a Committee from an Assembly Concerning the free-dome of Elizabeth Key

It appeareth to us that shee is the daughter of Thomas Key by severall Evidences and by a fine imposed upon the said Thomas for getting her mother with Child of the said Thomas That she hath bin by verdict of a Jury impannelled 20th January 1655 in the County of Northumberland found to be free by severall oathes which the Jury desired might be Recorded That by the Comon Law the Child of a Woman slave begott by a freeman ought to bee free That shee hath bin long since Christened Col. Higginson being her God father and that by report shee is able to give a very good account of her fayth That Thomas Key sould her onely for nine yeares to Col. Higginson with severall conditions to use her more Respecfully then a Comon servant or slave That in case Col. Higginson had gone for England within nine yeares hee was bound to carry her with him and pay her passage and not to dispose of her to any other For theise Reasons wee conceive the said Elizabeth ought to bee free and that her last Master should give her Corne and Cloathes and give her satisfaction for the time shee hath served longer then Shee ought to have done. But forasmuch as noe man appeared against the said Elizabeths petition wee thinke not fitt a determinative judgement should passe but that the County or Quarter Court where it shall be next tried to take notice of this to be the sence of the Burgesses of this present Assembly and that unless [original torn] shall appear to be executed and reasons [original torn] opposite part Judgement by the said Court be given [accordingly?]

Document 5: Rachel Mordecai: "We Find the Jews to Form a Respectable Part of the Community"

Rachel Mordecai (1788–1838) was born in Goochland County, Virginia, and moved to Warrenton, North Carolina, with her family about 1792. A few years later her father opened a school for girls, which became an immediate success. The acceptance of the school and of the Mordecai family illustrates the degree of religious toleration in North Carolina. Rachel's letters to Maria Edgeworth also demonstrate her ethnic pride and sense of religious identity. The first extract is from a letter written in 1815, after Rachel had read The Absentee. *Rachel wrote the second letter two years later, after the publication of* Harrington *in which Edgeworth had used a passage from the earlier letter.*[18]

Relying on the good sense and candour of Miss Edgeworth I would ask, how it can be that she, who on all other subjects shows such justice and liberality, should on one alone appear biased by prejudice:

should even instill that prejudice into the minds of youth! Can my allusion be mistaken? It is to the species of character which wherever a *Jew* is introduced is invariably attached to him. Can it be believed that this race of men are by nature mean, avaricious, and unprincipled? Forbid it, mercy. Yet this is more than insinuated by the stigma usually affixed to the *name.* In those parts of the world where these people are oppressed and made continually the subject of scorn and derision, they may in many instances deserve censure; but in this happy country, where religious distinctions are scarcely known, where character and talents are all sufficient to attain advancement, we find the Jews to form a respectable part of the community. They are in most instances liberally educated, many following the honourable professions of the Law, and Physick, with credit and ability, and associating with the best society our country affords. The penetration of Miss Edgeworth has already conjectured that it is a Jewess who addresses her; it is so, but one who thinks she does not flatter herself in believing that were she not, her opinion on this subject would be exactly what it is now. Living in a small village, her father's the only family of Israelites who reside in or near it, all her juvenile friendships and attachments have been formed with those of persuasions different from her own; yet each has looked upon the variations of the other as things of course—differences which take place in every society. . . .

We have read both Harrington and Ormond with much satisfaction; the former will, I hope by asserting the cause of toleration, reward the benevolent intentions of its author. In England, where from circumstances related in that work, we must believe prejudices carried to an excess, hardly conceivable by us in America, it will doubtless be productive of much good. If by scrutinizing the conduct of Jews, they are proved to fulfill in common with other men every moral and social duty, it is to be hoped that the stigma which habit has associated with the name will lose its influence. The eagerness with which Miss Edgeworth has sought for such characters, and such incidents, as were honourable to our unfortunate nation, evinces the sincerity with which she undertook their defence. It is impossible to feel otherwise than gratified by the confidence so strongly, yet so delicately manifested, by the insertion of a passage from the letter in which I had endeavoured to give an idea of their general standing in this country.

Document 6: Eliza Lucas Pinckney: A Rational Piety

Eliza Lucas Pinckney's (1722?–1793) religious sentiments especially demonstrate the rational piety favored by many southern Anglicans before the American Revolution. In the following document, the first passage is from a letter to her brother, written when she was about twenty years old, and illustrates her thoughts on religion, which remained essentially unchanged the rest of her life. The latter passage, written to her mother shoftly after her husband's death, reaffirms her conviction that Christian beliefs grow out of reason.[19]

I have been thinking, My Dear brother, how necessary it is for young people such as we are to lay down betimes a plan for our conduct in life in order to living not only agreeably in this early season of it, but with cheerfulness in maturity, comfort in old age, and with happiness to Eternity; and I can find but one scheme to attain all these desirable ends and that is the Xtian scheme. To live agreeably to the dictates of reason and religion, to keep a strick gaurd over not only our actions but our very thoughts before they ripen into action, to be active in every good word and work must produce a peace and calmness of mind beyond expression. To be consious we have an almighty friend to bless our Endeavours and to assist us in all difficulties, to be consious We have to the utmost of our power and ability endeavoured to please him, and shall finally injoy Him for ever, who is infinite perfection it self, gives rapture beyond all the boasted injoyments of the world—allowing them their utmost extent and fulness of joy.

Let us then, my dear Brother, set out right and keep the sacred page always in view. You have entered into the Army and are not yet sixteen years of age. Consider then to how many dangers you are exposed, (I dont now mean those of the field) but those that proceed from youth, and youthful company, pleasure, and disipation. You are a Soldier, and Victory and conquest must fire your mind. Remember then the greatest conquest is a Victory over your own irregular passions. Consider this is the time for improvment in Virtue as well as in every thing else, and tis a dangerous weakness to put it off till age and infirmities incapacitates us to put our good designs in practise. But old age, you will say, is a long way off from you and me. True, and perhaps we shall never reach it. 'Tis then an additional reason why we should make use of the present and remember no time is ours but the present—and that so fleeting that we can hardly be said to exist.

Excuse my fears, my much loved brother, and believe they are excited by the tenderest regard for your welfare, and then I will inform you I am in some pain (notwithstanding your natural good sence, for the force of Example is great) least you should be infected with the fashionable but shameful vice too common among the young and gay of your sex. I mean pretending a disbelief of and ridiculeing of religion; to do which, they must first Enslave their reason. And then where is the rule of life? However it requires some degree of fortitude to oppose numbers, but cherish this most necessary virtue; tis so to all mankind, particularly to a soldier. Stand firm and unshaken then in what is right in spite of infidelity and ridicule. And you cant be at a loss to know what is right when The Devine goodness had furnished you with reason, which is his natural revelation, and his written word supernaturally revealed and delivered to mankind by his son Jesus Christ.

Examin carefully and unprejudicedly, and I am persuaded you will have no doubts as to the truth of revelation. For my own part I am so happy in the belief of the Xtian scheme that I cant help adopting an expression I have some where mett with, that if 'tis a delusion tis so pleasing a one that I would not be undeceived for the whole world. For if we lead a life of piety here, 'tis a life of all others the most pleasing and agreeable. And if there is no future state we are in as happy a situation as the irreligious. But if there should! with what dreadful astonishment must they cry out in Solomons words, we fools counted his life madness and his end to be without honour. How is he numbered among the children of God and his lott is among the saints. But say these wise heads, these pretenders to reason, how can we believe the scriptures when there are things contained therein contrary to reason! Were it really so the objection would be just, but upon examination you will find reason in the manner they use it is but another name for their prejudices.

God is Truth it self and cant reveal naturally or supernaturally contrarieties. The Christian religion is what the wisest men in all ages have assented too. When I speak of religion I mean such as is delivered in the scripture without any view of any particular party with exclusion of all the rest. It has been acknowledged by the greatest men of our nation and many others have revealed religion is consonant to the most exact reason tho some things may appear at first sight contrary to it. But you must observe there may be things above, tho' not contrary to reason. . . .

His had been the life of a constant steady active Virtue with an habitual trust and confidence in as well as an intire resignation to the Will of the Deity, which made him happy and cheerful through life and made all about him so, for his was true religion free from sourness and superstition; and in his sickness and death the good man and the Christian shined forth in an uncommon resolution and patience, humility, and intire resignation to the Devine Will.—My tears flow too fast. I must have done; 'tis too much, too much to take a review of that distressful hour!

Document 7: Religious Instruction in the Home: Devereux Jarratt Discovers True Religion

The Reverend Devereux Jarratt, the prominent Episcopal clergyman from Dinwiddie County, Virginia, and an early friend to Methodists, attributed his first experience with experimental religion to a Mrs. Cannon, a Presbyterian. At the time (about 1753), he was a young schoolmaster boarding in various households. During his stay with the Cannon family, he observed every night Mrs. Cannon's religious instruction of the family. Much to her great joy, Jarratt became an avid listener and convert.[20]

It was on a Sunday, P. M. when I first came to the house—an entire stranger, both to the gentleman and his lady. Though they had sent their niece and daughter to me, for about three months, yet I had no personal acquaintance with them, as the school had been made up, without my presence. The interview, on my part, was the more awkward, as I knew not how to introduce myself to strangers, and what style was proper for accosting persons of their dignity. However I made bold to enter the door, and was viewed, in some measure, as a phenomenon. The gentleman took me, (if I rightly remember) for the son of a very poor man, in the neighbourhood, but the lady, having some hint, I suppose, from the children, rectified the mistake, and cried out, *it is the school-master.*

I found her reading a religious book, and the gravity of her appearance, gave me an unusual feeling, which, perhaps, might increase the disadvantage, under which I appeared. I felt miserable, and said little, the whole evening. I was truly out of my element, and was glad, when the morning arose, to get off to my little school, that I might, once more, be from under the eye of restraint.

The custom of this lady was, as I soon discovered, to read a sermon, in *Flavel,* every night—to which she wished me to attend. I had, indeed, little relish for such entertainment, yet, agreeable to my purpose of playing the hypocrite, and gaining a favourable opinion, I affected a very close attention. And that I might excel in this art, and more effectually answer my purpose, I would sometimes, after a long discourse was finished (Flavel's sermon's being all lengthy) ask her to read another—though, probably, I understood not the tenth part of what was read. Flavel's sermons are too experimental and evangelical, for one, so ignorant of divine things, as I was, to comprehend. When she was weary of reading, she would ask me to read in my turn. But so poor a hand did I make of the business, that reader and hearer were rather abashed, than edified. Yet I could not decently refuse. She soon desisted asking me to read, and took the whole task on herself. This custom continued for six or eight weeks, without any other effect on me, but fatigue and drowsiness, which I supported with much fortitude and self-denial, rather than give the least reason for suspicion, that I could be weary of good things. I should, no doubt, have eloped some nights, and passed the evening at my former stand, but as I was to carry the two little girls to school, every day, on horse back, one behind and the other before me, I was obliged to stand to my charge.

But it pleased God, on a certain night, while she was reading, as usual, to draw out my attention, and fix it on the subject, in a manner unknown to me before. The text of the sermon was, "*Then opened he their understanding:*" From which words were pointed out, what new discoveries would open to the eye of the mind, by means of spiritual illumination, &c. The subject was naturally as dark to me, as any of the former, and yet I felt myself imprest with it, and saw my personal interest in the solemn truths—and truths I believed them to be: But, at the same time, I was conscious, that I was a stranger to that spiritual illumination and its consequent discoveries, and, of course, was yet in a dark and dangerous state. I must have known before this, that I was a sinner, and all things were not right with me, but nothing ever came home to my heart, so as to make a lasting impression, till now. The impression followed me to bed—arose with me in the morning, and haunted me from place to place, till I resolved to forsake my sins, and try to save my soul.—But my resolution was made in my own strength, for I had not yet learned how weak and frail we are by nature, and that all our suffering is of God.

It may be worthy of remark, that my distress, then, did not arise from a painful sense of any particular sin, or sins in general, but from a full persuasion, that I was a stranger to God and true religion, and was not prepared for death and judgment. The alteration, in my conduct, effected by these impressions on the mind, soon became visible to my benefactress, which was matter of great joy.

Document 8: "Virtuous Women are the Sweetness, the Charm of Human Life"

One of the best examples of eighteenth-century advice literature, Dr. James Fordyce's Sermons to Young Women, *first published in 1765, was widely read in both England and the American colonies. Colonial bookstores and newspaper printers often advertised it in their lists of books for sale. Although Fordyce (1720–1796) was a Scottish Presbyterian minister, his audience included members of various denominations. His sermons not only emphasized the proper conduct for young ladies, but also described their desired intellectual attainments and religious behavior.*[21]

When a daughter, it may be a favorite daughter, turns out unruly, foolish, wanton; when she disobeys her parents, disgraces her education, dishonors her sex, disappoints the hopes she had raised; when she throws herself away on a man unworthy of her, or if disposed, yet by his or her situation unqualified, to make her happy; what her parents in any of these cases must necessarily suffer, we may conjecture, they alone can feel.

The world, I know not how, overlooks in our sex a thousand irregularities, which it never forgives in yours; so that the honor and peace of a family are, in this view, much more dependant on the conduct of daughters than of sons; and one young lady going astray shall subject her relations to such discredit and distress, as the united good conduct of all her brothers and sisters, supposing them numerous, shall scarce ever be able to repair. But I press not any farther an argument so exceedingly plain. We can prognosticate nothing virtuous, nothing happy, concerning those wretched creatures of either sex, that do not feel for the satisfaction, ease, or honor of their parents.

Another and a principle source of your importance is the very great and extensive influence which you, in general, have with our sex. There is in female youth an attraction, which every man of the least sensibility must perceive. If assisted by beauty, it becomes irresistable in the first impression. Your power thus far we do not affect to conceal. He that made both you and us manifestly meant it should be so, from having attempered our hearts to such emotions. Would to God you know how to improve this power to its noblest purposes! . . . Youth and beauty set off with sweetness and virtue, capacity and discretion—what have not they accomplished? . . .

Men, I presume, are in general better judges than women, of the deportment of women. Whatever affects them from your quarter they feel more immediately. You slide insensibly into a certain cast of manners; you perceive not the gradations. You do not see yourselves at a proper distance. If the effect produced be upon the whole disagreeable, self love will not be the first to discover it. Men, it is true, are often dazzled by youth, vivacity, and beauty; but yet at times they will look at you with a cooler eye, and a closer inspection, than you apprehend; at least, when they have opportunities of seeing you in private company. . . .

At any rate, the majesty of the sex is sure to suffer by being seen too frequently, and too familiarly. Discreet reserve in a woman, like the distance kept by royal personages, contributes to maintain the proper reverence. Most of our pleasures are prized in proportion to the difficulty with which they are obtained. The sight of beauty may be justly reckoned in that number. Nothing can be more impolitic in young ladies, than to make it cheap. . . .

. . . [If you lead too public a life, young men will find you pleasurable "companions of an hour."] Companions for life, if they ever think of such, they will look for elsewhere. They will then make the necessary discrimination; I mean, if they are wise and honest enough to marry from choice. They will then try if they can find women well bred and sober-minded at the same time, of a chearful temper with sedate manners: women of whom they may hope that they will love home, be attached to their husbands, attentive to their families, reasonable in their wishes, moderate in their expences, and not devoted to eternal show. Having found them, whether with or without fortune (that will never be their prime consideration) they will endeavour to gain them by another sort of style and behaviour than they used towards you. Far other sentiments, far other emotions, will then possess them. In short, their hearts will be then engaged; and if they are happy enough to obtain the much wished for objects, then, with a joy unfelt before, they will form the tenderest of all connections, leaving you where they found you, as widely removed as ever from the truest pleasures, and the fairest prospect, that humanity knows; the pleasures which are enjoyed at home, and the prospects which include a family. . . .

Your safety, I said before, lies in retreat and vigilance, in sobriety and prudence, in virtuous friendship and rational conversation, in domestic, elegant, and intellectual accomplishments: I add now, in the Guardianship of Omnipotence, as that which must give efficacy to all the rest, but which can only be obtained by something more and better than them all, I mean, True Religion. What reason indeed have you to [word blurred] for a privilege so great, if you do not ask it? What cause could you have to complain; if your righteous Creator, on whom every consideration ought to teach you dependance, were to leave you to yourselves amidst those dangerous attacks, or artful snares, which you presumptuously imagine you could resist by your own strength, or e[ls]e by your caution? That humility which does not depress, as Christian humility never can, is the best means of security. She who is most sensible of her hazard, is most likely to be on her guard. She who perceives her own inbecillity, will be glad to invoke a higher power. Nor will the Parent of all be deaf to one of his reasonable offspring, who, apprehensive of the difficulties to which her frame and situation expose her, heartily implores his help. . . .

In many instances men are attacked by folly, before they surrender; whereas women must generally invite it by art, or rather indeed take it by violence, ere they can possess themselves of its guilty pleasures. So far the Almighty, in consideration of their debility, and from a regard to their innocence, has raised a kind of fence about them, to prevent those wilder excursions into which the other sex are frequently carried, with a freedom unchecked by fear, and favored by custom.

Corrupt as the world is, it certainly does expect from young women a strict decorum, nor, as we have seen before, does it easily forgive them the least deviation. And then, while you remain without families of your own, few of you are necessarily so engaged, as not to have a large portion of time with daily opportunities for recollection, if you are inclined to improve them. I go farther and say, that your improving them by a piety the most regular and avowed, if withal unaffected and amiable, will be no sort of objection to the men, but much the reverse.

But let us turn to Scripture, and see what peculiar incitement you have from thence to the profession and practice of godliness. How encouraging to reflect, that the very first promise made to the human race destinguished your sex with a mark of honor, as signal as it was unexampled! Need I explain myself by saying, that the greatest personage who ever visited our world, he who came on the most important design, and who executed it in the most wonderful manner, none other, in short, than "the son of God, who was manifested to destroy the works of the devil," and on their ruins to raise an empire of righteousness and happiness elevated as heaven, and lasting as eternity—that He, I say, was from the beginning predicted under the singular and interesting character of "the seed of the woman"? How exalting a circumstance for your whole sex, that the Saviour of men, the admiration of angels, and the prince of heaven, was accordingly "in the fulness of time made of a woman"! And, Oh, my young friends, what dignity will it forever reflect on maiden virtue, that "a virgin conceived and bore a son, the only begotten of the Father, full of grace and truth?" Where is the religion, or the philosophy, that has lifted your nature so high, or placed the beauty of female purity and excellence in a light so conspicuous and noble?"

[Concerning private devotion:] It will not be learnt by those who have no relish for retirement. The Almighty's voice must be often attended to in the silence of the passions, and the secrecy of the soul. Those are yet strangers to their Maker, who cannot endure to think of him, or do not love to turn to him, when alone. Is the reverse of this your case, my dear hearer? Are your meditations of God sweet? Does your heart go out after him, as its best and greatest object? Is it your joy to pour it forth into his paternal bosom? Do you generally perceive your sentiment raised and refined by it, your ideas of your duty quickened and enlarged, your detestation of the contrary confirmed and heightened, your resolutions invigorated of course, your gratitude, humility, meekness, resignation, and good affections of every kind, improved? Then are you a true worshiper. These are some of the genuine workings of piety.

[Different minds require different kinds of devotion.] Besides the regular, invariable, and solemn performance of your morning and evening devotions, it would be well if now and then, especially on the day of sacred rest, you took repeated opportunities of entering into your closet, shutting your door, and praying to your father who sees in secret; according as you found yourself in a happier disposition for such employment, or were prompted to it by some peculiar occurrences in your situation, or exigence in your soul. And if at certain times of the year, pointed out by religious custom, or fixed upon by personal choice, you were to consecrate a whole day to holy retreat and devotional exercises, joined with prudent fasting; I am persuaded, you would find it as highly beneficial in your own practice, as it comes strongly recommended by the experience of the saints.

If you might be advised by me, you should in prayer neither trust wholly to your single fund of thought and expression, supposing it even rich and various, nor confine yourself entirely to forms, by whatever man or set of men composed; but use sometimes one, sometimes the other, and sometimes a mixture of both, just as the attraction of your mind seems to lead at the moment, or as any of these methods may on trial be attended with most satisfaction and advantage. In effect, I am convinced that of those who, in this kind of commerce, limit themselves to their own unassisted stock, the greater part will often, particularly in circumstances of bad health or spiritual dryness, be reduced to such straits as must produce a poverty of devotion which they could not suffer, did they proceed on a larger foundation. On the other hand, I cannot conceive, that, even amongst those who are most devoted to forms, any sincere worshipper should not by the swelling of sentiment, and the current of devotion, be frequently carried away into a freer and fuller effusion of the heart.

As to the length of those duties, I would only say, that you must be governed by your condition both outward and inward; . . .

For acquiring what is generally styled Religious Knowledge, reading the scriptures throughout and often large proportions at a time, may be perfectly proper. For improving in that which those scriptures speak of chiefly under this denomination, I mean a practical and vital sense of things divine and everlasting, a different method, as I conceive should be followed.

["On Female Meekness":] But that vigilance which is forced will be frequently suspended; and that gentleness which is put on will be always precarious. Therefore we wish you to acquire early the habits of self-controul, and to cultivate from principle a meek and quiet spirit. This you will do with success, if imploring and depending on the grace of God, you make conscience of curbing betimes the irascible passions of nature, of submitting calmly to the daily mortifications of life, of generously yielding to those about you, and particularly of condescending to persons of low estate.

I have never seen a woman eminent for the last of these qualities, who was not excellent in many other ways. Respect to superiors may be enforced by fear, or prompted by interest, and is therefore no demonstrative proof of a good heart. But habitual mildness to those of inferior rank, is one of its surest indications. That young lady cannot have a bad mind, who readily enters into the distresses, and affectionately contributes to the felicity, of those whom Providence hath placed beneath her. In reality, there is no such discovery of your tempers as your treatment of domestics. She is always the worthiest character who behaves best at home, and is most liked by the servants. They are the truest judges of a women's disposition, because to them disguise is laid aside, and they see her in all lights. An unaffected propension to use them well, without partiality and without caprice, argues a confirmed benevolence. . . .

Document 9: Martha Laurens Ramsay: "A Life of Prayer"

Martha Laurens Ramsay (1759–1811) demonstrated an intense religious faith from her childhood through her adult life. A daughter of the wealthy Charleston merchant Henry Laurens, Martha married Dr. David Ramsay in 1787. Although she had been raised an Anglican, she joined the Independent (Congregational) Church. Ramsay's memoirs of her life prove the perfect model for eighteenth-century advice literature. In addition to passages from the Memoirs, *an extract from her early "Religious Exercises" and an entry from her diary written in November 1797 are also included to illustrate this lifelong religious faith.*[22]

Miss Laurens, in her 12th year, began to be the subject of serious religious impressions. She was well instructed in the great gospel mystery of salvation by the atoning sacrifice of Jesus Christ for the sins of the world. And there is good reason to believe, that at a very early period she was brought by the grace of God cordially to accept of salvation freely offered, though early purchased.

In the 15th. year of her age in conformity to the advice of Dr. Doddridge, and in a form of words recommended by him, she prepared, and solemnly executed an instrument of writing, called by her with great propriety, "A self dedication and solemn covenant with God." In this, after a suitable introduction "she presents before her Maker the whole frame of her nature, all the faculties of her mind, and all the members of her body, as a living sacrifice holy and acceptable unto God." And "not only consecrates all that she was, and all that she had to his service, but humbly resigns to his heavenly will all that she called hers, to be disposed of as he pleased." . . .

In every period of her adult age, whether married or single, when, from accidental circumstances, she was the head of the family, and in health, she daily read to her domestic circle, a portion of the holy scriptures, and prayed with them; and frequently on particular occasions, with one or more individuals of it, and regularly, every Sunday, with her young white and black family, in addition to catechetical instructions given to both at the same time. . . . She prized prayer as the courtier does a key, that at all times gives him access to the presence of his sovereign; and in all the important transactions of her life, resolved on nothing till she had previously sought direction of God respecting it. She might be said to live a life of prayer, for she incorporated it with her daily business, and was so habituated to its constant practice, that prayers frequently constituted a part of her dreams. Believing most thoroughly that God's providence extends to every event and every circumstance of the life of every human being, and subscribing to the doctrine of Dr. Leechman, in his excellent sermon on prayer, which she highly prized, "that it is as absurd to expect we shall arrive at virtue and happiness without prayer, as it would be for the husbandman to hope he shall have his usual crop, though he bestow none of his usual labour and industry." She practically conformed to the apostolic precept "pray without ceasing," and daily brought before her Maker the cases of herself, family, friends, neighbours, and sometimes of strangers, whose situation was known to be interesting.

She was a constant and devout attendant on divine service; steadily recorded the text, and occasionally made a short analysis of the sermon. She generally spent a considerable part of the intervals of public worship, in catechising and instructing her children and servants; in reading with them the Bible and other good books, particularly "Burkitt's help and guide to Christian families." In performing this duty, she placed her children around her, and read alternately with them verses in the Bible, and Watts's Psalms and Hymns, or sentences in other religious books, so as to teach them at the same time, by her example, the art of reading with emphasis and propriety. The exercise was occasionally varied by reading in the same manner the New Testament in Greek, with her sons, and in French with her daughters. From the seventeenth year of her age, she was a regular, steady, and devout attendant on the communion. In this she found so much comfort, that she regretted absence from it, as a serious loss. She possessed herself of the names of the new members admitted to it from time to time, and recorded them as brothers and sisters in Christ, who broke with her the bread of life, at the same table of their common Lord, and prayed for each individual of them, whether she had any personal acquaintance with them or not, and took a particular delight in rendering to them and her other fellow communicants, every kind office in her power; for she had high ideas of the communion of saints among themselves, as being conjoined into one mystical body of Christ, throughout this world, and partly in heaven, all united under one common head, and bound to each other by peculiar ties.

In discharging relative duties, Mrs. Ramsay was exemplary. As a child, she had high opinion of parental authority; and to it she conceived herself as owing implicit obedience in every case not plainly inconsistent with the duty due to her God. It was therefore a standing order to her servants, without a moment's delay, and without announcing the circumstance, to call her, not only from business, but from her most private retirement whensoever her father called for her services. She had no scruple of doing that for him on Sundays, about which she had scruples of doing for herself. She reasoned thus; "Children, obey your parents in all things, for this is well pleasing to the Lord." Col. iii. 20. is a divine command. The same authority which enacted the fourth commandment also enacted the fifth, and the minor duty should yield to the major. Never was there a daughter more devoted, attached, and obedient to her parent than she was: and her conduct flowed not from instinct, accident, or example, but from principle. In the same manner she had determined what were her conjugal duties. She was well acquainted with the plausible reasonings of modern theorists, who contend for the equality of the sexes; and few females could support their claims to that equality on better grounds than she might advance; but she yielded all pretensions on this score, in conformity to the positive declaration of holy writ, of which the following were full to the point, and in her opinion outweighed whole volumes of human reasoning. "In sorrow, thou shalt bring forth children, and thy desire shall be to thy husband, and he shall rule over thee." Gen. iii. 16. "Wives, submit yourselves unto your own husbands as unto the Lord. For the husband is the head of the wife, even as Christ is the head of the church; and he is the Saviour of the body. Therefore, as the church is subject until Christ, so let the wives be to their own husbands in every thing." Eph. v. 22, 23, 24. In practice, as well as theory, she acknowledged the dependent, subordinate condition of her sex; and considered it as a part of the curse denounced on Eve, as being "the first in the transgression." 1 Tim. ii. 13, 14. The most self denying duties of the conjugal relations being thus established on a divine foundation, and illustrated by those peculiar doctrines of revelation on which she hung all her hopes, the other duties followed by an easy train of reasoning, and were affectionately performed. In this manner, the subject of these memoirs used her bible as a system of practical ethics, from which she acquired a knowledge of her true station, and also deduced such excellent rules of conduct in life, as might be expected from correct principles. As a parent who had brought children into a world of sin and misery, without their consent, she considered herself as bound, in common justice, to do every thing in her power for their comfort in passing through it. She thought no pains too great, no sacrifices too hard, provided her children were advanced by them. In addition to her steady attention to their education, she exerted herself to keep them constantly in good humour; gave them every indulgence compatible with their best interests; partook with them in their sports; and in various ways amused their solitary hours so as often to drop the mother in the companion and friend: took a lively interest in all their concerns, and made every practicable exertion for their benefit. From the bible she was taught. "Fathers, provoke not your children to anger, lest they be discouraged." Col. iii. 21. On this text she often commented verbally, and every day practically. From it she drew several rules of conduct in her behavior toward her children. As a child, she was for implicit obedience, but as a mother was very moderate in urging her parental rights, and avoided, as far as consistent with a strict education, every thing which might "provoke her children to anger." Under this general head she considered as forbidden, unnecessary severity, sarcasms and all taunting, harsh, unkind language; overbearing conduct, high toned claims of superiority; capricious or whimsical exertions of authority, and several other particulars, calculated to irritate children or fill them with terror. On the other hand, she considered parents as required by this precept to curb their own tempers; to bridle their passions; to make proper allowances for indiscretions and follies of youth; and to behave toward their offsprings in the most conciliatory manner, so as to secure their love and affections on the score of gratitude. These and several other rules of conduct in the discharge of relative duties were not taken up at random, but derived from reason and reflection, and especially from an attentive consideration of the perceptive part of the word of God. Happy would it be for society if all its members used their bibles for similar purposes.

Religious Exercises

Thursday, Dec. 23, 1773

BEING THIS DAY FOURTEEN YEARS AND SEVEN WEEKS OLD.

I Do this day, after full consideration, and serious deliberation, and after earnest prayer for the assitance of Divine Grace, resolve to surrender and devote my youth, my strength, my soul, with all I have, and all I am, to the service of that great and good God, who has preserved and kept me all my life until now, and who in infinite compassion has given me to see the folly of my ways, and by faith to lay hold on a dear Redeemer, and obtain peace to my soul through his precious blood.

Martha Laurens.

Shall not the Judge of the whole earth do right. O yes, he will. Shall not he, who freely gave his own Son for us, deal kindly by his redeemed ones. Oh yes, he will. Be not, therefore, cast down, Oh my soul, neither be thou disquieted within me, for I shall yet praise him who is the light of my countenance and my God; yes, I will even now praise him, for whether he gives or takes, he is still my God; and seeing the whole, while I see only in part, will always do better for me than I could for myself.

Resolutions made at this time.

To watch against my easily besetting sin.

To read the word of God with more meditation.

To lift up my heart to the Lord, whenever I awake in the night.

To encourage religious conversation in the family on all fit occasions, particularly with my beloved Miss Futerell.

To be more watchful and earnest in inward and ejaculatory prayer.

To be much in prayer for my dear husband, and to endeavour, to be to him a useful as well as a loving wife.

To endeavour to see the hand of God in every thing, and to undertake nothing without a dependance on, and a seeking of his blessing.

Not to let a spirit of indolence get the better of me in the education of my children; and in this matter, may God most especially help me; for I find when any thing presses much on my mind, I am very apt to be listless and inactive in the duty which I owe them.

Document 10: Elizabeth Foote Washington: "A Dutiful, Obedient Wife"

Elizabeth Foote Washington was a model of eighteenth-century wifely submissiveness, a role which, she believed, was dictated by the Scriptures. She yearned for a daughter, and when that seemed impossible, she desired the company of a female relative with whom she could share her religious faith. She was married to her cousin, Lund Washington, in 1779, and lived at Mt. Vernon until 1785, when Washington left his position there as manager and acquired his own estate.[23]

[November, 1779.] I have lately promised to enter into the holy state of matrimony & may a Blessing of the almighty attend this momentous step I have taken. . . . [She desires] to please my husband in every thing that is not against the divine Laws, & as there is a probability of my living in Houses not my own for some time—may the divine goodness assist me, so that I may study to live in peace & friendship with the family where I live,—may it be one of my daily petitions to the throne of grace to conduct myself as a dutyful obedient wife. . . .

I hope I have prepared myself for the worst that may happen—that is—if my marrige should prove & unhappy one—I trust I have so sincere a desire to please my Saviour that I hope I shall be enabled to bear with whatever is the divine will,—& as I believe nothing happens by chance, so it is my duty to bear with what the almighty permits with the same resignation as if . . . he had will'd it, but as my gracious God has been infinitely merciful to me, so I humbly hope my marriage may be an happy one—& hope my husband may never be against my being as religious as my inclination may lead me. . . .

[Summer, 1784.] I have now been married better than four years —& I think have had the satisfaction of conducting myself much to the approbation of my husband—& God grant I may continue to do it. . . . I can truely say I have never had cause to repent of my marriage. . . . [In this entry, Elizabeth now sets forth rules to] conduct myself in my family[:] by treating my domesticks with all the friendly kindness that is possible for me to do,—& never to think they were given me to domincer over—by treating them with expressions, because they are in my power,—such as fool—Blockhead—vile wretches, & many other names that I hope I shall ever think myself above using,—but on the contrary I will endeavour to do as follows,—first—never to scold at a Servant if it is possible to avoid it.—& I think if I endeavour to refrain from it—I shall be able to resist,—but when they do wrong talk to them in a kind & friendly way, pointing out their fault with calmness,—but at the same time with a steadiness that they may know I will not be impos'd upon—& I will endeavour to make them think I do not wish they should behave well for my sake, but because it will be pleasing in the eyes of the almighty—& that if they will do their business for his sake, I shall be well serv'd if they never think of me,—which is truly the case—I do most sincerely wish for their sakes—they may do their business with an earnest desire to please him—nothing would give me so great pleasure as having a truly religious family—not led away with Baptistical notions—but a religion that effectually touches the heart. . . .—rule the second—I will never find fault of a Servant before their master—ever to let them know that their master has the least idea that they ever offend me by any neglect of their business,—so that they shall never know he knows any of their faults—only just at the time that he may be oblig'd to speak to them,—as I suppose will be the case sometimes—for I do not expect they will always behave so as never to require his speaking to them. . . . it is my wish that my husband should court my company—not avoid it if he can—as must be the case with those men who has those teasing kind of wives,—or what else can be the meaning of men being so fond of going abroad . . . mine I thank God has hitherto appear'd always pleas'd with being with me—& I do hope I shall never disgust him by any conduct of mine . . . how much do I pity those women who has husbands that loves the gaming table—how often a fine woman is left at home to lament the loss of her husbands company, who is really not worthy of her. . . . It shall be my endeavour not to hurt the feelings of my servants—when I am oblig'd to find fault, I will take care not to find fault of one servant before another—but wait with patience till I have an opportunity of doing it alone,—if it should be even a day or two before I have one,—by that means I shall teach myself patience & forbearance—& avoid hurting their feelings . . . thirdly—if I should have children I will avoid if possible ever finding fault of a servant before them. . . .

[September, 1788.] It has pleas'd my good God to give me another sweet child—it is a girl—& nam'd Lucinda—& if it lives, I will strive to discharge the duty of a parent who wishes to glorify her Redeemer in every thought word & action of her life. . . .

& let me tell my dear child—that there is no real happiness without religion—a religion that effectually touches the heart—to conform to the outward ceremonies of religion is nothing, if it does not proceed from a sincere desire to please the almighty being,—there is no solidity—no comfort in the outward part of religion—if it does not proceed from a real principal of vertue—a sincere desire to please the Redeemer who has done so much for us, has a very pleasing feel,—& I sincerely hope my child—should she live, will make it her study to walk . . . pleasing in the eyes of her Saviour—never be ashamed of being religious. . . . endeavour to live in peace & friendship with every creature,—entertain a good will & fellow feeling for all mankind—be kind & good to everyone who is in want—never say or do any thing that will give another pain,—though your evil nature should want to do it.

[Spring, 1789.] As to my two girls—it is needless to say, what pains I have taken with their education,—because I have done every thing that a mistress could do for them, in every respect.—it is impossible to tell what I have done for them for if they had my Daughters I could not have given them better advice,—& I shall continue to do so as long as we live together,—I have taught them to read & write—there is few young Ladies ever had the same pain taken with them,—if they should not be such servants as one might expect,—I shall have the satisfaction of thinking I have done what I could do towards their happiness in this world, & in that which is to come. . . .

Within two years after we came home to live—I had prayers in my family, night & morning—& very constant—never failing if it was possible to get two or three together—& still continue to do it—but they do not seem fond of it—what is the cause I know not—human nature I believe is naturally averse to anything that is good. . . .

[She continues that one of the first resolutions she made after marriage was never "to contend" with her husband] in my opinion of things . . . if ever we differ'd in opinions not to insist on mine being right, & his wrong,—which is too much the custom of my Sex.—they cannot bear to be thought in the wrong.—which is the Cause where there is so much contention in the married state,—& the Lordly Sex—they can never be in the wrong in their own opinion—therefore cannot give up to a woman but I blame my sex most—it is their business to give up to their husbands.—our mother eve when she transgress'd was told her husband should rule over her,—then how dare any of her daughters to dispute the point,—I never thought it degraded my un[der]standing to give up my opinion to my husbands. . .-. I think a woman may keep up the dignity of a wife & mistress of a family—without ever disputing with her husband.

[July, 1792.] I am griev'd greatly to have this to set down—that my family is got so Baptistical in their notions, as to think they commit a crime to join with me in Prayer morning & evening—I have talked to every one of them separately—& seriously—endeavouring to convince them that they did not commit a crime by joining with me in Prayer—but all I can say, will not convince them—so that I am oblig'd to give out having Prayers in my family,—which has given me great concern—but I trust as my gracious God knows the desire I had to serve him daily in my family—that I shall not be answerable for not having family prayers.

[July, 1792.] When a person is accustomed to say only one particular prayer for a length of time, those who join them will be apt to repeat them & not think of them at the same time, having got them by rote, so that instead of praying it is but mere babbling. [She has written nine evening and morning prayers. She has nine manuscript books that include various private prayers] & for a person who prayers regular in their family to think that will excuse them from going to church, is extremely wrong—but indeed I do not think there can be an instance found of one who thought it their duty to pray in their familys that did not think it their duty to go to church. [In disagreeing with those individuals who say that they can read the Bible or a sermon at home as well as going to church, she asks] what right have they to expect a Blessing on their reading at home when they dispise going to church . . . we may be certain no one who dispises the priesthood on earth, can with truth be said to value Jesus Christ, the head of that holy order in heaven.

Document 11: Margaret Sharpe Gaston: A Model for Catholic Motherhood

In 1791, Margaret Sharpe Gaston sent her twelve-year-old son William Gaston, who would become one of North Carolina's most prominent statesmen, to Philadelphia for precollege education. From there, William moved to Georgetown in the fall as one of that school's first students. He also became a great favorite of the Jesuits. In the following document, the first two letters are from Francis Fleming, a priest in Philadelphia, and show his admiration for both William and Mrs. Gaston. The third letter, written by William, reveals his sensitivity to his mother's not being able to attend mass. The fourth letter, written by Margaret, expresses her concern for William's character while he is attending Princeton.[24]

I received great pleasure from your purpose of visiting Philadelphia next Spring on your way to Georgetown. It will be very agreeable to the Clergy of Philadelphia to see the mother of their beloved William. I had a letter from him a few days ago, which showed to what an eminent degree of piety he had reached. His mind was so full of Religion, when he wrote it, that after writing a few words to me, he took a flight to heaven & wrote a long & beautiful prayer to God. *I have a presentement, that the child, to whom you gave birth, will become your spiritual Father, & be a blessing to his native country.* [Letter from Francis A. Fleming to Margaret Gaston, October 5, 1792]

The Bearer young Mr oNeill is going to reside in Newbern, & I take the liberty of introducing him to you for the same purpose, which engaged me to use the same freedom before, in favour of another youth, that by your advice & exhortations he may preserve his religious ideas. He is indeed a fine youth, & if any of our Catholics assemble in your house on Sundays to pray, be pleased to admit the bearer. . . . [Letter from Fleming to Margaret Gaston, October 8, 1792]

Be assured that whenever I approach the holy table I do not forget to pray for you. No I do not. I earnestly entreat Almighty God that out of his goodness, he would not deprive you of that most Blessed Sacrament forever. My poor Aunt! how I pity her! I am in hopes, however, that a priest will be sent into North Carolina. It is the wish of the Bishop, who says that it is owing to the great want of them that he does not do it, but that as soon as one can be spared for that, he will send him there with all his heart. Oh what must be your situation never to approach the sacraments; never to hear mass; to have no one to administer Baptism. But dearest Mamma, you must suffer it patiently. Perhaps you have as many opportunities where you are, as if you were in the most Catholic country that is. This however is certain that God will give you grace enough to enable you to work out your salvation. [Letter from William Gaston to Margaret Gaston, November 24, 1792]

I shed tears of joy so young and so prudent thought I. What have I to fear, but O My Dr. Son So little Good Example and so seldom opportunity of practiceing your Religion and surrounded as you are with a set of wild youths fond of Gaming and all Sorts of Vice when absent from there Masters, how much I to fear of you being Corrupted, Consider my dr. the care, I have had of bringing you up in Virtue and the many pious lessons you have rec'd from the best of men this and your own Good Sense with the assistance of God's Grace I trust will preserve you from vice. [Letter from Margaret Gaston to William Gaston, July 8, 1795]

Document 12: Mrs. Anne Wager, Williamsburg Schoolmistress for Young Blacks

Dr. Bray's Associates, an English philanthropic society, was especially interested in the religious instruction of young blacks. The society attempted to set up schools in several towns in the southern colonies, and its major achievement was the school that it established in Williamsburg, Virginia. The success of this school, which was operated by Mrs. Anne Wager and directed first by William Hunter and later by Robert Carter Nicholas, can be directly tied to Mrs. Wager's dedication and teaching ability.[25]

The School was opened with 24 Scholars, (as many I think as one Woman can well manage)[.] Their Progress and Improvement in so short a Time, has greatly exceeded my Expectation, and I have Reason to hope that the good Intentions of the Associates will be fully answer'd by the Care and good Conduct of the Mistress. [William Hunter to Mr. John Waring, February 16, 1761]

I have had the Number of Children augmented [to] Thirty as you desired. The Mistress is very diligent and I am in hopes we shall be able to give you soon an agreeable account of the Progress They Make under her Care & Tuition. I must own to you that I am afraid the School will not answer the Sanguine Expectations the pious Founders may have formed but we endeavour to give it a fair Trial. [Robert Carter Nicholas to Associates, 1762]

[H]ave sent a list of the Black Children at present in the School, but can give no satisfactory account of those who have left the school the Mistress having kept no regular account. that a[t] a late Visition of the school they were pretty much pleased with the Scholars performances as they rather exceeded their Expectations, that They believe all the Chi[ldren] have been baptized & that it is general Practice in the Province for Negroe Parents to have their Children baptized that the many Difficulties They have to Struggle with in the Prosecution of this good Work make them Apprehensive the Success might not answer the Expectation of the Assoc[iates] but they shall think themselves very Fortunate if any Endeavours of theirs can contribute to the Spiritual Welfare & Happiness of the poor Negroes.—They hope, notwithstanding the several Obstacles to the Instruction & Reformation of the Negroes (which they enumerate) that this Scheme of Negro Schools properly conducted may have a good Effect. . . . [Robert Carter Nicholas to Associates, 1762]

[S]ent a List of thirty four Negro Children then at School in that City; tis, impossible for him to fix their Ages: but he Supposes them to be from about four to ten years, The Time of their Standing in the School, from the Mistress' Account which is not scrupulously exact, from about Six Months to Two Yrs & half. The Rules which He formerly drew up for the better government of the School, and which were approved of by the Associates, He wou'd gladly have observed, but soon found that the Masters & Mistresses were so averse to every

Thing that looked like Compulsion that He Thought it adviseable to relax a little in hopes that Things might be put upon a more agreable Footing. The present number exceeds what the Mistress stipulated to teach; for as it is not in her power to oblige them to attend constantly she is willing to instruct all such as offer themselves. The Owners, as soon as the Children are able to do little Offices about the House; either take them away from School entirely, or keep them from it at Times so that they attend only when there is no Employment for Them at Home. The Form He proposed for the Children to continue at school was three years at least, but few are allowed to stay so long; those who do generally learn to read pretty well, to say their prayers & the Catechism. He had lately visited the School and examined the Children, who seemed to have made a reasonable Progress. The Mistress is far advanced in years, & He is afraid the Business will soon be too laborious for Her: & how to Supply the school better He at present doth not know, for He is satisfied She takes a great deal of pains with the Children. He will not fail to encourage her and do everything he can to promote the success of so pious an Institution. [Robert Carter Nicholas to Associates, 1765]

[Advises the Associates of Mrs. Wager's death] & wishes he could have revived the Charity on such Terms as wou'd be agreable to the Associates, but seeing no Prospect of it at present He has discon[tin]ued the School till he can receive further Directions. [Robert Carter Nicholas to Associates, 1774]

Document 13: A Revival in North Carolina: A Black Woman and Her White Mistress Pray Together

The Reverend James McCorkle, a Presbyterian minister, described in vivid detail a series of revivals that were held in North Carolina in 1802. Of particular interest are the participation by both blacks and whites in these revivals and the effects on the women and children. McCorkle himself had doubts about the confusion and disorder of the revivals, but then decided that the outcome of this particular meeting had to be the work of God.[26]

I NOW set down to give you a Narrative of the transactions at Randolph, commencing on Friday January 1, 1802, and continuing until the ensuing Tuesday.

On Thursday, the last day of the last year, I set out from home for Randolph, and lodged in Lexington with some preachers, and a number of people, mostly from Iredel, going on to the same place. The evening was spent in prayer, and exhortation without any visible effect. Next day the preachers arrived at the Randolph-meeting-house; but the Iredel company lodged 5 miles behind.

On Saturday in the interval of two sermons, the congregation (near 2000) were informed that the Iredel company were religiously exercised, in a sudden and surprising matter, at evening prayer in the family or house where they lodged.

This struck, with seriousness every reflecting mind, because the effect did not appear to arise from oratory or sympathy, the causes commonly assigned for this work.

The second sermon was delivered, and the benediction pronounced as usual: but the people paused as if they wished not to part, nor go either to their homes or encampments.

Just then rose a speaker to give a short parting exhortation: but wonderful to tell, as if by an electric shock, a large number in every direction men, women, children, white and black, fell and cried for mercy; while others appeared, in every quarter, either praying for the fallen, or exhorting bye-standers to repent and believe.

This, to me perfectly new and sudden sight, I viewed with horror; and, in spite of all my previous reasoning on Revivals, with some degree of disgust. Is it possible, said I, that this scene of seeming confusion can come from the Spirit of God? or can he who called light from darkness, and order from confusion educe light and order from such a dark mental, or moral chaos as this! Lord God, thou knowest.

The first particular object that arrested my attention was a poor black man with his hands raised over the heads of the crowd, and shouting "Glory glory to God on high." I hasted towards him from the preaching-tent; but was stopt to see another black man prostrate on the ground, and his aged mother on her knees at his feet in all the agony of prayer for her son. Near him was a black woman, grasping her mistress' hand, and crying "O mistress you prayed for me when I wanted a heart to pray for myself. Now thank God he has given me a heart to pray for you and every body else.

I then passed to a little white girl, about 7 years old. She was reclining with his [her] eyes closed on the arms of a female friend. But O what a serene angelic smile was in her face! If ever heaven was enjoyed in any little creature's heart it was enjoyed in her's. Were I to form some notion of an angel, it would aid my conception to think of her.

I took her by the hand, and asked how she felt, she raised her head, opened her eyes, closed them, and gently sunk into her former state.

I met her next day with 2 or 3 of her little companions, I asked her how she felt yesterday? O how happy," said the dear little creature, with an ineffable smile, and I feel so happy now, I wish every body was as happy as I am."

I asked her several questions relative to her views of sin, a Saviour, happiness and heaven; and she answered with propriety, and as I thought rather from proper present feelings than from past doctrinal or educational information: for when I was afterwards called to examine her in order to communion. I found her defective in this kind of knowledge, and dissuaded her from communicating at that time, tho' she much desired it. This I have since regretted, for I do believe, on cool reflection that she possessed that experimental knowledge of salvation, which is infinitely preferable to all the doctrinal or systematic knowledge in the world without it. But to return.

I pressed through the congregation in a circuitous direction to the preaching tent, viewing one in the agony of prayer; another motionless, speechless, and apparently breathless; another rising in triumph, in prayer and exhortation. Among these was a woman 5 hours motionless, and a little boy under 12 years of age who arose, prayed and exhorted in a wonderful manner. After themselves I observed that their next concern was their nearest relations. . . .

Natural affections begin with self, and then spread around: so do the affections that shew themselves in this work. First what shall I do to be saved. Then O my child, my brother, or sister, "Repent and believe." Surely this must be the work of God, and marvellous in our eyes!

Black Women and Religion in the Colonial Period

LILLIAN ASHCRAFT WEBB

Black women, brought as slaves to North America in the seventeenth and eighteenth centuries, responded to conditions of servitude from perspectives of their West African cultural heritage. It is important, therefore, to understand this African background when assessing black women's interactions with religious forces in colonial America, particularly in English Protestant territories.

AFRICAN BACKGROUND

In most West African tribes, women were persons in their own right, with responsibilities and privileges not always based on their husbands' and fathers' patriarchal powers. Women controlled marketplaces, and their economic monopoly provided them with leverage for autonomous activity and with opportunities for leadership experiences.

In religious ceremonies, for example, women frequently were priests and leaders of cults. They sometimes maintained secret societies of their own. Whatever was the extent of West African women's participation in society beyond the marketplace and the immediate residential compound, it was based on realities of their economic initiative and contribution. These helped refine and solidify communal sharing and group identification.

Traditional religious systems permeated all facets of life in Africa, blurring distinctions between sacred and secular. Religious laws regulated sexual relationships, marriage rituals and responsibilities, and ceremonies of passage through puberty. They prescribed women's activities during pregnancy and shortly after childbirth, regulated dietary habits, and provided for lifetime continuance of sexual and other physical and psychological nurture.[1] Religious beliefs and practices primarily were localized tribally and were inherited from ancestors, but several tribes often shared similar elements and patterns of beliefs, practices, and rituals.

EUROPEAN REACTIONS

European Christians had inherited strict monogamous views on sexuality. Believing themselves to have a monopoly on virtue and right-living, they curiously devoured licentious travel narratives about life in Africa. People in Africa, unlike their European contemporaries, practiced pragmatic approaches to human sexuality such as arranging for the fulfullment of sexual needs "in absentia" when spouses were deceased or otherwise away. Some tribes adhered to a system of levirate—a widow's being inherited by her brother-in-law. This insured that: (1) widows would have "continuity" in "mating with the deceased husband," and (2) the children of the deceased would have the presence of a father figure and an assured share in the deceased father's inheritance (Document 1).[2] Several societies with disproportionately high female populations assured virtually all women benefits of marriage through polygamy.[3] (Polyandry was of negligible dimensions by the sixteenth century in Africa.) Such institutional practices as these offended Western Christian sensibilities, and explorers fueled European ethnocentrism by circulating narratives that described Africans as savages.

Religious fervor that had only smoldered in sixteenth-century Europe caught ablaze in the seventeenth century, and the African narratives had an especially disquieting effect upon English settlers in the American wildernesses.

> The age was driven by the twin spirits of adventure and control . . . [with] voyages of discovery overseas . . . [and] inward voyages of [self-]discovery. . . . [Within] this charged atmosphere of self-disocvery, . . . Englishmen . . . used peoples overseas as social mirrors, . . . and . . . they were especially inclined to discover attributes in . . . [those] they called savages which they found first but could not speak of in themselves.[4]

Although Winthrop Jordan made this statement to describe English religious zealots, it remains valid when applied to other seventeenth-century Euro-Americans.

The most probable frontal attack upon populations introduced into a male-oriented and -dominated society is that of denigrating the image of the "conquered" people's males. From that assault there follows aspersions upon the women. Europeans looked at blacks through stereotypes and not as human beings with individual strengths and weaknesses in character.

Prior to the importation of African women, settlers already had begun differentiating among character types when assigning work to European female servants (Document 2). Because of their own Christian piety, their acceptance of rumors that Africans were savage, and their need for cheap labor, colonists arbitrarily presumed that every black woman was "nasty' and "beastly." Consequently, the colonial mind was set early in the seventeenth century to be insensitive to individual black character or sex when assigning work.

SEVENTEENTH-CENTURY BLACK EXPERIENCES

African women's initial experiences with the "churched" in North America was one of exclusion from church membership. The Anglican-dominated legislature in Virginia, for example, enacted a law that distinguished between servants. European servants were designated "Christian," and African laborers were referred to as "Negro servants" (implying that they were non-Christian).[5] Colonists underscored the distinction by neglecting to bring "Negro servants" into the Christian church, sometimes legislating against black church attendance and discouraging black conversions. Settlors took these steps in an effort to protect their property (their black servants) since they were uncertain that Christianized servants could be held in bondage.

Ever since the Diet of Worms (1521), "the notion half-lurking . . . was that baptism and consequent conversion to Christianity affected the freedom of a slave." This posed a problem, but on the surface it seemed easily resolved. If masters did not teach Africans to be Christians, they could "justly" enslave them for the purpose of Christianizing them at some future, undesignated time. That way pious masters were less disturbed in their consciences, believing they had complied with the letter of the Diet and with the spirit of English Common Law by bringing Africans into geographical proximity to Christianity.[6] One clergyman's extrapolation was representative of that generation's thinking; according to him, "perpetual bondage among Christians made useful servants of savages."[7]

Whenever colonists introduced Christianity to Africans, black women quickly played a prominent role. Many already had Spanish Christian names when imported (Angela, for example). This indicated, according to one social scientist, that a number of Africans previously had been baptized. More recently, though, Murray Heller (editor of a study of black names) concluded to the contrary: "It appears . . . that whether or not baptism was involved, whites tended to supply their black slaves, to a great extent, with biblical and Christian names."[8] The second, recorded Spanish-christened woman imported to North America from Africa was Isabella. Her "brush" with Christianity is among the earliest written accounts mentioning an African woman. She arrived on the first shipment of African "servants" to dock at a North American port. (Anthony —also spelled variously—whom she later married, was also on that vessel, which sailed into Jamestown in 1619.)

A brief entry (1624–1625) in parish church records mentions: "Anthony, negro, Isabell, a negro, and William, her child, baptized."[9] Whether or not this was a family baptism into Christianity is unclear.

Probably William only was ceremonially baptized as the first child born to African parents in North America. St. George Tucker noted in his dissertation on slavery that whether baptized or not, Negroes were uniformly reported as infidels.[10]

Before African women were imported to America, adultery and rape were legally punishable by death and fornication by whipping. The legislation charged local church parishes with publishing and enforcing that code (Document 3). It is doubtful that the law ever was applied to curb the raping of black women by white men. Whipping was a common form of punishment during the colonial period, but local church parishes seemed less reluctant to whip black women than white men for sexual offenses. A point of reference is the 1640 Sweet case in which the white man (Sweet) was found guilty of getting a black woman servant pregnant. She was whipped, and he was sentenced to public penance.[11] The close association between church officials and unfair penal enforcements is not likely to have gone unobserved by black women, even those most recently arrived from Africa.

Massachusetts, though close on the heels of Virginia in practicing and instituting slavery, was the first recorded English colony to accept an adult of African ancestry into full fellowship among Christians. John Winthrop recorded in his memoirs that a black woman, after having proven her "true godliness" over many years, was baptized and communed into the Puritan congregation in 1641.[12] Black conversion to Christianity in North American colonies was token and generally without positive impact upon white attitudes towards Africans.

By 1660, Massachusetts, Virginia, and other English colonies already established at that time had taken steps to make slavery a legal, self-perpetuating institution. Intending to settle the question of whether or not converted slaves should be freed, Virginia passed legislation in 1662 which stated that children would inherit their mothers' social statuses—not their religious conditions.[13] Still not certain that Christians could be enslaved, for there was no English positive law to that effect, Virginia enacted legislation which prohibited a slave's status from being altered because he or she was baptized.[14]

The Church of England kept its distance while these disincentives to Christian conversion were imposed on African slaves. Their avaricious owners jealously guarded slave property against the potentially enlightening influences of Christian teachings. Eventually, an evangelizing unit was organized—the Council for Foreign Plantations—for the purpose of converting Africans and Indians. After 1660, the restored crown tried to centralize English authority. In 1661, 1680, and 1682, the crown urged royal colonies to support the council as it introduced ministers who would specialize in the work of converting Negroes and Indians to Christianity.[15]

Not even Quakers, however, expressed full awareness of the evils of slavery, although the system was crystallizing into an ominous institution by the mid-seventeenth century. Though Fox and other Quakers showed concern over the plight of slaves, they accepted slavery as a *fait accompli* and encouraged those of their faith to give slaves religious instruction and to take slaves to meetings.[16] In 1672, Virginia and other colonies enacted stalemating legislation that forbade Negro attendance at Quaker meetings.[17]

Black women more frequently were identified as converts than black men. Before the turn of the eighteenth century, "free" black women were motivated to join churches. Ginney Bess was one of the first identified by name to take her child for baptism. Her action, in 1683, probably indicates that she had been baptized at a time previous to presenting her child for this sacrament.[18] Reasons for joining churches were numerous. DuBois (and, more recently, Alex Haley) conjectured that African women usually made the initial breakthrough to "accept" Christianity, hoping their conversion would benefit them and their families. Masters of slaves commented that the birth of children (those born in America) motivated black women to embrace Christianity.[19]

Sometimes women as well as men sought asylum from harsh masters in Catholic Florida under the guise of being anxious for baptism and religious instruction. Spanish Florida was a refuge for the alert and enterprising from nearby colonies.[20]

"Witchcraft mania" spread throughout the Christian world during the seventeenth century. Congregationalists, believing "powers of the devil could be executed by human witches," seemed particularly prone to this witchcraft mania, and it assumed noticeable proportions beginning in 1647 in Connecticut and climaxing in 1692 at Salem. A black woman servant named Marja was one of its first victims. Marja was accused of conspiring with two men to burn down a building in Roxbury, Massachusetts. She alone was executed by burning at the stake because she did "not . . . have 'the feare of God before her eyes' [and her actions were] 'instigated by the divil.' " Her punishment was unusually harsh and of the genre mostly reserved for those thought to be devil-possessed. The severity of the punishment was an apparent indication that paranoia had set into the colony, that social instability prevailed there, and that a mind-set fixed on impending "spiritual" doom abounded.

In Salem, the epidemic was related to the failure of Puritans to put forth a concerted effort to Christianize African people. It was compounded by a decline in old-fashioned piety and by conflicting social interests. A major character in the Salem hysteria was a half-Indian, half-African slave woman named Tituba, whom the town's pastor had imported from Barbados. As she worked to complete household chores, Tituba unraveled tales about witches, demons, and ghosts, holding the pastor's daughter and other teenage girls in rapt attention. Soon the impressionable girls began to experiment with fortune-telling. Feeling guilty about their activities, the girls began to believe themselves to be punished for being "tools of the devil." They imagined themselves the victims of witchcraft and pointed accusing fingers at townsfolk, setting off a panic. The hysteria ended with trials, during which twenty residents were executed. One hundred fifty others, including Tituba and another Negro servant, Mary Black, were jailed. Both were later released, and Tituba was sold to pay for her jail expenses. Her quick confession "exorcised" the evil spirits from her body and saved her life. "Clemency" for Tituba suggests that the real source of the furor was elsewhere. It lends credence to recent interpretations which indicate that no small amount of the confusion was touched off by conflicting class interests and religious tensions in the Puritan town (Document 4).

EIGHTEENTH-CENTURY BLACK EXPERIENCES

In the wake of the Salem trials, a group of slaves in Massachusetts requested (in 1693) that Cotton Mather organize them into a body for weekly religious instruction and worship.[21] Only in 1701 did leadership within the Church of England form a united drive to evangelize and teach among slaves. This missionary band was called the Society for the Propagation of the Gospel (SPG). The SPG operated out of London and was financially independent of local church parishes. As a result, the SPG bypassed usual problems that individual pastors often had encountered and took its preachments more successfully into slave communities. The SPG appointed some 30 missionaries and catechists to preach and teach a gospel with emphasis on morality and ritual. Although the SPG owned slaves in its early years and took the position that emancipation was not a mandatory result of conversion, settlers were suspicious that the intentions of the society were to initiate the first step toward freedom for black slaves.[22]

The SPG was not intentionally sexist in its conversion program. But it did make special appeal to males and provided an all-male leadership role model. Moreover, missionaries and catechists sometimes directed lessons in reading and writing to particularly apt male youths, grooming them to become teachers (tutors) among other black slaves. Many women and girls, nevertheless, were numbered among SPG missionaries' acclaimed converts (Documents 5.)[23]

Missionaries soon became aware of African cultural retentions among slaves. Discussion of this problem took place in missionary reports to the SPG headquarters in London about, for example, polygamous tendencies, male separations from women who either could not or had not given birth as a result of their mating, and the women's frequent changing of "husbands." These reports revealed the cultural parochialism typical among Anglican clergy (Document 6).[24] Their consternation, however, inspired legislation to "regularize" marriage procedures and to control immorality among slaves.[25] The clergy complained that white settlers were poor exemplars of moral virtue.[26]

White women in New York City tried to alleviate social repression against women of African ancestry. Much of this repression was caused by the colonist's belief that African women could not become productive or responsible for their behavior outside of slavery. These white women reflected the influence of Enlightenment thought, which stressed possibilities for improving the social environment—both people and institutions.

In 1712, the white women opened a school to "train" black women, hoping they would be socially responsible and assimilable. Alleged "Negro plots" to burn down the city and massacre white colonists fueled fear of blacks and renewed urgency to restrict their social mobility. These controls apparently brought about the demise of the 1712 school movement, but several other schools for Negro women were opened in 1740 and later in the century.[27]

The Great Awakenings, which highlighted American sectarianism and fragmented Anglican SPG activity around mid-century, also gave Africans/Afro-Americans an opportunity for virtually unrestricted participation in Christianity in North America for the first time. During the religious ferment and widespread conversion experiences, white antislavery sentiment and black assertiveness intensified. In 1743, for example, a black woman and her husband sued a white man for trespassing upon her character. They made clear their understanding that a Christian woman's (including a black woman's) moral reputation should not be impugned without legal challenge. The suit also indicated the extent to which Christian puritanism had seeped into the black community, causing the ostracism of reputedly immoral black folk (Document 7).

Popular Great Awakening evangelists, such as George Whitefield, commented on the enthusiasm with which Negroes, particularly women, received the gospel and its messrngers (Document 8). John Wesley, himself an antislavery advocate, noted in his Diary that the first Negroes that he baptized into Methodism were two women slaves. Yet sentiment against slave conversions still abounded, and circuit riders had to urge owners to send slaves to religious instruction and to worship. Quakers and other antislavery groups increased their proclamations and other active challenges to the institution of slavery.

The best-known black Christian writer in the prerevolution decade was Phillis Wheatley. Her writings suggest that she had been accepted into membership in Boston's Old South Meeting House before 1769 when her pastor, Reverend Sewall, died.[28] By the time she was eighteen (1772), Miss Wheatley showed herself to be a fully converted, zealous Congregationalist. Her writings, when analyzed from the perspective of one's conversion, indicate that Phillis rejoiced in the psychological succor of her Christian faith and had little awareness of her African background. In this respect, hers was not a singular reaction, even among slaves. Missionaries of the period said of slave converts, "They will ever bless God for their knowing good things which they knew not before [their enslavement]." Phillis's letters—rather than her poems, which have been overly politicized by biographers—demonstrate her responsiveness to Christian conversion (Document 9).

In other ways, black women who came of age under the tutelage of American colonial evangelistic and missionary zeal, claimed rights to creative religious action (Document 10). Katherine Ferguson, organizer of the first Sabbath school for children in New York City, is one example. In her early years, Katy's mistress was a Christian woman who permitted the young slave girl to attend church services. This early involvement probably accounted in part for Miss Ferguson's later religious devotion and charitable efforts as much as her having been purchased by a sympathetic friend when she was sixteen. Although she herself never learned to read or write, she helped to make such learning available to children from the poorhouse without regard to race or color. Having been separated from her own mother at the age of eight, she expressed an affinity for reaching out to children from destitute backgrounds, to neglected youths and unwed mothers. Her "work contributed to the development of free secular education for the poor. For this reason, her name is noted among those considered pioneer educators in America. . . . In tribute to Katy and in recognition of her early contributions, a home for unwed mothers—the Katy Ferguson Home—in New York was named in her honor" (Document 11). Wives and women converts of pioneering black preachers and church pastors were among the more obscure missionaries and charitable workers at the turn of the century (Document 12).

Ironically, the century closed with discordant tones from the ranks of Quakerism. Several black women applied for membership into that faith. They were subjected to prolonged monthly, quarterly, and annual meetings where their applications were scrutinized, tabled, and kept in committee for months before the women eventually were admitted. It is possible that they never would have been admitted, except that they were mulattos (Document 13).

Sarah Johnson, who died in 1845 after a life that spanned more than a century, is an example of the black Christian of this period. The poignancy of black women's religious experiences in North American colonies is summarized in the black pastor's eulogizing at her funeral. In a manner characteristic of Christian clergy, her African Methodist Episcopal pastor referred continuously to what was commendable that he had observed in her outward behavior (Document 14).

Slave dance, possibly at a wedding. The use of canes and scarfs reflect African customs, and the head scarfs resemble West African Yoruba cloth. One musician plays an African molo, a precursor of the banjo, while another taps a gudu-gudu drum. The painting, circa 1700, is reproduced courtesy the Abby Aldrich Rockefeller Folk Art Collection, Williamsburg, Virginia.

English settlements in the West Indies, like their North American counterparts, occasioned black women active in religious affairs. One such was Maria, a Moravian missionary from St. Thomas. She died in 1749. [From *Herrnhut: Ursprung und Auftrag* (Hamburg: Friedrich Wittig Verlag, 1972), no. 39.]

Phillis Wheatley (1753–1784), poetess. This portrait appeared as the frontispiece of her poems published in 1773. [From Linda de Pauw and Conover Hunt, *Remember the Ladies: Women in America, 1750–1815* (New York: Viking, 1976), p. 141.]

Elizabeth Freeman (Mumbet), a slave in Massachusetts who won her suit for freedom under the United States Constitution, which says that all *men* are created free and equal. Portrait by Susan Sedgwick, courtesy the Massachusetts Historical Society, Boston.

Documents: Black Women and Religion in the Colonial Period

1. ***An African Leviratic Statement***
2. ***Kinds of Work for Servants***
3. ***Punishments Prescribed for Colonial Sexual Offenders***
4. ***Tituba's Testimony in the Salem Witchcraft Trials***
5. ***Black Religious Instruction in New York City: A Tally (1705)***
6. ***African Polygamy Versus Western Christianity: SPG Missionary Letters***
7. ***A Black Christian Woman Sues a White Man for Slander***
8. ***A Woman Convert Comforts George Whitefield***
9. ***Evangelical Zeal in the Letters of Phillis Wheatley***
10. ***A Pastoral Recommendation of a Black Woman***
11. ***Katherine Ferguson—Sabbath School Founder***
12. ***Defending a Corps of Black Nurses***
13. ***Quaker Reluctance to Accept Black Women into Membership***
14. ***Funeral Sermon for Sarah Johnson***

Document 1: An African Leviratic Statement

Leviratic customs, which once thrived across the continent, have been preserved in sections of East Africa (Tanzania and Kenya). The legal statement below is a contemporary Luo (Bantu descendants) expression of this centuries-old custom.[29]

When a husband dies his widow may either: (A) continue to live in her deceased husband's home, in which case she may cohabit with either (1) one of her dead husband's brothers, (2) one of her husband's male relatives, or (3) any man who has been adopted into the deceased husband's clan, though originally a stranger, e.g., a *Jadak Mocham Musuma*. However, her choice is subject to the approval of the family and clan elders . . . of her deceased husband. If she cohabits with a man of whom they do not approve, the man may be sued by the . . . [clan elders] for adultery.

The children of a levirate union belong to the family of the dead husband.

(B) return to her father's home. In such a case the . . . (bridewealth) may be returnable according to the number of children the widow has. . . . However, a widow may *not* return to her father's home before she first cohabits (even though for a very short period) with someone under (A) above, i.e., a leviratic union must be formed before a widow can sever her connections with the late husband's clan, and go back to her father.

Document 2: Kinds of Work for Servants

The tasks assigned to servants were among the Reverend John Hammond's several observations on the English colonial scene. In this excerpt, he specifies that women, more than men, were given tasks on the basis of their behavior and reputation.[30]

The labour servants are put to is not hard nor of such continuance as Husbandmen, nor Handecraftmen are kept at in England, I said little or nothing is done in winter time, none ever work before sun rising nor after sun set, in the summer they rest, sleep or exercise themselves five houres in the heat of the day, Saturdayes afternoon is alwayes their own, the old Holidayes are observed and the Sabboath spent in good exercises.

The Women are not (as is reported) put into the ground to worke, but occupie such domestique imployments and houswifery as in England, that is dressing victuals, righting up the house, milking, imployed about dayries, washing, soeing, &c. and both men and women have times of recreations, as much or more than in any part of the world besides, yet som wenches that are nasty, beastly and not fit to be so imployed are put into the ground, for reason tells us, they must not at charge be transported and then maintained for nothing, but those that prove so aukward are rather burthensome then servants desirable or usefull.

Document 3: Punishments Prescribed for Colonial Sexual Offenders

The punishments meted out for sexual infractions during the colonial period, particularly in early the Virginian settlement, are noteworthy because: (1) they were extended to masters and mistresses as well as to servants, and (2) local church parishes were the chief administrators of such applicable laws. These two points are evident in following codes, which were designated by settlers before they left England.[31]

11. He or she that can be lawfully convicted of Adultery shall be punished with death. No man shall ravish or force any woman, maid or Indian, or other, upon pain of death, and know ye that he or shee, that shall commit fornication, and evident proffe made therof, for their first fault shall be whipt, for their second they shall be whipt, and for their third they shall be whipt three times a week for one month, and aske publique forgiveness in the Assembly of the Congregation.

19. Every minister or Preacher shall every Sabboth day before Catechising, read all these lawes and ordinances, publikely in the assembly of the congregation upon paine of his entertainment checkt for that weeke.

Document 4: Tituba's Testimony in the Salem Witchcraft Trials

*Witchcraft trials began in Salem, Massachusetts, in 1692, when a black West Indian slave, Tituba, was accused of bewitching the children of Mr. Samuel Paris. Tituba testified that the devil, which at times appeared to her in the shape of various animals, had come to her as a man with white hair and dressed in black. He had told her that he was God and that she must serve him six years. He had shown her a book, and she had made a mark in it, "red like blood." There were nine other marks in the book, two of them made by Salem women, Good and Osborne. Tituba also described night-riding on the stick in the company of Good and Osborne and two other witches from Boston. This detailed confession set the stage for a proliferation of examinations and trials in Salem. Two different accounts of Tituba's testimony have been preserved. The following version was taken from two contemporary commentators on the Witchcraft trials at Salem: Robert Calef (*More Wonders of the Invisible World, 1700*) and John Hale (*A Modest Inquiry into the Nature of Witchcraft, *1702).*[32]

The first complain'd of, was the said Indian Woman, named Tituba. She confessed that the Devil urged her to sign a Book, which he presented to her, and also to work Mischief to the Children, etc. She was afterwards Committed to Prison, and lay there till Sold for her Fees. The account she since gives of it is, that her Master did beat her and otherways abuse her, to make her confess and accuse (such as he call'd) her Sister-Witches, and that whatsoever she said by way of confessing or accusing others, was the effect of such usage; her Mas-ter refused to pay her Fees, unless she would stand to what she had said . . .

I. In the latter end of the year 1601, Mr. Samuel Paris, Pastor of the Church in Salem-Village, had a Daughter of Nine, and a Neice of about Eleven years of Age, sadly Afflicted of they knew not what Distempers: and he made his application to Physitians, yet still they grew worse: And at length one Physitian gave his opinion, that they were under an Evil Hand. This the Neighbours quickly took up, and concluded they were bewitched. He had also an Indian Man servant, and his Wife who afterwards confessed, that without the knowledge of their Master or Mistress, they had taken some of the Afflicted persons Urine, and mixing it with meal had made a Cake, and baked it, to find out the Witch, as they said. After this, the Afflicted Persons cryed out of the Indian Woman, named Tituba, that she did pinch, prick, and grievously torment them, and that they saw her here and there, where no body else could. Yea they could tell where she was, and what she did, when out of their humane sight. These Children were bitten and pinched by invisible agents; their arms, necks, and backs turned this way and that way, and returned back again, so as it was impossible for them to do of themselves, and beyond the power of any Epileptick Fits, or natural Disease to effect. Sometimes they were taken dumb, their mouths stopped, their throats choaked, their limbs wracked and tormented so as might move an heart of stone, to sympathize with them, with bowels of compassion for them.

. . . Paris seeing the distressed condition of his Family, desired the presence of some Worthy Gentlemen of Salem, and some Neighbour Ministers to consult together at his House; who when they came, and had enquired diligently into the Sufferings of the Afflicted, concluded they were preternatural, and feared the hand of Satan was in them.

II. The advice given to Mr. Paris by them was, that he should sit still and wait upon the Providence of God to see what time might discover; and to be much in prayer for the discovery of what was yet secret. They also Examined Tituba, who confessed the making a Cake, as is above mentioned, and said her Mistress in her own Country was a Witch, and had taught her some means to be used for the discovery of a Witch and for the prevention of being bewitched, etc. But said that she her self was not a Witch.

... In a short time after other persons who were of age to be witnesses, were molested by Satan, and in their fits cryed out upon Tituba and Goody O. and S. G. that they or Specters in their Shapes did grievously torment them; hereupon some of their Village Neighbours complained to the Magistrates at Salem, desiring they would come and examine the afflicted and accused together; the which they did: the effect of which examination was, that Tituba confessed she was a Witch, and that she with the two others accused did torment and bewitch the complainers, and that these with two others whose names she knew not, had their Witch-meeting together; relating the times when and places where they met, with many other circumstances to be seen at large. Upon this the said Tituba and O. and S. G. were committed to Prison upon suspicion of acting Witchcraft. After this the said Tituba was again examined in Prison, and owned her first confession in all points, and then was her self afflicted and complained of her fellow Witches tormenting of her, for her confession, and accusing them, and being searched by a Woman, she was found to have upon her body the marks of the Devils wounding of her.

IV. Here were these things rendred her confession creditable. (1). That at this examination she answered every question just as she did at the first. And it was thought that if she had feigned her confession, she could not have remembred her answers so exactly.

... (2). She seemed very penitent for her Sin in convenanting with the Devil. (3.) She became a sufferer her self and as she said for her confession. (4.) Her confession agreed exactly (which was afterwards verified in the other confessors) with the accusations of the afflicted. Soon after these afflicted persons complained of other persons afflicting of them in their fits, and the number of the afflicted and accused began to increase. And the success of Tituba's confession encouraged those in Authority to examine others that were suspected, and the event was, that more confessed themselves guilty of the Crimes they were suspected for. And thus was this matter driven on.

Document 5: Black Religious Instruction in New York City: A Tally (1705)

On October 3, 1705, missionary and catechist Elias Neau wrote a letter to the headquarters of the Society for the Propagation of the Gospel (SPG) from his assignment in New York. In that letter, he included a chart that indicated the numbers of black women who had received religious instruction. Neau had been appointed to his position in April, and he went from door to door, trying to convince masters and mistresses to send their slaves and servants to catechism classes. His intention in constructing the following chart was to list for SPG officials the names of prominent whites who were supportive of the society's program, but in addition, Neau reveals that more women than men attended sessions.[33]

Master/Mistress	*Women Sent*	*Men Sent*	*Catechisms Given*	*Other Books*
My Lord Cornbury	1 Mulatress	0	2	2
Mr. Vesey	2 Negresses	0	2	2.2 letters
	2 Negresses	1 Indian	3	3.3 letters
	1 Negress	0	1	1 letter
Mrs. Widow Keep	1 Negress	0	1	1.1 letters
	1 Negress	0	1	1.1 letters
	1 Negress	0	1	1.1 letters
Mr. Joseph Smith	1 Negress	0	1	1.1 letters
	1 Negress	1 Negro	2	2.2 letters
	1 Negress	1 Negro	2	2.2 letters
	0	1 Negro	1	2.2 letters
	0	1 Negro	1	1.1 letters
	1 Negress	0	1	1.1 letter
	0	1 Negro	1	1.1 letter
Mrs. Jourdain	1 Negress	0	1	1.1 letter
Mr. Fauconnier	1 Negress	1 Negro	2	
		1 Negro	1	
		1 Negro	1	
		1 Negro	1	
		1 Negro	1	
Mr. Abraham Keep	1 Negress	0	1	
	1 Negress	1 Negro	2	
	1 Negress	0	1	
	1 Negress	0	1	
	1 Negress	0	1	
	1 Negress	0	1	
	1 Negress	0	1	
	1 Negress	0	1	
	1 Negress	0	1	
		1 Negro	1	
		1 Negro	1	
	1 Negress	0	1	
	1 Negress	0	1	
	1 Negress	0	1	
Mrs. Van Vosse		3 Negroes	2	
Mrs. Marcomb	1 she Indian	2 Indians	2	
Totals:	27 Negresses/ Mulatresses	15 Negros		

Document 6: African Polygamy Versus Western Christianity: SPG Missionary Letters

The Reverend Francis Le Jau was a missionary assigned to Goose Creek Parish Anglican Church in South Carolina from 1706 to 1717. He expressed his concern that slaves who had received rudiments of religious instruction often still did not fully understand the moral precepts of Christianity when they applied for baptism and communion. What he thought were polygamous practices that persisted among slaves who professed Christianity compelled him to present repeatedly the matter to SPG headquarters. The following excerpts from two letters written by Le Jau, dated 1708 and 1709, presents his views. In addition, a third excerpt, from a letter written by the Reverend Elias Neau (SPG missionary in New York) and dated July 4, 1714, also reflects Anglo-cultural perspectives via the medium of pastoral concern.[34]

. . . Whether or no we are not to answer for grievous sins dayly Committed by all our Slaves here & elsewhere, and tolerated or at least Connived at by us under a pretence of Impossibility to remedy them; tho' I'm sure we cou'd prevent all those evils if we wou'd take pains about it; . . . The evil I complain of is the constant and promiscuous cohabiting of Slaves of different Sexes and Nations together; When a Man or Woman's fancy dos alter about his Party they grow up one another & take others which they also change when they please this is a General Sin, for exceptions are so few they are hardly worth mentioning. [Rev. Francis Le Jau, September 15, 1708]

Since I came I baptised in all two adults and 47 children. . . . On Sunday next I design God willing to baptise two very sensible and honest Negro men whom I have kept upon tryal these two Years. Several others have spoken to me also; I do nothing too hastily in that respect. I instruct them and must have honest life and sober Conversation. . . .

One of the most scandoulous and common crimes of our slaves is their perpetual Changing Wives and husbands, which occasions great disorders: I also tell them whom I baptise, "The Christian Religion dos not allow plurality of Wives, nor any changing of them: You promise truly to keep to the Wife you now have till Death dos part you." [Rev. Francis Le Jau, October 20, 1709]

. . . A man married his Brother's Wife because said he she had no children by him. Now I humbly ask whether the ceremony can make such a Marriage Lawfull. My opinion is that it cannot be lawful and I will not commune them. [Rev. Elias Neau from New York, July 4, 1714]

Document 7: A Black Christian Woman Sues a White Man for Slander

During the fervor of the Great Awakening, a white man verbally attacked a black woman, calling her a "damned Negro whore." She and her husband filed suit, seeking payment for damages done to her Christian reputation in the black community. Unfortunately, the outcome of this case is unknown.[35]

Bucks County Courts September term in the Year of our Lord one thousand seven hundred and forty-five.

Adam Jourdan was attach'd to answer William Hood and Elizabeth his wife of a plea of trespas . . . and where upon the said William and Elizabeth by John Cox their attorney Complain that whereas the said Elizabeth is a good true faithfull and honest . . . Subject of our Lord the King . . . from her nativity hitherto hath behaved . . . herself and [is] of good name fame Creditt and reputation as well amongst her neighbours . . . with whom [she] allways hath been, free from all manner of Incontinence Adultery or the Suspicion thereof . . . not undeservedly obtained, Nevertheless the said Adam not being ignorant of the promisses but well knowing the same and Envying the happy State and Condition of her the said Elizabeth but Contriving and Intending . . . her good name, fame, Creditt and Reputation to hurt, and to bring her into the hate and Evil Opinion of all her Neighbours and other . . . Subjects of our said Lord the King but also innocently to Cause her to be brought into Danger of the pains and penalties Enacted and Proscribed by the laws of the province of Pennsylvania for the punishment of persons guilty of the Crime of Adultery the twenty fourth Day of June in the year of our Lord one thousand seven hundred and forty five at Newton in the County of Bucks and within the jurisdiction of this Court in the presence & hearing of severall . . . Subjects of our said Lord the King falsly Scandalously & publickly did say and with a loud voice publish malitiously to the said William Hood . . . of the said Elizabeth his Wife these false, Scandalous & Defamatory English Words Viz. Take your damned Negro whore . . . home with you, . . . upon which the aforesaid William Hood than & therebeing present, answering said, to the said Adam, No, I have no Negro Whore to take home, to which the said Adam then and there in the hearing of the Subjects aforesaid Said & replied "you, . . . Sent your damned Negro whore of a wife, . . . to abuse my folkes—go you son of a whore, . . . with her . . . to Maryland, and bring the Negro bastard home with [you]. . . , pronouncing and publishing of . . . English words, the same Elizabeth not only in her good name, fame, reputation Estimation, & Creditt amongst her aforesaid acquaintance is greatly hurt, Scandaliz'd, degenerated and . . . fell in great disgrace so that divers Creditable persons of her Neighbourhood and other faithfull Subjects of our said . . . Lord the King with whom the said Elizabeth before that had Conversation and Acquaintance, . . . have refused to have any further Conversation or Acquaintance . . . with her in any manner to Converse and have withdrawn themselves from the Conversation of the same Elizabeth as from a whore and more & more had kept themselves from the Conversation of the same Elizabeth with whom she had used to Converse . . . to the Damage of them the said William & Elizabeth forty pounds proclamation money and thereof they bring this Suit &C.

Coxe atty.

Document 8: A Woman Convert Comforts George Whitefield

During a return trip to North America in the late 1740s, George Whitefield suffered a grave illness. In the following passage, he tells of the loving concern a black woman convert showed for him and of her "prophecy" that he would recover.[36]

. . . Such affects followed the word, I thought it worth dying for a thousand a times. Though wonderfully comforted within, at my return home, I thought I was dying indeed. I was laid on a bed upon the ground, near the fire, and I heard my friends say, "He is gone." But God was pleased to order it otherwise. I gradually recovered; and soon after, a poor negro-woman would see me. She came, sat down upon the ground, and looked earnestly in my face, and then said, in broken language; "Master, you just go to Heaven's gate. But Jesus Christ said, Get you down, get you down, you must not come here yet; but go first, and call some more poor Negroes."

Document 9: Evangelical Zeal in the Letters of Phillis Wheatley

Phillis Wheatley (1753–1784) was bought as a child from a slave ship by the wealthy Boston merchant, John Wheatley. Recognizing the girl's precocity, John Wheatley educated her and treated her more as a daughter than as a slave. In her teens, she was touted as a prodigy by Boston society because of both her youth and her race. She was even entertained by the Countess of Huntingdon in England, who arranged for the publication of her verses, including her elegy on George Whitefield. But, with the scattering of the Wheatley family by death and marriage, Phillis was forgotten and she died in poverty. In these two letters written to her friend, Arbour Tanner of Newport, Rhode Island, when she was nineteen, we see her zealous evangelical Christianity.[37]

Boston, May 19th, 1772

Dear Sister,—I rec'd your favour of February 6th for which I give you my sincere thanks. I greatly rejoice with you in that realizing view, and I hope experience of the saving change which you so emphatically describe. Happy were it for us if we could arrive to that evangelical Repentance, and the true holiness of heart which you mention. Inexpressibly happy should we be could we have a due sense of the beauties and excellence of the crucified Saviour. In his Crucifixion may be seen marvellous displays of Grace and Love, sufficient to draw and invite us to the rich and endless treasures of his mercy; let us rejoice in and adore the wonders of God's infinite Love in bringing us from a land semblant of darkness itself, and where the divine light of revelation (being obscur'd) is as darkness. Here the knowledge of the true God and eternal life are made manifest; but there, profound ignorance overshadows the land. Our observation is true, namely that there was nothing in us to recommend us to God. Many of our fellow creatures are pass'd by, when the bowels of divine love expanded towards us. May this goodness & long suffering of God lead us to unfeign'd repentance.

It gives me very great pleasure to hear of so many of my nation, seeking with eagerness the way of true felicity. O may we all meet at length in that happy mansion. I hope the correspondence between us will continue, (my being much indispos'd this winter past, was the reason of my not answering yours before now) which correspondence I hope may have the happy effect of improving our mutual friendship. Till we meet in the regions of consummate blessedness, let us endeavor by the assistance of divine grace, to live the life, and we shall die the death of the Righteous. May this be our happy case, and of those who are travelling to the region of Felicity, is the earnest request of your affectionate

FRIEND & HUMBLE SERVANT

PHILLIS WHEATLEY.

Boston, July 19th, 1772.

My Dear Friend,—I rec'd your kind epistle a few days ago; much disappointed to hear that you had not rec'd my answer to your first letter. I have been in a very poor state of health all the past winter and spring, and now reside in the country for the benefit of its more wholesome air. I came to town this morning to spend the Sabbath with my master and mistress. Let me be interested in your prayers that God would please to bless to me the means us'd for my recovery, if agreeable to his holy will. While my outward man languishes under weakness and pa[in], may the inward be refresh'd and strengthen'd more abundantly by him who declar'd from heaven that his strength was made perfect in weakness! May he correct our vitiated taste, that the meditation of him may be delightful to us. No longer to be so excessively charm'd with fleeting vanities: but pressing forward to the fix'd mark for the prize. How happy that man who is prepar'd for the night wherein no man can work! Let us be mindful of our high calling, continually on our guard, lest our treacherous hearts should give the adversary an advantage over us. O! who can think without horror of the snares of the Devil. Let us, by frequent meditation on the eternal Judgment, prepare for it. May the Lord bless to us these thoughts, and teach us by his Spirit to live to him alone, and when we leave this world may we be his. That this may be our happy case, is the sincere desire of, your affectionate friend, & humble serv't,

PHILLIS WHEATLEY.

Document 10: A Pastoral Recommendation of a Black Woman

The Reverend Georgie Liele, a former slave who acquired his freedom after the Revolutionary War, was pastor of the first Negro Baptist Church in Savannah, Georgia. When one of his members went to London, Liele wrote the following brief recommendation for her. Although the woman's social status is not specified here, she probably was a slave who was being relocated in London with the family that owned her.[38]

Kingston, Jamaica, we that are of the Baptist Religion, being separated from all churches, excepting they are of the same faith and order after Jesus Christ, according to the scriptures, do certify, that our beloved *Sister, Hannah Williams,* during the time she was a member of the Church at Savannah, until the evacuation, did walk as a faithful, well-behaved Christian, and to recommend her to join any church of the same faith and order. Given under my hand this 21st day of December, in the year of our Lord, 1791.
George Liele.

Document 11: Katherine Ferguson—Sabbath School Founder

By 1793, when she opened New York City's first Sabbath School, Katherine Ferguson had suffered many personal losses and heartaches. She had grown up in slavery without knowing her mother, and she had given birth to two children who died young. Out of this suffering emerged a woman who empathized with neglected and orphaned children. She is remembered in the sketch below, which was written by a woman who had known her.[39]

Katy Ferguson was known to me from my very young days as a comfortable-looking colored woman of firm Christian faith and consistent and useful religious life. Her occupation was the making of excellent cake such as was found in the pantries of the Old Dutch housewives of New York, whose daughters alone were able to compete with her skill.

. . . Others besides my self must call her to mind. Her cheery look and talk, her devoted Christian spirit, her benevolence could not but elicit respect. She professed her Christian faith in early life and became a member in full communion in the Old Scotch Presbyterian

Church . . . then under the pastorate of the Rev. John Mason, D.D. At that time race prejudice was so prevalent that the prescence of a colored person sitting, even at the Lord's table, and partaking of the elements side by side with the white members was looked upon with offishness. As a rebuke to this spirit, on the first Communion Sunday after her reception, as she entered the church Dr. Mason walked down the aisle to meet her, and taking her by the hand led her up and placed her in her seat at the table. Her name must still be enrolled in the list of church members in that church, now of course uptown.

I can recall her now in my mind as she started out, the basket on her arm, her hands clasped before her, her peaceful countenance shining because of her loving spirit. Her Sunday school was, I think, established in her own neat home, which was not, as I remember it, in the mean portion of the city. Her scholars were many poor white children. . . . As a school girl I often called on her on my way from school to my home in Fulton Street. I think her home was on one of the side streets leading to Broadway. Her cakes and her kindly, wholesome talk were her attractions.

Document 12: Defending a Corps of Black Nurses

The corps of nurses supplied by the African Church to nurse the sick and dying during Philadelphia's yellow fever epidemic was accused of stealing from and neglecting patients. In excerpts below, Richard Allen and Absalom Jones publicize the health risks and personal sacrifices that the women undertook to serve the community. Here the women's sense of Christian mission often surfaces.[40]

Sarah Bass, a poor black widow, gave all the assistance she could, in several families, for which she did not receive any thing; and when any thing was offered her, she left it to the option of those she served. . . .

A woman of our colour nursed Richard Mason and son; when they died, Richard's widow considering the risk the poor woman had run, and from observing the fears that sometimes rested on her mind, expected she would have demanded something considerable, but upon asking what she demanded, her reply was half a dollar per day. Mrs. Mason, intimated it was not sufficient for her attendance, she replied it was enough for what she had done, and would take no more. Mrs. Mason's feelings were such, that she settled an annuity of six pounds a year on her, for life. Her name is Mary Scott.

. . . An elderly black woman nursed ——— with great diligence and attention; when recovered he asked what he must give for her services—she replied "a dinner master on a cold winter's day," and thus she went from place to place rendering every service in her power without an eye for reward. . . .

A young black woman, was requested to attend one night upon a white man and his wife, who were very ill, no other person could be had;—great wages were offered her—she replied, I will not go for money, if I go for money God will see it, and may be make me take the disorder and die, but if I go, and take no money, he may spare my life. She went about nine o'clock, and found them both on the floor; she could procure no candle or other light, but stayed with them about two hours, and then left them. They both died that night. She was afterward very ill with the fever—her life was spared. . . .

It has been alledged, that many of the sick, were neglected by the nurses; we do not wonder at it, considering their situation, in many instances, up night and day, without any one to relieve them, worn down with fatigue, and want of sleep, they could not in many cases, render that assistance, which was needful. . . . The causes of complaint on this score, were not numerous. The case of the nurses, in many instances, were deserving of commiseration, the patient raging and frightful to behold; it has frequently required two persons, to hold them from running away; others have made attempts to jump out of a window, in many chambers they were nailed down, and the door was kept locked, to prevent them from running away, or breaking their necks, others lay vomiting blood, and screaming enough to chill them with horror. Thus were many of the nurses circumstanced, alone, until the patient died, then called away to another scene. . . .

Document 13: Quaker Reluctance to Accept Black Women Into Membership

These excerpts from Quaker monthly, quarterly, and yearly meetings reveal that racial bias invaded even these quarters during the late eighteenth century. Two local Quaker groups hesitated to accept two mulatto women into fellowship.[41]

At the Concord Monthly Meeting 7th month 4th, 1781, a query came from the Birmingham (Pennsylvania) Meeting whether, if an applicant for membership is known or believed to be sincere, he or she should be rejected on account of color. This was referred to a committee of men and women and, subsequently, to the Quarterly Meeting. The latter appointed a committee "to inquire more minutely into the disposition, color and circumstances of the individual on whose account the application took its rise." The committee reported three months later that some of them had visited the young woman and that

> her disposition they apprehended to be worthy of Friends' notice; and her color appeared to them not darker than some who are esteemed white: and we find by inquiry that her great grandfather was an African

> Negro and her great grandmother an American Indian; her grandfather a descendant of them and her grandmother an Indian; her father a descendant of them and the mother a white woman.

The matter was, however, not settled even then, but referred to the Yearly Meeting, which, by minute of 10th Month 1st, 1783, recorded:

> The request of Chester Quarter last year respecting the application of a woman to Concord Monthly Meeting to be received into membership, and which was referred for further consideration to this or a future meeting being now revived, the subject opening with weight, it is the sense and judgment of the meeting that Concord Monthly Meeting may safely consider the application of the person on the same ground in common with other applications for admission into membership.

The minutes mentioned no opposition at any stage, but only "weighty and edifying deliberations and a spirit of condescension," "a weighty exercise," and "divers just observations." Evidently, there was doubt or objection. This was apparent in a personal letter of a friend of the applicant who, after the Yearly Meeting's decision, wrote "that the mountains of opposition are leveled before her." By the following May, Abigail Franks was accepted into membership in the Birmingham Meeting:

> Women Friends . . . inform that Cynthia Miers, a mulatto woman, had also requested to be joined in membership with Friends, but this being a case of a singular nature amongst us the meeting thinks it best to proceed very cautiously herein and therefore appoints to take the subject into their serious consideration and report to the next meeting —John Haydock [and eleven other men].

The next month's minutes reported progress of the committee and acceptance of its suggestion that some men be appointed to "join women Friends in a visit to her, they to report their sense of her disposition of mind to our next meeting." At the next meeting, the visitors reported that they believed "her to be convinced of the principles of Truth as professed by us and desirous of walking agreeable thereto"; but the meeting accepted the judgment of the original committee that the case should "go forward to the Quarterly Meeting for their advice and direction herein." A Scottish Friend, John Wigham, who was present in this monthly meeting, described the case in his journal as follows:

> The case of a Mulatto woman, who had applied for membership with Friends, came before the meeting: a committee had been appointed to visit her, and reported their satisfaction as to her convincement but thought it unsafe to receive her on account of her colour! After much discussion it was at last concluded to refer the matter to the Quarterly Meeting. How hard it is to overcome old prejudices.

The Quarterly Meeting adopted the following course:

> From Rahway and Plainfield [New Jersey] Monthly Meeting we are informed that Cynthia Myers, a Mulatto woman, had applied to be received into membership with them, had been visited by a committee from their meeting, who made a favorable report respecting her, yet as they could not fully unite in judgment in her case, it was referred to this Meeting where claiming our solid attention, and many friends expressing their sentiments thereon, it was thought best to refer it to the Yearly Meeting as friends here could not unite in the propriety of receiving The without the concurrence of that meeting.

The Yearly Meeting appointed a committee to consider the question, to which both women Friends and visitors from other parts were admitted. Their report, made in writing and accepted by the Yearly Meeting, stated:

> We are united in believing that our Discipline already established relative to receiving persons into membership is not limited with respect to Nation or Colour.

The Committee recommended that applicants for membership should be investigated as to their views and practices, and when the results of these investigations were satisfactory, monthly meetings "may in their freedom receive such with propriety without respect of persons or colour."

The minutes of the Rahway and Plainfield Monthly Meeting showed that in the next month Cynthia Miers's case was resumed and that, in the following month, she was received into membership.

Document 14: Funeral Sermon for Sarah Johnson

Sarah Johnson was 104 years old when she died in 1845. Her funeral sermon was preached by the Reverend J. N. M'Jilton, rector in charge of St. James' First African Church, Baltimore. The excerpts below from that sermon indicate the confident faith appropriate to such a believer.[42]

. . . It is not my purpose today, to speak of the just as a body. I esteem it a privilege to be able to delineate the character from *individual example*—example seen, and known, and admired among us. There was one, but recently in our midst, whose walk and conversation gave evidence that she had been washed in the waters of Regeneration. The proofs of her walk of faith were the fruits of a holy and devoted life. During her later years, the fear of God was continually before her eyes, and it appeared to be her steady aim to render such obedience to His commandments as would secure her peace of mind, and justify the hope, that when her worn out frame should be consigned to the earth, her spirit should be with God who gave it.

Sarah Johnson, the subject of my remarks, was born at Snow-hill, on the Eastern shore of Maryland, in the early part of the year 1742. She died on the night of the 4th of September, 1845, at the advanced age of nearly ONE HUNDRED AND FOUR YEARS.

She expressed the strongest confidence in God. . . . [A]fter the communion on Easter day, I asked her if she felt that she was getting near to Heaven, as she approached the grave. Her reply was the usual acknowledgment of her unworthiness. . . . "I am sinful, . . . but my Redeemer is all righteousness, in myself I am lost, but in Him I am safe. I pray that I may be faithful to the end and that my Saviour may be my portion forever."

The last time I saw her at home and in life, . . . she had not then a doubt but that she would be saved; and when I asked how that great work was to be accomplished, she answered, "Not by me, but by faith in Jesus Christ, my Saviour." I asked her if she was willing to die. She said with great animation, "My dear child, if it is my Saviour's will, I am not only willing to die, but I am anxious to be gone." I asked her if she was weary of the world in which she had lived so long. She replied, "Yes, I am really and truly weary of the world; I have lived so long in it and seen so much of its evil that I am sometimes impatient to leave it." I asked her if she was perfectly satisfied that she was safe, knowing that she had been sinful in the sight of God. "I am safe not in myself," she answered, "but in my Saviour; I know that my soul is safe in His hands. O I know it so well, . . . that I am anxious He should have it. Would that He might take it now!" A short time after I held this conversation with her, I was told that she was dead. . . . My inquiry . . . was, how the lamp of the aged Christian had expired. I was told that she had died as she had lived, an humble, self-accusing yet trusting disciple of the Lord Jesus Christ. Her exit was as peaceful as the passing of a lovely summer's eve. The sun of life went down without a cloud, and she laid as calm and still in dying as the smooth unruffled lake when the night shadows are slowly stealing over it. A friend at her side was reading to her the Word of God, and as she listened to the recital of the Sacred Record, her spirit departed to look upon the realities which were rehearsed in her ear of flesh. . . . Perhaps the first realities that broke upon the sight of her released soul, were those that confirmed the truth of what she had heard. She laid so still while the reader was performing his task, that one approached to look upon her to ascertain if she was not asleep. The examination disclosed what had hardly been indicated by suspicion. She was indeed asleep,—asleep to wake no more until the trump of the Archangel shall awaken the millions of the sepulchre for the judgment of the Lord.

. . . It is the example of the deceased's virtues that I would hold up to your sight, for your admiration and for your imitation. . . . her devotion to the church. . . . her integrity as a christian professor. . . . her ardent piety. . . .

Women in Sectarian and Utopian Groups

ROSEMARY RADFORD RUETHER AND
CATHERINE M. PRELINGER

In sixteenth- and seventeenth-century Protestantism in England and Germany, a number of radical movements emerged that rejected the continued alliance of magisterial Protestantism (Anglican and Puritan in England, Lutheran in Germany) with the state. For these representatives of radical, anabaptist, and mystical Protestantism, the state, and its ally, the state church, was Babylon, the enemy of Christ. The true church, the elect of Christ, must exodus from the state church and preach the transformation of humanity in anticipation of the coming Kingdom of God. The elect must be ready to suffer at the hands of false authorities, even to death.[1]

Such radical Christians often stressed mystical piety, relying on the direct authority of the Holy Spirit. This reliance on the Holy Spirit enabled them to validate the spiritual gifts of both men and women. It also allowed them to reject official ecclesiastical and civil authorities by claiming obedience to the higher authority of direct inspiration by God.

SEVENTEENTH-CENTURY QUAKERS

The Quakers, or Society of Friends, arose in England during the civil war era of the mid-seventeenth century. George Fox began the preaching of the Inner Light in 1648. In 1652, he visited the manor home of Thomas and Margaret Fell, having previously been apprised of the likelihood of a sympathetic reception from the mistress of Swarthmore Hall. Judge Fell was absent, but Fox soon won over Margaret Fell and her seven daughters. Several servants of the house, including a maid, Ann Clayton, were converted and left to become Quaker preachers. While the judge himself never joined the society, he protected it politically during his lifetime, until his death in 1658. In 1669, Margaret Askew Fell (1614–1702) married George Fox. She is known as the "mother" of the Society of Friends. Her manor at Swarthmore Hall was the organizing center from which funds, both for the missionary journeys of the Publishers of Truth and for the support of the many imprisoned Quakers and their families, were gathered. Letters and tracts streamed forth from her pen, defining the vision of the movement and supporting the missionaries in their far-flung endeavors that soon took them beyond England into North America, the Caribbean, and the Middle East.[2]

Women, as well as men, were understood to be empowered by the indwelling Spirit and commissioned to witness and to teach. Fox defended women's right to preach and also women's administrative role in the society through the Women's Meetings. Between 1663 and 1668, Margaret Fell was imprisoned, along with many other Friends, under the Quaker Act, which charged them with disloyalty to the crown for refusing to swear the oath of allegiance. During this imprisonment, Fell wrote *Women's Speaking Justified, Proved and Allowed of by the Scriptures,* which provided the theology and biblical hermeneutics for women's equal roles in the Society of Friends.

Early Quakerism was notable for its intrepid female preachers and missionaries who experienced continual floggings and imprisonments in their witness to the Light against the "hireling priests" of the "steeple-houses." Dauntless Quaker women, as well as men, made a particular point of traveling to the great universities of Oxford and Cambridge to witness against the monopoly of ministry by the university-trained clergy. They received many a blow from enraged theology students for their efforts. In Massachusetts, the Quakers fell into conflict with Puritan authorities who refused to allow them to preach or to settle in their territories. Quaker preachers returned again and again to pursue this "War of the Lamb" against the Puritan leaders (the struggle of the elect of Christ against the state church). Several were finally hanged (Document 1), but this spectacle of the persecution of Quakers was so generally repugnant that when word reached England, the king commanded Massachusetts authorities to rescind the death penalty for Quakers (1660). Yet the persecution continued intermittently until 1680.[3]

A controversial innovation in early Quakerism was the institution of Women's Meetings, which gave Quaker women an official role in the administration and government of the society. Women's Meetings both supervised internal morality and managed extensive works of charity. They gathered and administered funds for the relief of the imprisoned, of the poor, of the sick, widows, orphans, and the aged. They organized projects, such as spinning groups, for unemployed women and placed orphans in apprenticeships. They supervised marriages and the payment of tithes within the society.[4] Correspondence between Women's Meetings, particularly from the Women's Meeting at Swarthmore Hall, headed by Margaret Fell and later by several of her daughters, encouraged the development of such meetings throughout the Friends' societies in the American colonies (Document 2).

The eighteenth century saw a downplaying of the role of Women's Meetings and women as ministers. But the advocacy of women's spiritual and administrative powers remained strong enough in the nineteenth century to attract early feminist Sarah Grimké into the Quaker fold in Philadelphia in 1821.[5] It is no accident that a number of the early feminists and abolitionists of the nineteenth century, such as Lucretia Mott and Susan B. Anthony, were Quaker ministers.[6]

EPHRATA CLOISTER

Many of the sects that came to Pennsylvania during the great German migrations of the late seventeenth and eighteenth centuries shared a common religious orientation with the Quakers. Dunkers, Mennonites, Moravians, Seventh-Day Baptists, and the "Silent of the Land" made up an estimated one hundred thousand Germans seeking residence in William Penn's experiment between 1683 and the time of the revolution. Stirred by pietist revivalism on the continent, they were persecuted by the established churches and forced to flee. Like the Quakers, theirs was a commitment to continuing revelation, a belief that reduced the importance of traditional rituals as well as the authority of the clergy. The option of sexual egalitarianism is often implicit in this kind of Christianity, an option the German sectarians interpreted in various ways.

Ephrata Cloister was a community of Dunker enthusiasts established in 1732 in Lancaster county which ultimately became an independent sect. It was unique in its elaboration of the option of female celibacy within a communal society that also included male celibates and married people. Ephrata Cloister began when Pastor Conrad Beissel (1690–1768) broke with his Dunker congregation in Germantown, Pennsylvania, on the two issues of the superiority of celibacy and the observance of the seventh day as the Sabbath. First he set himself up as a hermit on the Cocalico Brook, where Ephrata would later be located. A band of followers was attracted by his faith and personal life.[7] Then a community was developed by Beissel that, at its height, consisted of between twenty-five and thirty-five celibate men, a somewhat larger number of celibate women, these groups being resident in the monastery, and a much larger circle of householders whose dwellings surrounded the cloister grounds.

Beissel drew the intellectual substance of his faith from the writings of Jacob Boehme (1575–1624), whose inspiration had led to Beissel's conversion and subsequent exile from Germany. Beissel accepted Boehme's view of the existence of three warring worlds: the temporal world, the realm of light, and the realm of darkness. As he saw it, the battle between these three cosmic forces is played out in every human soul. Through the exercise of the will in ascetic discipline, the community member could attain freedom from the flesh and the world and form a mystical union with God. Beissel adopted Boehme's concept of the divine

Sophia or Wisdom as the original ground of unconditional being. Sophia exists prior to and becomes coexistent with the male divine principle. Adam was created by the female principle, Sophia, and God, the male principle, and so Adam was androgynous. The original androgynous Adam was without either genital organs or digestive functions. The carnal appetites were introduced when Eve was separated out from Adam. Only by ascetic transcendence of sexuality and material demands can humanity return to unity with God.[8]

Beissel's preaching of celibacy was a particularly powerful attraction to women. Local hostility was aroused when a number of wives left their husbands to adopt the ascetic life at Ephrata. The Ephratines created a communal society based on two economies conducted independently by the celibate males and females. Especially under the leadership of Prior Onesimus (Israel Eckerling), Ephrata became a complex economy that offered opportunities to many specialized trades, maintaining active trade with the outside world and resulting in a prosperity that more than supported the intellectual and artistic lives of its members. Ephrata was particularly renowned for its printing. Much of the ink and paper for the entire provincial printing industry came from the Ephrata mills. The Mennonite *Martyrs' Mirror,* produced on their press, was the largest book published in Pennsylvania before the revolution.

The women of Ephrata lived by a written rule known as the Rose (Document 3). The women's economy depended on spinning, quilting, basketry, the preparation of home medicines, and the manufacture of sulphur matches, wax tapers, paper lanterns, and artificial flowers. The women chopped their own wood. They also cared for their own household, but not for that of the brothers. The sisters lived together in a three-story building that contained tiny sleeping cells and a number of large community rooms, including the refectory, rooms for caligraphy, for copying music, for needlework, and so forth. The sisters achieved their greatest distinction in the artistic and musical realms. Although they did not record their own views about life at Ephrata, a pride and sense of spiritual satisfaction marked their creative works, and one can still admire the beauty of their manuscript illustrations. Their special mode of singing, elaborated for them by Beissel, was so notable that efforts continue to revive it to this day (see Document 4, 5). Several contemporary travelers have left accounts that comment on the beauty of the sisters' singing (Document 6).

THE MORAVIAN BRETHREN

The Moravians, whose American headquarters at Bethlehem, Pennsylvania, was less than seventy miles from Ephrata, shared many similarities with the Dunkers. They, too, were German pietists and pacifists. Their Christianity was highly emotional, and they revived early Christian practices, such as the love-feast[9] and foot-washing. Unlike the Ephratines, the Moravians were activists and missionaries. They belonged to a worldwide network that stretched from Europe, to South Africa, Labrador, and the West Indies. They came to America to convert both the colonists and the indigenous Indian populations.

Historically, the Moravians trace their origins to the fourteenth-century Hussites. Fleeing persecution in their native lands of Moravia and Bohemia, the Brethren settled in the 1720s on the estates of Count Ludwig von Zinzendorf (1700–1760) at Herrnhut in Saxony, Germany. Zinzendorf, already influenced by pietism, gathered an ecumenical following of disaffected Lutherans, Reformed and Roman Catholics, as well as the Brethren. Herrnhut became the model community and administrative center for Moravian settlements throughout the world. Zinzendorf, who was called "the Disciple," was present at the founding of Bethlehem, Pennsylvania, in 1741. An earlier settlement in Georgia, under Augustus Gottlieb Spangenberg (1704–1782), had failed, and Spangenberg became the leader in residence at Bethlehem.

The Moravians were Christocentric, focusing particularly on a mystical adoration of the bleeding wounds of the crucified Christ. Their settlements were organized both to support the local congregation and to send forth missionaries as the "pilgrim" congregation. Property and production were owned and operated by the entire community, which was organized into sex and age cohorts called "choirs." Each choir worked, lived, and worshipped as a unit. There were choirs for single sisters, single brothers, widows and widowers, as well as for infants and children, and for married couples. Married women were thereby freed from childcare for productive work. As early as 1747, out of a population of about four hundred, the Bethlehem supported fifty members as missionaries.[10] By 1755, there were forty different crafts represented at Bethlehem. Fourteen buildings, as well as five mills, constituted an industrial quarter in addition to the choir residences.[11]

Women's occupations at Bethlehem were much less specialized than those of the men. Those women who were not engaged in the routine of communal laundry and food preparation were producers of linen. In 1747, 3,308 yards of linen were woven by the sisters because each member of the community needed three to four shirts a year.[12] Single sisters helped with the harvest; widows worked in the spinning and manufacture of cotton. These occupations of Moravian women differed little from those of other women at the time. However, Moravian women held significant managerial roles within the productive economy and in the residential and religious life of the community (Document 7).

The choirs were both economic and residential units and also worship groups. Each choir maintained a diary, and these show the strenuous religious life of the Moravians. Beginning at daybreak with morning grace and a Bible watchword and ending with evening Bible study, hymns, and fellowship, litanies celebrated each occasion of life. Women in the female choirs conducted these exercises, even composed them, and kept their diaries (Document 8).

Various committees administered a Moravian settlement. Each Sunday, following the morning service, all adult communicants convened as a community council. Women commonly belonged to both the Elders' Conference and the Supervisory Council, which reported to this assembly. Mary Spangenberg, Anna Nitschmann, Elisabeth Böhler, Anna Mack, and Anna Maria Lawatsch were among the notable women of early American Moravian annals (Document 9).

Evangelizing was the central purpose of the Moravian settlement. By 1748, the Bethlehem settlement and its sister community in Nazareth served thirty localities, mostly in Pennsylvania, New York, and New Jersey.[13] By 1753, a settlement was begun in North Carolina. The Moravians were particularly concerned to evangelize the American Indians. Zinzendorf himself visited a number of Indian settlements during his American sojourn. Women were highly valued for their work among Indians. Jeannette Rau, for example, developed a facility for various Indian dialects which made her invaluable (Document 10). Some Indians came to the Moravian settlements on their own initiative. The first volume of the Bethlehem Church Register records among the adult baptisms an account of Elisabeth, wife of Shawnee Chief Paxnou, who on a visit to Bethlehem declared "the desire for the Savior in her face and explained that for three years something was missing from her soul."[14]

By 1748, 500 Indian converts had been settled in a station called Gnadenhuetten, about thirty miles from Bethlehem. Gnadenhuetten was later raided by hostile Indians who set it afire. Eleven Moravian missionaries died, and four survivors and seventy Indians made their way back to the horrified community at Bethlehem. Moravian hagiography portrayed the deaths of such martyrs in the Indian missions as the ultimate service to the gospel for both women and men (Document 11).

Moravians developed an emphasis on the married couple as partners in mission. The concept of the "militant marriage" made possible a missionary partnership that could minister to both sexes. The sexes were strictly segregated until marriage, although any member of the single sisters' choir was eligible for the marriage lot. Moravians typically made important decisions by lot as a way of submitting themselves to the will of God and legitimating their self-concept as a theocracy. The drawings took place at the Elders' Conference and was used for such purposes as the selection of new members, assignment to choirs, choice of officers, and determination of economic policy. Recourse to the lot always occurred when consensus was lacking. All marriages were subject to the lot, although not in an identical manner (Document 12). In the Great Wedding of 1749, fifty-six members of the Third Sea Congregation submitted their names to the lot and married one another shortly after their arrival in Bethlehem.[15]

The Moravians were able to maintain themselves as a separate and distinct community through the American Revolution, although with difficulty. Their refusal to bear arms or take oaths and their ties with England and Germany made them suspect to the Americans. But the diplomatic skills of John Ettwein, their leader in the 1770s, won the respect of colonial authorities. Their role as noncombatants in offering provisions and nursing care when the fighting centered in Western Pennsylvania in the early years of the war earned them the gratitude of the populace at large.

FEMALE MESSIAHS IN THE REVOLUTIONARY WAR ERA

The Revolutionary War era stirred a new intensity in the prophetic traditions of American Protestantism, which saw the hand of God both as punishing corrupt religion and politics and as bringing about a new millennial society through this divine purgation. Among the religious phenomena of the period were two movements led by women who were acclaimed by their followers to be manifestations of the Second Appearing of Christ: Mother Ann Lee (1736–1784) and Jemima Wilkinson (1752–1819).

Mother Ann Lee, foundress of the Shakers, or the United Society of Believers in Christ's Second Appearing, attracted followers of theological and organizational talent who were able to develop her movement after her death into one of the most creative religious communities, theologically and culturally, in America. By contrast, Jemima Wilkinson, while initially she drew followers of greater wealth and social status than the Shakers, lacked heirs of theological and organizational abilities. Her movement was sustained by her personal charisma, which began to wane in her old age, and was already in decline at the time of her death.

Both women were targets for hostile attacks during their lifetimes, attacks that were inspired in large part by the scandal of women claiming high spiritual authority. However, the memory of Ann Lee has been shaped primarily by the testimonies of her religious heirs, whose faith in her spiritual authority was enshrined in a theological understanding of her unique mission as representative of divine wisdom in the last days. Jemima Wilkinson, on the other hand, was subject to sustained character assassination both during her lifetime and after her death. This hostile tradition, and the lack of availability of authentic records from her own community, has continued to shape her historical image, despite efforts of recent historians to correct it.[16]

Mother Ann Lee was the daughter of a working-class family in Manchester, England, and went to labor in the mills at the age of eight. She was illiterate all her life. Her marriage to Abraham Stanley, a blacksmith by trade, was not happy, and her four children all died in infancy or early childhood. In 1758, she joined a breakaway sect from the Quakers, the Wardley Society, which had been influenced by the French *Camisards,* a fanatical prophetic sect. Jane Wardley was an impassioned apocalyptic preacher who taught the androgyny of God. Jesus represented the male Messiah, and the Wardleys believed that a female Messiah would soon appear.[17]

Lee was subject to religious visions that often left her weak and emaciated. During an imprisonment in 1770, she had a vision that identified the sexual act as the cause of Adam and Eve's expulsion from paradise. From that time onward, she preached celibacy as a necessary condition of salvation. She also had a vision that she was Christ's anointed successor on earth, a revelation which Shaker tradition declares to have been confirmed by the Wardleys.

During this period, the Methodist preacher George Whitefield, recently back from a preaching tour of the English colonies in North America, declared that the true Church of Christ was to be established in America. Lee took this as a sign that she should take her movement and plant it in America. In 1774, a small band, which included her brother, William Lee, and her husband, departed for New York. The trip was a rough one, and the captain, annoyed by the ecstatic singing and dancing of the Shakers on shipboard, threatened to throw them into the ocean. But, according to Shaker tradition, at that moment a terrible storm arose, and a wave drove a hole in the side of the ship. Mother Ann prayed, and another wave snapped the loose board back in place, closing the hole. The captain no longer impeded the spiritual activities of the Shakers during the rest of the journey.[18] Mother Ann landed in America already confirmed in her destiny by this sign from heaven.

In New York, Mother Ann earned a living for a period by taking in washing. Her husband, Abraham Stanley, no longer able to tolerate his wife's spurning of the marriage bed, took off with another woman. By 1776, members of the society had been able to secure land in Watervliet near Albany, and Lee and her followers moved there. From this first settlement, Lee and the other early leaders conducted continual preaching tours in the northeastern colonies. They often met with hostility and persecution from townspeople, as well as colonial authorities. The testimonies of the early converts, gathered together in the 1820s from the memories of those still living then, describe the terrors of these persecutions, as well as the calm wisdom of Mother Ann. Her brother, William Lee, died after suffering a fractured skull from the beatings he received. Mother Ann herself never recovered her strength after a particularly savage beating she received in 1783 in Harvard, Massachusetts. She died in 1784 (Document 13).

Jemima Wilkinson was fifteen years younger than Mother Ann. Their preaching itineraries passed within a few miles of each other between 1778 and 1783 (Wilkinson won her converts mostly in Connecticut, Pennsylvania, Rhode Island, and New Jersey, while Ann Lee worked more in Massachusetts), and yet there is no evidence that the two women met or influenced each other, although they were sometimes popularly compared—and judged as two instances of female religious frauds. Wilkinson was the eighth of twelve children of a prosperous Quaker farmer of Cumberland, Pennsylvania, Jeremiah Wilkinson, and his wife, Amey Whipple. Unlike Mother Lee, Jemima was a fourth-generation American with ties to leading families in Rhode Island. She had little formal education, but was deeply grounded both in Scripture and in Quaker piety and martyrology. As a farm girl, she had a number of practical skills, including proficiency in medicine, and was an excellent horsewoman.

Wilkinson was left motherless at the age of twelve or thirteen (1764). She remained at home into her mid-twenties and in 1774 was converted during the New Light Baptist revival. This created a crisis with her Friends' Meeting, which expelled her for failure to attend. Her sister and several of her brothers were also expelled from the meeting at the same time, for various reasons, including active participation in the militia. In October of 1776, these events, as well as typhus fever, brought about a critical illness and a spiritual crisis for Jemima. She lay ill for six days. Then, on October 10, she suddenly recovered, believing that she had died and had been reanimated by a Spirit of (or sent from) Christ, which had descended into her body. She took the name of Universal Friend and, for the rest of her life, no longer allowed anyone to use her former name.

Jemima began her preaching career three days later under a tree at the Elder Miller Baptist meeting house. For several years, she conducted preaching tours in the vicinity, remaining based in her father's house. The family was a close-knit one, and four of her sisters and one brother were to join her movement. Her father accompanied her on her early trips and was disowned for this by the Quakers in 1777. Jemima was a striking beauty with dark eyes, glossy black curls, a deep voice, and a commanding appearance. She adopted a remarkable garb with a white cravat and flowing robes and wore a man's beaver hat when traveling. Her caravan usually consisted of twelve followers, with herself at the head on a spirited horse, seated on a blue velvet and white sidesaddle with silver stirrups. Jemima clearly had a sense for the theatrical and everywhere attracted large crowds of several hundred, many drawn by curiosity. Although hostile rumor always accompanied her, she was often able to dispel this by her serene self-confidence and sincerity. Contemporary accounts suggest a woman of powerful charisma, who excited both awe and anger because of her adoption of masculine clerical dress and authority.

Jemima's theology was not at all original. Basically, she preached a revival message of repentence, conversion to Christ, and adoption of the

Golden Rule in view of the shortness of the times and the transitoriness of life. She reflected her Quaker background in her belief in universal salvation, freedom of the will, direct spiritual relation with God, and a rejection of war and slavery. At her assemblies, she combined revival preaching with silent prayer meetings in which the gathered testified to their experiences of the Spirit. She relied, however, on dreams and visions and, in the early days, on faith healings.[19] The scandal of her movement lay primarily in her claim to unique spiritual authority as a resurrected prophet sent by (or as) Christ to preach conversion to humanity in the last days. At some point in the 1780s, she also adopted the doctrine of celibacy as the higher ethic for the converted Christian, although, unlike the Shakers, this was never imposed on all her converts as a condition of membership.[20]

For fourteen years, Jemima traveled constantly on preaching trips in New England and gathered several hundred converts, among them the wealthy Judge Potter of Narragansett planter aristocracy, as well as most of his family, and Thomas Hathaway of New Bedford, Connecticut. Judge Potter built a fourteen-room addition onto his large mansion in South Kingston and this became the center of her movement in the 1780s. She conducted several successful preaching tours of Philadelphia, holding forth to crowds of up to seven hundred in the Methodist St. George's Church and later in the Free Quaker Meeting House. (The Free Quakers were a group of Quakers who set up their own meetings after they had been expelled by the regular Friends' Meetings for participation in the American revolutionary army.

From 1785 through 1790, Jemima and two hundred and fifty to three hundred of her followers made plans to emigrate to the newly opened Seneca Indian territory of Genesee county. The dream of a communal society may have been inspired by both the Ephrata community and the Shakers. But the Universal Friends, as they called themselves, never intended to form a community where all property would be held in common. Rather, they wished to buy a large track of land where all could have individual farms and contribute to a central community that would house Jemima and a group of her immediate supporters, most of them celibate women. However, these efforts went awry, due to territorial disputes between Indians, Canada, and the United States, and between New York and Massachusetts. Many of the poorer members were defrauded of their land as a result of poor management by James Parker, the agent for the Universal Friends. Some of the wealthier members profited, including Judge Potter. Jemima moved her own house farther west in Genesee county, taking with her the poorer members of the society.[21]

These events marked the beginning of the decline of the society and the disaffection of the wealthier and more respected members who were to attack her viciously in her later years, although Jemima herself never became bitter toward them or lost her own self-confidence. In 1793, her closest friend and financial manager, Sarah Richards, died. Sarah Richards' daughter would later elope with Enoch Malin, a brother of two members of Jemima's female community, Rachel and Margaret Malin. Enoch Malin, together with a lawyer, Elisha Williams, conceived the plan of trying to obtain Jemima's property by claiming that it belonged to Sarah Richards. These litigations dragged on through the last years of Jemima's life and after her death. Although the case was finally settled in Jemima's favor, hostile stories that depicted her as a fraud, hypocrite, and golddigger were drummed up by the lawyers in an effort to win this case. One of the lawyers, David Hudson, published these stories in an account entitled *The History of Jemima Wilkinson, Preacheress of the Eighteenth Century* (1821).[22] Unfortunately, this biased account, filled with fictitious stories, became and has remained the primary source on the career of Jemima Wilkinson for American religious historians. Although Jemima was not an important thinker, she was a preacher and religious leader of considerable authority whose story deserves to be told from a friendlier viewpoint (Document 14).

Mary Dyer, seventeenth-century Quaker martyr for religious freedom. Bronze sculpture by Sylvia Shaw Judson, commissioned by the General Court of Massachusetts to be placed on Boston Common, where Dyer was hanged by Puritan authorities in 1660. A copy of the statue is located at the entrance of the Friend's Center in Philadelphia. [Courtesy the Philadelphia Annual Meeting of the Religious Society of Friends.]

Member of the Ephrata Sisterhood in the habit of the order. Sketch on flyleaf of manuscript hymnal, 1745. [From Julius Friedrich Sachse, *The German Sectarians of Pennsylvania, 1742–1800* (Philadelphia: Published by the author, 1900), p. 190.]

Saron sisterhouse and dining room, the cloister, Ephrata, Pennsylvania. Photo by Mel Horst. [Courtesy the Ephrata Cloister Associates.]

Hymnbook of the Ephrata Sisterhood, showing characteristic decorative motifs, by Petronella. [Courtesy the Historical Society of Pennsylvania.]

Anna Nitschmann (1715–1760), Moravian missionary to America and Zinzendorf's second wife. [From *Herrnhut: Ursprung und Auftrag* (Hamburg: Friedrich Wittig Verlag, 1972), no. 46.]

Moravian group wedding, 1758. Old Salem, Inc., Winston-Salem, North Carolina. [From Linda de Pauw and Conover Hunt, *Remember the Ladies: Women in America, 1750–1815* (New York: Viking, 1976), p. 77.]

Women's bands of the Moravian Brethren in footwashing ceremony, with a woman presiding. [From *Unitas Fratrum in Pictures, 1457–1957,* ed. Radim Kalfuss (Prague: Unitas Fratrum, 1975), p. 101.]

Shaker religious dancing, circa 1835. Courtesy the Shaker Museum, Old Chatham, New York. [From Linda de Pauw and Conover Hunt, *Remember the Ladies: Women in America, 1750–1815* (New York: Viking Press, 1976), p. 79.]

Jemima Wilkinson in 1816, painted by John L. D. Mathies. This portrait hangs in the Oliver House, Penn Yan, New York, in the collection of the Yates County Historical Society. [Courtesy the Village Board, Penn Yan, New York.]

Documents: Women in Sectarian and Utopian Groups

SEVENTEENTH-CENTURY QUAKERS

Document 1: Quaker Women Missionaries and Martyrs of the Seventeenth Century

In the first generation of the Society of Friends, women were very active as missionaries. They also endured their full share of the sufferings inflicted on the Quakers by the religious and civil establishments of England and New England. During the 1650s and 1660s, the Quakers engaged in repeated confrontations with the Puritan authorities in Massachusetts in protest against laws of Uniformity of Religion that banished religious dissenters from the colony under pain of death.[23]

The Act of Uniformity of Religion in the Massachusetts Bay Colonies (1646)

In that Province were sitting at the Helm of Government a Set of Men, making high Pretensions to Religion, and such as had loudly cried out against Tyranny and Oppression of the Bishops in *Old-England,* from whom they had fled, protesting themselves *pious and peaceable* Protestants, *driven by Severity to leave their Native Country, and seek a Refuge for their Lives and Liberties, with Freedom for the Worship of God, in a Wilderness in the Ends of the Earth;* yet, when invested with Power, we find them exercising a cruel Dominion over the Faith and Consciences of others; in which they appear not to us so inconsistent with themselves as some have thought, because when, under Oppression, they pleaded for *Liberty of Conscience,* they understood it not as *the natural and common Right of all Mankind,* but as a peculiar Privilege of the *Orthodox.*

The Case of Mary Fisher

Mary Fisher (1623–1698) was an intrepid Quaker missionary. She had been a serving girl who was converted by Fox in 1651. She was the first apostle to the Universities of Oxford and Cambridge, where she suffered beatings and imprisonments for her preaching against the clericalism of the divinity students. Her crowning missionary effort was a trip that took her 600 miles, alone and by foot, across Thrace to talk to the Turkish Sultan. After many missionary journeys and two marriages, she finally settled in North Carolina. In 1656, she arrived in Boston from Barbados. When news of their arrival came to the deputy-governor, Richard Bellingham, he immediately ordered Fisher and her companion, Ann Austin, detained on board ship and he sent officers to search their trunks. About 100 books were confiscated. Mary Fisher and Ann Austin were imprisoned and denied communication with anyone but the magistrates.

In consequence of this Order, their Books were burnt by the Hangman, in the Market-place, and they, being brought on Shore, committed by The Deputy-Governor to Prison as *Quakers,* of which all the Proof he had was, that one of them said *Thee* to him, whereupon he said, *Now he knew they were* Quakers. In Prison they were kept close, and an Order given that *none should speak with them,* no *not through the Window.* Their Pens, Ink, and Paper were taken away, and they suffered to have no Candle by Night. They were stript under Pretence of searching whether they were Witches, and on that Occasion barbarously and immodestly used. And to prevent any conversing with them, a Board was nailed up before the Window of the Goal. Their Case excited the Compassion of *Nicholas Upshall,* an old Inhabitant of *Boston,* and a Member of the Church there, so that he gave the Goaler five Shillings per Week for the Liberty of sending them Provisions, lest they should be starved. After about five Weeks Confinement, one *William Chichester,* Master of a Vessal, was bound in a Bond of one Hundred Pounds to carry them back to Barbadoes, and not suffer any to speak with them, after they were put on board; And the Goaler kept their beds, which were brought out of the Ship, and their Bibles, for his fees.

The Martyrdom of Mary Dyer

Mary Dyer had been a former member of the Massachusetts Bay colony before she returned as a Quaker to confront Puritan authorities. In 1635, she and her husband, William, arrived in Boston and were enrolled as members of the church. However, she and her husband were expelled from Massachusetts for supporting Anne Hutchinson in the Antinomian dispute. The Dyers moved to Rhode Island, where William rose to the rank of attorney-general of the colony. On a trip to England in the mid-1650s, she became a Quaker and was imprisoned in Boston in 1656 on her return to Rhode Island. Her husband had to pay a large sum to obtain her liberty under strict orders that she should never return to Massachusetts. Two years later in 1659, Dyer returned with two other Quakers, a London merchant, William Robinson, and a Yorkshireman, Marmaduke Stevenson, to protest the persecution of Quakers. The three were imprisoned and ordered to depart under pain of death. Robinson and Stevenson went only to Salem and were soon imprisoned again. Mary Dyer then returned and was also taken into custody.

On the 20th of October these three were brought into Court, where John Endicot and others were assembled . . . and Mary Dyer was called to whom Endicot spake thus: Mary Dyer, *You shall go to the Place from whence you came (to wit, the Prison) and from thence to the Place of Execution and be hanged until you are dead.* To which she replied, *The Will of the Lord be done.* Then Endicot said, take her away Marshall. To which she returned, *Yea, Joyfully I go.* And in her going to the

Prison she often uttered Speeches of Praises to the Lord; and being full of Joy, she said to the Marshall, *He might let her alone, for she would go to the Prison without him.* To which he answered, *I believe you Mrs. Dyer, but I must do what I am commanded.*

The Day appointed by the Court for the Execution of their bloody Sentence was the 27th of October 1659, when in the Afternoon the condemned Persons were led to the Gallows, by the Marshall Michaelson. . . . Glorious signs of heavenly joy and gladness were beheld in the countenances of these three persons, who walked hand in hand, Mary being the middlemost, which made the marshall say to her, who was pretty aged and stricken in years, 'Are not you ashamed to walk thus hand in hand between two young men?' 'No' replied she, 'this is to me an hour of the greatest joy I could enjoy in this world. No eye can see, nor ear can hear, no tongue can utter, and no heart can understand, the sweet incomes or influence, and the refreshings of the spirit of the Lord, which now I feel.'

William Robinson and Marmaduke Stevenson are hanged. . . .

Mary Dyer seeing her companions hanging dead before her, also stepped up the ladder; but after her coats were tied about her feet, the halter put about her neck, and her face covered with a handkerchief, which the priest Wilson lent the hangman, just as she was to be turned off, a cry was heard, *'Stop, for she is reprieved.'* Her feet then being loosed, they bade her come down. But she whose mind was already as it were in heaven, stood still, and said *She was there willing to suffer as her brethren did, unless they would annul their wicked Law.* What she said was little regarded, but they pulled her down, and the Marshall and others taking her by the Arms, carried her to Prison again. . . .

Being thus returned Home from Prison, she went afterwards to *Long-Island* and tarried there the most Part of the Winter, and then coming Home again found herself under a Necessity, laid on her from the Requirings of the Spirit of the Lord, to go back again to *Boston* in the Beginnings of the next Year; . . .

Anno 1660. On the 21st of the Third Month, she came again to *Boston,* and on the 31st of the same, was sent for by the General-Court; being come, Endicot the Governour said, *Are you the same* Mary Dyer *that was here before?* And it seems he was preparing an Evasion for her, there having been another of that Name lately come from *England.* But She, far from any Disguise, undauntedly answered, *I am the same* Mary Dyer *that was here the last General Court.* Then Endicot said, You will own yourself a Quaker, will you not? To which she answered, I own myself to be reproachfully called so. Then the Goaler, who would also say something, said, She is a Vagabond. Then Endicot said, The sentence was past upon her the last General-Court, and now likewise: You must return to the Prison, and there remain till To-Morrow at nine o'clock; then from thence you must go to the Gallows, and there be hanged till you are dead. To which she answered, This is no more than what thou saidst before. Endicot replied, But now it is to be executed.... She then spoke thus: *I came in Obedience to the Will of God the last General-Court, desiring you to repeal your unrighteous Laws for Banishment on pain of Death; and that same is my Work now, and earnest Request; although I told you, that if you refused to repeal them, the Lord would send others of his Servants to witness against them. Hereupon Endicot asked her, Whether she was a Prophetess? She answered, She spoke the Words that the Lord spoke to her, and now the Thing was come to pass.* And beginning to speak to her Call, Endicot cried, *Away with her, away with her.* So she was brought to the Prison-house, and kept close shut up until the next Day.

About the Time appointed ... Mary Dyer was brought forth, and with a Band of Soldiers, led through the Town, the Drums being beaten before and behind her, and so continued that none might hear her speak all the Way to the Place of Execution which was about a Mile. Thus guarded she came to the Gallows, and being gone up the ladder, some said to her, that *If she would return She might come down and save her Life.* To which she replied, *Nay, I cannot, for in Obedience to the Will of the Lord I came, and in his Will I abide faithful to Death.* ... Then Priest Wilson said, Mary Dyer, *O repent, O repent, and be not so deluded and carried away by the Deceit of the Devil.* To this she answered, *Nay, Man, I am not now to repent.* And being asked by some, Whether she would have the Elders pray for her? She said, *I know never an Elder here.* Being further asked, Whether she would have any of the People pray for her? She answered, *She desired the Prayers of all the People of God.* Thereupon some scoffingly said, It may be she thinks there are none here. To which she replied, *I know but few here.... Then one mentioned, that she should have said, She had been in Paradise. To which she answered, Yea, I have been in Paradise these several Days.* And more she spoke of Eternal Happiness, into which she was now to enter. Thus *Mary Dyer* departed this life, a constant and faithful Martyr of Christ....

The Sufferings of Elisabeth Hooten

Elisabeth Hooten (1600–1672) was one of the early converts to Quakerism (1647), having previously been a Baptist preacher. She was imprisoned several times for her preaching activities in England. From 1651 to 1653, she was imprisoned with Mary Fisher in York castle. In 1661, she came to Boston to protest the laws of uniformity of religion, being then an aged woman of sixty years. She and a female companion, Joan Broksup, were imprisoned and then driven out into the wilderness and left without provisions to make their way by foot to Rhode Island. After a journey to Barbados, they returned to New England. This time they were put on board a ship for Virginia, and from there Hooten returned to her home in England.

Some time afterwards, Elisabeth Hooten felt moved again by the Spirit to return to Boston to testify against the persecution there. But this time, she procured a license from the king to purchase a house there, which she intended to be a refuge for Quakers. She then sailed to Boston with her daughter of the same name:

> She applied herself again and again to the court at Boston, for Liberty to purchase a House there for herself to dwell in, and for her Friends to meet in, and a Piece of Ground to bury their Dead, strenuously insisting that she had a Right so to do, both by common Privilege as an *English* Woman and also by particular License from the King. But these Magistrates regarding not the King's grant, nor her Right, would neither suffer her to purchase nor hire an House, nor have any Habitation there. Thus repulsed, she traveled *Eastward* toward *Piscataqua* River. At *Hampton* she was imprisoned for testifying against a persecuting Priest there. At *Dover* she was set in Stocks and then kept four Days in Prison in cold Weather. At *Cambridge* being moved to exhort the People to Repentence as she passed through the Streets, she was imprisoned in a close stinking Dungeon, where there was nothing either to lie down or sit on, where she was kept two Days and two Nights without Bread or Water. . . .

On the third day she was brought before the court and pleaded her right to purchase a house.

> But they regardless of her Plea, though altogether just and reasonable, made a cruel Order for sending her out of their coasts toward *Rhode-Island,* and for whipping her at three several towns, . . .

Hooten was then whipped with ten stripes in Cambridge, then in Watertown, and finally in Dedham.

> Thus miserably torn and beaten, they carried her a weary journey on Horseback many miles into the Wilderness, and toward Night left her there among Wolves, Bears and other wild Beasts. . . . When those who conveyed her thither left her, they said, *They thought they should never see her more.* And indeed in all human Probability she must have perished, had not the providential Hand of God preserved her, and brought her safe through the dismal Desert, and many deep Waters, to a Town called *Rehoboth,* where she arrived next Day, neither weary nor faint, and then passed to Rhode-Island, Praising and Magnifying the Name of the Lord, whose Mercies endureth for ever and who had signally supported and strengthened her through such grievous Tortures and Sufferings, as to her Age and Sex, in all outward Appearance, were insupportable. . . .

After a short stay in Rhode Island, she returned to Boston, not at all terrified by her previous ill usage:

> There [she] publickly warned the People to *Repentence,* and of the *terrible Day of the Lord,* which would otherwise overtake them: This

> Message of hers was received with Scorn, her godly Admonitions rejected, and she herself sent to the House of Correction, and there whipt at a Whipping-post with ten stripes; thence she was sent to *Roxbury*, and there whipt at a Cart's Tail, and from thence to *Dedham*, where the same cruel Punishment was repeated: Thence she was had to *Medfield* and the same Night hurried into the Wilderness, and there left to pass above twenty Miles with her Body thus miserably torn and mangled. . . . She arrived the next Day at a Town, and after some Stay with her Friends there, she returned again to Boston, where she was again cast into Prison, and after two Days, whipt from the Prison-door to the Town's End, and then sent away for *Rhode Island*, with a Warrant to whip her from Town to Town, threatening withal, that *If ever she came thither again, they would either put her to Death, or brand her on the Shoulder.* But she continued stedfast and unmoveable in the Work of the Lord, and obedient to the Call and Requirings of his Holy Spirit, and to the Testimony given her to bear against an hypocritical Generation of hard-hearted Persecutors: But as in so righteous a Cause her *Afflictions* abounded, so her inward *Consolations* did much more abound; so that she was enabled in an Holy Triumph and humble Meekness to declare, *All this,* said she, *and much more, have I gone through and suffered, and much more could I, for the Seed's Sake, which is buried and oppressed, and as a Cart is laden with Sheaves, and as a Prisoner in an inward Prison-house: Yea, the Love that I bear to the Souls of all Men makes me willing to undergo whatsoever can be inflicted on me.*

Hooten survived this abuse and continued her missionary activity. She was imprisoned once more in Boston in 1665 for speaking out during Governor Endicot's funeral. In 1671, she sailed with George Fox on a mission trip to Jamaica where she died in 1672.

Document 2: The Women's Meeting in Early Quakerism

The following document was probably sent from the Swarthmore Monthly Meeting, led by Sarah Fell, the daughter of Margaret Fell, to all the women's meetings in England and America. A copy preserved in the depository of the Arch Street Friends' Meeting House in Philadelphia probably derives from an original sent to the Newport (Rhode Island) Meeting about 1675. The letter, which details the duties of women's meetings, also contains the militant theology of women's equality in Christ developed not only by Fox, but particularly in the writings of Margaret Fell (Women's Speaking Justified, Proved and Allowed of by the Scriptures, 1667).[24]

From our Country Women's meeting in Lancashire to the Dispersed abroad, among the Women's meetings every where.

Dear Sisters.
In the blessed unity in the Spirit of grace our Souls Salute you who are sanctified in Christ Jesus, and called to be Saints, . . . for as many

of us as are baptized into Christ, have put on Christ; for we are all the children of God by faith in Christ Jesus, where there is neither male nor female &c. but we are all one in Christ Jesus . . . the word of the eternal God that endures forever stands upon his (the Devil's) head, that the Seed of the woman should bruise the Serpents head, and this is—fullfilled and fullfilling, in the day of the lords power, and of the restoration, and redemption of his seed and body, which is his church, which is coming out of the wilderness, leaning on her beloved, who is coming in his power and great glory, . . .

So here is the blessed Image of the living God, restored againe, in which he made them male and female in the beginning: and in this his own Image God blessed them both, and said unto them increase and multiply, and replenish the earth, and subdue it, and have dominion over the fish of the sea, and have dominion over the fowles of the heavens, and have dominion over the beasts, and over the cattel, and over the earth, and over every creeping thing on the face of the earth. And in this dominion and power, the Lord God is establishing his own seed, in the male and female, over the head of the serpent, and over his seed, and power. And he makes no difference in the seed, between the male and the female, as Christ saith, that he which made them in the beginning made them male and female, &c. they were both in the work of God in the beginning, and so in the restoration, but if the work of the old serpent, put them out of the work of god, and as he did the beginning tempt them to sinne and transgression, and disobedience, so he would still keep them there, and make a difference, and keep a superiority one over another, that Christ the head should not rule in male and female: and so keep them in bondage, and slavery, and in difference and dissention one with another, and then they are fit for his temptations. . . .

Soe all Dear friends and sisters, make full proofe of the gift of God that is in you, and neglect it not, in this your day, and generation; but that you may be helps meet, in the Restoration, and Resurrection of the body of Christ, which is his Church . . . (give proof of God's gift) as did the Godly women under the law . . . who brought the Lord's offering to the works of the tabernacle. Exodus 35:25–26.

And likewise Miriam the prophetess . . . and all the women who went out after in triumph and singing prayse to the Lord . . . Exodus 15:20–21. . . . And like wise Hannah (who prayed powerfully in the House of the Lord) the Lord hath regard unto and takes notice of women and despises them not . . . you may read in (Isaiah) 32 . . . the Lord calls, Rise up ye women that are at ease . . . untill the spirit be poured on us from on high. . . . And also Jeremy, Chapter 9, . . . thus saith the Lord, call for the mourning women that they may come, for a voice of wailing, is heard out of Zion; yet hear the Word of the Lord. . . .

And Christ Jesus in the days of his flesh, had a dear and tender care and regard unto women, who received many gracious blessings and favours from him: he despised not the woman of Canaan, when she came unto him for her daughter that was vexed with a devil . . . when he saw her faith, he said woman great is thy faith. And also the woman of Samaria, John 4. Christ directed her to the gift of God. . . . See what love and plainess he manifested unto this woman, not dispising her, nor undervalluing her, in the least: . . .

All of those women that he healed, as peters wifes mother, which he healed of a feaver: And the woman that had an issue of bloud: And certain women that had been healed of evill Spirits and Infirmities . . . and many others which ministered to him of their substance. . . .

And all his acquaintance and the women that followed him from Gallilee stood afarr off beholding these things: and the women also that followed him from Gallilee, followed after, and beheld the sepulchre and how his body was layed . . . and upon the first day of the week . . . they came unto the sepulchre . . . behold two men stood by them in shining garments (and said) he is not here but is risen. . . .

And they returned from the Sepulchre and told all these things unto the eleven, and to all the rest, It was Mary Magdalen, and Joanna, and Mary the Mother of James, and other women that were with them, which told these things unto the Apostles, . . . So these women was the first preachers of the Resurrection of Jesus, And Jesus himselfe spake with Mary before he was Ascended to his Father, and said unto her, goe unto my Brethren, and say unto them, I Ascent unto my father, and your father, to my God, and your God, and Mary Magdalen came and told the disciples, that she had seen the lord, and that he had spoken these things unto her. Soe here the Lord Jesus Christ, sends his first message of his resurrection by women unto his own disciples: And they were faithfull unto him, and did his message, and yet they could hardly be believed.

And Paul and Sylas . . . went also among the women where they did usually meet together. . . . So wee having a cloud of wittness, at the order of the Gospell, and of the good works, and charitable practices which multiply in the Scriptures, and practise of the Saints in light, in the primitive times, (women as well as men) that is gone before us; we may be encouraged in the Lords name, power and spirit, to follow their examples and practises: . . . And let us Come into our practise, and into our possession of our portions, and inheritance, that we have of the lord. And let us stand faithfull, and true wittnesses for him in our day, against all deceit, and wickedness.

And let us meet together, and keep our womens meetings, in the name and power, and fear of the lord Jesus, whose servants and handmaids we are, and in the good order of the Gospel meet.

1st. And first, for the women of every . . . monthly meeting, where the mens monthly meetings is established let the women likewise of every monthly meeting, meet together to wait upon the lord, and to hearken what the lord will say unto them, and to know his mind, and will, and be ready to obey, and answer him in every motion of his eternal spirit and power.

2ly. And also, to make inquiry into all your severall particular meetings, that belongs to your monthly meetings, If there be any that walks disorderly, as doth not become the Gospell, or lightly, or wantonly, or that is not of a good reporte: Then send to them, as you are ordered by the power of God in the meeting, (which is the authority of it) to Admonish, and exhort them, and to bring them to Judge, and Condemn, what hath been by them done or acted contrary to the truth.

3ly. And if any transgression or Action that hath been done amongst women or maids, that hath been more publick, and that hath gott into the world, or that hath been a publick offence among friends; then let them bring in a paper of condemnation, to be published as far, as the offence hath gone, and then to be recorded in a booke.

4ly. And if there be any that goes out to Marry, with priests, or joineth in Marriage with the world, and does not obey the order of the Gospell as it is established amongst friends. then for the womens monthly meeting to send to them, to reprove them, and to bear their testimony against their acting Contrary to the truth, and if they come to repentance, and sorrow for their offence, and have a desire to come amongst friends again: before they can be received, they must bring in a paper of Condemnation, and repentance, and Judgment of their Action; which must be recorded in Friends Booke: And also to carry that paper to the priest, that married them, and Judge, and Condemn, and deny that Action, before him or any of the world before whome it shall come.

And dear sisters it is duely Incumbent upon us to look into our families, and to prevent our Children of running into the world for husbands, or for wives, and so to the priests: for you know before the womens meetings were set up, Many have done so, which brought dishonour, both to God, and upon his truth and people. . . .

5ly. And also all friends that keeps in the power of God, and in faithfull obedience to the truth, that according to the order of the Gospell that is established, that they bring their Marriages twice to the womens meetings, and twice to the mens: the first time they are to come to the womens meetings that the women of the meeting, do examin both the man and the woman, that they be cleare and free from all other persons, and that they have their parents, and friends and Relations, Consent; And that enquiry be made of their clearness in each particular meeting to which they do belong, before their next appearance in the womens meeting.

And if nothing be found, but that they come in clearness to the next monthly meeting, then they may proceed according to the order of the Gospell, and perfect their marriage in the meeting of friends, as friends which they belong to sees it Convenient: But if any thing be found that they are not clear, but that others lay Challenge, or Charge to them, either by promise or otherwise that then they do not proceed, till they have given satisfaction both to the parties, and friends, concerning that matter, according to the order of the Gospell; and that if any thing be amiss concerning the woman, examin it, and look into it, which may not be proper for the men.

6ly. And likewise, that the women of the monthly meetings, take care, and oversight of all the women that belongs to their several particular meetings, that they bring in their testimonies for the lord, and his truth, against tithes, and hireling priests once every yeare, Since the priests claimes, and challenges a tithe, which belongs to women to pay, as well as the men, not only for widdows, but them that have husbands, as piggs, and geese, henns and eggs, hemp and flax, wooll and lamb: all which women may have a hand in: Soe it concerns the womens meetings, to looke strictly to every particular meeting, that every woman bring in their testimony against tiths, and that those testimonies be recorded in the quarterly, or halfe yeares meeting book, once every year. . . .

8ly. And also all friends, in their womens monthly, and particular Meetings, that they take special care for the poore, and for those that stands in need: that there be no want, nor suffering, for outward things, amongst the people of God, . . .

And so let Care be taken for the poore, and widdows, that hath young Children, that they be relieved, and helped, till they be able and fitt, to be put out to apprentices or servants.

And that all the sick, and weak, and Infirme, or Aged, and widdows, and fatherless, that they be looked after, and helped, and relieved, in every particular meeting, either with clothes, or maintainance, or what they stand in need off. So that in all things the Lord may be glorified, and honoured, so that there be no want, nor suffering in the house of God, who loves a Chearfull giver.

And so here in the power and spirit, of the Lord God, women comes to be coheirs, and fellow labourers, in the Gospell, as it was in the Apostles dayes. . . .

So here was the womens meeting, and womens teachings, of one another, so that this is no new thing, as some raw unseasoned spirits would seem to make it:

And though wee be looked upon as the weaker vessels, yet strong and powerfull is God, whose strength is made perfect in weakness, he can make us good and bold, and valliant Souldiers of Jesus Christ, if he arm us with his Armour of Light, he who respect no persons, but chuseth the weak things of this world, and foolish things to confound the wise: our sufficiency is of him, and our Armour, and strength is in him:

This is given forth for Information, and Direction, that in the blessed unity of the spirit of grace, all friends may bee, and live in the practice of the holy order of the Gospell; if you know these things, happy are you if ye do them so.

THE EPHRATA CLOISTER

Document 3: The Spiritual Order of the Roses of Saron

The Rose, or the acceptable flower for Saron's Spiritual betrothal with their celestial Bridegroom, whom they have espoused as their King, Ruler, Spouse, Lord and Bridegroom unto all Eternity. Added thereto is the full allegiance and obedience to their Spiritual Mother and Vorsteherin, *and then of their fidelity and duty unto themselves and toward one another. Given of their Spiritual father and founder, as it was by his diligence that this whole spiritual Society was erected, as was also the no less worthy society in Zion. Ephrata, May 13, 1745.*

So reads the title page of the rule by which the solitary sisters lived at Ephrata. The sister's way of life was in contrast to that of the brothers, who conducted themselves by oral rule, which was subject to relatively frequent change and individual interpretation. The original copy of the sisters' rule is composed in fractur schrift *and is illuminated. The translation comes from Julius Friedrich Sachse, The German Sectarians of Pennsylvania,*[25] *a leading authority on the sect who apparently tried to reproduce the peculiar language of Canaan which the members affected.*

Applicants for the sisterhood were obliged to submit to a novitiate of a year and a day. Normally no one under eighteen years of age was admitted.

Under the leadership of this person, [Maria, one of two sisters who received Beissel's permission to start the sisterhood] it was never a question who was most competent in the Society to bear the honorable title of Spiritual Mother, for as soon as she entered upon that office all was changed. Now there came a demand for a life under rule and discipline (*regel u. Schrankenmässig leben*). Thus the above-mentioned wooer spent the time of her hard service among the sisterhood. Soon the longing came for a well ordered and circumscribed rule of table discipline. Then we sought well to discern the time for sleeping and waking, and as everything was viewed with moderate discreetness, it was sought to arrange the matter so that nature as a spiritual vessel and instrument was not blunted nor made uncomfortable, but rather willing and eager for the service of God.

Thus the hours for sleep amount to six hours, as after the evening meal it happens that from the second to the fourth hour (7 to 9 P.M.)

the time is occupied in school instruction and practice (*schülbungen*) (sic), be it writing, reading or singing, after which the three hours, fourth (9 P.M.) until the seventh (12 M.), are devoted to sleep. The seventh hour (12 to 1 A.M.) is devoted to the midnight mass (*nacht mette*), where the Christian and divine psalms and hymns are sung and the holy prayer attended until the ninth hour (2 A.M.) after which three hours, namely from the ninth until the twelfth hour (2 A.M. to 5 A.M.) are devoted to sleep. Thus the time is passed from night until morning, and everything is done within divine bounds and in regular order.

The awakening takes place at the twelfth hour (5 A.M.) and is done in the greatest order. The time being devoted to holy contemplation, until the first striking of the first hour (6 A.M.) then each and every one goes to their regular vocation or employment given them by the overseer until the fourth hour (9 A.M.), which hour is also devoted to spiritual and bodily refreshment. Little can now intervene to prevent us from keeping at our bodily employment until the twelfth hour (5 P.M.), then we again devote an hour to holy and divine contemplation until the first hour (6 P.M.), when our meal is prepared with great care and takes place, at which more attention is again given to obedience and moderation than to the kind of the viands. [The Sabbath commenced at the first hour of the sixth day, in other words on Friday at 6 P.M. and closed at the end of the twelfth hour of the seventh day, Saturday at 6 P.M., to conform to the letter of the New Testament.]

[The sisters were divided into seven classes to perform the round of the day's tasks, under the discipline of a seasoned sister. They all wore identical habits.]

Now we will describe the rule and use of our every day clothing, and in what manner they are to be worn. First, we have a knit gown of grey [unbleached] fabric, just as nature supplies it. To this gown belongs a hood of same fabric, only that it may be of coarse flaxen cloth. It is arranged as follows: it is to be deep over the face, so that the head may be covered and enveloped, from this a veil [apron] is to hang from the front and back, long enough to be caught by the waist girdle. In front under the chin there are to be two small lapels, to further hide the body. For daily use knit socks are to be worn in place of shoes, they are to be made like shoes, reinforced with a coarse woolen cloth or thin leather sole, so that our walk may be quiet and silent. Our every day clothing [meaning under clothing] is to be the same summer and winter. . . .

What shall we say more of the quiet and justly in God enamoured souls, how they arrange their lives and conduct, so as to please only and alone their King of Heaven, whose kingdom is not of this world. Therefor our life and conduct cannot agree or conform to the world, whether it be in eating and drinking,—sleeping or waking,—in clothing or other requisite things pertaining to the natural life. Thus we have taken it into hand to deny and refute such engagements, and have schooled ourselves to be moderate in our eat and drink, and subsist upon little, and that with scant preparation, not according to the usual desire of nature, but merely reflecting upon the necessity of human frailty, so that the spirit may the more readily accomplish its divine task. Our sleep we have also arranged so that we can without great difficulty keep the time of our midnight vigil. Thus we make no further preparation when retiring to rest, than to lay down in the clothing or habits, we wear during the day. Our couch is a bare bench, the pillow, a small block of wood, or small straw pillow,—more frequently neither,—in this matter every one has their option. . . .

As we have first renounced all vanities of the world, our future conduct will be guided according to the discipline of the body. We will begin by contracting to the utmost our eating and drink, sleep and waking. So that our whole life and conduct be that of a suffering and dying pilgrim upon earth, for which reason we have divorced ourselves from the ways and customs of this world, and daily and hourly learn the manner and laws of our crucified Jesus, who instructs us in all things and taught us abnegation of self, and to take up the cross and follow him.

Then again it is to be mentioned what is requisite to keep duly and properly within bounds. Firstly, it is meet that we keep proper order with our eating. As it is set inevitably that there is to be but one meal a day, it will be held in the evening, and great stress is laid that the entire Society assemble at it. [Besides bread, this meal might consist of barley boiled in milk, pumpkin mush and cheese curds; there was a strong sentiment against meat in the Ephrata community.] It may happen during the day that one perhaps takes a bite of bread, owing to our weakness, this is not prohibited to such as feel the necessity of it. Let them partake of the same as a special gift, and acknowledge themselves a debtor unto God, and pray for him to grant the strength yet wanting. . . .

What then further concerns our intercourse with and toward one another, is this: It is to be striven in all seriousness and diligence, that our life be modest, quiet, tranquil and retired, so that each becomes an example for the other, and exemplifies the secret course of life and communion with God. All levity and needless gossip with one another, or light laughter, is not to be thought of, nor shall it occur in this spiritual society. Therefor it is unnecessary to make much of this rule, as it is not considered and much less likely to occur.

It is further to be said of the mood of the hearts and souls who have sacrificed their whole life unto God, and live for him in the silent contemplation of their heart, and walk in his ways.

[The conclusion of the rule deals with how the overseer of each class of sisters is to determine the legitimacy of requests for visits into the outside world. Although these visits were carefully restricted, the sisters did earn a wide reputation for errands of mercy to the sick and needy.]

Document 4: The Single Sisters' Music

The Chronicon Ephratense, *however biased in favor of Beissel, provides the best account of the beginning of the singing school at Ephrata and the development of the sisters' choir.*[26] *Beissel himself had known nothing about music except whatever he remembered from his youth in Germany when he played the fiddle. He engaged a master-singer, Ludwig Blum, from among the householders to instruct the sisters, and as other accounts claim, he himself told the sisters to "steal" Blum's art. Beissel not only took over the choir, but wrote the earliest known American treatise of music, the* Turtel-Taube *or* Turtle-Dove, *many of whose principles are also summarized here.*

Now those of the Solitary, of whom about seventy of both sexes were in the Settlement, were selected who had talent for singing, and the above mentioned Ludwig Blum, together with the Superintendent, arranged a singing-school in the Settlement, and everything prospered for a time. But the Sisters at last complained to the Superintendent that they were sold to one man, and petitioned him to manage the school himself, saying that they would steal the whole secret of the schoolmaster and hand it over to him. The Superintendent soon perceived that this advice came from God, for as the event proved, quite different things were hidden under it, for which the good school-master's hands were not made. And now the Sisters told the Superintendent everything they had learnt in the school, and as soon as they saw that he had mastered the art, they dismissed their schoolmaster. . . .

Before the commencement was made, he [Beissel] entered upon a strict examination of those things which are either injurious or beneficial to the human voice, in consequence of which he declared all fruit, milk, meat, to be viands injurious to the voice. One might have thought that he borrowed this from the teaching of Pythagoras, in order to break his scholars of the animal habit of eating meat, of which habit he was never in favor. When bringing all this before the Brethren for examination, they observed that he crossed some words with his pen, by which he had declared the love of women as also injurious to the voice. When asked why he did this, he answered that some might take offence at it. But the sentence was retained with full consent of the Brethren, and the writing was added as preface to the hymn-book. This was but fair, for who does not know that carnal intercourse stains not only the soul, but also weakens the body, and renders the voice coarse and rough; so that the senses of him must be very blunt who cannot distinguish a virgin from a married woman by her voice. . . .

The singing-schools began with the Sisters, lasted four hours, and ended at midnight. Both master and scholars appeared in white habits, which made a singular procession, on which account people of quality frequently visited the school. The Superintendent, animated by the spirit of eternity, kept the school in great strictness and every fault was sharply censured. The whole neighborhood, however, was touched by the sound of this heavenly music, a prelude of a new world and a wonder to the neighbors. . . .

After the Superintendent had with much trouble broken the ice, and taught the first principles of singing to the scholars, he divided them into five choirs with five persons to each choir, namely, one air, one tenor, one alto, and two bass singers. The Sisters were divided into three choirs, the upper, middle and lower; and in the choruses a sign was made for each choir, when to be silent and when to join in the singing. These three choirs had their separate seats at the table of the Sisters during love-feasts, the upper choir at the upper end, the middle at the middle, and the lower at the lower end; in singing antiphonally, therefore, the singing went alternately up and down the table. Not only had each choir to observe its time when to join in, but, because there were solos in each chorale, every voice knew when to keep silent, all of which was most attentively observed. And now the reason appeared which induced him to establish such choirs of virgins. It was with him as with Solomon, he was zealous to make manifest the wonderful harmony of eternity, in a country which but lately wild savages had inhabited; for God owed this to North America as an initiation into the Christian church, therefore these choirs belong to the firstlings of America. The contents of these songs were entirely prophetic, and treated of the restoration of the image of Adam before his division, of the heavenly virginity, the priesthood of Melchizedek, etc. The gift of prophecy overflowed the Settlement like a river at that time; and close observation showed that the beautiful sun of Paradise had then already reached its meridian, but afterwards inclined towards its setting, and was at last followed by a sorrowful night, as will be shown in its place. This wonderful harmony resounded over the country; whoever heard of it, wished to see it, and whoever saw it, acknowledged that God truly lived among these people.

Document 5: Hymns by Women at Ephrata

The talent of the Ephrata Sisters for illuminating and copying music is well known; many of the manuscripts are still extant today. What is less well known is that many of the hymns which they sung were of their own composition. An entire section of the Paradisisches Wunderspiel *("A Pleasant Fragrance of Roses and Lilies, which grew forth in the valley of humility among the thorns, all from the Sisters Society of Saron") was devoted to the verses of hymns composed by women—thirty-five were published there, written by twenty-three different sisters.*[27] *Much of their lyricism and rhymed rhythm is unfortunately lost in translation.*

Now there I walk along in hope and carry my trespasses
in pain there blossoms my reward: thus will I gladly suffer.

And even if I find myself alone on my pilgrim's ways
God will provide for me all along many a comfort and blessing.

Thus I look forward to that world which be a new beginning,
that is the aim I set myself, that's why I fear no hardship.

The pure thought of my God above makes all the darkness flee;
that's why in following my path I'll reach my righteous goal.

This now is here my pilgrim's staff on which I can rely;
although I have no other goods nor property to hold.

Thus is my luck in the hand of God, to him I will submit:
and since already he has claimed me in this present life.

Thus I am very well supplied with God's mercy and grace:
since they have healed all my pains and freed me from all cares.

The comfort often handed me whenever I sat sadly:
that is what carries me to God and has my peace restored.

Therefore when all the strife is done and done are all my trials,
there will in all eternity and without end I praise Him.

Document 6: Comments of Visitors

There are a number of descriptions of Ephrata Music.[28] *One appears in a letter of Reverend Jacob Duche, son of the mayor of Philadelphia who visited Ephrata in 1771, while another description is given in Dr. William M. Fahnestock's early nineteenth-century account.*[29]

The music had little or no air or melody; but consisted of simple, long notes, combined in the richest harmony. The counter, treble, tenor and bass were all sung by women, with sweet, shrill and small voices; but with a truth and exactness in the time and intonation that was admirable. It is impossible to describe to your Lordship my feelings upon this occasion. The performers sat with their heads reclined, their countenances solemn and dejected, their faces pale and emaciated from their manner of living, their clothing exceeding white and quite picturesque, and their music such as thrilled to the very soul.—I almost began to think myself in the world of spirits, and that the objects before me were ethereal. In short, the impression this scene made upon my mind continued strong for many days, and I believe, will never be wholly obliterated.

Their music is set in four, six and eight parts. All the parts save the bass are lead and sung exclusively by females, the men being confined to the bass, which is set in two parts, the high and low bass—the latter resembling the deep tones of the organ, and the first, in combination with one of the female parts, is an excellent imitation of the concert horn. The whole is sung on the *falsetto* voice, the singers scarcely opening their mouths, or moving their lips, which throws the voice up to the ceiling, which is not high, and the tones, which seem to be more than human, at least so far from common church singing appear to be entering from above, and hovering over the heads of the assembly. . . . often as I entered I became ashamed of myself, for scarcely had these strains of celestial melody touched my ear, than I was bathed in tears—unable to suppress them, they continued to cover my face during the service; nor in spite of my mortification could I keep away. They were not tears of penitence, for my heart was not subdued to the Lord, but tears of ecstatic rapture, giving a foretaste of the joys of heaven.

THE MORAVIAN BRETHREN

Document 7: The Religious Growth of a Moravian Woman: The Life Story of Martha Powell (1704–1774)

Most members of Moravian congregations wrote a Lebenslauf *or religious autobiography during the course of their lives. These autobiographies constitute an invaluable source of insight into the nature of the Moravian personality and experience. An individual believer would keep the account up to date to cultivate personal spiritual awareness and activity, and then at the time of death, the minister of the congregation would complete the record. There were five relevant stages of religious development: uneasiness over the condition of the soul, religious awakening, admission to the Brethren, life and work as a member, and death itself.* Lebensläufe *were delivered at funerals as obituaries, but they were much more than this: they were models of instruction to others, often included in congregational diaries, exchanged and circulated within the Moravian network.*[30] *The life story of Martha Powell (1704–1774) is particularly illuminating because it records the experience of an ordinary woman, rather than a member of the Moravian leadership, and suggests the immense emotional and practical commitment, including the extensive travels, of such a person who was herself of no special distinction in the community.*[31]

I was born the 12th of February 1704 at *Norby* not far from *Oxford* in *England.* My fathers name was *Prichard.* My Fathers greatest concern was to educate me after the way of the World, and had me taught Dancing and other Idle things customary in the same, but my Mother, who was brought up a Quaker, (tho she was baptized on her wedding day) was full of concern for her childrens Salvation, which she manifested more Particularly in her last Illness, when she frequently spoke of our Saviour's Merrits, as the whole of her dependance, and commended her children to his care with Prayers and Tears. I was in my 5th year when she dyed, and from my childhood I was quite taken up with the Pleasures of this world, nevertheless I frequently melted into Tears when I heard at church of our Saviour's suffrings.

In my 15th. Year My Father married a second wife, upon which I left his House and went to service at Oxford, and being a good Dancer was much respected among my companions. In my 31 Year I went accidentally to a meeting which was keept by a strickt preacher of the Law, and grew very uneasy at what I heard, the woman in whose service I was, observed it, and did all in her Power to bring me to a nother way of thinking, but when she found nothing had any effect upon me she became my Enemy, and I quitted her Service.

Not long after I was Persuaded to go to a Dance, scarce did I begin to dance, before I was overcome with such Terror, that I left the company immediately, returnd home and begd of God with thousands of Tears to have Mercy on me because I had acted against my better Knowledge and Conviction. This was the hardest Night I had ever had in my Life before, moreover I was soon after taken with the small Pox, and sufferd a great deal in that Disorder. By this means the world became so distasteful to me, that I thankd God with numberless Tears for his unspeakable Mercies, in setting me free from its delusions.

From this time forward frequented the Methodists Society Meeting,[32] keept by Mr. *Kinshin* and *John Gambold* and others, but did not attain to real rest of Soul. After some time the *Disciple* came to Oxford visited our Society, spoke all the awakend, and at his Return to Germany, sent Brother *Wing* to us, whose Testimony of Jesus Love to poor Sinners was greatly blessed to my heart. One time 14 of us being at a Love Feast, Brother Wing at the close of the Meeting fell on his knees and pray'd most fervently. In that Instant my dear Saviour! My Lord and my God! drew near my heart in his bleeding Form, and it was to me as tho he spoke audibly to me: *I have loved thee with an everlasting Love and none shall pluck thee out of my Hand.* This, which surpass'd by far all heavenly apearances that I could form an Idea of, sett me att once free from all Trouble Fear & condemnation, and my heart was easy and happy. It was Proposed to me, wether I would go to Germany, or rather stay in England, I chose the last, and removed to London where I was some time Labouress among the Single Sisters, and then on the 5th. of February 1742 was joined in Marriage to my dear Husband *Joseph Powell.*

In obedience to our call on the 4th. of March following, we saild with the first Sea Congregation to Pennsylvania, and landed in Philada. on Asscention day. Our joy was very great to find the Disciple here, and we followed him to Bethlehem as the first Beginners to this congregation. Soon after our arrival here, I was admitted to the Holy Sacrament with the congregation and received an accoluth [accolade]. I understand very little of the German Language, yet I felt very happy in the meetings, and that grace which reigned in this growing congregation, made me ready and willing to assist to the uttmost of my Power, wherever my Service was required. *The 24th. of Decr.* the same year my Husband and I travelled with the Disciple to Philadelphia, and from thence to *Schamini*[33] and after 3 Months stay there, returnd to Bethlehem where I enjoy'd unspeakable Blessings for my heart. In the Year *1744* my Husband and I was 4 Months in West Jerseys, and then sometime at our dear Captain Garrisons on *Staaten Island* and in the year 1746 we were at Dansbury.[34] In the year 1748 we were sent to Shemoho.[35] where I had a hard fitt of illness, and returnd to Bethlehem in November where the office of servant of the Church was committed to my charge.[36] In the year 1751 we was sent to Long Island and after a 7 Months stay there, was sent a 2d time to Dansbury. There we staid one year, and then returnd to Bethlehem, where my Husband began Storekeeping. In the year 1755 we were sent to Gnadenhütten on the Mahony, there we staid 9 Months untill the Terrible Attack of the Indians of which I was aprehensive some time before it came to Pass, which was on the 24th of November. Then we retreated to Bethlehem and after we had strengthned and refreshed ourselves some time here, we went to Sichem in New England. Here we staid 3 Years, and in that space of time had the comfort to see a little congregation settled there by our dear Brother Spangenberg.

In the Year 1759 we received a call to assist in the work of God among the Negoes in Jamaica and after a stay in Bethlehem of 8 Weeks we satt out on our Journey thither on my Birth day the 12th. of February. I lookd upon it as a peculiar Favour to serve the poor Negro Slaves. I loved them, and they loved me, but the excessive heat of the climate weakned my poor Tabernacle greatly. After we had been there near 6 Years we received our call to return home. I was very sea sick, and had very little hopes of outliving the Voyage, but yet I could not believe I should be Buried in the Sea, but that I should be permitted to lay my Bones to rest in the congregation.

The 27th of October I arrived at my beloved Bethlehem to my unspeakable Joy. I had now obtaind the uttmost of my wishes, and often said to our dear Saviour with Tears: "Now I am ready to quit this poor Mortal clay and sink into thy arms for thou has redeemed me with thy Precious Blood." However I recoverd thro the care and Tenderness of my dear Brethern and Sisters so far, that on the *30th.*

of May 1766 the Post at Carrols Mannour in Maryland was committed to our charge. We accepted the call with willing hearts, and arrived there on the *14th. of July.* Here we resided above 6 years wept with those that wept, and rejoiced with those that rejoiced, and our dear Lord and Saviour graciously acknowledged our poor Services. At length my strength decayed so fast, that in the Year *1772* we was obliged to quit this Post and came to Bethlehem on the *22d. of October.*

Thus far our dear Sisters own words.

Her Joy to find herself among her Beloved People before her End, was so great, that for a time she seemd to regain strength, so that she could frequent the Meetings and during her Husbands Absence (who in the Interim made a voyage to Barbadoes) she was able to go about her little Household affairs, but after his return her weakness increased daily and her longing after her eternal home increased from day to day, which was at length happily asswaged on the *6th. Instant:* a little before, her Husband ask'd her wether she had much Pain? O No said she smiling, now it will be soon over. After He had given her the last Blessing to her departure she said: my dear Husband now give me one kiss, he did so, and she instantly fell asleep as a Redeemed Sinneress, aged 70 Years, 2 Months and 24 days.

Document 8: Diary of the Single Sisters' Choir at Lititz

The following excerpt comes from the Diary of the Single Sisters' Choir at Lititz, Pennsylvania.[37] *Lititz was originally a congregation served by Bethlehem-Nazareth; today it is one of the most active and prosperous of contemporary Moravian communities. The diary, kept by the women themselves, is primarily a spiritual record; the intensity of religious life is suggested in this brief entry documenting the continuing sense of sisterhood maintained with decreased members, women of whom Christ is now the Bridegroom. Unfortunately, the idiosyncratic and sensual nature of Moravian language is almost impossible to capture in translation.*

19 August 1769 . . . Towards evening a storm developed so that the congregational hour was suspended. This gave us the most beautiful opportunity in our choir meeting to renew the memory of our dear blessed Charitas on this day [anniversary] of her Home-going [death]. Our dear Marie Magdlen offered a beautiful prayer as a prelude for this, in order [to establish] the eternal communion with the full Congregation of those departed [in death] and particularly with our dear sister Charitas. We offered ourselves in most deferential greeting before the Bride of our Saviour and then listened to a beautiful talk, appropriate to this occasion, of the dear blessed disciple on the words; His sick ones at the invalid pool all enter into the Kingdom of health; with which [text] we concluded the day and the week. . . .

Document 9: Female Leadership among the Moravians: The Autobiography of Anna Nitschmann

The life story of Anna Nitschmann (1715–1760), one of the most remarkable and influential leaders of the Moravians during their formative years in America, speaks for itself. Anna's father, David, was uncle of the David Nitschmann, the weaver, who became bishop. The vow of 1730 which she mentions here, taken with a number of other single women at Herrnhut, to renounce any idea of marriage and to devote her life exclusively to Christ, was apparently what made it possible for her to travel extensively in mixed company. Normally, Single Sisters were segregated at all times, but they were viewed as candidates for marriage by the community and the Elders. Nitschmann's life also demonstrates the socio-economic egalitarianism of the Moravians and the extraordinary opportunities available to women of energy and talent.[38]

I was born November 24th, 1715, at Kunewalde in Moravia. My father was David Nitschmann, a farmer and carpenter; my mother, Anna, daughter of Samuel Schneider, both natives of Zauchtenthal. From my early childhood the thought of God and divine things inspired me with reverential awe; and though I loved the world and felt almost tempted to join the ranks of its votaries, the unseen hand of my Heavenly Father mercifully preserved me. In my seventh year I was compelled to partake of the Holy Communion as administered in the Romish Church. I believed what I was told, that I received the real body and blood of Jesus Christ, and my heart was deeply moved. When I was eight years old—it was in the year 1724—the great awakening in Moravia began. In my father's house there were meetings attended by from 100 to 200 people. I was powerfully aroused, and began to pray in the public assemblies. This was in winter. During the summer months I tended my father's flock, singing in the fields our old Moravian Brethrens' hymns, . . .

[After her father and brother had been imprisoned a number of times for their religious activities, the family decided to emigrate to Herrnhut.]

At that time a great awakening took place in the whole congregation, more especially amongst the children, who often passed the night in the fields and in the forest of the Hutberg. I became anxiously concerned, and thought, 'What a sinful creature I am!' Our Saviour placed in a strong light before my eyes the grace which He had bestowed upon me from my infancy, and the unfaithfulness with which I had requited His love. My heart melted within me. I shed many tears. I began to seek the Saviour with all my heart, and earnestly implored His forgiveness. And He blotted out all my debt, though

I could scarcely believe it at the time, thinking it was too soon to expect such a blessing. Yet I felt confidence in Him, and enjoyed free access to the throne of grace. In the same year I was confirmed and admitted to partake of the Holy Communion. . . . Eternity was the sole object of my thoughts and aspirations. The work of guiding the souls of others and attending to their spiritual concerns brought me down in some degree from these soaring heights. I went to my work with a cheerful heart, and it was my greatest pleasure to watch the gradual progress of the souls entrusted to my charge. In the congregation I was as yet but little known, not being possessed of the gifts calculated to attract notice. I remained in retirement and laboured amongst the elder girls, nine in number. We had our regular offices and arrangements—elders, overseers, exhorters, sick nurses. I filled the office of exhorter. We treated all our little concerns with great seriousness; nor did our Saviour withhold His blessing from our feeble efforts.

On March 17th, 1730, I was chosen by lot, elderess of the congregation, contrary to the expectations of most, if not all, the members of the Church, and certainly to my own deep humiliation. Being at that time in a very childlike, obedient frame of mind, I did not raise many objections, but said, 'Behold the handmaid of the Lord; be it unto me according to Thy word.' I accepted the appointment, trusting in my ever faithful Friend, who, I felt assured, would help me through all my difficulties and 'graciously regard the low estate of His handmaiden.' [At the time of her appointment to this office, she was only fourteen and a half years old.]

. . . In the same year, on the 4th of May, it happened that all the unmarried women, eighteen in number, who loved the Lord Jesus, were assembled at a lovefeast in the house of David Nitschmann, the weaver. On that occasion they were led clearly to discern the duties and obligations peculiar to their position; and being desirous of living to the praise of the Lord and the joy of the congregation, they entered into a solemn covenant with each other to demean themselves as true virgins of the Lamb. Oh how delightful it was to me to witness this! . . . The third year of my office was, consequently, a season of trial. On the 26th of January, 1733, I moved into the sisters' house together with thirteen single sisters. I felt truly happy. We lived with each other in love and hallowed fellowship, and spent many a night in social prayer. At first we 'had all things common;' . . . [For a while in 1733, she suffered a period of anxiety and misgivings.] I felt deeply ashamed of my impatience and want of confidence in the wisdom of my Lord and Master, who assuredly knew best what would tend to advance my spiritual growth. More than ever did I feel the absolute need for a Redeemer in whose wounds I could find a secure resting-place. His death upon the cross came home to my heart with a power, an energy, and a freshness such as I had never before experienced.

I could firmly believe that He had laid down His life for my sins. If our Saviour had not thus had compassion upon me, I should have sunk into despair. During this chilling season of trial and inward conflict I often sighed, 'Oh Lord! where is my former strength, and where is the blessed simplicity I once possessed?' Oh! what did I experience during those two years! I cannot recount or describe all the troubles of my soul. My office was a heavy burden to me, and I sincerely wished to resign it into the hands of a more qualified person. The hand of the Lord, however, was clearly traceable in my leadings. My natural independence of character might easily have led me to leave the congregation, and thus to deprive myself of those blessings which God's children enjoy in fellowship one with another. But the office which I held bound me to the Church which the Lord had called me to serve; and I could not think of laying down my office without our Saviour's sanction. I therefore resolved to serve Him and His congregation as long as it should please Him to employ me in His vineyard. Gradually, after many an inward struggle, I was enabled to regain my former simplicity. It was my sincere desire to die to self and to live wholly to Him who died and rose again for me. He it was whom my soul had chosen. . . .

[During the late 1730s, Nitschmann established her capacity for leadership by ministering to converts in Holland and Germany in the company of Zinzendorf's family.]

In 1740, I was commissioned to accompany my father to America, in order to assist, in my small degree, in promoting the Lord's work in those parts. . . .

[After a stay in Holland and another in England,] we then embarked for America, and, after being detained for seven weeks in the channel, proceeded to Philadelphia, where we arrived in safety after a voyage of seventeen weeks. The period of my sojourn in that country was a season of peculiar blessing to my soul. I was privileged to win not a few souls for our Saviour, and spent many a happy hour in communion of heart with Him while we were roaming about in the forests. In 1741, Count Zinzendorf arrived with his daughter Benigna and the rest of his company, and on the 9th of December I had the pleasure of welcoming them in America. We proceeded together to Philadelphia, where we closed the year very happily. We spent the whole of the following year in America, and were three times among the heathen for forty-nine days, in the midst of wild beasts and venomous serpents. On that very spot a congregation was founded before the close of the year. The word of the cross sounded through the whole country. Bethlehem became a congregation in June, and is now a flourishing congregation of the Lord Jesus. I was very happy in America.

Document 10: Moravian Missions to the American Indians: J. Martin Mack's Recollections of a Journey from Olstonwakin to Wyoming (October 1742)

John Martin Mack (1715–1784) and his wife, Jeannette Rau (1722–1749), were among the foremost Moravian missionaries to the Indians. Mack himself was made Elder of the Heathen in 1745. Jeannette (or Johanna) Rau grew up near Shekomeko (Reinbeck, New York), an Indian settlement that became one of the very earliest Moravian missions. She knew the Mohican language, the medium of communication among many members of the Algonquin family, and a number of other dialects. Her linguistic skill made her invaluable. Mack was persuaded to write this account of Zinzendorf's journey to the western Indians during his American visit of 1741–1742. No white people, except adventurers, had previously made this trek into the wilderness. The very nonchalance of the account illustrates the habitual Moravian lack of concern with gender difference in the face of missionary dangers.[39]

As I recollect, you [Peter Böhler] accompanied the sainted Disciple [Zinzendorf] as far as Otstonwakin,[40] and then returned to Shamokin. From here my sainted Jeanette and myself, with Shikellimy[41] as guide, and a grandchild of his, set out for Otstonwakin on the next day, arriving there late at night.

The Disciple and Anna [Nitschmann] were rejoiced to see us. We remained there several days, and on two occasions held meetings, which were attended by Andrew Montour and his grandmother (?)[42] and some of the Indians. The services were conducted in French, which language the former understood.

Leaving Otstonwakin, our way lay through the forest, over rocks and frightful mountains, and across streams swollen by the recent heavy rains. This was a fatiguing and dangerous journey, and on several occasions we imperiled our lives in fording the creeks, which ran with impetuous current. On the fifth day, at last, we reached Wyoming,[43] and pitched our tent not far from the Shawanese town. The Disciple's reception by the savages was unfriendly, although from the first their visits were frequent. Painted with red and black, each with a large knife in his hand, they came in crowds about the tent, again and again. He lost no time, therefore, in informing the Shawanese chief, through Andrew Montour, of the object of his mission. This the wily savage affected to regard as a mystery, and replied that such matters concerned the white man, and not the Indian.

. . . One day Jeannette, on returning to the town from visiting the Indians, informed the Disciple that she had met with a Mohican woman in the upper town, who, to her unspeakable joy, had spoken to her of the Saviour. This intelligence deeply affected him. He rose up and bade us go with him in search of her, and in the interview that followed he magnified the love of Jesus to her in terms of most persuasive tenderness. This woman now became our provider, furnishing us with beans and corn-bread, until we could procure other supplies. . . .

One day, having convened the Indians in the upper town, he [Zinzendorf] laid before them his object in coming to Wyoming, and expressed the desire to send people among them that would tell them words spoken by their Creator. Most of these were Mohicans, and not as obdurately perverse as the Shawanese. Although they signified no decided opposition, they stated their inability to entertain any proposals without the consent of the lattér, according to whose decision they were compelled to shape their own. Should these assent, they said they would not object, but be satisfied. My Jeannette acted as interpreter of what passed during the meeting. . . .

From our first encampment . . . I once rode out with the Disciple and Anna. There was a creek in our way, in a swampy piece of ground. Anna and myself led in crossing, and with difficulty succeeded in ascending the farther bank, which was steep and muddy. But the Disciple was less fortunate, for in attempting to land, his horse plunged, broke the girth, and his rider rolled off backwards into the water, and the saddle upon him. It required much effort on my part to extricate him, and when I at last succeeded, he kissed me and said, "My poor brother! I am an endless source of trouble!" Being without change, we were necessitated to dry our clothes at the fire and then brush off the mud. Adventures of this kind befell us more than once.

Document 11: Massacre and Martyrdom at Gnadenhuetten in 1755

The instructive or propaganda function of the Lebensläufe *(life stories) is nowhere better illustrated than in the group entitled "Personals of our Brothers and Sisters Martyred November 24 1755 on the Mahony by Hostile Indians."*[44] *The episode could have seriously discouraged further missionary endeavors on the part of the Moravians. But the life stories of the martyrs were recorded in such a way as to reinforce the missionary commitment of the survivors and to suggest that those killed had anticipated—indeed, welcomed—their martyrdom as an opportunity.*

Anna Catharina Sensemann (1717–1755) had served as a missionary to Indians at Shekomeko and at Pachgotgoch before she was sent to Gnadenhuetten, where in the summer before her death, she was elected to the office of chairperson (Vorsteher). *She also had experience as a missionary to blacks in St. Thomas. During the intervals between her missions, she acted as a table-servant* (Tisch-Diener) *and hall-servant* (Saal Diener).

The day before her martyrdom, she held once again a particularly heartfelt devotional [*besonders herzl. Bande*][45] with her husband whom she had always particularly loved, and on the last morning ... she demonstrated her affection to him in the midst of his activities, kissed his head with great respect, and at the same time took leave of him, not knowing what would happen to her. For from then on they did not see one another again, but afterward she spent the whole day with the sisters at laundry. Thus in the evening she went in flames to the Lamb and to her Congregation. As she already sat in the flames, she folded her hands, held a heartfelt devotion with the Saviour and her last words were: "O now dear Saviour this is how I imagined it!" She brought 38 years, 1 month and 4 days to the day of her death. She then has appeared next to the other sisters with a loving gaze and in a white dress [perhaps in a dream] to Sister Partsehin and has said to her "Better the smaller portion than the larger."

Susanna Nitschmann (1721–1755), originally from Silesia, had been with her husband at Bethlehem and Nazareth in America since 1749 and at Gnadenhuetten since the summer of 1755.

She received the grace soon after [the martyrdom of] her husband to enter the arms of her Eternal Husband through the martyr's death at 34 years old. Before the end of her life for death she had a particularly heartfelt devotional [*Herzens-Bande*] with Sister Anna Maria and said: "I know for a certainty that I am on the Mahoney in order that I may come to know the Lamb so that Eternity and I and I and Eternity may be ever one heart." And she said that she well knew and was well satisfied that she truly knew the Saviour sought nothing more from her than to truly possess her.

Sister and Brother Nitschmann had only two sons with one another, Johannes and Martin, and both survive and are here [in Bethlehem].

Document 12: The Marriage Lot in Practice

When a Single Brother or Widower wanted to marry in the Moravian community, various circumstances of his situation were considered in the Elders' Conference. The marriage lot itself was devised in a variety of ways. Men who wished to marry were expected to be economically in a position to support a wife and children, notwithstanding the existence of a communal economy and the universality of women's work. Presumably a married woman did not contribute enough to the community to compensate for both her own and her children's maintenance.

In America, there was often a shortage of marriageable Single Sisters. As is apparent from the extracts that follow, women were assigned in marriage to men, never vice versa. The Moravian settle-

ments in North Carolina at Bethabara, Bethania, and Salem were founded between 1753 and 1766. During the period represented by the following selections, the Elders' Conference was responsible for all the congregations in Wachovia, as the Moravians called the tract they purchased in North Carolina.[46]

Minutes of the Aeltesten Conferenz Elders' Conference

Feb. 11, 1772. Br. Stockburger has notified this Conferenz in writing that he is willing to take charge of the plantation in Salem, and suggests that he keep his present position until August, in addition to the farming. The Conferenz does not think this wise, and would rather help him settle now. His marriage also comes into the question, and the Saviour's decision as to that will decide the plan for our Brother. So far the only one we have thought of for him is B____ E____, so it was asked with Yes and No: "Shall B____ E____ be suggested to Br. Stockburger?" Answer: "No."

Then it was asked "whether we should inquire whether he had himself thought of any one?" Answer: "No."

Then H____ L____ of Bethania was proposed, and it was asked: "Whether we should consider her in connection with this marriage?" Answer: "No."

Then M____ S____ and Catharina Christmann were discussed, and the question put as to the latter with Yes, No, and a Blank, and the "Yes" was drawn.

Now the suggestion will first be made to Stockburger, if he approves it then to Sr. Christmann, and if she accepts then George Schmidt [whose family she was then living with] must be notified.

Feb. 25. Br. Stockburger's marriage will take place in Salem next Sunday, Br. Tiersch officiating. On Monday the newly wedded pair will come to Bethabara.

April 13, 1773. As Johann Schaub has now been re-admitted to the Communion his marriage need no longer be delayed. The question was laid before the Saviour whether the proposal concerning Hanna Leinbach still held good, and the affirmative lot was drawn.

March 16, 1775. . . . Heinrich Spoenhauer, Jr. has told Br. Petersen that his circumstances require him to marry. His parents think the same and would be glad to see him do it. He and they have thought of Michael Hauser's daughter, Elisabeth, but do not wish to do anything without hearing from the Conferenz, as they do not wish to undertake it without the blessing of the Saviour and of the Brethren. The Aeltesten Conferenz sees no objection, and heartily wishes them the grace and blessing of the Saviour. On their next visit to Bethania Br. and Sr. Graff will speak with Br. and Sr. Spoenhauer about it, and if they both wish it Br. and Sr. Graff will take the proposal of marriage to the Michael Hausers, and if they approve they shall lay the matter before their daughter. If she accepts she and Heinrich Spoenhauer shall be betrothed by Br. and Sr. Ernst in the presence of their parents; and then Br. Ernst shall commend them to the Communicant members for their thoughts and prayers. All this was done on March 27th.

April 13. Heinrich Stöhr having returned from his journey Br. Graff will speak with him, and tell him that nothing can be done about his marriage until he has paid his debts in his Choir House, for we will not permit any Sister to be so unfortunate as to give herself unto poverty through his debts.

May 17. Concerning Heinrich Stöhr's marriage it was remarked that debts no longer stand in the way, so it will be taken up with him and Anna Dorothea Schutz.

May 24. Heinrich Stöhr and A. Dor. Schutz both accepted the proposal, and on May 21st they were betrothed by Br. and Sr. Graff, and it was announced to the Congregation in Salem. It will be announced in Bethabara and Bethania next Sunday.

Jan. 17, 1775. As Br. Nissen has accepted the call to Friedland, there was discussion concerning his marriage, and the following Sisters were inquired about:

a) The widow D. shall be suggested to Br. Nissen? The negative was drawn.
b) The Single Sister M.P. shall be suggested to him? The negative was drawn.
c) In similar manner the name of Single Sister Salome Meuer was considered, and the affirmative lot was drawn. *The Sr. Salome Meurer shall be suggested to Br. Toego Nissen.*

Jan. 24. Br. Nissen shall be married next Sunday.

FEMALE MESSIAHS IN THE REVOLUTIONARY WAR ERA

Document 13: Mother Ann Lee, the Word of Christ's Second Appearing

Mother Ann Lee (1736–1784), founder of the Shakers, left no writings of her own. The main sources of information about her life and character come from her early followers who often quoted her sayings, and these were written down many years later from memories shaped by pious devotion. Testimonies and personal remembrances of Mother Ann Lee were gathered from aged believers thirty-five years after her death and then published by the society.[47] *The following account of her life was drawn from such accounts taken down from the recollections of the first generation of believers.*[48]

This extraordinary female, whom, her followers believe God had chosen, and in whom Christ did visibly make his second appearance, was Ann Lee. She was born in the year 1736, in the town of Manchester, in England. Her father's name was John Lee; by trade a blacksmith; she had five brothers, viz.—Joseph, James, Daniel, William and George, and two sisters, Mary and Nancy. Her father, though poor, was respectable in character, moral in principle, honest and punctual in his dealings, and industrious in business. Her mother was counted a strictly religious, and very pious woman.

Their children, as was then common with poor people, in manufacturing towns, were taught to work, instead of being sent to school. By this means Ann acquired a habit of industry, but was very illiterate, so that she could neither read, nor write. She was employed, during her childhood and youth in a cotton factory, in preparing cotton for the looms, and in cutting velvet. It has been said that she was also employed as a cutter of hatter's fur, but this was probably afterward.

From her childhood she was the subject of religious impressions and divine manifestations. She had great light and conviction concerning the sinfulness and depravity of human nature, and especially concerning the lusts of the flesh, which she often made known to her parents, entreating them for that counsel and protection by which she might be kept from sin. . . .

But not having then attained to that knowledge of God which she so early desired, nor having any one to strengthen and assist her in withstanding the powerful examples and practices of a lost world, and the ensnaring temptations of a fallen nature, she grew up in the same fallen nature, and was married to Abraham Stanley, who was a blacksmith by trade, and lived with her, at her father's house, while she remained in England;—by him she had four children, who all died in infancy.

During this period of her cohabitation with her husband she fell under great exercise of mind, and, for a season, passed through excessive tribulation and sufferings of soul; without any mortal guide to instruct and lead her in the way of truth, till she became acquainted with James and Jane Wardley. She became a subject of the work of God under their ministration, and united herself to that society in the month of September, 1758, being then about twenty-two years of age.

As these people had been favored with a greater degree of divine light, and a more clear and pointed testimony against sin than had hitherto been made manifest, Ann readily embraced their testimony. And, as their light had led them to the open confession of every known sin, and to the taking up of a full and final cross against all evil in their knowledge, they were thereby endowed with great power of God over sin, by which means Ann found a good degree of that protection which she had so long desired, and so earnestly sought after. And, by her faithful obedience to the instruction of her Leaders, she attained to the full knowledge and experience in spiritual things which they had found.

But Ann was destined to still deeper sufferings, in order to prepare her for a far greater work, and therefore could not rest satisfied with what she had already attained....

As she was ordained of God, as her followers believe, to be the first Mother of all souls in the regeneration, she had, not only to labor and travel for her own redemption, through scenes of tribulation, and to set the example of righteousness, and mark out the line of self-denial and the cross of her followers, but also to see and feel the full depth of man's loss, and the pain and judgment which every description of lost souls were under....

Though Ann was wrought upon in this manner, more or less, for the space of nine years, yet she had intervals of releasement, and was, at times, filled with visions and revelations of God. By this means the way of God, and the nature of His work, gradually opened upon her mind, with increasing light and understanding. At length, about the year 1770, after a scene of deep tribulation, and the most excessive sufferings and cries to God, she received a full revelation of the root and foundation of human depravity, and of the very transgression of the first man and woman in the garden of Eden. Then, she clearly saw whence and wherein all mankind were lost and separated from God, and the only possible way of recovery.... She testified in the most plain and pointed manner, that no soul could follow Christ in the regeneration, while living in the works of natural generation, and wallowing in their lusts.

The light and power of God revealed in Ann, and through her revealed to those who received her testimony, had such sensible effect in giving them power over all sin, and filling them with visions, revelations, and gifts of God, that she was received and acknowledged as the first spiritual Mother in Christ, and the second heir of the Covenant of Life in the New Creation. She was often shamefully and cruelly abused, and a number of times imprisoned. But, her testimony continued to grow and increase in the hearts of Believers in England, till, by the special revelation of God, she embarked for America.

On the 19th of May, 1774, she sailed from Liverpool, in company with her husband (who then professed the same faith), her brother,—William Lee, James Whittaker, John Hocknell, Richard Hocknell,—son of John Hocknell, James Shepherd, Mary Partington, and Nancy Lee—a niece of Mother Ann. After enduring the storms and dangers of the sea, in an old leaky vessel, in which they came very near being shipwrecked, they all arrived safely in New York, on the 6th of August....

John Hocknell, soon after their arrival, went up the river, and purchased a place at Niskayuna, near Albany, for their future residence. . . . In the spring following, Mother left New York, and came up the river, and joined the rest of the society.

[The new sect soon fell under the suspicion of the American authorities.]

As their accusers well knew it to be contrary to the faith of the Believers to bear arms and shed human blood, they flattered themselves with the hope of confirming the charge of treason, by taking the advantage of this circumstance, and the minds of the Committee being previously impressed, they were ready to exert their authority according to their discretion. After some examination the Committee required them to promise obedience to their laws, without informing them what those laws should be.

The result was what might be expected, the prisoners, whose faith and conscience bound them to obey every just and righteous law, without any external observation, could not promise obedience to laws which were yet unknown, and which, in all probability, would be unjust, and oppressive; consequently, they could not comply with the demand of the Committee; they were, therefore, committed to prison. . . . [A]n officer was sent to take Mother Ann, Elder William and Elder James, and convey them to Albany. Calvin Harlow, being then at Watervliet, obtained Mother Ann's consent to go to prison with her. She also took Mary Partington with her, as a female companion. After a short examination, in which they were charged of being enemies to the country, and yet, without the smallest degree of evidence, they were also committed to prison. . . .

But the progress of the gospel was not to be arrested by these, nor any other means which its enemies could devise. The Believers were still zealous in assembling together, and supporting the testimony at all hazards; for no outward opposition could dampen the zeal of a people who had been awakened by the resurrection power of Christ, and who, by their obedience to the testimony, had been made partakers of the power of salvation from all sin. . . .

These things greatly increased the rage of Mother Ann's persecutors; for they viewed her as the grand actress in these movements, therefore it was against her their malice was principally directed. Hence they were very urgent to banish her to the British army, which then lay at New York. The committee, however, decided on sending her to Poughkeepsie; accordingly, about the middle of August, she was taken from the prison, conveyed on board of a sloop, and sent down to Poughkeepsie, and imprisoned in the jail of that town. Mary Partington, at her own request, was permitted to accompany her.

[The new American converts to Shakerism questioned Ann Lee's authority, as a woman, to represent Christ.]

Joseph Meacham and Calvin Harlow were among the first who

visited this little Church, for the purpose of searching out the truth of their religion. After much conversation, and many critical inquiries, in all of which they received plain and satisfactory answers, Joseph Meacham sent Calvin Harlow to Mother Ann with the following observation and query, namely: Saint Paul says, "Let your women keep silent in the Churches; for it is not permitted unto them to speak; but they are commanded to be under obedience, as also saith the law. And if they will learn anything let them ask their husbands, at home; for it is a shame to a woman to speak in the church. But you not only speak, but seem to be an Elder in your church. How do you reconcile this with the Apostle's doctrine"?

Mother Ann answered, "The order of man in the natural creation is a figure of the order of God, for man in the spiritual creation. As the order of nature requires a man and a woman to produce offspring, so, where they both stand in their proper order, the man is first, and the woman the second, in the government of the family. He is the father, and she the mother, and all the children, both male and female, must be subject to their parents; and the woman, being second, must be subject to her husband, who is the first; but when the man is gone, the right of government belongs to the woman; so is the family of Christ."

This answer opened a vast field of contemplation to Joseph, and filled his mind with great light and understanding concerning the spiritual work of God. He clearly saw that the New Creation could not be perfect in its order, without a father, and a mother. That, as the natural creation was the offspring of a natural father and mother, so the spiritual creation must be the offspring of a spiritual father and mother.

He saw Jesus Christ to be the Father of the Spiritual Creation, who was now absent; and he saw Ann Lee to be the Mother of all who were now begotten in the regeneration; and she, being present in the body, the power and authority of Christ on earth, was committed to her; and to her appertained the right of leading and governing all her spiritual children.

The opening of the gospel in America, and the mighty power of God which attended the subjects of it, excited great alarm among the enemies of the cross. The spirit of Anti-christ could not but view, with fearful apprehensions, this new and strange religion, attended as it was, with such extraordinary and unaccountable operations, and embraced with such enthusiastic zeal, by so many who had been anxiously waiting for the second coming of Christ. . . .

The first act of open persecution that took place, after the testimony was received in America, was in the month of July, 1780. As many people from New Lebanon, Hancock and other places resorted to Niskayuna to hear the testimony, those Believers who were able, found it necessary to take provisions for their support. This served as an occasion for some evil-minded men in and about New Lebanon, to accuse these innocent people of being enemies to the country, and to stir up those in authority to persecute them.

In December, 1781, Mother Ann and the Elders made a journey to Petersham; they arrived at Thomas Shattuck's late in the evening, and found the family waiting their arrival.

The next day, being Sabbath, many people of the world, came in to attend meeting. Elder James Whittaker preached the gospel from these words, "Cleanse your hands ye sinners, and purify your hearts ye double minded; be afflicted, and mourn and weep."

This being the first visit that Mother Ann and the Elders made in Petersham the inhabitants generally manifested a desire to see and hear for themselves, and as they pretended civility, they had full liberty. Accordingly, on Monday evening there came a considerable number of civil people, also a company of lewd fellows from the middle of the town, who styled themselves the blackguard committee. . . . entered three ruffians painted black and rushing forward, the foremost one seized hold of Mother, and, with the assistance of his comrades, attempted to drag her out, but Elizabeth Shattuck and several sisters instantly clinched hold of her, and held her, and Elizabeth being a large, heavy woman, and the passage narrow, the ruffians were not able to accomplish their purpose; and quitting their hold they suddenly fled out of the house. . . . Those who remained were about retiring to rest when Mother discovered, from the window, that her cruel persecutors were near, and made some attempts to conceal herself. The house was again assaulted by about thirty creatures in human shape; the doors being fastened, were burst open and broke, and these ruffians entered. . . . [T]hey seized fire brands, and searched the house, and at length, found her in a bedroom; they immediately seized her by the feet, and inhumanly dragged her, feet foremost, out of the house, and threw her into a sleigh with as little ceremony as they would the dead carcase of a beast, and drove off, committing, at the same time, acts of inhumanity and indecency which even savages would be ashamed of.

In the struggle with these inhuman wretches, she lost her cap and handkerchief, and otherwise had her clothes torn in a shameful manner. Their pretense was to find out whether she was a woman or not. In this situation, in a cold winter's night, they drove nearly three miles to Samuel Peckham's tavern, near Petersham Meeting-house. . . .

It appeared that Samuel Peckham was a Captain of militia, and had previously agreed with the ruffians who seized Mother, to give them as much rum as they would drink, on condition they would bring her to his house.

Being by this time ashamed of their conduct, and fearful of the consequences, they promised to release Mother Ann upon condition that David would sign an obligation not to prosecute them for what they had done. Being impelled by a feeling for Mother's safety, he reluctantly yielded to their demands, . . .

This being done, they released Mother Ann, and some time in the night some of them brought her and those with her back to David Hammond's. She came in singing for joy that she was again restored to her children, (meaning her spiritual followers). The men who brought her back appeared to be greatly ashamed of their wicked conduct, and confessed that they had abused her shamefully, said they were sorry for it, and desired her forgiveness. Mother Ann replied, "I can freely forgive you, I hold nothing against you, and I pray God to forgive you;" so they departed peaceably. After their departure Mother related the shameful abuse that she had suffered from these merciless wretches, and said, "It really seemed as if my life must go from me, when they dragged me out of my room, and threw me into the sleigh; besides they tore my handkerchief from my neck, my cap and fillet from my head, and even tore some of the hair out of my head. . . .

But so insidious were the inhabitants of Petersham, both priests and people, professors and profane, that it seemed as if nothing was too bad for them to say or do against the Believers in general, but more especially against Mother Ann and the Elders, against whom the most vile and vicious accusations that could be conceived, were uttered. Witchcraft and delusion was the general cry; even in their solemn assemblies of worship, the preachers would vent their malicious spleen, and mock and mimic the operations of the power of God, which they had seen or heard of among the people.

After the decease of Father William, Mother, who had been ably supported by him, in the vast weight of Believers brought upon her, now began to decline in bodily strength; and knowing that her work was nearly at a close, she accordingly endeavored to prepare the minds of the Believers for it. She repeatedly warned them to be faithful; for she was about to leave them.

Soon after Father William expired, Mother said, "Brother William is gone, and, it will soon be said of me, that I am gone too." She was afterward often heard to say, "Well, I am coming soon.'. She would then say to those who were present, "Brother William is calling me." Sometimes she would say, "Yea, Brother William, I shall come soon."

She continually grew weaker in body, without any visible appearance of bodily disease, til the 8th of September, 1784, between twelve and one o'clock in the morning, when she breathed her last without a struggle, or a groan. Before her departure, she repeatedly said to those around her, that she was going home. A little before she expired, she said, "I see Brother William, coming in a golden chariot, to take me home." . . .

At the grave Father James Whittaker spake as follows, "Here lie my two friends; God help me; as ever a man desires to eat, who is hungry, I desire to lie here with them! They are a part of myself! They are gone to that treasure which is my only interest." . . .

He then addressed himself to the unbelievers, saying, "This that we so much esteem, and so much adore, is a treasure worth the laboring for; it is the gospel of Christ's Second Appearance; it is the only means of salvation that will ever be offered to sinners; it is the last display of God's grace to a lost world."

Document 14: Jemima Wilkinson, the Universal Public Friend

Most of the accounts of Jemima Wilkinson's character and career in ministry came from hostile outsiders or apostates from her movement,[49] *rather than from her own pen or from those of her faithful followers. A balanced account of her story must be pieced together from a combination of these sources.*

Wilkinson described her dramatic conversion experience in 1776 as a literal death and resurrection in which her former identity was replaced by a Spirit sent from heaven by Christ. An account of this experience was found tucked in her Bible at her death:[50]

A Memorandum of the introduction of that fatal Fever, call'd in the Year 1776, the Columbus fever: since call'd the Typus, or malignant fever:—The Ship call'd Columbus, which sail'd out of Providence, in the State of Rhode Island Being a Ship of war, on her return brought with her Prisoners. This Awful, and allarming disease, Of which many of the inhabitants in providence died: And has Since spread more universally across the Country. And on the fourth of the 10th. Month, it reached the house of Jemima Wilkinson, ten Miles from Providence, In which this truly interesting and great event took place!

On the fourth Day of the 10th. Month, on the Seventh Day of the weak, at night, a certain young-woman, known by the name of Jemima Wilkison was seiz'd with this mortal disease. And on the 2d. Day of her illness, was render'd almost incapable of helping herself.—And the fever continuing to increase until fifth Day of the Weak about midnight, She appear'd to meet the Shock of Death; which [illegible] the Soul.

The heavens were open'd And She saw too Archangels decending from the east, with golden crowns upon there heads, clothed in long white Robes, down to the feet; Bringing a sealed Pardon from the living God; and putting their trumpets to their mouth, proclaimed saying, Room, Room, Room, in the many Mansions of eternal glory for Thee and for everyone, that there is one more call for, that the eleventh hour is not yet past with them, and the day of grace is not yet over with them. For every one that will come, may come, and partake of the waters of life freely, which is offered to Sinners without money, and without price.

And the Angels said, The time is at hand, when God will lift up his hand, a second time, to recover the remnant of his People, whos day is not yet over; and the Angels said, The Spirit of Life from God, had descended to earth, to warn a lost and guilty, perishing dying World, to flee from the wrath which is to come; and to give an Invitation to the lost Sheep of the house of Israel to come home; and was waiting to assume the Body which God had prepared, for the Spirit to dwell in. . . . And then taking her leave of the family between the hour of nine & ten in the morning dropt the dying flesh & yielded up the Ghost. And according to the declaration of the Angels,—the Spirit took full possession of the Body it now animates.

Ruth Prichard, a faithful follower of Jemima Wilkinson, described her own conversion and the early days of the preaching career of the Universal Friend.[51]

I was sincerely a Seeker; and did not mean to mock the Sacred Name. . . . But dear Soul, we must seek before we can find, we must knock before it will be open unto us. While I was thus a lost Enquirer, and as I was then must never have seen the Smiling Face of Jesus; Lo! The Universal Friend was to pass thro' Wallingford where I kept school: And I with some more went on First Day, (hearing the Friend was to Preach at such a House) about 7 Miles to hear. And blessed be the day I went; O! Blessed be the Lord for giving me this great Day of visitation: And I do testify unto Thee, my dear Friend it was the Voice that spake as never Man Spake. It is that which if obey'd will bring Light Life & Love unto the Soul; That peace that the world can neither give nor take away. And there is nothing below the Sun shall tempt me back, the Lord helping me.

The Friend of Sinners began to serve In the year 1777 When this Nation was still in arms and America had embroiled her hands in human blood. There appeared the Messenger of Peace going from City to City and from Village to Village proclaiming the News of Salvation to all that would Repent and believe the Gospel. The Friend was not staid by guards of armed men. She went through to visit the poor condemned prisoners in their Chains. Naked swords shook over the Friend's head, she was not in terror because of the mighty Power of the Lord. No storms or severity of weather could hinder the Friend's journey to speak unto Souls like the unwearied Sun, Determin'd its faithful race to run, spreading heavenly benediction far abroad that wandering sinners might return to God. And Traveling far & wide to spread the glad tidings & news of Salvation to a lost and perishing & dying World who have all gone astray like Lost Sheep;—The Lord has lifted up his Hand To the Gentiles and set his Hand the Second Time to recover the remnant of the lost Sheep of the House of Israel. He that hath ears to hear, let him hear.

The Marquis de Barbe-Marbois, head of the French delegation to the American revolutionary government, heard Wilkinson preach in Philadelphia in 1782 and described her appearance as a curious but sympathetic outsider.[52]

Jemima Wilkinson has just arrived here. Some religious denominations awaited her with apprehension, others with extreme impatience. Her story is so odd, her dogmas so new, that she has not failed to attract general attention. . . .

This soul sent from heaven has chosen a rather beautiful body for its dwelling and many living ladies would not be unwilling to inhabit that outer shell. Jemima Wilkinson, or rather the woman whom we call by that name, is about twenty-two years old. She parts her hair on top of her head, and lets it fall onto her shoulders. Her only care for it is to wash it every day in fresh water; she never powders it. She has beautiful features, a fine mouth, and animated eyes. Her travels have tanned her a little. She has a melancholy and thoughtful air, and no cultivated charm, but every charm that nature gives. She carries herself easily and freely, and at the same time with all imaginable modesty. She has a large gray felt hat with turned up edges, and she lays it on the desk of her pulpit when she preaches. She wears a kind of cloth smock tied under the chin like a dressing gown. It falls to the feet, without outlining her figure, and its sleeves reveal only the tips of her hands. . . .

I had sufficient curiosity to hear her. I went with seven or eight French officers, and as people were good enough to make way for us, we found ourselves fairly near the pulpit. In spite of their being quite a number of us, and in spite of the commotion which our unforseen arrival occasioned in the assembly, she did not seem to see us, for she continued to speak with ease and facility, her eyes lowered.

Her discourse seemed to us to be composed of commonplaces about the Bible and the Fathers. She enunciated so clearly, though without elegance, that I think she was reciting a prepared sermon, and it was difficult for me to believe that she was speaking from inspiration, or as the worldly say, extemporaneously. But, glancing at us Frenchmen, she seemed to notice us for the first time. As she spoke of the attachment people have for the things of this world, she continued thus:

"Amongst those who listen to me, how few have been led here by a desire for their salvation! Curiosity attracts them, they wish to be able to tell of extraordinary things when they return to their own country." I swear to you that at this moment I thought her a seer or a prohetess, and I expected to hear her mention my journal.

"Do these strangers believe that their presence in the house of the Lord flatters me? I disdain their honors, I scorn greatness and good fortune. Do not seek me, do not listen to me, unless you are touched by grace. Go away, no longer profane this temple, if you are still in the snares of the infernal angel. But if you are disposed to enter into the way of salvation, if my discourses have have softened your hearts, if I can snatch a single one of you from the danger which he runs, I have not come from too great a distance to bring light, and you have not traveled too long a road in seeking it."

She was so moved, talking thus, that she was obliged to stop, and took out her handkerchief to dry her tears. We were surprised at the apostrophe, but perhaps as hardened as before.

Jemima Wilkinson accepts no pecuniary gifts. She and her disciples possess nothing, but one must live, and they receive the gifts which the piety of the faithful presents to them. She lives soberly, her conduct is good, and her morals are irreproachable.

Women and Revivalism: The Puritan and Wesleyan Traditions

MARTHA TOMHAVE BLAUVELT AND
ROSEMARY SKINNER KELLER

The story of the Great Awakening and the origins of evangelicalism in early America has traditionally focused on two men, Jonathan Edwards and George Whitefield. Edwards revitalized Puritanism by restoring private experience to the center of religious faith, and Whitefield, as an Anglican follower of John Wesley, introduced American colonists to the Wesleyan strain of piety. Together, they made evangelicalism—the theological emphasis on conversion as essential to salvation—the dominant characteristic of eighteenth-century religion.

Yet however important Edwards and Whitefield were to religion, as men they are not entirely appropriate representatives of early American evangelicalism. Colonial revivalism was significant not only in bringing a great theologian and "field preacher" to prominence, but in expanding women's religious activities. That expansion was more dramatic in the Wesleyan tradition than in the Puritan, but in both cases evangelicalism was women's chief vehicle in enlarging their religious sphere.

This chapter explores how Puritan women, such as Sarah Goodhue, Deborah Prince, and Sarah Osborn—at first privately and tentatively, then publicly and more confidently—worked to spread the evangelical tenets of their faith. It shows women in the more activist Wesleyan tradition, such as Barbara Heck and Selina, Countess of Huntingdon, organizing Methodist societies, establishing chapels and seminaries for training Methodist preachers, directing missions, and performing many of the functions of evangelical ministers. The experience of the Spirit within enabled these women to pursue such activities despite the protests of male clerics who could not envision the radical implications of evangelicalism. In this sense colonial revivalism witnessed an awakening of women's power as well as of religion and prepared the way for women's much wider participation in evangelicalism in the nineteenth century.

PURITAN EVANGELICALISM

Puritanism began as a "revival" in the sense that the movement sought to revitalize and purify English Protestantism. Yet, as Rosemary Keller has shown, the Anne Hutchinson affair and the related experience of women in other New England towns quickly curtailed Puritanism's radical implications for women. The Hutchinson affair had implications for men as well:[1] it intensified clerical resentment against all challenges to authority. Puritan emphasis on the "new birth" was not to mean the overthrow of external authority by anyone, male or female. Although laymen maintained their power in secular matters, by the 1650s they found themselves silenced within many churches: ministers prevented them from asking questions after sermons and lectures, participating in disciplinary cases, or relating their own spiritual experiences before the church. The Hutchinson affair thus limited laymen's power as well as women's. Throughout colonial history, male and female lay authority would rise and fall together, as male laity attempted to retrieve power from ministers and women tried to share it with laymen. For both sexes, that rise and fall coincided with periods of revival and declension.

As lay ecclesiastical authority declined, fewer and fewer men joined New England churches, and by the late seventeenth century females dominated church membership rolls.[2] In any case, their life experience made women more likely than men to experience conversion. As historian Gerald Moran has shown, Puritan theology required the sinner to admit total helplessness, to give up all dependence on self.[3] Upon marriage, New England women underwent just such an experience: submission to their husbands and the prospect of death in childbirth reminded them of their lowliness and weakness. Men, in contrast, gained authority through marriage and found it correspondingly difficult to experience the humiliation necessary to conversion. As a result, the vast majority of seventeenth-century Puritan converts were married women, such as Mrs. Elizabeth White (Document 1).

During the late seventeenth century, Puritanism's evangelical tradition began to find expression in distinct religious revivals.[4] The political difficulties and Indian threats of the 1670s and 1680s encouraged many New Englanders to turn to God. In these revivals, men increased their representation in Puritan churches, but women did not lose their numerical advantage. What part women played in these revivals is obscure: little is known about their origins and effects. But these revivals mark the beginning of a new period in Puritan evangelicalism: thereafter, certain New England towns experienced periodic revivals as each generation came of age. These local revivals provided a forum for female religious activity and would, in time, merge with the First Awakening.

The one minimal evangelical role open to women in the late seventeenth century was preaching within the private circle. Anticipating death in childbirth, Sarah Whipple Goodhue wrote a *Valedictory* in 1681 that illustrates the limited religious roles women then had (Document 2). Goodhue spoke as an evangelist confident of her own election and authority; she urged her "Children, neighbours and friends" to "get a part and portion in the Lord Jesus Christ." It is clear from this document that female religious meetings did not totally disappear after Anne Hutchinson's banishment. What activities such "private Societ[ies]" engaged in is unclear, but given the sensitivity of ministers to male infringement on their authority, such meetings must have confined themselves to fairly innocuous matters. That they met at all, however, suggests that women had developed a means to activism and sisterhood.

During most of the seventeenth century, women received little public acknowledgment of their piety. Significantly, neither Sarah Goodhue's *Valedictory* nor Elizabeth White's conversion account were published until the eighteenth century. Beginning in the 1690s, however, such ministers as Cotton Mather began to praise female piety in funeral sermons and elegies (Document 3). By 1730, 40 percent of New England's extant funeral sermons were about women.[5] These sermons typically praised women who converted early, prayed and fasted, went to church faithfully, read the Scriptures, submitted to God's will, and managed their households well.

Puritan ministers accorded women this public attention for several reasons. First, they felt compelled to recognize a change in reality: that there were a great many pious women in New England—indeed, that more women than men were pious. As Mather observed, "Tho' both *Sexes,* be thro the Marvellous Providence of our God Born into the World, in pretty AEqual Numbers, yet, in the Female, there seem to be the Larger Numbers, of them that are *Born Again,* and brought into the Kingdom of God." In trying to explain this, Mather developed a new understanding of the fall and of women's nature. He interpreted Eve's seduction, which men had conventionally viewed as evidence of women's evil and weakness, as a blessing in disguise. The childbirth women experienced as Eve's punishment inclined them to religion: "the Dubious Hazards of their Lives in their Appointed Sorrows, drive them the more frequently, & the more fervently to commit themselves into the Hands of their Only Saviour."[6] Mather used Eve to exalt woman rather than to debase her, and in so doing he vastly upgraded the image of both Eve and woman.

But ministers may well have meant to do more than acknowledge a statistical change in church membership. During the last half of the seventeenth century, church membership declined in proportion to New England's population. At the same time, those few church members were being drawn from the less socially significant part of the population, the female half. In eulogizing women, ministers tried in effect to enhance the worth of that portion of their constituency that showed continued growth. At the same time, ministers hoped to reach the coming generation, especially New England's sons, through women. In short, ministers praised women in order to retrieve clerical authority.

Although turn-of-the-century ministers granted women unprecedented public recognition, they did not accord them qualities superior to those of men, as they would do in the nineteenth century. The premise of eighteenth-century sermons was that male and female natures were equally depraved; women were more religious than men because their *experiences* were different, not their natures. Women, such sermons insisted, were as good as men, not better. But the fact that ministers had to argue spiritual equality, and the care with which they cited example upon example of female virtue, suggests that many New Englanders needed convincing. The frequent reprinting of English misogynist literature throughout the eighteenth century suggests that clergymen had to deal with a still popular image of woman as the seductive Eve. Such tracts as Edward Ward's *Female Policy Detected: or the Arts of a Designing Woman* countered sermons on "The Good Works of a Vertuous Woman" and left colonists with an ambivalent attitude toward women that persisted throughout the colonial period.[7] The most important change between 1700 and the Revolution lay not in ideology, but in activity. And the movement that unleashed that activity was the First Awakening.

The First Awakening's converts differed from their Puritan predecessors in several respects. First, the proportion of men in the churches increased during the eighteenth-century revival, even though women remained in the majority.[8] Because of this, the association of femininity and piety was delayed until the revivals of the early 1800s, which women overwhelmingly dominated. Second, the First Awakening's subjects were younger than seventeenth-century converts.[9] In the 1600s, women had converted in their twenties or early thirties, after marriage. But Deborah Prince, a representative eighteenth-century revival subject, underwent conversion when she was single and still in her teens (Document 4). The power and pervasiveness of the Awakening, with its national scope and charismatic evangelists, pushed many people to convert earlier than they would have a century before. In short, the Great Awakening overwhelmed the patterns of everyday life.

Several traits distinguished the conversion of young people such as Deborah Prince. For example, Awakening converts typically experienced intense self-abasement. Prince described herself as a "vile Creature"; she wrote her cousin that "all my own Righteousness are but as filthy Rags. My Duties are specious Sins, guilded Iniquities." Such feelings were by no means unknown to seventeenth-century converts, but the Awakening's sermons emphasized self-abasement with unusually imaginative language and great drama: Prince quotes George Whitefield's declaration that "by Nature I am half a devil and half a Beast; I know that in me, that is in my Flesh, dwells no good Thing."[10]

This theme may have had special meaning to women, for their culture emphasized that they should not be selfish and should not rely on themselves. Society trained women to practice self-abasement, and the theological language of the Awakening echoed that message. Theological emphasis on humiliation may also have disproportionately attracted young people. Eighteenth-century Calvinist child-rearing practices stressed breaking the will and subordination to parental authority; perhaps these young converts were transferring their family experiences to the religious sphere.[11]

Precisely because of this stress on the sinner's "filthiness," Awakening converts found it difficult to believe that they were truly saved—a striking difference between Puritan and Wesleyan evangelicalism. The Awakening created tremendous anxiety over this issue, and four years after her conversion, Deborah Prince was still unsure about her spiritual state. Ministers such as Prince's father tried to relieve such fears by emphasizing Christ's love and uncritical acceptance—an almost maternal image of divinity that would become prominent in the nineteenth century. Clergymen also suggested that evangelical zeal characterized the regenerate. Prince offered as proof of his daughter's conversion "her peculiar Love to Those whom she apprehended to be most eminent for vital Piety; especially those ministers who most laid open the hypocrisy of the Hearts of Men, who made the Hypocrites and Formalists the most uneasy, and were most zealous for the power of Godliness. . . ."[12] Through its emphasis on the fruits of the Spirit, the activism of good works, preachers sought to relieve the anxieties the Awakening had aroused.

The most important expression of that activism was the rise of lay power. Laity not only attacked unregenerate ministers, but took over their clerical functions as well. Convinced that piety rather than learning qualified ministers, laymen began to preach. This resurgence of male lay activism and the Awakening's fervor emboldened women too, permitting them to criticize ministers openly.[13] It also allowed them to perform some clerical functions—always excepting preaching. While Sarah Goodhue had offered religious advice only to her "Children, neighbours and friends," the Awakening's female converts advised total strangers. And a few, such as Sarah Osborn of Newport, publicly displayed doctrinal knowledge in evangelical tracts; her *Nature, Certainty and Evidence of true Christianity* (1755) evinced an erudition equal to many ministers.[14] Women had begun to speak for themselves and no longer relied on male ministers for posthumous praise. Women also founded prayer societies, which gave their activities an organized basis.[15] Although the Awakening did not put ministers, laymen, and women on the same level, it at least expanded the functions of laymen and women and helped close the gap between laity and clergy.

In judging the unregenerate and in taking on clerical roles, women gained public religious functions. Before, their religious roles had been largely private: they gave spiritual advice within the home and experienced conversion "in the closet." But during the Awakening, conversion became a dramatic, public event. Women experienced "violent fits" and their cries might be heard far beyond the confines of their homes. As the revival rendered religiosity public and emotional, it drew women into the public sphere.

Women acted independently as well as publicly during the Awakening. Many believed that the Spirit within directed them to attack sinners, separate from established churches, and advise others on religion. A few women transferred this spiritual independence to everyday life. For example, when Hannah Harkum's anti-evangelical parents turned her out, she became a professional seamstress and developed the business acumen that made her an equal partner in her later marriage (Document 5).

These changes in women's religious functions were important, but they should not be exaggerated. Though women may have left the private religious realm somewhat, they by no means attained the prominence of even minor male evangelists. Thomas Prince's *Christian History,* which publicized virtually every revival in the Awakening, scarcely mentions women. And while Whitefield periodically noted women's activities in his popular *Journals,* most of his entries concerned his own evangelical gifts. No woman during the Awakening achieved the fame of Anne Hutchinson in the seventeenth century. And women who acted publicly or independently often had to defend themselves. Sarah Osborn of Newport was a devout, middle-aged, married schoolteacher. When she allowed her *Nature, Certainty and Evidence of true Christianity* to be published, however, she felt obliged to include an apologetic note on the title page: "Tho this *Letter* was Wrote in great *privacy* from *one Friend* to *another,* yet on representing that by allowing it to be *Printed,* it would probably reach *to many others in the like afflicted case,* and by the Grace of God be *very helpful to them,* the *Writer* was at length prevailed on to suffer it—provided her Name and Place of abode remained concealed." Similarly, when in 1766 and 1767 Osborn found hundreds pressing into her home for weekly religious meetings, she felt compelled to defend her behavior in an eight-page letter to a male critic (Document 6).

WESLEYAN EVANGELICALISM

John Wesley was introduced to the ministry of evangelical women through his mother, Susannah, and particularly through an experience of hers similar to that of Sarah Osborn. Wesley's father, Samuel, a clergyman in the Church of England, was away from home for an extended meeting of the governing body of the church in 1712. Susannah wrote Samuel in defense of the prayer meetings that she held in their home on Sunday evenings, meetings that drew as many as two hundred people, so that many had to be turned away "for want of room to stand."

Refuting charges that she was diverting people from the Sunday morning service, Susannah explained her own spiritual awakening: "At last it came into my mind, Though I am not a man, nor a minister, yet if my heart were sincerely devoted to God, and I was inspired with a true zeal for His glory, I might do something more than I do. I thought I might pray more for them, and might speak to those with whom I converse with more warmth of affection." Susannah claimed that the power of the Holy Spirit had been given directly to her and that she was actively responding with her personal commitment to service.

John Wesley was so moved by his mother's account of her role as an evangelist that he included her letter in his journal on the day of her death. Introducing the letter, which Susannah had written to Samuel when John was only nine years old, he stated that "even she [as well as her father and grandfather, her husband, and her three sons] had been, in her measure and degree, a preacher of righteousness."[16]

Susannah's experience raised an issue that would remain central for generations to come as women in the evangelical tradition continued to expand their ministries: how far could a proper woman extend her evangelical work into the public sphere? Susannah did not consider preaching sermons which she would write herself, but she questioned whether 'because of my sex it is proper for me to present the prayers of the people of God." Clearly, the people had been responding eagerly to the active presence of God they experienced through her: "Last Sunday I would fain have dismissed them before prayers; but they begged so earnestly to stay, I durst not deny them."[17]

While both Puritans and Wesleyans shared "generic marks of Evangelicalism," theological distinctions within the two traditions made Wesleyans, from the earliest days of the movement, more open than Puritans to the public ministries of women. These "generic marks" have been defined by Donald Mathews as belief

> that the Christian life is essentially a personal relationship with God in Christ, established through the direct action of the Holy Spirit, an action which elicits in the believer a profoundly emotional conversion experience. This existential crisis, the *New Birth,* as Evangelicals called it, ushers the convert into a life of holiness characterized by religious devotion, moral discipline, and missionary zeal.[18]

The focal point of one's life, then, was conversion. New birth was preceded by a complete breakdown of personal pride and self-possession and resulted in a new life of disciplined holiness centered in devotion and service to God in Christ.

Both the Calvinistic and Arminian heritages of the evangelical movement stressed the primacy of God's grace as the context within which persons make decisions. However, Puritans, in the Calvinistic tradition, continued to emphasize that the individual's role in the work of salvation was one of personal passivity and that humans could do nothing to affect God's determination of who was chosen. Methodists, on the other hand, stressed freedom of the will from their Arminian roots and rejected the Calvinistic God who left the sinner without assurance of salvation all his life while demanding strict obedience to an impossible ethic. Methodist doctrine allowed for the real possibility of backsliding and offered an endless number of chances to receive God's grace. Wesley's followers endeavored to present God's sovereign grace and human free will not as a paradox, but as complementary parts of the conversion experience. In actual practice, the emphasis was resolved in favor of commonsense belief in the ability to repent and to commit one's self to Christ.[19]

While such theological differences were real, the key distinction, according to Mathews, was the Puritan emphasis on the necessity of proper doctrinal identification and self-definition, in contrast to the Methodist belief that the fruits of the committed life were more important than prolonged efforts of self-definition. Methodists were concerned to be "out and about," reforming the nation and saving the world. The key ideological distinction was that the Puritans placed theological definition at the center while Methodists avoided it.[20]

A logical implication for evangelical women in both the Puritan and the Wesleyan traditions was that the Holy Spirit was given indiscriminately to men and women alike and that the chosen ones could not be identified by human eyes. Evangelical Puritan women, however, spent more time and energy in discerning the fine points and justifications of their new life in Christ. The more activist emphasis in Methodism resulted in an affirmation of their witnesses, both private and public, based on the criterion that God was "owning their ministry," that God was using women as agents of salvation.

John Wesley affirmed the spiritual independence of women from the time of his earliest experiences in ministry. He spent only two years in America, on an unproductive evangelical mission to Georgia (1736–1738) during the same period in which Edwards's work in Northampton was causing the first stirrings of the Great Awakening in New England. In Georgia, Wesley became involved in a personal and pastoral relationship with Sophy Hopkey, which he bungled. Even so, significant dimensions of his attitude toward women were already emerging in these early days of his ministry. According to Alan Hayes, Wesley affirmed Hopkey's spiritual independence from her husband, counseling her that she must make her own decisions regarding observance of fasts and attendance at dawn services and discussion groups. Hopkey told Wesley that her husband did not approve of his directing her spiritual life and that she should only obey her husband. Wesley responded with this principle: "In things of an indifferent nature you cannot be too obedient to your husband, but if his will should be contrary to the will of God, you are to obey God rather than man."[21]

His affirmation of the public ministry of women developed after Wesley returned to England where he worked closely with women in the Methodist movement throughout the latter half of the eighteenth century. His advocacy of women's public witness expanded as he observed their effectiveness in winning souls to Christ. As Earl Kent Brown's study shows, "Mr. Wesley's attitude began to liberalize under the impact of the evangelical success of several women friends. He was a pragmatist when it came to institutions through which the gospel was spread. What impressed him was that God was blessing the women's work with a harvest of souls. . . . God was 'owning' their ministry." While he never formally appointed a woman to the itinerating ministry, several women actually "traveled the connection," journeying hundreds and thousands of miles throughout England to bear witness and to preach to groups of all sizes.[22]

Hester Ann Roe Rogers was representative of Wesleyan women whose work was limited to England, but whose influence spread to America. Her letters and spiritual biography, like those of Mary Bosanquet Fletcher and others, were reprinted in the United States in the nineteenth century and provided obvious models of spiritual piety and activism for evangelical women (Document 7). Rogers's letters reflect the assurance of new birth in Christ, in contrast to the continued questioning by Puritans. Because Wesley allowed women to claim their direct spiritual experience of God's presence and to put it to use, they felt no need for ordination. Wesleyan women performed the public functions that evangelicals believed were essential for ministry—leading prayer and preaching services, and bringing converts to the altar to begin their journey toward perfect Christian love. However, because early Wesleyan women were not ordained, they could not be part of the governing structures of the Methodist Episcopal Church, which was organized in the United States in 1784.

The earliest impact of a Wesleyan woman on American soil was made by the Englishwoman Selina Hastings, the Countess of Huntingdon. Though she never realized her deep desire to come to the colonies, Selina was the first woman to establish the trans-Atlantic connection of the Wesleyan movement. Her life (1707–1791) virtually spanned the eighteenth century. Traditionally, she has been given minor recognition in the history of the Wesleyan movement as a wealthy benefactress to the Wesleys and to George Whitefield, one who founded colleges for the training of dissenting ministers and chapels for their active evangelical service.

Yet Selina's major contribution to the movement was not realized through her role as a patroness of its male leaders. More importantly, she was a forerunner of those Wesleyan women in the nineteenth century who would find their first public identity in the development of missionary societies and social reform organizations. As Mollie Davis's work has established, Selina herself personified the modern female reformer: a woman who in mid-life develops a new and independent identity that provides commitment and purpose for the second half of her life (Document 8).[23]

Selina's letters to John and Charles Wesley and to George Whitefield reveal that their relationship was a working one, characterized by collegiality and equality, rather than a relationship in which a wealthy benefactress simply supplied revenues for their ministerial operations. In seeking pastors to supply pulpits, Selina was clearly asking for their recommendations of able candidates to fill the chapels of which she was in charge. Further, Whitefield and the Wesleys accepted Selina's invitations to preach, thereby recognizing her authority as director of the parishes. She herself organized the mission of ministers to the Indians in Georgia. Though she was in charge of the enterprise from a distance, her vision was that "the Lord will have me there, if only to make coats and garments for the poor Indians." Selina's desire became the realized experience of female missionary society leaders and reformers of the next century, who immersed themselves in the day-to-day fieldwork of their projects.

As was true of evangelical women in the Puritan tradition, most Wesleyan women still performed their spiritual functions within their own homes. The belief that piety was rooted in woman's nature, which was fostered by the Great Awakening, flowered in late eighteenth-century Wesleyanism. The religious influence of female followers on their husbands and children gave women in the colonies their first evangelical roles and became the most immediate influence on early nineteenth-century Wesleyan women as well.

The experiences of two early Wesleyan women of the Baltimore area indicate the way in which beliefs in both the spiritual equality and the spiritual superiority of women in the Wesleyan movement became central to the purpose of the wife and mother in the home by the end of the eighteenth century. Perry Hall was the plantation of wealthy Henry and Prudence Gough. During the first days of Francis Asbury's superintendency of the Methodist Episcopal churches in America, the Gough estate became identified as the seat of major church planning, where much of the organizational work of early Methodism took place. Both Henry and Prudence Gough were Methodist followers, but Prudence was her husband's spiritual mentor. In a document written by the distinguished nineteenth-century Methodist historian, Abel Stevens, Prudence's innate piety is lifted up in contrast to her husband's weak religious nature. The message which the nineteenth-century historian wanted women to receive was that, again and again, Prudence bore with her husband's backsliding ways and led him toward regeneration (Document 9). Following the example of Susannah Wesley, Prudence Gough performed the widest range of evangelical functions *within the home:* she ministered to both her husband and her child, and she led religious services on the plantation when males were not present to do so.

The letters of Catharine Livingston Garrettson, wife of one of the first Methodist preachers on the Atlantic seaboard, suggest the function and legacy of early pastors' wives (Document 10). If not her husband's spiritual superior, Catharine was at least his equal, critiquing his preaching style and freely sharing her doctrinal interpretations with him. In one letter to her husband, Freeborn, Catharine summed up her self-understanding: as a woman and as a pastor's wife, she was to live her life through her husband and to press him to greater public service for both of them. For, she wrote, "I despair of ever being a shining light, but I would wish to see you the most pious man in the world."

CONCLUSION

When compared to the activities of nineteenth-century evangelical women, the efforts of women in the First Awakening and in the early Wesleyan movement in America seem minor. Both Puritan and Wesleyan women ran prayer meetings, but most eighteenth-century women dared to pray only before members of their own sex. Sarah Osborn and Prudence Gough, who held "mixed" meetings in their own homes, were rare exceptions. Even then Osborn and Gough prayed only before boys and black men and were careful not to assume a position of superiority over any white men who attended. "Mixed" prayer meetings would not become common for another hundred years. And unlike the nineteenth-century prayer societies, these eighteenth-century meetings rarely stimulated local revivals; colonial revivals seem to have occurred only in response to male preaching. Eighteenth-century evangelicalism produced no equivalents of Maggie Van Cott, Phoebe Palmer, and Amanda Berry Smith, who would become renowned evangelists and lead revivals throughout the world in the next century through the sanction of Methodism and the Holiness movement.

Eighteenth-century female evangelism was so limited largely because of ideological restraints. Women lacked a "Cult of True Womanhood" to give them confidence in female moral superiority and to unite them in a holy sisterhood. Further, they were not yet able to appropriate the implications of the Declaration of Independence—that they, too, had been endowed by their Creator with certain unalienable rights through the birthright of equality.

Few people, regardless of sex, accepted women's right to religious authority. By the time of the First Awakening, the image of woman as Eve had faded, but was still strong enough to undermine female religious authority. The general social and political confusion that accompanied the Awakening made the prospect of a sexual reordering seem more frightening. And even the more positive views of women were no less limiting to female evangelicalism. Jonathan Edwards suggested the constraints of the more "enlightened" eighteenth-century view of women (Document 11). Like Cotton Mather, Edwards did not attribute evil, seductive, Eve-like qualities to women, but he clearly expected women to continue Eve's subordination. Edwards allowed reason to men and affections to women, whom God had made "weaker, more soft and tender, more fearful, and more affectionate, as a fit object of [men's] generous protection and defense." This was a feminine ideal that notably lacked the vigor of Mather's "Amazons of Zion." When Edwards criticized women who were "rugged, daring and presumptuous," he denied them the characteristics that New Light Protestants demanded in their clergy. His definition of women, in effect, removed them from evangelical leadership and rendered them inconsequential. The most far-reaching of his views regarding women was that men were reasonable and women were affectionate as a result of distinct differences in their natures determined by God. This argument became the primary justification for the separation of men's and women's functions into public and private spheres during the nineteenth century.

The Great Awakening caused few immediate changes in women's lives, but it set in motion trends that would expand women's evangelical role in the next century. Despite the furor over the Awakening's excesses, its success in increasing church membership irrevocably committed Calvinist denominations to evangelicalism. The revival became so important to church growth that, by the nineteenth century, many ministers were willing to allow women a major role in revival creation; the desire for revivals would overcome social conventions. The Awakening also affected women's place in American ideology by exalting "Heart." "Heart religion"—that religion grounded in the affections—was the eighteenth-century synonym for evangelicalism. In the 1600s, "Heart" had been associated with women in a largely negative way: men's rationality made them strong, while women's emotionalism made them at best weak and at worst seductively evil. However, the Awakening gave "Heart" both a positive connotation and a central place in American culture, laying the foundation for women's evangelical triumph in the nineteenth century.

A study of nineteenth-century evangelicalism indicates that the Wesleyan movement proved the most liberating religious tradition for women in all areas of religious expression—preaching, missionary and missionary society organizations, deaconess societies, and social reform. Yet one must not minimize the struggles with established authorities that accompanied women's entrance into these fields.

Anne Hutchinson had made the same claim to spiritual authority—that the Holy Spirit was given to her directly and personally—which the circle of "Women in Mr. Wesley's Methodism" made in eighteenth-century England. Their legacy was carried through Selina Hastings, who moved into a "career" in social reform in mid-life, and Barbara Heck, who broke up a game of cards, threw the cards into the fire, and summoned her cousin with these words: "Philip, you must preach to us, or we shall all go to hell, and God will require our blood at your hands" (Document 12). Nineteenth-century evangelical women were distinguished because they held word and action in essential unity. Anne Hutchinson, Selina Hastings, and Barbara Heck were their spiritual foremothers.

Broadside cut for Rebekah Sewall, showing a winged death's head and other motifs characteristically found on New England gravestones. [From Allan Ludwig, *Graven Images* (Middletown, CT: Wesleyan University Press, 1966), p. 282.]

Lady Huntingdon, patroness of George Whitefield and the Methodist movement. [From Helen C. Knight, comp., *Lady Huntingdon and Her Friends* (New York: American Tract Society, 1853), frontispiece.]

Gravestone for Sarah Swan, 1767, Bristol, Rhode Island. The only extant example of the Adam and Eve story on a New England gravestone. The legend, "For in Adam all die so in Christ shall all be made alive" (1 Cor. 15:22), was cut into the stone. [From Allan Ludwig, *Graven Images* (Middletown, CT: Wesleyan University Press, 1966), fig. 13.]

Barbara Heck (1734–1804), the "Mother of American Methodism," helped to organize America's first Methodist Society in New York City in 1766. This portrait by Joseph Barnes (1773) hangs in the John Street Methodist Church, 44 John Street, New York City.

Hester Ann Roe Rogers was one of the early "women of Mr. Wesley's Methodism" who took the first public roles of evangelical women in leading prayer meetings and class and band meetings throughout England. This engraving of the pious Hester in prayer and Bible study represented a model to be emulated by nineteenth-century American women. [From Gabriel Poillon Disosway, *Our Excellent Women of the Methodist Church in England and America.* (New York: J. C. Buttre, 1861), between pp. 84 and 85.]

Documents: Women and Revivalism: The Puritan and Wesleyan Traditions

PURITANISM

1. ***"I Doubted Whether I Was Elected . . . yet I Was Unwilling to Perish": Conversion Account of Mrs. Elizabeth White***
2. ***"More Precious Than Gold Tried in the Fire": Valedictory of Mrs. Sarah Goodhue***
3. **"*THE AMAZONS OF ZION,* I Will Call Those Illustrious Heroines": Tabitha Rediviva, Funeral Sermon Praising Pious Women by the Reverend Cotton Mather**
4. ***"What a Vile Creature I Am": Funeral Sermon on the Death of His Daughter by the Reverend Thomas Prince***
5. ***"There May Be Mercy and Pardon There for You": Obituary Containing Account of the Conversion and Life of Hannah Harkum Hodge***
6. ***"My Resting Reaping Times": Sarah Osborn's Defense of Her Revival Activities, Written to Her Spiritual Adviser, Reverend Joseph Fish***

WESLEYANISM

7. ***"Come Just as You Are to the Open Fountain of His Precious Blood": Spiritual Letters of Hester Ann Roe Rogers to John Wesley and a Female Convert***
8. ***"The Mother in Israel, That Mirror of True and Undefiled Religion": Letters of Selina Hastings, the Countess of Huntingdon, to John and Charles Wesley, George Whitefield, and Others***
9. ***"O If My Wife Had Ever Given Way to the World I Should Have Been Lost": The Evangelical Witness of Prudence Gough***

PURITANISM

Document 1: "I Doubted Whether I Was Elected . . . yet I Was Unwilling to Perish": Conversion Account of Mrs. Elizabeth White

Little is known about the life of Elizabeth White, who died in 1669, but her spiritual memoir provides the only detailed conversion account of a seventeenth-century Puritan woman. That document shows her to have been a woman with intellectual leanings and a gift for expression, as she wrote of how she came to grips with the awesomeness of Calvinist theology and her own mortality. Elizabeth White's handwritten statement was discovered in her closet after her death and published almost seventy-five years later.[24]

From my Child-hood the Lord hath inclined my Heart to seek after the best Things, and my Father's choicest Care was to bring me up in the Nurture and Admonition of the Lord: My Nature being some-what more Mild than the rest of my Sisters, I was ready to think my self some Body, and with the proud Pharisee, to thank God that I was not as others, not considering that I was but like a Wolf chained up, which keeps its Nature still, as I by the Goodness of God have seen, since the Lord was pleased to lay his Eye Salve upon me. I was a great lover of Histories, and other foolish Books, and did often spar'd my sleeping Time in reading of them, and sometimes I should think I did not do well in so doing, but I was so bewitched by them, that I could not forbear. . . . I remember about a Month before I was married, my Father would have me receive the Sacrament of the LORD's Supper, and I was very willing to it; until I considered what was requisite to be in those which did partake thereof, and then I began to doubt that I had not those Things which were requisite wrought in me, as Knowledge, Faith, Love, Repentance, &c. And then this Scripture came into my Mind, *He that doubteth is damned if he eat, whatsoever is not of Faith is Sin:* When I had considered those Things I was filled with Sorrow, and could not tell what to do, I was loath to disobey my Father, and more loath to eat and drink my own Damnation; in this Perplexity I set my self to seek the Lord for his Grace, being at that Time somewhat sensible of the want of it; when I had thus done, I began to be comforted, verily thinking, now I had repented, and could believe in Christ Jesus: . . . and so unworthy I went to the Lord's Table. . . . But blessed for ever be the Lord, which broke my false Confidence. . . . and this was about a Quarter of a Year after I was married, in the Year, 1657. The Minister being upon this subject, Prov. 1.23. *Turn ye at my Reproof, &c.* Being upon the Use of Trial, whether indeed we had turned to God or no? He bid us examine our selves by some Marks which he then gave, and it was at this Time that God did begin to manifest his Love to me, as I trust, in my effectual Vocation; here the Lord was pleased to open my Heart, as he did the Heart of *Lydia;* so that I attended to the Things that were spoken, and I perceived my Heart was not right in the Sight of God, and that my Hope was but like that of the Hypocrite which perisheth; . . . [Three weeks later, the minister visited her.] O how loath was I to acquaint him with my sad State! I was ashamed to tell him that I was yet a Stranger to God and all Goodness, till it was forced from me. . . . then there came many Sins to my Remembrance, which I had taken no notice of before, counting them small Sins; now the Time which was spent in reading Histories, I remembered with bitter Grief, and I thought that there was no Mercy for me, but he perswaded me there was hope of Mercy for such as I, and that the Lord waited to be gracious to poor Sinners, and then I was a little satisfied for the present; but then I was troubled with Blasphemous Thoughts, which were very grievous to me: I thought I had a Heart worse than the Devil, and wondered that I was not consumed in some strange Manner. When I have seen a Spider, which of all Things is most loathsome to me, I have been ready to wish my self such a one, esteeming of it to be in a far happier Condition than I was; I was afraid to be in the Dark, lest I should meet the Devil; I doubted whether I was Elected, . . . but yet I was unwilling to perish, I could not be so satisfied, although I had but little Hope to obtain Mercy, yet I could not but ask it: . . . in this Condition I remained a great while, . . . I doubted much of my Sincerity, often saying, I was an Hypocrite, but if at any Time I was asked in what I was one, I could not tell; . . .

. . . [A]ll this while I did not set such a high Price upon the LORD JESUS as I should, but still I thought that I must do something to merit Salvation, not daring to venture my Soul with all its Concernments upon Christ, therefore I should tie my self to pray six times a Day, and then I should be satisfied, and think all was well with me then. But if I at any Time failed of my Number, then I was dissatisfied, and so in other Duties, so that my Comforts did not flow from the Blood and Righteousness of JESUS, but from my own Duties; but blessed by the LORD, who likewise shook this Foundation, even because he had a Favour to me: For being in Discourse with a Friend, he desire me to read *Sheperd's sincere Convert;* which I did, and here did I see as in a Glass my folly, for there were Signs given whereby I might try my self, whether I did rest in Duties. . . .

Now this I plainly say was my Condition, but how to get out of it I knew not, for now I was in a worse Condition than at the beginning, finding it abundantly more hard to deny righteous Self than sinful Self. I thought it wonderful Strange, that I must be saved by the Righteousness of another, if ever I were saved; O this my proud Heart was unwilling to yield to, and yet I was very desirous of Salvation: . . . once when I was in great Fear least my Heart should grow dead, and when I was with Child, I was much dejected, having a Sense of my approaching Danger, and wanting an Assurance of my everlasting Happiness; but whilst I was considering of these Things, I had this Scripture set home with abundance of Sweetness, Psal. 53. 15. *Call upon me in the Day of Trouble, and I will deliver thee, and thou shalt glorify me:* And in the Time of Extremity this Word was set home upon my Heart again, and my good GOD made me to Experience the Truth of it in a wonderful Manner, for I had speedy Deliverance beyond my Expectation, which filled my Heart and Mouth with Praises to the LORD; about three Days after a Friend coming to visit me, I related to her how good the LORD had been unto me, and how sweetly my Heart was established, but no sooner was my Friend gone, but I was tempted to think my Faith was false, but I laboured what I could to encourage my Self in the Lord my GOD.

But as I lay in my Bed, I thought I saw three Men before me, and it was presently suggested to me that these were the three Persons in the Trinity; O then I was very much troubled, but I knew I was under a Temptation, and therefore cryed to the LORD for help, . . . at last I resolved to try to Suckle my Child, which I did, and then lay down again, and found that I was pretty well freed from that Temptation, and finding my self much distempered in my Head, I desired the Lord to give me rest, and went about to compose my self to Sleep, but as I lay, I thought Satan stood before me, asking where I could find a Promise for Sleep, at present I could not think of any, but after some study this was brought into my Mind, *The Lord will give his Beloved Sleep:* This Word comforted me, but yet I could not all that night get any Sleep, but still I thought I saw Satan laughing at me, because I had no Sleep, and yet trusted in his Word; thus all the Night I continued weak in Body, and comfortless in Mind, so that in the Morning I expected nothing but Death, then beginning to think more seriously of my Change, Satan as I then thought, asked me where was my Assurance of my everlasting Happiness? . . . my Heart made Answer, it is true, I have no Assurance, but I have cast my self wholly upon the Lord Christ, and in him only is my Hope, and here will I rest, and if I perish, I perish, but sure I am such shall not perish, for Christ hath promised them eternal Life. Thus being assisted by the Lord, I vanquished Satan for that Time: And being thus at Peace, I quickly fell asleep, and dreamed there was a Ladder set upon the Earth, whose top reached to Heaven, and I thought I was to go up that Ladder into Heaven, and that as fast as I got up, I was pulled down again, which caused me to shed abundance of Tears, fearing that I should never get up, and I tho't something from above drew me by the Arms, but I could not see what, but at last I thought I was in Heaven, where all Tears were wiped from mine Eyes, and I was filled with Rejoycing, but when I had been there a little while, I thought I was to go back again to the Earth, and this very much troubled me: But then I thought I heard a Voice saying, it would be but for a little while, and. . .I should die in child-bed, [which she in fact did, twelve years after her marriage] and that the Night before I died, I should have full Assurance . . . when I did awake I was with inexpressible Joy, earnestly longing to be Dissolved, and to be with Christ, which was best of all, and yet willing if the Lord pleased to suffer any Thing which might be inflicted on me.

Document 2: "More Precious Than Gold Tried in the Fire": Valedictory of Mrs. Sarah Goodhue

Sarah Whipple Goodhue (1641–1681), the youngest daughter of a church elder and the wife of a minister, was a devout Puritan. On July 14, 1681, knowing that she faced a difficult childbirth at the age of forty, she wrote this Valedictory. *Twins were born to her on July 20, and three days later, she died. Her* Valedictory *testifies to the evangelical role that Sarah Goodhue exemplified toward family and friends in her private life.*[25]

Brothers and Sisters all, Hearken and hear the voice of the Lord, that by his sudden Providences doth call on you to prepare yourselves for that swift and sudden messenger of death; that no one of you may be found without a wedding garment, a part and portion in Jesus Christ, the assurance of the love of God, which will enable you to leave this world, and all your relations, though never so near and dear, for the everlasting enjoyment of the great and glorious God, if you do fear him in truth.

The private Society, to which while here I did belong, If God by his providence come amongst you, and begin by death to break you, be not discouraged, but be strong in repenting, faith and prayers, with the lively repeatal of God's counsels declared unto you by his faithful messengers: O pray each for another, and with one another; that so in these threatning times of storms and troubles, you may be found *more precious than gold tried in the fire.* Think not a few hours time in your approaches to God mispent; but consider seriously with yourselves, to what end God lent to you any time at all. This surely I can through grace now say, that of the time that there I spent, through the blessing of God, I have no cause to repent, no not in the least.

O my children all, which in pains and care have cost me dear, unto you I call to come and take what portion your dying mother still bestows upon you; many times by experience it hath been found, that the dying words of parents have left a living impression upon the hearts of Children: O my children, be sure to set the fear of God before your eyes consider what you are by nature, miserable sinners, utterly lost and undone; and that there is no way and means whereby you can come out of this miserable estate, but by the Lord Jesus

Christ; He died a reproachful death, that every poor, humbled and true repenting sinner by faith on God through him, might have everlasting life. O my children, the best counsel that a poor dying mother can give you is, to get a part and portion in the Lord Jesus Christ: that will hold when all these things will fail; O let the Lord Jesus Christ be precious in your sight.

O Children, neighbours and friends, I hope I can by experience truly say, that Christ is the best, most precious, most durable portion, that all or any of you can set your heart's delight upon. . . . To that end, my children, I do not only counsel you, but in the fear of the Lord I charge you all, to read God's word, and, pray unto the Lord that he would be pleased to give you heart and wisdom to improve the great and many privileges that the Lord is at present pleased to afford unto you, improve your youthful days unto God's service, your health and strength whilst it lasteth, for you know not how soon your health may be turned into sickness; your strength into weakness, and your lives into death. . . . Endeavour to learn to write your father's hand, that you may read over those precious sermons that he hath taken pains to write and keep from the mouths of God's lively messengers, and in them there are lively messages. I can, thro' the blessing of God along with them, say, that they have been lively unto me; and if you improve them aright, why not to all of you? God upbraideth none of the seed of Jacob, that seek his face in truth. My children, be encouraged in this work; you are in the bond of the covenant—altho' you may be breakers of covenant, yet God is a merciful keeper of covenant. Endeavor as you grow up, to own and renew your covenant, and rest not if God give you life, but so labour to improve all the advantages that God is pleased to afford you, that you may be fit to enjoy the Lord Jesus Christ in all his ordinances. What, hath the Lord Jesus Christ given himself for you, if you will lay hold upon him by true faith and repentance? And what, will you be backward to accept of his gracious and free offers, and not to keep in remembrance his death and sufferings, and to strengthen your weak faith? I thank the Lord, in some measure I have found that ordinance, a life making ordinance to my soul.

Oh the smiles and loving embraces of the Lord Jesus Christ, that they miss of, that held off, and will not be in such near relation unto their Head and Saviour. The lord grant that Christ may be your portions all.

Document 3: "THE AMAZONS OF ZION, I Will Call Those Illustrious Heroines": Tabitha Rediviva, *Funeral Sermon Praising Pious Women by the Reverend Cotton Mather*

The Reverend Cotton Mather (1663–1728) was the most prominent Puritan divine of his day. A prolific writer, he had a special interest in women. He developed the funeral sermon that praised the pious woman, of which Tabitha Rediviva *is a typical example. Mather's sermon represents an important turning point in the changing public attitude toward women from the earlier Puritan emphasis on women's innate spiritual inferiority to the nineteenth-century view that females were inherently more religious and more pious than males.*[26]

We must now go on to take Notice, That there are *Vertuous Women* to be found, (even Dorcas's as well as Peters,) among the Disciples of our Saviour, who by being Full of Good Works approve themselves the *Children of God.* It was once demanded; Prov. XXXI. 10, *Who can find a Vertuous Woman; For her Price is far above that of Pearls.* The Name of a Margarite, which imports, A Pearl, were very proper for such an One; And if she wear it, yet she her self conveys a Lustre to it, Exceeds the Lustre of it. Our God has blessed Mankind in this thing, that many such have been found; May He increase the Number of them! And indeed, if such could not have been found, we should not have bewayl'd the Loss, of which our Neighbourhood this day are sensible. The Gentlewomen at Bethlehem, was not the only one, who has deserved such a Testimony as that; Ruth III. 11. *All the City of my People does know, that thou art a Vertuous Woman.* The Grace of God is not Confined unto Our Sex alone; so that indeed it is from such a Confinement, that the Instances of it seem to be more Numerous in the Other Sex than they are in Ours. Tho' both Sexes, be thro' the Marvellous Providence of our God, Born into the World, in pretty AEqual Numbers, yet, in the Female, there seem to be the Larger Numbers, of them that are *Born Again,* and brought into the Kingdom of God. Among the many Circumstances in which they are more prepared for a Godly Life, it may be this may deserve to have a Remark more particularly made upon it; The Curse is turned into a Blessing unto them. God Sanctifies unto them their Fear of Death, and thereby renders them the more acquainted with the way of Living unto Him; the fitter to Dy, and by consequence the fitter to Live. They are in Deaths often; This prepares them to Dy, and this teaches them to Live. The Dubious Hazards of their Lives in their Appointed Sorrows, drive them the more frequently to commit themselves into the Hands of their Only Saviour. They are Saved thro' Child-bearing; inasmuch as it singularly obliges them to *Continue in Faith, and Charity, and Holiness, with Sobriety.* . . .

Yea, The *Women full of Good Works,* have illuminated all Ages of the World; when some have Set, others have Rose and Shone, in every Generation. We read, I Pet. III. 5. *In Old Time, there were Holy Women, who trusted in God.* As far as we can Learn, the *First Believer* on our Saviour, that ever was in the World, was, *A Woman.* And that brave Woman, being Styled, *The Mother of all the Living,* it has induced

Learned Men to conceive, that EVE was, by being the First of them all, in a peculiar manner, the *Mother of all that Live unto God;* and that she was on this Account, [oh! most Happy Woman!] a Mother to her own Husband, and the Instrument of bringing him to Believe in the Great Redeemer. Both Testaments of the Bible have celebrated the Vertuous Women in the following Ages; Women that were Strong in Faith, and gave Glory to God our Saviour; Women that were Leaders to others in the Praises of God; and that were mighty Blessings to all the People of God; Women, that were filled with the Holy Spirit of God, & Exemplary for the Things that are Holy, and Just, and Good. . . . THE AMAZONS OF ZION, I will call those Illustrious *Heroines,* who have made so great a Regiment in the Army of *Martyrs,* and having the Mother of the Maccabees for their Leader, make such a figure in the Glorious Catalogue of Overcomers! . . . At the same time, there have been Women who have not been inferior to them for the Piety of their Lives, and yet have passed silently thro' the World, without so much as an Epitaph at their Deaths bestow'd upon them. No History or Poetry, has preserved their Memory, it was enough to them, that the Great God has a *Book of Remembrance* for them. And as it was thus Of Old Time, thus also it has been In Our Time. Very many of those Matrons who chearfully born their part, in the terrible Transportation over the huge Atlantic Ocean, into this horrid and howling Wilderness, were such Patterns of *Patience* and of *Courage* in going thro' that Glorious Undertaking to take Possession of these Uttermost parts of the Earth, for our Saviour, that wherever the Gospel is Preached in Foreign Countries, what they have done ought to be told for a Memorial of them. And the Remainder of their *Pilgrimage* which they passed in this Wilderness, they spent in a Conspicuous *Fear of God,* & the actions of a Prayerful, Watchful, Humble Walk with Him, wherein they obtained a Testimony that they pleased Him, and this Wilderness became on the noblest Accounts in the World, a Fruitful Field. They are gone, and their Daughters have Rose up, and called them Blessed. The Two Succeeding Generations have been also Brightened with Numbers of their genuine Daughters, who have Walked in the Steps of that Faith, and that Zeal for Good Works, which they have been in those that went before them. . . .

And this brings me to a Finishing Stroke, on the Pourtraiture which I am now drawing of.

Finally, EXPENCES ON PIOUS USES, are such Orient and Brillant *Gems,* in the Golden Bracelet of Good Works, that One who appears without them, cannot walk with any Decency among the Disciples of the Lord. Of a *Dorcas* if it be said, *This Woman was full of Good Works,* it must have this Addition to Explain it, *And of Almsdeeds which she did.* You know what is added yet more particularly; The Widows that stood by, weeping, shewed the Coats and Garments, which Dorcas made, while she was with them. It seems, that being loth to mispend any Time, she would at her Leisure, use her Needle, whereof she was a Mistress, to prepare Garments for the Poor that wanted them; and, no doubt, the Garments that came from such an Hand, were worn by the Poor, with the more of Satisfaction, for the Hand that had afforded them.

There are Women, who have Revenues at their own Disposal; & these Daughters of Abraham, will not be so bound, but that they will count a Tenth part, the Least that they owe to the King of Righteousness. When also the Men are not Churlish and Sordid Nabals, the Women of any Sense at all, are allow'd such a competent share in the Revenues of their Husbands, that they may fairly apply something to Pious Uses, and the Left Hand not know, what the Right Hand has done. Women may become full of Good Works, by animating their Husbands to be so; & indeed their Opportunities to Do Good this way, if the men are not Intractable Children of Belial, are such as none else can pretent unto. But then, there are many other Opportunities for *Good Works,* which may more immediately with their *Own Hands* be managed by the Handmaids of the Lord. They may Devise Liberal Things, for the Propagation of Piety, among all the People. They may with a Bountiful Eye, (and the Sharp-Eyed Charity of a Dorcas,) be on the Look-out for Objects, whose Cry may be, *Have Pity on me; for the Hand of the Lord hath touched me!* When they may not be in Stock with *Money,* on such Occasions, yet they may *Cloath,* or they may *Feed* the Miserable; give Honey to Bees that have lost their Wings; they may *Visit* them, and *Watch* with them; and may do many *Kindnesses* for them; and may with a most Courteous Affability ask them, *I pray, What is there to be done for you?* . . .

It is well known, to this whole Congregation of the lord, that there has been the Last Week a DORCAS taken from us, who was a *Blessing* and an *Honour* to the Church, in the Communion whereof she Led a Religious Life, no Less than Forty years together; & (since her First year were, Sine Culpa, fine Fabula, and Fame was then even afraid of Beyling her) I may say, One in Esteem among the People of God in the Town, for more Years than I have been in the World; who yet am arrived unto a Jubilee. . . .

We have Lost One, of whom it might be very emphatically said, *She was One that Chose the Best Part.*

One, who both maintained the *Religion of the closet,* and also *Loved the House of God,* . . .

One, who was very Conscientious of Relative Duties, and so Prudent, so Helpful, so Honourable towards her several Relatives, that of these, she nearest, *He praises her;* the rest, *Rise up and call her Blessed.*

One who in some heavy Afflictions, which in the Dayes of her Pilgrimage, came upon her, glorified God, with a most holy Resignation; gave her self up in a most ardent Supplication; . . .

One, who for Good Works in the strict sense of the Term, tho' she was far from affecting Ostentation in them, yet made the Vicinity sensible, that they were beholden to God for her. All that wanted any Help, which lay in her power for them, repaied unto her, as unto a *Common Mother;* and at her Decease, they are, (according to the Language of the Psalmist,) Bowed down heavily, as one that mourneth for his Mother.

Document 4: "What a Vile Creature I Am": Funeral Sermon on the Death of His Daughter by the Reverend Thomas Prince

This funeral sermon given by the Reverend Thomas Prince on the death of his daughter, Deborah, reveals the tormenting faith experiences that wrenched her life—their resolution being unclear until her "deathbed scene." Finally relieved of her guilt and accepting salvation immediately before death, she proved herself as "fervent. . . in exhorting and expostulating with Sinners" as her father. The writings of Prince (1687–1758), the New Light pastor of Boston's "Old South" Church, helped publicize the First Awakening. His revival accounts in his son's Christian History *(Boston: 1744, 1745), advertised the Awakening's successes, as did his funeral sermon for his daughter, who lived from 1723 until 1744.*[27]

And this brings me to the known Occasion of this Discourse, *the Death of my Dear and eldest Daughter*. . . .

It was on Dec. 23, 1723, when He Gave her to me. . . . As she grew up, he was pleas'd to restrain her from youthful Vanities, to make her serious, and move her to study the BIBLE and the best of Authors both of History and Divinity: Among the latter of which, Dr. *Watts* and Mrs. *Row's* Writing were very agreeable and familiar to Her. The SPIRIT of GOD was also pleas'd to work on her Heart by, Dr. *Sewall's* Ministry, for whom she had a high Esteem, and by other Means of Grace: Especially when she came to be about Fourteen Years of Age, 'convincing and humbling her (as in a Paper of hers she represents it) of all her Sins both Original and Actual, of their Greatness and Heinousness, and of her Need of a SAVIOUR: enabling her, as she hoped, to repent of her Sins and forsake them; to look on CHRIST as a compleat Redeemer; to renounce her own Righteousness, and depend on his only; and making her willing to accept Him as offer'd in the Gospel, as her Prophet, Priest and King, to instruct, intercede for and rule over Her.'

Upon this she was desirous of Renewing her covenant in Publick, and coming up to all his Ordinances: But Apprehensions of her own

Unworthiness and Fears of Eating and Drinking Judgment to herself, discourag'd and prevented her; till July 18, 1739, when she narrowly escaped being drowned. . . .

Being affected with this great Danger and Deliverance, she seem'd to be further awakened and stirred up to her Duty of Devoting Herself to her DIVINE PRESERVER, of walking in all his Commandments, and living to his Glory. And in consequence of this, at her own Motion, she was on Lordsday the 5th of the following Month, Propounded; and the 19th Publickly Gave Herself to GOD in Covenant, and came into full Communion with us.

When Mr. *Whitefield* came and preached in the Fall of the Year ensuing; she, with Multitudes of Others, was excited to a livelier View of Eternity, to a greater Care of her immortal Soul, to a stricter Search into Herself, and a more earnest Labour after vital Piety and the Power of Godliness, and to make them more the Business of her Life. And now such Experimental and Searching Writers as Mr. *Shepard* of Cambridge, Mr. *William Guthry* of Scotland, Mr. *Flavel* and *Mead* of England, Mr. *Stoddard* of North-Hampton and Mr. *Mather* of Windsor in New-England, &c, were more diligently read and highly valued.

She now suspected all her former Experiences; that her Heart remain'd unrenewed, and that she had not rightly received CHRIST: until Dec. 13, 1740: When on a Day of Private Prayer and Fasting, those Divine Passages were set home with surprizing and overcoming Power on her distressed soul in *Mat.* viii, *Mark* i, and *Luke* v. And there came a Leper to Him, full of Leprosy, who seeing JESUS, fell on his Face and besought Him, saying, 'Lord if Thou WILT, Thou CANST make me clean:' And JESUS moved with Compassion, put forth his Hand, and touched Him, and saith unto Him," I WILL!—Be Thou clean!" And as soon as He had spoken, immediately, the Leprosy departed from Him, and He was cleansed. With those Passages of Grace, there came into her such a sweet and raised View both of the *Power, Willingness* and *Will* of this DEAR REDEEMER, to cleanse her from the Leprosy of Sin and save Her; as to satisfy her of it, and draw her to him in such a Manner as she never felt before. And she told her younger Sister, that if ever she rightly embraced the SAVIOUR and was converted; she thought it was at that happy Season. Tho' this I never knew 'till since her Funeral; it being one of her Infirmities to be too reserved.

Mr. *Tennent's* Searching Preaching raised in Her, as in many Others, a great and constant Jealousy of being Deceived: And upon every spiritual Declension, a cloud of Darkness overwhelm'd her and inclin'd her to judge she was. His insisting also that without *sanctifying Grace,* our BLESSED SAVIOUR gives none a *Right* to Partake at his Table, occasioned her much Perplexity. For from thence she argued; that unless she *knew* she had *sanctifying Grace,* she cou'd not *know* she had a *Right:* And to Partake without *knowing* she had a *Right,* would be not to Partake in *Faith,* but in *Presumption,* and this she had no Right to do. And hence, when Doubts of her State of Grace arose, she dare not Participate; but only attended with Desire, and I believe with deep Regret and Self-abasement. So though her Jealousies and Fears were troublesome; I am apt to think they were useful; not only to make her Look more into and see herself, and make her more broken, humble, and careful, but also excite her Prayers and Labours after livelier Degrees of Grace and the clearer Evidence of it.

Sometimes she had Light and Comfort: But I think oftner otherwise. And this seem'd to be another Infirmity; that she was afraid of Comfort, lest it belong'd not to her, and she should be thereby deluded. For I think she should have humbly received every Comfort which the Sovereigh GOD by the *Scriptures* offered her; to excite her Thankfulness, Love, Praise and Zeal, Encouragement to go on in her Christian Course, and Care to guard against ungrateful Negligence and Security.

In her lively and pleasant Frames she wrote her happy Ideas, and they were her choicest Writings; But afterwards in a Time of Decay she burnt them: And the Reason she gave to an intimate Companion and one of the Female Society to which she join'd for the most indearing Exercise of social Piety, was, because, in Case she should be suddenly taken away, her Friends would think Her to be as Good as those Writings represented.

But I now come to her *Sickness.*

On *Tuesday, May 29,* she was seized on a sudden with a slow Fever; And upon going up to her Chamber drop'd a Word, as if she should never come down alive.

From the Beginning she was much more apprehensive of *Danger* than any else: And though concerned about her Soul; yet complained of her Stupidity, Hardness of Heart, blindness of Mind, Impenitence and Unbelief; censuring and condemning herself of all Good, denying she had any sanctifying Grace, but judging she had been deceiving Herself with the counterfeit Resemblance of it.... And though I reasoned with her about her *former Experience,* yet all in vain. 'O Dear Father, (said she) you have better Apprehension of me than you should have: You don't know what a vile Creature I am: I have dreadfully apostatized from CHRIST, have grown exceeding negligent of religious Duties, and was returning to the World again.' I told her, we did not perceive it; that I could not see those Decays she spoke of, to be inconsistent with a regenerate State, though they were Matter of deep Abasement, and she should have a Care she denied not the gracious Work of GOD within Her....

I told Her CHRIST as a compassionate Saviour had revealed Hell to us on Purpose, that we might be afraid of it, and by the Fear be mov'd to fly to him to save us from it; and this must therefore be a dutiful Compliance with his gracious Purpose; that this Kindness in discovering Hell, with his Concern and willingness to save us from it, is a Part of his Amiableness, for which we ought to love and embrace him; though we should indeed be excited also with the higher Motives of *his Personal Excellancies:* . . .

I also argued from her Love to the house and Word of GOD, and to his People and Ministers; from her peculiar Love to Those whom she apprehended to be most eminent for vital Piety; especially those ministers who most laid open the Hypocrisy of the Hearts of Men, who made the Hypocrites and Formalists the most uneasy, and were most zealous for the power of Godliness: . . .

I then chang'd the Tenor of my discoursing from Day to Day. And *supposing she were not converted,* represented her Case as indeed very dreadful, but not as desperate: And at several Times, as she was through grievous Illness able to bear, endeavoured to set before her the infinite Fountain of Mercy and Grace in GOD; how this Fountain is open, free, and eternally overflowing; how He thereby glorifies every Person in the Godhead, both FATHER, SON, and SPIRIT, and how he would be so far from loosing any Glory, that he would glorify more of his Perfections in Forgiving and Saving her, than in Rejecting and Damning her. I endeavour'd also to set before her the wondrous Piety, Condescension, Offices, Humiliation, Sufferings, Sacrifice, Righteousness, Merits, Exaltation, Glory, Power, Grace, Calls and Promises of CHRIST: how touched with a fellow-Feeling of her Infirmities and Miseries; how tenderly compassionate; how open his Arms; how earnestly inviting and intreating; how ready to receive her; bestow his Righteousness on her, intercede for and reconcile her to the HOLY GOD: . . .

[But on her deathbed, she finally spoke a "new Language."] *O I love the* LORD JESUS *with all my Heart! I see such an Amiableness, such an* AMIABLENESS *in Him; I prize Him above a thousand Words! And the Delights and Pleasures of the World are nothing to* HIM! I ask'd her, If she could now Resign Herself to his arms? She replied—*O Yes! I Believe in Him! I rejoice in Him! And I rejoice in all the Agonies I have borne! And tell the young People of it:* Tell such a one, and such a one, and such a one, and all the Society, for the strengthening of their Faith and their Encouragement to go on! Tell such a one, Not to mind the Vanities of the World, but seek to make her Hope stronger Tell such a one, To live nearer to God, and live nearer to Him: Tell such a one, Not to be so careful about worldly Matters, but to be more careful after CHRIST and Grace. And having deliver'd the like pithy pertinent and pathetick Messages for 5 others, I then ask'd her—'Well, my dear Child! What have you to say to me?' *O Sir,* said she, *that you may be more fervent in your Ministry, and in exhorting and expostulating with Sinners!*

Document 5: "There May Be Mercy and Pardon There for You": Obituary Containing Account of the Conversion and Life of Hannah Harkum Hodge

In her youth, Hannah Harkum Hodge (1721–1805) attended Reverend Jedidiah Andrews's orthodox Calvinist services in Philadelphia and knew little of "heart religion." The arrival of George Whitefield changed entirely her understanding of piety and the character of her life. In contrast to Deborah Prince, Hannah Hodge lived a long time and was confident of her own salvation. Her conversion resulted in a life that embodied the prominent Puritan combination of evangelical zeal and worldly business enterprise, as her obituary here reveals.[28]

When Mr. Whitefield first visited America, she was deeply affected by his preaching, on which she assiduously attended. She has often told her friends, that after the first sermon which she heard him preach, she was ready to say with the woman of Samaria, "Come see a man who told me all things that ever I did." The preacher, she said, had so exactly described all the secret working of her heart, her views, her wishes, her thoughts, her imaginations, and her exercises, that she really believed he was either more than mortal, or else that he was supernaturally assisted to know her heart. . . .

The effects produced in Philadelphia, at this time, by the preaching of Mr. Whitefield, were truly astonishing. Numbers of almost all religious denominations, and many who had no connexion with any denomination, were brought to inquire with the utmost earnestness, what they should do to be saved. . . . So great was the zeal and enthusiasm to hear Mr. Whitefield preach, that many from the city followed him on foot to Chester, to Abingdon, to Neshaminy, and some even to New-Brunswick, in New-Jersey, the distance of sixty miles. She . . . gave the writer a particular account of an excursion of twenty miles, which she made to Neshaminy on foot, to attend a religious meeting there. But so far was she from applauding herself for it, that she condemned both herself and others, as chargeable with imprudence and extravagance. She said, that in these excursions, the youth of both sexes were often exposed to danger and temptation. . . .

After the first impressions made by Mr. Whitefield, four or five godly women in the city, were the principal counsellors to whom awakened and inquiring sinners used to resort, or could resort, for advice and direction. Even the public preaching of ministers of the gospel, some who were no doubt practically acquainted with religion, was not, it would seem, always the most seasonable and judicious. Mr. Rowland, a truly pious and eloquent man, being invited to preach in the Baptist church, proclaimed the terrors of the divine law with such energy, to those whose souls were already sinking under them, that not a few fainted away. . . . [T]he subject of the present memoir had been carried out of the church, in a swoon which lasted for a considerable time.

It had not been ascertained how long her mind remained subject to legal terror, without any measure of the comfortable hope of the gospel. Her exercises, however, are well known to have been of a very violent and distressing kind. At one time she was brought near the borders of despair, insomuch that she even refused to listen to the counsel of Mr. Tennant, or even to suffer him to pray with her, under an apprehension that it would but aggravate her future condemnation. In this state of mind she was visited by the Rev. Dr. Finley, who prudently waved a direct discussion of her case, but gradually and insensibly drew her attention to the all-sufficiency of the Saviour. "And who knows," said he, "but there may be mercy and pardon there for you." He then left her. But the words "who knows but there may be mercy there for you," melted her soul. . . .

It was at this period, that she, with a number of others, endured persecution for conscience sake, and were even excluded from their parents' houses, for considering and treating the salvation of their souls as the one thing needful. The subject of this narrative, during the time of her banishment from her home, supported herself by her needle. She had a sister who was similarly circumstanced with herself. They rented a room, and lived comfortably and reputably on the fruits on their own industry, and before their father's death, they had the happiness of seeing him fully reconciled to them, and of hearing him express his regret for the severity with which he had treated them. . . .

In 1745, as nearly as can be ascertained, the subject of this narrative was married to Mr. Hugh Hodge. He too was one to whom the labours of Mr. Whitefield had been remarkably blest. . . . On his side, as well as that of his wife, a regard to religious comfort and improvement had a governing influence in the choice which they made of each other as partners for life; and experience fully demonstrated, that on both sides a wise and happy choice had been formed. . . .

Coming together with a very small portion of wordly property between them, they had to provide for their subsistence by their own efforts. These efforts were mutual, strenuous, and constant; and by the smiles of Providence, such was their success in business, that they were able not only to live in a comfortable and reputable manner; but to show a most amiable example of hospitality, to perform numerous acts of charity and liberality, to be among the foremost in the support of the gospel, and, after all, to remain possessed of a handsome capital. . . .

During the life of deacon Hodge, his house was constantly open for the reception of all *evangelical* clergymen who visited the city. . . .

Such, indeed, was the deep interest which both Mr. and Mrs. Hodge took in every thing that related to the church, such their eminent piety, and such the influence of their opinion upon others, that their sentiments on many interesting subjects, were asked by their clerical visitors, and are well known to have had weight in several important public concerns.

Deacon Hodge died A.D. 1783. By his will he left the use of nearly his whole estate to his wife during her life. . . . The house of Mrs. Hodge, after the death of her husband, was the same hospitable mansion as before, the same place of sacred conferences, and meetings for prayer and religious improvement. . . . For many years after the death of her husband she likewise continued the business of shopkeeping, to which she had long been accustomed. . . . The income from her shop, which was considerable, was almost wholly applied to charitable uses. . . . She well knew that having long been accustomed to fill up a large portion of the day with active business, she would be likely to feel the want of it, both in body and mind, when it should be discontinued. Accordingly, when her infirmities at last compelled her to relinquish her employment, she declared that she regretted it, principally because she found it unfavourable to her religious state. "You are very fortunate, madam," said a friend to her pleasantly, "very fortunate, indeed, in having no care or anxiety about the world; no business to take up your time or attention; nothing to do from morning till night, but to read, and meditate, and pray, and converse with your friends." "For all that," answered she, "I have not half so much comfort, not even in religion, as when I was bustling half the day behind the counter. I need more variety than I now get. I become moped and stupified for the want of something to rouse me. Beside all this, vain, foolish, wicked, and vexatious thoughts are almost constantly working their way into my mind, because I have so much of that time, which you talk of, for meditation. And, in addition to all, I become lazy and indolent, and do nothing as I ought to do. No, I was a great deal better off when I have some worldly business to which I could attend moderately. It did me good in every way. I must get along as well as I can, now that I am incapable of business, but I find it no advantage, but the contrary, to be without it." It is believed that this was the language of truth, of nature, of experience. Those who have led a busy life should contract their business as age advances, but they will seldom find it beneficial, even to a life of religion, to be wholly unemployed in worldly concerns.

Document 6: "My Resting Reaping Times": Sarah Osborn's Defense of Her Revival Activities, Written to Her Spiritual Adviser, Reverend Joseph Fish

A widow of twenty-six when the Awakening began, Sarah Haggar Wheaten Osborn (1714–1796) of Newport, Rhode Island, found in evangelicalism a means to religious influence and a relief from a life of drudgery. But as her activities expanded from guiding a female prayer society to leading a revival, she met clerical opposition. Here she explains her role in Newport's 1766–1767 revival to her spiritual adviser, Reverend Joseph Fish of Stonington, Connecticut.[29]

Revd and Worthy Sir

. . . And now believing Zions cause is as dear as ever to my venerable friend, permit me to set my self as a child in the Presence of her Father to Give you the Most Satisfactory account of my conduct as to religious affairs I am capable. I will begin with the Great one respecting the poor Blacks on Lords day Evenings, which above all the rest Has been Exercising to my Mind. And first Let me assure you Sir it would be the Joy of my Heart to commit it into Superior Hands did any arrise for their Help. My Revd Pastor and Brethren are my wittnesses that I Have earnestly Sought, yea in bitterness of Soul, for their assistance and protection. [I] would Gladly be under inspection of Pastor and church and turn things into a safe channel. O forever blessed by my Gracious God that Has Himself vouchsaft to be my protection Hithertoo by Putting His fear into My Heart and thereby Moving me as far as possible in this surprizing day. To avoid Moving beyond my Line, while I was anxiously desirous the poor creatures should be savrd with some sutable one to pray with them, I was Greatly distresst; but as I could not obtain [help] I Have Given it up and Thay Have not Had above one [prayer] Made with them I believe Sir Since you was here. I only read to them talk to them and sing a Psalm or Hymn with them, and then at Eight o clock dismiss them all by Name as upon List. They call it School and I Had rather it should be calld almost any thing that is good than Meeting, I reluct so much at being that Head of any thing that bears that Name. Pray my dear Sir dont Look upon it as a rejecting your council; that I Have not yet dismist. It is Such a tender point with me while the poor creatures attend with so Much decency and quietness you Might almost Hear as we say the shaking of a Leaf when there is More than an Hundred under the roof at onece (I mean with the young Mens Society in the chamber) for all there was so Many. Yet was not the Net broken Has sometimes been a refreshing thot. They cling and beg for the Priviledge and no weathers this winter stops them from Enjoying it, nor Have I been once prevented from attending them. . . .

As to the young Men that did in sumer visit us on tusday Evenings and spend the Evening in religious Exercises, praying in turn etc. but as soon as time come to work on Evenings in Sept that ceasd. The Boys fills that vacancy now and the young Men Haven only the priviledge of Meeting in our chamber on Sabath Evenings. I Have no thing to do with them, only Have the pleasure of Seting my candlestick and Stool. This convenient retire Habitation God gave me in answer to prayer, and as soon as I removed to it I Solemnly dedicated it with all its conveniencies to his service, and I cant Help rejoicing in opportunities to improve it. So I dare not desire the young Men to remove from Hence as I know not that any one of them has conveniency and our female Society was broke up Many years on that very account. And as they will not invite Ministers disapprov'd of, Hope their Meeting here will be no ways offencive to any—

There is usualy 30 odd young garls every Monday Evening except and weather is excessive bad and indeed it is surprising to see their constancy thro almost all weathers—yet I know of no Extraordinary Effects but *Here* they behave quite serious and the Pashions are sometimes toucht I think. My companies are all Voluntiers—our Society on wensday Evenings is I Hope not on the decline but rather growing hand[ily?]— . . .

But I come now to answer your tender important Enquiry after approving of part of my work; viz. "Have you Strength ability and Time consistent with other Duties to fill a Larger sphere by attending the various Exercises of other Meetings, in close succession too. A Moses May undertake More (from a tender concern of the people too) then His Shoulders was able to bear; Jethros advice was Seasonable etc."

As to Strength Sir it is Evident I gain by Spending; God will in no wise suffer me to be a Looser by His Service. I am much confirm'd in My believe of that work, He that will Loose His Life for My Sake Shall save it, as I usd to Lie by, unable to sit up, usualy one day in the week for years together. I have Lain by but one this winter and comparatively know nothing about weariness to what I did when I Had so Great a School and ten or more children in family to attend. I always feel stronger when my companies break up then when they come in and blessed by God I have a Good appetite and sleep well, Except any Great pressure is on my Spirits. . . .

As to My ability I can only say I trust christs Strength is Made perfect in my weakness, and at sometimes am Made open to Glory Even in my infirmities, that the Power of christ May rest upon me and rejoice that I am nothing and can do nothing without Him. And yet tho I was born as the wild asses Colt and fit for nothing till brot too by soverign Grace, as mr Henry Notes, yet He can Serve Himself of me and Glorifie Himself in me and in His own way too, However Misterious to me and all around me—he Has chosen the weak things of this world etc.

As to time consistent with other duties it is Most true dear Sir that I am calld by the Providence of God as well as by His word to be a redeemer of time Precious time. And Ille tell my Worthy friend How I do My wakeing time, Except unwell or weary with Exercise Generaly prevents. The dawning of the day mr Osborn rises while it is yet dark, can Just see to dress etc. From which time I am alone as to any inturruption, for drive by infirmity and want to conveniency I was about a doz years ago constraind to Make my bed my closet, curtains drawd Except Just to Let in Light. I do not Lie there but turn upon my knees my stomach soported with bolster and Pillows, and I am thus securd from the inclemency of all Seasons and from all inturruptions from family affairs. There I read and write almost Every thing of a religious Nature. Thus I redeem an Hour or two for retirement without which I must *starve* and this priviledge blessed by God I Have been Enabled to Hold thro all my Seeans of business, sickness in family only Excepted. I never go down till breakfast is Near ready—after Breakfast family worship; then Giving Some orders as to family affairs, I apply to my School, to which you know Sir a kind providence Has Limited my Earning time for soport of my family. And if in this time I educate the children of poor Neighbours who Gladly pay me in washing Ironing Mending and Making, I Imagine it is the Same thing as if I did it with my own Hands. I think my family does not Suffer thro My Neglect tho doubtless if I Had a full purse and Nothing to do but Look after them some things Might be done with more Exactness then now, but Every dear friend is ready to set a stitch or Help me in any wise and all is well Here—my fragments in the intervails I pick up for keeping and drawing out accompts etc. or what Ever my Hand finds to do besides refreshing the body. . . .

sincier tho unworthy friend
S Osborn
March 7 1767

PS I Long to hear How you all do

WESLEYANISM

Document 7: "Come Just as You Are to the Open Fountain of His Precious Blood": Spiritual Letters of Hester Ann Roe Rogers to John Wesley and a Female Convert

Hester Ann Roe Rogers was one of the many "women of Mr. Wesley's Methodism" who "traveled the connection" for John Wesley, leading prayer meetings, class and select band meetings, and preaching throughout England. Though she herself does not appear to have preached, she represents those women who took the first public roles in the Wesleyan movement. Her spiritual biography and letters, like those of other early English Methodist women, were reprinted in the United States in the nineteenth century. These English Wesleyan women became models for their American counterparts who were venturing into public life through the church.

Hester Rogers's letters to John Wesley point to the extent and type of her work throughout England, the mutual support that she ex-

changed with him, and her own strong and clear articulation of the evangelical faith. The final letter included here, which Hester Rogers wrote to another woman, is an example of one of her most typical forms of ministry and enduring legacies—winning other women to Christ and supporting them in their faith through personal contact and correspondence.[30]

Hester Rogers to John Wesley, June 13, 1782

Rev. and Dear Sir,—I have been very ill, and my body brought very low since I saw you; but those sweet words continually applied, caused me to rejoice with joy unspeakable and full of glory, viz., "According to my earnest expectation, and my hope, that in nothing I shall be ashamed, but with all boldness, as always, so now also Christ shall be magnified in my body, whether it be by *life* or by *death;* for me to live is Christ, and to die is gain." O my dear sir, I never dwelt so much in God as I have of late. My whole soul has been swallowed up in communion with the eternal Trinity; and peculiarly within this last fortnight, with the Holy Spirit. I have been led to pray in faith for a universal and pentecostal outpouring of His divine fulness; and it surely will descend.

Being lately on a visit to Nantwich, the dear people there, who knew me formerly, flocked around me with eagerness, and I held a prayer meeting with twelve or fourteen of them, for which I believe we shall praise God through eternity. A poor backslider was restored, and all present were filled with humble love and joy. I left five or six earnestly crying for a clean heart, and determined to meet among themselves, for all the classes were broken up, or torn by divisions. When I came to Congleton, on my return home, I found a young man, who lately withstood cousin Robert Roe to his face, respecting sanctification by faith, now rejoicing in it, and declaring it boldly to all around. I spoke with several who felt the need of holiness, and two of them are able to testify "the blood of Jesus cleanseth them from sin."

In this place, those who enjoy Christian perfection have had much opposition from some of their brethren. Four or five met constantly together to revile cousin Robert and all who profess it. But one of them now has been truly humbled before God, and received it himself in the very way he so much reviled, even by simple faith. And another of them says in his class, and publicly to all, that, if he had continued to revile them, he believes he should have been damned for it; but he is now determined never to rest till he receives it himself. Since you were with us, six or seven have been justified, and four or five sanctified. Cousin Robert preached at Keethlesum, about eight miles off, where one was justified, and another sanctified. At Burslem he found many thirsting for holiness, some enjoying it, and others stirred up to seek it.

The children who professed sanctification when you were here, stand steadfast and unreprovable; though they have much opposition from those who do not believe the doctrine. Indeed I believe it is a means of good to them, constraining them to walk and cleave so much the nearer to God, that he may give them wisdom and strength. For my own part, I find every trial or affliction has this blessed tendency. Still pray for me, dear sir, and believe ever your affectionate, though unworthy child,

H. A. Roe

Hester Rogers to John Wesley, November 21, 1782

My Dear and Honoured Sir,—I have been much indisposed since I wrote last, but I think it is not wholly my old disorders. I believe since my cousin's death my nerves have been much affected, because any thing sudden will occasion tremours, which I can not otherwise account for, at the same time that my soul is in perfect peace and solidly happy; as also many times there is a dulness and stupidity, when at the same moment I feel a direct witness that it proceeds not from any abatement of the ardours of love divine. Glory be to God, I feel this as a well of water ever spring up afresh, and I know the work of his grace takes still deeper root than ever in my worthless heart; and though at times the enemy suggests, if this nervous disorder takes hold of me, as on my late dear cousin, I shall not rejoice evermore, as I have done hitherto; yet I am enabled to answer him, in the power of faith, "My strength shall be equal to my day." If he afflicts, I have his word of promise, "My grace is sufficient for thee." Nor can I have one painful fear: I know in whom I trust....

I was yesterday employed in visiting members of the classes with Mr. R.; a business which has been much neglected here of late, and which, I trust, will be made a blessing to many. I find it profitable. Mr. R. has suffered much through the prejudices of some; but he is as gold purified in the fire: It has been an unspeakable blessing. It has cut off his intimacy with those who would perhaps have proved snares and hinderances to his soul and his labours; and united him more closely to the little flock, who are rich in faith, and heirs of the kingdom. I believe he has acted faithfully to God, to souls, and to you.

The select band is now the most precious meeting in which I ever assembled. There are forty-eight members, all truly and happily walking in the narrow path: thirty-five, I have no doubt, enjoy perfect love. About six have enjoyed it before, and are now seeking it afresh, and the rest, who never enjoyed it, are thirsting for it more than gold or silver. We are all, too, united in one spirit. All in this little company are helpers of each other's joy.

I love Mrs. R. much: she is indeed one of the excellent ones of the earth. I feel much for you respecting the affair at Birstal: may the Lord strengthen your hands, and in doing so, defend his own cause. Your warfare shall surely yet be glorious, though it be through briers, or thorns, or scorpions. The Lord still reigneth, and will defend his dear servants. Surely he is purging his Zion, and will remove the chaff, and leave himself a pure and a peaceable remnant, whose motto shall be, "Holiness to the Lord."

The openness of my disposition has sometimes brought me into inconviences; but with you I believe it will not, and therefore I speak freely. I am very unapt to suspect any person of guile, but experience tells me all are not to be trusted. I feel I need the continual unction of the Holy One to teach me. O pray that this may be ever given to your ever affectionate, unworthy child in a precious Jesus,

H. A. Rogers

Hester Rogers "To one lately emerged out of Arian darkness," November 5, 1789

My Dear Miss D.,—I received the favour of yours, and rejoice that you know in whom you have believed, and that your face is now Zionward. Go on, my dear sister; it is a blessed path:—the goodly land is before—the land of sacred liberty, and glorious rest from all sin. O that you may soon prove, by happy experience, "perfect love casteth out all [slavish] fear!" and that the deepest humiliation before God, on account of our ignorance, helplessness, and unworthiness, is not only consistent *with,* but inseparable *from,* rejoicing evermore; for the ground of that rejoicing is, that he who hath loved, and wash me from my sins in his *own blood,* hath all the honour and glory, and is all in all for ever; while I sink a poor worm at his feet—overwhelmed at his free unmerited grace: grace that plucked me from the gulf beneath—reconciled a poor guilty rebel to her God—changed the lepard's spots, and made the Ethiop white. Thus, the more deep our sense of unworthiness, the more precious is Jesus, our interceding Advocate with the Father, who, in his exalted human nature, ever liveth to intercede for us, until that day when he shall deliver up the kingdom (viz., his mediatorial office) to God, even the Father, and the glorious Godhead of Father, Son, and Holy Ghost, shall be all in all for ever. O the preciousness of such a High Priest, such a Saviour, such a Counsellor, such a King! O for more heartfelt union with him—more of the power of his transforming love! Blessed promise, "He that hungereth and thirsteth after righteousness, shall be filled."

You have heard, I doubt not, of previous Mr. Fletcher's death, and how he proclaimed, with his latest breath—GOD IS LOVE! O that we may be filled, as he was, with his heavenly Master's Spirit. *There* was a witness of the power of grace! a living and a dying witness that Jesus can save to the uttermost. Let me exhort my dear friend to come just as you are to the open fountain of his precious blood; and how soon may you feel the merit of Him you were once taught to despise, made of God unto you not only *wisdom* and *righteousness,* but also *sanctification* and *redemption.*

You see how freely I write, as if I had known you seven years. I hope you will follow my example in this, and let me know the particulars of your spiritual state, that I may rejoice yet more in your joy. My love and my dear partner's attend you. "May He that liveth, and was dead, who is the First and the Last—the bright and the morning Star," be the portion of your happy soul, prays your invariable friend,

H. A. Rogers

Document 8: "The Mother in Israel, That Mirror of True and Undefiled Religion": Letters of Selina Hastings, the Countess of Huntingdon, to John and Charles Wesley, George Whitefield, and Others

Although little known in American history, Selina, the Countess of Huntingdon (1707–1791), was a prime mover of the early Wesleyan movement in Europe and America. This wealthy benefactress established chapels and seminaries for training preachers in the British Isles, and provided vision and funding for the first Methodist missionary work in Georgia. Her correspondence below with John and Charles Wesley and George Whitefield demonstrates her highly influential role as their lay colleague in mission work and social reform on both continents. Designating her in his will as "that mother in Israel, that mirror of true and undefiled religion," Whitefield bequeathed to her the Orphan House and all other buildings and land in his possession at Bethesda, Georgia, hoping that she might yet bring their dream of the orphanage to fruition. As her letter to George Washington attests, the Countess took her cause directly to public officials of rank.

In the nineteenth century, most Wesleyan women who became active in church work in the United States would follow in the footsteps of the countess. Their contribution and personal identity would be formed in organizing and developing powerful missionary societies and reform movements.[31]

The Countess of Huntingdon to Charles Wesley, June 18, 1746

I have written to my worthy friend, Dr. Doddridge, to assist in obtaining a pious, sensible man, one whose whole soul is alive to God and the concerns of eternity, and I have to solicit your assistance, my good friend, in aiding me in this matter. Amongst your very numerous connections, you may hear to some one suited to the situation, which is of great importance, as he will have four churches open to him, where the light of divine truth may be widely extended amongst a people hungering and thirsting after the bread of life.

Do aid me in this business with your willing services, your prayers, and your advice. I am but a weak instrument, and need the supporting care of my great Advocate every minute of my existence. Though I am hardly able to hold my pen, yet I am willing, thanks be to God, to be employed in any way that may conduce to the good of others. Pray for me, my good friend, that if it be the will of God and our Lord Jesus Christ, I may be strengthened for the work which is before me, and that which he has appointed for me on earth. I feel that flame still burning within me—the ardent longing to save sinners from the error of their ways. O, how does the zeal of others reprove me! O, that my poor cold heart could catch a spark from others, and be as a flame of fire in the Redeemer's service! Some few instances of success, which God, in the riches of his mercy, has lately favoured me with, have greatly comforted me during my season of affliction; and I have felt the presence of God in my soul in a very remarkable manner, particularly when I have prayed for the advancement of his kingdom amongst men in the world. This revives me, and if God prolongs my poor unprofitable life, I trust it will ever be engaged in one continued series of zealous active services for him, and the good of precious immortal souls.

Adieu, my most worthy friend. Let me hear from you soon, and give me some tidings to rejoice my heart. Your most faithful friend,

S. Huntingdon

George Whitefield to the Countess of Huntingdon, August 21, 1748

Honoured Madam,—I received your Ladyship's letter last night, and write this to inform you that I am quite willing to comply with your invitation. As I am to preach, God willing, at St. Bartholomew's on Wednesday, evening, I will wait upon you the next morning, and spend the whole day at Chelsea. Blessed be God that the rich and great begin to have hearing ears. I think it is a good sign that our Lord intends to give to some, at least, an obedient heart. Surely your Ladyship and Madam Edwin are only the first fruits. May you increase and multiply! I believe you will. How wonderfully does our Redeemer deal with souls. If they will hear the Gospel only under a cieled roof, ministers shall be sent to them there. If only in a church of a field, they shall have it there. A word in the lesson, when I was last at your Ladyship's struck me—"Paul preached privately to those that were of reputation." This must be the way, I presume, of dealing with the nobility who yet know not the Lord. O that I may be enabled, when called to preach to any of them, so to preach as to win their souls to the blessed Jesus! I know you will pray that it may be so. As for my poor prayers, such as they are, your Ladyship hath them every day.

That the blessed Jesus may make you happily instrumental in bringing many of the noble and mighty to the saving knowledge of his eternal self, and water your own soul every moment, is the continual request of, honoured Madam, your Ladyship's most obliged, obedient, humble servent,

G. Whitefield

The Countess of Huntingdon to John Wesley, September 14, 1766

My dear Sir,—I am most highly obliged by your kind offer of serving the chapel at Bath during your stay at Bristol; I mean on Sundays. It is the most important time, being the height of the latter season, when the great of this world are only in the reach of the sound of the Gospel from that quarter. The mornings are their time—the evenings the inhabitants chiefly. *I do trust that this union which is commenced* will be for the furtherance of our faith and mutual love to each other. It is for the interest of the best of causes that we should all be found, first, faithful to the Lord, and then to each other. I find something wanting, and that is a meeting now and then agreed upon that you, your brother, Mr. Whitefield, and I should at times be glad regularly to communicate our observations upon the general state of the work. Light might follow, and would be a kind of guide to me, as I am connected with many.

Universal and constant usefulness to all, is the important lesson. And when we are fully and wholly given up to the Lord, I am sure the heart can long for nothing so much as that our time, talents, life, soul, and spirit, may become upon earth a constant and living sacrifice. How I can be most so, that is the one object of my poor heart. Therefore, to have all the light that is possible, to see my way in this matter is my prayer day and night; for worthy is the Lamb to receive all honour and glory, and blessing.

. . . But so vile, and foolish, and helpless as I am, he keeps my heart full of faith that he never will leave me or forsake me: having neither help nor hope, but that he will each moment prove the Lord, the Lord full of mercy and compassionate love, to such a poor worm. Pray, when you have leisure, let me hear from you, and believe me most faithfully, your affection friend,

S. Huntingdon

The Countess of Huntingdon on the significance of the Georgia mission

America is honoured by the mission sent over. The province of Georgia have made proposals to build a church at their own expense, and present me with it, that the College of Georgia may have their ministry in that part honoured. The invitations I have for our ministry in various parts of American are so kind and affectionate, that it looks as if we were to have our way free through the whole continent. . . . My last letters from America inform me, our way appears to be made to the Cherokee Indians; and in all the back settlements we are assured the people will joyfully build us churches at their own expense, and present them to us, to settle perpetually for our use. Some great, very great, work is intended by the Lord among the heathen. Should this appear I should be rejoiced to go myself to establish a College for the Indian nations. *I can't help thinking but before I die the Lord will have me there, if only to make coats and garments for the poor Indians. I am looking when some from among us shall be called to the* JEWS—but the Gentiles by us will surely hear the voice of the Lord.

The Countess of Huntingdon to General George Washington, April 8, 1784, regarding her plans "to convert all the revenues of the Orphanhouse at Bethesda, and of her own estates, into a fund for the establishment of a mission to the Indians, on a grand scale"

Sir—I live in hopes that before this you must have received, by our mutual and most excellent friend, Mr. Fairfax, the grateful acknowledgements of my heart for your most polite and friendly letter; this further trouble arises from the kindness of Sir James Jay offering to take charge of my packets to the several Governors of those States of America, to whom I have applied on the subject of my most anxious wishes for the poor Indians; and I felt it quite impossible to let anything go out of my hands without communicating my intentions to you before all others. I have, therefore, taken the liberty of sending you with this a copy of my circular to the Governor of each State, together with a plan, or rather outlines of a plan, thrown together to convey some idea of my views. With my very best compliments to Mrs. Washington, I remain, with the greatest respect and esteem, Sir, your most obliged and most faithful and obedient humble Servant,

S. Huntingdon

Document 9: "O If My Wife Had Ever Given Way to the World I Should Have Been Lost": The Evangelical Witness of Prudence Gough

From its inception, Wesleyan evangelicalism opened public roles of leadership for women, which carried visions of equality for women with men in the church and in the world. Prominent also in evangelicalism, however, has been a strain that restricted women's religious influence to the home, since women were granted spiritual superiority over men but kept in social subordination to them.

The relationship of wealthy Henry and Prudence Gough of late eighteenth-century Maryland makes them striking forerunners of this modern-day legacy. The following account was written by the nineteenth-century historian of Methodism, Abel Stevens. The de-

scription of Prudence Gough's evangelical role within the home, particularly in bringing her husband to Christ, is notable for its nineteenth-century perspective.[32]

Perry Hall is still more historical in the Church, if possible, than the White Mansion, as a home of Asbury and his itinerant associates; and its lady, PRUDENCE GOUGH, gave it primarily its fame for Methodist hospitality, and maintained its enviable reputation to the last. No preachers' home is more frequently mentioned in our early literature. In the week before the memorable "Christmas Conference" of 1784 it sheltered Asbury, Coke, Whatcoat, Vasey, Black of Nova Scotia, and other eminent men, who prepared there the business of the conference. The constitutional organization of American Methodism may be said to have been constructed under its roof.

Asbury's usefulness in the Baltimore Circuit in 1775 had permanently important results. He gathered into the young societies not a few of those influential families whose opulence and social position gave material strength to Methodism through much of its early history in that city, while their exemplary devotion helped to maintain its primitive purity and power. Henry Dorsey Gough and his family were distinguished examples. Gough possessed a fortune in lands and money amounting to more than three hundred thousand dollars. He had married a daughter of Governor Ridgeley. His country residence —Perry Hall, about twelve miles from the city—was "one of the most spacious and elegant in America at that time." But he was an unhappy man in the midst of his luxury. His wife had been deeply impressed by the Methodist preaching, but he forbade her to hear it again. While he was reveling with wine and gay companions one evening, it was proposed that they should divert themselves by going together to a Methodist assembly. Asbury was the preacher, and no godless diversion could be found in his presence. "What nonsense," exclaimed one of the convivialists, as they returned, "what nonsense have we heard to-night!" "No," replied Gough, startling them with sudden surprise; "no, what we have heard is the truth, the truth as it is in Jesus." "I will never hinder you again from hearing the Methodists," he said as he entered his house and met his wife. The impression of the sermon was so profound that he could no longer enjoy his accustomed pleasures. He became deeply serious, and, at last, melancholy, "and was near destroying himself" under the awakened sense of his misspent life; but God mercifully preserved him. . . .

The wealthy converts erected a chapel contiguous to Perry Hall; the first American Methodist church that had a bell, and it rang every morning and evening, summoning their numerous household and slaves to family worship. They made a congregation; for the establishment comprised a hundred persons. The circuit preachers supplied it twice a month, and local preachers every Sunday. After some years of steadfast piety this liberal man yielded to the strong temptations of his social position, and fell away from his humbler brethren. But his excellent wife maintained her integrity, and her fidelity was rewarded by his restoration. Under the labors of Asbury, his "spiritual father," he was reclaimed in 1800, and applied for readmission to the Church in the Light-street Chapel, Baltimore. When the pastor put the question of his reception to vote, the whole assembly rose, and with tears and prayers welcomed him again. His zeal was renewed, his devotion steadfast, and his family built another chapel for the Methodists in a poor neighborhood. Their charities were large, and they were ever ready to minister, with both their means and Christian sympathies, to the afflicted within or without the pale of their Church. After his reclamation he exclaimed, "O if my wife had ever given way to the world I should have been lost; but her uniformly good life inspired me with the hope that I should one day be restored to the favor of God." . . .

"Perry Hall," says the Methodist chronicler, "was the resort of much company, among whom the skeptic and the Romanist were sometimes found. Members of the Baltimore bar, the *elite* of Maryland, were there. But mattered not who were there; when the bell rang for family devotion they were seen in the chapel, and if there was no male person present who could lead the devotions, Mrs. Gough read a chapter in the Bible, gave out a hymn, which was often raised and sung by the colored servants, after which she would engage in prayer. Take her altogether, few such have been found on earth." Asbury called her a "true daughter" to himself, and Coke, "a precious woman of fine sense." "Her only sister became a Methodist about the same time that she did; they continued faithful to a good old age, when they were called to take a higher seat. Most of her relations followed her example of piety. . . .

Their own child, Sophia, "was raised," says Lednum, "after the most religious order. It was a rule of Mrs. Gough not to allow her daughter to go into any company where she could not go with her, nor to join in any amusements that the pious mother could not, with a good conscience, join in. What was very remarkable, this well raised young lady was converted at her piano while singing, 'Come thou Fount of every blessing.' She bore the joyful news to her parents. The mother wept for joy, and the father shouted aloud. . . .

The venerable Henry Smith says of Prudence Gough: "I was with her a few days before her death. She was not in triumph, yet humbly and confidently waiting till her change came. Betsey Cassell, a preacher's widow, her faithful companion, was with her to the last. Some people marveled that she did not leave the world shouting; but it never staggered me in the least, for she was not of that cast of mind. Those who are created anew in Christ Jesus, and live right, are sure to die safe, no matter whether their sun sets fair or under a cloud. She was bold and zealous in the cause of God, yet humble and unassuming. I frequently heard her say, 'I have much severity in my nature.' That might have been so, but it was seasoned by grace. She seemed to have little patience with professors of religion who appeared to be ashamed of their religion before the people of the world. She never prayed in public till after Mr. Gough's death. But when she could get no one to pray with her large family, she took up the cross, read a chapter, and gave out a hymn, which was sung, (for she could not sing herself,) and prayed, and so led the worship of God in her family, no matter who was present. She was a woman of firmness, uncommon fortitude, and moral courage. Taking Mrs. Gough for all and all, she certainly was a Christian of a high grade. Always plain in dress; plain, yet dignified, in her manners; a decided Methodist, but a lover of good people of every denomination, she set an example worthy of imitation. To me she was like a mother for many years, and I think myself honored to be permitted to recall and record her example." Dr. Bond, late editor of the Christian Advocate, who knew her well, says: "Mrs. Gough survived her husband for several years, and still resided at Perry Hall during the summer seasons. During the whole of her widowhood she still held the family devotions in the chapel. O she was an Israelite indeed, in whom there was no guile! All, all she had, her fortune, 'her soul and body's powers,' were consecrated to the service of God."

Document 10: "They That Turn Many to Righteousness Shall Shine Like the Stars, Forever and Ever": Letters of a Pastor's Wife, Catharine Garrettson

The legacy of women's natural piety, which nineteenth-century Wesleyan women received from their eighteenth-century forebears, found its fullest expression in the person of Catharine Garrettson. She was born in 1753 and she died in 1849, her life evenly bridging the two centuries. A member of the wealthy and politically eminent Livingston family of New York, Catharine was married to the Reverend Freeborn Garrettson. Garrettson was a leading founder of Methodism along the Atlantic coast from Nova Scotia to North Carolina, "the first American Methodist preacher that proclaimed the doctrine of free, full, and immediate salvation in New England."

Catharine described her preeminent desire: "I want to be a shining witness of perfect love." Upon reading her letters, one may rightfully question whether her spiritual relationship with her husband was one of mutual equality or whether Catharine was indeed his superior and guide in matters religious. A good case might be made for either position.[33]

Catharine Livingston to Freeborn Garrettson, July 2, 1791

I thank you my Dear Sir for your favor of June 4th and am happy to hear you had so pleasant a meeting this last Conference. I trust the hopes of uncommon success, which you seem to look forward to, may attend your joint endeavors.

Yes, by Br. I think it is a great thing "To love the Lord with all the heart." And I trust this great thing the Lord has done for you and will one day do for me also. This much I can say, there is no earthly object that comes in competition with my love to God. All my happiness is in Him and all my future hopes I desire from him. I sometimes feel my trials too sensibly; but when I reflect that the way to glory is the way of the cross, I am encouraged to press forward and give myself anew into the hands of God, to be fashioned to his purpose and be made meet for glory. I do know that sublunary things are under my feet, that my love to God is supreme. And I think I may venture to say my intention is pure and my desire stronger and more to live to the glory of God than is consistent with my present low estate. The last week has been a season of uncommon peace and love. I have had much union and communion with the God of my spirit. All things are made easy to me. . . .

This is Sunday and I am going to hear Brother ______ preach. Last Sabbath we had Br Evereth, but this place knows no changes. The people set with attention; but no power follows the word. I hope and believe you have better success. I could not see that I should have done right in going to Conference, and therefore staid; though I believe my friends expected I would have gone. Mrs. Lewis mentioned to me her dining with you, and said she felt for you *that hot day.* I hope the Lord is with you in all your journeys to be "your sun and shield." And surely if the life you lead was not sweetened by the love of God, it would doubtless be the greatest drudgery you can perform. But what a reward is held out in these words, They that turn many to righteousness shall shine like the stars, forever and ever. That this will be your happy lot, my worthy friend, I do not entertain a doubt. Press forward then my dear Brother, for the attainment of every gift and grace that may make you a powerful Herald, to spread the glad tidings of salvation.

May I again presume in the name of a sister to mention what I think is a fault in your speaking? When you are earnest, you lose the natural tone of your voice. Everything that is unnatural seems to give pain. I always think you hurt yourself by the exertions you then make, and have no doubt but to do, though you may not be sensible of it at the time. The effect on your audience is disagreeable. It appears like anger. Speak strong words, they are proper, they are often necessary, but let it be in your own tone of voice, which is soft and persuasive. I do not think our brethren are attentive enough to little things. St.

Paul became all things to all men, that he might gain some. I know you too well to believe that this observation will give offence. If I am wrong in making it, the intention I know is right and that alone will justify me in your opinion. Sister Rutsen has spent some days at this place and is still with me. I find her a pleasing, profitable companion. She begs her love to you.

God bless you my dear Brother, and take you into his tenderest care, keeping from this time and forever more, prays your friend and sister

Catharine Livingston

Catharine Livingston to Catharine Rutsen, December 1791

My dear Sister:—

I send you the book I promised, and hope on Monday to hear from you by a person who will be at the store for two Files. Send by him if you please a piece of pocket tape for Mrs. T.

My mind has been deeply exercised ever since I saw you, but yesterday, when I felt the effects on this frail Tabernacle, and then my mind was somewhat more composed. I ardently long to be what the Lord would have me be. I want to be a shining witness of perfect love. Oh! that the Lord would give me faith to lay hold on the blessing he is willing to bestow, the time is *Now.* Why can I not fully believe. I dreamed once since I came home that I was going to be crucified, that they were raising the cross up on which I was stretched, and I was in expectation of great sufferings. The next night I dreamed I was dead, that I saw my own corps and was greatly shocked at the solemn spectacle. I thought I had another body and was soliciting the servants to remove the old one. Both times I awoke and slept no more during the night. That these things have a spiritual meaning I doubt not. Lord teach me to understand them aright. I have put my construction on them. Let me hear yours. There are many things that pass between you and I that I wish may go no farther, perhaps what I have written is among the number.

I have found the preachers experience very profitable and see many of them were in possession of that perfect love which I pant after. And they all received it by simple Faith. "Lord Jesus Christ my Master give this faith, that I may receive what thou art willing to bestow, without money and without price." The whole creation is blanck to me. I can truly say I take no pleasure in anything. There is a mighty void which God alone can fill. I have not slept this three nights, and still I am in tolerable health this day. O pray for me my Catherine, that "the Lord would suddenly come to his Temple" and cleanse me from evil, that no thing may reign in my heart but His pure love alone.

I feel little freedom in writing, therefore will conclude wishing you, near access to the throne of grace than I find, and sweeter communion with the God of your spirit, than is at present my experience. And yet, blessed be God, I feel no guilt. But am willing to be the Lord's on his own terms. Ah! may I be guided by his blessed Spirit in every step of my journey, not my will but thine O Lord! be done in me, and by me.

Give my love to all with you. And God of his great mercy grant that you all be in the spirit on the Lord's day. Farewell believe me your Friend and Sister

Cath Livingston

These Dreams were explained by the love of God being so shed abroad in my soul that I could rejoice in God with joy unspeakable, and a belief that I was cleansed from all sin.

Catharine Garrettson to Freeborn Garrettson, June 5, 1795

My dearest Friend:—

I am still where you left me, and I bless God in very tolerable health. On Sunday Mr. Mire drove me in the chair to church where I heard Mr. Wolsey. The first part of the sermon was dull enough but towards the latter part he was warm and animated. To be eminent in anything exertion is necessary. To be strong in the Lord, we must be unwearied in his service. If we would win souls we must learn from everything in creation and bring forth as occasion demands out of our treasury things new and old.

I hope my dear you find your soul more than ever engaged in the work of the Lord, and that you will improve every opportunity to bring glory to God. Keep ever in view the importance of every living soul you meet with, and let none pass without a word in season, tis expected from you, and God has laid it on you. I despair of ever being a shining light, but I would wish to see you the most pious man in the world.

I conclude you got to town by Tuesday. Let me know by the earliest conveyance when you return. I hope my dear you find a throne of grace acceptable at all times, and a constant disposition for prayer. Oh! when shall my soul breathe constantly the language of prayer and praise.

Sunday morning. I find myself in much heaviness. I am afflicted with the aspect of the times both in Europe and America. In this country wicked and designing men are rising daily in power and influence, and how matters may yet turn the other side the water we know not. We are guilty, and desire to be smitten and afflicted; but in the midst of all discouragements I endeavor to remember my peculiar wants, and trust in the promise of the dear Redeemer "That they who hunger and thirst after righteousness should be filled." I will try and go to Class this afternoon, perhaps I may leave my burden, and come back rejoicing. Oh! my dear let us be more than ever engaged with God. I fear we shall see sad times. . . .

Your affectionate wife
Catharine Garrettson

CONCLUSION

Document 11: "When Marriage Is According to Nature and God's Designation": Treatise on Marriage by the Reverend Jonathan Edwards

More than any other one person, Jonathan Edwards exemplified what has been traditionally interpreted as the spirit and vision of the Great Awakening. His belief that God spoke directly and personally to each individual could have led Edwards to affirm the spiritual and social equality of men and women—as Anne Hutchinson had sought to impress upon Puritan society one hundred years before. However, as his treatise on marriage indicates, Edwards took the other route. Here he compares the relationships between the soul and Christ with that of the husband and wife, maintaining the long-standing Puritan emphasis on the subordination of women. The thrust of Edwards's rationale—opposite and distinct natures of man and woman—foreshadowed the nineteenth-century thesis of the "Cult of True Womanhood." The argument for both the equality of the sexes and the spiritual superiority of women had roots in the Great Awakening and the revolution, the evangelical and enlightenment traditions, of the eighteenth century.

Edwards undoubtedly based this description of the ideal marriage on his relationship with his own wife, Sarah Pierrepont. And while he admired her piety, he never questioned her subordination to him.[34]

The soul is espoused and married unto Jesus Christ; the believing soul is the bride and spouse of the Son of God. The union between Christ and believers is very often represented to a marriage. This similtude is much insisted on in Scriptures—how sweetly is it set forth in the Song of Songs! Now it is by faith that the soul is united unto Christ; faith is this bride's reception of Christ as a bridegroom. Let us, following this similitude, that we may illustrate the nature of faith, a little consider what are those affections and motions of heart that are proper and suitable in a spouse toward her bridegroom, what are those conjugal motions of soul which are most agreeable to, and do most harmonize with, that relation that she bears as a spouse.

Now it is easy for everyone to know that when marriage is according to nature and God's designation, when a woman is married to an husband she receives him as a guide, as a protector, a safeguard and defense, a shelter from harms and dangers, a reliever from distresses, a comforter in afflictions, a support in discouragements. God has so designed it, and therefore has made man of a more robust [nature], and strong in body and mind, with more wisdom, strength and courage, fit to protect and defend; but he has made woman weaker, more soft and tender, more fearful, and more affectionate, as a fit object of generous protection and defense. Hence it is, that it is natural in women to look most at valor and fortitude, wisdom, generosity and greatness of soul these virtues do (or at least ought, according to nature) move most upon the affections of the woman. Hence also it is, that man naturally looks most at a soft and tender disposition of mind, and those virtues and affections which spring from it, such as humility, modesty, purity, chastity. And the affections which he most naturally looks at in her, are a sweet and entire confidence and trust, submission and resignation; for when he receives a woman as wife, he receives her as an object of his guardianship and protection, and therefore looks at those qualifications and dispositions which exert themselves in trust and confidence. Thus it's against nature for a man to love a woman as wife that is rugged, daring and presumptuous, and trusts to herself, and thinks she is able to protect herself and needs none of her husband's defense or guidance. And it is impossible a woman should love a man as an husband, except she can confide in him, and sweetly rest in him as a safeguard.

Thus also, when the believer receives Christ by faith, he receives him as a safeguard and shelter from the wrath of God and eternal torments, and defense from all the harms and dangers which he fears; Is. 32:2, "And a man shall be as an hiding place from the wind, and a covert from the tempest; as rivers of water in a dry place, as the shadow of a great rock in a weary land." Wherefore, the dispositions of soul which Christ looks at in his spouse are a sweet reliance and confidence in him, a humble trust in him as her only rock of defense, whither she may flee. And Christ will not receive those as the objects of his salvation who trust to themselves, their own strength or worthiness, but those alone who entirely rely on him. The reason of this is very natural and easy.

Document 12: "Preach to Us, or We Shall All Go to Hell": Barbara Heck Becomes the "Mother of American Methodism"

Debate continues today as to whether Robert Strawbridge, an early Methodist preacher in the Baltimore area, or Barbara Ruckle Heck should be credited as the true "founder of American Methodism." Their work led to the first Methodist societies in New York and Maryland at approximately the same time. One year after she migrated to New York City in 1765, Barbara Heck made a colorful evangelical witness that distinguished her as the "Mother of American Methodism." She was also the founder and architect of the earliest extant Methodist society in North America, the John Street United Methodist Church in New York City.[35]

Many of the Palatines who accompanied Embury and Barbara Heck from Ireland, had by this time lost even the form of godliness, and had become adept at card playing and other sinful amusements. Several of those who accompanied Paul Ruckle had but little respect for religion, and in the evenings, when both parties met after the day's labour, card-playing formed the staple amusement. There is not the slightest shadow of evidence that Embury ever played with them, or even witnessed them playing. One evening in the autumn of 1766, a large company were assembled playing cards as usual, when Barbara Heck came in, and burning with indignation, she hastily seized the cards, and throwing them into the fire, administered a scathing rebuke to all the parties concerned. She then went to Embury's house, and told him what she saw, and what she had done, adding, with great earnestness, "Philip, you must preach to us, or we shall all go to hell, and God will require our blood at your hands!" Philip attempted a defence by saying, "How can I preach, as I have neither house nor congregation?" "Preach," said this noble woman, "in your own house, and to your own company." Before she left, she prevailed on Philip to resolve to make the attempt, and within a few days, Embury preached the first Methodist sermon in New York, in his own hired house, to a congregation of five persons. Such was the origin of the Methodist Episcopal Church of the United States—now the largest and most influential church in the American Continent. "Who hath despised the day of small things."

Women, Civil Religion, and the American Revolution

ROSEMARY SKINNER KELLER

In January 1776, John Adams left his home in Braintree, Massachusetts, to begin his third year as a delegate to the Continental Congress in Philadelphia. During that session, he would be a major architect of the Declaration of Independence and a prime mover of the patriot cause. Immediately after John's departure, his wife, Abigail, wrote her close friend, Mercy Warren, describing the "contending passions dividing my heart":

> Our Country is as it were a Secondary God, and the first and greatest parent. It is to be perferred to parents, to wives, children, Friends and all things the Gods only excepted.
>
> These are the considerations which prevail with me to consent to a most painfull Seperation.[1]

Only a person who held a patriotic fervor amounting to religious ardor could express loyalty to her nation in such terms of exalted sacrificial commitment. Abigail Adams's sanctification of the American cause was not unique to her, however. It reflected the sentiments of a vast number of patriots throughout the colonies during the War for Independence.

The connection between national reverence and Christian piety, identified in our generation as "civil religion in America," has had the most far-reaching effect on America's religious life of all the revolutionary changes wrought by the War for Independence. After surveying the effects of the American Revolution on religious institutions—separation of church and state, religious freedom, rise of denominationalism, and voluntaryism in church membership and support—the distinguished church historian Sydney Ahlstrom wrote:

> Overarching all of the foregoing circumstances of the churches was the patriotic spirit which soon pervaded every aspect of the country's thought and feeling.... With the passing years a new kind of national feeling came into

existence. The Union became a transcendent object of reverence, a stern author of civic obligations as well as a source of faith and hope. Americans became stewards of a sacred trust, while the country's statesmen, orators, and poets gradually brought a veritable mystical theology of the Union into being. . . . From the start both national reverence and Christian piety came to be seen as intrinsic elements in the religion of Americans. It thus became the duty of the churches to uphold the sacred trust and yet avoid the temptations of idolatry; to remind men of the country's ideals and yet preach that the God of Israel is Judge of all nations. But in decade after decade the supreme difficulty of that task would be exhibited. Patriotism would protect and enliven the churches, yet threaten their integrity.[2]

The "real American Revolution . . . in the minds and hearts of the people" created by the War for Independence was a radical change in the purpose of the nation and its relationship to God—from the religious foundations sanctioned by early colonial Puritans to the secular grounding espoused by the citizens of the new republic at the beginning of the nineteenth century.[3] The American Revolution marked the turning point from the early Puritans' vision of their colony as a restored Jerusalem, committed to devotion and service to God, to the modern, nationalistic conception of the United States as a secular nation undergirded by religious principles of public morality and civic virtue.

When Robert Bellah introduced the phrase "civil religion in America" seventeen years ago, he conceptualized that religious dimension of political and cultural life which was intended by the founders of the country to reflect a prophetic understanding of God's judgment on the nation, but which at times has amounted almost to idol worship of the United States and to the "rightness" of its national and international causes. This sacred dimension of public life provided an intangible unity of spiritual principles that constituted an overarching "national religion" or religious sentiment transcending loyalties to the myriad denominations and sects which would arise in generations to follow.[4]

There is a sense, as Bellah has more recently pointed out, in which the American Revolution and American civil religion are one and the same. Religion as the basis of public morality and the necessary underpinning of a republican political order originated in the historical circumstances of the War for Independence and has remained an uninterrupted theme to inspire and energize an American sense of mission throughout our country's history. The founding fathers believed that religion, defined as morality, was the essential basis of public virtue—disinterested service dedicated to the well-being of the citizenry. The civil religion which they sought to instill in the populace was the commitment of citizens to sound moral principles and virtuous conduct for the good of the state.[5]

Norms for attaining a moral and virtuous citizenry were embodied in the founding documents of the American republic, the Declaration of

Independence and the Constitution. Norms, however, are abstract entities unless they become the driving force that provides vision for leaders and motivation for the masses. Thus, the values of the national faith were personified and personalized in the spirit of patriot leaders of the revolutionary period, notably those from New England and Virginia.

The espousal of civil religion as a faith commitment for public service, through the leadership and citizenship primarily of men, has been well established during the last fifteen years by sociologists, historians, and political scientists.[6] The relationship of women to civil religion in America has been different from that of men—but equally crucial in the shaping of American life and women's place in that society over three centuries. This chapter will focus on the foundations of the connection between women and civil religion which were laid during the revolutionary era. To understand the historic beginnings of this relationship is to identify the underlying religious persuasion that has determined much of the role and vision of women in the mainstream of American society.

The chapter first will describe the work of most women in New England during the revolution and their interpretation of those functions as patriotic contributions to the American cause. It will then consider the origins of civil religion through the perception and commitment of women to the patriot effort as a holy war growing out of Puritan and Enlightenment religious and political views. Further, the chapter will analyze the ways in which religious patriotism helped to mold a new role for women as wives and mothers in the young republic, to expand the boundaries of education open to them, and to create a vision of social equality in their minds. Finally, it will question the legacy of the War for Independence as a conservative or radical revolution for the future of women in American society.

I

The "plain duties and humble virtues," which characterized the experience of most New England women before the revolution, were hardly sufficient guidelines for the crises they had to confront during the war era. With men away from home serving in the armies for varying periods of time, women had to shoulder home-front responsibilities for which their typical domestic experiences had not prepared them. Further, these home fronts, which women were expected to keep stable, were very often battle zones themselves. Thus, women were required to exercise endurance, resourcefulness, and courage comparable to that of soldiers in armed conflict. As Mary Beth Norton has expressed it:

> Most narratives of the Revolutionary War concentrate upon describing a series of pitched battles between uniformed armies. Yet the impact of the conflict can more accurately be assessed if it is interpreted as a civil war with profound consequences for the entire population. Every movement of troops

through the American countryside brought a corresponding flight of refugees, an invasion of epidemic disease, the expropriation of foodstuffs, firewood, and livestock, widespread plundering or destruction of personal property, and occasional incidents of rape.[7]

Such terrors were the daily experiences of women minding their homes alone during the war. When fighting was taking place in nearby towns, they had to be ready, with little or no advanced warning, to convert their homes into hospitals for wounded soldiers or hostels for troops en route. But most women found that their primary patriotic responsibility was to assume their husbands' tasks of farm, business, and home management in addition to their own normal duties, a situation well described as "doubled in Wedlock." And so they maintained economic stability at home, disciplining or bargaining with troublesome hired hands, coping with financial crises created by inflation and scarcity, and even becoming small entrepreneurs themselves. Highly resourceful and efficient management by women saved countless families from destitution.[8]

At the same time, many women took part in activist protests for the patriot cause, a departure from their previous noninvolvement in public affairs. Spinning bees, held in the homes of local ministers, drew large numbers of women and were items of public news. After the women had spun all day and eaten a dinner of American produce, the pastor would conclude the gathering with an appropriate sermon, lauding the women that they "may vie with the men in contributing to the honor and prosperity of their country and equally share in the honor of it." Spinning bees enabled women to employ their traditional domestic enterprise while making political statements comparable to men's wearing of homespun on public occasions. Although their value as far as quantity of material produced was probably more symbolic than real, spinning bees dramatized the need for industry and frugality and encouraged cloth production in homes.[9]

A more marked departure from previous female activity were door-to-door campaigns by Daughters of Liberty to raise money for cloth to make shirts and other clothing for soldiers. The first campaign, for the benefit of Washington's army, was launched in 1780 in Philadelphia by the Ladies Association. Similar successful drives were waged in at least three other states.[10]

As early as 1767, women supported economic boycotts of tea and other items taxed by the Townshend Act of that year. They occasionally made formal agreements not to purchase or consume imported tea, as in February 1770 when more than three hundred "Mistresses of Families" pledged to "totally abstain" from the use of tea, "Sickness excepted." Increasingly activist expressions of female protest found women forcibly opening stores owned by Tory sympathizers, removing hoarded goods, and distributing them to patriot supporters and needy citizens of the town. Such efforts were given public recognition and praised as vital to the patriot cause, which again contributed to women's new sense of the worth and value of their work.[11]

But this sense of esteem that women gained from their war efforts was not simply the result of this recognition and appreciation granted to them. Even more, women came to believe that they had contributed a genuine public service to their country, less dramatic but in some way parallel to that of their husbands. Characteristic of most New England women, Abigail Adams saw her own patriotic duty as tending the family's private affairs with frugality and economy and, in the process, releasing her husband for service on a high level and in distant places. "All domestick pleasure and injoyments are absorbed in the great and important duty you owe your Country," she wrote John, expressing her continued understanding of living her life through his. But also, she evaluated her responsibilities at home during the war: "I hope in time to have the Reputation of being as good a *Farmeress* as my partner has of being a good Statesmen." Abigail Adams, symbolic of many women of the American Revolution, was coming to a new perspective of herself as an autonomous being in an equal and interdependent relationship with her husband.[12]

II

Before the American Revolution, no one seriously believed that women, as well as men, could have ideas on political subjects and desire to discuss them. Educated women might admire the British historian and political writer Catharine Macauley, but they would not have seen her as a possible model for themselves.

When women first began to share their views on war conditions and issues of the revolution, they did so either in private circles with other women or in an indirect manner with their husbands. Women had taken seriously John Fordyce's rationale that they had both the ability and the right to influence men in a seductive and manipulative manner as the "power behind the throne." In a letter to Catharine Macauley, Mercy Warren, wife of Massachusetts legislator James Warren, stated the accepted belief and strategy that women could exert as much influence by sharing their views through "the soft whispers of private friendship" as men could by thundering their ideas from a public platform.[13]

Mercy Warren and Abigail Adams are prime examples of the kind of women throughout the colonies who, in their own right, became political commentators on the revolutionary war. Both were well educated for their day, though that education had been gained entirely at home. They had grown up in homes of clergymen or lawyers and had been exposed to books and political discussions since early childhood. Further, they married lawyers who moved into politics and served in the Massachusetts

Bay colony and in the Continental Congress. Abigail Adams limited her judgments on political ideas to private conversation and personal letters. Mercy Warren wrote political satires in the form of plays, most of which were published anonymously during the war to expose the evil British designs to crush the liberties of American colonists.[14] *The Group,* one of her plays published anonymously in Boston in 1775, disguised the misguided and selfish Massachusetts Tories under such names as Judge Meagre, Brigadier Hateall, Hum Humbug, and Dupe (Document 1).

Yet the revolution became more than a patriotic cause for women. The war acquired a divine sanction that transformed it into a religious commitment for founding mothers, as well as fathers, of the republic.

Since the migration of Puritans to the Massachusetts Bay Colony in the 1630s, the New England clergy had held the accepted duty of translating political ideas into religious terminology. Regular Sunday sermons, and particularly fast, thanksgiving, and election sermons, sometimes sounded more like patriotic orations than religious addresses. Because they were given by clergymen, however, they were recognized as carrying divine authority.[15]

One of the key precepts correlating political and religious thought was the right of Christians, under stipulated conditions, to rebel. From the Bible and such Enlightenment political writers as John Locke and Algernon Sydney, the New England clergy had built a political philosophy that justified resistance to invasion of natural and civil rights by those in authority, foreign armies, or mobs. This philosophy stressed that rulers existed for the sake of their subjects and that the happiness of leaders and the happiness of the people were intimately bound together. Besides the sacredness of the compact between ruler and subjects, those divinely ordained rights included the choice of officials by the people, freedom of speech, trial and appeal, and taxation by representatives elected by the people. Before the revolution, these sermons did not hint at popular discontent but were unimpassioned expositions of Puritan political theories on government. By 1750, however, the sermons were officially sanctioned by legislative resolve in Massachusetts as a source of political instruction to be published and distributed in the province.[16]

During the revolution, Boston's clergymen, including Jonathan Mayhew, Charles Chauncy, Samuel Cooper, and Andrew Eliot, were among the leading propagandists and clerical spokesmen of the patriot cause, not only in the Boston area but throughout the colonies. They preached that subjects were to be dutiful and peaceable, never using their liberty as a cloak for licentiousness. On the other hand, the primary loyalty of the Christians was "to the supreme RULER of the universe, by whom kings and princes decree justice." Submission of the citizen was a criminal act if the ruler usurped unwarranted power and oppressed the people. After careful and rational deliberation, the true patriot might be required to rebel. Clergymen laid the demand for divine approval, the most powerful sanction for rebellion in the eyes of a religious person, upon their congregations.[17]

The religious sanction of revolution provided biblical and divine approval of the Enlightenment political principle: that governmental authority was based upon a social contract between rulers and the people. Therefore, the tyranny of British rule was a violation of Americans' natural right to a role in legislation and taxation. Clergymen both recast Enlightenment thought and drew upon past Puritan political ideas in stating that God demanded allegiance of the chosen people to earthly rulers, but commanded them to rise against earthly rulers if their rights were violated.[18]

The interpretation of the war as the Lord's battle, of the patriots as God's chosen people, and the British as agents of evil carried tremendous force in mobilizing support both on the home front and in battle. Women as well as men, living out of a Puritan heritage, wrote and circulated political propaganda pieces that reflected a strong religious persuasion.

Such efforts were not simply the work of women in politically oriented families, such as the Adamses and the Warrens. A popular form of propaganda was the broadside, which was posted on trees and buildings in town squares where it would be read by many people. Two such broadsides, written by Daughters of Liberty of Massachusetts—women who boycotted tea, raided stores owned by Tory merchants, conducted money-raising campaigns for patriot supplies, and spun cloth in church spinning bees—indicate an ideology of religious patriotism held by large numbers of patriot women (Documents 2, 3). Both anonymous writers placed the cause of the war in the sins of the people. The colonists' sins of vice, ostentatious living, and "whoring from thy God" caused the Lord to turn against them. Britain became an instrument to inflict God's wrath upon the colonists. Only as the colonists themselves repented would the Lord withdraw the scourge of England. But the Lord is ever faithful to his chosen ones and would again make the land to blossom.[19]

The Daughters of Liberty called the people to repentance, using words strong as any Puritan preacher had ever used—and their promise of forgiveness to God's special people was equally compelling:

Should we go on our sinful course,
Times will grow on us worse and worse.
Then, gracious God now cause to cease,
This bloody war and give us peace!
And down our streets send plenty then
With hearts as one we'll say Amen![20]

III

The way in which religious patriotism helped cast a new mold for women's lives in New England during the American Revolution can be understood most clearly by tracing the change in the life of a representative woman. The experience of Abigail Adams provides such a focal point (Document 4). The letters which she exchanged with her husband during the war years contain the fullest description of any correspondence extant from the revolutionary era of how the struggle for independence affected the inner lives of individuals and families. Her journey is representative of the origins of civil religion in relationship to women and reveals how the revolution became the catalyst to redirect the values and self-understanding of women from early to modern American life.

Like so many New Englanders of the revolutionary generation, Abigail and John Adams's forebears were among the early Puritan settlers in Massachusetts Bay. Abigail's original American ancestors migrated from England in 1633 in the Puritan settlement led by church divine John Cotton. They became members of the First Church of Boston, of which Cotton was the teacher. John's ancestors arrived in Boston five years later. During the generations that followed, their subsequent forebears actively participated in and assumed leadership of the church and political life of the Boston vicinity. Some of Abigail's Quincy relatives were elected representatives to the Massachusetts provincial government. Abigail's father was the minister of the Congregational Church in Weymouth for forty-four years. When John Adams selected law as a career, he viewed it as a means of expressing both his religious and his civic commitments.[21]

The letters that Abigail wrote to John while he was serving in the Continental Congress and other governmental posts during the revolution express her deepest convictions, which she shared with other Daughters of Liberty and gained from preachers of her own day and past generations.[22] Writing on June 17, 1766, she described American patriots engaged in a holy war and fighting on the Lord's side: "The remarkable interpositions of Heaven in our favour cannot be too gratefully acknowledged. He who fed the Israelites in the wilderness, who cloaths the lilies of the Field and feeds the young Ravens when they cry, will not forsake a people engaged in so righteous cause if we remember his loving kindness."

"Doubled in Wedlock," Abigail Adams raised their children and managed their home and farm alone while John was away in governmental service for over ten years during the 1770s and 1780s. In her own political commentaries that fill her letters, Abigail speculated with discernment on the future of the new nation and the need for sound laws and strong government as its foundation. Even more significant are the implications for the rights and role of women which she drew from the Declaration of Independence, the meaning of Liberty, and the part women had played in the war. Interwoven with her political principles are the religious beliefs upon which her understandings of patriotism and the future of women were based.

Abigail is best known today for her foresight in applying the principle of natural rights contained in the Declaration of Independence to the condition of women, even before that historic document passed the Continental Congress. In one now-famous letter to John, written on March 31, 1776, she urged him to "Remember the Ladies" as the delegates developed new codes of law and to incorporate independence for women into the laws. She recognized that, during her day at least, men held in their hands the fate of subordinated women. As an enlightened Christian would have stated it, she urged the delegates "in immitation of the Supreme Being [to] make use of that power only for our happiness."

Her most eloquent application of the "patriotick virtue" of women to their lack of rights, however, came in a statement that she wrote near the end of the war, on June 17, 1782 (Document 4). Here she seemed resigned to the expectation that women would have a long road to travel before their own sacrifices for the welfare of their country would be duly affirmed, because the nation remained unmindful of the hand of God guiding it.

Along with her discernment of the far-reaching implications of women's rights growing out of the American Revolution, Abigail Adams's letters illuminate the way in which this religious and patriotic cause led her to a new role of republican womanhood that would characterize the lives of most women in generations to come. One of the most pervading themes of her correspondence is Abigail's recognition that she found her meaning and identity in life through her husband. Her function was a sacrificial one in which she released him from the cares and responsibilities of the home and family so that his life could be given to the "Secondary God" of country. The honors that public service brought to John were to Abigail "badges of unhappiness" from which she gained "a pleasure in being able to sacrifice my selfish passions to the general good, and in imitating the example which has taught me to consider myself and family, but as the small dust of the balance when compared with the great community."

Republican womanhood carried with it the dual role of mother as well as wife. The secularized meaning of the home in the new republic was central to Abigail's understanding of motherhood. While her Puritan ancestors had described their home as a "little church" with religious training at its core, the revolutionary generation began to envision the home as the primary institution for training their sons and daughters in the ways of good citizenship. Abigail knew that much of her own satisfaction in life would come through raising her sons to be worthy public citizens as voters and leaders of the country. To men and women of the revolution, good citizenship was grounded in virtue, disinterested public service growing out of honesty, integrity, and sound moral values. "The only sure and permanent foundation of virtue is Religion," Abigail told her son, John Quincy, when he was only thirteen years old. As she trained him from his earliest years to become a great statesman, she instilled in him the belief that "every new Mercy you receive is a New Debt upon you, a new obligation . . . in the first place to your Great Preserver, in the next to Society in General, in particular to your Country, to your parents and to yourself."

Abigail also felt great personal investment in the upbringing of her one daughter, Nabby, and strongly advocated a more liberal and comprehensive education for girls. However, even with her far-reaching vision of political, economic, and social rights for women, she believed that young women's primary purpose in the new nation, at least for many years to come, would be realized in standing behind, rather than alongside men. As she put it: "If we mean to have Heroes, Statesmen and Philosophers, we should have learned women."

IV

Abigail Adams's letters reflect not only her own experiences and self-understandings, but also the experiences of a large number of New England women during the revolutionary era. And they point ahead to the way in which Enlightenment thinkers, writing after the war, would apply the meaning of the revolution to women's lives.

In the 1780s and 1790s, Benjamin Rush, Judith Sargent Murray, and Mary Wollstonecraft brought their enlightened viewpoints to bear on the issue of women's rights and role. Taken together, their writings present the strongest statement on women's equality with men to be published by the end of the eighteenth century. Rush used his pen and platform, while Sargent and Wollstonecraft employed their pens alone, to develop arguments grounded in religious patriotism for the education of women.

"Yes, ye lordly, ye haughty sex, our souls are by nature equal to yours; the same breath of God animates, enlivens, and invigorates us," stated Judith Sargent Murray in 1790 (Document 5). The equality sought was a recognition that women's mental capacities were equivalent to those of men and that only environmental differences and lack of educational opportunities had kept women from developing their natural and God-given abilities.

Rush delivered his "Thoughts Upon Female Education" at the graduation exercises of the Young Ladies Academy of Philadelphia in 1787 (Document 6). He emphasized that a curriculum should be accommodated to the state of society, manners, and government of a particular country at a given time. In his view, a principle share of the work of education should placed upon women who could mold the manners and character of a nation, as well as its laws, through their influence on young children. In identifying religion as the study that connected all other branches of education, he primarily meant, as did Abigail Adams, the inculcation of virtue, moral principles, into a generation that was becoming more secularly oriented.

A classic work, written in 1792 by the Englishwoman Mary Wollstonecraft and entitled *A Vindication of the Rights of Women,* was republished shortly thereafter in Philadelphia. Though condemned by many as the most radical statement on women ever written, it, too, was basically an argument for a more enlightened mother within the home (Document 7):

> And how can woman be expected to co-operate unless she knows why she ought to be virtuous, unless freedom strengthen her reason till she comprehend her duty and see in what manner it is connected with her real good? If children are to be educated to understand the true principle of patriotism, their mother must be a patriot; and the love of mankind, from which an orderly train of virtues springs, can only be produced by considering the moral and civil interest of mankind; but the education and situation of woman, at present, shuts her out from such investigations.

It remained, however, for an unknown young woman, Priscilla Mason, to extend the argument for women's education beyond the recognition of their equal mental abilities and their role of character training within the home. Delivering a graduation address for her class of 1793 at the Young Ladies Academy of Philadelphia, Priscilla Mason pressed the alternative goal of equality of rights and opportunities in the public sphere, as well as the private realm—as Abigail Adams had done (Document 8). The opportunities for public service open to men also should be made available to women, whether in the church, the bar, or the senate, Mason eloquently contended. Such opportunities would be open to women, and were already beginning to emerge, where females received the same education as men. She turned to the "enlightened and liberal Church" as the example of significant breakthroughs in opening doors for women: "They regard not the anatomical formation of the body. The look to the soul, and allow all to teach who are capable of it, be they male or female."

However, Priscilla Mason also recognized how the religious understandings of women had encouraged the constriction of women's role in church and society. In contrast to the way that "enlightened" churches, which emphasized women's rational equality with men, had helped to liberate females, many other religious bodies limited women to the domestic sphere and found justification for this in St. Paul, himself often a captive of his own culture, advocating celibacy for men of religious commitment and ordering women to keep silent in church.

Finally, Priscilla Mason lifted up her unique vision of women's role of religious patriotism in the new republic, which, in contrast to other postrevolutionary spokespersons, was to be expressed in the public, not the domestic, sphere. Women are the citizens who set the tone for manners and morals in a nation, she pointed out. Instead of leaving this responsibility to be fulfilled indirectly within the home, Mason called upon the federal government to establish a national congress of women who would establish the moral excellence, the public virtue, of the young nation. To remain independent and to grow in stature, the United States must set its own standards of fashions, morals, and manners, and not adopt European patterns of correctness. Mason sought to transfer the accepted private role of women in the home to a position of recognized public and political responsibility. Such an acknowledged political role, she told her audience,

> would call forth all that is human—all that is *divine* in the soul of woman; and having proved them equally capable with the other sex, would lead to their equal participation of honor and office.

V

Priscilla Mason idealized the effect that the education of women could have on their attainment of equal opportunities for service, sacred or secular, in the newly emerging republic of nineteenth-century America. Further, her congress of women, which would have amounted to public legitimization of women's accepted private role in promoting the civil religion of America, probably never gained a hearing beyond the audience at her graduation exercises.

The goal and the reality of women's role as carriers of civil religion in the next century is more rightly found in Abigail Adams. She envisioned a long struggle for equal rights in society that would lead to the goal of a public, political role for women. Yet, in her own life, she embodied the reality of republican motherhood, which would more closely approximate most women's actual experience. The American Revolution was the catalyst that redirected the role and vision of most women from early to modern American society.

Civil religion fused the patriotic and religious goals of men as public servants in the more secular society of late eighteenth- and nineteenth-century America. It also provided the means of understanding the new purposes and the two enduring legacies for women from the American Revolution—republican motherhood and equality of rights with men.

Both the revolution's radical implication of equal rights for women and its conservative consequence of republican motherhood resulted from the merging of religious and political aims. In its most immediate and direct influence on women, the civil religion growing out of the revolution created a conservative legacy. The political role of females—to raise virtuous sons for public service and worthy daughters who would support their husbands in the home and behind the scenes—was authenticated during the nineteenth century as an expression of piety to the glory of God and of man. Republican motherhood provided firm ground for domestic training during the early years of the republic, but at the cost of restricting men and women to separate spheres. Consequently, republican motherhood made it difficult, if not impossible, for either sex to gain the wholeness of experience within both the private and public worlds.

Generations would pass before the more radical of the revolution's two legacies—the struggle for equal rights with men in all institutions, including the church—would even begin to have its effect. Yet the leaders of the American Revolution and the founders of the republic had realized the radical implications of the war and of the Declaration of Independence. For they knew that, in its most essential form, the patriotic movement rested on the religious truth that human dignity is a natural right given by God to all created beings—and finally it cannot be denied to any human being by another on the basis of race, creed, or sex.

Abigail Adams. Pastel by Benjamin Blyth, 1766. [From Andrew Oliver, *Portraits of John and Abigail Adams* (Cambridge, MA: Harvard University Press, 1967), p. 7.]

John Adams. Pastel by Benjamin Blyth, 1766. [From Andrew Oliver, *Portraits of John and Abigail Adams* (Cambridge, MA: Harvard University Press, 1967), p. 6.]

Mercy Otis Warren, playwright and wife of Massachusetts legislator John Warren. By John Singleton Copley, 1763. Museum of Fine Arts, Boston.

Sarah Franklin Bache (1743–1801), daughter of Benjamin and Deborah Franklin, leader of the "Association," an interstate patriotic women's organization that supplied money and clothes for the American Revolutionary Army. Portrait by John Hoppner, 1797. Metropolitan Museum of Art, New York City.

Frontispiece from the *Lady's Magazine and Repository of Entertaining Knowledge*, volume I, Philadelphia, December 1, 1792. Depicts the presentation to Liberty of a bill of the Rights of Woman—probably an allusion to Mary Wollstonecraft's *Vindication of the Rights of Woman* (1792). The Library Company of Philadelphia. [From Linda de Pauw and Conover Hunt, *Remember the Ladies: Women in America, 1750–1815* (New York: Viking Press, 1976), p. 150.]

A NEW
TOUCH ON THE TIMES.
Well adapted to the distressing Situation of every Sea-port Town.
By a DAUGHTER OF LIBERTY, living in MARBLEHEAD.

Broadside by a Daughter of Liberty, Massachusetts, 1779. The New York Historical Society. [From Linda de Pauw and Conover Hunt, *Remember the Ladies: Women in America, 1750–1815* (New York: Viking Press, 1976), p. 94.]

Documents: Women, Civil Religion, and the American Revolution

1. ***"They Fight in Virtue's Sacred Cause"***
2. ***"New England, Now to Meet Thy God Prepare"***
3. ***"With Hearts as One We'll Say Amen!"***
4. ***"Patriotism in the Female Sex Is the Most Disinterested of All Virtues"***
5. ***"Yes, Ye Lordly, Ye Haughty Sex, Our Souls Are by Nature Equal to Yours"***
6. ***"The Female Breast Is the Natural Soil of Christianity"***
7. ***"If Children Are to Be Educated to Understand the True Principle of Patriotism, Their Mother Must Be a Patriot"***
8. ***"The Church, the Bar, and the Senate Are Shut Against Us"***

Document 1: "They Fight in Virtue's Sacred Cause"

Women who were members of families that actively supported the American patriot cause often became commentators and propagandists as they shared their spirited views in private correspondence. Mercy Otis Warren was one of the first and few to write for publication. Warren wrote several political satires in play form, written to be read, not performed. The Group, *published anonymously (as were her other plays) in Boston in 1775, characterizes the circle of Massachusetts Tories as evil and corrupt in contrast to the righteous patriots. Though Warren's plays, and later historical writings, are not works of considerable literary merit, they are outstanding examples of the way in which religious principles were used to undergird revolutionary political propaganda.*[23]

[In Act I, Scene i, "the Group" of Massachusetts Tory leaders are seated in a little dark parlor, with guards standing at the door. They are discussing the prospects of their cause.]

Brigadier Hateall:
Compassion ne'er shall seize my stedfast breast
Though blood and carnage spread thro' all the land;
Till streaming purple tinge the verdant turf,
Till ev'ry street shall float with human gore,
I nero like, the capital in flames,
Could laugh to see her glotted sons expire,
Tho' much too rough my soul to touch the lyre.

Simple Sapling:
I fear the brave, the injur'd multitude;
Repeated wrongs, arouse them to resent,
And every patriot like old Brutus stands,
The shining steal half drawn—its glitt'ring point
Scarce hid beneath the scabbard's friendly cell
Resolv'd to die, or see their country free.

Hateall:
Then let them die—*The dogs we will keep down*—
While N___'s my friend, and G___ approves the deed,
Tho' hell and all its hell-hounds should unite,
I'll not recede to save from swift perdition
My wife, my country, family or friends,
G___'s mandamus I more highly prize
Than all the mandates of th' eterial king.

Hector Mushroom:
Will our abettors in the distant towns
Support us long against the common cause,

When they shall see from Hampshire's northern bounds
Thro' the wide western plains to southern shores
The whole united continent in arms?—

Hateall:

They shall—as sure as oaths or bonds can bind;
I've boldly sent my new-born brat abroad,
Th' association of my morbid brain,
To which each minion must affix his name.
As all our hope depends on brutal force
On quick destruction, misery and death;
Soon may we see dark ruin stalk around,
With murder, rapine, and inflicted pains,
Estates confiscate, slav'ry and despair,
Wrecks, halters, axes, gibbeting and chains,
All the dread ills that wait on civil war;—
How I could glut my vengeful eyes to see
The weeping maid thrown helpless on the world,
Her sire cut off.—Her orphan brothers stand
While the big tear rolls down the manly cheek.
Robb'd of maternal care by grief's keen shaft,
The sorrowing mother mourns her starving babes,
Her murder'd lord torn guiltless from her side,
And flees for shelter to the pitying grave
To skreen at once from slavery and pain.

Lord Chief Justice Hazelrod:

But more compleat I view this scene of woe,
But the incursions of a savage foe,
Of which I warn'd them, if they dare refuse
The badge of slaves, and bold resistance use.
Now let them suffer—I'll no pity feel.

Hateall:

Nor I—But had I power, as I have the Will
I'd send them murm'ring to the shades of hell.

[In Act II, Scene iii, the play ends with Judge Meagre attempting to rouse the wavering and fearful members of "the Group" to greater courage and steadfastness to pursue the cause against the patriots.]

Judge Meagre:

Let not thy soft temidity of heart
Urge thee to terms, till the last stake is thrown.
Tis not my temper ever to forgive,
When once resentment's kindled in my breast.
I hated Brutus for his noble stand
Against the oppressors of his injur'd country,

I hate the leaders of these restless factions,
For all their gen'rous efforts to be free.
I curse the senate which defeats our bribes,
Who Hazlerod impeach'd for the same crime,
I hate the people, who, no longer gull'd
See through the schemes of our aspiring clan.
And from the rancour of my venom'd mind,
I look askance on all the human race,
And if they'r not to be appall'd by fear,
I wish the earth might drink that vital stream
That warms the heart, and feeds the many glow,
The love inherent, planted in the breast,
To equal liberty, confer'd on man,
By him who form'd the peasant and the King!
Could we erase these notions from their minds,
Then (paramount to these ideal whims,
Utopian dreams, of patriot virtue,
Which long has danc'd in their distemper'd brains)
We'd smoothly glide on midst a race of slaves,
Nor heave one sigh tho' all the human race
Were plung'd in darkness, slavery and vice.
If we could keep our foot-hold in the stirrup,
And, like the noble Claudia of old,
Ride o'er the people, if they don't give way;
Or wish their fates were all involv'd in one;
For iv'e a *Brother,* as the roman dame,
Who would strike off the rebel-neck at once.

Secretary Dupe:
Not all is o'er unless the sword decides,
Which cuts down Kings, and kingdoms oft divides.
By that appeal I think we can't prevail,
Their valour's great, and justice holds the scale.
They fight for freedom, while we stab the breast
Of every man, who is her friend profest,
They fight in virtue's ever sacred cause,
While we tread on divine and human laws.
Glory and victory, and lasting fame,
Will crown their arms and bless each Hero's name!

Meagre:
Away with all thy foolish, trifling cares,
And to the winds give all thy empty fears;
Let us repair and urge brave Sylla on,
I long to see the sweet revenge begun,
As fortune is a fickle, sportive dame,

She may for us the victory proclaim,
And with success our busy ploddings crown,
Though injured justice stern and solemn frown.
Then they shall smart for ev'ry bold offense,
Estates confiscated will pay th'e expence;
On their lost fortunes we a while will plume
And strive to think there is no after doom. Exit.

As they pass off the stage the curtain drawn up, and discovers to the audience a Lady nearly connected with one of the principal actors in the group, reclined in an adjoining alcove, who in mournful accents accosts them—thus—

What painful scenes are hov'ring o'er the morn,
When spring again invogorate the lawn!
Instead of the gay landscep's beautious dies,
Must the stain'd field salute our weeping eyes, . . .
Till British troops shall to Columbia yield,
And freedom's sons are Masters of the field;
Then o'er the purpl'd plain the victors tread
Among the slain to seek each patriot dead,
(While Freedom weeps that merit could not save
But conq'r Hero's must enrich the Grave)
An adamantine monument they rear
With this inscription—*Virtue's sons lie here!*

BRAVO! BRAVO!

FINIS

Document 2: "New England, Now to Meet Thy God Prepare"

One of the most popular means of reaching the masses in early America was through the use of broadsides—posters placed on buildings or trees where large numbers of people would see them as they passed by. The stern and sobering words of "An Address to New-England: Written by a Daughter of Liberty" in Boston in 1774 could have been preached from a pulpit in Boston by any Puritan preacher of the revolutionary generation. But the "Daughter" who composed these words remains anonymous.[24]

Mourn, mourn O heavens, and thou O Earth bewail,
And weep ye Saints, 'till all your Spirits fail!
Once happy Land, I grieve at thy sad Fate,
Thy Breach is like the Sea, exceeding great.
Boston! thou brave illustrious City fair,
How are thou on the Brink of black Despair?
I see thy Ruin where I turn mine Eyes,
Thy Trade is gone, thy gainful Merchandise.
Kind Heaven assist my Pen, inspire my Muse,

While I rehearse the melancholly News:—
Heaven cloaths itself in Blackness all around,
While I lament thy deep and dangerous Wound, . . .
The troubled seas with angry Billows roar,
That thy Destroyers now invade her Shore!
The angel strong foretold in holy Writ,
Has loos'd the Door of the infernal Pit.
See! how the Locusts in huge Swarms ascend,
New England's fall and ruin they intend
Thy passages are stopt,—this murd'rous Brood,
Thirst for our Lives to wash their Hands in Blood!
Devils incarnate, worst of human kind,
Who can in Hell such brutish Monsters find!
Witness, O King Street, how thy Sons once fell
A bleeding victim to those Hounds of Hell!
And wonder not if Earth with open Jaws,
Should vindicate God's broken injur'd Laws.
Their Vipers from our Bowels did proceed,
That first invented this black hellish Deed. . . .
Unhappy Boston! wherefore doth thy God
Thus scourge thee with a Tyrant's Iron Rod?
How art thou spoil'd, O City of Renown?
Thy sceptre broke, where hast thou Left thy Crown?
To deprecate thy Loss, who can refuse?
Is there no Balm in Gilead for thy Wound,
That thou sitt't desolate upon the Ground?
Consider now when God thus loudly calls,
Before the final Storm upon thee fall.
What Sins, what crying Sins did God provoke,
To cause his Wrath against this land to smoke?
Rejecting Christ when offer'd you refus'd,
His gracious Calls and Warnings you abus'd,
Like Sodom you declare your Sins at large,
An awful Roll is writ, an heavy Charge:
Among Professors and among Profane, . . .
Crushing the Poor and Needy to the Ground,
In every Place is common to be found:
These Sins have call'd for Vengeance from above,
Thy Glory stands just ready to remove.
Our Candlestick shall soon forsake its Place,
Too late we then shall prize the means of Grace.
Then Lord, ah Lord, what shall become of us?
When we shall feel that sore and heavy Curse!
Shook with Confusion then we trembling stand,
None of our Sons to hold us by the Hand.

The Clouds no Rain shall on the Vineyards shed,
Our starving Souls shall pine away for Bread:
Full fed, like Jethorun we wanton grew,
A sevenfold Punishment to us is due.
New England, now to meet thy God prepare,
Awake Repentance, Faith and earnest Prayer.
For who can tell but God may stay his Hand,
And send Salvation to our ruin'd Land. . . .
When we of human Succor shall despair,
And to the Lord alone for help repair
Now O New England, circumcise thine Heart:
No more provoke thy God then to depart:
The Wound is deep but God doth thee assure,
Attend the Lord's endearing gracious Call,
How shall I on thee let my Fury fall. . . .
How shall I lift thee up and make thee stand,
Like burning Sodom and Gomorrah's Land.
Thou hast destroy'd thyself, but yet return,
No more mind Anger shall against thee burn
Though thou hast gone a Whoring from thy God,
I'll be thy cov'ring and thy safe Abode:
I have not thee forsook nor from thee gone,
Though thou hast sinn'd against the Holy One.
Come poor Officers hide beneath my Wings,
I am the Lord of Lords, the King of Kings:
I am the Sovereign Prince who governs all,
I hear thy Cries, in Trouble on me call. . . .
Accept this Call and turn unto thy God,
Fear not the Tyrant's Yoke nor threatning Rod:
The Lord our Lawgiver our Judge our King,
Shall in the Mount appear and Succor bring.
Happy O People! Saved of the Lord,
He is thy Shield and Safety will afford:
Safely the People here alone shall dwell,
In vain shall rage the Sons of Earth and Hell:
We shall not fear although the Earth remove,
We lift our Eyes to him who dwells above;
This great Emmanuel, he shall be our Peace,
Soon shall he make the Indignation cease.

Document 3: "With Hearts as One We'll Say Amen!"

The following excerpt represents portions of a second broadside written in 1779, "A New Touch on the Times, Well Adapted to the distressing Situation of every Sea-port Town. By a Daughter of Liberty, living in Marblehead." The tone of this piece is softer than that of the former, though it, too, reflects God's judgment as well as forgiveness of the New Englanders. This broadside offers a striking picture of the day-to-day experiences and shortages of civilian patriots on the home front in the ravaged Massachusetts Bay area.[25]

Our best beloved they are gone,
We cannot tell they'll e'er return,
For they are gone the ocean wide,
Which for us now they must provide. . . .
It's hard and cruel times to live,
Takes thirty dollars to buy a sieve.
To buy sieves and other things too
To go thro' the world how can we do
For times they sure grow worse and worse
I'm sure it sinks our scanty purse.
Had we a purse to reach and sky,
It would be all just vanity,
If we had that and ten times more,
'Twould be like sand upon the shore.
For money is not worth a pin. . . .
And as we go up and down,
We see the doings of this town,
Some say they an't victuals nor drink,
Others say they are ready to sink.
Our lives they all are tired here,
We see all things so cruel dear,
Nothing now-a-days to be got,
To put in kettles nor in pot.
These things will learn us to be wise,
We now do eat what we despis'd:
I now have something more to say,
We must go up and down the Bay
To get a fish a-days to fry,
We can't get fat were we to die,
Were we to try all thro' the town,
The world is now turn'd up-side down.
But there's a gracious God above,
That deals with us in tender love,
If we be kind and just and true,
He'll set and turn the world anew.
If we'll repent of all our crimes,
He'll set us now new heavenly times,
Times that will make us all to ring,
If we forsake our heinous sins.
For sin is all the cause of this,
We must not take it then amiss,

Wan't it for our polluted tongues
This cruel war would ne'er begun.
We should hear no fife nor drum,
Nor training bands would never come:
Should we go on our sinful course,
Times will grow on us worse and worse.
Then gracious God now cause to cease,
This bloody war and give us peace!
And down our streets send plenty
With hearts as one we'll say Amen!

Document 4: "Patriotism in the Female Sex Is the Most Disinterested of All Virtues"

The letters of Abigail Adams provide greater insight into the lives of women in New England during the revolutionary era than any other source from that period. They are a compelling witness to the religious commitment underlying women's patriotic fervor and to the "patriotick virtue of the female sex" exhibited through the daily work of women during the war.

Abigail Adams has been remembered in American history primarily as the wife of the second president and the mother of the fifth. This identification most accurately reflects her own sense of purpose and her most enduring legacy. At the same time, however, her arguments for the rights of women are the first extant by a female in America and are a statement of prophetic judgment on her own generation's inability to confront the radical implications of their Declaration of Independence. Her own ardent advocacy of the patriot cause during the revolution was firmly grounded in her understanding of the conflict as a holy war and of God's will for an American triumph. Brief excerpts from her letters are given here:[26]

Abigail to John Adams, November 12, 1775

I could not join to day in the petitions of our worthy parson, for a reconciliation between our, no longer parent State, but tyrant State, and these Colonies.—Let us separate, they are unworthy to be our Breathren. Let us renounce them and instead of suplications as formorly for their prosperity and happiness, Let us beseach the almighty to blast their counsels and bring to Nought all their devices.

Abigail to John Adams, June 17, 1776

I feel no great anxiety at the large armynent designed against us. The remarkable interpositions of Heaven in our favour cannot be too gratefully acknowledged. He who fed the Isralites in the wilderness, who cloaths the lilies of the Field and feeds the young Ravens when they cry, will not forsake a people engaged in so righteous cause if we remember his Loving kindness.

Abigail to Mercy Warren, January, 1776

Our Country is as it were a Secondary God, and the first and greatest parent. It is to be preferred to parents, to wives, children, Friends and all things the Gods only excepted.

These are the considerations which prevail with me to consent to a most painfull Separation.

I have not known how to take my pen to write to you. I have been happy and unhappy. I have had many contending passions dividing my Heart, and no sooner did I find it at my own option whether my Friend should go or tarry and resign; than I found his honour and reputation much dearer to me, than my own present pleasure and happiness, and I could by no means consent to his resigning at present, as I was fully convinced he must suffer if he quitted.

Abigail to John Adams, March 31, 1776

I long to hear that you have declared an independancy—and by the way in the new Code of Laws which I suppose it will be necessary for you to make I desire you would Remember the Ladies, and be more generous and favourable to them than your ancestors. Do not put such unlimited power into the hands of the Husbands. Remember all Men would be tyrants if they could. If perticuliar care and attention is not paid to the Laidies we are determined to foment a Rebelion, and will not hold ourselves bound by any Laws in which we have no voice, or Representation.

That your Sex are Naturally Tyrannical is a Truth so thoroughly established as to admit of no dispute, but such of you as wish to be happy willingly, give us the harsh title of Master for the more tender and endearing one of Friend. Men of Sense in all Ages abhor those customs which treat us only as the vassals of your Sex. Regard us then as Beings placed by providence under your protection and in immitation of the Supreem Being make use of that power only for our happiness.

Abigail to John Adams, May 7, 1776

I can not say that I think you very generous to the Ladies, for whilst you are proclaiming peace and good will to Men, Emancipating all Nations, you insist upon retaining an absolute power over Wives. But you must remember that Arbitrary power is like most other things which are very hard, very liable to be broken—and notwithstanding all your wise Laws and Maxims we have it in our power not only to free ourselves but to subdue our Masters, and without violence throw both your natural and legal authority at our feet—

> "Charm by accepting, by submitting sway
> Yet have our Honour most when we obey."

Abigail to John Adams, July 21, 1776

Last Thursday after hearing a very Good Sermon I went with the Multitude into Kings Street to hear the proclamation for independence read and proclaimed. Some Field pieces with the Train were brought there, the troops appeard under Arms and all the inhabitants assembled there. The cry from the Belcona, was God Save our American States and then 3 cheers rended the air, the Bells rang, the privateers fired, the forts and Batteries, the cannon were discharged, the platoons followed and every face appeared joyfull. After dinner the kings arms were taken down from the State House and every vestage of him from every place in which it appeard and burnt in King Street. Thus ends royall Authority in this State, and all the people shall say Amen.

Abigail to John Adams, August 14, 1776

If you complain of neglect of Education in sons, What shall I say with regard to daughters, who every day experience the want of it. I most sincerely wish that some more liberal plan might be laid and executed for the Benefit of the rising Generation, and that our new constitution may be distinguished for Learning and Virtue. If we mean to have Heroes, Statesmen and Philosophers, we should have learned women. If much depends as is allowed upon the early Education of youth and the first principals which are instilld take the deepest root, great benifit must arise from literary accomplishments in women.

Abigail to John Quincy Adams (age thirteen, while traveling in Europe with his father), March 20, 1780

If you have a due sense of your preservation, your next consideration will be, for what purpose you are continued in Life? It is not to rove from clime to clime, to gratify an Idle curiosity, but every new Mercy you receive is a New Debt upon you, a new obligation to a diligent discharge of the various relations in which you stand connected; in the first place to your Great Preserver, in the next to Society in General, in particular to your Country, to your parents and to yourself.

The only sure and permanant foundation of virtue is Religion. Let this important truth be engraven upon your Heart, and that the foundation of Religion is the Belief of the one only God, and a just sense of his attributes as a Being infinately wise, just, and good, to whom you owe the highest reverence, Gratitutde and Adoration, who superintends and Governs all Nature, even to Cloathing the lilies of the Field and hearing the young Ravens when they cry, but more particularly regards Man whom he created after his own Image and

Breathed into him an immortal Spirit capable of a happiness beyond the Grave, to the attainment of which he is bound to the performance of certain duties which all tend to the happiness and welfare of Society.

Abigail to John Adams, June 17, 1782

Ardently as I long for the return to my dearest Friend, I cannot feel the least inclination to a peace but upon the most liberal foundation. Patriotism in the female Sex is the most disinterested of all virtues. Excluded from honours and from offices, we cannot attach ourselves to the State or Government from having held a place of Eminence. Even in the freest countrys our property is subject to the controuls and disposal of our partners, to whom the Laws have given a soverign Authority. Deprived of a voice in Legislation, obliged to submit to those Laws which are imposed upon us, is it not sufficient to make us indifferent to the publick Welfare? Yet all History and every age exhibit Instances of patriotick virtue in the female Sex, which considering our situation equals the most Heroick of yours. "A late writer observes that as Citizens we are called upon to exhibit our fortitude, for when you offer your Blood to the State, it is ours. In giving it our Sons and Husbands we give more than ourselves. You can only die on the field of Battle, but we have the misfortune to survive those whom we Love most."

I will take praise to myself. I feel that it is my due, for having sacrificed so large a portion of my peace and happiness to promote the welfare of my country which I hope for many years to come will reap the benifit, tho it is more than probable unmindfull of the hand that blessed them.

Abigail to John Adams, December 23, 1782

I cannot sometimes refrain considering the Honours with which he is invested as badges of my unhappiness.

If you had known said a person to me the other day, that Mr. Adams would have remained so long abroad, would you have consented that he should have gone? I recollected myself a moment, and then spoke the real dictates of my Heart. If I had known Sir that Mr. A could have affected what he has done, I would not only have submitted to the absence I have endured, painfull as it has been; but I would not have opposed it, even tho 3 years more should be added to the Number, which Heaven avert! I feel a pleasure in being able to sacrifice my selfish passions to the general good, and in imitating the example which has taught me to consider myself and family, but as the small dust of the balance when compared with the great community.

Document 5: "Yes, Ye Lordly, Ye Haughty Sex, Our Souls Are by Nature Equal to Yours"

Judith Sargent Murray is distinguished as probably the earliest American women to publish views of a feminist persuasion. With her father, a delegate to the Massachusetts Constitutional Convention of 1788, and her husband, a Universalist minister, Judith Sargent Murray extended the family's liberal religious and political ideas to the issue of women's equality.

Like Mercy Warren and Abigail Adams, she was moved by talk and action in her own patriot family to challenge traditional views on the status of women. Her essay, "On the Equality of the Sexes," was published in the Massachusetts Magazine *in 1790, but evidence indicates that it had been written in 1779. She argued that women's minds are by nature equal to men's and that women should be granted education to make them fitting companions of men.*[27]

Is it upon mature consideration we adopt the idea, that nature is thus partial in her distributions? Is it indeed a fact, that she hath yielded to one half of the human species so unquestionable a mental superiority? I know that of both sexes elevated understandings, and the reverse, are common. But, suffer me to ask, in what minds of females are so notoriously deficient, or unequal. May not the intellectual powers be ranged under their four heads—imagination, reason, memory and judgement. The province of imagination has long since been surrendered up to us, and we have been crowned undoubted sovereigns of the regions of fancy. Invention is perhaps the most arduous effort of the mind; this branch of imagination hath been particularly ceded to us, and we have been time out of mind invested with that creative faculty. Observe the variety of fashions (here I bar the contemptuous smile) which distinguish and adorn the female world; how continually are they changing, insomuch that they almost render the whole man's assertion problematical, and we are ready to say, *there is something new under the sun.* Now, what a playfulness, what an exuberance of fancy, what strength of inventive imagination, doth this continual variation discover? Again it has been observed, that if the turpitude of the conduct of our sex, hath been ever so enormous, so extremely ready are we that the very first thought presents us with an apology so plausible, as to produce our actions even in an amiable light. Another instance of our creative powers, is our talent for slander; how ingenious are we at inventive scandal? What a formidable story can we in a moment fabricate merely from the force of a prolifick imagination? how many reputations, in the fertile brain of a female, have been utterly despoiled? How industrious are we at improving a hint? suspicion how easily do we convert into conviction, and conviction, embellished by the power of eloquence, stalks abroad to the surprise and confusion of unsuspecting innocence. Perhaps it will be asked if I furnish these facts as instances of excellency in our sex. Certainly not; but as proofs of a creative faculty, of a lively imagination. Assuredly great activity of mind is thereby discovered, and was this activity properly directed, what beneficial effects would follow. Is the needle and kitchen sufficient to employ the operations of a soul thus organized? I should conceive not. Nay, it is a truth that those very departments leave the intelligent principle vacant, and at liberty for speculation. Are we deficient in reason? We can only reason from what we know, and if opportunity of acquiring knowledge hath been denied us, the inferiority of our sex cannot fairly be deduced from thence. Memory, I believe, will be allowed us in common, since every one's experience must testify, that a loquacious old woman is as frequently met with, as a communicative old man; their subjects are alike drawn from the fund of other times, and the transactions of their youth, or of maturer life, entertain, or perhaps fatigue you, in the evening of their lives. "But your judgment is not so strong—we do not distinguish so well." Yet it may be questioned, from what doth this superiority, in this discriminating faculty of the soul, proceed. May we not trace its source in the difference of education, and continued advantages? Will it be said that the judgment of a male of two years old, is more sage than that of a female's of the same age? I believe the reverse is generally observed to be true. But from that period what partiality! how is the one exalted and the other depressed, by the contrary modes of education which are adopted! the one is taught to aspire, and the other is early confined and limited. As their years increase, the sister must be wholly domesticated, while the brother is led by the hand through all the flowery paths of science. Grant that their minds are by nature equal, yet who should wonder at the *apparent* superiority, if indeed customs becomes *second nature;* nay if it taketh place of nature, and that it doth the experience of each day will evince. At length arrived at womanhood, the uncultivated fair one feels void, which the employments allotted her are by no means capable of filling. What can she do? to books, she may not apply; or if she doth, *to those only of the novel kind,* lest she merit the appellation of a *learned lady;* and what ideas have been affixed to this term, the observation of many can testify. Fashion, scandal and sometimes what is still more reprehensible, are then called in to her relief; and who can say to what lengths the liberties she takes may proceed. Meantime she herself is most unhappy; she feels the want of a cultivated mind. If she is single, she in vain seeks to fill up time from sexual employments or amusements. Is she united to a person whose soul nature made equal to her own, education hath set him so far above her, that in those entertainments which are productive of such rational felicity, she is not qualified to accompany him. She experiences a mortifying consciousness of inferiority, which embitters every enjoyment. Doth the person to whom her adverse fate hath consigned her, possess a mind incapable of improvement, she is equally wretched, in being so closely connected with an individual whom she cannot despise. Now she was permitted with the same instructors as her brothers, (with an eye however to their particular departments) for the employment of a rational mind an ample field would be opened. In astronomy she might catch a glimpse of the immensity of the Deity, and thence she would form amazing conceptions of the august and supreme Intelligence. In geography she would admire Jehova in the midst of his benevolence; thus adapting this globe to the various wants and amusements of its inhabitants. In natural philosophy she would adore the infinite majesty of heaven, clothed in condescension; and as she traversed the reptile world, she would hail the goodness of a creating God. A mind, thus filled, would have little room for the trifles with which our sex are, with too much justice, accused of amusing themselves, and they would thus be rendered fit companions for those, who should one day wear them as their crown. Fashions, in their variety, would then give place to conjectures, which might perhaps conduce to the improvement of the literary world; and there would be no leisure for slander or detraction. Reputation would not then be blasted, but serious speculations would occupy the lively imaginations of the sex. Unnecessary visits would be precluded, and that custom would only be indulged by way of relaxation, or to answer the demands of consanguity and friendship. Females would become discreet, their judgments would be invigorated, and their partners for life being circumspectly chosen, an unhappy Hymen would then be as rare, as is now the reverse.

Will it be urged that those acquirements would supersede our domestic duties, I answer that every requisite in female economy is easily attained; and, with truth I can add, that when once attained, they require no further *mental attention.* Nay, while we are pursuing the needle, or the superintendency of the family, I repeat, that our minds are at full liberty for reflection; that imagination may exert itself in full vigor; and that if a just foundation early laid, our ideas will then be worthy of rational beings. If we were industrious we might easily find time to arrange them upon paper, or should advocations press too hard for such an indulgence, the hours allotted for conversation would at least become more refined and rational. Should it be vociferated, "Your domestick employments are sufficient"—I would calmly ask, is it reasonable, that a candidate for immortality, for the joys of heaven, an intelligent being, who is to spend an eternity in contemplating the works of Deity, should at present be so degraded, as to be allowed no other ideas, than those which are suggested by the mechanism of a pudding or the sewing of the seams of a garment? Pity that all such censures of female improvement do not go one step further, and deny their future existence; to be consistent they surely ought.

Yes, ye lordly, ye haughty sex, our souls are by nature *equal* to yours; the same breath of God animates, enlivens, and invigorates us; and that we are not fallen lower than yourselves, let those witness who have greatly towered above the various discouragements by which they have been so heavily oppressed; and though I am unacquainted with the list of celebrated characters on either side, yet from the observations I have made in the contracted circle in which I have moved, I dare confidently believe, that from the commencement of time to the present day, there hath been as many females, as males, who, by the *mere force of natural powers,* have merited the crown of applause; who *thus unassisted,* have seized the wreath of fame. I know there are who assert, that as the animal powers of the one sex are superiour, of course their mental faculties also must be stronger; thus attributing strength of mind to the transient organization of this earth born tenement. But if this reasoning is just, man must be content to yield the palm to many of the brute creation, since by not a few of his brethren of the field, he is far surpassed in bodily strength. Moreover, was this argument admitted, it would prove too much, for occular demonstration evinceth, that there are many robust masculine ladies, and effeminate gentlemen. Yet I fancy that Mr. Pope, though clogged with an enervated body, and distinguished by a diminutive stature, could nevertheless lay claim to greatness of soul; and perhaps there are many other instances which might be adduced to combat so unphilosophical an opinion. Do we not often see, that when the clay built tabernacle is well nigh dissolved, when it is just ready to mingle with the parent soil, the immortal inhabitant aspires to, and even attaineth heights the most sublime, and which were before wholly unexplored. Besides, were we to grant that animal strength proved anything, taking into consideration the accustomed impartiality of nature, we should be induced to imagine, that she had invested the female mind with superiour strength as an equivalent for the bodily powers of man. But waving this however palpable advantage, for *equality* only, we wish to contend.

Constantia

In an addendum to the above article, Murray attached a section of a letter that she wrote to a friend in 1780. Here she puts forth woman's thirst for knowledge as a "laudable ambition" for Eve to have had when she received the apple from the serpent, in comparison to the sensual appetites of man, his "bare pusillanimous attachment to a woman!"

AND now assist me, O thou genius of my sex, while I undertake the arduous task of endeavouring to combat that vulgar, that almost universal errour, which hath, it seems enlisted even, Mr. P—— under its banners. The superiority of your self hath, I grant, been time out of mind esteemed a truth incontrovertible; in consequence of which persuasion, every plan of education hath been calculated to establish this favourite tenet. Not long since, weak and presuming as I was, I amused myself with selecting some arguments from nature, reason and experience, against this so generally received idea. I confess that to sacred testimonies I had not recourse. I held them to be merely metaphorical, and thus regarding them, I could not persuade myself that there was not propriety in bringing them to decide in this *very important debate.* However, as you, sir, confine yourself entirely to the sacred oracles, I mean to bend the whole of my artillery against those supposed proofs, which you have from thence provided, and from which you have formed an intrenchment *apparently* so invulnerable. And first, to begin with our great progenitors; but here, suffer me to promise, that it is for mental strength, I mean to contend, for with respect to animal powers, I yield them undisputed to that sex, which enjoys them in common with the lion, the tyger, and many other beast of prey; therefore your observations respecting *the rib, under the arm, at a distance from* the head, &c, &c, in no sort militate against my view. Well, but the woman was first in the transgression. Strange how blind *self love* renders you men; were you not wholly absorbed in a partial admiration of your abilities, you would long since have acknowledged the force of what I am now going to urge. It is true some ignoramuses have, absurdly enough informed us, that the beauteous fair of paradise, was seduced from her obedience, by a malignant deman, *in the guise of a baleful serpent;* but we, who are better informed, know that the fallen spirit presented himself to her view, *a shining angel still;* for thus, saith the criticks in the Hebrew tongue, ought the word to be rendered. Let us examine her motive—Hark! the seraph declare that she shall attain a perfection of knowledge; for is there aught which is not comprehended under one or other of the terms *good* and *evil.* It doth not appear that she was governed by any one sensual appetite; but merely by a desire of adorning her mind; a laudable ambition fired her soul, and a thirst for knowledge impelled the predilection so fatal in its consequences. Adam could not plead the same deception; assuredly he was not deceived; nor ought we to admire his superior strength, or wonder at his sagacity, when we so often confess that example is much more influential than precept. His gentle partner stood before him, a melancholy instance of the direful effects of disobedience; he saw her not possessed of that wisdom which she had fondly hoped to obtain, but he beheld the once blooming female, disrobed of that innocence, which had heretofore rendered her so lovely. To him then deception became impossible, as he had proof positive of the fallacy of the argument, which the deceiver had suggested. What then could be his inducement to burst the barriers, and to fly directly in the face of that command, which *immediately* from the mouth of Deity *he* had received, since I say, he could not plead the fascinating stimulus, the accumulation of knowledge, as indisputable convention was so visibly portrayed before him. What mighty cause impelled him to sacrifice myriads of beings yet unborn, and by one impious act, which *he saw* would be productive of such fatal effect, entail undistinguished ruin upon a race of beings, which he was yet to produce. Blush, ye vaunters of fortitude; ye boasters of resolution; ye haughty lords of the creation; blush when ye remember, that he was influenced by no other motive than a bare pusillanimous attachment to a woman! by sentiments so exquisitely soft, that all his sons have, from that period, when they have designed to degrade them, described as highly feminine. Thus it should see, that all the arts of the grand deceiver (since means adequate to the purpose are, I conceive, invariably pursued) were requisite to mislead our general mother, while the father of mankind forfeited his own, and relinquished the happiness of posterity, merely in compliance with the blandishments of a female.

Document 6: "The Female Breast Is the Natural Soil of Christianity"

Benjamin Rush well personified the "Enlightened Christian" of postrevolutionary America—a contributor to science, government, and education, a believer in goodness and progress, and a fervent evangelical Christian. Rush was also one of the foremost advocates of an expanded education for women based on principles of Enlightenment and religious patriotism. His address, "Thoughts upon Female Education," delivered at the 1787 graduation exercises of the Young Ladies Academy in Philadelphia, is a classic statement of its day envisioning the education of women to meet the needs of the emerging secular order of the new nation, an education that gave them both a religious and political calling to provide a domestic foundation for a virtuous society.[28]

Gentlemen,

I have yielded with diffidence to the solicitations of the Principal of the Academy, in undertaking to express my regard for the prosperity of this Seminary of Learning, by submitting to your candor, a few Thoughts upon Female Education.

The first remark that I shall make upon this subject, is, that female education should be accommodated to the state of society, manners, and government of the country, in which it is conducted.

This remark leads me at once to add, that the education of young ladies, in this country, should be conducted upon principles very different from what it is in Great Britain, and in some respects different from what it was when we were part of a monarchical empire.

There are several circumstances in the situation, employments, and duties of women, in America, which require a peculiar mode of education,

I. The early marriages of our women, by contracting the time allowed for education, renders it necessary to contract its plan, and to confine it chiefly to the more useful branches of literature.

II. The state of property, in America, renders it necessary for the greatest part of our citizens to employ themselves, in different occupations, for the advancement of their fortunes. This cannot be done without the assistance of the females of the community. They must be the stewards, and guardians of their husbands' property. . . .

III. From the numerous avocations to which a professional life exposes gentlemen in America from their families, a principal share of the instruction of children naturally devolves upon the women. It becomes us therefore to prepare them by a suitable education, for the discharge of this most important duty of mothers.

IV. The equal share that every citizen has in the liberty, and the possible share he may have in the government of our country, make it necessary that our ladies should be qualified to a certain degree by a peculiar and suitable education, to concur in instructing their sons in the principles of liberty and government.

V. In Great Britain the business of servants is a regular occupation; but in America this humble station is the usual retreat of unexpected indigence; hence the servants in this country possess less knowledge and subordination than are required from them; and hence, our ladies are obliged to attend more to the private affairs of their families than ladies generally do, of the same rank in Great Britain. . . .

The branches of literature most essential for a young lady in this country, appear to be,

I. A knowledge of the English language. She should not only read, but speak and spell it correctly. . . .

II. Pleasure and interest conspire to make the writing of a fair and legible hand, a necessary branch of female education. . . .

III. Some knowledge of figures and bookkeeping is absolutely necessary to qualify a young lady for the duties which await her in this country. There are certain occupations in which she may assist her husband with this knowledge; and should she survive him, and agreeably to the custom of our country be the executrix of his will, she cannot fail of deriving immense advantages from it.

IV. An acquaintance with geography and some instruction in

chronology will enable a young lady to read history, biography, and travels, with advantage; and thereby qualify her not only for a general intercourse with the world, but, to be an agreeable companion for a sensible man. To these branches of knowledge may be added, in some instances, a general acquaintance with the first principles of astronomy, and natural philosophy. . . .

V. Vocal music should never be neglected, in the education of a young lady, in this country. Besides preparing her to join in that part of public worship which consists in psalmody, it will enable her to soothe the cares of domestic life. The distress and vexation of a husband—the noise of a nursery, and, even, the sorrows that will sometimes intrude into her own bosom, may all be relieved by a song, where sound and sentiment unite to act upon the mind. . . .

VI. Dancing is by no means an improper branch of education for an American lady. It promotes health, and renders the figure and motions of the body easy and agreeable. . . .

VII. The attention of our young ladies should be directed, as soon as they are prepared for it, to the reading of history—travels—poetry—and moral essays. . . .

VIII. It will be necessary to connect all these branches of education with regular instruction in the christian religion. For this purpose the principles of the different sects of christians should be taught and explained, and our pupils should early be furnished with some of the most simple arguments in favour of the truth of christianity. A portion of the bible (of late improperly banished from our schools) should be read by them every day, and such questions should be asked, after reading it, as are calculated to imprint upon their minds the interesting stories contained in it.

Rousseau has asserted that the great secret of education consists in "wasting the time of children profitably." There is some truth in this observation. I believe that we often impair their health, and weaken their capacities, by imposing studies upon them, which are not proportioned to their years. But this objection does not apply to religious instruction. There are certain simply propositions in the christian religion, that are suited in a peculiar manner, to the infant state of reason and moral sensibility. A clergyman of long experience in the instruction of youth informed me, that he always found children acquired religious knowledge more easily than knowledge upon other subjects; and that young girls acquired this kind of knowledge more readily than boys. The female breast is the natural soil of christianity; and while our women are taught to believe its doctrines, and obey its precepts, the wit of Voltaire, and the stile of Bolingbroke, will never be able to destroy its influence upon our citizens. . . .

. . . those christians, whether parents or schoolmasters, who neglect the religious instruction of their children and pupils, *reject* and *neglect* the most effectual means of promoting knowledge in our country.

IX. If the measures that have been recommended for inspiring our pupils with a sense of religious and moral obligation be adopted, the government of them will be easy and agreeable. . . .

. . . To be the mistress of a family is one of the great ends of a woman's being, and while the peculiar state of society in America imposes this station so early, and renders the duties of it so numerous and difficult, I conceive that little time can be spared for the acquisition of this elegant accomplishment. . . .

I am not enthusiastical upon the subject of education. In the ordinary course of human affairs, we shall probably too soon follow the footsteps of the nations of Europe in manners and vices. The first marks we shall perceive of our declension, will appear among our women. Their idleness, ignorance and profligacy will be the harbingers of our ruin. . . . The prospect is so painful, that I cannot help, silently, imploring the great arbiter of human affairs, to interpose his almighty goodness, and to deliver us from these evils, that, at least one spot of the earth may be reserved as a monument of the effects of good education, in order to show in some degree, what our species was, before the fall, and what it shall be, after its restoration. . . .

But the reputation of the academy must be suspended, till the public are convinced, by the future conduct and character of our pupils, of the advantages of the institution. To you, therefore,

YOUNG LADIES,

An important problem is committed for solution; and that is, whether our present plan of education be a wise one, and whether it be calculated to prepare you for the duties of social and domestic life. I know that the elevation of the female mind, by means of moral, physical and religious truth, is considered by some men as unfriendly to the domestic character of a woman. But this is the prejudice of little minds, and springs from the same spirit which opposes the general diffusion of knowledge among the citizens of our republics. If men believe that ignorance is favourable to the government of the female sex, they are certainly deceived; for a weak and ignorant woman will always be governed with the greatest difficulty. I have sometimes been led to ascribe the invention of ridiculous and expensive fashions in female dress, entirely to the gentlemen, in order to divert the LADIES from improving their minds, and thereby to secure a more arbitrary and unlimited authority over them. It will be in your power, ladies, to correct the mistakes and practice of our sex upon these subjects, by demonstrating, that the female temper can only be governed by reason, and that the cultivation of reason in women, is alike friendly to the order of nature, and to private as well as public happiness.

Document 7: "If Children Are to Be Educated to Understand the True Principle of Patriotism, Their Mother Must Be a Patriot"

A Vindication of the Rights of Woman, *written by Mary Wollstonecraft in 1792, shocked genteel Englishmen and Americans "with the most indecent rhapsody . . . ever penned by man or woman." However, it was "so run after" that at times there was "no keeping it long enough to read it leisurely."*

What appeared shockingly radical in its own day is revered today as the breakthrough in advocacy of woman's rights in its generation. The book is a classic statement of Christian Enlightenment, arguing that a benevolent Creator endowed woman with a reasonable nature along with man. At the heart of her thesis is the belief that men need to become more attentive fathers and women more patriotic mothers in order to raise good citizens.[29]

Contending for the rights of woman, my main argument is built on this simple principle, that if she be not prepared by education to become the companion of man, she will stop the progress of knowledge and virtue; for truth must be common to all, or it will be inefficacious with respect to its influence on general practice. And how can woman be expected to co-operate unless she know why she ought to be virtuous, unless freedom strengthen her reason till she comprehend her duty and see in what manner it is connected with her real good? If children are to be educated to understand the true principle of patriotism, their mother must be a patriot; and the love of mankind, from which an orderly train of virtues springs, can only be produced by considering the moral and civil interest of mankind; but the education and situation of woman, at present, shuts her out from such investigations. . . .

Consider, sir, dispassionately these observations—for a glimpse of this truth seemed to open before you when you observed "that to see one half of the human race excluded by the other from all participation of government was a political phenomenon that, according to abstract principles, it was impossible to explain." If so, on what does your constitution rest? If the abstract rights of man will bear discussion and explanation, those of woman, by a parity of reasoning, will not shrink from the same test, though a different opinion prevails in this country, built on the very arguments which you use to justify the oppression of woman—prescription.

Consider—I address you as a legislator—whether, when men contend for their freedom and struggle to be allowed to judge for themselves respecting their own happiness, it be not inconsistent and unjust to subjugate women, even though you firmly believe that you are acting in the manner best calculated to promote their happiness?

Who made man the exclusive judge, if woman partake with him the gift of reason? . . .

For surely, sir, you will not assert that a duty can be binding which is not founded on reason? . . . The more understanding women acquire, the more they will be attached to their duty—comprehending it—for unless they comprehend it, unless their morals be fixed on the same immutable principle as those of man, no authority can make them discharge it in a virtuous manner. They may be convenient slaves, but slavery will have its constant effect, degrading the master and the abject dependent. . . .

I have repeatedly asserted, and produced what appeared to me irrefragable arguments drawn from matters of fact to prove my assertion, that women cannot by force be confined to domestic concerns; for they will, however ignorant, intermeddle with more weighty affairs, neglecting private duties only to disturb by cunning tricks the orderly plans of reason which rise above their comprehension. . . .

Let there be then no coercion *established* in society, and the common law of gravity prevailing, the sexes will fall into their proper places. And now that more equitable laws are forming your citizens, marriage may become more sacred: Your young men may choose wives from motives of affection, and your maidens allow love to root out vanity.

The father of a family will not then weaken his constitution and debase his sentiments by visiting the harlot nor forget, in obeying the call of appetite, the purpose for which it was implanted. And the mother will not neglect her children to practise the arts of coquetry when sense and modesty secure her the friendship of her husband.

But till men become attentive to the duty of a father, it is vain to expect women to spend that time in their nursery which they, "wise in their generation," choose to spend at their [looking] glass; for this exertion of cunning is only an instinct of nature to enable them to obtain indirectly a little of that power of which they are unjustly denied a share; for if women are not permitted to enjoy legitimate rights, they will render both men and themselves vicious to obtain illicit privileges.

I wish, sir, to set some investigations of this kind afloat in France; and should they lead to a confirmation of my principles, when your constitution is revised, the Rights of Woman may be respected, if it be fully proved that reason calls for this respect and loudly demands JUSTICE for one half of the human race. . . .

Moralists have unanimously agreed that unless virtue be nursed by liberty, it will never attain due strength—and what they say of man I extend to mankind, insisting that in all cases morals must be fixed on immutable principles and that the being cannot be termed rational or virtuous who obeys any authority but that of reason.

To render women truly useful members of society, I argue that they should be led, by having their understandings cultivated on a large scale, to acquire a rational affection for their country, founded on knowledge, because it is obvious that we are little interested about what we do not understand. And to render this general knowledge of due importance, I have endeavored to show that private duties are never properly fulfilled unless the understanding enlarges the heart and that public virtue is only an aggregate of private. But the distinctions established in society undermine both by beating out the solid gold of virtue till it becomes only the tinsel covering of vice; for whilst wealth renders a man more respectable than virtue, wealth will be sought before virtue; and whilst women's persons are caressed when a childish simper shows an absence of mind, the mind will lie fallow.

Document 8: "The Church, the Bar, and the Senate Are Shut Against Us"

The Young Ladies Academy of Philadelphia, opened in 1787, was one of the pioneering educational institutions for women in postrevolutionary America. Attended by young women from affluent New England families, it provided instruction for them in the same academic areas in which young men could be trained, including grammar, arithmetic, geography, and oratory.

The commencement addresses of most students reveal the contradiction in their lives between the stimulation of the education they were receiving and the lack of vision of life after their graduation. Priscilla Mason, who delivered the "salutatorian addression" in 1793, envisioned a purpose, however: a society of women in the "Church, Bar, and Senate." Yet Priscilla knew that even the equal education of women could not break down the cultural barriers that kept public power in the hands of men.[30]

Venerable Trustees of this Seminary, Patrons of the improvement of the female mind; suffer us to present the first fruits of your labours as an offering to you, and cordially to salute you on this auspicious day. . . .

A female, young and inexperienced, addressing a promiscuous assembly, is a novelty which requires an apology, as some may suppose. I, therefore, with submission, beg leave to offer a few thoughts in vindication of female eloquence. . . .

Our right to instruct and persuade cannot be disputed, if it shall appear, that we possess the talents of the orator—and have opportunities for the exercise of those talents. Is a power of speech, and volubility of expression, one of the talents of the orator? Our sex possess it in an eminent degree.

Do personal attractions give charm to eloquence, and force the orator's arguments? There is some truth mixed with the flattery we receive on this head. Do tender passions enable the orator to speak in a moving and forcible manner? This talent of the orator is confessedly ours. In all these respects the female orator stands on equal, —nay, on *superior* ground. . . .

Our high and mighty Lords (thanks to their arbitrary constitutions) have denied us the means of knowledge, and then reproached us for the want of it. Being the stronger party, they early seized the sceptre and the sword; with these they gave laws to society; they denied women the advantage of a liberal education; forbid them to exercise their talents on those great occasions, which would serve to improve them. They doom'd the sex to servile or frivolous employments, on purpose to degrade their minds, that they themselves might hold unrivall'd, the power and pre-eminence they had usurped. Happily, a more liberal way of thinking begins to prevail. The sources of knowledge are gradually opening to our sex. Some have already availed themselves of the priviledge so far, as to wipe off our reproach in some measure. . . .

But supposing now that we possess'd all the talents of the orator, in the highest perfection; where shall we find a theatre for the display of them? The Church, the Bar, and the Senate are shut against us. Who shut them? *Man;* despotic man, first made us incapable of the duty, and then forbid us the exercise. Let us by suitable education, qualify ourselves for these high departments—they will open before us. They *will,* did I say? They have done it already. Besides several Churches of less importance, a numerous and respectable Society, had display'd its impartiality.—I had almost said the gallantry in this respect. With others, women forsooth, are complimented with the wall, the right hand, the head of the table,—with a kind of mock pre-eminence in small matters: but on great occasions the sycophant changes in his tune, and says, "Sit down at my feet and learn." Not so the members of the enlightened and liberal Church. They regard not the anatomical formation of the body. They look to the soul, and allow all to teach who are capable of it, be they male or female.

But Paul forbids it! Contemptible little body! The girls laughed at the deformed creature. To be revenged, he declares war against the whole sex: advises men not to marry them; and has the insolence to order them to keep silence in the Church—: afraid, I suppose, that they would say something against celibacy, or ridicule the old bachelor.

With respect to the bar, citizens of either sex have an undoubted right to plead their own cause there. Instances could be given of females being admitted to plead the cause of a friend, a husband, a son; and they have done it with energy and effect. I am assured that there is nothing in our laws or constitution to prohibit the licensure of female Attornies; and sure our judges have too much gallantry, to urge *prescription* in bar of their claim. In regard to the senate, prescription is clearly in our favour. We have one or two cases exactly in point.

Heliogabalus, the Roman Emperor, of blessed memory, made his grandmother a Senator of Rome. He also established a senate of women; appointed his mother President; and committed them the important business of regulating dress and fashions. And truly methinks the dress of our country, at this day, would admit some regulation, for it is subject to no rules at all—It would be worthy the wisdom of Congress, to consider whether a similar institution, established at the seat of our Federal Government, would not be a public benefit. We cannot be independent, while we receive our fashions from other countries, nor act properly, while we initiate the manners of the governments not congenial to our own. Such a Senate, composed of women most noted for wisdom, learning and taste, delegated from every part of the Union, would give dignity and independence to our manners; uniformity, and even authority to our fashions.

It would fire the female breast with the most generous ambition, prompting to illustrious actions. It would furnish the most noble Theatre for the display, the exercise and improvement of every faculty. I would call forth all that is human—all that is *divine* in the soul of woman; and having proved them equally capable with the other sex, would lead to their equal participation of honor and office.

Notes

American Indian Women and Religion

1. For perspectives on the extent and reliability of this literature, see Robert F. Berkhofer, Jr., *The White Man's Indian: Images of the American Indian from Columbus to the Present* (New York: Alfred A. Knopf, 1978). See also Francis Jennings, *The Invasion of America: Indians, Colonialism, and the Cant of Conquest* (Chapel Hill: University of North Carolina Press, 1975); Bernard Sheehan, *Savagism and Civility: Indians and Englishmen in Colonial Virginia* (Cambridge, England: Cambridge University Press, 1980); and Cornelius J. Jaenen, *Friend and Foe: Aspects of French-Amerindian Cultural Contact in the Sixteenth and Seventeenth Centuries* (New York: Columbia University Press, 1976).
2. See, for example, Selwyn Dewdney, *The Sacred Scrolls of the Southern Ojibway* (Toronto and Buffalo: University of Toronto Press, 1975).
3. Just as the fragility of the documentary record renders interpretations of American Indian women especially tentative, application of the term *religion* to the sacred beliefs and practices of North American tribal peoples is also problematic. Although traditional Indian "religious" beliefs and customs are still only partially understood by non-Indian observers and Indian nonparticipants, it now seems clear that the majority of traditional believers in North America conceived of religion differently and perhaps more broadly than did Euro-Americans during the seventeenth and eighteenth centuries. For an overview of North American Indian cosmologies, see Ake Hultkrantz, *The Religions of the American Indians,* trans. Monica Settlerwall (Berkeley: University of California Press, 1979). See also Dennis Tedlock and Barbara Tedlock, eds., *Teachings from the American Earth: Religion and Philosophy* (New York: Liveright, 1975); Walter H. Capps, ed., *Seeing with a Native Eye* (New York: Harper & Row, 1976); Elisabeth Tooker, ed., *Native North American Spirituality of the Eastern Woodlands: Sacred Myths, Dreams, Visions, Speeches, Healing Formulas, Rituals and Ceremonies* (New York: Paulist Press, 1979); and Sam D. Gill, *Native American Religions: An Introduction* (Belmont, CA: Wadsworth Publishing, 1982).
4. Hultkrantz, *The Religions of the American Indians,* pp. 27–28. Cosmological beliefs varied widely. See, for example, Alfonso Ortiz, *The Tewa World: Space, Time, Being and Becoming in a Pueblo Society* (Chicago: University of Chicago Press, 1969); A. Irving Hallowell, "Ojibwa Ontology, Behavior, and World View," reprinted in Raymond D. Fogelson, ed., *Contributions to Anthropology: Selected Papers of A. Irving Hallowell;* (Chicago: University of Chicago Press, 1976); Gladys A. Reichard, *Navaho Religion, A Study in Symbolism,* 2 vols., Bollingen Series XVIII (New York: Pantheon Books, 1950); and Gene Weltfish, *The Lost Universe: The Way of Life of the Pawnee* (New York: Basic Books, 1965).
5. For the concept of "other-than-human person," see Hallowell, "Ojibway Ontology, Behavior and World View." See Gill, *Native American Religions,* pp. 15–26, for a brief introduction to Zuni, Navajo, and Seneca creation traditions. The classic work on the Trickster cycle is Paul Radin, *The Trickster: A Study in American Indian Mythology* (New York: Philosophical Library, 1956).
6. Paul Radin, *Primitive Man as Philosopher* (New York: Appleton, 1927).
7. The concept of power is central to a number of traditional North American religious belief systems. See Lowell John Bean, "Power and Its Application in Native California"; Mary B. Black, "Ojibwa Power Belief Systems"; Raymond J. DeMallie, Jr., and Robert H. Lavenda, "*Wakan: Plains Siouan Concepts of Power*"; and Hope L. Isaacs, "*Orenda and the Concept of Power Among the Tonawanda Seneca.*" In Raymond D. Fogelson and Richard N. Adams, eds., *The Anthropology of Power: Ethnographic Studies from Asia, Oceania, and*

the New World (New York: Academic Press, 1977). A book-length study of this subject is being prepared by Clara Sue Kidwell.

8. See Lynn Ceci, "Watchers of the Pleiades: Ethnoastronomy Among Native Cultivators in Northeastern North America," *Ethnohistory* 25 (Fall 1978): 301–317.

9. The classic work on the spiritual relationship between hunting peoples and their animal relatives is Frank G. Speck, *Naskapi: The Savage Hunters of the Labrador Peninsula* (Norman: University of Oklahoma Press, 1935). Renewed interest in this relationship has been stimulated by Adrian Tanner, *Bringing Home Animals: Religious Ideology and Mode of Production of the Misstassini Cree Hunters* (New York: St. Martin's Press, 1981), and Calvin Martin, *Keepers of the Game: Indian-Animal Relationships and the Fur Trade* (Berkeley: University of California Press, 1978). Scholarly debate surrounding Martin's thesis can be seen in Shepard Krech III, ed., *Indians, Animals, and the Fur Trade: A Critique of Keepers of the Game* (Athens, GA: University of Georgia Press, 1981).

10. See James Axtell, ed., *The Indian Peoples of Eastern America: A Documentary History of the Sexes* (New York: Oxford University Press, 1981), for a useful introduction to the traditional roles of Eastern Woodlands women. See also Elisabeth Tooker, *The Iroquois Ceremonial of Midwinter* (Syracuse, NY: Syracuse University Press, 1970); Mary Jane Schneider, "Plains Indian Art," in W. Raymond Wood and Margot Liberty, eds., *Anthopology of the Great Plains* (Lincoln: University of Nebraska Press, 1980), pp. 197–211; and H. A. Dempsey, "Religious Significance of Blackfoot Quillwork," *Plains Anthropologist* 8 (1963): 52–53. The first scholarly book-length work on American Indian women has only recently appeared: Beatrice Medicine and Patricia Albers, eds., *The Hidden Half: Studies of Plains Indian Women* (New York: University Press, 1983), includes useful articles by Raymond DeMallie, Jr., Mary Jane Schneider and Patricia Albers, and Beatrice Medicine.

11. Jerald T. Milanich and William C. Sturtevant, eds., *Francisco Paraja's 1613 Confessionario: A Documentary Source for Timucuan Ethnography,* trans. Emilio F. Moran (Tallahassee, FL: Division of Archives, History and Records Management, 1972). See also Ruth F. Benedict, "The Concept of the Guardian Spirit in North America," *American Anthropological Association Memoirs* 29 (1923), and Patricia Albers and Seymour Parker, "The Plains Vision Experience: A Study of Power and Privilege," *Southwestern Journal of Anthropology* 27 (1971): 203–233.

12. See Thomas Buckley's provocative "Menstruation and the Power of Yurok Women: Methods in Cultural Reconstruction," *American Ethnologist* 9 (February 1982): 47–60.

13. Denis Raudot, cited in Vernon Kinietz, *The Indians of the Western Great Lakes, 1615–1760* (Ann Arbor: University of Michigan Press, 1940), p. 353; Jacqueline Peterson, "Women Dreaming," in "The People in Between: Indian-White Marriage and the Genesis of a Metis Society and Culture in the Great Lakes Region, 1680–1830," Ph.D. diss., University of Illinois at Chicago, 1981, pp. 58–102.

14. See, for example, Calvin Martin, "The Four Lives of a Micmac Copper Pot," *Ethnohistory* 22 (Spring 1975): 111–133, and Calvin Martin, *Keepers of the Game,* pp. 58–59.

15. A useful introduction to the voluminous literature on missionary activity among North American Indians is James P. Ronda and James Axtell, *Indian Missions: A Critical Bibliography,* The Newberry Library Center for the History of the American Indian Bibliographical Series (Bloomington: University of Indiana Press, 1978). See also Henry Warner Bowden, *American Indians and Christian Missions: Studies in Cultural Conflict* (Chicago and London: University of Chicago Press, 1981).

16. See the articles on the Luiseno by Lowell John Bean and Florence C. Shipek, and on the Tipai and Ipai by Katharine Luomala, in Robert F. Heizer, ed., *California,* vol. 8 of William C. Sturtevant, ed., *Handbook of North American Indians* (Washington, D.C.: Smithsonian Institution, 1978).

17. *Palou's Life of Fray Junipero Serra,* trans. and annotated by Maynard J. Geiger, (Washington, D. C.: Academy of American Franciscan History, 1955), pp. 118–119.

18. *The Discoveries of John Lederer, in Three Several Marches from Virginia, to the West of Carolina, and other Parts of the Continent, Begun in March 1669, and ended in September 1670,* collected and trans. by Sir William Talbot (London: Printed by J. C. for Samuel Heyrick, 1672), pp. 8–9.

19. Frank J. Kingberg, ed., *The Carolina Chronicle of Dr. Francis Le Jau 1706–1717* (Berkeley and Los Angeles: University of California, 1956), pp. 67–68, 80.

20. Louis Hennepin, *A Description of Louisiana,* trans. John Gilmary Shea (New York: John G. Shea, 1880), pp. 278–280.

21. Hennepin, *A Description of Louisiana,* pp. 333–334.
22. Mark van Doren, ed., *Travels of William Bartram* (New York: Dover Publications, 1928). (Originally published under the title *Travels Through North and South Carolina, Georgia, East and West Florida* . . . by William Bartram [Philadelphia: Printed by James Johnson, 1791]).
23. Deliette, "Memoir of De Gannes Concerning the Illinois Country," in Theodore C. Pease and Raymond C. Werner, eds., *The French Foundations, 1680–1693,* Collections of the Illinois State Historical Library 23 (Springfield: 1934): 352–354. (The original Memoire concernent le pays Illinois, Montreal, October 20, 1721, signed De Gannes, is in the Edward Everett Ayer Collection, Newberry Library, Chicago, IL.)
24. Edwin James, ed., *A Narrative of the Captivity and Adventures of John Tanner (U.S. Interpreter at the Saut de Ste. Marie) During Thirty Years Residence Among the Indians in the Interior of North America* (New York: G. & C. H. Carvill, 1830; reprint edition, Minneapolis: Ross & Haines, Inc. 1856), pp. 31–34.
25. Claude Dablon to Rev. Father Francois le Mercier, Relation of the Mission to the Outaouaks (Sault St. Marie), n.d., in Relation of 1669–70, in Reuben Gold Thwaits, ed., *The Jesuit Relations and Allied Documents: Travels and Explorations of the Jesuit Missionaries in New France 1610–1791,* vol. 54 (Cleveland, OH: The Burrows Brothers, Co., 1896–1901), pp. 139–143.
26. Anna Brownell Jameson, *Winter Studies and Summer Rambles in Canada,* ed. James J. Talman and Elsie McLeod Murray (Toronto: Thomas Nelson and Sons, Ltd., 1943), pp. 214–215. (Excerpted from the original three-volume edition published in 1838).
27. Daniel Gookin, *Historical Collections of the Indians in New England* (Massachusetts Historical Society Collections, First Series, vol. 1, 1792).
28. Memoir of De Gannes Concerning the Illinois Country," pp. 369–371.
29. Hennepin, *A Description of Louisiana,* pp. 328–329.
30. *Le Clercq: New Relation of Gaspesia,* facsimile edition (New York: Greenwood Press, 1968), pp. 229–233. (Originally published as Champlain Society Publications V.)
31. *Palou's Life of Fray Junipero Serra,* p. 112.
32. Frederick Webb Hodge, George P. Hammond, and Agapito Rey, eds., *Fray Alonso de Benavides' Revised Memorial of 1634* (Albuquerque: University of New Mexico Press, 1945), p. 53.
33. Thwaites, ed., *The Jesuit Relations and Allied Documents,* vol. 41, pp. 177–179.
34. Hennepin, *A Description of Louisiana,* pp. 330–332.
35. *Indian Converts: or, Some Account of the Lives and Dying Speeches of a Considerable Number of the Christianized Indians of Martha's Vineyard, in New England, by Experience Mayhew* (London: Printed for Samuel Gerrish, Bookseller in Boston in New-England, and sold by J. Osborn and T. Longman in Pater-noster-Row, 1727), pp. 175–179.
36. James Dow McCallum, ed., *The Letters of Eleazar Wheelock's Indians* (Hanover, NH.: Dartmouth College Publications, 1932), pp. 230–231.
37. *A Journal of the Life, Travels and Religious Labors of William Savery* (London: C. Gilpin, 1844), pp. 66, 68–70.
38. Walter Pilkington, ed., *The Journals of Samuel Kirkland* (Clinton, NY.: Hamilton College, 1980), pp. 351–353.

Women and Religion in Spanish America

1. John H. Elliot, *Imperial Spain, 1469–1716* (New York: St. Martin's Press, 1964), pp. 87–99; Antonio Domínguez Ortíz, *The Golden Age of Spain, 1516–1659* (New York: Basic Books, Inc., 1971), pp. 199–228; P. Tarsicio de Azcona, O.F.M., *La elección y reforma del episcopado espanol en tiempos de los Reyes Católicos* (Madrid: Consejo Superior de Investigaciones Científicas, Instituto "P. Enrique Flores," 1960).
2. Sebastian V. Ramge, O.C.D., *An Introduction to the Writings of Saint Teresa* (Chicago: Henry Regnery Company, 1963); Elgar Allison Peers, *Mother of Carmel. A Portrait of St. Teresa of Jesus* (New York: Moorehouse-Gorham Co., 1946); Father Thomas, O.D.C., and Father Gabriel, O.D.C., eds., *St. Teresa of Avila. Studies in her Life, Doctrine and Times* (Westminster, MD.: The Newman Press, 1963).
3. Josefina Muriel, *Conventos de monjas en la Nueva España* (Mexico: Editorial Santiago, 1946), pp. 16–17.

4. Melquíades Andrés, *Los recogidos: Nueva visión de la mística española, 1500–1700* (Madrid: Fundación Universitaria Española, 1976).
5. *Alumbrados* advocated the direct union of man and God through the mystical experience. When this union was achieved, the soul was saved, without pious deeds or the intervention of the church as an intermediary between man and God. The *quietists* were a seventeenth-century version of the *alumbrados,* inspired by the works of Miguel de Molinos. Their aim was to suppress the will and to receive God in a state of passivity. See Antonio Márquez, *Los alumbrados: Orígenes y filosofía. 1525–1559* (Madrid: Editorial Taurus, 1972); Alvaro Huerga, *Historia de los alumbrados* (Madrid: Fundación Universitaria Española, Seminario Cisneros, 1978); and Domínguez Ortiz, *The Golden Age of Spain,* pp. 225.
6. Manuel del Socorro Rodríguez, *Fundación del monasterio de la Enseñanza* (Bogotá: Empressa Nacional de Publicaciones, 1957); *La Provincia eclesíastica chilena: Erección de sus obispados y división en parroquias* (Friburgo: Casa Editorial Pontificia de B. Herder, 1895), pp. 348–356, 404–409.
7. J. Lloyd Mechan, *Church and State in Latin America* (Chapel Hill: University of North Carolina Press, 1966), pp. 3–37; Rodolfo Quezada Toruño, "A propósito del monasterio de Nuestra Señora del Pilar (Capuchinas)," *Anales de la Sociedad de Georgrafía e Historia,* Guatemala, vol. XI, año XL (enero-junio 1967): 156–191.
8. Bernardo de Torres, *Crónica Agustina* (Edición de Ignacio Prado Pastor), vol. II (Lima: Copyright Ignacio Prado Pastor, 1974), pp. 878–880; Murdel, *Conventos de monjas,* pp. 26–27.
9. Asunción Lavrin, "Women in Convents: Their Economic and Social Role in Colonial Mexico," in Berenice A. Carroll, ed., *Liberating Women's History: Theoretical and Critical Essays* (Urbana: University of Illinois Press, 1976), pp. 256–257.
10. Josefina Muriel, *Las indias caciques de Corpus Christi* (Mexico: Universidad Nacional Autónoma de Mexico, 1963), pp. 243–294. (The author of the biographies of the Indian nuns remains anonymous.)
11. Pilar Foz y Foz, *La revolución pedagógica en Nueva España (1754–1820),* vol. II (Madrid: Instituto de Estudios Americanos "Gonzalo Fernández de Oviedo," 1981), p. 187.
12. Asunción Lavrin, "In Search of the Colonial Woman in Mexico: The Seventeenth and Eighteenth Centuries," in Asunción Lavrin, ed., *Latin American Women. Historical Perspectives* (Westport, CT.: Greenwood Press, 1978), pp. 23–59.
13. Fr. Diego de Córdova Salinas, O.F.M., *Crónica Franciscana de las provincias del Perú* (1651) (Washington, D.C.: Academy of American Franciscan History, 1957), pp. 949–952, (New edition with notes and introduction by Lino Canedo, O.F.M.) 938–948. See also Josefina Muriel, *Los recogimientos de mujeres* (Mexico: Universidad Nacional Autónoma de Mexico, 1974); Cayetano C. Bruno S.D.B, *Historia de la iglesia en la Argentina,* vol. II (Buenos Aires: Editorial Don Bosco, 1970), p. 78; and R.P. Fr. Alonso de Zamora, *Historia de la Provincia de San Antonino del Nuevo Reino de Granada* (Caracas: Parra León Hermanos, Editorial Sur America, 1980), pp. 37–75.
14. Asunción Lavrin, "La Congregación de San Pedro. Una cofradía urbana del Mexico colonial, 1640–1730," *Historia Mexicana,* vol. XXIX (abril-junio 1980), pp. 562–601.
15. Francis Parkinson Keyes, *The Rose and the Lily: The Lives and Times of Two South American Saints* (New York: Hawthorn Books, Inc., 1961).
16. Salinas, *Crónica Franciscana,* pp. 831–32, 875, 902; Juan B. Díaz de Gamarra y Dávila, *Ejemplar de religiosas. Vida de la R.M. Sor María Josefa Lino de la SSMA Trinidad* (Mexico: Imp. de A. Valdés, 1831); Antonio de Miqueorena, *Vida de la V.M. Micaela Josefa de la Purificacion* (Puebla: Vda. de Miguel de Ortega y Bonilla, 1755).
17. Richard L. Kagan, *Students and Society on Early Modern Spain* (Baltimore: Johns Hopkins University Press, 1974), pp. 27–29.
18. Isaac Barrera, *Prosistas de la Colonia: Siglos XCV–XVIII,* Biblioteca Ecuatoriana Mínima (Puebla, Mexico: Editorial J.M. Cajica Jr., S.A., 1960), pp. 135–143.
19. Barrera, *Prosistas de la Colonia,* pp. 282–284.
20. Mariana de Santa Pazis, *Carta Pastoral,* in Madre Josefa de la Providencia, *Relacion del origen y fundacion del origen y fundacion del monasterio de Sr. San Joaquin de religiosas Nazarenas, Carmelitas Descalzas de esta ciudad de Lima . . .* (Lima: Imprenta Real de los Niños Expósitos, 1793).
21. Sor Juana Inés de la Cruz, *Obras Completas* (Mexico: Editorial Porrúa, S.A., 1969).
22. Sor Juana Inés de la Cruz, "Respuesta a Sor Filotea de la Cruz," in *A Woman of Genius:*

The Intellectual Autobiography of Sor Juana Inés de la Cruz, trans. and intro. Margaret Sayers Peden (Salisbury, CT.: Lime Rock Press, Inc., 1982), pp. 44, 64, 66, 68, 70, 80–81.

23. Sor Paula de Jesús Nazareno, "Coloquios con Dios," Section VI, in Rubén Vargas Ugarte, S.J., *Rosas de Oquendo y otros,* Clásicos Peruanos, vol. 5, trans. Ruth Moroles (Lima: n.p., 1955), pp. 159–165.

24. "Coloquio que compuso la R.M. Maria Vicenta de la Encarnacion para la profesion de su discipula la hermana Maria de San Eliseo, Carmelita Descalza en el convento de Santa Teresa la Antigua," (1804). Manuscript at the Collection of the University of Texas, Austin.

25. Madre Francisca de la Concepción Josefa de Castillo, *Obras Competas,* vol. II (Bogotá: Talleres Gráficos del Banco de la República, 1968), pp. 47–48, 283–284, 346–347, 484.

26. Foz y Foz, *La revolución pedagógica,* vol. II, pp. 65–66. See also Bruno, *Historia de la iglesia,* vol. VI, pp. 450–55.

27. Asunción Lavrin, "Women in Convents," pp. 262–270.

28. Claudio Jiménez y Vizcarra, "Dignatarios y reglamento de gobierno del convento de religiosas recoletas agustinas de Santa Mónica de Guadalajara," *Estudios Históricos,* III epoca, (septiembre 1977), pp. 143–146.

29. Asunción Lavrin, "Ecclesiastical Reform of Nunneries in New Spain in the Eighteenth Century," *The Americas,* vol. XXII (October 1965), pp. 182–203.

30. Juan Manuel Pacheco, S.J., *Historia eclesíastica,* vol. XIII of *Historia Extensa de Colombia,* Academia Colombiana de la Historia (Bogotá: Ediciones Lerner, 1975), p. 523.

31. Zamora, *Historia de la Provincia de San Antonino,* pp. 323–324 (notes); Fr. José Maria Vargas, O.P., *Historia de la iglesia en el Ecuador durante el patronato español* (Quito: Editorial "Santo Domingo," 1972), pp. 298–306; *La Provincia eclesíastica chilena,* p. 359.

32. Nancy M. Farriss, *Crown and Clergy in Colonial Mexico, 1759–1821* (London: The Athlone Press of the University of London, 1968).

33. See the works on the Inquisition by José Toribio Medina, which are still useful sources for this topic: *Historia del Tribunal de la Inquisición en Lima (1569–1820)* (Santiago de Chile: Fondo Histórico y Bibliográfico J.T. Medina, 1956); *Historia del Santo Oficio de la Inquisición en Chile* (Santiago de Chile: Fondo Histórico y Bibliográfico J.T. Medina, 1952). See also Richard E. Greenleaf, *The Mexican Inquisition in the Sixteenth Century* (Albuquerque: University of New Mexico Press, 1969).

34. Noemí Quezada, *Amor y magia amorosa entre los aztecas* (Mexico: Universidad Nacional Autónoma de Mexico, 1975).

35. Genealogical Society of Utah, Archivo Histórico del Antiguo Obispado de Michoacán, Section 4, Leg. 44, Microfilm 785793.

35. Genealogical Society of Utah, Archivo Histórico del Antiguo Obispado de Michoacán, Section 5, Leg. 253, Microfilm 753973; Cathedral of Mexico, Archivo del Cabildo, Borradores, 34 (1730s).

37. Toruño, pp. 176–178.

38. Muriel, *Las indias caciques de Corpus Christi,* pp. 243–294.

39. Foz y Foz, *La revolución pedagógica, vol. II, p. 187.*

40. Córdova Salinas, *Crónica Franciscana,* pp. 949–952.

41. Córdova Salinas, *Crónica Franciscana, pp. 938–948.*

42. Excerpt from Jesús Herrera, *Secretos entre el alma y Dios,* in Barrera, ed., *Prosistas de la colonia, Siglos XV–XVIII, pp. 282–284.*

43. Santa Pazis, *Carta Pastoral,* in Providencia, *Relación del origen y fundación del monasterio de Sr. San Joaquin de religiosas Nazarenas, Carmelitas Descalzas de esta ciudad de Lima . . .*

44. Inés de la Cruz, "Respuesta a Sor Filotea de la Cruz," pp. 44, 64, 66, 68, 70, 80–81.

45. Jesús Nazareno, "Coloques con Dios."

46. Madre Francisca Josefa de Castillo, *Obras Completas,* vol. II, *intro. Dario Achury Valenzuela* pp. 47–48, 283–284, 346–347, 484 (excerpts from *Afectos Espirituales*).

47. Foz y Foz, *La revolución pedagógica,* vol. II, pp. 65–66.

48. Jiménez y Vizcarra, "Dignatarios y reglamento de gobierno del convento de religiosas recoletas agustinas de Santa Mónica de Guadalajara," pp. 143–146.

49. Genealogical Society of Utah, Archivo Histórico del Antiguo Obispado de Michoacán, Section 4, Leg. 44, Microfilm 785793.

50. The first four letters are found at the Genealogical Society of Utah, Archivo Histórico del Antiguo Obispedo de Michoacán, Section 5, Leg. 253, Microfilm 753973 (Peticiones

Sueltas del Gobierno de los Illmos, Señores Escalona y Elizacochea, circa 1720s and 1750s). The last letter is found at the Cathedral of Mexico, Archivo del Cabildo, Borradores, 34 (1730s).

Women in Colonial French America

1. Jean Delumeau, *Catholicism Between Luther and Voltaire: A New View of the Counter-Reformation* (Philadelphia: Westminster Press, 1977).
2. For example, in 1590, Henri Boquet published *An Examination of Witches.*
3. See, for example, St. Theresa of Avila, *Life,* in *Complete Works,* vol. I, trans. and ed. E. Allison Peers (New York: Sheed and Ward, 1963). Marie of the Incarnation mentions the possession at London in her Relation of 1654, printed as *The Autobiography of Venerable Marie of the Incarnation, O.S.U.: Mystic and Missionary,* John J. Sullivan, S.J. (Chicago: Loyola University Press, 1964), pp. 84–85.
4. Carolyn C. Lougee, *Le Paradis des Femmes: Women, Salons, and Social Stratification in Seventeenth-century France* (Princeton: Princeton University Press, 1976); Dorothy Anne Liot Backer, *Precious Women* (New York: Basic Books, Inc., 1974); Eva Jacobs et al., *Women and Society in Eighteenth-century France* (London: The Athlone Press, 1979).
5. Marie de Jars de Gournay wrote *Egalité des hommes et des femmes* in 1622, and Anna Maria von Schurman wrote *The Learned Maid* in 1641.
6. For ridicule, see Moliére's *L'école des femmes* (1659) and *Les femmes savantes* (1672). For the first major work on the equality of the sexes, see Poulain de la Barre *De l'égalité des deux sexes* (1673).
7. The two major texts that were written in the shadow of the French Revolution were Olympe des Gouges's *Declaration of the Rights of Women* (1791) and Mary Wollstonecraft's *A Vindication of the Rights of Women* (1792). See also Darline Levy et al., eds., *Women in Revolutionary Paris 1789–1795* (Urbana: University of Illinois Press, 1979).
8. Christine Allen, *The Concept of Woman from 700* B.C. *to 1300* AD: The Aristotelian Revolution (forthcoming).
9. There are several other women who also bear careful study: Madame de la Peltrie, Sr. Catherine St. Augustine, and Sr. Marie Morin.
10. The first English settlers arrived in Jamestown, Virginia, in 1607.
11. Madame de la Peltrie probably ought to be recognized as the first lay woman missionary. She was the patroness of the Ursulines and insisted on coming to New France to live near them. When Jeanne Mance arrived, Madame de la Peltrie decided to accompany her to Montreal. This caused some consternation among the Ursulines, who feared the loss of their financial backing. However, Madame de la Peltrie found the Montreal colony not to her liking; she returned to Quebec City and remained faithful to the Ursulines.
12. It is very possible that Marguerite Bourgeoys modeled her vocation after the pattern established by St. Vincent de Paul (1580–1660). He was the first to found an uncloistered society of sisters of charity in France; women religious had been strictly cloistered since the thirteenth century.
13. For a detailed description of their backgrounds, see the *Dictionary of Canadian Biography* (Toronto: University of Toronto Press, 1966). The maiden names of the women considered were: Marie of the Incarnation—Marie Guyart, Marguerite D'Youville—Marguerite Dufrost de La Jamerais.
14. The Jesuit Relations were first published in France between 1632 and 1673. The seventy-three-volume work was edited by Rueben Thwaites and published as *Jesuit Relations and Allied Documents,* ed. S.R. Mealing (Toronto: McClelland and Stewart, Ltd., 1963).
15. Cornelius J. Jaenen, *Friend and Foe: Aspects of French-Amerindian Contact in the Sixteenth and Seventeenth Centuries* (Toronto: McClelland and Stewart, Ltd., 1976) pp. 12–40.
16. Diamond Jenness, *The Indians of Canada* (Toronto: University of Toronto Press, 1977).
17. Jaenen, *Friend and Foe,* pp. 98–119.
18. Thwaites, ed., *The Jesuit Relations and Allied Documents.*
19. Louise Duchêne, *Habitants et marchands de Montréal au XVII*[e] *siècle* (Montreal: Plon, 1974) pp. 77–80.
20. Mason Wade, *The French Canadians 1760–1967,* vol. I (Toronto: Macmillan Company of Canada, 1968) pp. 1–46.

21. Hugh MacLennon, *Two Solitudes* (New York: Duell, Sloan, and Pearce, 1945). This novel about Canada made the phrase "two solitudes" popular in describing French and English relations.
22. For the specific details about availability of sources, see the notes attached to each section of documents.
23. This turn toward modern spirituality was most clearly articulated in the *Autobiography of St. Thérèse of Lisieux.*
24. I am much indebted to Dom Guy-Marie Oury, O.S.B., for permission to use the letters of Marie of the Incarnation. Don Oury is the editor of *Marie de l'Incarnation Ursuline (1599–1672): Correspondence* (Solesmes: Abbaye Saint-Pierre, 1971). The documents used in this section were translated by Odile Hellman. Don Oury is also the author of the major English biography of Marie of the Incarnation: *Marie Guyart,* trans. Miriam Thompson, O.S.U. (Cincinnati, OH: Speciality Lithographing Company, 1978). He is presently chaplain at the new Benedictine contemplative monastery, The Priory of the Immaculate Heart of Mary, Westfield, Vermont. An English version of selected letters of Marie of the Incarnation is available: *Word from New France: The Selected Letters of Marie de L'Incarnation,* trans. and ed. Joyce Marshall (Toronto: Oxford University Press, 1967). An English version of the Relation of 1654 is also available as *The Autobiography of Venerable Marie of the Incarnation: Mystic and Missionary,* trans. John J. Sullivan, S.J. (Chicago: Loyola University Press, 1964).
25. *Marie de l'Incarnation Ursuline (1599–1672): Correspondance,* Letter XVII, pp. 39–41.
26. Ibid., Letter XLIII, pp. 94–101.
27. Ibid., Letter LXXX, pp. 218–226.
28. Ibid., Letter CX, pp. 323–337.
29. Ibid., Letter CLXI, pp. 542–547.
30. Ibid., Letter CC, pp. 677–680.
31. Ibid., Letter CC, pp. 681–682.
32. Ibid., Letter CCLXX, pp. 915–919.
33. Ibid., Letter CIX, pp. 316–321.
34. Sr. Marie Morin, *Des Annales,* transcribed by S. Julienne Boisvert, r.h.s.j. and published in *Le Bulletin de la Province Ville-Marie des Hospitalières de Saint-Joseph* (Montreal: Maison mère des Religieuses Hospitalières). The *Annals* were originally written by Sr. Morin between 1697 and 1727. I am grateful to the Sisters of St. Joseph for allowing me to use this manuscript. The extracts have been translated by Odile Hellman. For further information, see Esther Lefebvre, *Marie Morin: premier historien canadien de Villemarie* (Montreal: Fides, 1959); Marie-Claire Daveluy, *Jeanne Mance* (Montreal: Editions Albert Levesque, 1934); Robert Lahaise, ed., *L'Hôtel-Dieu de Montréal (1642–1973)* (Montreal: Les Cahiers du Québec, 1973); Yvonne Estienne, *Undaunted (The Hospitaller Sisters of St. Joseph)* (Montreal: Palm Publishers, 1973); and F. Dollrer Casson, *A History of Montreal, 1640–1672,* trans. R. Fienly (Toronto: J. M. Dent and Sons Ltd., 1928).
35. Sr. Marie Morin, *Des Annales,* pp. 14–15, 26.
36. Ibid., pp. 27–30.
37. All of these documents were taken directly from *The Writings of Marguerite Bourgeoys: Autobiography and Spiritual Testament* (Montreal: Congregation of Notre Dame, 1976). I am grateful to Sr. Florence Bertrand, Archivist of the Congregation of Notre Dame, Montreal for her help in securing original sources. See also Margaret Mary Drummond, *The Life and Times of Margaret Bourgeoys: The Venerable* (Boston, MA.: Angel Guardian Press, 1907).
38. *The Writings of Marguerite Bourgeoys,* pp. 164–166.
39. Ibid., pp. 33–34.
40. Ibid., pp. 30–31.
41. Ibid., pp. 113, 201.
42. Ibid., pp. 49–50.
43. Ibid., pp. 48, 170–171, 176–177.
44. This document is taken from "Letter and Life of Katharine Tekakwitha, first to vow virginity among the Iroquois barbarians" (1715) by Father Cholenec. This work is available in *The Positio of the Historical Section of The Sacred Congregation of Rites on the Introduction of the Cause for the Beatification and Canonization and on the Virtues of Katharine Tekakwitha: The Lily of the Mohawks* (New York: Fordham University Press, 1940). This volume also contains "The Life of the Good Katharine Tegakouita, Now Known as the

Holy Savage" (1685, 1695) by Father Chauchetiere; "The Life of Katherine Tekakwitha, First Iroquois Virgin" (1696) by Father Cholenec; and various testimonies of miraculous cures attributed to her intercession. It is available at the Vanier Library, Loyola Campus, Concordia University, Montreal. See also Ellen H. Walworth, *The Life and Times of Katiri Tekakwitha: The Lily of the Mohawks* (Buffalo: Peter, Paul and Brother, 1891).

45. *The Writings of Marguerite Bourgeoys,* p. 136.

46. Marie Morin, *Des Annales,* pp. 40–41.

47. *L'Ange de Ville-Marie: Jeanne Le Ber* Montreal: Le Bureau des Archives de la Congrégation de Notre Dame, 1948), p. 13. I am grateful to Sr. Florence Bertrand, Archivist of the Congregation of Notre Dame for giving permission to use this document. Translated by Odile Hellman.

48. Ibid.

49. Reprinted from Sister Mary Pauline Pitts, G.N.S.H., *Hands to the Needy: Blessed Marguerite D'Youville Apostle to the Poor* (Garden City, NY: Doubleday and Company, Inc., 1971), pp. 57–58. See also Estelle Mitchell S.M.G., *Marguerite D'Youville Foundress of the Grey Nuns* (Montreal: Palm Publishers, 1965). I am grateful to Sr. Mitchell, Historian of the Grey Nuns, Montreal, for her invaluable information about documents for Marguerite D'Youville.

50. L'Abbé d'Youville Dufrost, *Vie de Madame d'Youville* (Levis: Archives Srs. Grises de Montréal, 1930). I am grateful for the help of Sr. Gaétane Chevrier, Archivist of Les Soeurs Grises, Montreal, for access to this document. In a later account of the life of Marguerite D'Youville by her son, Charles, he deletes the phrase "more by reason than inclination" to reflect his later view that his mother really loved her husband. Also, the deed to the house rented by Mme. D'Youville reads 1737, not 1738, as written by Charles. Finally, the first foundling was registered in 1754, and nineteen more were admitted in 1759, not 1760 as stated by Charles.

51. The Letters of Marguerite D'Youville have been taken from Albertine Ferland-Angers, *Mère D'Youville: Fondatrice des Soeurs de la Charité de l'Hôspital-général de Montréal, dites Soeurs Grises* (Montréal: Centre Marguerite-D'Youville, 1977), pp. 222–223, 226, 235–236, 259, 262.

New England Women: Ideology and Experience in First-Generation Puritanism (1630–1650)

1. See note 37 (for Document 3) and note 38 (for Document 4).

2. See note 38 (for Document 2).

3. Elizabeth Clark and Herbert Richardson, eds., *Women and Religion: A Feminist Sourcebook of Christian Thought* (New York: Harper & Row, 1977), pp. 116–120; Rosemary Ruether, "The Persecution of Witches," *Christianity and Crisis* (December 23, 1974); H. R. Trevor-Roper, *The European Witch-Craze of the Sixteenth and Seventeenth Centuries and Other Essays* (New York: Harper & Row, 1969); Alan MacFarlane, *Witchcraft in Tudor and Stuart England* (New York: Harper & Row, 1971); E. William Monter, *Witchcraft in France and Switzerland: The Borderlands during the Reformation* (Ithaca, NY: Cornell University, 1976); H. C. Erik Midelfort, *Witch Hunting in Southwestern Germany,* 1562–1684: The Social and Intellectual Foundations (Stanford: Stanford University, 1972).

4. J. Sprenger and H. Kramer, *Malleus Maleficarum,* trans. Montague Summers (London: Pushkin, 1948).

5. Rosemary Ruether, "Misogynism and Virginal Feminism in the Fathers of the Church," in Rosemary Ruether, ed., *Religion and Sexism: Images of Woman in the Jewish and Christian Traditions* (New York: Simon and Schuster, 1974), pp. 150–183.

6. Martin Luther, *Lectures on Genesis, Luther's Works,* vol. 1, ed. Jaroslav Pelikan (St. Louis: Concordia, 1958); Martin Luther, "The Estate of Marriage," *Luther's Works,* vol. 45, ed. Walter I. Brandt (Philadelphia: Muhlenberg, 1962).

7. See note 37 (for Document 1).

8. Carol F. Karlsen, "The Devil in the Shape of a Woman: The Witch in Seventeenth-Century New England," Ph.D. diss., Yale University, 1980, chap. 1. I am indebted to Karlsen throughout this essay for her highly significant recent study of New England witchcraft, particularly regarding the relationship between religion and sexuality, and her demographic analyses.

9. David D. Hall, *The Faithful Shepherd* (Chapel Hill: University of North Carolina Press, 1972), Ch. 4, 5.
10. Ibid., p. 87.
11. Gerald F. Moran, " 'Sisters' in Christ: Women and the Church in Seventeenth-Century New England," in Janet W. James, ed., *Women in American Religion* (Philadelphia: University of Pennsylvania Press, 1980), pp. 47–65; See also the important modern classics on this subject: Edmund Morgan, *The Puritan Family* (New York: Harper & Row, 1966); John Demos, *A Little Commonwealth* (New York: Oxford, 1970); and Lyle Koehler, *A Search for Power* (Urbana: University of Illinois Press, 1980).
12. Karlsen, "The Devil in the Shape of a Woman," p. 267.
13. Ibid., p. 268.
14. See note 41 (for Document 5).
15. See note 42 (for Document 6).
16. Moran, " 'Sisters' in Christ," pp. 48–54, and note 10 on p. 54; Mary Dunn, "Saints and Sisters: Congregational and Quaker Women in the Early Colonial Period," in James, ed., *Women in American Religion,* pp. 35–37, and Karlsen, "The Devil in the Shape of a Woman," pp. 238, 239.
17. Barbara Welter, "The Feminization of American Religion: 1800–1860," in Barbara Welter, ed., *Dimity Convictions: The American Woman in the Nineteenth Century* (Athens: Ohio University Press, 1976), pp. 83–102, and Ann Douglas, *The Feminization of American Culture* (New York: Avon, 1977).
18. *Winthrop's Journal: History of New England, 1630–1649,* vol. 2 (New York: 1908), p. 225, reprinted in Aileen S. Kraditor, *Up from the Pedestal* (Chicago: Quadrangle, 1968), p. 30.
19. Dunn, "Saints and Sisters," p. 30.
20. See note 43 (for Document 7); David D. Hall, *The Antinomian Controversy, 1636–1638: A Documentary History* (Middletown, CT: Wesleyan University, 1968); Lyle Koehler, "The Case of the American Jezebels: Anne Hutchinson and Female Agitation during the Years of Antinomian Turmoil, 1636–1640," Ben Barker-Benfield, "Anne Hutchinson and the Puritan Attitude Toward Women, *Feminist Studies* 1 (Fall 1972); Karlsen, "The Devil in the Shape of a Woman," p. 176.
21. Ibid.
22. Koehler, "The Case of the American Jezebels."
23. Koehler, "The Case of the American Jezebels," pp. 69, 70.
24. See note 44 (for Document 8).
25. See note 45 (for Document 9). My excerpt is taken from Nancy Cott, ed., *Root of Bitterness, Documents of the Social History of American Women* (New York: Dutton, 1972), pp. 47–64.
26. Koehler, "The Case of the American Jezebels," p. 70.
27. Richard Gildrie, *Salem Massachusetts, 1626–1683, A Covenant Community* (Charlottesville: University of Virginia Press, 1975), Ch. 5.
28. See note 46 (for Document 10).
29. Gildrie, *Salem Massachusetts,* p. 81.
30. Koehler, "The Case of the American Jezebels," pp. 70–72.
31. Rev. Newman Smyth, D.D., ed., "Mrs. Eaton's Trial (in 1644); as it Appears upon the Records of the First Church of New Haven," *Papers of the New Haven Colony Historical Society* (New Haven, CT), pp. 134, 135.
32. See note 47 (for Document 11).
33. Ibid.
34. Karlsen, "The Devil in the Shape of a Woman," pp. 18–28.
35. See note 48 (for Document 12).
36. See note 49 (for Document 13).
37. "An Homily of the State of Matrimony," *Certain Sermons or Homilies Appointed to be Read in Churches* (London: 1562), pp. 530–537, 541, 544, 545.
38. William Perkins, *A Discourse of the Damned Art of Witchcraft* (London: 1596).
39. William Perkins, *Christian Oeconomie* (London: 1590).
40. William Gouge, *Of Domesticall Duties, Eight Treatises* (London: 1622), excerpts from "The Epistle Dedicatory," and pp. 4–7, 25, 26, 132, 133, 135, 136, 149.
41. John Robinson, *The Works of John Robinson, Pastor of the Pilgrim Fathers,* vol. I (Boston: 1851), pp. 236–242.

42. Robert C. Winthrop, ed., *Life and Letters of John Winthrop,* vol. I (Boston: 1869), pp. 160, 161, 163, 164, 178, 179.
43. Thomas Hutchinson, *History of the Colony and Province of Massachusetts Bay* (Boston: 1767), Appendix: Number 11.
44. Richard D. Pierce, ed., *The Records of the First Church in Boston, 1630–1868,* vol. 39 (Boston: Colonial Society of Massachusetts, 1961), p. 25.
45. Reprinted from the manuscript of Robert Keayne's "Notes on John Cotton's Sermons," in Cott, ed., *Root of Bitterness,* pp. 47–58.
46. James Kendall Hosmer, ed., *Winthrop's Journal, "History of New England," 1630–1649* (Boston: 1638), pp. 285–286.
47. Charles J. Hoadley, ed., *Records of the Colony and Plantation of New Haven, from 1638 to 1649* (Hartford: Case, Tiffany and Co., 1857), pp. 242–245, 253–257.
48. John Brinsley, "A Looking-Glasse for Good Women" (London: 1645).
49. John Cotton, "Singing of Psalms a Gospel-Ordinance. 1650," in Edmund Clarence Stedman and Ellean Mackey Hutchinson, eds., *A Library of American Literature from the Earliest Settlement to the Present Time,* vol. 1 (New York: Charles L. Webster & Company, 1888), pp. 254–270.

The Religious Experience of Southern Women

1. Susan Myra Kingsbury, ed., *The Records of the Virginia Company of London* (Washington, D.C.: U.S. Government Printing Office, 1906–1935), I:256; III:493.
2. Henry Foley, ed., *Records of the English Province of the Society of Jesus* (London: Burns & Oates, 1878), III:370–371.
3. William Hand Browne, ed., *Archives of Maryland* (Baltimore: Maryland Historical Society, 1883–1952), XLI:531.
4. Ibid., XXX:334–335.
5. Kenneth A. Lockridge, *Literacy in Colonial New England* (New York: W. W. Norton & Company, 1974), p. 97.
6. Elise Pinckney and Marvin R. Zahniser, eds., *The Letterbook of Eliza Lucas Pinckney, 1739–1762* (Chapel Hill: University of North Carolina Press, 1972), p. 40.
7. Benjamin Sheftall Diary, 1733–1800, Keith Read Manuscript Collection, University of Georgia, Athens.
8. Henry F. May, *The Englightenment in America* (New York: Oxford University Press, 1976), pp. 66–74.
9. Michelle Zimbalist Rosaldo and Louise Lamphere, eds., *Woman, Culture and Society* (Stanford, CA: Stanford University Press, 1974), pp. 25–26, 43–66.
10. The Journal of Betsy Foote Washington, October, 1789, Washington Family Papers, Library of Congress Manuscript Division, Washington, D.C.
11. William Gaston to Margaret Gaston, August 2, 1795, The William Gaston Papers in the Southern Historical Collection of the University of North Carolina Library, Chapel Hill. *The Guide to the Microfilm Edition of the William Gaston Papers,* printed by the Southern Historical Collection of the University of North Carolina Library in 1966, contains biographical information on the Gaston family.
12. Donald G. Mathews, *Religion in the Old South* (Chicago and London: University of Chicago Press, 1977), pp. 109–120.
13. Robert B. Semple, *A History of the Rise and Progress of the Baptists in Virginia* (Richmond, VA: John O'Lynch, 1810), pp. 5, 374.
14. Richard Allestree, *The Whole Duty of Man* (Williamsburg, VA: W. Parks, 1746), pp. 244–247.
15. Northampton County, Virginia, Order Book & Wills No. XV, 1683–89, p. 105.
16. Anna Sioussat, "Colonial Women of Maryland," *Maryland Historical Magazine* 2 (1907):225–226; see also *Archives of Maryland,* VIII:155, 226.
17. Warren M. Billings, ed., *The Old Dominion in the Seventeenth Century: A Documentary History of Virginia, 1606–1689* (Chapel Hill: University of North Carolina Press, 1975), p. 167.
18. Edgar E. MacDonald, ed., *The Education of the Heart: The Correspondence of Rachel Mordecai Lazarus and Maria Edgeworth* (Chapel Hill: University of North Carolina Press, 1977), pp. 6, 14–15.
19. Elise Pinckney and Marvin R. Zahniser, eds., *The Letterbook of Eliza Lucas Pinckney,*

1739–1762 (Chapel Hill: University of North Carolina Press, 1972), pp. 51–53; 100–101.

20. Devereux Jarratt, *The Life of the Reverend Devereux Jarratt* (Baltimore: Warner & Hanna, 1806), pp. 32–35.

21. James Fordyce, *Sermons to Young Women: In Two Volumes* (Boston: Mein & Fleeming, 1767), I:12–13, 73–76; II:86, 114–117, 151–154, 160, 208–209.

22. David Ramsay, ed., *Memoirs of The Life of Martha Laurens Ramsay . . .* (Charlestown: Samuel Etheridge, 1812), pp. 14–15, 28–32, 42–46, 64, 170–171.

23. The Journal of Betsy Foote Washington, Washington Family Papers, Library of Congress Manuscript Division, Washington, D.C.

24. The William Gaston Papers, Southern Historical Collection of the University of North Carolina Library, Chapel Hill (microfilm copy used).

25. American Correspondence, Dr. Bray's Associates, February 16, 1761, pp. 120–121; extracts of letters from Minute Book of Dr. Bray's Associates, I:180, October 7, 1762; 186, March 3, 1763; 243, April 3, 1766; II:71–72, March 2, 1775; photocopies in the Library of Congress Manuscripts Division, Washington, D.C.

26. James Hall, *A Narrative of a Most Extraordinary Work of Religion in North Carolina* (Philadelphia: William W. Woodward, 1802), pp. 20–22, 24.

Black Women and Religion in the Colonial Period

1. John S. Mbiti, *African Religions and Philosophies* (Garden City, NJ: Doubleday & Company, 1970), pp. 188–89, discusses levirate and sorotate arrangements. Refer to Cheikh Anta Diop, *African Origin of Civilization,* ed. Mercer Cook (New York: Laurence Hill & Co., 1974), pp. 142–145, for insights into African matriarchy.

2. Mbiti, *African Religions and Philosophies,* xiii, Chapter 1, and pp. 110–111.

3. Ibid., pp. 188–89, 192; Michael C. Kirwen, *African Widows* (Maryknoll, NY: Orbis Books, 1979), passim; and Jasper Gerhard, "Polygamy in the Old Testament," *African Theological Journal* 2 (February 1969): 27–57.

4. Winthrop D. Jordan, *White Over Black: American Attitudes Toward the Negro, 1550–1812* (Baltimore: Penguin Books, Inc., 1909), p. 40.

5. Roscoe E. Lewis, superintendent, *The Negro in Virginia* (New York: Hastings House, 1940), p. 11.

6. For quotation and expression of conclusive statement that follows, refer to Joseph B. Earnest, Jr., *The Religious Development of the Negro in Virginia* (Charlottesville, VA: The Michie Company, Printers, 1914), 21–22.

7. Lewis, *The Negro in Virginia,* p. 11.

8. See Murray Heller, *Black Names: Origins and Usage* (Boston: G. K. Hall & Co., 1975), p. 6; Jordan, *White Over Black,* p. 73.

9. Earnest, *The Religious Development of the Negro,* p. 16.

10. St. George Tucker, *Dissertation on Slavery* (Williamsburg, PA, 1796).

11. William W. Hening, *Statutes at Large: Laws of Virginia* I (New York: Barton, 1832), 552.

12. John Winthrop, *History of New England from 1630–1649,* ed., James Savage (Boston: Little, Brown & Co., 1852) II, 31 His note: "Similar instances have been common enough ever since."

13. Hening, *Statutes at Large,* p. 170, for Act XII.

14. Ibid., p. 260, for Act III.

15. Earnest, *The Religious Development of the Negro,* p. 20.

16. Henry J. Cadbury, "Negro Membership in the Society of Friends," *Journal of Negro History* 21 (April 1936): 324.

17. Ibid.

18. Earnest, *The Religious Development of the Negro,* p. 26.

19. Frank J. Klingberg, *Anglican Humanitarianism in Colonial New York* (Philadelphia: Church Historical Society, 1940); Klingberg, ed., *Carolina Chronicle of Dr. Francis Le Jau, 1706–1717* (Berkeley and Los Angeles: University of California Press, 1956). See also W. E. Dubois, *The Negro Church* (Atlanta, GA: Atlanta University Publications, 1968), no. 8, and Alex Haley, *Roots* (Garden City, NY: Doubleday, 1976).

20. "Dispatches of Spanish Officials," *Journal of Negro History* 9 (April 1924): 145–146, 150–153.

21. Mather referred to this group as his "black sheep"for whom he will send, "and pray with . . . , and preach to . . . , and inquire into their conduct, and encourage them, in the ways of Piety: A religious Society of Negroes," in his *Diary 1709–1724* (Norwood, MA: Plimpton Press), I: 8, and II: 364, 532.

22. Klingberg, *Anglican Humanitarianism.* For early religious instructions and "letters" among slaves, see The Reverend Samuel Thomas of Goose Creek Parish Church, South Carolina (1695); for general correspondence and history of the SPG in South Carolina, see Klingberg, ed., *Carolina Chronicle.*

23. See Neau (New York SPG missionary and catechist) and Le Jau (South Carolina SPG missionary and catechist.) correspondence with SPG headquarters in London, passim, in Klingberg volumes cited above and colonial church registers, passim.

24. See, for example, Neau letter dated July 4, 1714, in Klingberg, *Anglican Humanitarianism,* p. 132.

25. Lorenzo J. Greene, *The Negro in Colonial New England* (New York: Atheneum, 1971), p. 195; James A. Padgett, "Status of Slaves in Colonial North Carolina," *Journal of Negro History* 14, (June 1929), p. 300+; and Klingberg, volumes cited above.

26. John Thomas of Hempstead, New York, for example, noted his expenditure of energy in trying to bring white "infidels" to conversion in a letter dated June 12, 1709; see Klingberg, *Anglican Humanitarianism,* p. 131.

27. Maud Wilder Goodwin, "Negro Plots," *Dutch and English on the Hudson: A Chronicle of Colonial New York* (New Haven: Yale University Press, 1921) pp. 206–217; David R. Roediger, "Funerals in the Slave Community," *The Massachusetts Review* 22 (Spring 1981): 167.

28. Charles F. Heartman, ed., *Phillis Wheatley: Poems and Letters* (Miami: Mnemosyne Publishing Co., 1969), passim.

29. Michael Kirwen, *African Widows,* p. 30. Based on Law of Marriage and Divorce Meeting at Kiswuru, Kenya, April 1972.

30. John Hammond, "Leah and Rachel or . . . Virginia, and Maryland" (London, 1656), in Peter Force, collector, *Tracts and Other Papers, Relating Principally to the Origin, Settlement, and Progress of the Colonies in North America From the Discovery of the Country to the Year 1776,* vol. 3 (New York: 1947), p. 12.

31. Sir Thomas Dale Knight, Marshall and Deputie Governour, "Articles, Lawes, and Orders, Divine, Politique, and Martiall for the Colony in Virginia" (June 22, 1611), in Force, collector, *Tracts and Other Papers,* vol. 2, p. 10.

32. Reprinted from Calef's and Hale's accounts, in George Lincoln Burr, *Narratives of the Witchcraft Cases,* 1648–1702 (New York: Scribner's and Sons, 1914), pp. 343, 413–415. Two somewhat different versions of Tituba's actual court testimony have been preserved. See *Records of Salem Witchcraft* (Roxbury, 1864), I: 41–50, and William Samuel Drake, *The Witchcraft Delusion in New England* (Roxbury, 1866), III: 185–195.

33. Elias Neau, in Klingberg, ed. *Anglican Humanitarianism,* p. 137.

34. Francis Le Jau to secretary of SPG (London), September 15, 1708, and October 20, 1709, in Klingberg, ed., *Carolina Chronicle,* pp. 41–42, 60–61; Neau to SPG Headquarters, July 4, 1714, in Klingberg, ed., *Anglican Humanitarianism,* pp. 339–344.

35. Court record of case of *William and Elizabeth Hood versus Adam Jourdan,* Bucks County Pennsylvania, Court of Quarter Session (September 1745), from Historical Society of Pennsylvania.

36. Reverend George Whitefield, *Memoirs* (London, 1772), p. 143.

37. Heartman, ed., *Phillis Wheatley,* p. 23.

38. Letter of recommendation from George Liele, dated December 21, 1791, for woman who moved from Savannah to London, in *Baptist Annual Register, 1790–1793.*

39. Mrs. John W. Olcott, "Recollections of Katy Ferguson," *The Southern Workman* 52 (September 1923): 463. Refer to same journal for article on the Katy Ferguson Home in New York City. Refer also to "Catherine Ferguson: She Had Compassion for Poor Children," *Philadelphia Inquirer Magazine* (June 21, 1970).

40. Absalom Jones and Richard Allen, "A Narrative of the Proceedings of the People, During the Late Awful Calamity in Philadelphia, in the Year, 1793," in Dorothy Porter, ed., *Negro Protest Pamphlets* (New York: Arno/*New York Times,* 1969), p. 9.

41. Cadbury, "Negro Membership," p. 171.

42. Sermon on death of Sarah Johnson (1845), preached at St. James First African Methodist Episcopal Church, from Historical Society of Pennsylvania.

Women in Sectarian and Utopian Groups

1. Franklin Littell, *The Anabaptist View of the Church* (Hartford, OH: American Society of Church History, 1952).
2. Isabel Ross, *Margaret Fell; Mother of Quakerism* (London: Longmans, Green and Co., 1949).
3. William Sewel, *The History of the Rise, Increase and Progress of the Christian People Called Quakers,* vol. 1 (London: James Phillips, 1799), p. 126, for Quaker confrontations at Oxford. Throughout the volume, Sewel covers the conflict of Quakers with Massachusetts authorities. See also George Bishop, *New England Judged by the Spirit of the Lord* (part I, 1661; part II, 1667), for an early account. For the story of Mary Dyer, see Horatio Rogers, *Mary Dyer of Rhode Island. The Quaker Martyr that was Hanged on Boston Common, June 1, 1660.* (Providence, RI: Preston and Rounds, 1896).
4. Isabel Ross, *Margaret Fell,* pp. 283–302. Also Mabel Brailsford, *Quaker Women, 1650–1690* (London: Duckworth and Co., 1915), pp. 268–289.
5. Sarah Grimké fled to Philadelphia in 1822 from South Carolina and joined the Quakers there. Her sister, Angelina Grimké, followed her in 1829, and the two women began a lifelong commitment to abolitionism and women's rights. See Gerda Lerner, *The Grimké Sisters from South Carolina* (New York: Schocken, 1971), pp. 57–59, 86.
6. Oteia Cromwell, *Lucretia Mott* (Cambridge, MA: Harvard University Press, 1958.)
7. The *Chronicon Ephratense* is an apologia for Beissel's religious career and for the community that gathered around him (see note 26).
8. Eugene E. Doll, *The Ephrata Cloister: An Introduction* (Ephrata, PA: Ephrata Cloister Associates, 1958–78), p. 22; Catherine F. Smith, "Jane Lead: The Feminist Mind and Art of a Seventeenth Century Protestant Mystic," in Rosemary R. Ruether and Eleanor McLaughlin, *Women of Spirit: Female Leadership in the Jewish and Christian Traditions* (New York: Simon and Schuster, 1979), p. 189; Walter C. Klein, *Johann Conrad Beissel: Mystic and Martinet 1696–1768* (Philadelphia: University of Pennsylvania Press, 1942), pp. 195, 127.
9. What actually constituted a love-feast differed among the sects and also within any given sect from time to time. William M. Fahnestock, commenting in the early nineteenth century on the practice, said that the Dunkers, like the Moravians, served rusk and coffee, preceded and followed by singing and prayers, and afterwards gave the kiss of charity to one another. In the early days of the society at Ephrata, he writes, the meal in the evening after the close of the Sabbath was regarded as a love-feast. Additionally, the sect at Ephrata and other German Seventh Day Baptists also celebrated a festival form of love-feast that was preceded by extensive preparations, included the entire neighborhood, and took place in the spring and fall. See *Milton H. Heinicke's History of Ephrata,* Booklet II, Historical Society of the Cocalico Valley, pp. 20–21.
10. Gillian Gollin, *Moravians in Two Worlds: A Study of Changing Communities* (New York and London: Columbia University Press, 1967), p. 157.
11. Hellmuth Erbe, *A Communistic Herrnhut Colony of the Eighteenth Century.* Publications of the German Foreign Institute of Stuttgart: A Cultural Historical Series, vol. 24 (Stuttgart: Foreign and Home Publication Joint Stock Co., 1929), p. 62.
12. Ibid., p. 65.
13. John R. Weinlick, "Moravianism in the American Colonies," *Continental Pietism and Early American Christianity,* ed. R. Ernest Stoeffler (Grand Rapids, MI: Wm. B. Eerdmans Publishing Co., 1976), pp. 150–151.
14. *Bethlehem Church Register,* vol. I (1742–1756), p. 127, from The Moravian Archives, Bethlehem, PA (translation by this author).
15. A sea congregation: "In the eighteenth century when a group of Moravians traveled together on shipboard, they permitted their usual activities to be interrupted as little as possible. Thus they organized themselves as a congregation, maintaining services, discipline, physical care of individual travelers, etc." *The Bethlehem Diary, vol. I: 1742–1744,* ed. and trans. Kenneth G. Hamilton (Bethlehem, PA: The Archives of the Moravian Church, 1971), p. 23. The first sea congregation, under the leadership of Peter Böhler, arrived in the spring of 1742 and participated in the early organization of Bethlehem. The third sea congregation arrived in New York in May 1749 and soon made its way to Bethlehem.
16. The original papers of Wilkinson's movement were kept in the family of the last leader

of the Universal Friends, James Brown, Jr. A descendent, Arnold Potter, deposited these papers in the Cornell University Collection of Regional History in 1946 and was engaged in writing a biography of Jemima Wilkinson from these papers (unpublished). But when Arnold Potter died in 1953, a niece claimed the papers and seems to have destroyed many of them before her death. Some papers and an original portrait of Wilkinson were turned over to the Yates County Historical Society of the village of Penn Yan. The Cornell University library, however, retained a microfilm of many of the Wilkinson papers that were later destroyed. Herbert Wisbey, Jr., used this material, as well as careful research into other contemporary accounts, to reconstruct a more favorable portrait of Wilkinson in *Pioneer Prophetess: Jemima Wilkinson, The Publick Universal Friend* (Ithaca, NY: Cornell University Press, 1964), pp. 217–225 (bibliographical essay).

17. Nardi R. Campion, *Ann the Word, Founder of the Shakers* (Boston: Little, Brown, 1976).

18. *Testimonies of the Life, Character, Revelations and Doctrines of Mother Ann Lee and the Elders with Her, Through Whom the Word of Eternal Life Was Opened This Day of Christ's Second Appearing,* Collected from Living Witnesses in Union with the Church, ed. S. Y. Wells (Albany, NY: Lackard and Benthuysen, 1827), pp. 53–54.

19. Wisbey, *Pioneer Prophetess,* pp. 27–35. Jemima's title of the "Public Universal Friend" was adopted from Quakerism. "Public Friends" in the Quaker tradition were those members commissioned to preach and travel from meeting to meeting. Jemima added to this the word Universal to indicate a wider mission.

20. Ibid., pp. 68–69, 94–95.

21. Ibid., pp. 97–118.

22. Ibid., p. 150. Hudson's book was published in Geneva, New York, by S. P. Hull in 1821 while the litigations over her property were still going on (these were not finally settled until 1828). It was reprinted under the title, *Memoir of Jemima Wilkinson* (Bath, NY) in 1844. Despite the Wisbey book exposing the inaccuracies of Hudson's account, Hudson has continued to be used by scholars of American utopianism as the primary source for Wilkinson's life and character.

23. Joseph Beese, *A Collection of the Sufferings of the People Called Quakers for the Testimony of a Good Conscience, 1650–1689,* vol. II (London: Luke Hinde, 1753), pp. 177–178, 198–206, 228–231.

24. Edited by Milton Speizmann and Jane Kronick, *Signs* (Autumn 1975): 235–245.

25. Julius Friedrich Sachse, *The German Sectarians of Pennsylvania 1742–1800: A Critical and Legendary History of the Ephrata Cloister and the Dunkers,* vol. 2 (Philadelphia: privately printed, 1900), pp. 176–196.

26. Lamech and Agrippa, *Chronicon Ephratense: A History of the Community of Seventh Day Baptists at Ephrata, Lancaster County, Penna,* trans. J. Max Hark (Lancaster, PA: S. H. Zahm, 1889), pp. 160–5, from the Pennsylvania Historical and Museum Commission, Ephrata Cloister.

27. A Pleasant Fragrance of Roses and Lilies, which grew forth in the valley of humility among the thorns, all from the Sisters Society in Saron. *Paradisisches Wunder-Spiel, Welches sich in diesen letzten Zeiten und Tagen denen Abendländischen Welt-Theilen, als ein Vorspiel der neuen Welt hervorgethen . . . ,* Ephrata, 1766, p. 360, from the Pennsylvania Historical and Museum Commission, Ephrata Cloister; translated for this volume by Ernst Prelinger.

28. Felix Reichmann and Eugene E. Doll, *Ephrata as Seen by Contemporaries,* Pennsylvania Folklore Society, XVII (1952), p. 57, for example.

29. Quoted in Klein, *Johann Conrad Beissel,* pp. 146–8.

30. R. B. Ludewig, "On the Tender Wings of Blessed Death: Moravians and Death in Two Generations 1740–1820." A Thesis submitted to the Honors Committee of Moravian College in partial fulfillment of the requirements for the Honors Program 1980, p. 22–23.

31. *The life story of Martha Powell (1704–1774). Personals of our dear Sister Martha Powell who entered the Joy of her Lord the 6th of May 1774.* The Moravian Archives, Bethlehem, PA.

32. The Methodists and Moravians were always close to one another during the eighteenth century, beginning when John and Charles Wesley voyaged to Georgia in 1735—John as incipient Anglican rector in Savannah, and Charles as secretary to General Oglethorpe. The faith of the Moravians at sea profoundly impressed John, and Spangenberg had a great impact on the young pastor, which ultimately culminated in his conversion experiences at Aldersgate back in London in 1738 and the formulation of the doctrine of perfection.

33. Probably Neshaminy in Pennsylvania.

34. Captain Nicholas Garrison organized a congregation of Moravians on Staten Island. He had known Zinzendorf in the West Indies. Later he was skipper of a Moravian vessel called the *Irene,* which was used to transport Moravians to America.

35. Shekomeko (variously spelled), near Reinbeck, New York, was a major Indian station of the Moravians, with a filial station at Pachgatgoch near New Milford, Connecticut. The settlements were viewed with hostility by the white settlers of the area, in part because the Moravians discouraged the use of liquor by the Indians while the local white inhabitants profited from its sale.

36. "Servant of the Church" or *"Diener"* was used for various offices, and usually signified an individual in charge of temporal affairs, a warden or supervisor of a choir. See Kenneth G. Hamilton, ed. and trans., *The Bethlehem Diary, vol I: 1742–1744* (Bethlehem, PA: Archives of the Moravian Church, 1971), pp. 230–231.

37. *Diarium dess Ledigen Schwestern Chors in Lidiz, Angefangen den lsten Juli 1768.* The Moravian Archives, Bethlehem, PA. (translation by this author).

38. "Anna Nitschmann," *The Messenger: A Magazine of the Church of the United Brethren,* New Series, XV: 419–427, 447–455.

39. William C. Reichel, ed., "J. Martin Mack's Recollections of a Journey from Otstonwake to Wyoming, in the Wilds of Skehandowana, in company with Count Zinzendorf and Anna Nitschmann, and of his Sojourn in the latter place in October of 1742," *Memorials of the Moravian Church,* vol. I, (Philadelphia, PA: Lippincott, 1870), pp. 100–11.

40. Otstonwakin is present-day Montoursville, Pennsylvania, on the west branch of the Susquehanna in Lycoming County.

41. Shamokin is south and slightly east of Sunbury, Pennsylvania, where the west and east branches of the Susquehanna River diverge. Shikellimy was an Indian chief, friendly to the Moravians who subsequently urged Mack to found the mission at Shamokin in 1746–1748.

42. Andrew Montour was the son of an Iroquois chief, Carondowa, and Madam Montour, a French woman who is probably meant by "grandmother." (The question mark is in the original text.) Montour was a noted chief in colonial times and a friend of Great Britain rather than of France.

43. Wyoming, Pennsylvania, is between present-day Scranton and Wilkes-Barre.

44. "Personals of our Brothers and Sisters Martyred," *Personalia, Unserer am. 24ten Nov. 1755 an der Mahony von denen feindlichen Indianern martyrisirten Geschwister,* from The Moravian Archives, Bethlehem, PA (translation by this author).

45. *Herzliche Bande* and *Herzens-Bande* on the next page are clearly a derivation from the conception of Bands, defined in Hamilton, *The Bethlehem Diary,* p. 231, as "small groups . . . intended to foster spiritual growth . . . . They met informally for prayer and intimate discussion of personal experience." Here I have taken the concept to mean a devotional or inspirational moment between as few as two people.

46. Adelaide L. Fries, Douglas LeTell Rights, Minnie J. Smith, and Kenneth G. Hamilton, eds., *Records of the Moravians in North Carolina,* vol. II (Raleigh, NC: North Carolina Historical Commission, 1922–69), pp. 715, 767, 825, 826, 827, 895. See also Clarence E. Beckel, "Early Moravian Marriage Customs . . . ," *Pennsylvania German Folklore Society* III (1938): 6–7.

47. *Testimonies Concerning the Character and Ministry of Mother Ann Lee and the First Witnesses of the Gospel of Christ's Second Appearing, Given by Some of the Aged Brethren and Sisters of the United Society* (Albany: Packard and Van Benthuysen, 1827).

48. Excerpts are taken from the *Testimonies of the Life, Character Revelations and Doctrines of Mother Ann Lee,* pp. 2–6, 16–17, 53–55, 73–77, 274–275.

49. Several brief firsthand accounts of Wilkinson are available. Benjamin Brownell, a former member of the Universal Friends, wrote a hostile account, primarily to justify his own apostasy, entitled, *Enthusiastical Errors, Transpired and Detected* (privately printed, 1783). A brief account of Wilkinson's preaching in Philadelphia appeared from an author called "Lang Syne," reprinted in John F. Watson, *Annals of Philadelphia and Pennsylvania,* vol. I, (Philadelphia: Carey and Hart, 1845) pp. 553–555. William Savery, a Quaker missionary who regarded Wilkinson as a deluded heretic, wrote an account of her household and also her preaching at the Council of the Seneca Indians and the

U.S. Government in Canandaigua in 1794: *A Journal of the Life, Travels and Religious Labors of William Savery* (London: C. Gilpin, 1844), pp. 58–9, 66–71.

50. Wilkinson Papers, Cornell University Archives, film 357.

51. Ibid. See also Wisbey, *Pioneer Prophetess,* pp. 18, 30.

52. Eugene P. Chase, ed., *Our Revolutionary Forefathers: The Letters of Francois, Marquis de Barbe-Marbois,* (New York: Duffield and Co., 1929), pp. 162–166.

Women and Revivalism: The Puritan and Wesleyan Traditions

1. The effects of Anne Hutchinson's trial and banishment are discussed in Chapter 4 and in Lyle Koehler, *A Search for Power* (Urbana: University of Illinois Press, 1980), pp. 227–234, and Mary Dunn, "Saints and Sisters," pp. 37–38, in Janet W. James, ed., *Women in American Religion* (Philadelphia: University of Pennsylvania Press, 1980).

2. Gerald F. Moran, " 'Sisters' in Christ: Women and the Church in Seventeenth Century New England," in James, ed., *Women in American Religion,* pp. 48–53.

3. Ibid., pp. 57–61.

4. Robert G. Pope, *The Half-Way Covenant: Church Membership in Puritan New England* (Princeton: Princeton University Press, 1969), pp. 209, 217, 222, 229, 245–246; Michael J. Crawford, "The Invention of the Anglo-American Revival," paper presented at the American Historical Association Convention (December 1977), pp. 4–5, 10.

5. Emory Elliot, "The Development of the Puritan Funeral Sermon and Elegy: 1660–1750," *Early American Literature* 15 (1980): p. 161. Cotton Mather's role in this development is discussed in William D. Andrews, "The Printed Funeral Sermons of Cotton Mather," *Early American Literature* 5 (1970): pp. 24–44. The meaning of this change for women is dealt with in Laurel Thatcher Ulrich, "Vertuous Women Found: New England Ministerial Literature, 1668–1735," in James, ed., *Women in American Religion,* pp. 67–87, and Lonna M. Malmsheimer, "Daughters of Zion: New England Roots of American Feminism," *New England Quarterly* 50 (1977): pp. 484–505.

6. See note 30 (for Document 3). Portions referred to here are from pages 2 and 22 of the original text.

7. Ward's tract, originally published in England in 1695, maintained that women were a "deceitful, false and inconstant sex" and that "there scarce happens any notorious murder, cheat, or villany, throughout the world, but a woman is to be found at the bottom of it." See Edward Ward, *Female Policy Detected: or the Arts of a Designing Woman Laid Open* (New York, 1794), pp. 66, 42, 43.

8. Gerald F. Moran, "The Puritan Saint: Religious Experience, Church Membership and Piety in Connecticut, 1636–1776, PhD diss., Rutgers University, 1973, p. 326.

9. Ibid., p. 278.

10. See note 31 (for Document 4).

11. Philip Greven, *The Protestant Temperament: Patterns of Child-Rearing, Religious Experience, and the Self in Early America* (New York: New American Library, 1977), Part 2.

12. See note 30 (for Document 3).

13. William McLoughlin, *New England Dissent, 1630–1833; the Baptists and the Separation of the Church and State* (Cambridge: Harvard University Press, 1971), pp. 102, 181, 182, 248.

14. *In a Letter from a Gentlewoman In New-England, To Another her dear Friend, in great Darkness, Doubt and Concern of a Religious Nature* (Boston, 1755).

15. For example, Sarah Osborn of Newport founded a female prayer society in about 1741, which met weekly under her guidance until her death in 1796. See note 29.

16. John Wesley, *Journal,* ed. Nehemiah Curnock, vol. III (London: Epworth, 1909–1916), p. 31.

17. Ibid., pp. 32–34. See also Frank Baker, "Susanna Wesley: Puritan, Parent, Pastor, Protagonist, Pattern," in Rosemary Keller, Louise Queen, and Hilah Thomas, eds., *Women in New Worlds,* vol. II (Nashville: Abingdon, 1982), pp. 112–131.

18. Donald Mathews, *Religion in the Old South* (Chicago: University of Chicago Press, 1977), p. xvi.

19. Ibid., Chs. 1, 2, particularly pp. 31, 60.

20. Ibid., Chs. 1, 2. See also Sydney Ahlstrom, *A Religious History of the American People,* vol. I (New York: Doubleday, 1975), Chs. 18, 20; Frederick Norwood, *The Story of American Methodism* (Nashville: Abingdon, 1974), Chs. 1, 4.

21. Alan Hayes, "John Wesley and Sophy Hopkey: A Case Study in Wesley's Attitude Toward, Women," in Keller, Queen, and Thomas, eds., *Women in New Worlds,* vol. II, p. 37.
22. Earl Kent Brown, "Women of the Word: Selected Leadership Roles of Women in Mr. Wesley's Methodism," in Thomas and Keller, eds., *Women in New Worlds,* vol. I, p. 74.
23. Mollie Davis, "The Countess of Huntingdon: A Leader in Missions for Social and Religious Reform," in Keller, Queen, and Thomas, eds., *Women in New Worlds,* vol. II, pp. 162–175; Mollie Davis, "The Countess of Huntingdon and Whitefield's Bethesda," *Georgia Historical Quarterly* 56 (Spring 1972): pp. 12–82; Zechariah Atwell Mudge, *Lady Huntingdon Portrayed* (New York: Carlton & Porter, 1857); Reverend Alfred H. New, *Memoir of Selina, Countess of Huntingdon* (New York: Protestant Episcopal Society, 1859); Abel Stevens, *The Women of Methodism* (New York: Carlton & Porter, 1866).
24. *The Experiences of God's gracious Dealing with Mrs. Elizabeth White. As they were written under her own Hand, and found in her Closet, after her Decease, December 5, 1669* (Boston, 1741), pp. 3–8, 10–13.
25. *The Copy of a Valedictory, and Monitory Writing, Left by Sarah Goodhue, Wife of Joseph Goodhue, of Ipswich, in New-England; and found after her Decease* . . . (New London, 1773), pp. 3, 4.
26. Cotton Mather, *Tabitha Redivivia, An Essay to Describe and Commend the Good Works of a Vertuous Woman; Who therein approves her self a Real Disciple of a Holy Saviour. With some Justice done to the Memory of that Religious and Honourable Gentlewoman, Mrs. Elizabeth Hutchinson. Who Expired 3.d.12.m 1712, 13. In the LXXI Year of her Age* (Boston, 1713), pp. 20–26, 43–45, 52–54.
27. [Thomas Prince], *The Sovereign God Acknowledged and Blessed, both in Giving and Taking away. A Sermon Occasioned by the Decease of Mrs. Deborah Prince On Friday, July 20, 1744. In the 21st Year of her Age. Delivered at the South Church in Boston, July 29* . . . (Boston, 1744), pp. 20, 21–29, 31.
28. Obituary of Mrs. Hannah Hodge, *General Assembly's Missionary Magazine* 2 (1806): pp. 45, 46, 92–94.
29. Sarah Osborn to the Reverend Joseph Fish, February 28–March 7, 1767. Osborn Collection. American Antiquarian Society, Worcester, Mass. Reprinted with permission of the Society. Excerpts are from Mary Beth Norton, ed., " 'My Resting Reaping Times': Sarah Osborn's Defense of Her 'Unfeminine' Activities, 1767," *Signs* 2 (1976): pp. 522–529.
30. *An Account of the Experience of Hester Ann Rogers; and her Funeral Sermon, by Rev. Dr. Coke to which are added Her Spiritual Letters* (New York: Lane & Scott, 1849), pp. 253–255, 267–269, 283–285.
31. Aaron Crossley Hobart Seymour, *The Life and Times of Selina Countess of Huntingdon* (London: William Edward Painter, 1840), vol. I, pp. 73, 74, 89, 475, 476; vol. II, pp. 257, 258n, 262, 273.
32. Stevens, *The Women of Methodism,* pp. 235–240, 243–246. See also Edward T. James, Janet James, and Paul Boyer, eds., *Notable American Women,* vol. II (Cambridge, MA: Belknap Press, 1971), pp. 174, 175.
33. Manuscript Collection of Catharine Garrettson correspondence, Drew University.
34. Jonathan Edwards, "Miscellanies," no. 37 on "Faith," typed ms., pp. 169–171. From the Beinecke Rare Book and Manuscript Library, Yale University. Used with the permission of Thomas Schafer.

Women, Civil Religion, and the American Revolution

1. Abigail Adams to Mercy Otis Warren, January 1776, in L. H. Butterfield, ed., *Adams Family Correspondence,* vol. I (Cambridge: Harvard, 1963, 1973), pp. 422, 423. I am indebted to Linda Kerber whose conceptualization of republican motherhood in *Women of the Republic: Intellect and Ideology in Revolutionary America* (Chapel Hill: University of North Carolina, 1980) is integral to my formulation of the relationship between women and civil religion during the American Revolution.
2. Sydney E. Ahlstrom, *A Religious History of the American People,* vol. I (Garden City, NY: Image, 1975), pp. 464, 465.
3. John Adams to Hezekiah Niles, 1818, quoted in Bernard Bailyn, *The Ideological Origins of the American Revolution* (Cambridge, MA: Belknap, 1967), p. 160.

4. Robert Bellah's classic article on "Civil Religion in America" was first published in *Daedalus* 96 (Winter 1967): 1–21.
5. Robert Bellah, "The Revolution and the Civil Religion," in Jerald C. Brauer, ed., *Religion and the American Revolution* (Philadelphia: Fortress, 1976), pp. 55–73. Henry May's *The Enlightenment in America* (New York: Oxford, 1976) is an important study of the relationship between the Enlightenment and religion and considers the significance of public morality and virtue.
6. An excellent collection of essays that brings together these perspectives is Russell E. Richey and Donald G. Jones, eds., *American Civil Religion* (New York: Harper & Row, 1974). It includes a significant bibliography on the subject.
7. Mary Beth Norton's *Liberty's Daughters: The Revolutionary Experience of American Women, 1750–1800* (Boston: Little Brown, 1980), p. 195, is, along with Kerber's work, the most important volume on women in the revolutionary era. Nancy Cott's *The Bonds of Womanhood: "Woman's Sphere" in New England, 1780–1835* (New Haven, CT: Yale, 1977) extends into the early republic and is also essential.
8. Abigail Adams to Mercy Otis Warren, April 13, 1776, in Butterfield, ed., *Adams Family Correspondence,* vol. I, p. 377. Primary accounts of such home-front experiences are found in Oliver M. Dickerson, comp., *Boston under Military Rule, 1768–1769 as revealed in A Journal of the Times* (Boston: Chapman and Grimes, 1936); Anne Rowe Cunningham, ed., *Letters and Diary of John Rowe, Boston Merchant, 1759–1762, 1764–1776* (Boston: W. B. Clarke, 1903), pp. 177, 179, 194, 202, 218; and Winthrop Sargent, ed., *The Letters of John Andrews, esq. of Boston, 1772–1774* (Cambridge, MA: J. Wilson and Sons, 1866) pp. 32–84.
9. Norton, *Liberty's Daughters,* pp. 167, 168.
10. William Reed, ed., *The Life of Esther DeBerdt, Esther Reed* (Philadelphia: C. Sherman, 1853), pp. 315–324; Frank Moore, comp., *Diary of the American Revolution,* vol. II (New York: C. Scribner, 1860), pp. 203–298, 341, 342. See also Norton, *Liberty's Daughters,* pp. 177–188.
11. Abigail Adams to John Adams, July 30, 1977, in Butterfield, ed., *Adams Family Correspondence,* vol. III, p. 295, and note 2, p. 296; D. Hamilton Hurd, *History of Essex County, Mass.,* vol. I (Philadelphia: J. W. Lewis and Co., 1888), p. 704; Edwin Stone, *History of Beverly, from its Settlement in 1630 to 1842 (Boston: J. Munroe and Co., 1843), pp. 83, 84; Norton, Liberty's Daughters,* pp. 156, 160, 161.
12. Abigail Adams to John Adams, June 3, 1776, in Butterfield, ed., *Adams Family Correspondence,* vol. II, p. 4; Abigail Adams to John Adams, April 11, 1776, ibid., vol. I, p. 375; Abigail Adams to John Adams, May 7, 1776, ibid., vol. I, p. 402; Abigail Adams to Mercy Otis Warren, April 11, 1776, ibid., vol. I, p. 377. See Rosemary Keller, *Abigail Adams and the American Revolution: A Personal History* (New York: Arno, 1982), for a study of the effect of the American Revolution on her life and personal identity.
13. Mercy Otis Warren to Catherine Macaulay, December 29, 1774, Mercy Warren Papers Microfilm Edition, Massachusetts Historical Society (Boston: 1968), Reel I.
14. For short and well-done biographical sketches of Abigail Adams and Mercy Otis Warren, see Edward T. James et al., eds., *Notable American Women,* vols. I and III (Cambridge, MA: Belknap, 1971), I: 6–9, III: 545–546.
15. Philip Davidson considers the significance of the church as an agent of propaganda for patriots in *Propaganda and the American Revolution* (Chapel Hill: University of North Carolina, 1941), Ch. 5. See also Harry P. Kerr, "Politics and Religion in Colonial Fast and Thanksgiving Sermons, 1763–1783," *American Journal of Speech* 66 (1960): 372–382.
16. Alice M. Baldwin, *The New England Clergy and the American Revolution* (Durham, NC: 1928), and Claude H. Van Tyne, "Influence of the Clergy and of Religious and Sectarian Forces on the American Revolution," *American Historical Review* (1913): 64, have particularly stressed the continuity of religious and political thinking throughout the development of the New England colonies.
17. Good examples include Andrew Eliot, "A Sermon Preached before his Excellency Francis Bernard, Esq.; Governor, The Honorable, His Majesty's Council, and the Honorable House of Representatives, of the Province of the Massachusetts Bay in New-England, May 29, 1765 (Boston: Green, 1765); Charles Chauncy, "Civil Magistrates must be just, Ruling in the Fear of God" (Boston: House of Representatives, 1749); Samuel Cooper, "A Sermon upon Occasion of the Death of our late Sovereign,

George the Second, Preach'd before His Excellency Francis Bernard, Esq." (Boston: John Draper, 1761); and Jonathan Mayhew, "A Discourse concerning Unlimited Submission and Non-Resistance to the Higher Powers" (Boston: Fowle and Gookin, 1750).

18. These arguments are developed in secondary sources, including John Wingate Thornton, *The Pulpit of the American Revolution* (Boston: Sheldon and Co., 1860); Perry Miller, "The Moral and Psychological Roots of American Resistance," in Jack P. Greene, id., *The Reinterpretation of the American Revolution, 1763–1789* (New York: Harper & Row, 1968); Bernard Bailyn, "Religion and Revolution: Three Biographical Studies," *Perspectives in American History,* vol. IV (Cambridge, MA: Harvard 1970), pp. 85–169; Nathan L. Hatch, "The Origins of Civil Millenialism in America: New England Clergymen, War with France, and the Revolution," *William and Mary Quarterly,* 3 (July 1974): 407–430; Davidson, *Propaganda and the American Revolution;* Van Tyne, "Influence of the Clergy"; Baldwin, *The New England Clergy.*

19. See note 24 (for Document 2).

20. See note 25 (for Document 3).

21. See Keller, *Abigail Adams and the American Revolution,* Chs. 1 and 2.

22. See note 26 (for Document 4). Quotations from Abigail Adams on these pages are found in Document 4.

23. [Mercy Otis Warren], "The Group" (Boston: Edes and Gill, 1775).

24. *An Address to New England: Written by a Daughter of Liberty,* broadside, 14-3/4 × 8-1/4 in., Boston, 1774 (Historical Society of Pennsylvania, Philadelphia).

25. *A New Touch on the Times: Well adapted to the distressing Situation of every Sea-port Town. By a Daughter of Liberty, living in Marblehead,* broadside, 13 × 8-1/4 in., Massachusetts, 1779 (The New York Historical Society).

26. Selections are from Butterfield, ed., *The Adams Family Correspondence,* vols. 1–4.

27. Judith Sargent Murray, "On the Equality of the Sexes," *The Massachusetts Magazine,* (March 1790) pp. 132–135 and (April 1790) pp. 223–226; *The Gleaner* vol. II (Boston: 1798), No. xxxxv, pp. 5–8.

28. Benjamin Rush, "Thoughts upon Female Education" (Philadelphia: 1787).

29. Mary Wollstonecraft, *A Vindication of the Rights of Woman* (New York: Norton, 1967; first published 1792), pp. from "Dedication," and 283–284.

30. From the salutatory oration, delivered by Miss Priscilla Mason, May 15, 1793, in *The Rise and Progress of the Young-Ladies' Academy of Philadelphia* (Philadelphia: Stewart and Cochran, 1794), pp. 90–95.

Index